Internal Auditor's Manual and Guide

The Practitioner's Guide to Internal Auditing

Milton Stevens Fonorow

PRENTICE HALL
Englewood Cliffs, New Jersey 07632

Prentice-Hall International (UK) Limited, *London*
Prentice-Hall of Australia Pty. Limited, *Sydney*
Prentice-Hall Canada, Inc., *Toronto*
Prentice-Hall Hispanoamericana, S.A., *Mexico*
Prentice-Hall of India Private Limited, *New Delhi*
Prentice-Hall of Japan, Inc., *Tokyo*
Simon & Schuster Asia Pte. Ltd., *Singapore*
Editora Prentice-Hall do Brasil, Ltda., *Rio de Janeiro*

"This publication is designed to provide accurate and authoritative information in regard to the subject matter covered. It is sold with the understanding that the publisher is not engaged in rendering legal, accounting or other professional service. If legal advice or other expert assistance is required, the services of a competent professional person should be sought.

. . . *From the Declaration of Principles jointly adopted by a Committee of the American Bar Association and a Committee of Publishers and Associations.*"

10 9 8 7 6 5 4

Library of Congress Cataloging-in-Publication Data

Fonorow, Milton Stevens, 1919–
Internal auditor's manual and guide: the practitioner's guide to internal auditing/by Milton Stevens Fonorow.
p. cm.
Includes index.
ISBN 0-13-471194-7
1. Auditing, Internal—Handbooks, manuals, etc. I. Title.
HF5668.25.F66 1989
657'.458—dc20 89-8794
CIP

ISBN 0-13-471194-7

90000
9 780134 711942

PRENTICE HALL
Career & Personal Development
Englewood Cliffs, NJ 07632
A Simon & Schuster Company

Printed in the United States of America

Acknowledgment

Thanks to members of my family for their continued support, particularly our sons, Richard and Roger, for their useful suggestions in their fields of expertise.

I also wish to express my appreciation to the editorial staff at Prentice Hall, especially to Bette Schwartzberg for her encouragement and for the many hours she gave to this undertaking.

About the Author

Milton Stevens Fonorow is a Certified Internal Auditor and as a Certified Public Accountant, earned his MBA from the University of Chicago. He joined the newly formed three-man internal audit staff at the Kraft Foods Company division of National Dairy Products Corporation. As the department grew, Mr. Fonorow became its manager and held the position until his retirement. By that time Kraft Foods had over two hundred sales branches, distribution centers and processing plants as well as over twenty major administrative offices and a corporate headquarters office employing more than one thousand people. The internal audit staff was responsible for auditing all of the company's locations and operations.

Milton wrote all of Kraft's internal audit programs and manuals and was responsible for all the audits conducted by his department. He wrote necessary programs and instructions, and helped train the audit managers for newly formed staffs in the larger International Divisions of Kraft, including England, Australia and West Germany.

As audit manager, he conceived and initiated the management and operational audit concepts that became an accepted phase of internal auditing at Kraft. He originated necessary audit forms and programs, trained the auditors and personally supervised in-depth reviews.

To cover interim periods between internal audits, he conceived, designed and implemented a Self Audit Program for use by management at major company locations. Responding to the data processing challenge, Milton selected, trained and supervised a designated group of specialists to audit Kraft's EDP operations. This group became a separate part of the staff, with the responsibility for auditing data processing operations. The EDP group was ultimately assigned to work directly with computer application programmers. Milton served as task force chairman for a computer project he conceived and implemented. This project brought all of Kraft's finished-goods inventory records onto a real time system. The program required the creation of a large data used to process millions of inventory transactions.

Milton formed another group of specialists to audit and control construction expenditures. He selected, trained and provided working guidance to these auditors, some of whom were assigned full time to a single major construction project. This Construction Audit group reviewed all projects and participated in the preparation of plans and specifications, selection of bidders, receipt and analysis of bids and in the final preparation of the award documents. Serving as coordinator for company-wide cost-control programs, Milton was personally responsible for annual savings of millions of dollars without a mass firing of personnel.

Milton Fonorow took an active interest in professionalizing the field of Internal Auditing. He organized many professional seminars and was frequently a session leader or the featured speaker. While serving as the Education Chairman of the Chicago Chapter of the Institute of Internal Auditors, Milton initiated and spearheaded the first course in Internal Auditing ever offered at a university in the Chicago area. He designed the course, prepared the lecture outlines and delivered many of the lectures. He has served on several governmental study groups, organized by the business community to help public officials streamline and reduce personnel and associated operating costs.

Mr. Fonorow presided as President of the Chicago Chapter of the Institute of Internal Auditors and served many years as a governor of that chapter. He acted as Program Chairman for many innovative and successful Area and International Conferences run by the Chicago chapter for the Institute of Internal Auditors.

Contents

What This Book Will Do for You

When the board of directors selects a member to chair the audit committee, the selected board member can refer to this Manual to find out what internal auditing is all about. What are the auditor's professional standards? How does an auditor perform the job? What methods are employed by auditors to evaluate operations and risks? To whom should the head auditor report? What type of information should be included in an audit report, and who should receive copies of these reports? How should audit points be followed up and resolved? How does internal auditing differ from the external audits conducted by the outside accountants? Is there an advantage in having the company's international operations audited by the home office internal audit staff? What other management services should be expected from the internal audit staff? These, and many other questions, are answered in this Internal Auditor's Manual and Guide.

The director of internal auditing will find many ideas about organization and administration of this area of responsibility. There is helpful information on such questions as: how to structure an internal audit department; where to recruit personnel; how to train and upgrade auditors and how to evaluate their performance. Possible new areas or approaches for audit activities may be discovered. This book points out activities of a business operation that are frequently overlooked, and it contains detailed programs for operational audits of departments that frequently spend a large percentage of incoming dollars. Many cost savings ideas are included throughout the text, and a list of tips for successful internal auditing management is contained in Chapter 31.

Internal audit managers will find a wealth of useful information at their fingertips. A manager frequently is brought into a company from the staff of the public accountant with little experience in the field of Internal Auditing. This manual points out the differences in approach between the internal and external auditor and can also be useful in helping a manager control and use internal audit time.

When fraud rears its ugly head, this book will provide many useful tips to help investigate and resolve the problem. When the manager is directed to audit an unfamiliar department, this book provides many sample audit programs with significant instructions for approaching and conducting the audit. There are many programs here that can be used to help audit managers prepare unique audit programs required for specific operations or departments, or the manger might wish to compare them to audit programs that he or she is currently using.

Internal audit supervisors should carry this book with their other manuals, controller bulletins and procedure write-ups. It can provide answers when a new situation is encountered. The detailed audit programs and audit instructions contained in this manual point out the significant areas to be studied in business operations.

The supervisor will find important tips for utilizing an auditor's time, and in using statistical sampling or computer assisted audit programs to achieve the maximum results with a minimum of effort. Supervisors can examine sample audit reports for format and to see how significant audit findings are presented. Audit supervisors will have at their fingertips a valuable training instrument to aid in instructing the internal audit staff.

Internal auditors will find this *Manual and Guide* indispensable during their careers in the internal auditing profession. They will have at their disposal the routine audit techniques that have been designed and used by their predecessors. By using these techniques, auditors can avoid many pitfalls. The few minutes spent in reading a particular page or chapter, will be repaid by having the tasks performed more reliably and efficiently. The reasons for selecting an audit step will become apparent, making the work more understandable.

How Is This Book Organized?

The manual is divided into four parts. Part I and sections of parts II and IV are directed toward the needs of the *Audit Committee Chairman* and the *Director of Internal Auditing.* Part II is primarily written with the *Audit Manager* and *Supervisor* in mind. They will also be interested in Part IV. Part III is devoted to instructions and programs for performing audits of most of the customary business operations. This information will be most useful to the practicing working auditor, who will also find much useful information in Part IV, even though that material is directed primarily to audit management.

More specifically, Part I deals with the *profession* of internal auditing, how it differs from external auditing, the customary responsibilities of a department and where the Internal Auditing Department should fit into an organizational structure. It briefly deals with internal controls and describes how to establish a self audit program.

Part II covers *administration* of an Internal Auditing Department. It also includes information useful in preparing internal audit manuals as well as audit programs and instructions. It contains detailed audit programs for management or operational audits of selected activities, as well as helpful information regarding audit files, forms, supplies and preparation of audit working papers. It tells how to plan an audit schedule, and then how to prepare for and start an internal audit. Finally, it deals with completing the audit assignment, writing the audit report, conducting the windup meeting and obtaining and following up on management comments.

Part III covers the customary types of operations that are audited, and contains *audit instructions, samples of programs, internal control questions, and critical points* that can be useful when conducting these particular reviews. Included are programs for the audits of purchasing, engineering, marketing, and advertising departments, computer centers, research departments, construction sites, international divisions, and security departments. These audit programs and instructions contain much detailed information, and readers must grasp the intent and apply the basic thinking to the comparable operations in their own organizations. The critical points are based on actual cases, which the author has personally experienced.

Part IV covers some of the *special facets* of the internal auditing profession. It describes special audit tools that are available to the staff, such as computer audit programs, special statistical sampling techniques and the use of contract audit agencies and consultants. Many unusual types of problems are covered including instructions for dealing with employee fraud, conflicts of interest, insider trading and confidential information. Part IV ends with some helpful hints and a long list of potential cost cutters.

The reader will, of course, benefit from reading this manual from cover to cover, but the book's organization is such that a complete reading is not required to understand material in a particular chapter. Some chapters do contain references to other parts of the book.

How Can This Manual Be Used to Your Greatest Advantage?

A reader who has just been asked to *form an Internal Audit Department* in an organization will turn to the second section of this manual which deals with the *administration of the internal audit function.* There lies a variety of information on the many facets involved in initiating, organizing and administering an Internal Audit department. If an *Audit Manager* is told to *review the* company's *Engineering Department,* the manager can turn to the chapters labeled *Auditing An Engineering Department* and *Auditing A Construction Project* to find detailed instructions and programs for conducting such reviews. If an auditor encounters a situation in which a *fraud* is likely to have been perpetrated, the chapters labeled *Auditing a Security Department* and the one dealing with *Employee Fraud* each contain useful information on the determination, investigation, interrogation and resolution of such an eventuality. If an auditor is told to review *advertising costs,* the chapter labeled *Auditing Advertising Expenditures* contains a sample of an audit program and instructions for auditing such activities.

During the author's work experience, he developed many timesaving audit techniques and approaches which are included in this book. Some internal auditing challenges are widespread and occur in almost all audits, such as cash, receivables, inventory and property. Basic internal audit approaches to these areas are described in detail. Some commonly used audit techniques, such as statistical sampling, flow charting and circularization of accounts are covered.

Audit programs are preceded by a section of instructions, which explain any unusual audit step. Most of the audit directions outline a common sense approach. The programs call for work which is routinely performed by auditors in the due course of an examination. These steps appear as checklists.

Why There Is Some Duplication of Information?

This manual contains information relating to the internal audit of most of the customary departments in a business enterprise. There is some duplication of information, deliberately so, in order to make this manual a useful audit tool. For example, the chapter on cash covers most audit routines commonly employed in auditing normal cash transactions, and some of these routines are repeated or referred to in chapters dealing with specific location audits. If an auditor examines a program designed for the audit of a sales branch, all necessary audit routines will be listed in that program, including some audit steps for verifying cash receipts at the sales branch.

However, it will be necessary for the reader to refer to the chapter on Internal Auditing of Cash Transactions where extensive detailed information of a specialized nature has been covered. The author may repeat brief audit steps or instructions, but has referred to material in other chapters when considerable information is involved.

Are All Internal Auditing Questions Answered?

It is often said that one person's meat is another person's poison, and some of the activities that the author inherently believes to be self-evident and require no explanation, might be foreign to a particular reader. If this occurs, the author can only suggest that the reader seek further data by attending a meeting of the local chapter of the Institute of Internal Auditors.

A Note from the Author

Internal auditing is a form of self appraisal. It is a review of an entity's organization and behavior, conducted by employees.

The modern concept of internal auditing began when the internal staffs broke away from the published statements, or the public accountant's approach to audit assignments. The principle of verification was retained, but the audit examination was extended to render a service that management could use to effect efficient administration and a more profitable operation. Auditors not only verified authenticity and validity of charges, but began using their broad knowledge of company operations to challenge amounts and necessity. They began auditing for profit and were just as much interested in internal controls to eliminate waste and inefficiency as those controls maintained to detect theft and fraud.

This approach, revolutionary at the time, has become widely accepted and has benefited both the profession and the companies served. Some internal audit directors are reluctant to perform management audits for fear that this type of approach might lead them into becoming a part of an operation, and thereby remove the reviewing pedestal. But this apprehension has been proven groundless, and the venturesome staffs have succeeded in separating recommendations from the implementation responsibility and have thereby provided a wide range of internal audit services.

Purpose of Internal Auditing

The primary purpose of internal auditing is to determine that the organization's stated policies and procedures are being followed by employees at all levels of operations. Management may prescribe policies, regulations, rules and procedures but all of these are subject to individual interpretation and personal whim as to the execution or implementation of management's stated desires. The internal auditor's job is to examine all operations and determine that the letter and intent of management's directives are being followed by all employees.

Forms of Internal Auditing

Auditing within an organization takes many forms. There are

1. Department auditors responsible for seeing that employees in their department follow certain prescribed rules and regulations.

2. Quality control auditors who specialize in evaluating the quality of products produced by their company.
3. Accounts payable auditors who review every disbursement before a check is released.
4. Pricing auditors who ensure that invoices are correct.
5. Many other specialized auditors who concentrate on one important sphere of their company's business.

Each of these auditors has limited activity and authority unlike the professional internal auditors who report to top management on their reviews of all aspects of their company's operations.

The Internal Audit Staff

An internal audit staff in an organization generally has authority and responsibility relating to all activities. But it is essential that the authority and responsibility of the staff be spelled out and approved by the highest level of management. Without top management support, the internal auditing function cannot provide the services that an organization should learn to expect.

This book covers all the usual, and many of the unusual, phases of internal auditing activities. An audit staff creates its own place in an organization. Its contribution to an enterprise is determined by the intelligence, application and initiative of all staff members.

Contents of This Manual

The information in this book has been accumulated during almost *40 years of working experience in the internal auditing profession.* During this period the profession has gained acceptance and has developed and grown into an important instrument for reviewing an organization's activities—be it in government, charity or business. *Working auditors, learning while performing appraisals, verifications and confirmations, developed their profession to its present status.*

There are *no great universal truths that apply to the profession,* neither are there any *secret formulas or fast solutions that ease the pressure* of an internal auditor's job. *There is no substitute for hard work, no labor saving devices nor deep insights that enable an auditor to master the profession.* The ingredients necessary to produce a successful internal auditor are *honesty, diligence, intelligence, knowledge* and *common sense.* An auditor must study everything available about a subject before starting an audit; for once the assignment is begun, the auditor is traveling on unchartered ground. Every operation is unique; the physical locations and layouts differ, volumes and timing differ and numbers and capabilities of personnel are never the same.

No great internal auditing experts stand out as beacons; just a great many competent, honest, intelligent, hard working auditors who are devoted to their profession lead the way.

This book is intended for use by all practitioners. It contains many new ideas and approaches that can help you work more effectively.

Milton Fonorow

Part 1

What Internal Auditing Is All About

Chapter 1

The Internal Auditing Profession

WHY INTERNAL AUDITING

Internal auditing deals mainly with the appraisal, analysis, interpretation and reporting of economic activities as shown by the relationships of numbers. The "number system" is to the auditor what oils are to the artist. The absolute values represented by the numeric symbols, and the relationships of numbers to other numbers, present a clear picture to a trained eye. To the internal auditor these numbers depict physical activities that have taken place. If the system of recording these numbers is efficient, accurate and well-controlled the numbers themselves remain as a permanent, concise record of economic activity.

Management at all levels is absorbed with operations and rarely can spare the time required to make a detailed study of any procedure or system. To obtain an objective, analytical review of a specific operation, management turns to the professional trained in the art of analyzing records, controls and procedures—the internal auditor. Calling for audit assistance is not a reflection on the ability of any manager but is rather the use of the proper tool to appraise an operation, isolate and identify problem areas and obtain help in improving controls and operations.

In order to effectively manage any operation, timely, accurate and complete reports are a necessity. This is the area where internal auditors provide a vital service to management.

Internal auditing has been defined as the eyes and ears of owners or management. This is a fair statement since the internal auditor, thinking and acting like the owner, looks at every part of a company's business from the standpoint of increasing efficiency and profits.

FIVE CRITICAL TASKS

Internal auditing is an appraisal, by trained company employees, of the accuracy, reliability, efficiency and usefulness of company records and internal controls. Typically the internal audit objectives will be stated somewhat as follows:

Internal auditors examine every phase of operations to insure that all company assets are properly recorded and safeguarded and that company operations are conducted in an efficient and businesslike manner. Auditors are responsible for performing the following tasks:

1. Determine that company policies are followed.
2. Determine that internal controls are adequate.
3. Suggest improvements in practices and procedures to obtain increased efficiency or to lower operating costs.
4. Detect fraud or manipulation of records.
5. Determine that all laws are being obeyed.

HOW INTERNAL AUDITORS HANDLE ILLEGAL ACTIVITIES

Routine internal audit procedures are directed toward the first two tasks of evaluating controls and determining that company policies are followed by all employees. Operational or management audit techniques are used to evaluate and improve operating and clerical efficiency. The fourth and fifth tasks are more difficult to accomplish.

Internal auditors are continually on the alert for any thefts, frauds or misrepresentations or any activities that may result in a loss. They must investigate all suspicious transactions to the degree possible with available records. Auditors work closely with outside police authorities and with legal representatives in the investigation and apprehension of wrongdoers within an organization.

The internal auditor *is ever watchful* for any activity or failure that could cause the firm to become party to a lawsuit or to be subject to punitive action by a government agency. Like the external auditor, when an unusual transaction concerning a high level executive is noted, the internal auditor must bring the matter to the attention of higher management. If the action is condoned by top management, the internal auditor drops the matter, providing it is not an obviously dishonest act or violation of a criminal law.

If an established illegal or dishonest act is committed or condoned by the top management of the entity, the auditor is placed in a difficult position. The auditor must carefully document and prepare notes of the incident and place these records in the audit work papers; and the auditor must then decide whether or not to remain with the company.

An experienced internal audit manager *will not normally remain with a firm that condones dishonesty or illegality.* The auditor must also decide whether to turn the matter over to the proper outside legal authorities, taking into consideration the possibility that ignoring the situation might have legal implications.

However, the audit manager must be very careful to refrain from acting hastily and perhaps erroneously. Consider these two examples:

EXAMPLE 1: An auditor, while reviewing executive expense reports, notes that the executive vice-president has been reimbursed for obvious personal expenditures. Charges for travel expenses incurred for the executive's wife have been submitted and paid, despite a company policy that prohibits such costs being charged to the firm. The information is presented to the president who advises the auditor that the charges are proper and had been approved in advance.

There is a good working relationship between the top executive and the internal audit staff, and the president volunteers additional information. The vice-president attended a trade conference because many of the firm's customers were present. An accidental death in the vice-president's family had left his wife in a state of shock, and she could not be left alone.

The president persuaded his chief aid to have his wife accompany him on the trip so that the firm would be represented. In the opinion of the president, an intelligent decision had been made that was well within his authority. Whether or not the auditor agrees with the decision, it is obvious that the president had merely exercised proper authority in making an exception to a formal policy. There is certainly no evidence of dishonesty or intent to defraud.

Now let's consider a different case:

EXAMPLE 2: An auditor notes that materials and manpower have been used to construct a building on the personal property of the president of the firm. These costs have been absorbed and charged to company expense, upon the instructions and approval of the president. The auditor requests an explanation from the president who tells the auditor that the charges are proper and have been approved. PERIOD! Thousands of dollars of company funds were used for the personal gain of an executive. They had not benefited stockholders and also had not been recorded as additional salary. The auditor is faced with the appearance of fraud. What should the audit manager do?

The audit manager is obligated to bring the information to the Legal department, or the Chairman of the Audit Committee or the Chairman of the Board. If proper action is not taken, then the audit manager is faced with a difficult decision. The Certified Internal Auditor, at this point, will probably discuss the matter with the public accountants and determine their position on the matter. If they are aware of and condone the acts, they should be willing to discuss their reasoning. They may merely consider the payments for goods and services as an additional perq for the top executive and point out that many company presidents receive expensive perqs, such as yachts, airplanes, expensive apartments or other items of value that are never reported as additional salary for the executive.

In such a case the audit manager must then struggle with conscience and self respect and decide on a course of action. The mere fact that one person breaks the law, does not justify another in doing the same. Caught in a situation of this type, the Certified Internal Auditor who wants to abide by the Code of Ethics, should resign the position and seek employment elsewhere.

NOTE: *An audit manager would be unwise to remain with a company under the above described conditions.* Effectiveness as an internal audit manager has been lost through the knowledge of the fraud perpetrated by the president. In future audits, the manager would be haunted by the knowledge of the abuse and could not, in good conscience, take action against an errant employee who had pilfered a few dollars from the till. *The audit department's relationship with the top executive would be strained, and the auditor would be reluctant to bring matters to that level of attention.* The manager should best retain self-respect by changing jobs at the earliest opportunity. There is a brief reference to this type of dilemma in the Certified Internal Auditor's Code Of Ethics which appears as an appendix to this book.

HOW INTERNAL AUDITING DIFFERS FROM EXTERNAL AUDITING

Though the techniques of examination and verification used by both the internal and external auditors are almost identical, there is a basic distinction in approach and objective. The internal auditor starts with original transactions and examines, verifies and appraises procedures, policies, controls and employee job performances. The internal auditor assumes that if all these factors are accomplished satisfactorily, the end result will be accurate operating statements. But the Certified Public Accountant (CPA) starts by verifying the end results and works backward by testing controls and examining transactions until satisfied that the results have been fairly and accurately stated.

As an example of the difference in approach, let's look at a cash audit. The CPA is concerned with the following:

1. Verifying that all cash accounts are accurately reported.
2. Establishing that procedures provide for proper authorization, that all

exceptions are properly approved and that all entries have proper explanations and approval.

3. Determining that internal controls are adequate to insure proper handling and reporting of cash transactions and that adequate safeguards exist against fraud and error.

The internal auditor approaches a cash audit from an in-house viewpoint. Cash is one result of sales activities and is itself a commodity. The audit takes the entire sphere of activities into consideration. The internal auditor examines all the elements that are reviewed by the CPA, and in addition determines the following:

1. Cash is received for all sales transactions, and is properly handled, safeguarded and promptly deposited. Where possible, incoming checks are mailed directly to a lock box at the bank.
2. Cash is moved promptly to reduce holding excess funds and to use those funds to produce revenue or reduce costs.
3. Cash is paid out in an efficient manner that levels employee work loads, takes advantage of cash discounts (when they are greater than the interest that could be earned by using funds), and assures that all payments are proper.

HOW TO COORDINATE INTERNAL AUDITING WITH EXTERNAL AUDITING

An important phase of internal auditing is the relationship of the work to that of the external auditor. The engagement of a CPA firm requires that they be free to examine any phase of a client's financial operations. It is, therefore, understood that any agreed upon division of work between the internal and external auditor is subject to the whim of the external auditor. The CPA may, without offering an explanation, decide to cover an area that was originally assigned to the internal auditor. **KEY POINT:** *Because of this proviso, the CPA and the internal auditor should each have their separate audit schedules.*

With proper coordination, each group supplements the other and benefits from the work of the other. The CPA must recognize the value and validity of the internal auditing work, and the internal auditor should arrange his or her schedule around the planned visits of the public accounting firm. **TIP:** *By working with each other, maximum coverage can be obtained, and duplication of routine auditing work can be minimized.*

PEER REVIEW

A peer review is an excellent tool for keeping the internal audit staff up-to-date on new auditing approaches and new areas for audit examinations. Every internal audit operation should be periodically reviewed by objective outside experts, to determine that the staff is efficiently performing audit reviews and that it is using appropriate audit programs. Such reviews not only examine what the audit accomplishes, but also what else should be done.

The Optimum Timing for Peer Reviews

Peer reviews are usually sought by the following people:

1. New internal audit managers who want an evaluation of their staff's expertise and work methods.
2. The Chairman of the Audit Committee for the Board of Directors. The public accounting firms employed by the corporation are usually engaged to conduct these reviews. This might not produce the best results, unless the public accounting firm utilizes specialists who have had years of experience in managing an internal audit staff.
3. Internal auditing experts. After a newly formed internal audit staff has been operating for a year or two, a peer review conducted by an internal auditing expert can materially assist in preparing appropriate audit manuals and in developing efficient audit techniques. In such situations, yearly reviews by the same expert might be the best approach. This enables the advisor to measure progress while reducing the time required to appraise the audit operation. But once a staff has settled down into a successful routine, peer reviews should be performed at three to five year intervals and by a different expert each time. This variety of reviewers will bring new ideas and approaches to the attention of the Director of Internal Audits.

What Should Be Reviewed?

Peer reviews can consist of the following:

1. Limited areas of examination, such as audit programs or audit schedules in which the review is conducted in the home office.
2. The entire audit activity, with the examiner visiting audit staffs as they perform their routine reviews. In such cases the examiner is usually present during the start of an audit, may visit for a day or two in the middle

of the audit, and then will return several days before completion to review work papers, the audit windup meetings and report writing techniques.

Using Questionnaires

Another approach uses questionnaires, which are sent to employees who were audited for their comments and their appraisal of audit personnel and the techniques used. This approach also uses questionnaires or interviews to learn the views and attitudes of the audit staff members. Reviewers then base their findings on an analysis of this subjective information.

Some audit managers use a modified form of the questionnaire approach to conduct their own "peer reviews." They send questionnaires to department heads and supervisors to solicit their comments on the professionalism and approach of auditors who participated in recent reviews. **TIP:** *This information can be very useful in evaluating the audit staff and the audit program.*

Chapter 2

Explicit and Implicit Responsibilities of Internal Auditors

Since internal auditing is a management advisory service, it has no line authority or responsibility. Normally authority must go hand in hand with responsibility if anything is to be accomplished, but such is not the case in the internal auditing activity. The manager of an internal auditing staff has management, or line, authority over all the members of the audit staff but no authority outside of the audit department. The manager of internal auditing does, however, have a great many responsibilities, many of which are spelled out in top management statements of policy covering the internal auditing activity. Additional responsibilities, implicit in the audit function, are rarely spelled out in a policy statement. If mentioned at all, they are couched in general terms such as, "whatever is necessary." This chapter will cover both explicit and implicit responsibilities of the internal auditing function.

OBJECTIVES OF AN INTERNAL AUDITING FUNCTION

To start an internal audit operation it is necessary to establish the objectives of the internal auditing department. The following is a sample of a statement of objectives:

Statement of Objectives

The Internal Audit Department is responsible for reviewing all books, records, operations and activities of the XYZ Corporation. It is their responsibility to determine that all company policies and procedures are being followed and to report deviations to management.

Auditors will determine that company personnel obey all laws, both in word and intent. The auditors will review all company operations and employee performances to determine that established procedures are being followed and operations are performed promptly and efficiently. The auditors are responsible for determining that all reports are legitimate, accurate and timely.

Auditors shall evaluate and appraise the organization's system of internal controls to insure that all information is properly, promptly and accurately processed. The audit group will perform special studies as requested by management and, upon the behest of an incoming manager, will conduct an audit of the department to verify that everything was in order up to the time of the change in management.

The Director of Internal Auditing will report to the Executive Committee and/or to the Board of Directors on any matters of significance that require that level of attention.

EXPLICIT RESPONSIBILITIES

At some point in the life history of an internal audit department, a decision is made as to where the audit staff fits into the company's organization chart. As time passes, the audit function is reevaluated and the position on the chart may become questionable because the audit scope may have been extended by executive fiat, without any written directives. To avoid confusion and potential controversy, management should issue a formal statement of policy outlining the audit function.

Need for a Formal Statement of Policy

An organization's formal policy statement concerning the internal auditing function spells out the explicit responsibilities of the staff. Those companies that do not issue formal statements limit the responsibility of the audit staff to assigned projects. Each audit assignment carries with it the authority to perform customary, routine work necessary for the review.

KEY POINT: *On each assignment, the responsibility for accomplishing the audit implicitly carries with it the authority to review and evaluate the records and procedures used in the department being audited.* When a manager questions the right of an auditor to examine certain records or activities, the matter is referred to top management. At that point the top executive must make a decision to either support the internal auditor or to ask the auditor to withdraw. If the top executive supports the internal auditor, from that moment on the audit staff has been given explicit responsibility and the related authority over a particular record or activity. The question originally raised, as well as the top executive's decision, may become generally known throughout upper management, but that type of question will probably be raised again.

To eliminate the need for making individual decisions, top management issues a formal statement of policy to clear the air and establish the guidelines for the internal auditing function. Such policies usually state that the Internal Auditing Department is responsible for reviewing all company operations and records. It means that the internal auditor can review, appraise, investigate or challenge all records, policies, operations or activities that are performed by company employees.

Sometimes, stated responsibilities are limited to accounting and financial activities within the organization. In such companies the auditor's responsibilities are limited to financial and accounting records, systems, procedures, policies and personnel. The auditor has no responsibility or authority to review other operations.

When top management decides to request the audit staff to review a specific operational department or activity considered outside of the financial sphere, it requires special handling. If such a request is accepted, a formal meeting ensues between the top executive requesting the audit and the department head of the operation to be reviewed. The Manager of Internal Auditing is often asked to attend the meeting. The department head is requested to give full cooperation to the audit staff and is reminded that the staff conducts the review for the benefit of the department. The request is always accepted and acted upon.

The department head calls a meeting of supervisors and tells them to cooperate with the auditors. Meetings are then held in which all personnel are appraised of the coming review and are asked to cooperate.

These special requests effectively extend auditing responsibility beyond the financial field, even though the first such ventures are considered as exceptions. After a few successful reviews of nonfinancial activities, the acknowledged scope of the internal auditing function is expanded.

A formal statement of policy spells out the exact responsibilities of the Internal Auditing Department. It may state that the department is only responsible for reviewing, appraising and reporting on all accounting and financial records, systems and controls. Or it may assign a much wider area of responsibility, and eliminate the need for pre-audit executive meetings. **KEY POINT:** *Much depends upon the caliber and experience of the audit staff, and the confidence of top management in the internal auditing function.*

What Policy Statements Often Omit

Policy statements often fail to explicitly mention the subject of special assignments. The formal statement may cover the subject with broad language, but it may not spell out specifics. Policy statements rarely mention internal auditing's responsibility in regard to the following:

1. Audit duties relative to the investment portfolio.
2. Reviewing operations in a joint venture or in another company in which a substantial investment has been made.
3. Potential buy-outs or acquisitions.
4. International operations.
5. Subsidiary companies.

The above areas are usually considered as special audits to be assigned to the staff as the occasion arises. Special assignments are top management's way of taking advantage of the internal auditor's specialized knowledge of the business.

In addition to the situations in the above list, the audit department may be asked to study specific policies or procedures or interdepartmental relations and organizations. These requests arise from audit recommendations, and many times they result in actual money savings to the company. This contrasts with auditing's protective reviews, which carry an expense without showing demonstrable results.

Two Special Areas

There are two other related areas that require mentioning: (1) freedom of access and movement, and (2) the treatment of confidential information. These will be discussed in the next chapter, but there are associated responsibilities that need to be pointed out here.

1. *A manager of internal auditing must keep in mind that the authority of unlimited access carries with it the responsibility for any improper use of information examined by staff members.* If information is improperly used or distributed, top management may well reconsider the policy that permits unlimited access to the internal auditing department. With this in mind, the manager must be careful in authorizing any member of the audit staff to look at classified information. If such examination is considered absolutely necessary, it should be done by a top supervisor.
2. *Audit managers may be designated as custodians of important documents that are considered secrets of the organization.* This vital, confidential information should be retained in an envelope or folder that can be sealed so that any tampering with the outer shell of the container will become immediately apparent. The external wrappings should be marked or initialed in some manner so that the custodian will notice any attempt to gain entry.

If documents must be moved, the assistance of another top executive should be enlisted to verify the existence and movement of the documents. The Secretary, the Treasurer, the Chief Financial officer or the head of security should be willing to act as a witness to this important movement. A certification stating the date, time, document contents, locations from which and to which the documents are moved, and the names and job titles of all parties who witnessed the transfer should be prepared and signed by all parties witnessing the transfer.

SCOPE OF INTERNAL AUDIT ACTIVITIES

An internal audit department must spell out its statement of purpose. Why does it exist, what does it hope to accomplish? What are its responsibilities? An answer could lie anywhere between the following two statements.

> The internal audit function, operating within the Comptrollers Department, is responsible for making such test checks and verifications as required or requested by the corporation's public accounting firm.

or

> The internal audit function will assist management in improving operating efficiency and strengthening internal controls. Auditors will determine the accuracy and reliability of data furnished to management and will supplement the work of the public accountants and coordinate effort with that group.
>
> Auditors will report deficiencies noted during their reviews, and follow up with appropriate management to insure that necessary corrective actions are taken.
>
> Auditors will verify company assets and determine that they are properly safeguarded. In the event of improper use or loss of company assets, auditors will see that the situation is corrected and take steps to recover any losses and report those responsible.
>
> Auditors will check for compliance with company policies and procedures as well as for compliance with public laws and regulatory commission regulations. Auditors will cooperate with outside law enforcement agencies as required to protect corporate assets.
>
> Auditors will continually review data processing programs as they are written and will be responsible for determining that adequate security is built into the systems. Auditors will make special studies at the request of executives or directors of the corporation.

The second stated scope of responsibilities includes almost all of an internal audit staff's expertise. **REMEMBER:** *Internal auditors normally do not perform operational activities, and they have no line authority.* They must be free to make recommendations at any level but line management is responsible for implemented changes. Management must agree and accept responsibility for all audit suggestions used.

KEY POINT: *This limitation on the auditor's authority is important because the operation, when reviewed later, could disclose an audit deficiency caused by a decision which auditing had forced on line management.*

In unusual circumstances—when management at a particular operation is discovered to be guilty of fraud and must be immediately replaced, for example—an internal auditor might assume responsibility and operate as line management *until a replacement is appointed and installed.* Such cases are rare, but they do occur.

FORMAL STATEMENT OF POLICY

The best starting point for any internal auditing operation is a formal statement by top management outlining the organization's policy regarding the internal auditing function. The audit staff may start off as a small group operating in the financial department under a controller's bulletin which states its functions and responsibilities. As the function takes hold, the scope of auditing operations may expand until the staff is serving all the company's needs. At this point the formal statement, which the Chairman of the Board issues to the executive staff, might read as follows:

> *To Executive Staff For Dissemination To All Personnel*
> Subject: *INTERNAL AUDITING*
>
> THE Internal Audit Department of XYZ Corporation has been an important element of our total management control system for a number of years. Recently we updated our policy statement on Internal Auditing and I believe it appropriate for each of you to have a copy so that you will be familiar with it.
>
> AS the policy statement indicates, the basic purpose of the Internal Auditing Department is to provide objective and professional evaluations of the corporation's activities.
>
> TO accomplish this, the auditors review our operating controls to insure that our policies and procedures are being followed in line with our stated objectives.
>
> EACH of you should view an internal audit review as an opportunity to improve the overall effectiveness and efficiency of your area of responsibility. Our auditors review all departments and operations and, accordingly, can be the instrument for an exchange of good operating techniques between different companies or locations.

IT is also of vital importance that all operating personnel be aware of and follow all laws and regulations that pertain to our operations, and this fact only reinforces our opinion that a strong Internal Auditing Department is a necessity.

THANK you for your continued cooperation and support for our internal auditing activities.

The above letter contains an attachment of the formal corporate statement of policy as it relates to the internal auditing activity. The formal statement reads as follows:

XYZ CORPORATION FORMAL CORPORATE POLICY STATEMENT

Subject: *INTERNAL AUDITING*

Objective:

THE objective of this policy is to state the corporate audit policy and set forth certain guidelines and responsibilities with respect thereto.

Policy:

THE Internal Auditing Department's primary purpose is to provide objective and professional evaluations of company activities to assist management in controlling areas of responsibilities and to ensure that company policies and procedures are followed in line with stated objectives.

Scope:

IN order to accomplish their objective, the scope of internal audit activities is necessarily broad and includes reviews of accounting, administrative and operational controls. The audit scope changes as the business needs of management and the company change. Internal auditor's functions are staff and advisory and they have no authority or responsibility over the activities they audit; these remain with line management.

SO that the Internal Auditing Department can fulfill its responsibilities, they have full, free and unrestricted access to all company activities, personnel, records and property. The complete cooperation of company personnel ensures that the Internal Auditing Department can fulfill its responsibilities in an effective and efficient manner.

THE scope of responsibilities of the Corporate Internal Auditing Department extends to XYZ's worldwide operations.

Reporting Responsibilities

THE Director of Internal Auditing reports to the Chief Financial Officer. However, the Director of Internal Auditing has the responsibility to report matters that he or she believes are not satisfactorily resolved to the President, the Chairman of the Audit Committee, and, if he or she believes it necessary, to the Chairman of the Board and/or the full Board.

WHERE an international subsidiary has its own internal auditing department or function, it reports to the designated financial officer of that company, who has a functional responsibility to the Corporate Comptroller. Accordingly, copies of internal audit reports are sent to the Corporate Comptroller and/or Director of Internal Auditing, as instructed.

Operations of the Internal Auditing Department

THE Director of Internal Auditing develops a comprehensive audit plan to ensure that internal controls in the company are reviewed at appropriate intervals, and organizes the department to fulfill the plan.

RESULTS of examinations made by internal auditors and their recommendations or suggestions are promptly reported to appropriate management personnel who have the authority to provide management's comments and initiate corrective action. Management is responsible for appropriate action in respect to each recommendation included in the report.

GROUP controllers, or their approved designees, have the responsibility for ensuring that corrective action is taken on a timely basis on all reported audit recommendations. This management employee submits a written follow-up report of action planned or completed to the Director of Internal Auditing within sixty days of the audit report. If a plan for action is reported, a second follow-up report is made promptly upon completion of the plan.

ANY actions or plans to correct reported deficiencies are evaluated by the Internal Auditing Department. If the plan or action is considered unsatisfactory by Internal Auditing, the Corporate Comptroller directs that further action be taken to achieve satisfactory resolution.

THE Chief Financial Officer and the Corporate Comptroller are immediately informed of all audit findings deemed to be materially significant, all defalcations, any infractions concerning the internal security of company formation or violations of the Corporate Code of Ethics. Additionally, a summary of significant audit findings and audit activities, completed each month, is submitted by the Director of Internal Auditing to the Chief Financial Officer for distribution to the President, the Chairman of the Board and any others concerned.

In summary, the explicit responsibilities enumerated in statements of formal policy dictate that internal auditors perform the following:

1. Review all company records, reports and activities of the department or operation under review.
2. Review all policy statements and procedure bulletins relating to the subject being audited.
3. Verify that company employees, in the audited activity, perform their tasks honestly, correctly and efficiently, and that they are present and working at their assigned station as reported.
4. Report deficiencies to the proper level of management.
5. Perform special assignments as requested by management.

Some statements include many other specific responsibilities, and all policy statements that outline the scope of the internal auditing function are unique to the particular organizations that issue them. Some are brief and cover the subject in broad general terms, while others outline minute detail. The statements reflect management's experience with internal auditing activities and the reaction of the organization's employees to internal audits.

Most statements leave a great deal unsaid, assuming that certain internal audit activities are so well understood that they need not be mentioned. These are the implicit responsibilities that attach to any internal audit review.

IMPLICIT RESPONSIBILITIES

In addition to the explicitly stated responsibilities of the internal auditing department there are implicit responsibilities that are generally acknowledged as a part of the internal auditor's job. The internal auditor is looked upon as an extension of top management by all of the company's employees. Since internal audits cover all levels of management, and audit reports are circulated at the top level, the auditor is generally acknowledged to have the authority to act in management's behalf.

Auditors are not ordinarily authorized to make operating changes or management decisions. However, there are times when an internal auditor must take over an operation and act as a line manager. Such instances occur when a manager is suddenly incapacitated and an internal auditor is asked to run an operation until a new manager can be assigned. In such cases, the internal auditor usually issues instructions through supervisors or lead employees and avoids the appearance of having taken over as an operating manager. If an audit discloses that the manager of a field operation is dishonest, the internal auditor may be the only management representative available to run the operation temporarily.

Internal auditors have the implicit responsibility to appraise any information or company activity for propriety and legality. **NOTE:** *An auditor who notes an employee committing an illegal or dishonest act is obligated to make a full report of the matter and to take action to forestall, correct or resolve the action.* The implicit obligation to act when dishonesty or illegality is noted does not stop at company employees. Any threat, illegality or theft involving company property or operations, no matter the source, implicitly gives the auditor responsibility for taking preventive or corrective action.

The Manager of Internal Auditing is ultimately responsible for the actions of any auditor. **NOTE:** *Staff members act as agents of the manager when they take action based on implicit responsibilities.*

Implicit responsibilities of internal auditors are similar to those of any supervisor or manager, and they extend to all company operations, locations and activities. These implicit responsibilities include the following:

1. Bring to proper management attention any gross injustice in pay scale or wage payments made to an individual or group of employees or outside contractors.

2. Bring to management's attention ideas or suggestions of employees that seem to warrant management consideration, even if they had already been rejected by immediate supervisors.
3. Determine that errors are corrected.
4. See that measures are taken to prevent theft or dishonesty.
5. Determine that assets and confidential records are protected.
6. Determine that company personnel are adequately protected while on company premises.
7. Cooperate with authorized public officials when approved by management.
8. Determine that employees adhere to public laws and to the regulations of authorized public agencies.

These tasks sometimes present a problem to the internal auditor who must use caution and restraint in exercising these implicit responsibilities. **KEY POINT:** *When any doubt exists as to the proper course of action, the auditor must discuss the matter with the supervisor before an act is irrevocable. This admonition applies particularly in the protection and dishonesty area, for appearances can be misleading and auditors must be careful in making accusations.*

The subject of audit reports and follow-up are sometimes ignored in formal policy statements. The writing of an audit report is implicit in the internal audit activity, but follow-up work may or may not be an audit responsibility. Some companies rely on line management to make necessary corrections without being prodded by auditors.

REPORT OF AUDIT FINDINGS

Many statements of policy related to internal auditing spell out the procedure for handling audit reports. The statement may designate the employees responsible for following-up on reported deficiencies and sometimes even set a time limit for corrective action. Statements may also specify the job titles of recipients of audit reports. When the policy contains such information, the questions of addressing and circularizing audit reports and the follow-up on audit points are resolved. Where no formal policy decision is stated, the questions are considered individually, case by case.

When the audit work has been completed on an assignment, it then usually becomes the responsibility of the Internal Auditing Department to take timely action to ensure that deficiencies noted during the audit are brought to the attention of appropriate managers. The audit group uses the audit report and audit-related correspondence to discharge this responsibility.

Addressing the Report

There are some fine distinctions in addressing and circulating audit reports. When the audit is conducted in the same department that contains the audit staff, the potential problem of addressing the report is minimized. For example, if the audit department is organizationally a part of the Controller's department and a review is conducted of Accounts Payable, then the report can be addressed to the Controller. Even then it probably would be best to address the report to the supervisor of the section that had been audited. But when auditors step over department lines and into a different area, then the best addressee for an audit report can be up for grabs.

It is easy to suggest that internal audit reports should be addressed to the executive that has the responsibility and authority to correct deficiencies pointed out in the report. It is sometimes difficult to identify that executive, since many problems noted by auditors result from confusion in the organization or because certain activities are not clearly delineated as belonging to a specific department. In such cases the report must be addressed to a higher level of management, where a decision can be made.

In an operational audit of an advertising department, for example, the report should be addressed to the executive in charge of the advertising department, even though the auditing function may report to an executive in the financial department.

Some of the larger audit staffs work their way around the touchy question of who the addressee should be by having the audit report signed by an audit supervisor and addressed to the Manager of Internal Auditing. The Audit Manager then writes a covering letter addressed to all parties concerned, and attaches a copy of the report.

The recipients of the covering letter are listed in alphabetical order. This avoids upsetting some executives who might resent having others listed ahead of them. Some audit managers prefer to list first the top executives where authority is crystal clear and then list the remaining recipients in alphabetical order. The audit manager's covering letter spells out by job title the appropriate managers that are responsible for taking action on specific audit points.

It is a quirk of human nature that people who have not been recognized as decision makers will not make decisions or take action until they are formally requested to do so. If a report or letter is not addressed to them, they feel slighted and resentful. They assume they are to do nothing until the addressee of the report asks them for their opinion or action.

Since most internal audit reports contain a variety of items that may concern different operations or sections of a department, the problem of deciding on a single supervisor who can take action on all of the noted audit deficiencies is sometimes impossible. In such cases the report may best be addressed to the department head. If the report merely relates to a particular phase within a department, it should be addressed to that supervisor.

Distribution of Audit Reports

Audit management decides who is affected by the contents of the report and then circularizes the report to all concerned parties. The nature of an audit and the activity reviewed are of prime importance in deciding who should read the report; but the contents also play a major role in deciding leadership and responsibility of corrective action.

When an audit report is finalized, duplicate copies are prepared and a distribution list is compiled. The list appears on the audit manager's letter of transmittal so that all recipients know who else is receiving a copy of the report. **TIP:** *When an addressee notes a superior as the recipient of a copy, there is a strong likelihood that immediate action will be taken on the report.*

The full report, or excerpts from it, may be circulated within a department or operation by the line manager. Such action is common and does not usually require that the audit manager be informed as to the identity of all readers.

> **EXAMPLE:** An Advertising Department audit report is sent to the vice-president in charge of advertising. The executive may elect to circulate the report to the advertising manager, the advertising production manager and the administrative assistant. Any of these managers may elect to excerpt a specific audit point to be called to the attention of a specific employee or to an outside agency or supplier. The decisions prompting corrective action on deficiencies are made by the executives receiving the report.

Audit findings are normally circulated to all management personnel who have an interest in the activity studied or who have similar operations or problems that might be affected by resulting decisions. Internal audit reports are also sent to the public accounting firm, to the executive to whom the Manager of Internal Auditing reports, and possibly to the Executive Vice-President, the President, the Chairman of the Audit Committee, the Chairman of the Board or the full Board. Distribution to top executives and board members is dependent upon the nature and significance of the audit findings.

An internal audit manager may decide to exclude certain items from the final report that is printed for circulation. *These subjects, sometimes highly controversial, may be covered in a separate letter to the audit manager's superior.* This executive will then decide the distribution to be made of the letter containing controversial items.

The points may include the following:

1. Ignored and no further action taken,
2. Directed to specific executives, or
3. Excerpted from the audit manager's letter and distributed to interested executives.

The key question that decides the distribution of an internal audit report is, "How can management best be served?" The answer usually lies in a limited distribution to those employees who can benefit from reading the audit report and who are responsible for taking corrective actions.

Follow-Up on Reported Deficiencies

When an audit report lists deficiencies that should be corrected, the audit function is not discharged until corrections have been made.
KEY POINT: *Auditors are implicitly responsible for bringing such matters out in the open and for prompting management to take corrective action.* In some organizations it is fully understood that writing and circulating an audit report relieves the audit staff of any further responsibility.

Operating management is paid to run an efficient and effective department and will most assuredly correct any deficiencies that are brought to their attention. If proper corrective action is *not* taken, the internal auditors will discover the oversight during their next audit visit, which may begin at any time. If auditors find that an audit point has not been satisfactorily resolved, the next audit report emphasizes and explains the importance of the point and notes that it had been reported previously and corrective measures agreed upon but that no action was taken. When such reports reach top management, the derelict managers must defend or explain their lack of action.

Some companies formally state that the Internal Auditing Manager is responsible for following-up on all reported deficiencies. The manager is assigned the responsibility for deciding whether adequate corrective measures have been taken. **REMEMBER:** *Though the audit manager has the responsibility for both prodding line management into taking action and for evaluating the changes that they institute, the audit manager does not have the authority to personally make any changes.* Instead of any line authority, the audit manager is given the responsibility to notify top executives that significant deficiencies have *not* been corrected. Formal statements of internal auditing responsibility sometimes spell out the time interval permitted between the issuance of an audit report and appropriate corrective action. The audit manager is frequently required to report to top executives if a deficiency is not corrected within a specified period of time.

If an audit-noted deficiency requires a period of time to correct, a plan for correction might be accepted as appropriate. The Audit Manager monitors the situation until agreed changes are in place.

When line management states in writing that a particular deficiency has been corrected, the audit department accepts the statement and is relieved of further responsibility. Evidence of correction may be a letter, policy statement or a directive issued by appropriate management that outlines the corrective action or states a revision or addition to existing policies or procedures. Should the next audit visit disclose that corrective action had not been taken as reported, the manager who wrote the erroneous letter may find it hard to explain. **KEY POINT:** *Some reported deficiencies may be of such importance that the audit manager may schedule a revisit to an operation as a follow-up to learn whether actions promised, or reported as in place, have actually been accomplished.* Operational management is aware that the audit staff may return at any time, without advance notice, and are therefore very careful in reporting their corrective actions or plans.

Too frequently, however, the importance of an audit point may be lost in the language and planned corrective changes might be set aside in the confusion of everyday business events.

Chapter 3

Organizing an Internal Auditing Department

The organization of an internal auditing staff depends upon these variables: the size of the enterprise, the geographic distribution of operations, the budget allocated to internal auditing, and the responsibilities assigned to the internal audit staff.

This book describes all of the usual, and many of the unusual, internal audit activities that are required to handle assigned responsibilities. An audit staff carves out its unique niche in an organization. This placement is determined by the intelligence, application and initiative of the internal audit staff members and their supervisors and the contribution of the function to the success of the enterprise. **NOTE:** *The internal auditing function is assigned a position according to what is expected of it. The broader the internal auditing scope, the higher the position on the chart.*

HOW TO SELECT AND ORGANIZE YOUR STAFF

When the function of internal auditing is first introduced into an organization, it begins on a trial basis with a minimum staff. An internal auditing manager is selected to organize the function and perform the audit reviews. The selection of personnel is most important, for these individuals must be considerate, courteous and tactful in order to gain respect and inspire confidence. In addition to their knowledge and skills in internal auditing techniques, they must have self-assurance and poise in order to interact with managers who have much experience and hold important positions. Staff members must have a good command of the language and be able to communicate effectively so that the tangible product of their work, their audit findings, will be accepted.

As responsibility grows, so does the size of the audit staff. The Audit Manager gradually limits his or her field time to reviewing the audit work, participating in final audit reviews and spearheading required follow-up action on audit-noted deficiencies.

In larger staffs, the title of Audit Manager may change to that of Director of Internal Auditing. When the Director title is assumed, the manager is far removed from the repetitious, bleary-eyed tasks of routine internal auditing. Managers of specialized audit activities are appointed to assume segments of responsibility, and most of the time of the Director of Internal Auditing is spent attending meetings and handling the public relation and administrative duties of the position.

Your Company's Operating Credo

The real starting point for determining the organization of an Internal Auditing Department is the company's Statement of Purpose, or an Operating Credo that states the organization's approach to its customers and its business.

> We are in business to serve our customers, our employees and the general public by providing high quality products at fair prices.
>
> We are the leaders in our field in innovations and providing services.
>
> We will not be undersold.
>
> Customer satisfaction is guaranteed.
>
> Quality is our number one consideration.

Each of the above affects the organization and operations of the business, which are designed to accomplish the stated objective. These slogans, or public relation statements, play an important role in the organization and day-to-day running of a business and, by their very nature, spell out many important policy decisions.

KEY POINT: *These company goals affect internal auditing activities, and the audit staff becomes an important aide in management's efforts to achieve stated goals.*

SCOPE OF INTERNAL AUDIT ACTIVITIES

An internal audit department must decide its scope of operations and its purpose. Why does the department exist and what is it expected to accomplish? The scope of the internal audit function determines the size and organization of the staff. Two extremes in audit staff responsibilities are stated below, most internal audit scopes lie somewhere between these statements:

1. The Internal Auditing Department reviews financial records and procedures and makes such verifications as requested by the accounting firm that certifies our financial statements.

or

2. The Internal Auditing Department assists management in improving operating efficiency, strengthening internal controls and performing special studies as required by management. They check for compliance with company policies and procedures as well as compliance with public laws and regulations. They report to management on significant items noted during their reviews, and are responsible for insuring that appropriate corrective action is taken.

   The Internal Auditing Department coordinates with the public accountants in testing and verifying information used in the published financial statements and determine the accuracy, reliability and appropriateness of information furnished to management. They insure that adequate internal controls are in effect over all operations and activities.

   The Internal Auditing Department verifies that company assets are properly reported, used and safeguarded. In the event of loss, the auditors supervise recovery actions as well as punitive and corrective measures. They cooperate with outside public agencies as required to protect company assets, personnel and reputation.

The second stated scope of internal auditing responsibilities includes almost all of an internal audit staff's expertise. Most internal auditing functions lie somewhere between these two extremes.

KEY POINT: *An internal auditor's main concern is to learn what actually and factually occurred, so that the reliability and accuracy of records and reports can be established.*

Even if someone vouches for an act or record, the statement does not necessarily establish it as a fact. An auditor seeks analytic or historic confirmation, which usually comes from a study of comparative numbers. Perhaps that is the reason that auditing falls naturally into the financial department of business organizations. Auditors recognize the absolute nature of numbers, can evaluate their reliability and meaning and can translate their analysis into projections of potential problems or into problem-solving possibilities.

Both of the above stated scopes assign financial responsibilities to the internal audit activity, but the organization of the staff set up to accomplish the first scope will be materially different from the staff assigned to accomplish the second statement. And the position of the Internal Auditing Department on the company's organization chart will reflect the significance of assigned responsibilities.

INTERNAL AUDITING'S PLACE ON THE ORGANIZATION CHART

The greater the responsibilities and expectations, the higher the place on the organization chart. It is more important, though, that the contribution of the internal audit function be recognized and supported. *The spot on the chart is not as important as the top executive's active support of the audit group.*

The function usually shows up somewhere in the financial area of the organization chart. Sometimes it appears in the administrative area at the top level, with the Director of Internal Auditing designated as a Vice-President and reporting to the President of the company. Or the Director of Internal Auditing may show up as reporting to the Chief Financial Officer who reports to the President.

Following are several sample organization charts, showing the different placements of the internal auditing function.

XYZ CORPORATION'S ORGANIZATION CHART

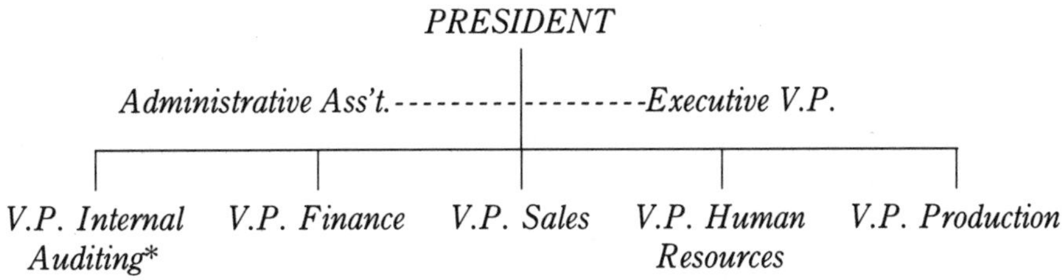

* On this chart the head of Internal Auditing holds the title of Vice-President and reports directly to the President of the company. The position is on a par with the Financial Vice-President.

If the internal auditing function were assigned to the financial department, the following chart would probably apply:

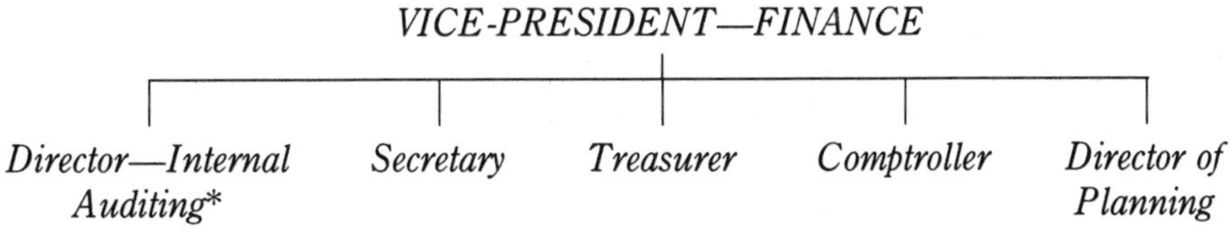

* On this chart Internal Auditing reports to the Vice-President of Finance and is headed by someone with the title of Director.

If the internal auditing function were assigned to a lower level of management it would probably fall under the Corporate Comptroller.

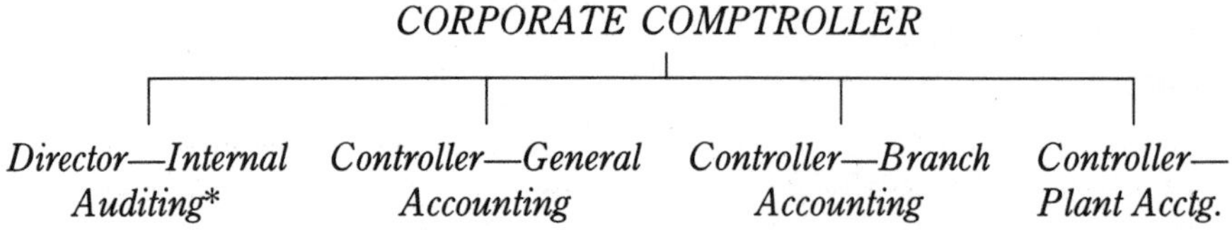

* In this position the top Internal Auditor would hold the title of Manager or Director and would report to the Corporate Comptroller.

An Internal Audit Department might report to the Controller of General Accounting, and this arrangement would appear as follows:

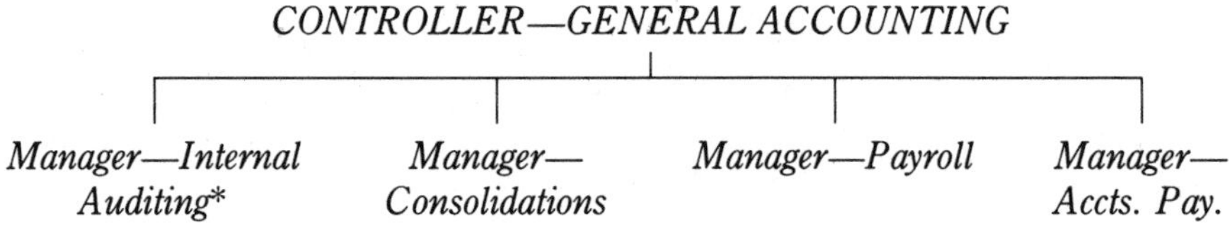

* On this chart the head of the Internal Auditing Department holds the title of Manager, and the audit function is usually limited to financial audits.

The above charts, reading from bottom to top, show a normal progression of an internal auditing function, starting as a small operation in the General Accounting Department and reporting to the Controller of that department. As the department increases its contribution to the success of the company, it gains recognition and stature and moves up the company's organization chart until the function reports to the President of the company.

ORGANIZATION CHART OF AN INTERNAL AUDITING DEPARTMENT

Some audit staffs have a simple organization, a Manager of the Internal Auditing Department together with a few lead auditors. The department is assigned some secretarial and clerical help.

The chart showing the department's organization looks like this:

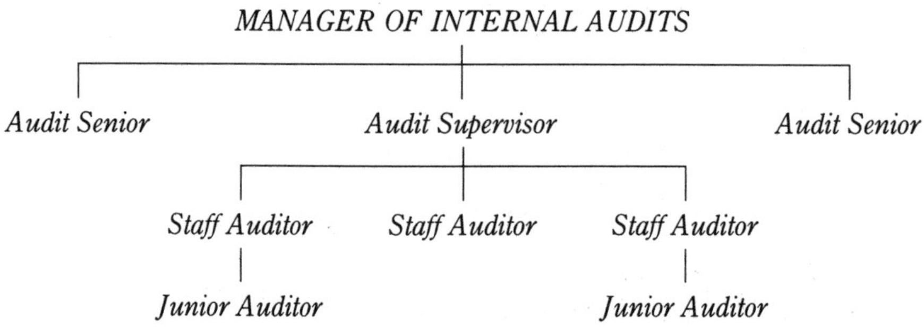

Then there is the large audit staff, operating in a multinational corporation with substantial responsibilities. This function requires a large, well-managed audit staff, which is represented in the Internal Auditing Department's organization chart that follows:

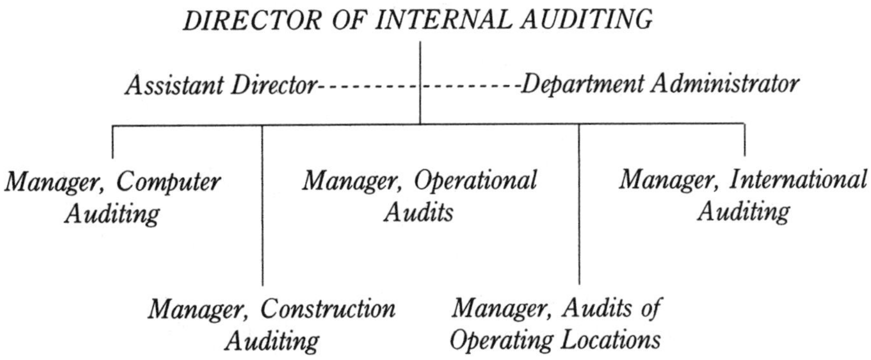

In the above chart the audit supervisors, audit seniors, staff auditors, audit juniors and audit trainees are not listed, though there is an abundance of these positions in the department.

The organization of an audit department, like any other department, must be regularly evaluated to ensure that it meets current needs. *Audit department management should periodically review their own operations with the same objectivity, if possible, with which they study other departments.* Many staffs become top heavy because of the desire to retain good people in the department who deserve recognition and require promotions to retain their enthusiasm. Sometimes this leads to a staff of many managers and supervisors and relatively few staff and junior auditors.

The result of this type of organization is that many routine audit procedures must be performed by high-priced and over-qualified personnel. Internal audit staffs, who provide their company's future executive pool, can use this potential for promotion to help keep the working auditors on the staff and on their toes.

JOB CLASSIFICATIONS FOR HIRING YOUR STAFF

Entry-level positions in the internal auditing profession may be called trainees, audit trainees or junior auditors depending on the organization of the internal audit staff. After rising above the entry level, there is some uniformity in classifying staff positions. Many staffs use the following classifications:

Trainees. Trainees hold entry-level position requiring no previous audit training. These individuals are usually brought into an audit staff on a *temporary* basis.

Trainees are frequently students who work on the staff during special work periods agreed to between the school, the audit staff and the student. Some trainees are selected from within an organization and given an opportunity to work with the audit staff.

KEY POINT: *All audit work performed by trainees must be carefully checked by the auditors who are assigned to supervise their training.*

Though exposed to staff operating philosophy, allowed to work in many areas of audit activity, and taught a variety of audit techniques, *they are NOT permitted to make auditing decisions.*

Junior Auditors. Junior auditors are sometimes called associate auditors and are at an entry-level position. They usually have completed some accounting and auditing classes and have earned their college degrees. Depending on ability, experience and education, the period that an auditor can expect to remain at the junior level varies from three to twelve months.

Junior auditors perform much of the routine work of the audit staff. They prepare schedules and audit forms, code and file work papers, add up and recheck columns of figures, count inventories and perform reconciliations, and are given an opportunity to work in most of the normal audit areas.

Staff Auditors. Staff auditors are the backbone of the internal auditing department. These auditors come from various sources, such as promotions from junior positions, hiring as graduates with advanced degrees, or by recruitment with good potential and previous auditing experience.

The work of new staff auditors is very carefully checked until audit management gains confidence in their reliability and auditing knowledge. They are then given full reign to examine, verify and appraise records, reports, systems and procedures as required by the audit assignments. They are trusted to perform important audit work, such as bank reconciliations, accounts receivable verifications and cash fund counts and reconciliations. Their work is frequently test-checked by audit supervisors to insure that they fully understand the audit phase they have been assigned to review. **KEEP IN MIND:** *Many auditors are content to remain at this staff level during their business career, possibly because of the minimum management responsibility attached to the job.*

Senior Auditors. Senior auditors are a step above the staff auditor level. They perform much of the supervisory work required on an audit assignment. Some staffs do not have specific auditors classified as seniors, but choose to appoint a staff auditor member of an assigned group to act as the audit senior on a specific job. They sometimes alternate the senior designation to give staff auditors some supervisory experience.

The audit senior allocates all of the audit work among all members of the crew. The senior reviews all work performed by other staff members and acts as liaison between the auditors and the home office. All audit questions and all problems encountered are brought to the senior's attention as the focal point for evaluating data and selecting items of importance to be covered in the audit report.

Audit Supervisors. Audit supervisors are usually given responsibility over several audit teams. Supervisors appoint an in-charge senior for each assignment, and they frequently accompany the staff to introduce the auditors to location management at the start of each job. The supervisor may decide to perform specific audit steps or may personally direct selected phases of the audit program in which the designated senior lacks experience. The supervisor returns near the close of the audit to review the audit work and to decide the points to be included in the final audit report.

Supervisors are generally responsible for the on-the-job training of staff assigned to them. They are also expected to lead some of the audit training sessions that are periodically presented to staff members. Audit supervisors rate performances of auditors assigned to them and are active members of the audit management team. They are good candidates for advancement up the audit management ladder.

Audit Managers. Audit managers head up specific sections of the larger audit staffs. They supervise all staff assigned to perform specialized audits, such as EDP, Construction, Operational Auditing or International Auditing. They make all decisions for their sections and report to the Director of Internal Auditing.

Assistant Directors or Managers. Assistant directors or managers act as the head of the department in the absence of the director or manager. Frequently the assistant acts as the person in charge of all auditing activities, while the titled head attends to administrative and interdepartmental duties. The assistant must be capable of acting in the absence of the director, but all such acts are subject to approval by the head of the audit department.

Director or Manager of Internal Auditing. The director or manager is the top company position in the Internal Auditing Department. This individual directs all internal auditing activities in the company and decides who and what to audit and when to do it. The director works closely with top management and all department heads. The extent of internal auditing activities is determined by the assigned scope and the place in the company organization chart.

To provide an example of the type of information that relates to the position of Director of Internal Auditing, a job description of the position, as drawn up by the mythical XYZ Corporation, is presented later in this chapter. This descriptive information is normally filed in the Personnel Department and is used when a new Director is being sought.

HOW TO SELECT A NEW INTERNAL AUDIT MANAGER

When the director, or manager, of an existing audit staff steps out of the position, there are usually many prospective replacements among the remaining audit supervisors. If one of the audit staff management members is considered acceptable, the change is made and the auditing activity proceeds as before.

Internal audit managers, for replacements or to head up newly created departments, frequently are drawn from among the managers of the CPA firm that audits the company's records. Since much of the internal audit work is identical with that of the external auditor, this is a logical choice.

Internal audit managers may also be located through want ads in financial papers and professional publications. Many local chapters of the Institute of Internal Auditing print help-wanted sections in their monthly letters to members.

After the scope of a newly conceived Internal Auditing activity has been agreed upon by top management, a manager for the department must be selected. The same executive search methods and sources are used as described above.

Finding an experienced manager can materially reduce the time frame required to start the actual internal auditing work of the department. Many organizational and procedural problems can be anticipated and avoided, but any new internal auditing operation will encounter resistance in an establishment because of the very nature of its scope. **REMEMBER:** *Internal auditors question any and all transactions and demand explanations of all activities.* This may antagonize any employee who has previously operated without being questioned and is accustomed to having his or her word or signature accepted at face value. **KEEP IN MIND:** *Even a completely honest and competent employee resents having his or her actions reviewed or questioned.*

It takes time before an internal audit staff is accepted as a part of, and as beneficial to, a company. This manual provides information which should enable auditors to reduce friction and enhance their position in an organization by constructive reviews and a cooperative approach.

The manager of a new internal audit staff should expect to operate as a working auditor until the department is accepted and is paying its way. While the department is small, the manager can also perform all administrative duties and thus can closely control costs and the work pace of the auditors. The manager must carefully evaluate the risk factor associated with all locations or operations subject to audit review and then select those that appear to offer the greatest opportunity for return on audit time employed. Some evaluation techniques are described in a later chapter dealing with administration.

JOB DESCRIPTION—DIRECTOR OF INTERNAL AUDITING

The job title of the person in charge of the internal auditing function is determined by the size of an organization, the position of the staff on the company's organization chart and the number of auditors on the staff. Job titles most frequently used are Manager of Internal Auditing and Director of Internal Auditing. No matter the title, the job is essentially the same.

Heading up an internal audit staff means selecting and training auditors; preparing manuals, programs and audit instructions; scheduling visits; supervising audit work and reviews; administering the staff and providing liaison between the staff and operating management. Following is a sample job description, used by the mythical XYZ Corporation, which outlines the audit scope.

JOB DESCRIPTION: Date ____________
Job Title: *DIRECTOR OF INTERNAL AUDITING*
Status: *Exempt—Executive*

Basic Purpose and Scope
Under the general guidance of the Financial Vice-President, directs all internal audit functions throughout the XYZ Corporation's worldwide organization. The internal audit group provides objective and professional evaluations of company operations and assists management to accomplish their assigned responsibilities. The audit group ensures that company policies and procedures are followed by all employees. The Director of Internal Auditing works closely with all functional departments and all organizational levels within the company and with outside agencies, as required.
Representative Functions and Duties

1. Responsible for all internal auditing activities.
2. Prepares and administers the department budget.
3. Responsible for selection, training and supervision of the audit staff.
4. Determines locations or operations to be audited and the frequency of visits.
5. Coordinates all audit activities with the Public Accountants.
6. Coordinates the program of self-audits conducted at specified field locations.
7. Recommends changes in policies or procedures to increase efficiency of operations or to improve safeguards over company assets.
8. Coordinates actions taken on product losses and employee fidelity cases, and acts as liaison with outside law enforcement agencies.
9. Conducts special studies as requested by top management.
10. Reports to Corporate President and to Chairman of the Audit Committee on matters which are not satisfactorily resolved.

Qualifications
Individual should possess a graduate degree in Business Administration or Industrial Management, with a strong background in accounting. Position requires extensive experience and accomplishment in auditing and a thorough understanding of business and accounting practices. Should have at least ten years of experience in internal auditing, some of which may be in the public accounting field. Experience in initiating, developing and monitoring accounting practices, internal control procedures and operating standards is required. Experience should provide familiarity with all company operations. Individual must be proficient in communicating and interacting with all levels of company management as well as outsiders.

FORMULATING THE DEPARTMENT'S BUDGET

After the internal auditing function is assigned a place in the company's organization chart, its scope established and a manager selected, the department's budget is worked out. The proposed audit work schedule is carefully considered. The manager prepares a tentative internal audit schedule after studying company policy and procedure statements, accounting and other manuals, comparative operating results, departmental expense estimates versus actual expenses, external auditor's audit programs and proposed visits, and previous internal audit work. Consideration must also be given to the geographic locations of company activities and to their effect on traveling time and expenses.

When all planned activities are tentatively agreed upon, the audit manager must place a dollar value on the resources required to accomplish the plan. To arrive at this figure, the manager reviews what is on hand. Such items as existing facilities; supplies; training aids; and resources, support and manpower available from other departments all carry a dollar value. Taking everything into consideration, including an estimate of audit time required to review each operation or location, the manager determines the size of the audit staff that will be needed.

If the work can be accomplished with the staff estimated in the agreed plan, it's full speed ahead. If additional auditors are required, the additional budget request must be explained and justified. When additions are authorized, the department prepares to recruit and train personnel and to put the plan into action.

FREEDOM OF ACCESS AND MOVEMENT

One of the major advantages of an internal audit staff is that it does not have routine, time-scheduled work that must be performed on a regular basis. **TIP:** *Much audit work is accomplished before or after normal working hours or on days when a location is shut down.* An internal auditor may show up at any location at any moment to start an audit review. This possibility is well understood by all employees of the firm. Auditors must have free access to all records and personnel and be free to move to any company operation or location in order to properly perform their job. The auditor is concerned with employee activities around the clock, regardless of whether a plant is in operation or closed down for cleaning or repairs.

Formal policies spelling out responsibilities of internal auditing departments state that auditors are to review all records, procedures, policies and activities. These statements effectively grant auditors the authority for free access, since that is required to discharge the stated responsibility.

Auditors must not be restrained in their movements within an organization, nor should they be denied access to any record or employee. *This, of course, does not give auditors the right to appropriate company property for their personal use,* but auditors do have the authority to verify that any item of company property exists and is in good condition.

Some movement restraint is imposed by the budget, but within that limitation, the auditors are free to move to any location or operation that they believe requires their attention. This is not to say that normal security measures should be ignored when an individual claims to be an internal auditor and demands free access to records and property.

CAUTION: *Auditors, newly arrived at a location, should be treated as any other outsider until their identity as company internal auditors is established.*

> **EXAMPLE:** People who seem to know their way around and who give the appearance of authority are rarely questioned. The author found this to be true during many years of auditing locations in many countries. He was rarely asked for identification and was only challenged once in all that time. The challenge occurred when he attempted to enter a room that was being used for secret research on a development project.
>
> There were "KEEP OUT" and "AUTHORIZED PERSONNEL ONLY" signs posted all over the area. The plant occupied a small portion of a major complex, and the author had not yet met the plant manager. Just as the author was entering the test room, the plant manager appeared and asked to see appropriate identification. This manager took his job seriously. Later he became an important executive with the company, not because of challenging the author, but because of his concern for protecting his company's interests and his willingness to act responsibly.

The Importance of Security

Internal security should not be imperiled by internal auditing activities. The two groups, Internal Auditing and Internal Security, when operating as separate entities, should work closely together to insure that adequate security exists to protect all company property and personnel.

Internal auditors should carry ID cards that contain their picture and a unique logo that is hard to copy. Since ID cards can be forged, or false, they should not be used as the sole means of identifying an employee. When internal auditors first arrive at a location they are scheduled to audit, they should show their ID cards and then wait in the reception room until location management can phone the head office and talk to auditing management to positively identify the individuals as internal auditors. Their identity established, the auditors are invited in and given free access.

> **EXAMPLE:** An incident occurred many years ago that supports the need to check identification. A two-man, internal audit team was sent to audit a small town dairy. They got off the train and without giving it any thought, entered a waiting cab and asked to be taken to the "dairy." The taxi dropped them off at a dairy building and the auditors entered the office, hung up their coats, shook hands with the local manager and were given work space in the conference room. They requested and received the general ledger and subsidiary ledgers and began their examination. In just a few minutes, they realized that they were looking at the books of a competitor. They closed up the records, gathered their belongings and asked the receptionist to call them a cab, telling her that they would be gone for awhile. Of course they never returned and they skipped the scheduled audit of their local dairy operation. Had that dairy used even the simplest security measures, the auditors would have discovered their error at the receptionist's desk and would have gone to the correct location.

Handling Classified Information

An important element of free access relates to confidential or secret information, processes or machinery. Freedom of movement and access is really granted to the head of the Internal Auditing Department who, in turn, delegates responsibility and corresponding authority to staff auditors as required. An audit manager must bear in mind the probability that not all staff members will spend their entire career working on the staff or even for the company. Some of these people may elect to change jobs and may even work for a competitor.

Some unscrupulous people resort to extremes to obtain confidential information. There is always the slight possibility that a private investigating company might place one of their agents in an internal auditing position to gain access to valuable trade secrets. This possibility makes it imperative that the audit manager be prudent in exercising free access and free movement rights.

To protect against unauthorized access to company secrets, a clear statement of policy relating to internal security should be issued to all concerned personnel of the internal auditing department.

KEY POINT: *Staff auditors must be cautioned that they not demand to examine classified information or operations until they have discussed their requirements with audit management.*

Employees responsible for the safekeeping of such information should only permit such access upon request from the manager or a specified assistant of the audit manager. *If the audit manager is satisfied that an examination of classified information is required to accomplish an important audit step, then such a review can be allowed.*

The next question is, "Who should examine the record or operation?" Under some conditions it might be wise for the manager or the top assistant to perform the work personally. Though a staff auditor may be chagrined at not being trusted to audit classified information, it is better to be safe than sorry. The security of vital information is of greater value to the company than the ego of a single staff member.

Secret Formulas, Drawings and Processes

The security over secret and confidential information should require that copies of secret documents be separated and retained in fireproof, safeguarded locations. One copy may be stored in a bank vault while another is held in the vault of the corporate attorneys or in a vault located in the company's headquarters. If either copy is destroyed, there will still be one copy available.

No matter where a record is kept, a corporate executive must be designated as the custodian of the vital record. In many companies, the designated individual will be either the Director of Security or the Director of Internal Auditing. The vital information should be retained in an envelope or folder that can be sealed so that any tampering with the outer shell of the container will become immediately apparent. The external wrappings should be initialed or marked in some manner so that the custodian will notice any tampering.

When a change of custodians occurs, the former custodian, if available, and the new custodian should review the data together and reseal and replace the documents. A certification should be written which relieves the former custodian of responsibility and notes the exact time that custodianship was transferred. A copy of the transfer certification should be given to the former custodian, and one copy of the transfer document should be retained by the new custodian.

KEY POINT: *When secret formulas are involved, a good procedure is to have the originator of the formula divide it into separate and distinct parts.* Each part should be capable of independent use and review without jeopardizing the integrity of the whole formula.

EXAMPLE: As an example, let's consider a secret formula for spaghetti sauce. The formula could be divided so that several mixes are blended together to make the final product. Each mix is given a name, letter or a number for identification. The mixes are prepared separately, hopefully in different departments or by different suppliers, and are only brought together at a controlled processing point. No single plant employee knows what ingredients are used in the mixes or how they have been prepared.

The auditors will ordinarily not need to know the specifics of the mixes, unless a major problem develops that makes it necessary to study their breakdown. In such case, the audit manager would be careful to use audit supervisors, or at least different auditors, to investigate the different mixes and would be certain that the audit working papers *did not* contain information that would enable *anyone* to figure out the exact formula.

REMEMBER: *Audit managers should strive to preserve the integrity of the system that provides security over confidential information.*

Auditors' Protocol

Freedom of movement and access carries with it the implicit restriction that internal auditors will use this authority in a considerate and respectful manner. An auditor should not break into a meeting, just to show that the authority exists. On the other hand, if the auditor knows that a meeting is in progress that might result in the endangerment of company assets or employees, the responsibility and accompanying authority could be used to enter the meeting room.

The same basic thinking applies to closed doors of private offices. If executive private office doors are normally open except when a meeting is in progress, common courtesy dictates that the closed door be respected, except for an emergency. If private offices are normally closed, the situation is different.

When department meetings are planned, it is proper for an auditor who is engaged in reviewing the department to request an invitation. In such conditions it should be normal practice for the department head to advise the auditor that a meeting on a specific subject is scheduled and allow the auditor to decide whether to sit in on the proceedings.

The authority for reviewing all activities, records, operations and personnel is a fragile one which could be revoked if the responsibility were abused. This is an area where the auditor must use common sense and discretion. In normal circumstances the auditor should respect the privacy of a closed door. This consideration should only be ignored in an emergency or if there is good reason to suspect that what is going on behind that closed door is not to the advantage or benefit of the company. The auditor who barges into a closed office must be prepared to defend the action if the intrusion is called to the attention of the top executive, and the auditor is asked for an explanation.

There is another restriction to the unlimited access stipulation. An auditor must not expect that all personnel will drop whatever they are doing in order to be available at the auditor's call. If a meeting is in progress, the auditor would be unwise to insist that an employee come out of the meeting room to discuss a minor problem or question. However, such a request would be proper if an emergency situation occurred or an immediate answer was required. On the other hand, an auditor would be properly irked if kept waiting by a manager or employee without a good reason. In such a case, the auditor would be fully justified in lodging a complaint with the supervisor of the employee who had been inconsiderate or disrespectful.

There is no substitute for common sense, and in this area logic must be combined with consideration for the rights of others and for their dignity and self-respect. Treat employees you audit as you would have them treat you, and respect their privacy. Phone or visit the individual that you want to interview and ask the employee to set a convenient time for your visit, giving the employee an estimate of the time that will be required. You should make it understood that time is an important factor and that since the time of both of you is valuable, the interview should take place as soon as possible. In many instances, the employee will make time for your questions.

Handling of Employees' Personal Files

In the area of unlimited access to information, there is always the factor of personal dignity and the right of confidentiality of personal information. The question sometimes arises as to whether the auditor has the right to examine personal files.

In the absence of a personnel policy statement dealing with this subject, auditors are authorized to examine any personal files held on company premises. However the auditor must exercise this right with a great deal of caution and respect for the rights and dignity of an individual. An employee who desires to keep personal records or correspondence in a company desk or file, risks the possibility that it may be examined by authorized company employees. The fact that these records are in the employee's desk, however, does not prove that the employee works on personal items during company time. The employee may do work during breaks, lunch periods, or before or after work hours.

When conducting a cash receipts audit during the period in which the auditor is controlling all incoming mail, the receipt of mail addressed to an individual may pose a problem. The envelope could actually contain company documents which an outsider merely addressed to the employee for expediting. **TIP:** *A safe procedure is for the auditor to deliver the unopened letter to the* *employee and request that the letter be opened in the auditor's presence.* If the letter is actually personal, and there are no enclosures that relate to the company, the auditor should not read the contents.

COORDINATION BETWEEN THE AUDIT GROUPS

The coordination and interrelationship between the internal and external auditing groups play an important role in determining the organization and administration of the Internal Auditing Department. Much of the internal staff's work affects the external auditor's work load and is relied on by the CPA firm. The internal audit effort in the area of verifications, takes a back seat to the responsibility of the external auditor. Plans and desires of the CPA firm determine how, and how much, work will be performed by the internal auditors.

Certification by a Public Accountant

A Certified Public Accounting firm is employed by management to review an organization's books, records, reports and statements and to certify to stockholders, government agencies, banks and lending agencies, potential investors and the general public that the published statements accurately reflect the financial activity and condition of an enterprise.

An accounting firm need not be certified to conduct such a review of an enterprise, but corporations listed on the major exchanges usually employ only the Certified accountants. In any event, the firm that acknowledges having audited an enterprise, states that they have satisfied themselves that all reviewed records and reports have passed the tests which they have conducted. The auditors work attests to the accuracy and reliability of the information issued by management and, by inference, assures interested parties that no material information is being withheld. A certified statement should mean that the information contained therein is accurate, timely and truthful, and discloses all pertinent data.

The public accountant frequently relies on the work of others when certifying statements. However, the CPA is obligated to review the work of others to determine that it has been reliably performed, and that it conforms to prescribed standards. Since much of the external auditors routine tasks are performed by internal auditors, it is essential that these two groups coordinate their efforts, and that the internal auditors use techniques and procedures that have been approved in advance by the public accounting firm that certifies their organization's published statements.

Exchange of Information

Some of the work of the internal auditor is similar to the verification work performed by the external auditor; thus, a close working relationship must be established between these two reviewing groups. External auditors should have access to the internal auditors work papers and reports so that they may gain confidence in the work.

A copy of all final audit reports are customarily sent to the external audit firm, and the internal audit files are open to inspection by the external auditors. For the same reason, a copy of every letter of comment, written by the external auditors, is sent to the manager of internal auditing. Frequent meetings are held between the managers of the two groups to discuss mutual problems and to plan the annual audit visits. **TIME SAVING TIP:** *Such coordination reduces duplication of effort and the upsetting of local management because of too frequent audit visits.* The external auditors have preference in selecting test locations for audit visits, with the internal group concentrating on the other locations or operations.

Money-Saving Through Cooperation

A close working arrangement will enable the external auditing firm to reduce the scope of their routine verification work and thereby reduce the fee. Such a reduction will pay for a good part of the cost of operating an internal audit department. Many companies have started an internal staff after discovering in discussions with their external auditors that they can materially reduce audit fees by establishing an internal group. The internal group is set up to review day-by-day transactions and perform many routine verifications, which enables the external group to reduce the frequency and scope of their audit at particular locations.

A good internal audit operation is the best insurance that an external auditor has in certifying the reports of a major corporation.

KEY POINT: *The work of the internal group can materially reduce the travel costs of the external auditors, as well as cut back the number of hours required for the certification review.*

With good coordination, the external auditors will be notified in advance of the locations that the internal group is planning to audit. They may elect to participate at the start or the close of an internal audit and to review the work done by the internal group to determine that it is of acceptable quality. The external audit firm may wish to assign their staff members to work with the internal auditors on selected reviews to perform specific audit steps or merely to evaluate the internal auditing approach and work.

Chapter 4

Appraising Internal Controls and Establishing a Self-Audit Program

APPRAISING INTERNAL CONTROLS

One of the most important tasks of the auditing profession is the determination, evaluation and testing of operating internal controls. Adequate internal controls are essential when line personnel must handle and control immense volumes of paper work while spending a minimum of time on individual transactions.

This chapter discusses the examination, evaluation and testing of existing internal controls, the elimination of unnecessary controls and the recommendation for and implementation of new controls.

Internal auditing appraises internal controls to determine that the following are true:

1. Internal controls are soundly conceived and operated and they fit into the established operating organization.
2. Management operating policies and established controls conform with the normal operating pattern of the business.
3. Internal routine procedures and checks are necessary, adequate and performed efficiently and correctly.

Modern business organizations, which utilize the separation of responsibilities, are based on the internal control concept. It is obvious that management controls are more effective when systems of checks and balances are established. Under such systems executive management operates as staff and develops general policies which are then coordinated into the line operations.

How Internal Controls Work

Internal controls are those systems, procedures and activities that are used within an organization to detect or prevent errors of commission and omission and to safeguard assets. Most internal controls are designed and used as timely measures to prevent mistakes from occurring or to correct operational and/or recording errors.

KEY POINT: *These controls only work if employees follow them, and almost all internal controls can be circumvented or nullified by negligence or complicity.* It takes two or more employees, working independently, to achieve an effective internal control. If these employees get too friendly or trusting of each other, or if they conspire together, any internal control may become worthless.

To add to the problem is the fact that internal controls are only as good as the operation's supervisors want them to be. *If a manager decides to steal, the internal controls under his or her supervision can easily be bypassed.* That is one reason why many employee defalcations involve supervisory personnel.

Forms of Internal Controls

Internal controls come in many forms; auditing is one. There is departmental auditing, quality control auditing, internal auditing and the external auditing performed by the public accountants.

Departmental and quality control auditing are exclusively control in nature, while the internal and external auditing provide additional services beyond the field of internal control. Other forms of internal controls are duplications of activities, records or reports; authorizations for intended actions; approvals for actions taken; routine supervision of critical activities and the circulation of reports to concerned employees. All of these controls make up an important and costly phase of internal administrative controls.

Internal auditing is a type of management control that functions by measuring and evaluating the effectiveness of other types of controls, primarily internal controls.

KEY POINT: *Internal control presupposes an adequate body of records kept accurately, consistently and systematically by alert, communicative and well-trained personnel.* Planning and related internal controls, involve recording, analyzing, interpreting, communicating, making decisions and taking action.

Importance of Communication

All management controls are important, but the timely dissemination of facts and the decisions for action are dependent upon communication.

Communication is a cornerstone of internal controls. It is the selling of ideas; it is simple language; it is arrangement of numbers on charts; it is an explanation on reports; it is friendliness, timing, forcefulness and many other things. *An internal auditor, to be effective and render a contribution to management, must be able to sell the concept of internal control so that all personnel cooperate in achieving meaningful controls.*

The auditor's sales pitch consists of a formal report, which avoids accounting terms and is simple and brief. Presentations are positive, well organized and limited to the matter under review.

KEY POINT: *If a decision on one point will automatically provide the basis for working out other problems, the presentation should only deal with the basic problem.*

Four Key Elements of Internal Control

Internal auditors must consider several elements of internal controls. These elements relate to organization, procedures, records and reports. Business operations begin with management's development of objectives, policies and plans. They then establish and maintain a functional structure that implements and promotes the attainment of their objectives. Let's consider some internal control elements.

1. *Organizational Controls*

   Adequate organizational control requires that all employees know their place in the organization and exactly what responsibility and authority has been assigned to their job. It also means that *adequate checks and balances, have been achieved by separating operating responsibility and accountability.* Controlled organization of an operation insures that the same individual is not authorizing and performing a task and also responsible for reporting results.
2. *Procedure Controls*

   Control through procedures involves the division and assignment of total work to be done. Limited by organizational checks and balances, *properly designed procedures divide tasks into logical, understandable sections that specify the work and responsibility of each employee.* Good procedural control divides the work so as to provide internal checks, without unnecessary duplication of records or effort. **NOTE:** *Control procedures must be codified and faithfully followed.* All employees should be informed of the procedures which govern their jobs.
3. *Control Through Records*

   Results of all business activities must be recorded promptly, completely and accurately. Sales, production, accounting and other records provide the means of retaining a history of past events for future study. These records serve as the basis for all reports issued.

   KEY POINT: *Every employee who prepares, approves, processes or summarizes a report must be made aware of the necessity for accuracy, timeliness and completeness of all records.*

4. *Control Through Reports*

   Reports of past events serve as the most significant control by management of its operations. These reports must be timely, complete, concise and accurate. They must also be impartial and present an accurate picture of what has actually occurred. The reports must be tailored to be usable by the administrators, and must fit the pattern of organizational responsibility.

   KEY POINT: *Employees preparing these reports must ever be aware of their significance.*

What Part Does the Internal Auditor Play?

All of the described elements of internal control contribute to the success of an enterprise. Where does the internal auditor fit in? During reviews the internal auditor tests and evaluates the operating controls to determine that they are necessary and cost effective, and that they are working as planned.

The auditor's visit is tangible proof that a particular location or operation has not been forgotten. The auditor provides a line of communication in the internal control chain. Local employees welcome an audit visit and feel free to discuss their problems, questions or suggestions. Auditors provide a medium for establishing contact between all levels of employees and can give proper attention to employee problems, suggestions or ideas that are not important enough for top management consideration.

In addition, internal auditors appraise the performance of staff and line personnel and organizations and review all activities for adherence to stated policies and operating procedures. They verify the information contained in the organization's records and also determine that reports are accurate, timely and truly reflect valid operations.

Internal Control and Duplication of Effort

Many companies duplicate work in their effort to achieve internal controls. *A good system employs a separation of activities into interrelated segments which must mesh at critical points. If one segment is off, the other parts should reflect the inbalance.*

Let's consider a common example of duplication of records. The following procedure is sometimes the result of company instructions, but more often the result of a supervisor's zeal.

> **EXAMPLE:** Warehouse managers personally maintain private notebooks listing every incoming and outgoing shipment made by the department, and the notebooks also list all merchandise received. *This handwrit-*

ten record is kept despite the fact that copies of all shipping and receiving documents are retained in the department's file. The notebooks are intended to provide a record in the event that someone removes the official documents.

When it is recommended that the handwritten notebook be discarded as a time-consuming duplication of records, the warehouse supervisor is apt to respond that it does not take any time to prepare or that the writing is done during break periods or after hours. These dedicated people only reluctantly will give up their notebooks.

As an example of the separation of required activities to achieve a degree of internal control over a common activity, consider the following:

EXAMPLE: The theater *box office cashier* sells tickets and reports total tickets used, by type, and total dollars received. The *ticket taker,* tears tickets in half, gives one half to patron and deposits the other half into a locked box. The *theater manager* compares the total stubs to the cashier's report and the figures must jibe.

Activities and responsibilities have been separated, with just a modicum of duplicate handling. (Cashier could just as easily have separated the ticket and deposited it into the control box.)

In the above example, the theater gained some internal control by adding a ticket taker to their operation. Part of their consideration was the desire to speed up the sale of tickets which this system accomplished. But have they established an airtight internal control over ticket receipts?

Suppose the cashier and ticket taker agreed that the cashier would retain the receipts from ten adult tickets and the ticket taker would palm off ten tickets and destroy them rather than place them in the stub box. The two employees would later split the proceeds. Now, has the addition of another person in the operation insured against employee theft? Obviously not. So how can management get assurance?

One way is to set up a surveillance camera and run it during the entire ticket selling period, then have management review the tape and count heads. This is possible, but time consuming and costly.

Another system is to print numbered tickets in a roll form, and have management check the first number to be sold, and then the last number that was used each day. As a control a turnstile is installed which counts each time the wheel is completely turned. At the end of the day, the number of tickets sold is compared to the number in the stub box, and then this agreed total is compared to the counter in the turnstile. If the turnstile counter doesn't jibe with reported ticket sales, a question arises as to which record is correct. Someone may turn the wheel without going through, or enter through a different door or jump over the railing. Or the ticket taker may fail to tear some tickets apart and return them to the cashier to be sold again.

In any case, it is difficult to establish an internal control that can prevent theft. Collusion between strangers is unlikely, so many organizations discourage the hiring of relatives. If relatives or friends are hired, they are usually not permitted to work together in the same department or in critical jobs which control one another. *Since collusion can negate the best controls, management settles for less than perfection and selects procedures which are most practical.*

Because collusion can bypass even the best of internal controls, internal auditors devote much of their effort toward determining that collusion has not occurred. Too many times, the auditors, in their frustration, introduce duplication of effort, in an attempt to achieve airtight controls. They choose duplication, which makes it necessary for several employees to conspire together to commit and attempt to hide a theft. They reason that if more than one employee is involved in a defalcation, there is a likelihood that one of the conspirators may confess to the actions.

How and When to Reduce or Eliminate Controls

Sometimes changes in an operation are such that the duplication of effort, which was originally introduced to improve internal control, is no longer necessary. In an obvious case, corrective action may be taken at once; but often a study is required to reach a decision.

> **EXAMPLE:** There is the classic case of the park bench in a Royal Court that was guarded night and day by assigned sentries. After many years, someone questioned the tight security over a park bench.
>
> Historians found that when the bench had been newly painted, a member of the queen's entourage sat on the bench and soiled her beautiful gown. The king immediately ordered that the bench be guarded to prevent a repetition of the incident. The order had never been rescinded. The story seems far-fetched, but it should make you wonder if there are such park benches in your organization.

A good example of an area where duplication of effort can be reduced is the standard auditor requirement for two independent counts of physical inventories. The two counts are normally compared, and any differences are then recounted by a supervisory team to learn the exact figure. When inventories are *not* EDP recorded, the two-count system does give a degree of assurance that the count is accurate. **TIP:** *When an EDP system computes a running balance of product on hand, the duplicate count procedure is unnecessary.* The computer control balance can be used to compare against a single count, and if the count matches then the figure is assumed to be correct. If the physical count differs, then supervisors can make a second and final count.

Physical counting of inventories requires much time and effort of both operating personnel and auditors. Much of the time is required to take advantage of the principle of internal control.

TIME SAVING TIPS:

1. *Some savings in time and effort can be realized by using the computer as a member of the internal control team that verifies inventory counts.* Under a computer real time inventory system, it is feasible to count and verify specific items, rather than to take a complete count of all items in the warehouse.
2. Additional savings can be realized by adopting a system that confirms stock-outs when such is reported by the inventory system. Items that are fast movers and are frequently scratched because of shortages do not need to be counted when the warehouse is loaded with the product, but instead the count can be confirmed at a low inventory point or when all the product has been shipped and the warehouse is waiting for a new order to arrive. This approach does not require that all product be counted at the same time since a perpetual record is separately maintained for each item.
3. Accounts receivable is another area where potential savings are available through reduction or elimination of certain internal control practices. Statistical sampling techniques, as well as computer programming of accounts receivable transactions, can materially reduce the effort required to confirm the A/R balance recorded in the General Ledger. The computer can be programmed to analyze and report transactions of exceptional accounts.

   KEY POINT: *This exception reporting technique narrows the audit work to those accounts requiring special attention.*

   Accounts which regularly pay outstanding balances are assumed to be correct, and the auditors concentrate on those accounts which have unusual transactions. A large part of the audit work is eliminated with a corresponding savings in time, effort and mailing costs.

Internal Control Recommendations

Auditors must examine and evaluate internal controls to determine if they actually operate as conceived. Every little detail of the control must be carefully studied. Too frequently a control is merely a window dressing that lulls supervisors into complacency. **REMEMBER:** *Auditors are apt to find, particularly in small offices, that separated tasks are interchanged among critical employees during coffee breaks, lunch periods, absences or vacations.* The net result is a complete breakdown in internal control. But this exchange of work assignments *also has a good point* in that the person taking over a missing employee's work may note inconsistencies indicating that records are being manipulated.

KEY POINT: *Before recommending the implementation of new controls, auditors should compare the cost to potential gains.* Costs of controls can be closely estimated, and those with a high price tag will be opposed by operating management. Benefits are often hard to gauge, but must be attempted. If a control results in dissuading one employee from going astray, how can one place a value on the savings? Internal auditors must be prepared to defend their suggestions for increasing controls, bearing in mind that it sometimes takes an employee defalcation to sell even a minor improvement in internal controls.

To illustrate the vast differences in internal control concepts, let's consider an example of cash sales in a warehouse operation.

> **EXAMPLE:** Customers wander through the warehouse and select items they desire. At the exit door they show their purchases to an employee who writes up a cash sales ticket and takes the money. The employee gives one copy of the ticket to the customer and retains one copy together with the cash. At the end of the day the employee turns over tickets and cash to the cashier in the office, who verifies that the total cash equals the total of the amounts shown on the invoices.
>
> *This system contains a number of control weaknesses.*
>
> 1. Pricing is not verified.
> 2. Quantities billed are not verified.
> 3. There is no assurance that all cash received by the warehouse employee was turned in to the cashier. And
> 4. There is no assurance that the office cashier did not destroy some of the sales tickets and keep the money.
>
> ***Control Suggestions.*** **(1)** A low cost internal control suggestion would be to use prenumbered invoices. They would be written in sequence and all numbers accounted for by an independent party. (Not the cashier!) This would give some assurance that all tickets were accounted for. (Unless the warehouse employee chose to risk detection and used a ticket from the bottom of the pile.) **(2)** Another control suggestion could be to increase the number of copies of the invoice to three. One to be given to the customer, one retained by the warehouse and the third to accompany daily receipts to the cashier. This suggestion would negate the possibility that the cashier might tear up a receipt and pocket the cash. (At least it would require collusion or the cashier would need access in order to destroy the warehouse control copy.) **(3)** A third possible control sug-

gestion, depending upon the physical layout of the warehouse building, would be to require that customers take their selections and two copies of the three-part invoice into the office. The third, customer-signed, copy remains in the warehouse. A pricing clerk completes the pricing, extends and totals the invoice and turns the copies over to the cashier. The money is collected and the cashier signs the invoices, retains the original and gives the other copy to the customer.

This suggestion brings another employee, the pricing clerk, into the act which provides an independent review of price, extension and addition. The system also removes funds from the warehouse, reducing the number of people handling cash and the opportunity for warehouse employees to misappropriate funds. The cashier's job is unchanged, and the warehouse is relieved of pricing and collecting.

The total amount of clerical work is not materially altered, but now requires the participation of a third party. Control is improved, providing the warehouse retains and safeguards their copies and that these are periodically compared to the cashier's reports. The cost of doing business is not increased, assuming that the volume is heavy enough to keep both the warehouse employee and the pricing clerk busy. A pricing clerk is added, but probably a warehouse job has been eliminated.

Now if we really want to introduce internal controls into the picture, consider the following: Customers must come into and remain in the office, where they place their order with an order clerk. The clerk prepares a four-part order and gives it to an order picker who selects the merchandise, checks off items as picked, records the order number on a pick sheet and then brings the order to a customer pickup dock.

The dock foreman checks the product against the order and retains one copy, returning the remaining copies to the order clerk. The clerk completes the invoice, noting quantities and exact description of items that have been pulled. The paper work is then given to a pricing clerk, who prices each item and turns the forms over to a calculator operator. The calculator operator extends and totals the invoice and notes the invoice number on a work sheet.

Invoices are then given to the cashier, who receives payment from the customer and receipts the invoice. One copy is retained by the cashier, and two copies are given to the customer. The customer then goes to the pickup dock, presents the two copies of the receipted invoice and is given the product. After checking items and quantity, the customer signs for receipt of the product and retains one copy of the invoice.

The warehouse now has two copies of the invoice, one is the original order and the other the completed invoice. The fully priced invoice is placed in a lock box to be picked up by a control clerk who will compare these copies to the cashier's daily report and then file the control copy by day's sales. The cashier's copy is filed by day's receipts and the other warehouse copy is retained in numerical order in a locked file in the warehouse.

Now there we have a complicated system, but one which can be justified by high volumes and values. The extent of controls that are necessary in any operation is a judgment call. If all workers were infallible and completely honest, then volumes of paperwork could be eliminated with resulting savings of billions of dollars.

Of course, in the above example the computer has taken over many of the tasks that were outlined. The order could be computer-produced and when filled would be priced, extended and totaled and the final invoice printed. A copy of the transaction would be retained in the computer's data base.

The computer then becomes an important element in the control picture, and the auditor must review the integrity of the computer program and the data base. But the computer is only as reliable as the information fed into it. In the above example, if the warehouse released more expensive product, or more product than the invoice called for, the computer would not spot the discrepancy. **REMEMBER:** *Any internal control can be bypassed or circumvented by dedicated and informed thieves.*

Getting Your Recommendations Accepted

Having an internal control recommendation accepted is the first hurdle to overcome; the remaining task is to be certain that line management understands the concept.

KEY POINT: *The recommendation must be explicit and not capable of misinterpretation.* Even after the most careful and detailed explanation, there is still the danger that a key element in the suggestion may be ignored or overlooked. You may later come back to an operation and discover that an audit-suggested control is mere window dressing because a vital part of the package is missing.

1. One way to reduce the possibility of misunderstanding is to work with line management in formulating the control and writing procedure instructions that spell out the work that each employee is to perform.
2. It can also be helpful to have a new procedure introduced before the audit is completed, so that auditors can determine that it is operating as planned and achieving its purpose.
3. Many audit suggestions are thrashed out during the audit windup meeting and suggestions are put into effect after the auditors have moved on to their next assignment. In these instances the writeup and associated instructions are forwarded to the audit department for review and comment,

usually before implementation. But the test of whether the new procedure is working as intended cannot be made until the next audit visit. If the potential problem is a major one, the audit manager may decide to send an audit supervisor to visit the location in order to evaluate the new procedure.

PAVING THE WAY FOR A SELF-AUDIT PROGRAM

Large organizations may have hundreds or thousands of operating locations, each containing several operations and numerous employees. The job of auditing all operations and activities is immense. Budget restrictions and availability of competent staff may make it difficult to accomplish internal auditing responsibilities within a reasonable time frame. Let's discuss a *Self-Audit Program* as an effective aid.

A self-audit program directs local management's attention toward areas of potential internal control weaknesses. By soliciting and obtaining the attention and cooperation of line management, the whole process of appraising internal controls is materially improved and raised to a higher level of management consciousness.

If top management wants every location to be visited at least once each year, they must be prepared to foot the substantial bill for audit time as well as travel time and costs. But when the internal audit budget exceeds a million dollars annually, top management may have second thoughts about the frequency of audit visits. To stretch audit resources over a risk area is a monumental task for the audit manager.

In any internal control situation, the key employee is the line supervisor, who continuously appraises internal controls and is responsible for their improvement. *Management personnel are interested and concerned in having a well-controlled operation.* One obstacle is that the supervisor lives with familiar systems, procedures and personnel and can, therefore, be lulled into a false sense of security.

Self-audit programs consist of one or more questionnaires relating to internal controls and routine operations. An effective self-audit program uses line management to objectively review their own operation and frankly answer the questions. **NOTE:** *At locations or operations using the self-audit approach, the audit interval can be extended and audit time required for a routine audit visit can be reduced.*

A self-audit program can be designed to fit almost any operation. It can be devised, installed and monitored to meet any requirement. An effective system which I devised was divided into two questionnaires. The first required management review of certain critical operations four months after the completion of an internal audit. The second questionnaire called for a review ten months after the first self-audit had been completed. This two-pronged approach effectively required a management review of all critical areas of the operation between internal audits. The audit visits were then spaced at twenty-four month intervals, rather than the twelve months that had been in effect before the self-audit program was initiated. **CAUTION:** *Naturally, a definite pattern of visits was not established for any location, and any activity could expect an internal audit visit at any time.*

How to Start the Program

A good way to start a self-audit program is to send a letter from top operating management to individual location or operation managers informing them of the introduction of the new system. Managers are told the reasons for the program and the objectives of the self-audit approach. The letter details how the program is to be handled at the local level and informs management that replies will be carefully read at headquarters and also reviewed and verified by the internal audit staff during routine visits. With these cautions in mind and the concern of local management for control of their own operations, the questions will probably be answered honestly.

Major problems with the program occur in the manner that local management decides to answer a particular question. **CAUTION:** *Too frequently the answer may be given by a local supervisor who believes that an operation is performed in the prescribed manner and doesn't bother to talk to the clerks performing the work.* The written response is the answer which the supervisor believes to be correct, but which is not factual. In such circumstances, when the internal auditors discover that wrong answers have been given to certain questions, the supervisor who provided the erroneous information is placed in a difficult position. After one such incident, all supervisors at a location will be very careful when responding to the questionnaire, and their approach to the self-audit program will improve materially.

Who Should See the Reports?

Completed copies of the self-audit programs are first processed through a division or subsidiary office and then sent to a head office designated point, such as the Internal Auditing Department. Full, or partial copies, are made and distributed to interested parties. An audit supervisor, preferably one who is acquainted with the operation, reviews the questionnaires and considers the answers. If any answer indicates a weakness in internal control, the audit supervisor is responsible for calling the oversight to the attention of appropriate line management. Concerned executives communicate with the location manager and order required corrections to be made. These letters of instructions become a part of the CAF for the particular location and all the answers to the items, as well as correspondence directing corrective actions, are reviewed and confirmed at the next audit visit.

KEY POINT: *Audit supervisors who review self-audit forms, should pay particular attention to repetition of weaknesses or problems which appear at more than one location.* These problems may become the subject of discussions and revisions of company policies or procedures.

Introducing the Program

The XYZ Corporation has decided to initiate a self-audit program. The following letter is written by top operating executives to the operation managers that are to install such programs:

> Subject: *Self-Audit Program*
> To: All Location Managers
>
> We are introducing a new control concept for the benefit of operating management which is called a Self-Audit Program. The program is being introduced and monitored by the Internal Auditing Department. You will shortly be receiving self-audit questionnaires for your location's use. Please answer the questions carefully and frankly after discussing the items with personnel who perform the work. You may change a weak procedure, and you may do so before answering the question. Your answer should reflect the procedure that you know to be in effect in your operation.
>
> The forms should be completed in duplicate, and signed and dated by appropriate managers. Retain one copy for your files and mail the original to the Manager of Internal Auditing at the home office. You have the prime responsibility for internal control over your operation and should be vitally interested in ensuring that adequate, complete and effective internal controls are in place. You may use your staff as necessary, but you are responsible for all reported answers.
>
> We expect that your operation will benefit materially from this program which should make all of your people more control-conscious. The internal auditors will review your answers when they visit your location, and we are hopeful that this program will enable us to reduce the frequency of audits and the time required for audit reviews.
>
> Your full cooperation in this program is anticipated.

Shortly after the above letter is distributed, the internal audit department sends out copies of the Self-Audit Questionnaire to affected locations with a short note referring to the earlier letter of instructions and stating the date that a reply is expected.

After the program is in operation, the audit department ensures that all locations have sufficient copies of the forms and relies on each location to monitor its own program. Auditing is usually responsible for the contents of the form and revises the questionnaire when necessary.

The audit department keeps a schedule showing all locations using the program, which lists the dates that reports are due and the dates received. If a self-audit report is not received within a few days of the due date, a form letter is sent to the location as a reminder that a report was due. This reminder, signed by the Manager of Internal Auditing, is usually sufficient to ensure that a self-audit report will be processed and sent to the auditing department.

Following is a sample of the XYZ Corporation's branch self-audit questionnaire that is to be answered by a location's manager four months after the last internal audit was completed.

Because personnel at all levels of management change periodically, the reason for the program is explained at the beginning of the form.

Branch Self-Audit Questionnaires

IA B01 XYZ CORPORATION

SALES AND DISTRIBUTION BRANCHES SELF-AUDIT PROGRAM

(To be completed 4 months after an internal audit)

Division ____________ Location ____________ # of office employees _____

The following check list is intended to direct the attention of local managers to areas of potential weakness in internal controls within an operation. This questionnaire presents an excellent opportunity to methodically review procedures, responsibilities and authority. Questions are not to be construed as statements of company policy, but are to be answered to reflect current practices in effect at the time the questionnaire is completed. The answers may point out policy or procedure oversights or may lead to revisions of existing policies. Please record the answers in the space provided alongside or below each question. Where a particular question is not applicable, please note "DNA" in the appropriate space.

A. Last Internal Audit

Review the last internal audit report for your location. What is the date of the last report? ____________________

1. (a) For those recommendations made and accepted, list each item's section letter and item number on the left-hand side of this page and describe the pertinent procedure now in effect after each such item listed. ____________________________________

B. Cash

1. Are adequate controls exercised over cash sales of:
   (a) Product? Yes _____ No _____
   (b) Property items and salvage materials? Yes _____ No _____
   (c) Does one person handle the complete transaction? Yes _____ No _____
2. Direct depositing: Do any employees make daily direct deposits of their cash receipts? Yes _____ No _____. If Yes:
   (a) Does responsible office clerk check off daily bank acknowledgments of employee direct deposits, against deposit slips submitted by employees? Yes _____ No _____
   (b) Are accounting adjustments of errors in direct deposits made daily? _______ Weekly? _______ Other? ______________

3. Does the bank promptly transmit all supporting documentation received in your bank lock box? Yes _____ No _____
4. Are all of your customers on lock box banking? Yes _____ No _____
5. Do you periodically review checks received in your office to determine if these accounts can be transferred to lock box banking? Yes _____ No _____
6. Does the bank always receive your daily deposit in time to credit our account the same day? Yes _____ No _____
   (a) If no, why not? ____________________
   (b) What exceptions, if any, during the past thirty days? Give the reasons. ____________________
7. Does someone other than the petty cash custodian periodically check the fund, and/or the petty cash bank account? Yes _____ No _____
   (a) How is the petty cash fund safeguarded? ____________________
   (b) Are all petty cash supporting documents promptly and properly canceled? Yes _____ No _____
   (c) Are all vouchers checked for proper approvals? Yes _____ No _____
8. Do you maintain a current list of employees who possess keys or combinations to safes, office and warehouse? Yes _____ No _____
   (a) Is this list and all combinations and keys properly safeguarded? Yes _____ No _____

C. Pricing

1. Is company policy being followed with regard to product pricing, freight expenses, unsaleable returns, etc.? Yes _____ No _____
2. Do you control the salesperson's orders on "deal" products to be sure they do not extend the period of the drive? Yes _____ No _____
3. Are pricing errors corrected in every case? Yes _____ No _____
   (a) If no, what is established limit? ____________________

D. Inventory Settlements

1. Does the office receive an independently prepared receiving report from the warehouse for comparison by the office to the shipping manifests (blind receiving), or do warehouse personnel check the product to the shipping papers as it is unloaded? _______
2. Does the office compare weights, shown on bills of lading and common carrier freight bills, to customer invoices? Yes _____ No _____
3. If merchandise is stored outside the branch warehouse, have adequate procedures been established to:
   (a) Take advantage of most favorable time to withdraw? Yes _____ No _____
   (b) Determine that stock is properly rotated and protected from abnormal changes in temperature or humidity? Yes _____ No _____
   (c) Prevent withdrawal without written authorization? Yes _____ No _____
   (d) Protect merchandise from contamination? Yes _____ No _____
4. How do you determine the minimum and maximum quantities of finished goods to be carried in each warehouse? ____________________

5. List names of outside storage locations and state what is stored at each location. ______
   (a) Why is outside storage necessary? ______

E. Shipping
   1. Who is responsible for spotting freight cars and trucks for loading and unloading? ______
   2. What is the job title of the loading supervisor? ______
   3. Are all copies of invoices available to the loader? Yes ____ No ____
   4. Is product loaded on trucks and/or freight cars checked by an independent checker? Yes ____ No ____

F. General
   1. When did you last review your files to be sure that the record retention schedule is being followed? ______
   2. When did you last review the security over your outer perimeter fencing and control over access to the premises? ______

Questions answered by ______ Date ______
Report reviewed by ______ Date ______

The second self-audit report, sent out ten months later is similar in critical areas, but differs in that local management is asked to look at some of the other items. A sample questionnaire follows.

IA B02 XYZ CORPORATION
SALES AND DISTRIBUTION BRANCHES SELF-AUDIT PROGRAM
(To be Completed 14 Months After Last Internal Audit)

Division ______ Location ______ # of office employees ____

The following check list is intended to direct the attention of local managers to areas of potential weaknesses in local internal controls. This affords an excellent opportunity for management to methodically review procedures and separation of authority and responsibilities. The questions are not to be construed as statements of company policy, but are to be answered to reflect current practices in effect at the current time. Your answers may point out policy or procedure oversights or may lead to revisions of existing corporate policies. Please record answers in the space provided alongside or below each question. If a question is not applicable, note "DNA."

A. Cash
   1. Does daily deposit include all mail-in checks and collections received up to the time of the deposit? Yes ____ No ____
   2. Does the bank always receive your location's daily deposit in time to credit our account the same day? Yes ____ No ____
      (a) What exceptions during the past thirty days, and reasons? ______
   3. How does the office insure that all salespeople and deliverypeople who make collections are submitting their collections promptly? ______
      (a) Does a clerk *periodically compare the keying of collections from the office copy of the deposit slip to the applicable collection report?* Yes ____ No ____

(b) Are dates shown on money order receipts periodically compared to the reported collection dates? Yes _____ No _____

(c) Does an office representative periodically contact the bank to compare listings of details of deposits as received by bank to the office copy of the deposit slip? Yes _____ No _____

4. Are petty cash slips prepared and approved in ink? Yes _____ No _____
   (a) Are monthly *petty cash summaries and all supporting papers routed to location manager for approval?* Yes _____ No _____
5. What precautions have been taken to preclude the possibility of the cashier, or anyone else, misappropriating cash receipts and then adjusting pertinent records to cover withholdings? __________
6. Do you periodically check the armored car pickup procedure to insure that all controls are being adhered to? Yes _____ No _____
7. Are customers required to sign for cash refunds? Yes _____ No _____
   (a) Are customers periodically contacted by the office to verify a sampling of these cash refunds? Yes _____ No _____
8. *Do controls over local purchases make it impossible for one person to order and receive merchandise, and then approve the covering invoice for payment?*
   Yes _____ No _____
   (a) What amount is stipulated as ceiling for local purchases? __________

B. Accounts Receivable

1. *How often are accounts which have been written off as not collectible, reviewed for change of status?* __________
2. Are customers who remit NSF checks promptly placed on a C.O.D. status? Yes _____ No _____
   (a) Do your procedures require salespeople to sign for NSF checks when they are directed to return them to customers? Yes _____ No _____
   (b) *Do you follow up to ensure return of these checks?* Yes _____ No _____
3. Describe program for verifying past due accounts. __________
4. Do you maintain a record of which salesperson's past due accounts have been verified? Yes _____ No _____
5. What system do you use to ensure that daily credits to A/R files are balanced to your daily control of debits and credits? __________
6. Does the A/R bookkeeper have:
   (1) Access to the daily receipts? Yes _____ No _____
   (2) Authority to issue credit memos? Yes _____ No _____
   (3) The task of preparing the daily summaries? Yes _____ No _____
   If yes, does the office manager, or a third party, have preliminary control figures for sales and cash? Yes _____ No _____
   (a) Is proper follow-through made daily to clear small pending differences on payments? Yes _____ No _____ By whom? __________
   (b) Is daily attempt made to clear unmatched payments?
   Yes _____ No _____
7. What is the current dollar variance between the control and the accounts receivable detail total? __________
   (a) When was detail last in balance with the A/R control? __________

(b) List the dates and amounts of each adjustment to A/R control since the last internal audit. ____

8. Are there any credits in the receivable file that cannot be identified with a specific customer? Yes ____ No ____ If yes:
   (a) Explain how such credits are handled. ____

C. Inventory Control

1. Who is responsible for investigating variances? ____
   (a) How are large inventory variances investigated? ____
   (b) *Are EDP variance reports regularly reviewed?* Yes ____ No ____
      (1) Do they accurately reflect product losses? Yes ____ No ____
2. Do you check to verify that all orders transmitted to the computer are properly billed? Yes ____ No ____
3. *Do you require supervisory approval for all adjustments entered into EDP?* Yes ____ No ____ If yes, who approves? ____
4. What procedure do you use to determine the accuracy of billings to accounts that are shipped directly from other locations? ____
5. Are control copies of invoices properly safeguarded after product is loaded? Yes ____ No ____
   (a) Does the office follow through to ensure that all invoices are accounted for? Yes ____ No ____
   (b) *Does your system ensure that all shipments are released to EDP for invoicing?* Yes ____ No ____
6. How often do office personnel participate in the physical count of finished goods inventory? ____
   (a) What is your present frequency of inventory settlement? ____
   (b) Do you regularly take two independent counts? Yes ____ No ____
   (c) Explain your procedure for comparing separate counts and reconciling differences. ____
   (d) Do procedures ensure that the consolidated inventory includes merchandise stored or carried at all locations under your control? Yes ____ No ____
   (e) Does your warehouse have written instructions describing your procedures for inventory counts? Yes ____ No ____
      (1) *Are these procedures followed?* Yes ____ No ____
7. If salespeople carry car stock, how do you verify that stocks as shown on inventory are actually held by salespeople? ____

D. Credits to Customers

1. Do zone managers or sales supervisors receive a copy of all C/M's issued by salespeople? Yes ____ No ____
2. *Do supervisors personally spot check customer stock* to determine if unsalables are sold, and not destroyed as reported? Yes ____ No ____
3. What procedures are in effect to *determine that credits for unsalable pickup are not for price concession or fraudulent use?* ____
   (a) Do you periodically examine first party checks to see if they agree with reported total amount collected? Yes ____ No ____
   (b) Does the office occasionally call customers to verify that they actually received reported credit? Yes ____ No ____

E. Pricing
1. Are adequate measures taken to ensure that there are no violations of our pricing policies? Yes ____ No ____
   (a) Do you check to determine that all orders meet the minimum weight requirements? Yes ____ No ____
   (b) What controls ensure that override prices are correct? ________
2. Do you periodically request and review an EDP printout of the price audit program for your location? Yes ____ No ____
3. *Is management approval required on sales tickets covering sales of close dated merchandise at reduced prices?* Yes ____ No ____
   (a) If no, how are these sales controlled? ________

F. Shipping and Receiving
1. How many days normally elapse between date *order is written* and date *product is delivered?* ________
2. Are truck driver movements watched in warehouse area? Yes ____ No ____
3. Do your controls eliminate the possibility of a duplicate freight bill being approved for payment? Yes ____ No ____
   (a) Are all freight bills for incoming shipments posted to receiving reports? Yes ____ No ____
4. *Is someone assigned to guard the docks during all periods of operations?* Yes ____ No ____
   (a) Are all incoming vehicles checked for proper identification and proper authority before entering the docks? Yes ____ No ____
   (b) *Before truck doors are opened are seals checked for tampering and compared to numbers recorded on the B/L?* Yes ____ No ____
5. Are all "scratched" items reviewed by management? Yes ____ No ____
   (a) Who decides what will be back-ordered when sufficient stock is not available?
   (b) Are summaries of all "back-ordered" items routed to management daily? Yes ____ No ____

G. Payroll
1. Are changes on employee's time cards made in ink? Yes ____ No ____
   (a) Who approves the changes? ________
2. *Are vacations taken by everyone entitled to them?* Yes ____ No ____
3. Does the person who enters the payroll data into the computer also distribute the payroll checks? Yes ____ No ____
   (a) How do you handle employee paychecks that could not be distributed because of absenteeism or vacation?

H. General
1. Does your location have vending machines? Yes ____ No ____
   (a) Who handles and controls the receipts from the machines? ________
   (b) Who receives the profits? ________
2. How many *extra cars* are assigned to your location? ________
   (a) How many *extra trucks* are assigned to your location? ________
3. Are controls over gas, oil and other miscellaneous supplies adequate to prevent unauthorized use? Yes ____ No ____

4. This questionnaire will be reviewed at higher headquarters. In these reviews, what other matters do you wish to direct to management's attention. ____________
5. Review your answer to question A of the last Self-Audit Report and list any items that are still pending. When will these items be completed?

____
6. What other items, not specifically covered, do you plan to follow up for improvement? ____________

____

Questions answered by ____________ Date ____________
Report reviewed by ____________ Date ____________

Plant Self-Audit Questionnaires

The same general approach is used for self-audit questionnaires designed to be used at production plants. Distribution center questionnaires are similar to the branch examples. Plant programs contain some of the same questions, but also have many variations that relate to the production processes.

The headings and opening paragraphs are identical to those just shown, so we will not bother to repeat that information. (Naturally, the heading will state Production Plant instead of Branch.) In the following examples we will start with item A on both the four and the fourteen month self-audits. We will cover the four-month report first.

A. Last Internal Audit
Review the last internal audit report. What is the date? ____________
1. For those recommendations made and accepted, list each item's section letter and item number on the left hand side of this page and describe the pertinent procedure now in effect after each item listed. ____________

____

B. Cash
1. Are adequate controls exercised over cash sales of:
   (1) Product? Yes ____ No ____
   (2) Property items, scrap and salvage materials? Yes ____ No ____
   (a) Does one person handle the complete transaction? Yes ____ No ____
2. Does someone other than the petty cash custodian periodically check the fund and the petty cash bank account? Yes ____ No ____
   (a) Are all supporting documents promptly and properly canceled? Yes ____ No ____
   Are they properly approved? Yes ____ No ____
   (b) How is the petty cash fund safeguarded? ____________

C. Inventory Controls
1. Is the office given independently prepared receiving reports by the warehouse to compare to shipping manifests, or do receiving personnel check

items to the shipping papers while unloading? ____________

2. Does office compare weights shown on bills of lading and carrier freight bills to supplier's billings? Yes _____ No _____
3. Are raw materials rotated in storage so that product is used on a first in, first out basis? Yes _____ No _____
4. Are freezers and coolers kept at correct temperatures? Yes _____ No _____
5. Are all incoming raw materials checked for proper quality and quantity before being accepted and moved into warehouse? Yes _____ No _____
6. Do you use your weigh scales according to policy? Yes _____ No _____
   (a) *When were your weigh scales last tested for accuracy?* ____________
7. If items are held in outside storage, do your procedures insure:
   (a) That withdrawals must be authorized in writing? Yes _____ No _____
   (b) That stock is properly rotated and protected from abnormal changes in temperature and humidity? Yes _____ No _____
   (c) That timing of withdrawals take into account the dates that lots were stored, so as to save on storage charges? Yes _____ No _____
8. Are all packaging supplies tested upon receipt for conformance to specs? Yes _____ No _____
   (a) Is usage on a FIFO basis? Yes _____ No _____
9. List names of outside storage locations and state items stored.
   (a) Why is outside storage necessary? ____________

D. Shipping
1. Who is responsible for spotting freight cars and trucks for loading and unloading? ____________
   (a) What is job title of employee who supervises loading? ____________
2. Are all copies of shippers available to loader? Yes _____ No _____
3. Is product independently checked before shipment? Yes _____ No _____
4. *Are all vehicles sealed after loading?* Yes _____ No _____
   (a) If no, describe exceptions. ____________

E. Processing Department
1. Are quality controls tests made as per policy? Yes _____ No _____
   (a) *Is product kept on "hold" until cleared by lab?* Yes _____ No _____
2. Are products requiring cooling moved into coolers immediately after casing? Yes _____ No _____
3. Are adequate records kept of transfers to processing? Yes _____ No _____

F. General
1. Are all confidential formulas kept under lock and key? Yes _____ No _____
2. Is cleanup crew properly supervised? Yes _____ No _____
   (a) *Is care taken to prevent cleanup crew from entering confidential areas?* Yes _____ No _____
3. Do you maintain a current list of employees possessing keys to the buildings and to restricted areas or safes? Yes _____ No _____
   (a) Is this list and all keys properly safeguarded? Yes _____ No _____
4. Do you enforce visitor control regulations? Yes _____ No _____

Questions answered by ______________________________ Date __________
Report reviewed by ________________________________ Date __________

Assuming no intervening internal audit, another self-audit report is sent to the plant ten months later. A sample of this fourteen month self-audit questionnaire follows:

A. Cash
  1. Are monthly petty cash summaries, and all supporting papers, routed to location manager for approval? Yes ____ No ____
     (a) Are petty cash vouchers prepared in ink? Yes ____ No ____
     (b) Who approves petty cash vouchers? ____________________
     (c) Is petty cash fund periodically counted and reconciled by someone other than the fund cashier? Yes ____ No ____
  2. Does an independent party periodically check vending machine receipts and compare to previous recordings? Yes ____ No ____
  3. Are receipts from miscellaneous sales adequately controlled and properly safeguarded until deposited? Yes ____ No ____

B. Finished Goods Inventory
  1. *Is supervisory approval required for any adjustment to inventory that is entered into the EDP system?* Yes ____ No ____
  2. How often do office personnel participate in the physical count of inventory? ________________________________
     (a) Do you regularly require two independent counts? Yes ____ No ____
     (b) Explain your counting and reconciling procedures. ____________
     (c) Do procedures ensure that your consolidated inventory figure includes items stored at all locations you control? Yes ____ No ____
     (d) Do you have written instructions describing your procedures for counting inventories? Yes ____ No ____
        (1) *Are these procedures followed?* Yes ____ No ____
  3. *Does office check to insure that all shipments entered into the computer terminal are properly processed?* Yes ____ No ____
     (a) Are hard copies of shippers filed so that they are readily available to support batch reports? Yes ____ No ____

C. Raw Materials
  1. *Are delivery trucks and tank cars weighed both before and after unloading.* Yes ____ No ____
     (a) Do your systems ensure that we are not paying for wash water, but only for quantity of goods actually received? Yes ____ No ____
        (1) Does your testing include moisture checks? Yes ____ No ____
        (2) Do you check for extraneous matter in bulk shipments, or boxes or crates when items are bought by weight? Yes ____ No ____
  2. Explain your system for reconciling R/M usage? ____________
     (a) *Are all adjustments to R/M approved by manager?* Yes ____ No ____

(b) List dollar value of R/M adjustments by month for last ten month period. ______

3. Are R/M stored as required by quality control SOP's?
Yes ____ No ____

D. Lab Testing

1. *When were lab instruments last checked for accuracy?* ______
2. Does lab supervisor periodically review testing procedures with every lab technician? Yes ____ No ____
3. Are lab supplies properly safeguarded? Yes ____ No ____
4. Are samples pulled and tested as prescribed by quality control testing procedures. Yes ____ No ____
   (a) What happens to product falling outside of specs? ______
      (1) Where applicable, does management supervise destruction of product? Yes ____ No ____
      (2) If reworked, are records properly adjusted? Yes ____ No ____
5. *During night shifts, do line foremen check to see that lab technicians actually draw samples and run tests?* Yes ____ No ____

E. Payroll

1. Are all written entries on time cards made in ink? Yes ____ No ____
   (a) Who approves these entries? ______
2. Do you periodically distribute paychecks to verify that checks are only written for legitimate employees? Yes ____ No ____
   (a) *Are checks normally distributed by someone other than clerk who enters data into the payroll system?* Yes ____ No ____
   (b) How do you handle paychecks that were not distributed due to absenteeism or vacation? ______
3. Are vacations taken by everyone entitled to them? Yes ____ No ____
4. Do you regularly review your labor variance report? Yes ____ No ____

F. Property

1. When was the last time you reviewed your listing of active property items?
   ______
   (a) Are there any items listed that you do not have? Yes ____ No ____
   (b) If yes, list them. ______
2. *Is your list of idle equipment accurate?* Yes ____ No ____
   (a) List and show date of record of all idle equipment still at your plant that you reported over six months ago. ______
3. When you dispose of property items, *do you obtain three bids* as required by policy? Yes ____ No ____
   (a) If no, why not? ______

G. General

1. Are machine shop purchases adequately controlled? Yes ____ No ____
   (a) *Do your systems ensure that the same employee does not order items, receive the merchandise and approve the invoice for payment?*
   Yes ____ No ____
2. Are high-cost machinery items properly tagged when received at the plant.
   Yes ____ No ____

3. Have you *designated specific management personnel to question any strangers* wandering around the building? Yes _____ No _____
4. Do you have adequate security over your property perimeter and over movements into and out of your plant? Yes _____ No _____
   (a) Do you require all visitors, including manufacturer's reps, to sign the visitor registration book and to fill in all of the requested information? Yes _____ No _____
5. Are maintenance work orders required for all work performed by the maintenance crew? Yes _____ No _____
   (a) Are these work orders properly authorized and retained in numerical order? Yes _____ No _____
   (b) Do supervisors periodically check to see that *machinery or tools are not removed from the machine shop?* Yes _____ No _____
6. Review your answer to Question A of your last self-audit report. List any items still pending and state when they will be completed. __________
7. What other points, not specifically covered, do you plan to follow up for improvement? ______________________________
8. In the review of this report at headquarters, what other matters do you wish to direct to managements attention?

Questions answered by ______________________________ Date __________
Report reviewed by ______________________________ Date __________

When a self-audit program is accepted by line management and operating satisfactorily, a general increase in awareness of internal controls occurs at all levels of management. Not only do the local managers benefit, but their counterparts in division or headquarters offices also become more conscious of the benefit of internal controls. As they read the reports and comments that are referred for their attention or action, they become active participants in the concept of initiating, monitoring and expanding operating internal controls.

Part 2

Managing the Internal Auditing Department

Chapter 5

Administering an Internal Auditing Department

The approach to internal auditing, the tenor of auditing activities, the way in which internal auditing is perceived in the organization, and the reaction of employees to the internal auditing function and staff are all dependent upon the internal audit manager.

Each audit manager has a unique approach. Some managers believe that they are merely the eyes and ears of top management, and not part of the brain. They believe that their job ends with a presentation of the facts and that all decisions are to be made by top management. While it is true that top management is responsible for decisions, they want suggestions and alternative solutions from the experts.

KEY POINT: *An internal audit manager is derelict who does not offer thoughtful recommendations.*

What operating management wants is *information.* Internal auditors can utilize their time and talents to meet management's operating information needs. They can help by:

1. Examining and evaluating the effectiveness and efficiency of all administrative and accounting operations.
2. Submitting audit reports that summarize findings and include objective and independent opinions.
3. Offering constructive criticism where necessary.
4. Recommending actions for tangible improvements.

POINTS TO KEEP IN MIND

The audit manager and staff influence the direction and approach to audit reviews of operations and departments. The audit staff can be a valuable assistant to operating management or it can be an internal police force. The administration of the audit staff is critical in determining the actual and perceived approach used by staff members.

A successful internal auditing operation requires a competently administered department. The smooth operation of a large audit staff requires a full-time, knowledgeable administrator.

THE DEPARTMENT ADMINISTRATOR

A new internal auditing department starts with a manager and a few staff auditors. The manager selects and trains the staff, supervises their field work, authors all the manuals and audit programs, and handles all of the administrative details of the department. As the audit scope increases, and more staff members are added, the manager works the position of administrative assistant into his budget request. At first the job may be held by an audit supervisor who continues to work on audit assignments, while assisting in administrative and clerical work in the department. The next step in a large staff is a full-time administrator, who may or may not be a professional auditor.

The administrator's job qualifications do not necessarily include previous internal auditing experience. The job of administering an audit staff is no different than that of any other traveling group. All tasks are performed as a service to the audit manager who is responsible for all of the administrator's actions.

As the audit function settles into place in an organization, the administrator becomes a combination department office manager and aide to the audit manager. The audit manager may also designate one of the supervisors as the assistant audit manager to directly supervise the internal auditing activities and to act as head auditor in the absence of the audit manager. The staff administrator's responsibilities are limited to specifically enumerated tasks that may have nothing to do with the internal audit work. However, in the absence of audit department management, the administrator acts as the recipient of all questions directed to the audit manager's office. An audit supervisor, performing the duties of an administrator, can effectively field questions and contact appropriate supervisors to obtain answers which are then forwarded to the appropriate party.

An audit department administrator's duties are not technical and need not consume the time of a professional auditor. The administrator handles many or all of the delegated duties in the following list.

Administrative Duties

1. Supervise all secretarial and clerical personnel in the department and take responsibility for performance of clerical work.

2. Be available at all times to handle inquiries directed to the audit manager's office.
3. Assist the manager in preparing the department's annual budget.
4. Prepare and process payroll notices, salary adjustments, time reports, expense reports and termination notices.
5. Conduct termination interviews with departing auditors and recover all company property in their possession.
6. Procure necessary audit forms and supplies, and keep audit teams supplied with forms or equipment as required.
7. Act as home office contact for field auditors as required.
8. Handle the details associated with audit conferences or meetings.
9. Keep the audit manual up to date. Issue manual pages that deal with administrative matters, and process pages written by audit department management.
10. Process audit reports. The administrator does not make decisions concerning changes in report content, but may suggest changes to the writer. Such changes usually concern sentence structure, spelling or choice of words. Any disagreements on significant items are covered with the audit manager.
11. Perform such other duties as directed by the manager of the internal auditing function.

FORMULATING A BUDGET

One of the first hurdles to overcome in establishing an internal auditing operation is the operating budget. A new staff is frequently set up to reduce the cost of the CPA firm's audit. Often, the amount that the financial officer hopes to save, out of the external auditor's fee, becomes the maximum cost figure for an internal staff. Most executives will hesitate to increase their costs by creating a new department which, in concept, is not revenue producing or does not seem necessary for conducting business in the usual way. If the company has had some large or unusual losses and the financial executive believes that an internal auditing department can help prevent future losses, then the budget for the department's operation is open to negotiation.

The auditing department's budget estimates the dollars required to operate a professional audit staff to accomplish the stated objectives of the function. Major factors include the following:

1. The number of auditors;
2. The salaries projected for the year;

3. The traveling and training expenses;
4. Other variable factors, such as illnesses, vacations and meetings.

A condensed sample budget may read as follows:

PROPOSED ANNUAL BUDGET FOR THE
INTERNAL AUDITING DEPARTMENT

Administrative Salaries		$____		
Staff salaries		$____		
Vacation costs	$____			
Sickness and accident costs	$____	$____		
Travel expenses		$____		
Insurance costs		$____		
Total personnel costs			$____	
Supplies		$____		
Meeting expenses		$____		
Office services		$____		
Space costs		$____		
Postage		$____		
Telephone		$____		
Miscellaneous		$____		
Total other costs			$____	
TOTAL DEPARTMENTAL BUDGET				$____

Size of Staff

Staff size is determined by adding the audit time required for each activity to be audited during the year and dividing this sum by the annual number of work hours available per staff member.

The audit manager must consider all activities of the company and draw up a matrix of all auditable locations and operations. A condensed sample matrix is illustrated below. Audit time is estimated for each activity, and this figure is entered into the matrix. The time estimate should include an estimate of travel time required to reach the activity. Next the manager must decide and enter the frequency of audits for each activity. When making this last estimate the manager takes into consideration the reviews by the CPA firm. Finally the internal audit manager estimates lost audit hours through preparation and start-up time, illnesses, vacations, meetings and unforeseen events.

A CONDENSED SAMPLE MATRIX (In Audit Hours)

Locations	Est. Audit	Trav.	Date, last	Est. Start	Interval	cont'cy	Total
New York	720	32	2/22/7	6/14/8	16 mon.	36	788
....	....	....	....	....	....	....	....
....	....	....	....	....	....	....	....
Chicago	580	26	11/13/6	4/5/8	17 mon.	29	635
Total Audit Hours Required for Schedule							16,250
Total Hours for Meetings and Training Sessions							1,320
Grand Total of Audit Hours							17,570

Taking all variable factors into consideration, the number of staff auditors required is determined and matched against existing staff. If the staff is not large enough, the manager must make a choice. There are three options available:

1. Attempt to gain approval to increase the size of the staff;
2. Extend the time interval between audits;
3. Change the time requirements for audits so that the available audit hours will stretch over the estimated audit time requirements.

If options 2 and 3 have been worked down to their bare bones, then the manager must push for an increase in staff auditors.

Location and Frequency of Audit Visits

Most audit departments, though limited by available funds, have unlimited responsibilities. **REMEMBER:** *The job of the audit manager is to stretch a thin web of audit resources over a vast geographic and complex operational organization.*

Very simply, selection of locations to be audited is determined by assigning a risk factor to all activities subject to audit and then selecting those that offer the best chance for a tangible return on the audit time required. The problem arises in determining the risk factor, which changes with the passage of time, and then estimating the number of activities that the existing audit staff can review.

In establishing the annual schedule of locations to be audited, the major considerations are the total number of activities that the staff must review, total audit time required for each review, the importance of each activity, and the period of time since the last audit visit. Some organizations, by policy, simplify the problem of selecting locations for audit. They decree that all company locations be audited at least once per year. This leaves the problems of timing and audit scope. If that same requirement applies to all departments in the administrative offices and to other special audits, then these too must be added to the schedule, at a time selected by the audit manager.

If the organization demands annual visits to all locations, then top management must permit staffing to accomplish this degree of audit visitation. In these circumstances the audit manager merely plans all the visits so as to minimize travel time and audit costs.

KEY POINT: *Good planning of itineraries can reduce travel costs.*

Assignment of teams to work in a given geographic area can help reduce travel distances, time and costs. Each team is given a certain area and travels from one location to another until it completes the audits of all locations in the assigned area. **KEEP IN MIND:** *Though travel costs are reduced, there is the disadvantage that all locations in the area are alerted that the internal auditors have appeared, and it is likely that they will soon be visited.* A modification of this approach, is the use of an area audit office which is discussed later in this chapter.

Sweeping an audit area is one way of scheduling audits that uses the element of surprise as an audit tool. Under this approach, several audit teams are assigned to a given geographic area and they start their audits on the same day and cover all locations in the area, thus catching all activities by surprise. **KEY POINT:** *The trick is to attempt to reduce travel time while retaining, as much as possible, the element of surprise.* Audit visits should usually be unexpected, except when responding to a request.

The surprise element is important because employees who engage in illegal acts sometimes plan their manipulations so as to avoid audit visits and/or the periods that auditors will study. **CAUTION:** *After a few audit visits, local supervisors become aware of audit routines and programs and have a good idea as to what records the auditors examine and the periods of time that are usually covered.* When any of these people decide to steal from their employer, they select a time when they are quite certain that internal auditors will never look at the records for that period. Some of these people may be caught during surprise internal audits.

> **EXAMPLE:** A defalcation was discovered because of an anonymous phone call in which the caller suggested that "something might be wrong" at a company location. An audit team was dispatched and the office manager's manipulations were discovered in short order.
>
> The manager admitted that he had started withholding office collec-

tions six weeks after completion of the last internal audit, and had continued for six months until detection. He planned to stop stealing several months before the start of the next audit. During interrogation he stated, "Internal auditors never return until at least twelve months after the completion of an audit." He therefore thought that he had several more months to act, because the auditors "never reviewed records that were more than two or three months old."

EXAMPLE: In another case, a division assistant-controller was tripped up by an audit visit that came as a surprise to local management. The culprit admitted that he had been manipulating bank accounts for over three years. He knew exactly when the external auditors would come in for their preliminary review and for their year-end audit. He confined his manipulations of about six months per year, to periods that he knew would not be looked at by the auditors.

This manager was caught because the internal audit staff decided to audit a location, normally only visited by the CPA firm, and timed their visit so as not to interfere with the public accountant's routine.

KEY POINT: *Surprise audits are designed to review records and activities before someone has the opportunity to hide or alter records that contain evidence of their defalcation.*

In organizations where there are no set criteria governing the frequency of audit visits, the audit manager decides what activities to audit and when. The manager must be flexible in his management of resources. The audit interval provides some flexibility. Planned intervals may be changed for a variety of reasons, such as:

1. An internal audit may require a follow-up visit after only a few months, to determine whether adequate corrective action has been taken.
2. An external audit report may dictate an immediate visit by the internal staff.
3. A location may be skipped because of a recent review by the CPA's.

Often the planned interval is changed at management's request or because of a change in the evaluation of management at a location. **KEEP IN MIND:** *Locations with good management and personnel, who intelligently follow established policies and procedures, need not be audited as often as operations of a similar nature with less diligent personnel.* Audit management's judgment is the deciding factor.

Evaluating Risk Factors

Following is a list of reports and other information used in evaluating the risk factor associated with individual locations or departments. Some are objective, some subjective and the relative importance may differ for each activity. At times the audit manager's intuition will outweigh all other considerations. Important reports and other considerations that can affect a schedule include the following:

1. Comparative operating results. Where such reports are truly comparable, the poor operations deserve attention.
2. P/L statements. Look for activities that show profit reductions.
3. Operating expense statements. Activities that report budget overruns or certain expenses that are disproportionate or out of line with related activities should be added to the schedule.
4. Variance reports. Locations that report above average variances that were written off during the year should be included in the list of locations to be audited.
5. Inventory loss reports. Locations experiencing large shortages of inventory must definitely be visited as soon as practical.
6. Self-audit programs, if the system is used. A study of these reports may point out significant problems to be explored.
7. Evaluation of management personnel. Those activities managed by questionable supervision should be high on the list for audit.
8. Evaluation of organization charts. Operations with top-heavy or insufficient supervision, or complex organizations may be studied.
9. Period since last audit. Any activity that has not been visited by any audit group during the past three years is ripe for audit.
10. Past auditing experience at the activity. Poor experience, or an absence of good internal control concepts, should place the operation on the current audit list.
11. Presence on the department's management team of an ex-auditor who has been promoted to the operation. Such transfers may give the audit manager confidence that internal controls are followed, and the time interval may be extended.

Sample Approach to a Formalized Risk Evaluation Program

A sample of a formalized approach that may be used to evaluate audit risk factors follows. This program can easily be adapted to a personal computer and, when so established, can be frequently reviewed and updated as required. Most of the ratings are of a subjective nature and for best results should be determined by an experienced audit supervisor. The same forms and general approach may be used to estimate audit man-hour requirements.

Naturally, the elements of risk and the assigned valuations will vary between companies. But each studied operation should be rated on a consistent basis, so that they may be accurately compared. The audit manager in charge of the risk assessment program establishes the guidelines for the assigned ratings. Two examples will demonstrate.

> **EXAMPLE 1:** In the handling of finished goods inventory the company experiences customary losses of product. The audit manager, aware of such losses, decides that annual losses of $5,000 are to be expected at the average branch. A designation of "good" is given to locations that are near that figure.
>
> Any location achieving a loss of less than $2,000 is considered to be superior. Any location experiencing a loss in excess of $100,000 is a MUST for an audit visit.

> **EXAMPLE 2:** In the normal course of business it is necessary to write off some open accounts receivable as bad debts. Past operating experience shows that an annual write-off of $10,000 is common at the average branch location. A designation of good is given to those locations, while a MUST assessment would be given for any location exceeding a write off of $75,000.

In the following sample form, we have used the assigned numbers in XYZ's chart of accounts to designate appropriate areas of review. A unique series of letters is used to designate operational activities that do not appear in the accounting statements. The actual program covers the full range of audit activities and all company locations or operations. We are presenting a condensed version to convey the idea.

Explanation of Form Entries

The following evaluation form can be used for a department, an operation or a complete location audit. The rating values remain the same for all assessments. The number of vertical columns is flexible, depending on the number of significant rating factors but the number of columns used should be consistent for all assessments.

In the sample, the column titled *"Element of Risk"* provides space for a description of each significant risk element. The following items are included in the form:

- The first element of risk is Coll. (ections) and the line is devoted to a risk rating for the cash collections activity.
- The second line, also for cash, provides space for the assessment of the Dep. (ositing) activities. In the actual form many other activities relating to cash, such as petty cash, cash advances, stamp funds, fees, and like items, would follow.
- Line 3, Secur. (ity) refers to the physical security, in this case, over investment documents.
- Line 4, Invoice, refers to preparation of sales invoices.
- Line 5, Admin. (istration) calls attention to the general field of administering the affairs of the Ohio Branch.

The second column is titled, Code No. (Number). In the sample, the accounting codes are used to designate an activity.

- Number 100 refers to Cash.
- 150 designates Investments.
- 400 is assigned to Sales Activities.
- AD is used to cover the general field of Administration at the operation being assessed.

The next column labeled "Date Last Audited" refers to the date that the particular activity was last reviewed by professional auditors.

The next columns (six in the sample) provide space for inserting and totaling the assigned risk rating for each of the listed items.

- Oper. (ating) Stat. (istics) refer to reports and statements relative to the operation being rated. Assigned values are frequently based on comparative results from similar operations.
- Manag. (ement) Eval. (uation) is a subjective appraisal of the managers who control an activity.
- Internal Controls is self-explanatory.
- Past Perf. (ormance) is a subjective rating based on previous audit reviews of the activity.
- Audit. (or) Rating gives the appraiser an opportunity to assess an activity based on personal knowledge or intuition.
- Total is self-explanatory, and provides an individual risk total for each activity. These total figures are very useful in deciding the activities to be reviewed in a *high point* audit.

The Grand Total value is used to determine an operation's place in the audit schedule. The higher the total value, the higher the risk factor. The pages can then be sorted in value order and *used as a basis* for determining an audit schedule. When used to estimate required audit hours, the same procedure is followed and the pages are totaled for the operations selected for audit.

The sample form follows:

Sample Form

XYZ CORPORATION
IA RA INTERNAL AUDIT DEPARTMENT
Location or Operation (Ohio Branch) Assessment Date (1/1/89)

Ratings: 1=Superior; 2=Excellent; 3=Good; 4=Poor; 5=Dangerous 6=Must

Element of Risk	Code No.	Date Last Audited	Assigned Risk Factors					
			Oper. Stat.	Manag. Eval.	Internal Controls	Past Perf.	Audit. Rating	Total
Coll.	100	5/6/87	2	1	1	2	2	8
Depos.	100	5/6/87	2	1	2	2	2	9
Secur.	150	5/6/87		2	3	3	4	12
Invoice	400	3/2/86	2	1	1	1	1	6
Admin.	AD	5/6/87		1	2	2	2	7
Grand Total								42

An audit manager who allows long intervals between audits for specific activities must remain alert for changes in management or operations that might affect the decision. The audit department must receive a copy of every notice of management or operating change that occurs, and the audit department must consider this information when deciding audit intervals.

KEY POINT: *The key to the preparation of the audit schedule is the evaluation of the risk of potential loss versus the cost of an audit.*

Unless there is a requirement that every activity be audited annually, the audit manager has the prerogative of determining the frequency of audit visits. Even under an annual requirement, the manager may elect to visit certain activities more frequently than once a year and can also control the audit scope used for each visit.

An audit approach is determined by the nature of the operation, the degree of risk involved and staff availability and cost. Some staffs perform a full and complete audit every time they visit an activity. Audit time requirements can vary from one day to several months depending upon the size and complexity of an operation.

High Point Audits

A high point audit approach is one method used to save audit time. For small, simple activities, the full audit program is always run, but the more complex operations can be approached in a different manner.

Locations that normally take several weeks or months to complete the full audit program can be switched over to a high point audit approach which divides the total program into several major sections. Each of these sections then becomes a complete audit program to be covered during a single visit. The sections can be set up to run in sequence so that section one is completed during the first visit, section two on the second visit, and so on. Each section contains a portion of the total audit program, but the critical areas of high risk appear in several, or all, of the sections.

Under a high point approach, audit management evaluates and rates each audit step and includes the critical ones in all programs. The next lower rated points appear every other visit, while the least important items appear for review every second or third year. Each program section contains a fraction of the total audit requirement; however, the audit frequency is increased under this concept.

> **EXAMPLE:** An audit of a location that usually required one month for three auditors may be divided into two separate sections with the same number of auditors working about two weeks per visit. The visits are now only nine months apart, however, instead of one year apart.
>
> Over a three-year period, the location will have been visited five times, as opposed to four under the old system. But the total audit time required is about eleven weeks, whereas under the usual system it would have required sixteen weeks.
>
> **KEY POINT:** *Audit frequency is increased, but the annual audit work load is reduced.*
>
> Critical areas are reviewed more frequently, while the other areas are skimmed over. The approach does increase travel time and mileage, and these factors must be taken into consideration.

Time Requirements for Audits

There are several ways to estimate the amount of audit time that will be required to review a particular activity. If the staff has audited an operation before, the same audit time may be assigned. If it is a first time audit but similar to operations that have been reviewed, then the average time taken for previous audits becomes the starting point for the new estimate. But any estimate based on past experience must be modified to consider other factors, such as:

1. The operating results of the location,
2. A comparison of business volume and size,
3. Comparison of actual to budgeted results,
4. A review of the comparative expense analysis, and
5. Any other information relating to the specific activity.

If the operation has never been audited by the staff, any estimate of required audit time is a pure guess, made by the audit manager.

Time assignments are used when there is insufficient information to make a good estimate. If it turns out that the allotted time is not sufficient, the audit supervisor must be given more time or permitted to omit some of the audit program.

IMPORTANT: *Audit time requirement for an individual location can be reduced:*

1. By use of a *Self Audit Program* which is described in Chapter 4.
2. By use of *Computer Assisted Audit Programs* or *Statistical Sampling Techniques* to perform some of the audit work. Discussions of these techniques are contained in Chapter 30.
3. Expensive auditor time can be saved by using local clerical help or outside temporaries to perform routine repetitive work that can be quickly reviewed and verified.
4. By using a *High Point Audit Approach* in which total audit programs are sectionalized based on a comparative analysis of the cost and value of audit steps as just described.

Stumbling Blocks

In estimating audit hour requirements, you will encounter some frequent stumbling blocks, such as the following:

1. The unexpected and unplanned work that is necessary when a large loss situation or an employee defalcation is detected.
2. Disruptions by specific requests for audits from executives who cannot be refused or put off.

3. Anonymous information or tips from employees that indicate the possibility of a problem in an operation or location that was not included in the current schedule.
4. A routine review of variance or inventory loss reports that makes it advisable to revise the audit schedule.

NOTE: *When enough of these types of incidents occur the manager must either cancel, revise or delay planned work or increase the size of the audit staff and the operating budget.*

Another important factor is the work performed by the external auditors. If the internal staff cannot handle all of the assigned work load that was agreed between the staffs, the external group may decide to cover the omitted activities. **KEEP IN MIND:** *This results in an increased fee for the CPA firm, but it enables the internal staff to stay within their budget.*

How to Check on Audit Performance

Too frequently an auditor skips over or fails to perform specific audit checks and does not make note of the oversight. The auditor merely initials the audit program, giving supervisors the impression that the work has been accomplished. These acts may come home to haunt the audit manager if something occurs that makes the oversight evident. There can be serious consequences if a major problem would have been disclosed if the work had been performed. **KEY POINT:** *Failure to note that work had been omitted could cause an auditor to be questioned as a possible accessory to a defalcation.*

As a cross-check on audit work performed and to provide a tool for the economical use of audit time, some staffs use an *auditor's time report program.* This program resulted from audit time analysis studies which centered on the audit program, time intervals between audits and the time required to perform each audit step.

Auditor's Time Reports

One way to learn how much auditing time is spent on each item and section of an audit program is to require that each auditor report the division of time spent on an assignment. Audit management then has a handle on the amount of time and related costs associated with audit routines and can, thus, better decide how to revise audit programs to reduce time requirements.

The *Time Report Program* uses an audit check list form that is coded to an audit program. The check list, given to each assigned auditor, contains an estimate of audit time required to perform each step as described in the audit manual. Some estimates of time needed to examine a single report are given, and these must be multiplied by the number of reports reviewed. These estimates are useful for planning and allocating field audit work. Auditors insert, in an appropriately headed column, their best estimate of total time actually required to perform the audit work. Time spent in waiting or because of unusual occurrences is eliminated. The sum total of all hours reported is not expected to equal total audit time spent.

Auditor's time reports serve a threefold purpose.

1. They give supervisors an estimate of the amount of time probably required to perform each audit step, which can be used when planning or allocating audit effort.
2. They can be used to find areas in which particular staff members need additional instructions.
3. They are useful in evaluating whether specific audit steps can be reduced or eliminated as too expensive for the risk involved.

Following is a sample of the form used by the XYZ Corporation:

XYZ CORPORATION
AUDITOR'S TIME REPORT

LOCATION .... DATE STARTED.............
NAME OF AUDITOR.................. DATE COMPLETED ....

This report is to be filled in as the audit progresses. When you complete each audit step, enter an estimate in minutes of the time required to perform the work. This is not a time study, nor will it be used to judge your efficiency. We require good estimates in order to evaluate each audit step to determine if changes are in order. These reports also help in establishing the number of audit hours normally required for a review of specific activities.

Note the time you start and stop a specific audit step. Ignore normal interruptions, but deduct such stoppages as lunch periods and coffee breaks. Your time should be close to the time estimate which appears in the first column. If something unusual requires time, make note in the comments column—for example "visited customer" or "visited bank." Your total reported time will not add up to the total time you actually spent on the job. Report all times in minutes.

	Est. Time	Time Req.	Comments
1. CASH—Petty Cash			
A. Count and reconcile petty cash fund.	30		
B. Review vouchers as directed.	30		
C. Check prior reconciliations.	20		
2. CASH RECEIPTS			
A. Control incoming mail.	150		
B. Review for proper endorsements.	60		
C. Review for proper keying.	120		

3. ACCOUNTS RECEIVABLE

A. Balance detail to control. (per control)	20
B. Prepare statements. (per statement)	5
C. Analyze replies. (per reply)	3

The information from auditors' time reports can be useful when estimating audit time required to review specific locations. Activity information files must contain statistical information such as the following:

1. Sales volume;
2. A breakdown of numbers of employees, such as office clerks, salesmen, deliveryman, and cashiers;
3. Number and size of petty cash funds and number of bank accounts;
4. Value of inventories and the locations of all outside storages; and
5. Other types of information that apply to a specific activity.

REMEMBER: *Estimates of audit time for any operation must be periodically reviewed and updated.*

Travel Time and Vacations

Other important considerations in estimating total annual audit time requirements are vacations and travel time. Both variables can be fairly well estimated, but travel time is affected by special requests or by unusual problems that occur during the year.

A large staff eats up many audit hours in traveling between assignments. Some staffs attempt to reduce travel time in a variety of ways, some of which are covered in the forthcoming section titled, "Travel Expenses." Reducing travel distances and associated time and costs may not appear to be important, but for a large audit staff the savings can be appreciable. In any event, the time required to move audit staff from one location to the next assignment must be calculated and included in the annual estimate of required audit time.

Audit schedules must also consider vacations, meetings, lost time through illness, unforeseen delays and special requests for audits. Vacations should be requested by staff auditors well in advance of the planned starting date so that their schedules can be arranged to wind up an assignment near their home base. The same planning can be used to reduce travel distances to meetings. Illness and requests for special audits cannot be anticipated, for they may come at any time. **REMEMBER:** *There is no way to estimate the amount of audit time overruns that are required to handle start-up time, significant errors or time spent handling employee frauds.* Internal audit managers must include an educated guess of the contingent audit hours that will be required to accomplish their audit schedule.

SALARIES

The major costs of an internal auditing department are the salaries and traveling expenses of the staff. Planned salary costs are sometimes skewed when across the board adjustments are required or when key staff members become dissatisfied with their salary and must be given substantial increases in order to keep them on the staff. Or the staff may require a specialist or expert in a particular field and may be required to pay salaries in excess of the plan. When such things occur, they are discussed with appropriate executives and if the budget cannot be increased, the manager must reduce either the size of the staff or other departmental expenses.

The audit staff administrator informs the manager of current salaries being offered by other audit staffs in comparable companies, industries and positions on company organization charts. This data is supplied by the Personnel Department, and is also periodically printed in financial publications and in surveys conducted by the Institute of Internal Auditors (IIA).

Auditors, like all other employees, exchange confidences with their peers, and after a short period of familiarization, the new staff member becomes aware of the salary rate of all other auditors. Payroll records are regularly audited by staff members, and new personnel soon learn where their starting salary fell in the established range. **TIP:** *With this in mind, audit managers should consider a hiring policy that sets a definite salary for every new entry at a given level.* After the first evaluation of the new member, an appropriate adjustment can be made. In any event, the starting salary for staff auditors should be high enough to attract good people. The audit manager should periodically meet with each staff member and discuss his or her salary, work evaluation reports and personal goals.

Wages and Hours Regulations

Another salary consideration is the classification of the work performed by a staff member. Staff members who perform most of the clerical routines required during an audit are classified as nonexempt employees and must be paid time and a half for overtime hours. This classification would certainly apply to audit trainees and junior auditors, and perhaps to some staff auditors. Auditors who perform clerical work sometimes receive bigger paychecks than the in-charge audit senior. This is true in spite of the fact that the supervisor may have actually worked more hours than the staff auditor. **TIP:** *Audit supervisors, fully aware of this inequity, can determine and set the overtime hours to be worked by an employee and can often find ways of reducing the overtime hours of nonexempt employees.*

A possible solution to the problem of job classification is to use the computer to perform much of the clerical work required in an audit assignment. The auditor's job then changes to one of analysis, rather than a clerical one. This approach can affect staff auditors, not trainees.

Another method is to hire temporary help from a local office services agency. These people can do the routine time-consuming tasks that would otherwise be performed by higher paid staff auditors.

Moving Expenses

Moving expenses can become a significant cost factor. Hiring new auditors and moving them to their new place of employment is costly, particularly when married people are involved and the movement includes a full family. **REMEMBER:** *New hires expect to be reimbursed for all costs of traveling to the new location and also expect to be given time to locate a new residence.* Each move of a household can cost thousands of dollars.

One way of reducing moving expenses, when a large increase in staff is planned, is to establish regional offices. New hires can be sought in the vicinity of the regional audit office, using that office as their base. This approach reduces moving and traveling expenses and attracts prospective employees residing in that particular area.

Some companies use an allowance basis for controlling moving expenses. A definite sum of money is allocated to each new hire to cover any and all expenses associated with the move. This is a fair approach for unmarried hires since they have the option of deciding what furniture to move and how to move it. Other companies utilize in-house services to make all arrangements for moves. All associated costs are paid for directly by the company. Removing this worry from the new employee, enables the auditor to concentrate on the new job.

TRAVEL EXPENSES

Traveling expenses are the other major cost area of an internal auditing function. Policies governing reimbursement of travel expenses are set by each organization. Normally, companies pay for all transportation costs which are processed through the employee's personal account. The audit manager must decide such things as the following:

1. Should the staff travel by air, and if so, what class of fare should be used?
2. Should schedules be firmly set so that advance tickets may be purchased at substantial discounts?
3. Can the audit staff be ordered to travel by bus?

4. Should use of private automobile be authorized, and if so, what mileage rate should be used for reimbursement?
5. What lodgings should the staff use, and are there limits to how much the company will pay?
6. How will expenses for food be controlled?

Decisions on any of the above items can affect travel expenses, and staff morale.

Per Diem Vs Actual

A *per diem* approach is frequently used for controlling food and lodging costs. A daily rate, designed to pay for decent accommodations in a good hotel and for three meals in a moderately priced restaurant, is established for each city that the staff visits. These rates are usually suggested by site supervisors and accepted by the home office.

KEY POINT: *Individual auditors may overspend or under-spend the per diem allowance but the difference is the responsibility of the auditor.*

Some staffs reimburse for *actual costs* and require receipted bills for all expenses. Staff auditors are expected to exercise moderation in incurring food and lodging costs. Staff administrators negotiate room rates with hotels located in cities which are regularly visited by the staff, and auditors are required to reside at those hotels.

A modified, actual reimbursement plan requires the auditor to use a company-supplied credit card for all company-related outlays on the trip. In such cases, travel advances are unnecessary, and an element of control over travel expenses is introduced. The employer pays the credit card company directly for all properly supported company expenses incurred by authorized employees.

Under any system, the staff administrator reviews all expense reports and works at controlling the free spenders on the staff.

Private Auto or Company Car

Some audit staffs attempt to save on travel expenses by allowing auditors to use their personal cars for traveling and by planning assignments so that auditors travel on weekends as much as possible. Under such conditions, the auditor is allowed a one-day travel period, which is the time that would be required to travel by air. It would be unwise for the audit manager to insist that staff auditors must use air transportation. Some staffs provide company cars, others permit the use of employee owned vehicles. It is a matter of economics.

When personal cars are used, the company establishes a flat per mile reimbursement rate. Mileage distances may be actual or based on the computed distances between company locations. A set amount may be computed on the standard distance times the rate for a stipulated mode of travel, or it may simply be the prevailing air fare. Staff members are then allowed to travel in any manner they choose.

Even though auto travel may take more time than air travel, there is a compensating payoff in that much of the excess travel time is spent during the weekend so that no work time is actually lost. In addition the auditor has a car available at the audit location which is frequently required to accomplish an audit task.

Some companies that permit auditors to use personal cars, study the comparative cost of supplying a company car against the cost of reimbursing for use of a personal car. **REMEMBER:** *There is always a mileage figure beyond which it is more economical to supply the car.* An estimate is made of the annual expected miles of travel and if this exceeds the economic break-even point, then the company supplies the car and pays for all operating expenses. The auto remains the property of the company and is merely assigned to the employee for business use.

Regional Audit Offices

No matter the travel method used, the finalized audit schedule should minimize the distance and related lost time required to travel between assignments. This can be done by scheduling audits to follow a geographic sequence. For example, an auditor's itinerary starting from the home office would lead toward audit locations at the outer extreme of the assigned area, and then return, picking up operations on a route back to home base in time for a planned audit activity or vacation.

Larger audit staffs sometimes establish *regional audit offices* to which they assign a number of auditors. The regional office, usually located in a major company complex, becomes home base for assigned auditors and *they are not on expenses while working in that city.* The office becomes the center of the area assigned to the audit group and results in reduced travel time and expenses. It has the advantage of enabling an assignment of personnel in or near their home towns.

Regional audit offices usually contain a minimum of permanent staff. The office gets the most use when one or more audit teams are auditing company operations located in the vicinity. If possible, each auditor should be assigned working space, a listed telephone and periodic office help. They also need file space, working tables and an up-to-date library containing auditing books and periodicals, and company policy and procedure manuals.

Monitoring the Budget

After the budget is approved, the administrator carefully monitors expenditures and reviews, line by line, actual expenses incurred versus budgeted estimates. **NOTE:** *The audit manager is immediately advised of any expense items that are exceeding estimates.* When the manager decides to take corrective action, the administrator works with audit supervisors and staff members to put the new directives into effect.

The manager must prepare a proposed work schedule within the agreed budget and select staff members needed to accomplish the approved plan. But first, an audit manual is required that spells out audit routines.

Need for a Manual

Staff auditors must have written instructions designed to enable them to perform assigned duties. An audit manager may write these instructions or may supervise their creation. Newly organized departments sometimes use their CPA firm's audit program as the starting point for in-house internal auditing work. In any case, the manager decides what material to prepare, how it will be organized and then approves the contents. This section deals with the administrative aspects of an audit manual. Chapter 6 considers the technical contents.

What Should an Internal Audit Manual Contain

The audit manual is a device for explaining audit routines and operating procedures to the staff. The manual should be complete enough to answer most questions that will arise, but it should still be flexible enough to encourage internal auditors to think problems through.

1. State audit objectives clearly, fully and concisely in the body of the audit program.
2. Aim basically for meaningful results. This means that your audit will produce more efficient operations and profits, will prevent losses or will reduce operating costs.

An internal audit manual may be limited or unlimited in its range, depending upon the desire of the department's administration. A limited manual only contains administrative information, such as pertinent personnel and audit department administrative policy and procedure bulletins. The pages originate in the Personnel Department or the administrative section of the Auditing Department. An unlimited, internal auditing manual contains all administrative material and also includes audit forms, programs and related audit instructions that are necessary for staff auditors to accomplish an audit of any company location or operation.

Limited manuals are light and easily handled. They contain information concerning company insurance and compensation policies, auditing department administrative matters and other items of this nature. Staff members soon master all the administrative directives that they consider important, and then they keep the manual at home, unless this practice is forbidden. They know that all the personnel policy statements are available at every location they audit, and they are continually confronted with all the audit administrative directions. These light booklets are rarely carted around by staff auditors. They know that audit supervisors usually carry one in their briefcase, just in case an unusual question arises.

When the condensed manual is used, staff members often carry a book of instructions that contains technical instructions associated with the audit programs. Some staffs include specific instructions in the body of the audit program and do not require a separate book. Audit programs are printed for all auditable locations, and the supply of forms is controlled by the audit administrator. Programs and necessary instructions are doled out as jobs are assigned.

Some staffs prefer to have a single internal audit manual of the *unlimited* variety. Each auditor carries a large, heavy manual which contains all information that audit management believes the staff auditor will need to accomplish any assignment. In the early period of employment, the staff auditor frequently refers to this manual. As time goes by, the important information is memorized, and the book is then rarely opened. But the information contained therein must be kept up-to-date and that becomes the responsibility of the audit department administrator.

Who Writes the Material

The audit manager is responsible for the preparation of all audit material included in the manual. Audit department administrative instructions and directives are usually conceived by the department administrator. Required technical information, such as the programs and related instructions, are written by audit supervisors.

Specific supervisors are selected to write or revise sections of programs relating to the audit of operations that they have already reviewed. The draft is studied by other knowledgeable staff members who suggest revisions or alterations. A revised draft is then prepared and recirculated to the original author and editors. The overseeing of the revision work is usually handled by the staff training supervisor.

After all parties agree on the draft, the audit manager finalizes the material and turns the matter over to the staff administrator.

Keeping Manuals Current

When a detailed technical writeup has been completed, the staff administrator handles all of the mechanical detail necessary to print and distribute the pages. The administrator is then responsible for keeping all manuals up-to-date and for insuring that old copies of revised instructions and programs are destroyed. A simple system is used to accomplish this task.

1. All manuals are numbered.
2. All employees who receive these books are listed in a register which is used to insure that all authorized holders receive additions or revisions.
3. Changes are mailed to registered holders with a covering letter to each holder, containing the assigned number of the manual.
4. All recipients are requested to sign and return the covering letter to insure that they received the mailed data. The letter may request that all removed pages be mailed back to the audit office for destruction. **IMPORTANT:** *This procedure insures that all old copies are destroyed, and it proves that field auditors received the data and at least removed the rescinded pages.* It does not insure that the correct pages had been properly placed in the manual.

   REMEMBER: *Audit supervisors are responsible for checking field manuals periodically to determine that all copies are current.*

Where there is a separation between administrative matters and auditing instructions, the same general approach to changes is applied. Limited manuals, carried by staff members, are numbered, assigned and controlled as above. As auditors move to various assignments, they are sent copies of programs and instructions required. When forms are changed, a clerk replaces the central stock with revised materials.

Central supplies of manuals, forms, programs and instructions are monitored by the staff administrator. Minor revisions are usually accumulated and made when the reorder point is reached.

When audit programs and instructions are originally written and sent out to the field, the users immediately play back any questions, errors or inconsistencies that they note. If the comments are important, the writeups are revised and the material is reissued.

KEY POINT: *When any material becomes outdated, audit supervision must advise the administrator so that the items can be deleted.*

How are Programs and Instructions Supplied to Field Staff

Internal audit staffs that use manuals make certain that they are carried by auditors, and send out working copies of required programs.

Staffs that use a *limited* manual send necessary supplies of forms, programs and instructions to audit teams. If the staff uses a book of audit instructions, each auditor is assigned a book which is controlled in the same manner as the audit manual. Otherwise a few copies of instructions, applicable to a specific activity, are sent out and used jointly by team members.

Individual audit programs are sometimes given to each auditor with specific work assignments checked off on each program. Sometimes, one master program is shared by all team members and the supervisor places appropriate initials before each audit step to show who is to perform the work. As work is completed, the program is initialed by the auditor who reviewed the specified records or procedures. **KEEP IN MIND:** *Sharing of audit programs and instructions may create some discomfort, but it can materially reduce the amount of paper carried during an extensive audit swing that covers many locations and activities.*

RECRUITING STAFF

A major administrative task is to select new personnel and then prepare them to fit into the audit staff organization. After the recruits are selected, an audit administrator schedules training programs that are designed to acquaint the new staff auditors with the company, the responsibilities of their new assignments and with the internal auditing profession.

The ideal internal auditor is a person who can interact with others on a basis of equality. One who is able to take control without rubbing people the wrong way. The individual must have the ability to express ideas intelligently and clearly, both in conversation and in writing. The potential auditor must have an analytical and enquiring mind with good professional training. Finally, the individual should be persistent and able to spot evasiveness.

Where shall we look and how do we find this person?

1. An obvious source for staff additions is among the graduating class of a good college or university.
2. A company personnel department can assist in the search.
3. Employees of other departments may be attracted to the internal auditing profession and may want to transfer to the audit staff.

Let's consider each of these sources.

Colleges and Universities

Some staffs send representatives to visit their alma maters during designated career days to interview interested students and to establish contact with faculty members who may be persuaded to identify good prospects. These faculty members are also asked to inform their students that the internal auditing profession is a good career field.

Other staffs send posters and brochures to be displayed and given out during career days to the college placement offices. Some staffs also provide application forms with accompanying instructions to be given to graduating seniors, and they are sometimes offered to lower-class students who are interested in apprenticeship programs.

Apprenticeship Programs

Under an apprenticeship or summer training program, potential staff members are identified by audit supervisors during their visits to the schools. In some cases a summer work program is offered to a likely prospect who opts for an advanced degree before leaving school. Some staffs limit their summer work programs to students who are working on their advanced degrees.

KEY POINT: *There is ample evidence that a well-designed summer work program can attract good prospects to an audit staff.* Audit managers hope these students will be persuaded to continue their education with the objective of becoming internal auditors and joining the staff that is providing the summer training.

During apprenticeship training programs, the staff administrator works with audit supervision in planning a training program and in monitoring the progress of the student. Trainees are required to prepare periodic progress reports as they move through their training program. These reports, which contain critical reviews of the training program, the auditing department's work approach and the personnel assigned to supervise the trainee provide a good insight into the thinking and ability of the student. They also serve, in a sense, as a critique of the auditing function by a nonprofessional.

KEY POINT: *Audit staffs do not generally benefit when trainees are assigned to perform routine tasks in various operating departments.* They only remain on a specific job for a few days and are then moved to another desk. Trainees are moved from department to department until they understand the company and its business; then they are assigned to work with an audit team.

KEY POINT: *When using trainees, the staff supervisor must be careful to keep these people away from confidential information, processes or trade practices.* The limitation of access is necessary, and should not be a surprise to an intelligent trainee, but it should be handled tactfully in a polite manner.

How to Use the Personnel Department Most Successfully

The company personnel department is a service-oriented operation, like the audit department, and the costs of the operation are included in overhead assessments. Personnel departments use their contacts with employment agencies to locate likely prospects. Sometimes, outside head hunters can find management types who are interested in changing jobs.

Personnel specialists use the local, regional and national publications to reach likely prospects. Unsolicited résumés are usually received by personnel, screened and routed to the audit manager. Final decisions on all audit job requests are made by the audit manager.

Transfers From Within the Company

Another source for entry-level auditors is the existing company work force. Some current employees may have the ability, intelligence and desire to become internal auditors. This source offers the advantage that such people already know the company, may not have to be moved and can be transferred to the staff for evaluation.

KEY POINT: *This existing employee pool can be particularly useful when the audit staff is assigned to perform an operational audit of an activity that has never been audited before.* For example, if a first time review of the Engineering Department has been assigned, the audit manager might consider adding an engineering expert to the staff.

Instead of an outsider, the manager might transfer a manager or an administrative supervisor who works in the Engineering Department. Such an individual will have a background of experience with the company and in the engineering field *and could be useful to the staff in providing technical information required for an operational review of the engineering function.*

This type of transfer must be handled so as to avoid the appearance that the added auditor is merely an informant. Such people should not be sent into sections where they formerly worked, but instead they should be used as consultants to review work papers and to advise on technical approaches.

TRAINING PROGRAMS

When likely prospects have been identified and hired, they must be indoctrinated into the organization and trained to do their jobs. Training can be accomplished in many different ways, and much depends on whether the approach is short range or long range.

Short range aims to get a specific job done accurately and quickly, and most auditors become specialists in the routine everyday assignments that are required for almost all audits.

The *long range* approach trains auditors thoroughly in many areas so that they will be prepared for future difficult assignments.

Much of the training of the staff is of an informal, long range nature. Important bulletins, general information letters, directives, policy statements, and company publications are routed through the department and wind up in the audit library. The library also contains audit and accounting textbooks and professional publications. Business magazines and newspapers are also available for reference purposes.

Audit department administration supervises the training of the staff. Internal auditors, just as any other professionals, require continuing education programs. Company training concentrates on increasing the employee's knowledge of company operations, policies, procedures and operating results. Special programs are usually designed to explain important changes in existing policies or to introduce significant new policies and may be only offered to selected employees. **NOTE:** *The audit administrator must schedule staff member attendance in a way that minimizes disruption of audit work.*

The type and extent of continuing education is dependent upon the auditors' previous experience, knowledge of the profession and familiarity with the employing company. Continuing training of internal auditors usually takes one of the following forms:

1. On-the-job training,
2. In-house training classes,
3. Courses at neighboring colleges or universities,
4. Correspondence courses,
5. Seminars or conferences sponsored by outside professional or educational organizations, and
6. Vacation relief of supervisory personnel.

Each of these training approaches offer unique challenges and benefits. Let's consider some of the specific training programs that are used by internal audit staffs.

On-The-Job Training

Probably the most extensively used method of training staff auditors is on-the-job training. All internal auditors receive some of this type of training at one time or another, usually in an informal fashion. People generally are more interested in an actual, rather than a theoretical, problem and will give their attention when they encounter such a situation during an audit.

Formalized on-the-job training programs utilize audit seniors or supervisors to train juniors or staff auditors as the work progresses on an audit assignment. The trainer not only explains what must be done, but why it is necessary and how best to accomplish the task.

On-the-job training is a low-cost teaching method, but it may also be the poorest. Under this approach, the trainer and student continue to do their work and the training is accomplished in as little time as possible—specifically, until the trainer thinks that the student understands what is to be done. The amount of know-how garnered by the trainee is entirely dependent upon the knowledge and capability of the trainer. If the trainee is fortunate enough to be instructed by a knowledgeable individual who also has some expertise in teaching, then the student will probably learn the job. **CAUTION:** *Any bad habits, poor approaches or false impressions that were in the teacher's mind will be passed on to the student.* Training of new people should be assigned to the most competent supervisors.

The experienced instructor assigns audit steps to the novice and then either leads the beginner through the maize, or walks away until asked for help. The approach varies with the trainee. Supervisory review of work papers discloses whether the novice grasped the intent of the audit step, or whether additional instructions are required. **TIP:** *The supervisor tells the trainee what is going to be explained, then offers the explanation and then summarizes what has just been explained.* The trainer gives detailed, step-by-step instructions and answers all questions until satisfied that the point is understood.

On-the-job training includes supervisory review of an auditor's work in all of the following areas of the profession:

1. Trainee's write-ups of operations,
2. Interview techniques,
3. Preparation of flow charts,
4. Preparation and coding of audit work papers,
5. Verification procedures,
6. Safeguarding of audit working papers and schedules,
7. Adherence to local rules and regulations, and
8. The novice's general decorum.

Corrections are discussed during private, personal interviews. Handled expertly this training system can get the job done.

In-House Training

All audit staffs conduct formal or informal in-house long range training sessions. These *formal approaches* consist of the following:

1. Familiarization sessions where the newcomer meets managers and top executives of the organization;
2. Review of organization charts, annual reports, accounting and audit manuals, financial bulletins and other pertinent information;
3. Formalized courses that are given to new hires. These courses cover basic audit policies and routines; review of company directives, organization charts, published policies and procedures; corporate goals and personnel policies;
4. In-house courses of a continuing nature for which auditors attend sessions during their "between audit" time. Here the basic courses are completed before the first audit assignment and remaining subjects are worked on when the auditor has time available.

Much information is disseminated in an *informal manner:*

1. Staff member "buzz sessions" spread interesting auditing experiences around the department,
2. Attendance at operating department meetings where educational information is presented to employees,
3. Management training seminars or courses given by company employees.

Periodic Meetings of the Audit Staff

A major training program is the periodic meeting of the full audit staff. Sessions are scheduled monthly, quarterly, or annually. The frequency of such meetings determines their length and format. The more frequent, the shorter and less detailed is the material covered.

The purposes of these gatherings include the following:

- Present an opportunity for staff people to intermingle with top executives and some of the managers who provide services to the group;
- Give auditors an opportunity to rub shoulders with the brass and hear top executives describe their management philosophy, and the operating policies of their department. This gives the staff a better understanding of the company, its goals and its executives;

- Enable auditors to get better acquainted with their co-workers and with auditing management.

Preparation for a departmental meeting requires planning. Travel plans must be adapted to the audit schedule, reservations must be made and menus and social affairs planned. The staff administrator handles all the details necessary for holding a successful meeting, but the subject matter of the training classes is handled by audit supervisors chosen to handle selected subjects. They prepare materials and lead the classes or panel discussions. **KEEP IN MIND:** *These sessions are designed as training aids, so audit supervisors must spend a great deal of time in lesson preparation, presentation, discussion and testing.*

The subjects at these sessions concentrate on areas in which the audit staff has shown some weakness. Case studies of actual events that staff auditors have encountered, are often used as examples. This approach is effective because it strikes close to home and holds the interest of auditors who may expect to encounter similar situations. Other staffs opt for the conventional lecture or panel discussion approach, while others combine the various formats. **REMEMBER:** *These meetings are designed to help train the staff, so that they will perform their work intelligently and efficiently, and to increase the morale of people who may feel far removed from the decision-making office.*

In addition to audit techniques and special instructional periods, such meetings also include administrative subjects of interest to staff members. Personnel policies, changes in company organization or policies, forthcoming changes in audit management personnel or assignments and other items of this nature are of interest to auditors, who spend so much of their working hours on the road.

Larger audit staffs use a training supervisor to achieve the following:

1. Determine the training needs of each staff member,
2. Work with staff auditors to fill training needs,
3. Select training materials and procure supplies,
4. Select subjects and design course materials,
5. Choose instructors to make presentations at staff meetings,
6. Act as an administrative assistant in working with staff members, and
7. Serve as the staff representative who visits schools during their career day activities.

Staff meetings can be quite expensive in money outlays as well as lost audit time. When considering the length of proposed meetings, or whether they need to be held at all, audit managers should compare the costs to the anticipated gains. Anticipated gains are listed next:

- Better trained and informed auditors,
- Improvement of morale and attitude of staff members, and
- Better acceptance of the audit staff by executives who are given an opportunity to visit with them.

Training of Audit Management

An audit staff's training program should include training sessions aimed at senior auditors and supervisors. Materials covered include the following:

1. Administrative problems of running an internal auditing department.
2. A detailed discussion of the operating budget so that each attendee is made aware of the costs of running the department.
3. An in-depth review of field problems. Suggestions for changes in audit instructions, internal control questionnaires or field manuals are considered and finalized.
4. A review of the audit schedule, with time estimates being revised as necessary.
5. Major audit findings are described and all supervisors told of danger signals that need to be checked.
6. Deciding whether it is necessary or desirable to hold meetings of the entire staff, or of certain sections. If meetings are agreed upon, the supervisors prepare the necessary plans.

Audit managers use these meetings to insure that the management team understands the philosophy and approach of the audit function and is aware of problems that might affect the staff.
KEY POINT: *These meetings help the seniors and supervisors feel that they are a part of the audit management team and give them information that improves their job performance.*

Courses at Neighboring Schools

Other training facilities are available at the local colleges. These schools offer courses, some of which are designed to aid in training auditors. Such classes are often held at night and scheduled for a one-night, four-hour session, so that the working auditor need only be in town one night per week. **NOTE:** *A working* *auditor who enrolls in such a course does so upon the advise or the consent of the supervisor of training who can arrange to adjust the auditor's work schedule.*

Most of these courses are accredited, and college credits are awarded upon satisfactory completion. Many company policies offer to reimburse employees for costs of approved courses, when they submit proof of satisfactory completion. **NOTE:** *This type of training is useful for auditors who are working for an advanced degree, but these courses are rarely helpful in solving immediate training problems.*

Correspondence Courses

Another useful training facility is a home study program offered by many colleges and universities. Staff-training supervisors may suggest that certain members take specific correspondence courses to help them understand various phases of business activities.

KEY POINT: *This training device is only as good as the caliber of course material and of the proctor who reads submitted assignments and comments on the answers.* The correspondence course approach can be modified, as follows, to improve it as a company teaching aid.

When the student receives a graded assignment, the entire material, including the proctor's comments are reviewed with an audit supervisor. Questions, answers and comments are discussed and considered from the standpoint of the auditing profession and the particular employer.

KEY POINT: *The course is thus brought into a working perspective.*

A major drawback to the correspondence school approach is the time factor involved in completing a necessary course. If an auditor is weak in a particular area, there usually is not enough time to complete a correspondence course. **NOTE:** *This approach is applicable to long range planning, rather than to the solution of an immediate problem.*

Conferences and Seminars

Other educational programs useful to internal auditors, or to other management personnel, are offered by the American Management Association, the American Institute of Certified Public Accountants, the Institute of Internal Auditors, and many private training companies. All of these conferences, seminars, courses or training sessions are designed to provide education for the business community at a reasonable price. Many organizations have specially designed courses, which are regularly offered, or seminars, which travel from city to city. Some public accounting firms have developed training programs that are available to clients or business organizations.

Many IIA conferences are run by chapters located in the larger cities, and are open to members, prospective members and guests. Some of these conferences present excellent training programs for selected subjects, and all offer an opportunity for professional people to rub shoulders and exchange ideas and experiences. **NOTE:** *Program contents are aimed, specifically, at auditing management or staff members.*

Vacation Relief

Another training opportunity is presented when line managers take their annual vacations. Some audit staffs use their personnel to fill in for office supervisory personnel who are on vacation.

KEY POINT: *This gives the auditor an opportunity to observe first hand the problems of operating supervision.* It also helps make the auditor more understanding of management problems. **MONEY SAVING SUGGESTION:** *Vacation relief is also an effective method of accomplishing a low cost audit review of an activity.* While serving as an operating manager, the auditor is able to evaluate procedures and personnel in a working environment. This subtle approach is most useful when an auditor substitutes at the office manager's job.

CIA and CPA Examinations

Good staff auditors are interested in improving their knowledge and their professional standing. Training aids and work assignments help improve knowledge of the trade; participation in professional conferences and seminars improve the auditors' professional standing.

Further improvement can result from earning certification through successful completion of recognized tests. The Certified Internal Auditor (CIA test), controlled by the IIA, and the Certified Public Accountant (CPA) test, sponsored by the American Institute of Certified Public Accountants, are the most widely recognized and accepted examples of professional certification examinations.

Both of these tests have prerequisites that must be satisfied before an applicant is eligible to take the exam. These tests, which delve deeply into the applicant's professional knowledge, require several days to complete and may be repeated at specified intervals.

To help pass one of these exams, an applicant must review a variety of subjects. Many organizations offer refresher courses designed as study aids for these tests. Some audit staffs reimburse their members for the costs of such courses and encourage their staff people to earn these certificates. **NOTE:** *They reason that their employees are working at improving their minds and increasing their knowledge and that they are bound to learn something that will aid in their job performance.*

SCHEDULING AUDIT ASSIGNMENTS

After the annual audit schedule is finalized, the audit manager sets the date for an activity to be audited and then selects the right internal auditor for each job. Every audit assignment presents a different challenge, and the manager is aware of the capabilities of staff people and the unique features associated with each assignment. In the selection of individual auditors, their training and past experiences are major factors in the consideration.

EXAMPLE: The monthly audit schedule contained three production plants, seven sales branches, the Research Laboratory and the Engineering Department. All staff members had successfully audited sales branches, but only four had worked on production plant assignments. One supervisor had worked on a previous audit of Research, and another had been used in an Engineering audit.

After due consideration, the assignments were made as follows:

1. Production plants: These were small plants and were assigned to be handled by two three-person teams. It was estimated that each plant would need a two-week audit period. Two of the four staff auditors with previous plant experience were selected to act as seniors and head up the teams. The other two auditors of each team were selected from the staff *to broaden their experience.*
2. Sales branches. Six were of normal size that normally required *five audit weeks* to complete. Three teams were assigned to audit these locations—each was composed of two experienced branch auditors, one named as senior, and one junior. Each branch was allocated two weeks for a total of *six audit weeks. The additional time was specified to provide for staff training.*

   The seventh branch was a larger operation that consistently experienced control problems. A normal operation of that size would have required ten audit weeks; *but because of the past history,* fourteen audit weeks were allocated. The audit team, composed of three staff auditors and one junior, was scheduled to spend four weeks at the location. One of the staff auditors was assigned to only spend two weeks at the location.
3. Research Laboratory. One audit supervisor, who had previously performed operational studies and had completed college courses in Chemistry, Physics and Advanced Mathematics, was selected to head up the audit team. The goal was to complete the review in four weeks. One of the experienced plant auditors was assigned as was one junior auditor who had a suitable education.

In addition, arrangements were made to transfer an employee from a major production plant who had worked as the plant laboratory supervisor for several years. This was a permanent transfer, and the employee was added to the audit team. *The audit staff utilized in-house experience.*

4. Engineering Department. The audit staff contained a group of specialists used exclusively to audit construction jobs. The manager of this group was selected to head up the review team. A one-month period was estimated to complete the job, and the audit team was made up of one experienced plant auditor, one experienced sales branch auditor, and a recent addition to the staff who had a background which included experience as an administrative manager of a medium-sized engineering firm. *In this instance, outside experience was advantageous.*

Rotating Work Assignments

When deciding who to send out on a job, the manager prefers an auditor who has had some previous experience in the applicable audit routine and/or the specific type of activity to be reviewed. Someone who understands all audit instructions and their underlying reasoning. **NOTE:** *Sometimes an auditor is selected who has NOT audited the type of operation, and the assignment helps round out the auditor's experience level.* Another factor is the need to challenge the thinking of staff members so that they don't become lulled because of examining the same type of activity over and over again. *These same considerations apply when assigning specific sections of the audit program during the audit.*

Large internal audit staffs that contain specialized groups for reviewing specific activities have an opportunity of moving staff people in and out of these special areas. **KEY POINT:** *Such movement makes the staff auditors job more interesting and broadening and brings fresh thinking into the special sections of the staff.*

Avoiding Set Pattern for Visits

Audit schedules can be easily handled by establishing a working routine and consistently following it. Though the easiest, this system is far from the best. Staff members like a consistent schedule that informs them well in advance where they will be working during the coming year. Audit administrators are in favor of routine because it makes their jobs much easier. The audited locations like it because they know well in advance when to expect the audit visit and can prepare for it. *This last element is the main reason that it is not a good idea.*

One of the main intangible elements of control is the psychological advantage gained from surprise audit visits. The routine year-end visits by outside auditors are examples of established schedules which conform to external audit goals. Clients know when to expect these visits and prepare in advance, so that the CPA firm will be able to perform their required work in a minimum of time. **CAUTION:** *This kind of reasoning does NOT always apply to the internal audits.*

Responding to Requests for Audits

As the audit function gains stature and acceptance, the staff is looked upon as management's appraisal expert and is often requested to look into special areas of operations. Employees feel free to openly discuss any business matters with auditors, and they freely voice their misgivings about certain activities, records or personnel.

Special audits or investigations are difficult to administer since the audit time requirement is often underestimated. **CAUTION:** *Specials always require top audit supervision and some staff auditor time.*

In a tightly scheduled program, these specials mean that something must give somewhere, and the audit manager's ingenuity is challenged. The manager may increase staff, delay other planned reviews, reduce the scope of certain audits or use some type of audit assistance. **NOTE:** *Help can come from computer-assisted audit programs, outside contract audit agencies or extensive use of statistical sampling techniques.*

To grow in stature and acceptance, audit managers must strive to perform these special requests. Successful accomplishment of a special assignment leads to other such requests. **NOTE:** *The word spreads quickly among top executives and soon the internal audit staff is performing management or operational audits, adding to its prestige.*

Executives may request a special audit of their full departments or of specific operations within their area of responsibility. When top executives consider reorganizing an operation, they seek an outside expert appraisal which will either confirm the action or point out why it should not be done. **CAUTION:** *The executive request is usually vague, and the audit manager must determine the scope and depth of a review.*

An executive who requests an audit review wants it done yesterday. Rarely will a request be received that may be satisfied by scheduling an audit for next year. **CAUTION:** *Delay in responding may antagonize the executive and lead to the employment of an outside consultant to perform the study.* If the audit staff is too busy to handle the request within a reasonable period of time, the executive should be told so that other arrangements may be made.

An incoming executive may ask for an audit so that responsibility for all previous actions can be pinpointed. **IMPORTANT:** *These requests are often* *made when the former department head has left the company for any reason other than retirement or death.* The new executive may also intend to alter the operation, recognizing that changes are best accepted when a new department head takes over. **CAUTION:** *Some executives may attempt to steer the direction of the audit, which is tolerable, but what cannot be tolerated is an attempt to influence audit findings or the writing of the audit report.*

A well-established audit function frequently receives "tips" or "leads" from sources within and outside the company. Internal auditors must protect their sources of information, and they must develop evidence independently with no preconceived conclusions. Many leads come from employees who have incomplete information or who are passing on a rumor.

Most requests for special audits come from top executives. Sometimes they request special studies that are far removed from the normal routine audit reviews. Some of these special investigations are discussed in detail in Chapter 29.

EVALUATING THE WORK OF STAFF AUDITORS

Internal auditors, like other employees, need to know that their work is being monitored and their efforts appreciated. Many staffs use an evaluation program that records the progress of each staff member and gives all employees an opportunity to review and discuss their personal ratings. Individual auditor's ratings are prepared by the most knowledgeable supervisors. One important phase of a supervisor's job is the evaluation of staff auditor's work.

Job Performance Reports and Reviews

Job evaluation reports are prepared either at the completion of each audit or monthly. The first-line supervisor who has worked closely with the auditor prepares the evaluation.

Job evaluation report forms are designed as a multiple choice selection to reduce writing and detailed explanations. The supervisor checks off the applicable answers.

Following is a brief sample of several sections of such a report.

XYZ CORPORATION
EMPLOYEE JOB ANALYSIS REPORT
(Supervisors: Place a check mark in the box that applies. For any "Below Average" rating, explain in comments line.)

Employee ________________________________ Date ____________
Prepared by ______________________________ Title ____________

	Excellent	Good	Average	Below Average
ASSIGNED WORK				
CASH:				
Count of funds	____	____	____	____
Auditing cash receipts	____	____	____	____
Bank reconciliation work	____	____	____	____
Keying collections to accounts	____	____	____	____
RECEIVABLES:				
Reconciling to controls	____	____	____	____
Circularization work	____	____	____	____
Contact with customers	____	____	____	____
Contact with salesmen	____	____	____	____
GENERAL:				
Attitude toward work	____	____	____	____
Responds to instructions	____	____	____	____
Appearance	____	____	____	____
Neatness of work	____	____	____	____
Interaction with others	____	____	____	____
COMMENTS				

Job performance reports indicate the expertise level of a staff member in specific areas of audit activity. The reports show areas of strength and weakness and are useful to supervisors when deciding specific activities to be assigned during an audit. **NOTE:** *They help to identify areas of audit examinations where the auditor might benefit by more working experience or closer supervision.*

Audit managers should personally review job analysis reports with the supervisors who prepared them and with the individual auditors. Staff auditors should be given an opportunity to explain or challenge any detrimental comments or low ratings. These interviews can help staff members become aware of any of their work habits or approaches that need improvement. **KEY POINT:** *These reports also give the training manager a basis for scheduling training classes or advising individual auditors to further their education in particular subjects.*

RESPONSIBILITIES OF SITE SUPERVISORS

Every audit assignment requires an objective review and appraisal of specific activities. **NOTE:** *Each audit reflects on the ability and professionalism of the audit staff.* To insure that staff work is accurate, objective and complete all audit papers must be reviewed by competent audit management.

Supervision is necessary when any group of people work together to accomplish a common goal. A general axiom holds that an individual's span of control be limited to about twelve people, and this is a rule of thumb used to determine the number of supervisors required. Audit teams may consist of two to ten or more auditors, and each team must have a leader. For smaller teams one of the staff auditors is named as the senior, while on the larger teams an audit supervisor may be the site leader. Some staffs use area supervisors who move among teams as required, and they appoint a site senior to head up each team.

The audit supervisor, or site senior, is in charge of the audit and assigns specific parts of the audit program to each team member. Audit supervisors perform specific audit steps and also review all work done by staff members to insure that each audit point is correctly interpreted and appropriately performed. The supervising auditor is available to each team member for consultation or to give instructions and to act as a funnel to the home office.

Contact Between Field and Home Office

Audit supervisors act as channels of communication between the home office and field auditors. They perform the following functions:

1. Process all questions to and answers from headquarters. Only in an emergency or for personal communications, is there direct contact.
2. Keep audit management informed as to the progress of each audit and appraised of any problems that arise. Report anything out of the ordinary that comes up as the audit progresses.
3. Process administrative problems of staff auditors. These are accumulated and the head office is contacted several times a week to get information and answers. The same method is used for information going in the other direction. Personal questions or emergencies are handled directly from headquarters with the staff member concerned.
4. Follow up on deficiencies noted during the audit study. *If they are significant, the audit manager is consulted for appropriate action.* The supervisor may be directed to discuss the deficiency with local management and perhaps to recommend corrective action even though the audit is still in progress. **CAUTION:** *Major problems may dictate that the audit manager personally visit the operation for a first-hand look.*

   Some audit observations can get very touchy and need to be handled diplomatically by a ranking member of management who has an overall grasp of the operation and its place in the company's organization.

TRANSFERS BETWEEN STAFF AND OPERATING DEPARTMENTS

Many audit staffs are looked upon as an executive training ground. Bright young prospects are brought into the company and work on the audit staff for a short period of time. When they are indoctrinated and are familiar with operating procedures, the prospects are placed in management positions. Any audit staff runs the risk of having one of their people pulled out for a management position when an opening occurs and when a particular auditor has the expertise to handle the job.

Transfers From Audit Staff to Operations

Auditors that perform functional audits frequently learn more about an operation than anyone else in the company. These auditors can be very valuable as administrative managers or even department heads. An auditor may be offered the top position when a manager retires or leaves the company. Such transfers improve the audit status and give operating departments knowledgeable and productive managers.

Many transfers from the staff to operations occur because personal problems require that an auditor stop traveling. When such a request is made, it enables the audit manager to place an internal control specialist into a critical management position. The ex-auditor moves to the operating department and all ties with the Auditing Department are severed.

However, the personal relationships and confidences that have been built up over the years cannot be easily shed. They can be used to good advantage by both the ex-auditor and the audit staff. The staff will have a higher degree of confidence in work supervised by the former auditor, and the ex-auditor will recognize danger signals and may advise the audit manager when those signals are flashing.

Transfers From Operations to Audit Staff

Transfers between audit staffs and operating departments move in both directions. Transfers from operations to audit staff can be initiated by the audit manager who needs specialized expertise for a particular assignment. An employee may be borrowed temporarily for a specific job or may be reassigned for a set period of time.

Temporary transfers may be made without preparing a payroll notice, but a transfer notice is usually processed to formalize the arrangement. Transfers may not require salary adjustments, but the transferred employee is subject to audit department rules regarding travel and entertainment expenses. Transfers covered by a formal payroll notice should not result in a salary decrease, since auditors are usually paid more than line supervisors. If audit staff salaries are artificially low because of high travel expense allowances, some adjustment in the newcomer's base pay may be required.

Temporary assignees should be closely supervised. They must not be treated as outsiders, but their work assignments should be selected with care. Sometimes these people have problems when they return to their old jobs, particularly if they worked with the audit staff in a review of their department. This problem can be reduced by promoting the employee to a higher level than their departure assignment.

Some audit managers are reluctant to add temporaries to their staff, particularly if they come from other departments. These managers prefer to employ outside consultants or experts to assist on problems that require special expertise, even when such knowledge is available within the company.

Terminations

Despite the best screening procedures, some people who are hired as internal auditors will not be successful at the job. Sometimes the inherent conflicts do not surface until after a few years of service on the audit staff. It may then be apparent to the audit manager that the employee should be separated from the staff. By that time the company has invested in the employee, and both parties may be better off if the individual can be transferred instead of fired.

The audit manager may seek a transfer to another department where the employee's temperament and interests are better suited. Such transfers can have beneficial results. Although the audit manager may deal directly with a department head in placing these individuals, the final agreement is worked out by others.

Chapter 6

Writing an Audit Manual: Program and Instructions

CONTENTS OF AUDIT MANUALS

All members of the internal audit staff carry with them the *information that the audit manager knows will be needed during the course of an audit visit.* This information is contained in an audit manual that is prepared by audit administration. Data in these manuals relate to the employing organization, to the auditing department and to the job of reviewing specific company activities.

This chapter discusses the types of information required by internal auditors and the various ways that the data are accumulated, composed, edited and then presented to the staff members. The word *"program"* here means the working audit checklist that auditors use when examining an activity. Examples of audit programs and instructions are given, together with explanations of the thinking behind the audit points and the intent of the audit approach.

Let's assume that the audit manager has decided to use a full manual. All items in the audit manual must be accurate, current, and contain all of the pertinent company policy and procedure statements that relate to the internal auditor's job.

KEY POINT: *An audit manual remains company property and is not the personal property of the auditor to whom it has been assigned.* These manuals are usually numbered and controlled and are returned to the auditing department by all departing employees.

Manuals are usually held in loose-leaf form so that revisions, additions or deletions can be easily handled. An expandable page numbering system is used that consists of letters that signify the sections and numbers that identify pages. They contain a Table of Contents that is revised each time pages are added or deleted.

The first part of an audit manual contains data written by company Personnel, Financial and Auditing Departments, and by top corporate executives. The other sections provide audit programs and audit instructions and copies of various pertinent audit forms. We'll consider each separate segment of the manual's content.

Personnel Policies and Company Directives

Opening pages of the manual may contain statements of the organization's goals and possibly a brief history of the company. Important directives are included in the audit manual, or selected portions may be extracted and placed in the manual or included in specific audit points in applicable audit programs. This approach enables the audit manager to remind staff members of important policy, procedure or operating directives. Audit managers receive copies of all new or revised policy and procedure statements, and they determine the information that needs to be given to the audit staff. **NOTE:** *They also determine if programs or instructions need to be revised so that auditors can insure that the new thinking is properly implemented.*

Audit administration handles such matters in a variety of ways:

1. Pertinent directives may be passed on to the auditors with the assumption that the staff will read the material and act accordingly.
2. Extracts of significant matter may be taken from such writings and included in the audit program or instructions.
3. Programs may be revised to refer to applicable directives, and the auditor is then expected to read and apply the material as required.

The really important directives usually are included in the first part of the audit manual, which also contains a variety of statements by top executives that are of significance to internal auditors. Such statements contain policy proclamations relating to the following:

- Adherence to public laws and regulations of government agencies,
- Conflicts of interest,
- Gratuities, gifts and entertainment,
- Confidential information,
- Discussions with competitors,
- Internal security matters and other special items.

This portion also contains selected personnel policies that pertain to the internal auditor's job and that can affect any staff member. These Personnel Department policy statements describe company programs for the following:

1. Vacations and paid holidays;
2. Employee benefits including medical programs, group life insurance programs, and retirement benefits;
3. Stock options, savings and profit sharing, or work incentive plans;

4. Military or jury duty;
5. Sickness programs; and
6. Reimbursement of tuition costs.

The manual will contain information issued by either the Personnel or Auditing Department that deals with rules and regulations applying to the work place. This data will cover such items as the following:

- Dress codes, working hours, and time reports;
- Authorizations for payroll withholdings;
- Company policy statements dealing with moving expenses for new hires and transfers to other locations within the organization.
- It can also describe termination procedures which emphasize responsibilities for the return of company property.

Auditing Department Administrative Matters

All of the above information is of personal interest to an auditor and is also useful as source data while conducting audit reviews. Information and directives prepared by the auditing administration are a significant part of the manual. These policy statements deal with the following:

- Auditors' traveling expense reports. They show sample reports and detail the type of expenses authorized and define established limits.
- Modes of travel that are acceptable, and dependents' travel and the responsibility for their expenses.
- An outline of proper procedure for submitting expense reports. They describe the supporting receipts and required approvals that must be obtained before reports are submitted for payment.
- An explanation of the Auditor's Time Analysis Report. The write-up contains a copy of the form being used and a full explanation of the purpose of the report and its preparation and submission.
- A description of the auditor's report of daily time worked.
- Vacation policy, outlining the advance notice requirement.
- Information relating to continuing education.
- The purpose and frequency of audit department meetings.
- Preparation and sitting for the CIA and/or the CPA examinations.
- Department policy for reimbursing tuition expenses, usually requiring advance approval to take courses and specific evidence of satisfactory completion of the training program.

A major segment covers the area of work assignments, practices and performance. It details the following type of information:

1. Who decides job assignments and how auditor schedules are posted.
2. When staff members are to arrive at new locations and the correct procedure to be followed upon arrival at a new job.
3. Authority and responsibilities of on-site supervisors, or seniors.
4. Dress requirements and on the job behavior of staff members are spelled out to avoid embarrassing situations.

KEY POINT: *Auditors are cautioned to conform to company regulations and practices, as they serve to provide good examples to other employees.*

5. Communication channels for use between staff members; between staff and operating employees; and also for passing information through the various levels of audit management.
6. Details for the preparation, coding and approval of work papers.
7. Writing of the formal audit report, with tips for formatting these reports and for determining what types of items are good subjects for comments. The write-up describes how the final report is prepared, discussed, processed and then circulated.
8. An explanation of the audit forms and supplies available. It also describes how they are to be obtained and used.
9. The procurement and care of items of equipment is covered as is the personal responsibility of staff members for these items.

   Briefcases, manuals, cameras, portable computers, calculators and other such equipment are assigned to staff members for use while on the staff. These items must be returned upon leaving the staff, and the procedures for the return and release of liability is described in detail.

Another part of the administrative section deals with audit files. This section tells what the files contain, where they are located and who is to have authorized access to them. The Continuing Audit File (CAF) is described, its contents listed, and responsibility for use and update is spelled out.

A description of the filing system used for the audit manual is included which tells how the manual is revised, who issues revisions, how old sheets are to be disposed of, who has access to the manuals and how the manuals are to be safeguarded.

A section of the manual deals with the general subject of security over audit information. **KEY POINT:** *All information obtained during an audit review is restricted to those employees who have the right and the need to know. Audit* *observations, findings and suggestions are not fit subjects for general conversations with employees who are not members of the auditing department.*

The items described above need to be included in any audit manual, and are usually found in the administrative section. A third section of the manual contains the technical information that an auditor requires to conduct an audit. Here will be found the audit programs and audit instructions that relate to specific operations or activities within the organization. The section may contain all audit programs, but for the larger audit staffs where special audit groups are used for specific types of assignments, the manuals are usually made up of the unique programs that are used by each special group.

For example, the Computer Audit Group may be given manuals that contain only the programs that relate to computer audits, and Operational Auditing specialists may find the third section of their manuals have only the operational programs and instructions. Each internal auditing staff has its own unique operating problems to solve.

Following is a *condensed sample* of the Table of Contents of a typical Audit Manual.

XYZ CORPORATION—INTERNAL AUDIT MANUAL
TABLE OF CONTENTS

INTRODUCTION
- Description of Department
- Operating Philosophy
- Formal Statement of Audit Scope
- Corporate Goals
- Greetings from the Chairman of the Board of Directors

SECTION I. PERSONNEL POLICIES
1. Working Hours, Dress Code and Office Decorum
2. Recognized Holidays and Vacation Policy

SECTION II. CORPORATE POLICIES AND PROCEDURES
1. Conflicts of Interest and Outside Interests
2. Corporate Code of Conduct

SECTION III. AUDIT DEPARTMENT ADMINISTRATIVE MATTERS
1. Preparation for an Audit Visit
2. Expense Account Procedures

SECTION IV. DETAILED AUDIT INSTRUCTIONS
1. General Instructions for Any Audit
2. Cash Examination
3. Receivable Examination

This Table of Contents is a bare bones example, showing the type of information presented in the various sections of an Audit Manual. The remainder of this chapter will be devoted to the last portion of the audit manual, the technical sections which contain the audit programs and the associated instructions.

INTERNAL AUDIT PROGRAMS

An Audit program is used as a device to guide an internal auditor through a department or activity. The program may either be prepared in advance, a "canned" program, or may start out as a broad outline and be crystallized on the job as the work progresses. **CAUTION:** *Canned audit programs are a threat to a good auditor's ingenuity since they spell out all of the audit steps that are to be accomplished.* But these planned audit programs are necessary when managing a large audit staff, since they define in advance the areas to be examined.

Statement of Audit Objectives

To prepare an internal audit program, you must understand certain things about the activity being audited.

- What are the operation's goals, and how is it progressing toward those goals?
- How well does it service its intended customers?
- What is *really* being performed within the department?
- What reviews or tests must be made for an effective evaluation of the operation?

Ask yourself these questions:

1. Is what they are doing working?
2. Is there any reason it shouldn't be done that way?

3. Does each person and operation make a direct or indirect contribution?
4. Can inefficiencies be eliminated?
5. Can specific losses be controlled?
6. Can poor results be hidden? And
7. Are bad results reported up?

The first item to be decided in writing an audit program is the scope of the audit. It must be clearly defined. A good scope will ensure a clear understanding of both the purpose and direction of the audit. It will force your staff to answer specific questions that are of interest to management. It provides a built-in scheduling control of audit time with work loads cut into manageable pieces. **IMPORTANT:** *It enables you to know when the audit has been completed.*

Programs should ensure that all areas of concern are adequately reviewed. Emphasis should be placed on three areas, which are (a) *adequacy of internal controls,* (b) *adherence to prescribed managerial policies,* and (c) *general operating procedures and efficiency.*

When the scope has been established, you are ready to draw up an internal auditing program. Programs are illustrated later, so for now we'll merely consider the manner in which a program is created.

Standard Audit Programs

A prerequisite for the efficient operation of an audit staff is the audit program which details the reviews that are to be performed in every section of the activity. It contains narrative instructions coupled with a questionnaire that directs attention to important operations and requires auditors to obtain specific answers to pertinent questions. It usually takes the form of a checklist of the audit work that is to be performed in a particular operation.

Programs are frequently drawn up in a form that permits the working auditors to note applicable dates of the data reviewed and to place their initials opposite each audit point as it is performed. The form also provides spaces for signatures of in-charge supervisors and the dates that their examinations were performed.

Each audit staff designs its own program, and the organization of the material varies from staff to staff. There is an area of general agreement and we'll consider those uniform elements.

To provide a good working tool, the complete audit program is divided into operating sections. Each section contains:

1. An appropriate and complete audit routine.
2. All audit steps relating to a specific department or operation.

3. Major headings such as *Cash, Receivables, Inventory, Property, Sales, Production, Advertising* and *Data Processing.*
4. All questions or reviews relating to each major subject.

Programs are preprinted, containing as much information as the audit manager believes necessary. Spaces are provided for answers or comments. Each printed program provides heading space for identifying the location and operation under review as a filing aid and for ready identification. There must also be provision for recording pertinent dates and names of the auditors who performed the specific reviews.

Heading

The heading of the program should contain the following items:

1. The name and location of the operation that is being audited.
2. Provision for the dates that the audit started and was completed.
3. Names of assigned auditor and supervisors.

All of this information will facilitate ready identification when searching for the appropriate program. Other information may be required depending on the size and complexity of an organization. A sample heading follows:

XYZ CORPORATION—INTERNAL AUDIT PROGRAM
LOCATION ADDRESS ....
ACTIVITY REVIEWED...
DATES: STARTED.................. COMPLETED.................
ASSIGNED AUDITORS ....
SUPERVISOR(S) ....

Each specific audit program is assigned a unique form number which is printed in the heading. After the heading, a brief opening paragraph is printed which outlines the scope of the audit review.

Opening Statement

Opening paragraphs may contain general instructions, or outline the scope of the audit, or may contain a combination of the two. The opening statements are tailored to fit a particular audit approach. Sample of opening paragraph follows:

CAREFULLY REVIEW GENERAL INSTRUCTIONS (Form IA GI1000)
The following program is intended to lead the auditor into all of the operational phases of Distribution Center activities. The auditor should examine each phase

to insure that all company assets and records are properly recorded and safeguarded and that the Center is operating in an efficient and businesslike manner. Audit responsibilities are to do the following:

1. Evaluate internal controls,
2. Determine that company policies are being adhered to,
3. Suggest improvements in procedures that will increase efficiency or reduce operating cost,
4. Detect fraud or record manipulation, and
5. Determine that no laws are being violated.

IMPORTANT: *Auditors must be certain that all required audit checks have been performed before placing their initials in the proper block.*

A sample of a more detailed opening statement follows:

INTRODUCTION

In an audit your general objectives are to do the following:

1. Determine the adequacy of internal controls and procedures, and if appropriate, to recommend ways to strengthen the system of internal controls.
2. Recommend changes in procedures when, in the opinion of the Internal Auditing Department, such changes would result in more efficient operations.
3. Check for compliance with Divisional and Corporate policies and procedures.
4. Supplement the work of our CPA's and coordinate their activities.
5. Determine the reliability of accounting and financial data furnished to management.
6. Verify the existence of the company's assets; see that proper safeguards for such assets are maintained and prevent or discover irregularities or misappropriations.
7. Review development of computer programs to protect against the company losing management or accounting controls.
8. Check compliance to regulatory commission regulations such as FTC, Wages and Hour Law, and so on.
9. Check for Federal Income Tax problems and ascertain areas or transactions for possible follow-up by the Tax Department.
10. Provide general assistance to management.

This audit program is designed as a general guide to assist you in meeting the above responsibilities; it is not to be construed as an all inclusive check list. All "in-charge" auditors must use their judgment in determining the extent of expansion or limitation of the internal auditing program.

> If there should be any deviation or change in conditions, which would require changes in this program, such changes should be cleared by the regional supervisor prior to implementation. At the end of each audit, these program changes should be written up so that they can be considered for revisions to this program.
>
> If, during the course of the audit, you learn that some company policies no longer apply due to changed conditions, write the matter up and send your comments to the regional supervisor.

After the opening statement, the audit program leads into those audit areas which the auditor should examine first. Let us now consider the body of the audit program.

Special Programs

One method of approach to the design of an internal audit program, which is useful in any application, is to home in on key points in the administrative and control systems. Direct audit attention toward the following:

1. Reviewing the division of duties.
2. Reviewing the important control files.
3. Evaluating the supervisory follow-up of key items.
4. Resolving the cause of recurring errors.
5. Examining the basis for supervisory approval of significant transactions.
6. Reviewing document accountability.
7. Reviewing the general security over paperwork and property.

A general program applies across the board to all operations and is often used as a starting point in an audit of an activity that has never been audited before. The general program leads the auditor into areas of activities that occur in all operations, but it does not serve as a complete audit program. It is expected that the auditor will expand the scope of the program as the work progresses and will have a specific program at the completion of the first audit.

Special programs are designed to deal specifically with a certain type of operation or location and contain all important audit steps required to effectively appraise the activity. But these programs must also be modified each time an activity is revisited.

Specific programs instruct auditors to review particular forms, procedures and operations. They spell out the detail of the work to be performed, instead of merely calling attention to a general area and relying on the expertise of the auditor. Audit manuals mainly contain specific rather than general types of audit programs.

Technical auditing materials contained in the special programs are written by audit supervisory personnel. Though the audit manager has the final word on program and instruction contents, the actual writing is frequently done by a designated audit supervisor. Certain materials are often included at the express request of operating executives who want the audit staff to examine specific items.

The selected authors of audit instructional data, whether it is new material or major revisions, send their write-ups to the head office where the material is reviewed, revised, finalized, printed and distributed. When the material is distributed, a covering letter lists revisions and the general nature of material added or deleted.

Audit Time Considerations

An audit program outlines the scope of work to be accomplished by staff members. It determines the areas and the depth of the audit examination. *Each item listed requires time and effort of an auditor and is therefore a cost-consuming study. Audit management must be sure that specified work is necessary and is efficiently performed.*

In answer to the rhetorical question, "Who audits the auditor?", the answer is *everyone.* Since the business of auditing entails the critical review of the work of all employees, it is only natural that other employees carefully watch all the actions of all members of the audit staff. Not only the activities of the internal auditors, but the department's budget is subjected to close, continuous scrutiny. It is therefore important that all audit activities and expenses be carefully considered.

The only physical attribute that the internal auditing department contributes to an organization's well being, is the audit time supplied by its staff. Audit time is expensive and must be wisely used. As a means of intelligent use of audit time, audit managers prepare and adopt an internal audit program. Most of these programs are based on a "worst scenario" assumption. Audit attention is directed toward those operations or activities that present the greatest risk of loss. This basic assumption sometimes can lead to excessive use of the time required to accomplish an audit.

> **EXAMPLE:** Let's consider the simple audit of a petty cash fund. Audit programs are usually designed to carefully review all aspects of the fund's operations. Some funds may have an imprest balance of over $5,000 and yearly expenditures exceeding half a million dollars. The audit program provides for an in-depth review of the handling of such a fund.
>
> Now assume that the same program is used to review a petty cash fund of $25, with annual expenditures of less than one thousand dollars. How much time should be allocated to petty cash?
>
> The first fund may justifiably require several days of audit work,

while the second would not warrant spending more than an hour of audit time. Yet each review uses the same program.

KEY POINT: *Audit supervisors need to evaluate each operation and determine how much audit time is justified.* To efficiently use audit time, supervisors must have a good idea of the amount of audit time that is required to properly perform each audit step.

In order to get this information, some staffs use the *Auditor's Time Report* which was described in the preceding chapter. As noted, the total reported audit time does not add up to the total time spent on an audit. For example, time spent in writing up and reviewing audit points is not included in the analysis. But the form does provide general data as to the amount of audit time required to accomplish a specific audit routine.

No one can foretell what unusual conditions may be encountered in a specific assignment so it is difficult to produce an accurate estimate, but an average of time actually reported for specific audit steps in similar operations should contain some of these variables. If the activity is operating as desired, the time required to perform an audit should be minimal. **CAUTION:** *If fraud or extensive errors are encountered, then much additional audit time will be needed.*

Audit programs are designed on the worst scenario assumption, but audit schedules assume the average time required for past audits of similar operations. If a sales branch audit normally takes six auditor weeks, then the audit manager assumes that the same amount of time will be required for future audits and schedules are prepared on that basis. Audit supervisors are then expected to perform a complete branch audit in two weeks with a three-auditor team.

There is an implicit authorization to exercise discretion in reviewing all items in the audit program. The audit manager assumes that if any work is omitted or skimmed over, it will be the low risk, relatively minor items. The in-charge auditor is expected to note on the audit program all of the audit steps that have been omitted. In addition, a note is placed in the audit work papers that describes the audit points skipped and the reasons for the omissions.

Using a Unique Design for the Audit Program

A good audit program follows operational work flow, as much as possible. The program should lead through an audit routine in an efficient and complete manner. **KEY POINT:** *Where practical, an auditor should be required to examine a particular type of record only one time during an audit. At that time, all pertinent data that relates to any required audit routine should be reviewed and scheduled.* This approach minimizes the duplication of effort that occurs when the same record is again searched out and reexamined to satisfy another audit step in a different section of the audit program.

This ideal approach is easier to preach than practice, since the program must cover all facets of a particular review at the time when an auditor has the pertinent records under examination. One record may contain discrepancies that lead the auditor to other records which explain the questions that arose. These other records may become the subject for an audit routine that appears later in the program.

Once an auditor knows and understands all of the steps of an audit program, he or she will be able to accomplish several audit points simultaneously as the work progresses.

KEY POINT: *The audit program must be constructed to cover all of the risk factors of a given activity.* To design a complete program, the author must know everything that is processed in that operation as well as the intent behind all proscribed records and procedures. **TIP:** *An approach to this type of problem is to prepare a full and complete write-up of every activity which takes place in the operation.* The write-up may be in narrative form; it may be prepared as a standard flow chart describing each form, record and activity; or it may be a combination of the two.

Procedure Write-Ups

Form and procedure write-ups are usually prepared by using standard flow chart symbols and methods. All incoming records are flowed through the activity and all records prepared in the department are flowed from origination to their final file resting place. Major activities of all employees are also flowcharted in order to have a complete record of all of the important transactions that occur.

Flow charts may be symbolic, narrative, or a combination of the two. And the markings used may be the standard symbols used by systems and procedures analysts or those uniquely designed by the auditor to meet a particular set of conditions. Standard symbols and flow charting techniques can be studied in any of the many books which describe flow charting procedures.

For your write-ups, you must first conduct a survey to determine the answer to some important questions:

- *What is the paper flow?*
- *What controls exist?*
- *What happens when a problem is encountered?*
- *How does the manager keep informed of progress toward the stated goals?*

Most of the information obtained for the initial survey comes from talking to managers and supervisors. The information is recorded in flow charts, internal control questionnaires and/or narrative procedure write-ups as appropriate.

For the high risk areas of activities that have been audited before, flow charts are usually contained in the CAF, and need merely be updated to serve as the basis for a revised audit program.

Using the information obtained from the initial survey, an audit program can be designed to cover all of the risk areas. **KEY POINT:** *The sensitive points, those in which internal controls are apt to break down, are located and become the focus of audit attention.* The degree of coverage should be proportionate to the degree of risk. **TIP:** *First rough out audit steps for providing minimum coverage.* This helps assure that important areas are not overlooked, *then allocate available audit hours to the more important activities.* **REMEMBER:** *Your purpose is to help management control the operation and achieve its goal.* The operation should be improved because of your visit.

As your audit progresses, you will find important functions being performed that you were not aware of when you developed your program. You may find that management people didn't know the specifics involved in particular jobs in their department. This means that your audit program and procedures will probably need to be updated.

An audit program should be designed to tell an auditor what records to look at and what to look for, and it is not a substitute for common sense and creative thinking. Part III of this manual contains many specific audit programs and related instructions, all of which were developed by using a basic approach.

For now, let's consider a general approach to designing a specific audit program. Any operation is viewed in the same basic way, regardless of the type of activity that is to be audited.

Constructing and Using a Specific Audit Program

As an example, we'll consider a common activity and design an audit program for reviewing cash receipts in a supermarket.

First let's consider the risks involved in cash receipts.

1. Product may be removed without cashier ringing up sale.
2. Cashier may ring up lower amount than product should sell for.
3. Cashier may give customer wrong amount of change.
4. All transactions may be proper, but cashier extracts cash from register.
5. Cashier's work is proper, but store supervisor extracts cash.
6. All work proper, but someone extracts cash from manager's drawer or steals a deposit envelope from safe.
7. All work at store is proper, but cash pickup service loses an envelope on its way to the bank.

The above is merely a sampling of the risks that are involved in a relatively simple cash transaction, but it is a good illustration of risk identification. **NOTE:** *An element of risk occurs at every point that cash is handled, and* the risk *factor does not end when cash leaves the location of receipt.*

An audit program which reviews the above risks is spelled out in the following pages. To relate the audit points to applicable risks, each number identifying an audit step is the same as the above risk identification number. The parenthetical comments within an audit step are examples of the type of audit recommendations that might help to improve controls. The program should require internal auditors to do the following:

1. Determine that all transactions that require payments are properly handled to insure prompt and accurate recording of the transaction.
   (a) Determine that all passage of product though a check out line is observed for proper handling.
   (Roving supervisors, optical scanners, TV cameras and placing the manager's booth close to check out lines all help control this risk.)
2. Determine that profit analysis reports are prepared for examination by managers.
   (a) A good system should be in effect for checking price lists and for spot checking price markings on product.
   (Risk is reduced by using optical scanners, but possible bypassing of the scanner and undetected errors in the master price list can cause substantial losses. All the other controls mentioned in point 1 above can also be useful.)
3. Determine that the system insures that a cashier has sole control of an assigned cash drawer and is responsible for all shortages. (Automatic change machines and the use of registers that compute and tell cashier the amount of change due, help control this risk.)
4. Determine that all registers are checked and readings recorded at each change of cashier.
   (a) All registers should be reconciled at the completion of each shift change, with all cashiers responsible for shortages.
   (Use of a TV camera and roving supervision would discourage cashiers from extracting cash.)
5. Determine that the system insures that each cashier is given a pre-numbered receipt for cash turned in. The receipt should be signed by the cash recipient, who should retain and safeguard a duplicate copy of each receipt.
   (a) Auditors should account for all receipts issued during the current and previous month, and they should reconcile total of all receipts to cash deposited. For any missing receipt, auditors should determine the

identity of cashier involved and request employee to produce a copy of the receipt in question.

(From receipt sequence number determine the day the receipt was written and check payroll record for that day to learn which cashier's receipt was missing in the original check.)

6. Determine that the system requires daily reconciliation of cash receipt turn-ins to daily deposits.
   (a) In the event of mysterious disappearance of funds, can the point of loss be pinpointed?
   (b) Determine that cash is prepared for deposit as soon as practical, and that deposit envelopes are adequately identified and placed in the safe when the deposit slip is completed.

   (In cases of mysterious disappearance, management should consider polygraph tests for all employees who have access to the area where cash was last stored. Changing critical safe combinations or locks might prevent mysterious disappearances from recurring.)
7. Determine that the system requires that the cash pickup service sign a receipt that shows the number of envelopes taken from the safe.
   (a) For the current and previous month, reconcile total of reported cash receipts to bank acknowledged receipts and track down any differences.

   (If a signed receipt is available which supports a claim that an envelope was picked up but never delivered to the bank, the cash handling service is liable for the loss.)

Note that the internal auditor is concerned that certain important elements of risk involving cash are examined. These risks follow:

1. That products are removed without proper payment.
2. That cash receipts may not be properly and promptly reported or properly safeguarded.
3. That cash may be lost or extracted at every point of storage or movement.
4. That cash may not be promptly deposited and credited or that once available it is not used promptly and properly to reduce costs or produce revenue.

In the above cited example, the audit trail traveled through the company operation to an outside carrier and then on to a bank. The audit research would normally continue from the bank to the company's Treasurer and then to the transfer of funds to the department responsible for the use and application of funds.

Going a step further, an audit program for cash receipts at a sales branch would cover the in-house transactions that preceded the receipt of cash. It would then cover all of the above enumerated risk points and carry the audit on to the bank. From there the program would require an audit review of the recording and reporting to the Treasury Department of cash deposited in the depository account. That would complete the portion of the risk area covered in a branch audit.

The audit program for the Treasury Department would require that all reports received in the department be compared to all branch reports of deposits, that all depository transfers be audited; that bank accounts be reconciled and that the system for putting excess funds to prompt and intelligent use be reviewed.

We have demonstrated a simplified version of the approach to preparing a specific audit program. In Part III of this manual you will find audit programs covering many areas that are frequently subject to audit review. These sample audit programs were conceived and prepared in a manner similar to that just described.

Summary for Designing and Using an Audit Program

Let's recap the steps for preparing and using an audit program.

1. Study all reports relating to the audit subject.
2. Review operating procedures at the activity to be audited.
3. Study organization charts and job descriptions.
4. Prepare flow charts of all activities, records and reports.
5. Read and understand all related audit programs and instructions.
6. Locate the significant risk points in the operation.
7. Determine the areas of internal control weaknesses.
8. Formulate a unique audit program that emphasizes a detailed examination of the areas of potential weakness in internal control.
9. Evaluate each significant risk. Determine whether activities of some employees have caused losses which were not detected because of weaknesses in operating procedures and controls.

Using the approach as outlined, you will wind up with an acceptable audit program. The program should be improved with every subsequent audit, for as staff members work through audit assignments they will find areas that were not properly covered, and some audit steps that are no longer required. These observations will lead you to revise and improve your instructional materials. **KEY POINT:** *Your audit programs should be altered to take advantage of improvements in audit techniques and to stay abreast of changes in social conditions and your business's activities and environment.*

Various Ways of Presenting Program Information

Some audit manuals contain samples of all audit programs that a staff member may be required to use on an assignment. Others are reduced in size by omitting individual audit programs and instead including a schedule showing what audit programs are available and the appropriate form numbers. Auditors order particular audit programs to meet their needs. The actual programs are stored and controlled by the auditing administration.

Some audit programs are printed on legal-size paper containing a continuous listing of audit points. One section immediately follows another until all of the audit steps have been listed. This minimizes the total number of pages required to print a particular audit program.

Another approach is to use a loose-leaf system and print the major sections on separate pages. Miscellaneous items are combined on the final page of the program. Each major section starts with a new sheet bearing a subject identity heading and a letter and subnumber for each sheet in the section. This system makes it easier to revise or expand parts of a program without disturbing those pages that are unchanged.

We have discussed the approach to locating areas of risk, deciding what audit steps should be included and then designing an appropriate audit program. Now let's consider the related auditing instructions that are required to enable staff auditors to discharge their obligations in a professional manner.

INTERNAL AUDITING INSTRUCTIONS

Audit managers are responsible for providing their staff with *all the information they will normally need to efficiently perform their job. A good set of audit instructions clarifies all of the unusual audit work that is called for in a specific program.* The information presented is the result of the many questions that were asked over the years of auditing particular operations. When audit supervisors note that some portions of the program cause confusion, they try to clear up the problems by issuing detailed instructions. In time, the accumulated correspondence is sifted through, analyzed and then brought together in a book of instructions.

A free exchange of information between audit management and staff auditors encourages questions that can disclose errors or ambiguities in written instructions. **CAUTION:** *The natural reluctance to ask questions must be overcome, so that an auditor does not elect to skip an audit step rather than show ignorance by asking a question.* Supervisory review and approval processes may discover the omission during a review of the audit working papers, but it is far better to learn of the problem before any audit work is undertaken. Any audit oversights or misunderstandings that come to light must be carefully evaluated

to determine if revisions or additions to the audit instructions are required.
NOTE: *If one auditor cannot understand an instruction, it is possible that others will also be confused.*

Audit instructions are confined to necessary information that an auditor may need to perform the specific audit steps that are called for in the program. The instructions may provide guidelines or specialized information that a new auditor is not expected to know.
KEY POINT: *They frequently describe or explain company operations or activities that are unique to the industry.*

Organizing the Material

Audit instructions may be incorporated into the audit program and placed at the beginning of each section of the form, or they may be bound together in a book entitled "Audit Instructions." Some audit staffs gather all necessary information into one "Audit Manual."

Separating audit instructions from the audit program reduces the size of the programs and eliminates duplication of printed matter in the audit files. Combining all audit information into an audit manual enables audit administration to limit the distribution of the data by controlling the issuance of copies of the manual. Copy control improves security over the information and also provides a means to insure that a manual is returned to the department when an auditor leaves the staff.

Before any of the audit routines are listed, the program should clearly state the scope of the audit to be performed and should provide general instructions as to the method to be employed in the audit work. These opening statements are sometimes considered as part of the heading of the program, or they may be contained in a separate section or in the book of instructions.

Following the opening statements, instructions detail the preparatory work that the auditors must accomplish. The records and reports that are vital to a review are listed so that the auditors will study and extract pertinent information before starting the audit work. A checklist is sometimes provided as an aide to staff members.

After preliminary instructions are detailed, specific material relates to the major segments of a particular audit program. The body of the book of instructions, containing important cautions or requirements, becomes the reference library for the operating auditor. Let's first consider the opening information, then we'll discuss the written instructions that are designed to serve as a reminder and an aid to working auditors.

Preliminary Instructions

Every audit function reminds their personnel of the type of material that the auditor will require to conduct an examination. Some checklists are short and simple, some are more complex. First let's look at an example of a simple checklist.

PRELIMINARY INSTRUCTIONS

Before you leave the home office to start an audit assignment, you should do the following:

1. Review previous audit reports and correspondence.
2. Review previous work papers for the location to be audited.
3. Review current audit programs and instructions for the type of operation to be audited.
4. Review pertinent flow charts and procedure write-ups.
5. Review pertinent, current, Comptroller bulletins.

Another simple statement follows:

PRELIMINARY REVIEW

A. Establish objectives of activity to be reviewed.
B. Determine place in the organization.
C. Review pertinent company policies and manuals.
D. Review external audit program and reports.
E. Review previous internal audit work.
F. Locate geographic areas of related company activities.

A more involved approach is demonstrated by the following extract from a program that contains much of the above information and in addition requires the following:

PRELIMINARY STUDY

The in-charge supervisor should attempt to develop the following statistics unless they are prepared by the branch to be audited.

For the audit period, compare to other branches for reasonableness, and plan the audit review work accordingly.

A. Petty Cash
   1. Normal amount of reimbursement. ____
   2. Amount of Imprest fund. $____ Frequency of reimbursement. ____
B. Cash General
   1. Average daily collections. ____
   2. % of cash collections to sales dollars for latest month. ____
C. Accounts Receivable
   1. % of total $ sales to ending receivable balance. ____
   2. A/R turnover. ____
   3. A/R write-offs. ____
D. Inventory and Warehouse
   1. Inventory $ variance between book and physical. ____
   2. % of warehouse dumps, by $ value. ____
   3. Sales to inventory, turnover ratio. ____

E. Sales
   1. Average monthly sales dollars. ____
   2. $ difference between EDP and manual sales figures. ____
F. Net profit
   1. Latest available net profit for the location. ____

Specific Instructions

Following the preliminary information, the specific instructions directly related to the audit programs are gathered together in one section of the audit manual. This section may be organized in a variety of ways. It may be divided by specific types of locations or by particular types of operations. Material is then subdivided into specific activities within an operation or location.

For audit routines that apply across the board, the instructions are labeled so that they can be identified and used whenever the audit routine is required in any review.

> **EXAMPLE:** A set of instructions to cover the audit program for sales branches, distribution centers, plants and administrative offices will require some description of cash work. The instruction section of the manual may have a separate section dealing with cash transactions. This section is referred to whenever an auditor has a question relating to a cash routine called for in an audit program. This same approach applies to other areas such as Receivables, Payables, Inventory, Payroll and Property.

KEY POINT: *Universal instructions are not repeated in write-ups relating to individual location or department audits, as the auditor knows where the information is filed and can refer to it when necessary.* The remaining specialized instructions are placed so that they are readily available for reference during specific reviews of locations or departments. Where applicable, audit instructions may be coded to the specific audit points printed on the programs.

Some staffs include detailed instructions written into the audit program checklist, making the instructions available to the auditor performing the work. Other staffs provide separate instructions that describe audit routines that are to be used in the work. In the latter companies the audit program serves merely as a checklist of the audit work to be performed. Auditors that are not familiar with a particular routine must refer to the audit instructions and read the details concerning the actions to be taken.

Instructional Language

Audit instructions are not written in minute detail because it is presumed that they will be used by knowledgeable professionals. Staff auditors are familiar with the basics involved in internal audit work. Written instructions, therefore, merely detail particular procedures, forms or idiosyncrasies that one can expect to encounter in a review of a specific activity.

But while the language of the writings is simple and clear enough for any auditor to understand what is to be done and why, it is written for a certain level of expertise of the reader. Information is presented to an audience of trained auditors and is not designed as a learning tool for people who are not familiar with accounting or business routines or the internal auditing profession. Sometimes, the language may be vague or subject to misinterpretation, and in such cases the real intent of the instruction is learned through experience and discussions with audit supervisors.

Audit instructions are written clearly and concisely, using as few words as possible to adequately cover the subject. Technical words, abbreviations, and professional nomenclatures are used extensively to reduce verbiage. These instructions are not intended as entertainment or for leisure reading but are designed to tell professional auditors what must be done to accomplish a set goal. They go hand in hand with the audit program and are used as reference by an auditor working through the assignment. Instructions are labeled and subheaded so that they can be clearly and rapidly related to specific audit points.

Now that we have considered some approaches to the selection and description of materials to be used in audit programs and in books of audit instructions, let's put the information together and look at some examples of working programs.

Putting Program and Instructions Together

There are many ways to present instructional material to professional auditors. We've mentioned that some staffs use manuals which contain all auditing instructions, and the program is used as a checklist; other staffs include all instructional material in the audit program to explain each audit step.

Still other staffs use a middle ground approach, they provide a separate book of audit instructions, but also include vital data in their checklists to insure that auditors have the information at hand when considering the work to be performed. To illustrate the extremes in approaches, consider the following examples of extracts from Cash Receipts sections of audit programs for such reviews, as used by the ABC Corporation and the XYZ corporation.

ABC CORPORATION

A. CASH RECEIPTS
   1. Determine that there are adequate controls over incoming cash.
   2. Determine that office processing of cash is fully controlled.
   3. Determine that adequate controls exist over cash deposits.
   4. For a test period, tie in cash receipts to deposit records.
   5. For a test period, tie in cash receipts to accounts credited.

Let's examine how another audit staff handles the same type of instructions for performing the audit of Cash Receipts. The following XYZ Corporation's audit program covers the same ground *as only the A.1 portion* of the ABC Corporation's audit program.

XYZ CORPORATION

A. CASH RECEIPTS
  1. Review flow charts, procedure write-ups, and accounting manual instructions for the handling of cash receipts.
  2. Control all incoming mail.
     a. Have mail delivered directly to auditor, or if location has a separate mail room, assign an auditor to work there.
  3. Perform the following checks on incoming mail.
     a. Determine that all company mail is opened by objective party.
        (1) Employee opening mail should not be connected with either Accounts Receivable or the Cashier.
        (2) Observe mail opening routine. If personal mail is received, have auditor deliver mail and request that mail be opened to determine whether envelope contains payment.
        (3) Insure that each remittance is properly stamped "For Deposit Only," at the earliest opportunity.
        (4) Determine that each remittance is properly and adequately listed, before mail is distributed.
        (5) Determine that all remittance advice is removed from each check and is attached to the appropriate envelope. If payment data is noted on check, such information should be written on the covering envelope.
  4. Observe distribution of mail.
     a. Checks, or other forms of payment, should be delivered directly to the Cashier.
     b. Remittance advice should be delivered directly to the Accounts Receivable bookkeeper.
  5. Review handling, safeguarding and reconciling procedures for the list of receipts prepared by mail department. These lists, after reconciliation by responsible supervisor, should be locked in a file or safe in the mailing department and should never be given to the Cashier or the Accounts Receivable Department.
     a. For the month immediately preceding the start of your audit, obtain the prelisting prepared by the mail department and compare this list to deposit records to determine that all remittances were properly deposited. Follow up on any discrepancies by interviews with supervisory personnel and by contact with payers if advisable.
     b. For the same period and in the same manner as 5.a. above, determine that all listed receipts were properly applied to outstanding accounts receivable. Review any discrepancies with supervisory personnel and contact customers if necessary.

(1) Carefully review supporting documentation for any credits or adjustments made to receivables to bring accounts into balance with receipts. If foreign exchange is involved, contact our local bank to ascertain the effective rate of applicable currency at date of transaction.

The difference in approach between the ABC Corporation and the XYZ Corporation is obvious, but each may be perfect for their particular operation. The XYZ program contains much of the detailed instructions that you might expect to find in a separate book.

ABC may have a staff of career auditors who have been with the firm for many years and/or who may have a separate book of audit instructions covering all the special features of their operation which could be of interest to auditors. On the other hand, XYZ may use their audit staff as a training group for potential executives and, therefore, experience a high turnover of personnel. Or XYZ may not use a separate book of audit instructions and desires to have all pertinent information available in their audit program.

Still other staffs may use a middle ground approach which uses an audit program containing some instructions but also provides a book of instructions for required reference materials. **NOTE:** *There is no right or wrong way; each audit manager must decide which approach is most appropriate for his or her operation.*

Approval of Contents and Handling Revisions

In the early stages of development of an organization's audit function, their audit programs and instructions are frequently revised as the staff learns new audit approaches and discovers new areas to be studied. Each discovery leads to revisions of existing materials. As the staff becomes established, there is less need to revise audit instructions and programs, and an audit manager may believe that revisions are no longer required. **REMEMBER:** *In any organization, changes come with time and new technology.* Business operations, procedures and policies change as personnel and business climate changes. Audit management needs a good system for identifying materials that require revisions, and for taking prompt remedial action.

All audit materials should be critically reviewed by knowledgeable audit management at established intervals. A set schedule should be established to study all instructions and program audit steps to determine that they conform to the latest thinking in audit techniques. At the same time, obsolete materials should be located and deleted from the audit manual and associated forms.
KEY POINT: *Supervisors must periodically review program contents and the associated instructions and bring the material up-to-date.* As they review staff auditors' work, they become aware of unnecessary or obsolete audit steps and

they are responsible for calling these to the administrator's attention for corrective revisions.

Signing Off on Audit Work

Staff members who perform specific audit steps should be instructed to initial appropriate spaces on the program, only after they have completed all of the required work. When supervisors review the audit work papers and the audit program, their attention will be drawn to any items which have not been signed-off. They then decide whether to omit the points or assign an auditor to perform the work.

KEY POINT: *Supervisors should not initial their approval of staff work until they are completely satisfied with the scope and accuracy of the audit review.* If any significant unanswered questions are generated during the supervisory review, answers should be obtained before the auditors who performed the work are sent off on their next assignment. This procedure helps in the training of staff members and in insuring that the auditor who performed the original work has an opportunity to study any related reports or records.

Chapter 7

Auditing for Profit Through Operational and Management Auditing

AUDITING FOR PROFIT

The term "Auditing for Profit" was coined to differentiate the normal auditing of financial records and controls from an approach aimed at increasing the profitability of an operation. Audits for profit emphasize an examination of the caliber of line management, the appropriateness of their decisions, and the operating efficiency of a department or activity.

This chapter is devoted to operational and management auditing. It contains audit programs designed for a general approach to any operational or management type of audit assignment. These programs will be helpful as a starting point for any specialized operation.

Several later chapters deal with this special type of audit review and its application to specific operational departments. Part III contains special programs for operational reviews of Engineering, Distribution, Advertising, Marketing and Purchasing.

Background

Early movement into the field of management auditing was labeled "Operational Auditing." Later the terms "Management Auditing" and "Auditing for Profit" appeared in the literature. All were used to describe the work that internal auditors performed as in-house professionals to help increase their company's profitability.

As internal auditing review systems developed, a distinction became apparent in the type of evaluation that was conducted. All internal auditing is basically aimed at increasing profits, but the scope and direction of an audit review determines the name by which it is called. *Operational Auditing* has come to mean a profit audit of the operating policies and procedures of a complete operation or department regardless of organizational lines and location boundaries. *Management Auditing* concentrates on a management review of the decision-making process within a particular operation or activity.

Application

No matter the title or the audit program used, the basic determinant is one of approach to an assignment. In an audit for profit the auditors place themselves in the role of major stockholders who are primarily interested in the profitability of the organization. Every production process, every sale, every purchase and all related activities are critically evaluated to determine whether any changes could be conceived that would result in an increase in profits.

Though the approaches which are labeled, "Operational Auditing" and "Management Auditing" have more similarities than differences, we'll consider them separately.

OPERATIONAL AUDITING

Financial auditing concentrates on the past; operational auditing is concerned with the future. Financial auditing verifies profits; operational auditing tries to increase them. Financial auditors point out areas for improvement but do not become associated with decisions; operational auditors suggest improvements and help make the suggestions work. Financial auditors review decisions after the fact; operational auditors are members of the management team helping to make decisions, though all decisions remain the responsibility of line management. Financial auditors generally review all operations at a given location; operational auditors review a function, wherever it is in operation.

Management expects that an operational audit review will not only verify records but will also lead to more efficient operations, a reduction in costs, prevention of losses and an increase in profits.

Operational Auditing Tools

A staff performing operational audits needs three elements:

1. Competent personnel;
2. Good audit programs; and
3. Top management support, without which the first two are wasted.

The staff should have competent financial auditors supported by personnel who have had experience in diverse fields. When considering staff additions to handle operational auditing work, audit managers should look for people with varying backgrounds, such as engineers, salesmen, production technicians, EDP specialists, or people who have worked on construction jobs. **NOTE:** *Auditors who have had specialized experience can give a staff flexibility* and possibly shorten the time period required for familiarization with a specific operation.

Audit programs used for operational auditing are composed in the same manner as that described in the previous chapter. The same basic approach is used as that which builds a financial audit program, and the same general questions apply. **IMPORTANT:** *Operational audits must have top management support,* and at the direction of such management need not be limited to a particular location, department or activity. There are no boundaries to such a study.

Audit Scope

In an operational review, auditors examine all facets of a particular operation wherever it occurs. Let's look at an example.

> **EXAMPLE:** An audit staff is requested to review and appraise company policies and activities relative to the distribution of finished product. Such a review entails an examination of handling product from the point of production through storage to sales and then on to the customer's dock. The study evaluates the following:
>
> 1. Method of recording the original receipt of product;
> 2. In-house method of palletizing, handling, and checking of product; and
> 3. Shipping of product and the mode of transportation selected.
>
> It compares costs of shipping by common carrier to shipment by company-owned conveyances. It evaluates relative costs of shipping by: (a) truck, (b) rail, (c) air, (d) water, or (e) any combination of these methods.
>
> An operational audit of distribution is concerned with every aspect of the distribution process and the ways that necessary work can be accomplished. It could lead to the creation of a new department charged with supervising all distribution activities in the company. It might make significant recommendations relating to the creation of an in-house fleet of transport trucks or rail cars.

KEY POINT: *There are no limits placed on an operational audit.*

With this unlimited consideration in mind, let's look at a sample internal audit program for operational auditing that applies to any department or activity that has not been previously studied.

Sample of a General Operational Audit Program

The following approach is general in nature and *intended to provide a starting point program which leads an auditor into an operation and becomes a base upon which a detailed specific type of program can be constructed.* This type of a general approach program is used when internal auditors first attempt an operational audit.

Audit programs are similar to those used for financial reviews. But there are fewer specific instructions and more of the type that require an auditor to do some creative thinking. However, the program formats are identical and conform to those described in the previous chapter.

Following is a sample of material taken from an operational audit program. We will skip the introductory material and move directly into the language contained in the body of the program.

AD GO2000 XYZ CORPORATION
OPERATIONAL AUDIT PROGRAM—GENERAL

1. Determine the type and extent of work performed by reviewing written job descriptions and policy and procedure statements. Discuss purpose and goals of department with manager and supervisors.
   A. Prepare an organization chart of the department. The chart should include the areas of responsibility in relation to other departments.
   B. Discuss purpose and objectives of the department with all levels of management. Are these thoroughly understood?
   C. Prepare a write-up listing all personnel with a brief but complete job description. If written job descriptions are available, they may be used, but determine that these write-ups are accurate and up-to-date.
2. Determine the cost of the operation from department expense summaries. Review statements to determine the types and amounts of the various expenses incurred.
   A. Review each major expense item to determine authenticity, application, necessity and economy.
   B. Review each major expense item for proper internal control and authorized approval of expense disbursements.
   C. Also consider unapplied costs to arrive at the total cost.
   D. Determine the operation's tangible and intangible benefits and compare to costs and alternative methods of obtaining benefits.
3. Determine if the overall operation (and each individual) is performing required duties in the most effective and efficient manner. Note especially, those duties which are duplicated within or outside the area, and those duties which could be eliminated without affecting the operation.
   A. Obtain answers to the following questions:
      - Is what they are doing working?
      - Is there any reason it shouldn't be done that way?
      - Does each person or operation make a direct or indirect contribution?

- Can inefficiencies be eliminated?
- Can specific losses be prevented?
- Can poor results be hidden?
- Are bad results reported up?

4. Determine that lines of authority are clearly established and followed.
   A. Are there excessive layers of supervision?
   B. Review "areas" of supervision for overlap or duplication.
   C. Look for areas "in between" various managers or departments!
   D. Are there areas of insufficient supervision?
5. If possible, make cost and efficiency comparisons between similar operations at other locations or other companies.
6. Flow chart records relating to the department's activities.
   A. Determine if each record prepared serves a useful purpose commensurate with the costs required to keep such record.
   B. Determine that work flows smoothly and evenly and that excessive handling and transportation is not present.
   C. Determine that controls are adequate for the risks involved.
7. Review records maintained in the department for accuracy, necessity, and efficiency.
   A. Is extent of checking for accuracy consistent with the importance of the information and cost of checking?
   B. Review those records maintained for internal control purposes.
      (1) Are they doing the job for which they were intended?
      (2) Are costs of maintaining these records offset by the degree of risk incurred by their elimination?
      (3) Can these records be "doctored" by unauthorized personnel?
   C. Should any of the records be transferred to another department to improve efficiency or internal control?
8. Review reports prepared by the department to determine their necessity, appropriateness and accuracy.
   A. Review distribution to determine that all departments that can use the information are obtaining it.
   B. Do the prepared reports duplicate information gathered by any other department?
   C. Is the duplicating process efficient and economical? Are all copies necessary?
   D. Can some information flow now being handled by written reports be handled on an oral or phone call basis more economically?
9. Review files and filing system.
   A. Are files current?
      (1) Determine that record retention program is being followed.
      (2) Are files weeded periodically and regularly?
   B. Review filing system. Would a "central file" be appropriate?
      (1) Are any files duplicated in another department?
      (2) Is file usage restricted?
      (3) Is "confidential" matter adequately controlled?

   C. Are files orderly and is information readily available?
   D. Can file space or required filing time be reduced?
10. Determine that office equipment is efficient and working properly.
   A. Are service contracts necessary, competitive and current?
   B. Is company receiving the servicing of equipment that it's paying for? Are controls adequate?
   C. Are all machines required? Report any excess equipment.
11. Review office layout and facilities.
   A. Is space utilized intelligently to facilitate efficiency?
   B. Does layout aid in flow of work between related sections?
12. Determine that office supplies are adequately controlled.
   A. Are supplies purchased competitively? Are requirements of several operations combined for quantity discounts? Is the quality of supplies necessary for purpose intended?
   B. If practical, review periodic usage of supplies.
   C. Is a requisition system used? Is it worth continuing?
   D. Review system and controls used by stationery stock room.
      (1) Do we need a full-time stock room attendant?
      (2) Would it be cheaper to establish small inventories readily accessible to users?
13. Are working hours and break periods closely controlled and do they conform to established policy?
14. If overtime is worked in department, is the overtime necessary or could it be eliminated by "cycling" work, shifting tasks to other departments or by employing temporary help from outside agencies?
   A. What is employees' attitude toward overtime?
      (1) Is there a system of allocating it? If so, it is likely to be considered a regular portion of compensation.
15. Determine that the salary structure is periodically reviewed by responsible management.
16. If department morale is low, attempt to learn the reasons and if appropriate, discuss observations with responsible management.
   A. Can work simplification be developed that will increase efficiency and yet not harm morale?
   B. Do employees appear to be truly functioning as a team, or are conflicting informal groups present?
   C. Do employees have goals for self-enhancement that are consistent with company objectives?

The above type of operational audit program provides a good start for a review of an activity that has never been audited before. As the audit progresses, a specific type of program is created by modifying the general approach and adding items as they are encountered.

KEY POINT: *When the audit review is completed, you should have a detailed audit program that can be used for future operational audits.*

MANAGEMENT AUDITING

The growth of management auditing followed the path of operational auditing. The extension of the auditing function was not the result of a long range plan, but rather came from the desire of top executives to use all of their resources to full advantage. They merely added the internal auditing staff to the operating management team.

Background

Internal audit staffs were gradually forced to move into the area of management auditing. They began by critically reviewing line management decisions, recognizing that some were made in haste or without full, complete and accurate information. A review of certain types of management decisions had always been a part of any internal audit. In practice, audit comments were largely criticisms of management decisions or oversights. In financial auditing, such criticism was limited to management neglect in the area of financial or internal controls, but even operational decisions became subject to scrutiny by management auditors.

At the direction of top management, audit staffs were assigned to review the operational management of specific departments, usually those that were not meeting their established goals. In this work the auditors paid more attention to the management aspects of the operation than to the recording and reporting features and adherence to internal controls, though they used records and reports to help analyze the problems. At the completion of such reviews the reports emphasized management approaches and activities and recommended action to improve the management and ultimately the profitability of the department. This activity became known as Management Auditing.

Management auditors are concerned with the manner in which work is accomplished as well as with the end results. They not only verify validity and authenticity of charges, but sometimes challenge amounts and the necessity for the expenditure. They are as much interested in internal controls to eliminate inefficiency and waste as in those maintained for the prevention or detection of errors or employee defalcations.

Types of Management Audits

Management audits come in a variety of categories. A major division uses the terms "responsibility" and "functional" to differentiate the approach used. A responsibility audit covers all matters within the jurisdiction of a specific department, while a functional audit is an in-depth review of a particular phase within the responsibility. The responsibility audit reviews all activities, records, reports, policies, procedures and personnel that are under the control of a single individual, the manager responsible for the operation. Most internal audits fall into this category.

Functional audits may be confined to a phase within a single department or division or may be extended to cover the function within the entire organization. **NOTE:** *When used across the board, the study can better determine weaknesses in internal control and can more readily locate unnecessary duplications of records and effort.* Techniques used in the functional type of audit tend to lead the audit reviews and appraisals into non-accounting areas.

Functional Auditing

Internal auditing normally follows jurisdictional lines. An audit is scheduled and performed of a department that reports to a single executive. For example, a production plant is audited and the report is directed to the plant manager and to the top production executive.

But sometimes it becomes necessary to ignore jurisdictional lines and review all activities of a particular type.

> **EXAMPLE:** Auditors may be requested to determine compliance with the Wages and Hours Laws, or they may be asked to determine if company policies are followed concerning the reporting of working time or travel expenses or personal auto reimbursement expenses.
>
> In such cases the audit staff must cut across departmental lines and audit an activity or function no matter where it takes place. The audit report is directed to the top executive and to the vice-president responsible for setting the policy that governs the way the function is handled. A copy is also sent to the financial executive responsible for reporting of function activities and the policing of the related records and reports.

Functional audits may be utilized at all levels of an organization, and may be confined to one location or be companywide. There are no legal or academic restrictions on the use of a functional audit, and the definition is established by the user. Common sense frequently dictates such an approach even though audit objectives may not have considered such use. Sometimes a functional audit approach is ignored or properly rejected because of the lack of available audit hours. *Audit managers must equate audit costs against potential gains before deciding to go ahead with a functional approach when it will obviously require more audit hours than were originally scheduled for the review.*

In a functional audit all aspects of an activity are minutely studied and justified. A value analysis type of approach is used to evaluate the significant cost elements. Each activity is broken down into its component parts and each part separately analyzed. If the purpose of the activity is essential and cost justified, then the audit examines the manner in which the goal is achieved. **KEY POINT:** *Nothing is taken for granted, and everything is questioned.*

Example of a Functional Audit Program

Following is a sample abstracted from an audit program designed to lead an auditor into a functional audit. As the audit progresses, this general-approach program is modified to fit a particular activity. In practice the full working program, from which this sample is taken, covered specific audit considerations and audit steps which have been eliminated to suit our purpose.

IA PM3000 XYZ CORPORATION
PROGRAM FOR AUDIT OF FUNCTIONAL ACTIVITY

Description of activity ______________________ Date start. ________
Locations visited ______________________ Date comple. ______
Assigned auditors ______________________ Work reviewed by ____________

PURPOSE OF REVIEW:

This program will guide you into some of the important areas of an activity but is not all inclusive. You must expand this program as required. The major purpose of your review is to determine that all personnel, controls, activities, procedures and forms meet the following requirements:

1. Necessary and consistent with established instructions.
2. Performing assigned duties efficiently and properly.
3. Cost effective and are all cost justified.
4. Performing in the best possible manner consistent with the purpose of the activity.

HOME OFFICE PREPARATION:

Before you depart on the assignment you must accomplish the following:

1. Review all policy statements relative to the activity.
2. Obtain copies of all national forms used in the activity.
3. Obtain copies of all procedure descriptions of the activity.
4. Review last five years operating statements, and next year's budget estimates as they relate to the activity. Work out a reasonable estimate of the company-wide cost of performing the work required by the activity.
5. Discuss with concerned top executives, the purpose of, and any future plans for, the activity.
6. List all locations where the activity is performed. Show number (approximate) of employees required and the total cost (estimate) of the activity at each listed location.
7. Determine, from list prepared in 6 above, the locations to be visited by auditors. Confine visits to major cost locations.
8. Set up audit schedule, and arrange visit with local management.

FIELD WORK:

A. Meet with location manager and with supervisors of the activity and explain the purpose of the audit. Ask management for their suggestions and make notes of their comments.

B. Prepare an organization chart of the activity, indicating its area of responsibilities in relation to other activities.

C. Request top supervisor of the activity to schedule a meeting of all employees concerned and explain purpose of review. Emphasize that the audit is aimed at improving the operation and if any changes result, they will not affect employee job security.
   1. Meet individually with each employee involved in the function and prepare a complete job description.
      a. If written formal job descriptions are available, compare your notes to write-ups and determine that official reports are accurate and up-to-date.
   2. Determine if employees know their job assignments and the purpose of their work.
   3. Are formalized procedures clear? Are they followed?
   4. Are established rules and regulations relating to the function being followed? Who enforces them? How?
   5. Give employees an opportunity to offer their suggestions or ideas for improving the function.

D. Flow chart significant records and operations.
   1. Determine if work is being duplicated somewhere else.
   2. Determine that work flows smoothly and evenly. Note where there is excessive handling or movement.
   3. Determine if each record prepared and operation performed serves a useful purpose.

E. Review the cost data that you obtained from headquarters.
   1. Are there any hidden costs?
      (a) Consider unapplied costs, such as wasted space, utilities, telephones, office and services from other departments.
   2. Could this work be performed at a lower cost?
      (a) Are outside services available to perform this work?
         (1) Would such an approach be more economical?
      (b) Could the function be better performed by changing the company's organizational concepts?
      (c) Is location necessary to perform this function?
      (d) Would a central handling point be possible? Beneficial?
   3. Is the function cost justified? Should it be discontinued?

A Case Study in Management Auditing

In auditing for profit, the auditor reviews every item that affects profit. The study must include costs and expenses and also every aspect of income generation. It can be a time-consuming, arduous and frustrating task. Let's view some highlights of a hypothetical in-depth management audit while working alongside the auditors and considering their approach and findings.

EXAMPLE: Our management audit team has been assigned to determine why a certain product line is no longer profitable. The audit department has been asked a series of questions.

1. Why is the product line losing money?
2. Is poor management to blame? Shall we change management?
3. Do we want to continue to handle the product?
4. Is there any way to turn the operation around?

There are no restrictions on the audit; all management wants are answers to the specific questions. We know that the operation's responsibility encompasses the production, selling and distribution of a product line to their customers. Where do we start the review?

First, remembering an earlier caution that auditors should not start an audit with preconceived answers, we begin by objectively amassing all the available information about the operation. We gather data dating back to the period when the product was producing a satisfactory profit and work forward to the present. Then we study the data, paying particular attention to any cost and expense items that have increased disproportionately and to any revenue items that have declined over the years.

We must keep in mind an elementary accounting concept. Net profit results from revenues minus costs. Revenues result from the pricing and movement of total product. Costs include that of production, storage, selling, distribution, administrative charges and higher office overhead allocation. So we divide the problem into the following:

1. The revenue producing elements,
2. The costs that are incurred to produce product,
3. The expenses necessary to run the business, and
4. The overhead allocations from higher offices.

Let's consider the elements in that order.

Income Considerations

Revenue is the result of two forces, sales volumes and sales price. There is usually an inverse ratio involved in this equation. As price increases, volume usually decreases; as prices go down, volume tends to increase. *The trick is to produce the greatest revenue, and the starting point is the selling price of the product.* Auditors are not expected to be pricing experts, but they can analyze sales statistics and determine the effect that marketing promotions have on movement of product.

Marketing managers may sometimes overlook an element of the profit equation. They use various methods to arrive at a selling price for their product. In some companies there is a "traditional" selling price, that being the price at which the product achieved success. Having once been set, marketing managers are reluctant to tamper in any way with a successful product, so the selling price remains constant.

Some companies use marketing surveys to learn the prices their competitors are charging for similar products. Products are then priced to compare with items that are of a similar quality. Marketing may have a preconceived notion of the comparative quality of their product which may not accurately reflect the attitude of large numbers of consumers. When this occurs, marketing may price their product above similar competitive items which they believe to be inferior.

Our audit team will obtain market analysis studies that not only tell us what competitors are charging, but also how consumers view our product in comparison with competition. Then they will persuade our marketing managers to make small adjustments in the selling price of the product while carefully reviewing the relative sales volumes resulting from these price modifications. Any upward movement in selling price that does not result in falling sales will be helpful. Though the possibility is not always apparent, a *decrease* in sales price may sometimes result in a *material increase in profit.*

A substantial increase in quantity sales should result in a per unit reduction in expenses. So if we can increase sales volume, we can reduce unit expense. A substantial increase in production volumes should result in reducing the per unit cost of production, since set up and clean up costs are spread over a wider base and idle time may be reduced, enabling us to achieve a higher rate of plant utilization.

Now to get to the audit at hand, our study shows that our marketing managers are doing a competent job in staying abreast of the consumer market. Product pricing is right in line with comparable competition, and any price increases would seriously deflate our quantity sales. Price decreases would result in increased sales, but marketing management is reluctant to take such action since they've been told that the current unit selling price is below our costs.

We note some areas where improvements could be made in sales policies and procedures. Our in-depth financial audit approach has located areas of poor controls that may have caused losses; such as the following:

1. Marketing uses periodic drives to hype the sale of products. During these drives a variety of incentives are used, including price reductions, rebates and contests. These promotions are successful as they do stimulate the sale of product.

   Several of these promotions have been repeated consistently over the years, and major customers look forward to them as the time to store up on our product. The net effect is that many of the major customers only buy our products during promotion periods and at that time buy in sufficient quantities to last until the next promotion is offered.

2. There were instances of product returns from a major customer that were priced at the date of return price, which was higher than any price paid by the customer during the year. Since our sales policy guarantees sale or full purchase price refund, the product returns had been valued at the then current price.

3. Some customers have been profiting by buying during promotion periods and returning some of their purchases a month or so later and receiving a higher credit for the product than they paid for it. This type of problem may remain unnoticed unless an in-depth study is performed.

   Management instructed that accounts be billed for the discrepancies noted in (2) and (3) above.

4. Another area of profit loss was related to quantity discounts. The pricing policy used a price bracket system that offered a substantial discount to customers that ordered a full carload of merchandise. Some of these major customers frequently returned large quantities of product and received their full price refund.

   In these cases the refund price was the same as the customer had paid for the product, but the excessive order quantity enabled the customer to buy actual quantity requirements at the lowest possible price. This type of transaction also resulted in additional costs of handling returned product and the associated paperwork.

   Management justified their actions, not penalizing customers for large returns from carload shipments, by stating that customers had incurred additional handling and storage costs and further that the customers had expected to sell all the product ordered. They had merely overestimated their sales potentials.

   Permitting customers to over order had resulted in losses to the operation. *Sales management elected to cope with the problem by cautioning salespeople to actively control the quantities of product ordered by individual customers.* Orders were to be accepted only for reasonable quantities of product so as to minimize sales returns.

Cost Considerations

Other areas of intensive study by the management audit team were the costs of distributing products to customers. Each item of cost was studied to determine whether it was necessary and cost justified. Alternative methods and sources were reviewed and their associated prices considered. Some audit findings could indeed reduce costs.

KEY POINT: When auditing for profit, *the auditor must consider the costs of distribution as a major factor.* The company published a price list which stated a national delivered price. This price applied wherever the customer was located and included all delivery charges up to unloading the product at the customer's dock. If the price list had been based on an FOB shipper's dock, and sales tonnage not been affected, the savings to the company would have been substantial.

Management argued that their approach gave every customer an opportunity to buy specific products at the same price. There could be no question of unfair price discrimination. They pointed out that competitors had producing plants located throughout the country, and they made delivery from the closest point to the customer. If the pricing structure were changed, we would lose sales in all areas where customers were located closer to a competitor than to our plant.

The pricing system as it relates to delivery of product results in penalizing customers located near the shipping points and subsidizing customers located at great distances from the point of shipment. It costs much less to deliver to a customer located a mile from the plant then it does to deliver product one thousand miles away.

Auditors pointed out that some companies adjust the distance inequity by establishing zones and only maintaining an identical price within a zone. Thus, they stayed within the limits of national laws regulating unfair pricing practices and reduced some of the inequities which exist in a national price policy.

The auditors felt that a fairer and more beneficial approach would be to set a uniform price for product, FOB shipping point, with the customer paying the freight. They acknowledged that the approach might overprice product to customers located away from the plant, but argued that it would gain sales from competitor's customers located nearby. As an alternate, auditors suggested that a pickup allowance be offered which might encourage customers who owned captive fleets to use their trucks that otherwise would be deadheading or sitting idle.

Management is considering all alternatives.

Another major cost consideration was the agreed labor rate that was negotiated at the last bargaining session. The plant is located outside a medium size town, and is surrounded by industrial complexes that produce heavy industry items. Our neighbors produce relatively few custom-made items, and their labor rates are much higher than the normal rate for our industry. Labor unions have established area wage rates and our plant labor is, therefore, overpriced. The situation is desperate.

Other than moving the plant location, there does not appear to be any solution to the high labor rate. Auditors offered some suggestions to reduce plant labor requirements, such as the following:

1. The plant used line workers to perform plant security duties. Twenty full-time employees were used to guard the premises. Auditors suggested that outside agencies be considered to replace the present staff. Contact with local agencies established that the services could be obtained on an "as required" basis at considerable savings.
2. In the same vein, the plant cafeteria was switched over to an outside service company, and eighteen employees were taken off the plant payroll. Plant operating costs have been reduced, since the cafeteria service company agrees to operate without a subsidy providing they are free to adjust prices to allow a reasonable profit.
3. *Higher volumes of sales would increase production demands and would succeed in lowering the per unit production costs* since the plant is only operating at 76% efficiency. Auditors suggested to top management that adding compatible products to the line might increase total sales and better utilize plant capacity. *Marketing will consider the problem, and an audit staff member will participate in the study.*
4. Other costs of production were reviewed in detail, and auditors found that studies by local management had effectively corrected many problems. Value analysis of purchased items had been ably performed.

Overhead Expenses

Confusion arose in the *audit analysis of overhead expenses* because of certain accounting practices. The use of outside services for both security and cafeteria resulted in reducing direct labor costs and increasing overhead. The net effect was a decrease in total costs.

An important factor in our profit analysis is the sales commission policy. Salespeople, in addition to their normal salary, are paid a commission on total sales as an incentive to move product. Some salespeople become friends with the buyers of major customers and may sometimes persuade these buyers to order more product than they need. Since product can be returned at full credit, the customer cannot lose by increasing an order which may qualify the purchase for a lower price. Much of the product may be returned later, as mentioned in an earlier paragraph, but the salesperson's commission is not reduced for the sales return.

Marketing management immediately corrected this oversight, and in the future all returns will be deducted from a salesperson's total sales figure when computing commissions.

Another similar problem surfaced concerning Marketing's practice of *conducting sales contests to stimulate sales.* Contest winners are determined when sales figures are reported at the close of the contest period. No adjustments were made for product returned after the contest ended. In many cases the winning salesperson or sales manager did not really earn the prize. As mentioned earlier, large returns of product were not taken into account that would have resulted in changing the winner of the contest.

Many hours were spent in establishing the facts and convincing sales management. Sales decided that *all returns would be considered* in determining the contest winners, and the final decision would not be posted until sixty days after completion of the contest period.

Other overhead expense items had been studied by local supervisors who had succeeded in making substantial reductions in overhead costs.

Main Office Overhead Allocations

The management auditing group decided to curtail their *examination of the system of allocating Division and Headquarter Office expenses* in order to complete their review and submit their formal report. The entire area of overhead allocation will be studied in the near future.

Allocation of overhead costs can materially affect the unit cost of a product, (particularly if by-products are involved), and can affect the paper evaluation of the profitability of an operation. **BEAR IN MIND:** *Such allocations can be particularly tricky when a conglomerate is involved or when rates for a public service are set by a public body. These allocations can be used to improve the profitability of certain operations at the expense of others.*

There are many ways to distribute local and head office overhead, and the distribution can be of significance in a profit analysis study. Cost allocation is a major subject of study in business schools, and the subject is briefly discussed in Chapter 21 titled, "Auditing Production Operations and Cost Accounting." **CAUTION:** Be reminded that *auditors should look into the allocation of all costs relating to any product or activity that is being studied.*

SUMMARY

Operational and Management Auditing offer an inviting challenge to resourceful internal auditors. All activities are studied in minute detail, and important management decisions are evaluated. Although internal audit programs are designed and used in such reviews, they should not interfere with the creative thinking of the auditor.

Why not consider applying your operational auditing concepts to your own department?

KEY POINT: *Challenge everything you take for granted.*

Measure your own procedures and practices. What do they cost? Are they worth it? Analyze your audit routines, step by step. Time study your own staff. Apply the approach we have just outlined.

We discussed the process of creating appropriate audit programs and presented some samples to serve as a starting point for operational or management audits. The growth and acceptance of this type of auditing shows a significant need for such services. Many of the larger internal audit staffs have specialized sections that devote their full time to this type of activity. Auditors assigned to operational and management auditing must be encouraged to rely on their own intelligence and common sense and not be bound by the printed word on an audit program.

In closing this chapter, let me remind you of a classic case that may demonstrate the danger of restricting the thinking of people who work for you.

> A railroad agent in Africa had been often criticized for doing things without orders from headquarters. One day his boss received the following startling telegram. "Tiger on platform eating conductor. Wire instructions."

Chapter 8

Writing Work Papers and Controlling Forms and Supplies

AUDIT WORKING PAPERS

This chapter is devoted to some of the technical problems that are encountered in internal auditing work. It considers the manner in which audit working papers are prepared and supporting information obtained and cross referenced. And in it we'll show examples of the type of audit observations that should be written up, and how to best document audit findings. We'll also discuss the CAF, and audit files, forms, and supplies and show samples of common audit forms.

As an auditor, you are also an historian. **KEY POINT:** *Your work papers become a permanent record of what occurred during the period of your audit.* They also document selected occurrences during the period after the previous audit to the beginning of the current one. Your audit papers spell out the following:

- What you expected to find and what you did find.
- What work you performed.
- What exceptions you noted.
- What actions you took.
- What impressions you gathered during your visit.

Work paper files also contain the permanent audit file.

CONTINUING AUDIT FILE (CAF)

Continuing audit files consist of the records relating to a particular location that remain fairly constant from year to year. The information in this file is updated during each audit visit. The file contains the following types of information:

1. Organization charts and job descriptions.
2. Flow charts of procedures and important record preparation.
3. Procedure write-ups.
4. Special directives and bulletins.
5. A physical description of the location, often with photos.
6. Other pertinent permanent information concerning the location.

Information in the CAF is reviewed by the supervising auditor prior to the start of any audit, and applicable items are brought to the attention of staff auditors assigned to specific audit steps.

KEY POINT: If time permits, *all staff members should be allowed to examine the contents of the file. It will give them a good idea of what to expect and who to talk to when they arrive at the location.*

A review of these files should reduce the time required for auditors to become acclimated to a specific location and the volume of auditor's notes explaining the operations. Familiarity with the file will shorten the question-and-answer period and help the internal auditor perform an examination with knowledge and dispatch.

WRITING INTERNAL AUDIT WORKING PAPERS

Audit working papers must show the audit work that was actually accomplished during the visit. They must contain clear and complete evidence supporting all findings that are reported to management. Normally the papers do not require complete transcripts or copies of everything examined. Internal auditors customarily review a location's or department's records which remain available in the file. The papers, therefore, need only show the work actually performed on those records.

Work Paper Headings and Codings

Handwritten notations should be made on a uniform standard, or legal size, sheet so that it can be readily identified. Any paper that is to be included in the work paper files should contain a proper heading. Headings should show such things as the following:

- The exact location that was the subject of the audit,
- The date the paper was prepared,
- The subject matter,
- The initials of the author, and

- An alphanumeric code designation that ties in to the applicable section of the audit program.

A typical heading of an audit working paper would look like this:

XYZ CORPORATION—AUDITING DEPARTMENT A 1.(c) page 1
DAYTON, OHIO Sales Branch Jan.20, 1990
Review Of Cash Handling In The Mail Room (Auditors initials)

Work papers must be carefully coded so that they can be readily found when needed. For working papers bound on the left side, the upper right hand corner should be numbered to correspond to the audit program. Coding should be written using a unique, noticeable color. The coding may need to be written over existing printed matter, so the same distinguishing color should be used to code all work papers.

Page coding should contain an alphanumeric reference, which is identical to the applicable point on the audit program. Within that specific grouping the pages should be numbered in succession. The page number assigned to an important document will be noted next to the relevant audit point in the discussion copy of the audit report. This will enable the auditor to readily locate pertinent data if and when required at the windup meeting.

The final numeric succession in the alphanumeric coding, the page number, should not be placed on audit work papers until the audit is completed and comments for the audit report have been decided. The numbers are placed on the sheets when they are sorted into a logical sequence that relates to the organization of the formal audit program.

For example, the working paper containing the listing of items found in the petty cash count would be labeled as follows:

I. (Where I corresponds to the Cash section of the audit program.)
I.C (Where C contains the audit points relating to Petty Cash.)
I.C.1 (Where 1 is the first page covering finding in Petty Cash.)

When the final coding has been established, work papers should be checked to be certain that they correspond to the coding listed on the audit program and that they are correctly noted on the control copy of the audit report. Careful preparation insures that a specific paper is readily available at the review or at a later date.

When to Write Up Audit Work Papers

Routine audit work, described and requested in the audit program, need not be written up unless something out of the ordinary comes to light. The auditor's initials in the appropriate box on the program signifies that the work has been done. If the program calls for a schedule, or a write-up, then an appropriate working paper is prepared using the heading just described. Any work performed that is not called for in the program or instructions should be written up noting what was done, the reason it was done and the results of the work.

Auditor's handwritten notes should be in sufficient detail to enable anyone reading them to retrace, step by step, the work that was performed. Any records reviewed should be positively and specifically identified, so that a future reader could obtain and view the exact record originally examined. **NOTE:** *Observations and interpretations should be described in detail and, where possible, documented with clear references to any other substantiation or witnesses.*

Types of Working Paper Data

Current audit work papers consist of the audit program, schedules, reports, copies of correspondence, confirmation requests and replies, auditor's pertinent notes and letters written during the audit. The file also contains the preliminary and final audit report, management responses and any correspondence resulting from the audit. Internal audit working paper files are not suspended from audit to audit, but rather are continually active with additions of correspondence and directives issued after the audit has been completed.

The file is an historical record of what the audit staff did on a particular visit and can sometimes be helpful, or even necessary, in establishing facts required during litigation. Audit work papers can be used to refresh the memory of an auditor or may contain information that is legally acceptable as evidence in a court of law.

KEY POINT: *Audit working papers should be treated as confidential material, should be properly safeguarded against fire and theft and should not be made available to unauthorized individuals.*

Normally work papers consist of SCHEDULES AND ANALYSIS prepared by the internal auditors as requested by the audit program. These papers must be complete and accurate and should tie-in to a formal summary record or final account balance. The records tied into should be period-ending, posted records that can be verified by reference to reports, schedules or statements. **NOTE:** *When significant, a copy of the record examined should be included in the working papers.*

PHOTOGRAPHS make excellent audit working papers. A good picture can take the place of several pages of narrative. If you found that a warehouse was in sloppy condition with goods piled up all over the place, any narrative that you wrote would create as many questions as your write-up answered. Your narrative would convey a different mental picture to each reader. If you included photos clearly showing the mess in the warehouse, your pictures would command attention and would clearly establish the actual condition.

Photographs can be used when auditors visit offices of outsiders and need detailed lengthy records which are on file in those offices. If duplicating machines are not available, and the outsiders are reluctant to permit records to leave their office, an auditor with an instant camera can obtain necessary information in a fraction of the time that would be required to hand copy the detailed data. The photo would eliminate the possibility of transcription error. The instant picture could be examined before the auditor left the premises.

Inclusion of photos in audit reports can command attention and should be carefully considered as a graphic means of demonstrating audit points. **TIP:** *In addition, photos can play an important role in investigating and legally proving the perpetration of theft or fraud.*

FLOW CHARTS can be important working papers. In flow charting an operation, procedure or record, the auditor may select any signs or symbols to signify specific activities. It is only important that these symbols be used with consistency so that they may be correctly deciphered at a later date. Flow charting techniques are consistently used by forms and system designers and by data processing analysts. A degree of uniformity has been achieved in flow charting symbolism, which enables strangers to understand the charts. These techniques are the subject of numerous books which are readily obtainable.

Audit work papers may also contain copies of LETTERS, BULLETINS, PERSONNEL NOTICES, INVOICES, CHECKS or DRAFTS, VERIFICATION REPLIES, major asset or liability ACCOUNT SCHEDULES and BALANCES and pertinent COMPUTER PRINTOUTS. To keep the work paper files orderly, it may be helpful to attach selected documents to the standard audit note paper.

Applicable records should all be clear and legible copies of information that can be verified through examination of the original records. These original documents may be on file at an outlying company location, at an identified and readily accessible outsider's office or at the company's headquarters office. **NOTE:** *Handwritten auditor notes can contain either matters of fact or expressions of opinions. Work papers should be clearly marked so as to differentiate fact from opinion.* Factual information should be separated from auditor's interpretations of the data. When you feel that your personal opinion should be included in the work papers, clearly label it "Auditor's Opinion." When you state an opinion give your reasons and detail the supporting documentation, also be certain to include any information you have that might lead someone else to a different conclusion. After completely stating the opposing side, explain why contra information has not changed your thinking.

AUDIT PROGRAMS are an important part of any set of audit working papers. Along with the program are PROCEDURE WRITE UPS, FLOW CHARTS, pertinent SCHEDULES and RECONCILIATIONS, and any special information that is called for by the formal audit program. The program contains spaces for the dates that work was accomplished and for initials of auditors that did the work and supervisors who reviewed the papers.

In addition to all the standard data contained in the file, there will also be SPECIAL NOTES or SCHEDULES that EXPLAIN DISCREPANCIES or POTENTIAL PROBLEMS that may become the subject of audit comment. Let us now consider these special working papers.

Material for Audit Comments

When an internal auditor notices material of record that indicates a failure to follow company policy, or a potential or actual loss, the auditor should make appropriate notes for the working papers. *Even if the matter is immediately corrected by appropriate management, the auditor must describe what had occurred and what action was taken.*

Auditors must decide what information to place in working papers. **KEY POINT:** *For actual or potential legal matters, the best information is an original copy of the pertinent data.* When originals are not available, photostats or photographs are acceptable. If it is not possible to get exact copies, handwritten notes prepared by the auditor who viewed the documents may have some credibility.

If an important and necessary document is filed in the dead file section of the file room, you may elect to take the original for the working papers and to make a replacement copy to be inserted in the proper place in the dead files. When such a replacement is inserted in the file, a note should be attached to the copy showing your name and the date of removal. A similar note should be prepared and attached to the original document in your work papers. Your note should also describe the exact location from which the original was removed. This information may be useful if it becomes necessary to produce associated documents resting in the dead files.

If an important document is located in the active files you will normally make a photocopy, and return the original to its proper place. **TIP:** *If the document is likely to become necessary evidence in a court of law, it should be removed and a photocopy made to replace it in the active files.* A note, attached to the photocopy, should show your name and the date you removed the original.

Notations may ordinarily be written on photocopies of routine documents taken to be included in the working papers. You should note the date the copy was made, and the location of the original in the files. Important documents should not be written upon, rather a separate note containing the desired data should be made and attached.

Examples of the type of documents that would be duplicated and placed in the audit working papers include the following:

1. Important forms that do not contain appropriate approvals;
2. Billings that contain obvious errors in extensions or footings;
3. Disbursements that were based on prices other than those stipulated in the Purchase Order or that did not take advantage of discounts or terms offered on the face of the invoice;
4. Standard reports, schedules or statements that are erroneous; and
5. Any evidence of a fraud or an employee defalcation.

The purpose of audit working papers is not only to indicate the work accomplished but to provide documented proof of discrepancies or unusual or unauthorized transactions. *The proof must be presented, identified as coming from a specific location in company files and established as being contained in the organization's business records.*

Anything that establishes or supports proof of a discrepancy, difference or error should be copied and placed in the working papers. Auditors should note all related information establishing that a relevent document had actually been used in the organization's records and reports. For example, if a voucher is removed from a batch, the auditor should schedule all other vouchers in that batch showing pertinent identification numbers, dates and amounts so that the total figure, including the extracted document, equals the batch total. Batch totals are then scheduled to tie-in to the daily report, thus establishing that the document was used in that day's business.

KEY POINT: *Working papers should leave no doubt as to their authenticity, accuracy and applicability. An auditor must not tamper with any of the information.* The notes in the audit working papers should enable an auditor to answer the following questions:

- Where did you get this information?
- When did you get the information?
- Why did you get the information?
- How do you know the information is accurate and legitimate?

To be able to answer these questions, an auditor must accurately note the identification numbers, dates, dollar amounts, approvals and other significant or unusual data about the pertinent information.

Auditors must assess information being viewed and recognize where it fits into the organization's activities and records. The record must also establish whatever it is that an auditor believes should be reported and proven. **KEY POINT:** *If the matter is important and other records are required to establish reliability, accuracy or authenticity, then the other required records must be able to be located or must become a part of the audit working papers.*

Reviewing Working Papers

As assigned work is performed, the auditor obtains necessary information in conformance with the audit program and prepares audit working papers showing the results of the examination. These notes must be carefully reviewed as soon as possible after their preparation to determine that all questions are answered.

All internal auditing working papers are reviewed and approved by the in-charge auditor and by audit supervisors before an audit is completed. Some papers are studied as soon as they are prepared, while other routine papers may not be examined until the final review.

REMEMBER: *The review consists of an examination of specific audit information to determine that it is legible, accurate, understandable and pertinent to the audit assignment.* Audit files should not be cluttered up with unnecessary or superfluous records. Supervisory approval of work papers signifies that the papers meet the established criteria. If an extracted copy of a document is interesting, but not necessary for the files, the supervisor should instruct the appropriate auditor that the information be returned to the files or be destroyed.

The review of an auditor's handwritten notes is a different matter. The review is to determine that the assigned auditor understood the audit point and approached the problem in the correct manner, that the auditor reviewed the correct records for the proper time period and that schedules, notes and comments are appropriate.

KEY POINT: *An in-charge auditor does not ordinarily have the authority to destroy any note written by a member of the audit staff.* If a supervisor disagrees with any opinion written by a staff member, the objections should be noted on the same work paper. The objections should be clearly identified as to author and date of notation and should clearly state the reasons for taking exception to the auditor's comments. Both the auditor's and supervisor's comments should remain in the audit working paper files, unless the originating auditor elects to withdraw the comment and destroy the handwritten workpaper.

If audit supervision finds that an auditor made errors or failed to understand the suggested audit approach, the auditor must be instructed in the correct procedure and asked to reexamine records. If time constraints prevent a reaudit of the activity, a decision may be made to forgo the corrective work.

NOTE: *Such decision must be properly approved and noted in the audit work papers.* The audit program should also be clearly noted that applicable work was not satisfactory, or that it was omitted. Audit supervisor's written comments should point out on the program, schedules, reports, or a separate page, why the work performance was not satisfactory.

After review by job audit supervision, the work papers are studied by the audit manager or an area supervisor who is assigned to wind up the audit. This final review of the staff auditor's work and first line supervisory review, consists of an in depth study of working papers and the audit program to assure that all of the audit points were satisfactorily performed and documented.

KEY POINT: *Working papers must contain necessary references and proof that the audit work was performed, and every audit point must be documented and proved beyond question.*

The purpose of this final review is to prepare for the audit windup meeting where the audit report is discussed with concerned line management. Audit management needs to be certain that documented answers can be supplied for all questions raised by management.

Binding Work Papers

At the completion of an audit all audit work papers, containing all the information relating to a specific audit should be brought together and bound in a hard cover binder. The binder should be properly labeled to show the audited location and the starting and completion dates of the audit. The CAF should be transferred to the current working paper file, so that all information relating to the last audit of the activity is together in one binder.

The sequence of filing working papers within the activity binder varies at the whim of audit management. Following is a sample:

1. A Table of Contents should be near the top of the file, to facilitate locating necessary information.
2. The last audit report is close to the top of the file, together with management's letters and directives resulting from the last review.
3. Follow-up letters and directives written by the audit staff are close to the top of the file, though some staffs elect to place such information in the related sections of the current working papers.
4. Immediately below are the most recent audit working papers.
5. The CAF may be near the top, or it may be near the bottom of the file.

Photographs may be used as evidential working papers, in the same fashion that photostats are used. Photographs should be clearly identified as to subject, location and the date that the picture was taken. Photos should be attached to standard work paper sheets. The use of a transparent wrap to enclose the photo will preserve the image.

Filing Work Papers

All audit working papers should be held in a fireproof, burglar proof vault or file case. Working papers may be filed by location or by type of activity audited, usually in alphabetic order or in numeric order if all activities are assigned a unique number. **REMEMBER:** *Files are confidential and access is restricted.*

Audit managers should establish a time retention period for audit working paper files. The established time period is affected by the space available for audit files, the time intervals between audits and the frequency of requests for audit information held in the files. **TIP:** *To save filing space, it is suggested that the audit working paper files be confined to the last two audits.* Under this system, the older audit working papers are carefully reviewed before the file is authorized for destruction. Any important and applicable information is transferred to current files, and the remaining bulk is destroyed.

The same basic approach is used for file control of self-audit reports when an organization uses such a program. Self-audits may be retained in a separate file apart from the audit working papers. The last two full self-audit reports should be held in file, and the oldest one discarded when a new report is received.

AUDIT FORMS AND SUPPLIES

Audit administration is responsible for stocking all forms and supplies required by the audit staff. The in-charge auditors are responsible for drawing forms and supplies that are needed for specific assignments. Each staff member is responsible for drawing the standard items of equipment that are normally assigned and for keeping these items in good condition.

Auditor's Equipment and Supplies

Following is a sample list of standard audit equipment that may be assigned to individual auditors, and for which they remain personally responsible.

1. Auditor briefcase. Good construction and large enough to carry working papers and auditing supplies.
2. Calculator. Good quality, preferably solar powered so that batteries are not required.
3. Camera. Small enough to carry in the briefcase.
4. Micro recorders. Good quality, supplied with high quality tapes.
5. Portable computers.

6. Stamping devices and pads. For use when sending out large quantities of written matter.
7. Other special devices, such as optical readers or data entry devices that are used by audit staffs in particular companies.

Other audit supplies of a general nature that are used in quantity are issued to staff members as required. Among these items are such things as staplers, paper clips, file folders, file binders, rulers, stationery, padlocks with keys, ink correcting fluid, erasers, auditor note and analysis pads, pens, pencils and other miscellaneous items of this nature. Most supplies are readily available in the average office, but an auditor may need them while away from a working office.

In addition to this general group of supplies, an internal auditor frequently must carry certain audit supplies and forms that are intended for specific use. When A/R verification work is to be performed, auditors require self addressed envelopes and reply cards, perhaps postage stamps and index cards. Auditors also carry audit programs and instructions and the audit manual.

Determining Need

Audit supervisors are responsible for determining the quantity and type of audit supplies that will be needed for a specific job or an audit swing. They may decide to draw all supplies that will be required for an audit tour, or they may elect to carry a minimum of supplies and have their remaining needs mailed to them at designated locations along their route. If the tour takes in many locations with only a day or two spent at each site, all supplies are usually carried by the audit team. **TIP:** *If some audits require a week or longer, the supplies may be mailed to specified locations on agreed dates.*

Working copies of audit programs, as well as final copies for the audit working papers, will be required for each activity audited. If the staff uses a loose leaf program system, then a minimal supply of audit programs is required since the program can be pulled apart and doled out to the working auditors. After auditors perform the work they then initial the formal working paper copy of the program, but do not mark up the copy with which they are working.

Under this approach, only a few copies of the audit program are required per location to be audited. One as a final copy, and the others to be separated and distributed among the working auditors. If the program is continuous and bound together, individual copies are given to each auditor for every job, plus one final copy is needed for each set of working papers.

The audit administrator is aware of the audit schedules and of the number of auditors assigned to each job and is, therefore, able to judge the quantity of audit programs, and other forms and supplies, which will be needed during the coming year.

Ordering of Forms and Supplies

Every audit supply item should have a reorder point that allows for normal usage during the time required to process an order and have it delivered to stock. Each item may have a different time frame to be considered. The reorder point must assure that supplies will be available until the new stock is received. **TIP:** *If, during the year, it becomes apparent that an audit form must be radically changed, the resupply time interval should be increased accordingly.*

Quantities of forms and supplies needed for a lengthy series of audits can be difficult to judge. Particularly if the staff uses a form for A/R verifications that is not produced by the computer. Reply envelopes can also be a problem, since these are usually postage metered and addressed to the PO Box at the home office.

Audit staffs use local duplicating machines and supplies where possible instead of carting tons of paper around the country. When such resources are locally available, the staff need only carry master copies of the forms to be used.

Special Audit Equipment

Any special equipment is usually carried by members of the audit team. If special measuring, marking or stamping devices are needed, they are carried by the auditors even though such items may be available at some of the locations to be visited. Let's consider some of the costlier equipment items that may be assigned to auditors.

Audit briefcases should be strong enough and large enough to hold all of the manuals and supplies that an auditor must carry on a field assignment. Cases must have a good strong lock, so that any tampering will be evident. Since briefcases carry manuals, postage stamps, verification forms, office supplies and audit work papers, they must be closely watched. Briefcases should not be left unattended, but it is customary to leave cases containing supplies in a locked office overnight, providing all important work papers have been removed. **KEY POINT:** *Auditors should be constantly on the alert for potential security problems.* They should realize that their briefcases may contain information of great importance to certain individuals. Materials in these cases should be considered as confidential and should not be shown to unauthorized personnel.

At least one member of each audit team should be assigned a good small camera. Preferably one that takes and produces instant pictures that can be viewed within a few minutes of the snapshot. The camera may be used to illustrate an unusual condition, or it might be used to photograph documents that are required for audit work papers.

Cameras are usually assigned to supervisory auditors who are responsible for insuring that an adequate supply of film is on hand and that the camera is only used for company business.

Each auditor should be supplied with a good quality microcassette recorder and a supply of high quality tapes for the instrument. These recorders may be used during travel periods to dictate observations or thoughts that the auditor wishes to include in the working papers. They are also valuable for agreed use during some interviews instead of writing out notes that can interfere with a normal conversation.

The recorder can also be useful during windup meetings to record management's responses to audit points, as well as any agreed changes in the audit report that were decided upon at these meetings. Custodians of recorders should be certain to carry a supply of suitable batteries.

Portable, lap top computers can be a useful audit tool. Depending on the programs in use and the access controls, the audit team might use a computer for access to the corporate data base to check on specific customer accounts, inventory transactions or other areas that are processed by the corporate Electronic Data Processing (EDP) Department.

Such a computer might also be useful for creating disks of data to be verified by the computer department, or perhaps for writing up the internal audit report on site. These portable computers can be battery operated or plugged into electrical outlets, and can use normal phone lines for access to the data base.

Control of Staff Property

Audit manuals, books of instructions, company bulletins, brief cases, other equipment and auditing supplies remain the property of the auditing department and do not become the personal property of the auditor in possession. **NOTE:** *Manuals and books of instructions should be numbered and accounted for, and a part of the procedure for terminations should require that all such documents be returned.*

Other company property, such as brief cases, audit equipment and office supplies should also be recovered from departing staff members.

Unique Audit Forms

Internal auditors, routinely working in the environment of their company, soon learn what letters and forms they use regularly. They are especially interested in forms that are several pages long. As auditors become aware of frequent usage, they may consider designing standard forms for use in future audits. Under this approach the common language is preprinted with appropriate blank spaces for insertion of the variable information. The variables can then be stamped, typed or handwritten in the appropriate spaces.

Accounts Receivable Verification Request

An accounts receivable verification request is a good example of a standard audit form. Following is a sample, hand-prepared accounts receivable verification request used by the XYZ Corporation auditors to circularize their open accounts receivable as of a certain date.

IA RV01 XYZ CORPORATION No. ________

Office Location ______________________

THIS IS NOT A REQUEST FOR PAYMENT

To Be Used For Auditor's Information Only

PLEASE USE ENCLOSED SELF ADDRESSED POSTCARD

FOR YOUR REPLY

Name ______________________________________

Street ______________________________________

City ______________________________ State ______________

Dear Customer:

Our records are being audited in accordance with our desire to keep customer accounts accurate. We show the following charges as unpaid on the following date. Date ________

Inv. Date	Inv. No.	Amount	Inv. Date	Inv. No.	Amount
					TOTAL OPEN

This is not necessarily your present balance. It does not include payments, credits or charges received after the above date. Would you please let us know if our records are correct or incorrect by filling in the enclosed reply card and returning it promptly. Please do not discuss this matter with anyone but the auditors. XYZ Corp.

The company location is stamped in, but the detailed information is either handwritten or typed. The form has been designed so that the name of the customer will be positioned into the proper space of a window envelope, thus eliminating the need to recopy the customer's name and address. The form is prenumbered and written in triplicate.

Auditors use the forms sequentially and account for all of the requests mailed. The original copy is mailed to the customer, the second copy is preprinted with the words "Second Request," and the third copy is retained as a control and later placed in audit files.

Many receivables are carried in a computer data base, and in these operations the auditor uses data processing to prepare statements to be used for accounts receivable verifications.

Verification Reply Cards

With each positive verification statement, a reply letter or post card is enclosed. Each reply bears a unique number which enables the audit staff to identify the customer replying. When customers are requested to reply and indicate whether the statement is correct or incorrect, a post card similar to the following example may be used.

IA RV01A XYZ CORPORATION No:________

PLEASE RETURN THIS CARD AS SOON AS POSSIBLE. THANK YOU.

The balance as shown on the enclosed statement corresponds with my records as checked below:

1. *Correct* and unpaid as of date shown on statement. ☐
2. *Incorrect*—paid *before* date shown of statement. ☐

(If any invoices on enclosed statement have been paid, please give the following information):

Invoice ________ Date paid ________ By cash ☐ or check ☐

Invoice ________ Date paid ________ By cash ☐ or check ☐

3. *Incorrect*—no record of invoice(s): ________ ☐

OTHER REMARKS ________

________ SIGNED ________ DATE ________

Verification of Sale of Property

The following standard letter is used to verify that the sale of property reported as sold by your company to individuals or other companies was accurately recorded. The form contains a unique number and is printed on company stationery; it appears to be a personal letter. The body of the letter reads as follows:

A routine audit is being conducted of selected dispositions of XYZ Corporation property. In connection with this review, we ask that you furnish the auditors with the following information pertaining to your recent purchase of ________ which was made on your behalf on (Date) ________.

Date Rec.	Quantity Rec.	Item name	Brass tag #.	Unit pr.	Total Pd.
___19__	______	______	______	$____	$____
___19__	______	______	______	$____	$____
___19__	______	______	______	$____	$____

Remarks________

Please insert the information requested in the appropriate spaces and return this request promptly to the auditors. Please use the enclosed self-addressed envelope for your reply. *Do not discuss this request with anyone except the auditor.*

Your cooperation is appreciated.

XYZ Corporation, by ________

Verification of Branch Warehouse Sales

When a location makes sales directly out of a warehouse operation, it is difficult to maintain adequate internal control over these transactions. The following postcard verification form is used by the XYZ audit staff to determine that warehouse sales are all properly reported. The auditors observe sales for a period of time, and then select a sampling of customers to circularize.

A two-part postcard is used; one contains the auditor's address, and space on the reverse side for the information that the customer is requested to supply. The account fills in the blank spaces in this card and mails it to the auditors. The second card, attached to the first, is addressed to the customer and its reverse side explains the purpose of the mailing.

The card explaining the purpose of the confirmation request is filled in by auditors and reads as follows:

IA WSO1V XYZ CORPORATION Date ________

VERIFICATION OF BRANCH WAREHOUSE SALES

Dear Customer:

In our desire to keep our records in agreement with those of our customers, we periodically check our records against customer records.

At this time we are interested in compiling statistics on the volume of product that our customers pick up directly at our branch.

We would appreciate your completing the attached card by listing all purchases that you picked up from our branch warehouse at ________________ ________________, during the period starting ________________, to ________________.

Your cooperation will aid us in our efforts to provide the best possible distribution of XYZ merchandise.

Respectfully.
XYZ CORPORATION

The second postcard attached to the above card is to be filled out by the customer. It provides columns for Dates, Invoice Numbers, and dollar amounts. It also contains a unique identification number and spaces for Remarks, Signature and Date the card was filled out.

Verification of Issued Credit Memos

When internal auditors verify the accuracy and appropriateness of credit memos, they either use a postcard or letter approach. The auditors at the XYZ Corporation use a letter approach. A two-copy set of the following letter is mailed to selected accounts, together with a self-addressed reply envelope. The customer is expected to fill in the lower portion and return one copy of the letter to the auditor. The letter on company letterhead contains a control number, is addressed to the customer and reads as follows:

Gentlemen:

In accordance with our desire to keep customer's accounts accurate our corporate audit department periodically verifies credit memos which we have issued to our customers.

They are currently conducting this examination and would appreciate your confirmation of the following credit memo.

Credit Memo # ____________ Date ____________ Amount ____________

Please indicate in the space provided below for your reply, whether this information is correct. If a difference exists, please give our auditors any information which might aid them in reconciling the difference.

Your reply should be mailed directly to the XYZ Corporation Audit Department using the stamped, addressed envelope which is enclosed for your convenience.

Very truly yours,
XYZ Corporation

The above credit memo dated ____________ in the amount of $__________ is correct and was part of our current balance with XYZ Corporation as of ____________. The reason the credit was issued was ____________

____

Date ____________ Signed ______________________

Your above information is incorrect and the following exceptions apply: ______

____

Date ____________ Signed ______________________

Audit Administrative Forms

In addition to the many forms that are conceived and designed to aid the staff auditor in performing assignments, audit management also creates many administrative forms, such as the following:

1. Standard covering letters for sending out supplies or equipment.
2. Standard receipts to be signed by auditors as evidence that they were issued certain items of equipment for which they are personally responsible.
3. Transmittal letters for audit reports or extracts of reports sent out by staff administrators.
4. An audit schedule which lists all assignments for each staff member for a definite period of time. Usually the formal issued schedule covers only a one-week period, though a tentative standard monthly schedule is also prepared.

   The internal audit assignment sheet lists all department personnel on the left hand side of the sheet, separated by job classification. Days of the week are listed at the top of the sheet, and pertinent information is entered showing the job location of each employee for each day of the week. The form also provides spaces for entry of information showing dates that audits are to be started or reviewed.

5. A supervisor's report to the audit manager which is prepared at the completion of each audit assignment. This report shows the location audited, the names of the auditors that participated and the supervisor's evaluation of each auditor's work. It contains space for the supervisor's personal observations and suggestions for revisions of the audit program or instructions.

Each audit staff creates its own forms as required. Most of these forms are merely reminders of specific information that is needed to aid in administering the audit department.

Chapter 9

Preparing for and Performing the Internal Audit

PREPARING FOR AN INTERNAL AUDIT

The first challenge in preparing for an internal audit is the selection of an auditor to take charge of the assignment. If the project is routine, the audit manager may elect to appoint a staff auditor as the in-charge supervisor. If the project is complicated the audit manager will select an experienced audit supervisor or the assistant audit manager to head up the audit team.

The assigned supervisor assembles all the necessary related data and studies all available information. This examination determines the audit scope, enables an estimate of audit hour requirements, and plays an important part in selecting audit personnel for the assignment.

Assembling Data

In-charge auditors assemble available records and correspondence relating to the location to be reviewed. These include the following:

- Previous audit reports, if the activity has been audited before;
- Previous audit working paper, including the CAF;
- Recent applicable letters of comment from outside auditors;
- Pertinent financial, operating and comparative analysis reports;
- Correspondence relating to previous audits, if available; and
- A summary of the information to be verified during the audit.

Before starting an internal audit, the supervising auditor also assembles and arranges for shipment of all of the necessary forms, supplies, programs and instructions that will be required.

How to Determine Your Audit Scope

From an analysis of the preliminary information, you should be able to determine the activity's size, volume of business, number of employees, types of operating problems and the relative success of the managers. Your study of comparative statistical results may disclose the areas where the activity is not performing up to expectations. If the operation has been audited before, the previous audit notes, program and follow-up correspondence should help you to establish the scope of the proposed review.

If the activity has not been audited before, your audit scope must be adjusted as the work progresses. The starting plan should conform to the explicit scope of the internal auditing function. If the assignment calls for an operational audit, you may wish to review the General Audit Program for operational audits in Chapter 7. For a normal financial audit, use the same scope that applies to an audit program for similar operations. Any program used will probably be modified as the audit progresses.

How to Estimate Audit Hour Requirements

If the last audit of the location had been routinely accomplished, the time spent on that previous audit is a good guide to the present assignment. It need only be adjusted for changes in the operation, in the audit program, or in the experience level of the assigned auditors.

Auditor Time Reports, described in Chapter 5, can be useful in estimating time requirements for an upcomimg review. Taking the norm of audit time for particular operations and applying it to available information should enable you to arrive at a good estimate of audit time that will likely be required for the present assignment.

When it is impossible to estimate accurately the time required for an audit assignment, it is best to err on the low side. Even if it is grossly wrong, it will serve as a bench mark for staff auditors and assist supervisors in allocating time to specific areas. Then, when staff members request more time, you'll know that their plea has merit. **POINT TO CONSIDER:** *If your estimate of audit hour requirements turns out to be considerably understated, it may be best to omit complete sections of the audit program during the present visit, and schedule a revisit in a few months to audit the sections that were skipped.* The revisit will come as a complete surprise, and your time estimate will be more accurate since you'll have the previous audit hours as a guide.

How to Assign Audit Personnel

Estimating hour requirements and deciding on the assignment of personnel is actually a simultaneous equation. The ability, previous experience, and work speed varies from auditor to auditor. You may set a time period and then select auditors who will do the job in the specified time, or you may assign specific auditors to a job and then gauge the amount of audit time that they will require to do the job.

KEY POINT: *If it is important to get the job done accurately and speedily, then assign your best, most experienced auditors.* Assigning auditors to new experiences may slow up the work on this job, but it will prepare the auditors to do a better job in the future. Most assignments are a compromise, mixing experienced auditors with novices.

KEY POINT: *The opportunity for on-the-job training should not be overlooked.* Bear in mind that *on-the-job training is an inexpensive way to teach auditors, but it is better not to train at all than to train improperly.*

Preliminary Work in Head Office

Audit staffs use a check-off chart that lists everything necessary to start the audit. Forms and supplies can be obtained from the audit administrator, while other necessary data are gleaned from a study of pertinent records and reports. The in-charge auditor is responsible for getting the requirements together and for distributing materials.

The following sample check-off chart lists requirements for a Distribution Branch audit. The form is used by XYZ Corporation's audit staff to prepare for an assignment. The letter bears an Audit Department Form Number, is dated and shows the location to be audited. The form is sent to the Audit Department administrator who obtains all the necessary papers and information, most of it from the Corporate Comptroller's Department. The form is designed so that the last two columns on the right (not shown), can be checked off by the administrator to indicate whether the requested data is enclosed or will be mailed to the auditor at a later date.

Please obtain and forward the following information:

	(Date or Per. of Data)
1. Last two self-audit programs and related follow-up correspondence.	Current
2. Copies of available daily, weekly, or monthly "Summary of Cash Receipts and Sales" through auditor's A/R and Inventory cutoff date.	Up to cutoff dates given by auditor
3. Depository transfer account cutoff statement.	Per auditor request
4. Copy of petty cash account reconciliation.	Last month-end
a. Amount of authorized Petty Cash fund is	$__________
b. Reimbursement summaries for prior periods.	6 week before audit
5. Month-end balance of A/R-Trade.	Last month-end $____
Detail listing of A/R-Employee.	Last month-end
6. Copy of monthly aging schedule of A/R-Trade.	Last month-end

	(Date or Per. of Data)
7. List of bad debt write-offs and recoveries.	Since last audit
8. Copies of F/G and supplies inventories.	Last period-end
9. Schedule of reported inventory O/S's.	6 mo. before audit
10. Inventories reported in outside warehouses.	Last month-end
11. Representative number of vouchers paid on branch approval prior to audit.	Selected at random
12. Property list in duplicate.	Current
13. List of payroll terminations by name and date.	Since last audit
14. Copy of branch payroll and rates.	Last payroll period
15. Employee time cards.	Last 2 pay periods
16. List of Sickness and Accident payments.	Previous 3 months
17. List of Hospital and Surgical claims paid.	Previous 3 months
18. List of locations leased or owned within a fifty mile radius:	

The above form assumes a repeat audit of a continuing operation and lists the type of information that is verified by auditors during a routine visit. In addition to the above, the auditors carry the previous audit working papers containing the CAF, operating reports, correspondence relating to the previous audits and the necessary forms and supplies that will be needed to conduct the audit.

The ABC Corporation's internal audit staff has a somewhat different approach. They use a national form bearing an internal Audit Department code and intended for audit supervisors. The form is headed "Preliminary Instructions" and reads as follows:

Prior to arriving at the audit location, the following should be done:

1. Review previous audit report and correspondence.
2. Review previous work papers.
   (a) Can any be brought forward?
   (b) Any problem areas?
   (c) Roughly determine what confirmations will be required.
3. Review various statistical reports of comparative operations. Compare this location with others that are similar. Use analysis to modify scope and audit program as required.
4. Review current audit program and related instructions.
5. Review location flow charts and procedure write-ups.
   (a) Obtain copies of standard flow charts where appropriate.
6. Plan timing of work required at location and prepare time budget.
   (a) Review the above with the regional manager.
7. The regional manager should inform supervisor of the following:
   (a) Any special areas to be investigated.
   (b) Results of outside auditor's visits and their future plans.
   (c) Any recent changes in procedures, operations or personnel.

8. Gather together necessary supplies for the assignment.
   (a) Distribute among audit team and arrange for additional needs.
9. Request regional manager to inform Division Controller of start of audit on morning of arrival.

Forms and Supplies

Another preliminary requirement form is used to request the forms and supplies that will be needed for the audit visit. This form lists on the left-hand side of the page the national form number of the item requested, and provides space for insertion of the desired quantity on the right-hand side of the form. The following forms would be needed by the ABC audit staff for an audit of a sales distribution branch:

1. *Receivable Confirmation Letter.*
   To be mailed to customers to confirm invoices in the A/R files.
2. *Credit Memo Confirmation Letter.*
   To confirm with customer, credit memos in the A/R files.
3. *Confirmation Statement.*
   To confirm customer's account containing an old balance.
4. *Customer Reply Cards.*
   To be mailed with above statement for customer reply.
5. *Verification of Branch Warehouse Sales.*
   To confirm customer pick-up of product at the warehouse.
6. Verification of Credits Paid by Salesman's Draft.
   To confirm selected accounts where credit was paid by draft.

In addition to the above forms, other requirements include working papers and audit supplies such as work sheets, analysis pads, and other miscellaneous items.

Audit forms and supplies are controlled by each job supervisor, who estimates and draws the total needs before leaving the home office.

Travel Arrangements

Just before each move, an audit team is informed of the address of the next location to be audited and of the time that they are to arrive at the job site. Using this information each auditor is expected to make whatever travel arrangements are necessary. Actual reservations may be made by the auditor, the administrator or an outside agency; but no matter who makes the arrangements, or what carriers are used, each auditor is responsible for arriving at the appointed time.

Staff members stay at the same hotel when possible and usually share rides to the office building. The in-charge auditor's hotel is the customary meeting place for the audit team, and the appointed meeting time is either the night before or at breakfast on the day the audit is scheduled to start. The team arranges to travel from the hotel to the assigned location, so that the supervising auditor arrives with or ahead of the other staff members. This enables the team to start the audit soon after arrival.

STARTING AN INTERNAL AUDIT

The start-up procedure used depends on the nature of the audit. For example, if an operational audit is scheduled for an activity that has never before been audited, the opening session will be different than that used in a regularly audited operation. In the new audit, the supervisor may elect to meet with all employees of the activity and introduce all staff members and then outline the work that is to be performed. This ice breaking meeting can be beneficial, but is not warranted at locations that are regularly audited.

First Time or Repeat Visits

When the audit team arrives at the location to be audited they introduce themselves, *have their identity and authority checked with the home office and start the audit review.* At this point the approach is different if the visit is a routine reaudit of a regularly visited location, as opposed to the first time audit of an activity.

On a first-time audit, local management is gathered together in a meeting where they are informed that an audit is to begin and are requested to cooperate with the audit team. The audit supervisor may also ask the activity manager to hold a short meeting of all department employees to introduce the auditors and briefly explain the purpose of the visit. Such a session can clear the air and cut down on rumors. It will also reduce friction between clerical employees and the audit staff. As the audit work progresses, each manager and supervisor is interviewed individually by a member of the audit team.

On repeat visits, general group meetings of employee or management personnel are not required, though all managers and supervisors are interviewed during the course of the audit. Individual interviews, in either case, are for discussions of the audit responsibilities and approach. Local management is asked for suggestions and auditors note their comments. **TIP:** *Flow charts of all significant activities are either prepared or updated during these discussions.* And these introductory sessions are used by staff auditors to prepare, or obtain and review, applicable systems and procedure write-ups.

Using the Element of Surprise

Before the audit group enters a location, the audit supervisor has already decided the sequence in which the critical activities will be reviewed. A decision has also been reached concerning any activities that are to be audited on a surprise basis.

KEY POINT: *By the term surprise, we mean that auditors try to get to critical records before custodians have an opportunity to alter, make extractions or insert any data that was not there before the auditors arrived on the scene.*

Since it is not wise to show personnel that certain activities are considered high risks, your work should flow in a normal fashion. A common auditing joke asks the question, "Should an auditor remove his coat before or after counting petty cash?" It is best that the coat be removed first and that the auditor then move gracefully, but with some dispatch, to the petty cash fund.

Routine audit visits are handled in the established effective manner. *Where the element of surprise is an important factor,* the auditors enter unannounced and, after proper identification, take possession of the most critical records that are to be verified.

Audit staff members proceed to their priority assignments as soon as possible in order to review records taken over on a surprise basis.

KEY POINT: *Records should be verified quickly and then returned to the responsible employee so as to reduce interruption in normal activity.*

Records that are usually examined on a surprise basis are cash registers and funds; accounts, notes and employee receivables; certain inventory records and perhaps warehouse cash sales reports in some operations. **REMEMBER:** *Audit supervision must decide in advance what records or activities, if any, are to be immediately examined so as to gain the advantage of a surprise review.*

> **EXAMPLE:** I recall an incident where I agreed to postpone audit work until the following Monday, because the controller pleaded for a delay, allegedly because of a shortage of personnel.
>
> The controller used the period to draw up a full new set of books in which records had been altered to hide a defalcation. The records were drawn up in such haste that they contained errors which led to an early discovery of the manipulation and the apprehension of the culprit. From that time on, I never delayed an audit start or announced in advance when an audit was to begin.

Confidentiality of Information and the Source

All audit notes and correspondence should be considered as confidential information. In addition, the source of critical information may also demand anonymity. **KEEP IN MIND:** *The audit staff must establish a reputation for shielding* *individuals that volunteer information on the condition that their identity not be disclosed.* If an auditor agrees to hold an identity in confidence, every effort should be made to keep that promise.

When such information is obtained, an auditor should try to gather some other independent proof rather than quote the original data. If use of the original information will readily identify the informant, the auditor should not use the information unless and until permission is granted by the employee who disclosed the facts.

If the data are readily available from other sources, the auditors are free to use the information, since they will not be required to identify the original informant.

Assignment of Working Space

Upon proper confirmation from the headquarter's office, auditors are assigned working space and immediately begin their examination. Locations that are frequently audited often have private offices for the exclusive use of auditors. At other locations the manager may assign a private office or a conference room for the auditor's use. **KEEP IN MIND:** *It is a good practice for at least one member of the audit team to work at an open desk in the general office area of the operation.* This makes the audit team accessible, and leads to better acceptance of the audit work, particularly in locations that are being audited for the first time.

Private offices offer the advantage of enabling the auditors to work in a secure environment, but it also removes the audit staff from working employees and sets up a mental barrier to free communication. If all members of the audit team must work in a private office, the members of the team should spend as much time as possible in the open general office area. When practical, interviews with employees should be held at the employee's desk, rather than in a private office.

Meeting with Employees to be Audited

In a normal audit sequence, the audit team prepares for the review by studying important available information, then the team travels to the audit location and meets the employees who are to be audited.

At the earliest opportunity, the in-charge auditor should discuss the study with the local operating and financial managers. The scope of the review should be outlined, and local management asked for their suggestions as to special areas that the auditors should study. **KEEP IN MIND:** *This does not necessarily mean that the audit team will follow the suggestions, but it does give the audit-senior a good idea of the areas that local management think need improvement.* There is always the danger that a manager might not mention an area in which a major problem exists. But if several managers agree that an operation needs study, the auditors are well-advised to examine that activity.

Auditors may conduct their study using one of two approaches. 1) An auditor may elect to sit individually with each supervisor and then with the section's employees and review their job assignments, records and procedures. At that time the auditor makes a preliminary analysis of work routines and paper flow in an attempt to identify duplication of effort, unnecessary procedures, inefficiencies, poor internal controls, high risk areas and time wasting "make work." During this process the auditor compares the location's work routines, as described by employees to nationally prescribed company standards. 2) An auditor immediately takes possession of important records and proceeds to critically examine them. During this examination the appropriate employees are questioned about work flow, office routines, and individual responsibilities. If records or postings are unclear or contain questionable entries, the auditor first talks to the employee responsible and then, if necessary, to the appropriate supervisor. **REMEMBER:** *One way or another an auditor should arrange to meet with and discuss job assignments and work procedures with each employee working in the activity.* At the completion of the audit, at least one member of the audit team should know the name and job title, and have a general idea of each employee's work habits, procedures and ability.

During meetings with employees the auditor must make notes of the conversations, and be certain that the notes are accurately written and can be correctly interpreted. If a microcassette is permissible and agreed to by the employee being interviewed, use it.

How to Assign Audit Tasks

Each member of the team is assigned a specific portion of the audit program. To increase audit efficiency, items are assigned on a related record basis. For example, the auditor assigned the cash count would also work on bank reconciliations, warehouse sales, and deliverypeople's and salespeople's collection reports. The auditor verifying disbursement records also reviews receiving and purchasing procedures. Auditors who work on inventory reconciliations, also handle billing procedures.

The audit supervisor may elect to divide up all of the work in advance, making each auditor responsible for certain sections of the program. Or the critical first items may be assigned, and as these are completed and staff auditors complete assigned work, other sections are doled out.

Another common method of distributing the work load is to use a chronological approach. This system requires that each audit step be considered as to the timing sequence of the audit work. The first work covers portions of the audit program that must be performed soon after arrival. When an auditor completes an audit phase, the audit supervisor reviews the work and, if satisfactory, assigns the section that follows next in sequence. For example, an auditor who has completed a review of the handling of salespeople's orders might next be assigned the shipping and billing activities. The auditor who completed a review of the cashier's cage might then be assigned the job of reconciling bank accounts. The sequence procedure is followed until all related audit reviews are completed.

When assigning audit tasks, the supervisor matches each audit step to a particular staff member. The supervisor then will check the auditor's progress at regular intervals to be sure that the work is progressing and that no problems have developed. **IMPORTANT:** *Supervisors must see that time is not wasted on insignificant items.*

PERFORMING THE AUDIT WORK

Under any method of assigning audit work, the supervisor is held responsible for ensuring that each audit point has been correctly interpreted and performed. Each auditor discusses the approach used and presents documented work papers. If the supervisor is satisfied, the papers are taken and placed in the "work completed" file; if not, the auditor is advised to use a different approach to accomplish the required task. When the work is satisfactory, both the auditor and supervisor initial the audit program.

When all of the audit steps have been signed off by the supervisor, the audit work is completed. As the staff nears the audit completion point, the in-charge auditor advises audit management of the progress of the work. A date for the windup meeting is set. When the meeting date arrives, the audit team moves on to their next assignment, leaving designated audit personnel to conduct the final meeting.

Before the windup meeting, a member of top audit management reviews all audit findings and the related documentation. The review might take place over the telephone, but if significant items are involved, an audit manager will usually travel to the location to participate in the final meeting. The audit manager, in these cases, decides when all loose ends have been tied down and the audit work completed. The audit manager schedules the windup meeting, and invites appropriate line and staff managers and audit department personnel to attend.

Auditor's Work Progress Checklist

Some internal audit staffs use a checklist form, to remind the audit staff of items to be accomplished. Following is a sample form used by the XYZ Corporation's audit staff. A column on the right-hand side (not shown) is to be checked off as the audit supervisor completes the item. The form is numbered, titled and contains some descriptive language. We'll start with the body of the form that covers actions starting at arrival at the assigned location.

A. Upon arrival at the location to be audited the supervisor should do the following:
   1. Introduce self and staff to local management.
   2. Work out arrangements with office manager with regard to these:
      (a) Work space.
      (b) Report requests.
      (c) Plans for inventory taking. (If appropriate)
      (d) Possible office help for clerical operations.
      (e) Discussions with local management as audit work progresses.
      (f) Arrangements for final audit review.
   3. Review the Self Audit Questionnaire with the office manager.
      (a) Note areas of potential weaknesses in internal controls that are apparent from answers. Carefully examine these areas during your audit.
      (b) Determine that local managers fully understand the implications of all of the self-audit points.
      (c) Review answers to questionnaire for accuracy and completeness. *Any evidence that answers have been deliberately falsified should be documented in the W/P's.*
      (d) Review all self audit correspondence to determine that follow-up is proper and timely.
      (e) In areas where the self audit indicates good controls and recent review by local management, the related audit work should be de-emphasized or perhaps entirely eliminated.
      (f) Discuss program and forward any suggestions or criticism to audit manager.
   4. Review standard flow charts and procedural write ups and update where necessary.
   5. Review company manuals that are maintained at the location.
      (a) For completeness, and timeliness.
      (b) For effect on related audit work.
   6. Review location's operating expense statements and compare expenses with historical pattern. Analyze large fluctuations.

B. Attempt to develop the following statistics where appropriate, and compare to other similar operations for reasonableness.
   1. Petty Cash
      (a) $ value of imprest fund.
      (b) Normal amount of reimbursement.
      (c) Frequency of reimbursement.
      (d) Annual disbursement through fund.
   2. Cash General
      (a) Average daily deposit.
      (b) Monthly recap to sales.

3. Accounts Receivable
   (a) Average month-ending balance.
   (b) Total dollar sales to ending balance.
   (c) Percentage of past dues to current accounts.
   (d) $ value of write-offs and percentage to total A/R.

C. Inventory
   1. Dollar value of month-ending finished goods inventory.
   2. $ and quantity variance between book and physical inventory.
   3. By major account designations, relate sales to inventory.
   4. Ratio of dumps and obsolete product to sales dollars.

D. Payroll
   1. $ monthly payroll.
   2. Employee count.
   3. Review work-efficiency reports.

E. Property
   1. $ value of property assigned to activity.
   2. $ value of Capital and Repair budgets.
   3. Number of automotive vehicles assigned.
   4. Obtain and review the Idle Equipment list.

The above checklist serves as a reminder to study statistical reports that could influence the direction of an audit.

Work Hours and Breaks

Auditors conform to the audited location's work rules and regulations. No matter how many hours of overtime were worked the previous night, or what time the audit staff closed up shop, some members of the audit team should put in an appearance at the office at the regular starting time. All staff members should follow local practices regarding work hours, lunch periods and coffee breaks.

If the location uses a flex-hour system, the audit staff need not be concerned about adhering to an established work period. But even in a flex-hour environment, the staff should have at least one auditor in the office from the time that doors open until they close for the day.

Staggering staff auditor's break periods has the effect of having an auditor present in the audit work area at all times to safeguard audit records. It also enables staff members to become acquainted with more of the office employees, since offices employees normally take staggered break periods.

Internal Auditing Routines

Knowing in advance what the first assignment will be, the auditors should have read all the important information concerning that task before reaching the job site. **IMPORTANT:** *If time permits, each auditor should read the full audit* *program, and should review all of the pertinent audit instructions.* This might save audit time if an auditor notices, while performing a routine task, a report or record that is scheduled for a later examination. Such observation might enable the auditor to accomplish two separate audit steps at the same time.

Audit supervisors may not always be able to assign all work in advance of arriving at an audit location. In such cases the work load is divided up immediately upon arrival. The audit supervisor decides what work will be done, who will do it and how much time will be spent on each point. Supervisors know that the audit program is a checklist concerned with the high risk areas and is to be used as a guide. The program is used as an aide in selecting the best way to study and resolve an issue.

NOTE: *Auditors are free to look into any activity or record at the location being audited, even those that are not mentioned in the audit program.* The supervisor is responsible for including these overlooked items in the audit review, and for reporting these oversights to audit management for consideration as future revisions of the program.

Preparing Auditor's Schedules

When performing audit work, you normally follow the directions contained in the audit program and associated instructions. When the program calls for the review of a specific period of time, you should cover that requirement. If the original time period studied leaves you with a feeling of having overlooked something, expand the period of the study until satisfied that all important matters have been examined.

Audit analysis schedules are usually necessary for all studies of high volume areas of activities. The analysis sheets should contain enough columns so that all important information can be handwritten on a single line. **TIP:** *When preparing such schedules you should first scan several of the documents in the file to be reviewed.* This will indicate the types of oversights, discrepancies and questionable transactions that will be encountered and should enable you to head up columns to classify important observations. After the preliminary review, go back to the first documents and start entering pertinent information in the appropriate columns.

Start your schedule by listing sufficient data so that anyone can find the document you are examining. For example if you are reviewing accounts payable, you might start your schedule by listing the voucher number and date; then perhaps you might list the batch number and date the data was entered into the computer system; then you might list the name and address of the payee and then the amount of the disbursement. With this information you can be certain that you are looking at the same document if you have to refer to it at a later time.

You then set up columns to classify the type of discrepancy or error noted. For example, discrepancy columns might be headed:

1. Lacking approvals.
2. Earned discounts not taken.
3. Paid price exceeds P/O price.
4. No receiving report.
5. No proper P/O.
6. Invoice terms not followed.

And so on and so forth. Leave a few blank columns on the right-hand side of the page for later comments on your findings. Your spread sheet will look something like this version, which is condensed from a fourteen column work sheet. The left-hand part contains the following:

XYZ CORPORATION—AUDIT SCHEDULE
REVIEW OF SUPPORTING DOCUMENTATION
FOR CASH DISBURSEMENTS

Col. 1	Col. 2	Col. 3	Col. 4	Col. 5	Col. 6	Col. 7
Payee	Address	Vou. #	Date	Batch #	Date	Amount
ABC CORP	Dayton, Ohio	3247-160	3/17/92	3-19-21	3/19/92	1,522.
EX CORP	Rio, Texas	3247-28	3/17/92	3-19-21	3/19/92	785.

Columns 8 to 14 are used to list the types of discrepancies. Note that the last two columns are used for miscellaneous comments:

Col. 8	Col. 9	Col. 10	Col. 11	Col. 12	Col. 13	Col. 14
Approvals	Rec. Rep.	P.O.	Price	Terms	Misc.	Comments
None	—	—	—	—	R.R. no proper approv.	
—	—	none	Seems high	—	No P.O. Check price!	

After reviewing the selected documents and making the appropriate notations in your audit schedule, you decide on the best approach to use to investigate the discrepancies. You may decide to retain all vouchers that have been listed and return the others to file. Then you sort the vouchers by type of discrepancy. Some vouchers will contain several discrepancies and each of these is placed into the group that coincides with the most seriously noted problem.

The next step is to select the most important group, seek out employees or supervisors who are responsible for the oversights and ask for explanations. Note applicable explanations in the appropriate space in your "Comments" column. If explanations are not satisfactory, the documents and offered explanations are discussed with the next level of management. Once again the statement of the responsible employee is written up.

This procedure is continued until an acceptable reason is found.

KEY POINT: *Regardless of the level at which a satisfactory answer is given, you are responsible for verifying that the explanation is accurate and complete.* It may be necessary to check related records and reports or to talk to other employees to verify that statements of personnel are truthful. If no reasonable answer can be found for significant discrepancies, a separate working paper should be prepared that sets out the problem and your step by step investigation.

KEY POINT: *No matter the item or the outcome, each discrepancy that you see should be recorded in the audit work papers.* Most of them will be a one-line notation in a working schedule. Sometimes an apparently minor discrepancy can lead to the disclosure of a major problem, as when an audit supervisor who may be aware of information not generally known, finds that a minor item fits into a larger picture.

Each audit note should indicate the nature of a discrepancy and when, how and by whom it was noted. **IMPORTANT:** *The working paper should also record what action was taken to resolve the problem, and identify the parties involved and the time frame.*

How to Handle Major Discrepancies

If evidence suggests a possibility of fraud, employee defalcation, theft, significant breakdown in internal controls, failure of company procedures or policies, or the potential loss of property or income, the matter must immediately be brought to the attention of appropriate management. **KEY POINT:** *In such cases it is important that the records and other evidence relating to the activity be immediately confiscated by the auditor.* Copies of the records should be made and inserted in the proper place in the files, with a note attached stating the date and the name of the auditor who removed the original documents.

IMPORTANT: *These records must be protected from destruction, and labeled so that they can be readily identified and enable an auditor to testify as to when and where they were located.* Auditors should not write on such documents nor mar any information contained therein. In necessary interviews concerning these important matters, the auditor should be careful of the language used in any preliminary discussions, and *should NOT make any accusations or infer that anything illegal has transpired.*

When important statements are made by responsible personnel, the auditor should attempt to record the statements or to write them up verbatim. If it becomes necessary to make a full investigation, the audit manager will consult with the legal department or with outside experts. In very important matters, it may be best to have depositions taken before a licensed court reporter.

How to Handle Minor Discrepancies

If audit noted discrepancies are the result of minor errors of a non-repetitive nature or minor deviations from policy or procedures, they can usually be handled at the local level without creating a major issue. **TIP:** *The more of these items that are disposed of locally and not mentioned in the formal audit report, the better will be the reception given to the audit staff at their next visit.* Supervisors should exercise good judgement when making such decisions.

Many noted discrepancies concern the failure of local personnel to follow nationally prescribed policies or procedures. **KEY POINT:** *These oversights are frequently the result of the failure of local people to understand and appreciate the significance of the issued directives.*

In such circumstances the auditor serves as an instructor in clarifying the material for local management. When correct procedures are pointed out, local management immediately rectifies the situation. Some of these failures to understand instructions can result in serious problems and must be treated accordingly. But if the oversight is not significant, the matter is merely written up for the audit work papers and need not be mentioned in the formal audit report.

If a noted discrepancy resulted in an accidental or unintentional loss to the organization, the matter must be brought to the attention of the responsible local supervisor. *The internal auditor should insure that proper action is taken to correct the problem and to recover any losses where possible and appropriate.* The matter should be discussed with the audit manager, but would not normally require intervention at that level of management.

Audit work papers should note the problem and the action taken by the auditors. Names of supervisors who took action, dates and the results should also be noted. Whether such items are included in the final audit report depends on the wishes of the audit manager.

Keep Audit Goal in Mind

When performing an internal audit you must always keep your purpose in mind. *Why is the audit being conducted, and what do you hope to accomplish?* Here are a few well chosen questions to keep in mind as your audit progresses.

1. Are internal controls well thought out and working?
2. Are personnel honest, competent and sufficiently informed?
3. Are all personnel necessary?

4. Is all work necessary and efficiently performed?
5. Is work flow logical and well timed?
6. Are working conditions conducive to efficient operations?
7. Are company policies and procedures followed by all employees?
8. Are records and reports accurate, complete and timely?
9. Is company property adequately protected?
10. Are all necessary activities being correctly performed?

If your answers to the above questions are all "Yes," you are looking at an exceptional operation.

Auditor Working Techniques

First the auditor must understand what an audit point means. What is the significance of the record or report that is to be examined? Why is it important and where does it fit into the activity's operations?

Then the auditor must understand the intent of the audit point. What am I to do? Why am I asked to do it? How shall it be done?

A good audit program, coupled with appropriate audit instructions, should provide answers to the above questions that can be readily understood by professional internal auditors. Let's watch closely while an auditor works on an audit assignment.

The audit program calls for the verification of a report and its supporting schedules. The auditor elects to make a copy of the report rather than hand copy the significant information. Each item on the report is then verified against the supporting schedules. Every item on the schedule is later verified against original source documents.

As each item on the report is verified, the auditor places a tick mark after each verified figure on the audit copy of the report. A unique tick mark is used to signify that an audit verification has been made. This procedure is followed until all of the items on the report have been ticked off, at which time the report is considered as verified against the supporting schedules.

As discrepancies are noted, the auditor writes up an audit work paper. For minor items, the auditor elects to prepare a nine-column schedule to list the items as noted. The first column identifies the source of information, the next columns describe the type of noted discrepancy. For example, a column is headed, "Approval not legible," another, " P/O not attached" and so on.

For major discrepancies, a separate audit work sheet is prepared. The write-up is headed to show the type of discrepancy discovered and is noted with the identifying location, the auditor's initials and the date the note was written. *All details of the irregularity are fully described, and a notation made of the actions taken by the auditor.* As these major discrepancy work papers are prepared they are shown to the audit supervisor who decides what action should be taken.

The audit supervisor may elect to make notations on the work paper or may start a new sheet that outlines recommended action. Results of these actions are noted on the sheet. **NOTE:** *Each irregularity is noted in the work papers, with a description of the observation, the actions taken and the results of such action.* The work paper is then ready for review by the area supervisor or the audit manager, who will decide if further action is necessary and if the item will be included in the final audit report.

Example of Handling a Major Discrepancy

As an example of the above technique, let's work through what appears to be a major discrepancy noted during a review of cash handling procedures. A staff auditor notes that the January month-ending summary of Daily Cash Deposits does not include one salesperson's cash report of January 16, in the amount of $47. *After rechecking to make certain that the audit work is correct,* the auditor prepares an audit working paper as follows:

> Chillicothe Sales Branch (Auditors initials and date)
> January Summary of Cash Receipts—current year.
>
> Auditor verified all daily receipt reports of salespeople for the month of January and tied these reports in to the monthly summary. All reports were handled properly except for salesperson #101's report for January 16th of current year. (Copy attached). This collection of $47 was not included in the 16th daily summary or in the monthly summary for Jan.
>
> The matter was brought to the attention of supervisor J. Doakes on Feb. 11th of current year.

The note is turned over to the in-charge auditor, who notes the following on the same sheet of paper:

> Feb. 12, year. Discussed discrepancy with the office manager (I.M. Smart), who explained as follows: Snow storm had shut down head office for two days which caused petty cash reimbursement check to be delayed. Branch ran out of petty cash and decided to use the $47 in cash collected by salesperson #101. A special entry was made that transferred the funds from cash receipts to petty cash. I personally verified that the head office was closed and that the transaction was handled properly. Signed J. Doakes.

The work paper was later reviewed by the audit manager during the windup work, and the following notation added on the sheet:

> Handling was proper. *We do not have a policy that covers this problem.* Do NOT include in audit report. Will discuss matter with corporate Comptroller and

have a policy statement issued regarding the intermingling of petty cash and cash receipts. U.R. Boss Feb. 22, year.

The Audit Manager made a copy of the audit work paper as a reminder to discuss the matter with the Corporate Comptroller, and the manager will participate in the drafting of a national policy statement that spells out the acceptable handling of problems of this type.

Request For Study

During the routine of business activity, the audit department receives many bulletins, directives and letters that relate to specific types of operations and activities. Audit administration uses a follow-up file system that contains a general subject file and files for specific locations or operations within a general subject.

If the department receives correspondence that specifically concerns one location, the material is placed in that location's file. If the letter concerns all locations of a special type, the letter is placed in the proper general file. If the letter mentions two or three locations, but the audit manager thinks it might be applicable to all similar locations, the letter is placed in the appropriate general file with a copy in the file of each location mentioned.

Executive comments or requests for auditing department studies of particular operations or problems are placed in these follow-up files. If audit management feels that a particular problem warrants auditing attention, a special form is prepared. This form titled, "Request for Study" is initialed and placed in the specific follow-up file for the location(s) affected.

When preparing for an audit visit, the in-charge auditor reviews all records and correspondence relating to the location to be audited, removes the "Request for Study" form and adds it to the list of items to be examined.

Let's follow a sample request from origination to completion.

EXAMPLE: The audit manager has received a request from the VP Sales to look into a matter during the next audit of the Almira Sales Branch. A late delivery problem surfaced in the area, and the branch manager has stated that the condition is under control. The Vice-President wants to know if the matter has been satisfactorily corrected. The letter from the VP is the basis for preparing a Request for Study form and the letter, together with a copy of the form, is held in Auditing's follow-up file.

The Request for Study is extracted from the Almira branch file by the in-charge auditor and assigned to a specific staff member for review. The auditor investigates the problem, writes the appropriate comments which are reviewed by the audit supervisor and forwarded to the audit manager.

The form itself then serves as the basis for a reply to the VP Sales. The audit manager may elect to send a copy of the request form or may decide to extract some of the information and include the extract in a separate reply letter. The results of the study might wind up as an audit point in the formal audit report, or simply be used to provide information and support the audit manager's reply to the Vice-President of Sales.

Following is an example of the form and a descriptive account of the applicable procedure:

Form IA SR5000 XYZ CORPORATION
INTERNAL AUDITING DEPARTMENT—REQUEST FOR STUDY
Study requested by: ____________________ Request date:
Subject: ____
Suggested approach: ______________________________________
Study assigned to: ____________________________ by: __________ on: ....
Results: ____
Work completed on: __________ Approved by: ________________ on: ....
Form forwarded to audit manager by: __________________________ on: ....

The first section of the form is completed by audit administration and reads as follows:

Study requested by: A. B. Coe, VP Sales Request date: March 3, year.
Subject: Is the Almira branch adhering to company policy of delivering product within two working days? Customer complaints have been received.
Suggested approach: Study delivery receipts and note dates orders are taken, entered into system and delivered to customers. Any that exceed 2 working days from date order taken to delivery must be investigated and reason for delay noted. If problem exists, analyze and recommend improvements.

(The study is assigned by the in-charge auditor)

Study assigned to: I. M. Smart By: T. Super On: 5/1/yr.

(The problem is studied and the auditor notes findings)

Results: Examined one full week of delivery documents; no exceptions noted. Only deliveries not made within 2-working-day policy were those where customer requested a specific delivery date which exceeded normal time span. Local management stated the problem had arisen because of illness and excessive absences of former data entry clerk. Job assignments were changed, and backup provided for order entry. No problems since changes were made.

(Answer is reviewed by audit supervisor and form completed)

Work completed on: 5/3/yr. Approved by: T. Super On: 5/5/yr.
Form forwarded to Audit manager by: T. Super On: 5/7/yr.

The audit manager decides that the matter will not appear in the formal audit report, but a copy of the Request for Study form is retained in the audit working papers. The audit manager writes to the Sales VP, and uses an extract of the last three sentences of the auditor's comments in the results section. The file is closed.

Security Over Audit Work and Records

Audit work papers should be treated as confidential information, only to be viewed by authorized individuals. Normal routine reports and schedules that belong to the operation being audited need not be treated as confidential *unless they are so classified or unless they contain evidence of improper handling or of a misappropriation.* In such cases the papers become the responsibility of the audit staff and should not be available to outsiders. Confidential papers should not be placed on top of a desk where they can be seen by passersby.

Audit working papers should be placed in file folders and held in a fire-proof, burglar-proof file or carried in the internal auditor's briefcase and locked when the responsible auditor leaves the work area. At the end of each working day, auditors should carry with them any briefcases that contain audit work papers and valuable equipment or supplies. Briefcases which only contain inexpensive supplies and standard forms may be locked and left in the work office overnight.

Any work papers carried to hotel rooms should be locked in briefcases and stored out of sight whenever the auditor leaves the room. Auditor briefcases kept in personal cars should be locked in the car trunk.

Chapter 10

Completing the Audit: Final Review and Writing the Audit Report

COMPLETING THE AUDIT

As the audit reaches its final stage, the payoff for all the audit time and effort is about to be reached. You, the audit manager, have decided to personally supervise the final stages of the review. Arriving several days before the date set for the windup meeting you can examine all of the audit work performed, pick up the loose ends, answer all questions raised, and determine what items to include in the final audit report. You must also finalize the details of the forthcoming audit meeting with management and decide who should attend the meeting and where and when it will be held. These considerations are all covered in this chapter.

Your audit will be completed successfully, and will produce the *best* results if you keep the following three important things in mind as you prepare your audit report.

1. *Answer all the questions posed by management* prior to the start of your audit.
2. *Emphasize only those deficiencies that are crucial* to operations.
3. *Ensure that local management is involved and agrees to the changes* that the auditors recommend.

FINAL REVIEW OF WORKING PAPERS

Your review of the audit working papers is designed to evaluate the quality and quantity of the audit work performed. Following is a checklist of questions for evaluating the audit work:

a. Have all the audit points been covered satisfactorily?
b. Did the staff auditors understand their assignments?
c. Do the work papers show that the proper records were examined for the specified time period?
d. Do work papers show who performed audit work and when it was done?
e. Do tick marks clearly indicate which figures were tied-in to permanent records?
f. Do audit notes show clear reference to documents in file, and can documents be easily located?
g. Was arithmetic checked, and do the totals tie-in to other independent summaries?
h. Did auditors write a separate note for each major discrepancy that they found during their examinations?
i. Are minor discrepancies properly described in the working papers?
j. Did the staff properly initial each point on the audit program?
k. If a notation, "DNA" appears on the audit program, is that decision appropriate?
l. Have any audit steps been omitted; do you agree with the decision?
m. Are all audit notes properly coded, legible and easily understood?
n. Are all copies of records, reports, schedules and correspondence necessary for the working papers?

In addition to evaluating the auditor's techniques, you must also ensure that the important activities were properly audited. Following is a list of questions to help you ensure a proper audit:

1. Do the work papers show the type of work that is done by the audited department or location? Do they indicate how well this work is done?
2. Do W/Ps contain suggestions for improving the way things are done, or is there convincing evidence that operations should remain as is?
3. Have possible alternatives been considered?
4. Are all reports generated in the activity, accurate and complete?
5. Can poor results be hidden?
6. Are bad results reported to higher headquarters?

These are some of the questions that should be answered in the audit working papers.

Opportunity For Training

The review of auditors' working papers offers an excellent opportunity for on-the-job training of both staff auditors and the audit supervisors. If your thinking does not coincide with that of your staff members, take the time to explain your thinking and point out why their actions or decisions should have been different.

You need to handle criticisms diplomatically. **CAUTION:** *Before criticizing a staff auditor, discuss the matter with the supervisor;* you may find that the auditor was merely following directions and that the audit supervisor might be responsible for the problem. Allow the supervisor to handle any corrective instructions and explanations.

Praise is another matter; it can be spread around to all deserving staff members, and a little praise goes a long way. Look for things that are commendable. Well thought-out recommendations, creative thinking, neat appearing work papers, clear and accurate page coding, constructive criticism of the audit program or instructions are all praiseworthy actions that deserve notice.

Picking Up Loose Ends

Any schedules that have not been completely tied-out should be pointed out to the audit supervisor so that the work can be completed with dispatch. A missing tick mark may signal the oversight. Sometimes a tie-in may be made to daily reports, but in the rush atmosphere of last minute work, the required tie-in of daily to month-end summaries may be overlooked.

There are times when an auditor is pulled away from an assignment just as it is being completed. After working on another problem, perhaps one that is more interesting, the auditor returns to the original work and forgets the final tie-in, but initials the audit point as being completed.

KEY POINT: *Audit working papers need to carefully reviewed.* Frequently there are important questions that are not answered in these papers. Look for the following customary oversights:

1. Records may be referred to, but they may not be clearly identified.
2. Copies of important documents that are necessary to support audit observations may not be in the file.
3. Notes may not spell out the location of old records in the files.
4. The names and addresses of important witnesses may not be included.
5. Photographs may not be properly labeled as to location, subject matter and time.

To summarize your approach to a review of audit working papers, keep in mind that it is necessary, to review each audit working paper:

- To understand its significance and relevancy.
- To insure that all data are legible and understandable.
- To determine that each note is worth keeping in the working paper files.
- To see that the sheets are properly coded and sorted so that they will be readily available when required.

Who Should Review Audit Working Papers

An audit staff may require that each audit be reviewed by the audit manager or the assistant before the final windup discussions and the writing of the audit report. In these cases, top audit management visits each location when the audit reaches its final phase, reviews the audit work accomplished, decides on the audit points to be discussed, conducts the windup review and determines the contents of the final report. The audit supervisor works with the manager in reviewing the work papers and assigning auditors to tie-up loose ends that were noted. The audit manager may sit on the sidelines and give the supervisor the experience of conducting the windup meeting.

Larger audit staffs rely on regional managers or supervisors to put the finishing touches on routine audits. They study all of the audit findings and discuss these matters and appropriate actions with top audit management before the windup meeting and finalization of the report. The Director of Internal Audits is thus made aware of the audit points that are to be discussed at each windup meeting and is in a position to decide whether to participate.

The discussions between site supervision and the home office also determine whether or not certain items are to be omitted from the report, and if so, how they are to be handled. If a supervisor feels that some of the audit findings are of major importance, the Director of Internal Audits may decide to sit in on the windup meeting in order to get firsthand knowledge of all the details involved in the audit findings and of management's responses to the auditor's comments.

When all the questions have been answered and loose ends have been tied together, the staff audit work is completed. All audit points are reviewed and the preliminary audit report is ready to be prepared.

One of the purposes of an audit report is to *inform concerned management* that the auditors have completed a study of a particular operation or department. Another purpose is to *apprise management of the condition* of the activity reviewed. A third objective is to *point out to management the deficiencies that were noted* by the internal auditors. And finally, the report should *indicate the corrective action taken or planned* by local management.

How to Achieve the Four Objectives of the Report

1. *Description of Audit Activity.*

   To accomplish the first objective, a simple standard opening paragraph will be sufficient. The paragraph need merely identify the activity audited and the time period of records that the audit review covered. The paragraph closes with a final sentence, such as: "As a result of this examination we offer the following comments: . . ."

   The first requirement of the audit report has been satisfied.

2. *General Appraisal of Activity Audited.*

   The second purpose can also be accomplished by a standard type paragraph. The wording will read somewhat as follows:

   Required work was conducted properly within the generally prescribed company policies and procedures. A number of minor deviations, noted during the audit, were corrected by local management. Other items of significance are listed in the following report. We believe that the following items require management's attention and action.

3. *Major Audit Comments.*

   In the third objective, we enter an area of potential controversy. What audit points should we list in the body of the report? Is the report designed to show management how efficiently and thoroughly the audit staff performed their review? If so, the report may list many deviations, oversights and discrepancies, some of which may have been corrected. If some changes are significant, the major points are listed *first* in the report. Most executives have little time for recreational reading and if the report starts out with minor problems, many will toss it aside after only reading the first minor point.

4. *Local Management's Actions.*

   The final purpose of the report is to present the reactions of local management to the audit findings and recommendations. This is where the responsible line supervisors explain, take exception to or defend the acts that are the subject of audit remarks. Audit reports may provide space for management's reply, immediately after the audit comment, or a separate letter containing the replies may be attached to the audit report when it is circulated or distributed.

Preliminary Audit Report

Assigned auditors are expected to make recommendations as to which audit points should be brought up for discussion at the windup meeting. However, the audit supervisor should exercise discretion in screening out insignificant or minor points. A verbal recitation of these items at the windup meeting, while excluding them from the formal report, can often satisfy all parties.

KEY POINT: *All listed audit exceptions should be followed by recommendations.* Each audit suggestion should be pertinent, practical and well thought out. The report should be written as though it were a verbal response to an executive who asked for observations and thoughts. If the staff has performed a professional internal audit, there will be sufficient facts to support the opinion and recommendations. All comments should be kept short and accurate.

The first draft of the preliminary audit report is written by the job supervisor and usually contains all audit comments that the staff considered important enough to write up as work sheets. This draft is discussed among the audit group, and minor and questionable items are deleted, and a revised second draft is written. This draft, after further revision by an area supervisor or the audit manager, is approved by audit management and becomes the preliminary draft used during the audit windup meeting. During those discussions, some wording in the report may be changed and some items dropped until a final draft is agreed upon. Management comments are added and the result is the formal audit report.

The Formal Audit Report

KEY POINT: *The final audit report should represent the best thinking of the audit staff. It should be written in a concise fashion, must be factual and may contain local management's replies to audit points.*

The audit report frequently points out problem areas that have a universal tone and are probably occurring at other locations with similar operations. Or the report may serve as a protective device for mentioning signs of serious problems, which the auditors were not able to track down.

When used as a protective device, the report lists discrepancies, even those of a minor nature, which may be indicative of a major problem. Sometimes, line management or operational executives might recognize a specific deficiency as a potential major problem, and they might be able to take corrective action across the board. **NOTE:** *Because of this possibility, auditors should be very careful when deciding to exclude items from the final report.* An audit manager must use intuition, as well as common sense, when deciding if something may be significant.

Examples of Audit Comments

The way a comment is worded is very important in conveying a message; choose your words carefully so that they are not ambiguous and so that they convey your true meaning. By choosing your language with care, you can appreciably reduce the size of your report.

Let's consider a few examples of how audit points may be handled in the final audit report.

> **EXAMPLE 1:** The audit working papers contained the following notation, properly headed and coded:
>
> Salespeople are not stamping all checks that they pick up from customers with the XYZ bank endorsement stamp, as required by company policy. Following work sheet contains stats of checks as they were received in branch in salespeople's envelopes. Note that they are not stamped!
>
> Talked to salespeople J. Doer (rt.33) and S. Jones (rt.42) on 6/2; both claimed they had never received an endorsement stamp nor heard of policy.
>
> On 6/3. spoke to office manager M. James who has been with company for three months. He never heard of policy.
>
> Branch manager, J. Adams, also was not aware of policy.

Based on this audit working paper, the following comment was written up for inclusion in the audit report.

> During the audit it was noted that salespeople were not immediately applying the XYZ bank endorsement stamp to checks collected from customers. Failure to restrictively endorse checks upon acceptance makes second party checks negotiable by finder in the event of loss. It also opens all checks to the possibility of a misapplication of funds. Stamping checks upon acceptance reduces the negotiability of the instrument since it can legally be deposited only to the account of the XYZ Corporation.
>
> Location management had not been aware of company policy in this regard, and had not supplied salespeople with endorsement stamps.
>
> It is suggested that all salespeople be supplied with the the proper XYZ bank endorsement stamp and that they be instructed to use them at the customer's location where checks are accepted. It is further suggested that the branch management team read and follow all prescribed procedures in the Sales Branch Procedures Manual.

The above example explains what the auditors found, the seriousness of the oversight and why it should be corrected. The audit comment contains corrective suggestions, and local management agrees to take the corrective action as suggested.

When the report is reviewed at headquarters level, top sales and financial management think that the same conditions may exist at other branch locations and decide to issue a reminder to all branches so that the procedure will be read and followed at all company locations.

EXAMPLE 2: In the following, the audit work paper reads as follows:

Reviewed customer remittances for the second week in the month of June. See schedule A. 2 (b). Remittances include mail-ins, driver collections, and collections made by salespeople. Collection summaries, samples attached, do not code checks to paying account as per prescribed procedure.

Discussed oversight with the office manager, B. Smart, who was not aware that procedure was not being followed. The branch manager, I. Care, stated that this is an office problem and should be handled with the office manager. Both discussions were held on June 27th.

The audit supervisor decided that the failure to follow procedures should be included in the audit report, and the audit point was worded to read as follows:

> Auditor's review of cash collections revealed that branch personnel were not following the prescribed policy of coding all checks received to the applicable customer's account. The policy is designed to enable ready identification of a second party check so that if it is returned by the bank we can readily identify the source from whom it was received.
>
> Such coding on first party checks, enables the office supervisors to note if cash receipts are not properly applied. If an invoice has been properly processed, and a customer's first party check pays for more than the open item it allegedly covers, the coding and verifying of the check's application, would make the discrepancy apparent.
>
> It is suggested that all branch employees who receive customer's checks, be reinstructed to code each collection to the customer from whom received. We further suggest that the office manager initiate a procedure of test-checking this coding to insure that it is being properly done and that obvious discrepancies are followed up.

The above describes the deficiency, a violation of stated policy, points out the reason for the directive, and recommends that the policy be followed. Management may either agree to conform or else point out that other controls are operating, which make the suggested procedure unnecessary.

If other controls are satisfactory, the audit department may determine that the procedure is unnecessary and recommend that the policy be rescinded. For instance, if all invoices are prepared by computer, and the system design makes it impossible for an invoice to be deleted, then the amount of any invoice could not be easily altered.

If the system also required that all payments be made by first party check, the potential problem posed by second party checks would be eliminated. If all checks were entered into the system and matched by the computer, and a list generated daily of all mismatches, the manual coding would not be necessary.

> **EXAMPLE 3:** In this case the audit working paper contained the following notation:
>
> Examined all time cards for production employees for month of April. Over ten percent of these cards did *not* contain the required supervisory approval. (See samples on following page.)
>
> Some line foremen and the office manager felt that such approvals were unnecessary. All supervisors know their workers and are aware of absentees. Each line supervisor has no more than ten employees and would know if any employee's time card had been punched in by someone else.

The audit point was written up for the final review meeting and appeared as follows:

> During the review it was noted that over ten percent of the plant production employee's time cards were not approved by the immediate supervisor. It is recommended that all clocked cards be approved by the line supervisor as evidence of the fact that the employee actually worked the reported periods and that the card was properly punched.

Management's reply to the audit comment, later verified by auditor, stated that the location used alternate means to verify work time.

> Any employee arriving late is required to sign in at the guard desk as they enter the building, and the daily late sheet is sent to the payroll department. We also require all supervisors to prepare a weekly summary of hours worked by everyone under their supervision. The summary is brought up to date daily.
>
> Supervisory initialing of time cards is used as a cross check by some supervisors while posting to weekly summaries.

Further audit check verified that all time cards for a one-month period had been correctly reported on the weekly summary. Management response at the windup meeting questioned the necessity of supervisory approval on individual time cards. The comment was excluded from the final report.

The above examples illustrate a few of the many problems that are involved in determining what should be included in an audit report and whether an item should be emphasized or downplayed. *The last example indicates an error by the audit group in not adequately discussing the matter with local management when the problem first arose.* A study at that time could have determined the facts and kept the discrepancy from being a point of discussion at the audit windup.

Some audit staffs list, as a protective device, every discrepancy noted. These reports are usually organized in order of audit point importance, with the minor items listed at the end of the report.

Other staffs comment only on significant deficiencies, and do not specifically mention each minor item. They use a standard closing sentence or paragraph that reads something like this:

> In addition to the discrepancies enumerated above, the auditors pointed out a number of minor problem areas which local management immediately corrected.

Another type of audit comment concerns the failure of an operation to take action on a previously reported deficiency. **NOTE:** *This type of problem can be delicate, but auditors cannot ignore such oversights.* In such a situation an audit report was worded to read as follows:

> As reported in the previous audit, the warehouse manager is not using the dual count system for counting finished goods inventories in the warehouse. This was pointed out in the last audit report, and the location manager agreed to make dual counts as spelled out in procedure manuals. As of the completion of the current audit, a dual count system has not been instituted.

The local manager replied to the audit comment and explained the failure to take the action that had previously been agreed upon.

> We had intended to install a dual count procedure, and we had instructed our warehouse manager to put it into effect. The manager was transferred before he could initiate the change and the new manager didn't know of the requirement. We will immediately comply with the procedure manual.

This case presents a problem for staff management, since local management failed to take agreed action.

The oversight might have been compounded if the location used a self-audit program, which asked local management to review the previous internal audit and comment on actions taken regarding open audit points. If the location had not reported the continued omission, it would indicate carelessness or delinquency.

But suppose that in the above case, management's reply had read:

> Immediately following the last audit our branch went on to the National Finished Goods Inventory System. Under this computerized program we receive a daily Stock Status Report which we use as a guide in counting our physical stock. We blind count all inventory, and compare counts to the computer report. *If they agree, the count is final.* If they don't agree, we send a different count team, with a supervisor, to recount. Very few recounts are required, and we did not have to recount a single item of the inventory the auditors reviewed.
>
> To double-count all product is a waste of labor, and we believe that our record of a negligible inventory variance supports our decision to save money.

Thorough work by the internal audit staff would have disclosed all this information before the audit report was written, and the item would have been handled in an entirely different manner.

Supporting Documentation for an Audit Comment

When you have decided upon the items to be included in the final audit report, you must make certain that each point is adequately documented. **KEY POINT:** *Every audit comment must be factual and supported by evidence in the work papers.* It is not enough to say that an employee told the auditor that the location was not following company policy of obtaining three bids for the disposal of company property. You must take the time to examine the equipment disposition files, locate and then make copies of all records relating to several transactions that support the assertion. In this way you develop a valid audit point.

Supporting documentation can be found in the organization's files and in the reports or statements that are regularly issued. Problems may occur when an attempt is made to prove an official report by examining supporting detail. Detail is tied-in to sub-accounts or summaries that combine to equal a reported figure. If the figures don't jibe, you need only keep copies of the detail that does *not* equal a specific summary. This reduces the quantity of evidence required to be placed in your work papers. *But you must be able to prove that you used the exact summaries that tied-in to the official reported figure.*

In many cases the supporting documentation may consist of copies of documents that have been received from customers, suppliers or from employees. You must be able to prove that these are actually copies of distributed company documents and must establish where and when they were originally prepared.

Organizing the Report's Contents

If a long audit report is necessary because of many violations of policy and numerous discrepancies, the formal report may require ten or more pages of audit comments and management replies. While the full report will be read by personnel immediately concerned, it is bound to contain many minor items that can alienate some readers.

KEY POINT: *When a lengthy report is necessary, it's a good idea to use a summary containing briefs of important points as the first page.* This makes the sheer volume of data less cumbersome and emphasizes the key points. Supporting data should be organized into titled subsections that tie into the summary page.

When writing long audit reports, the most significant items should appear at the beginning. A well-written report groups subject matter together by type of activity and order of importance. When applied to an audit report, this means that if there are ten comments concerning cash processing, they will all be contained in the cash section of the report. If two of the items are significant, and the others are of minor importance, ask yourself if they should all be grouped together. If this approach is used and there are six different major subjects, it would be necessary for a reader to study the full report in order to spot all important items.

Executives are reluctant to spend their limited time reading a lengthy audit report, particularly if most of the report elaborates on minor issues. They prefer to read a summary that contains only the major points. **KEY POINT:** *Recognizing this preference, many audit managers have adopted a procedure for transmitting audit reports with a covering letter containing a one-page or at most a two-page summary of the most important points covered in the audit report.* Some use a summary for all reports, even if the summary merely states that "The attached report does not contain any significant findings."

The Windup Meeting with Managers

Formal audit reports should be supplemented by meetings and discussions with all interested and concerned levels of management. Management comments and replies will affect the contents and the wording of the final audit report.

An audit report tells top management what activity was reviewed and what the auditors found. **KEY POINT:** However, *a report is not really complete until it contains operating management's explanations and comments.* Technical problems arise when trying to include management responses in the body of an audit report. The audit report must be written before the windup meeting is held, and at that point there is little indication of what management is going to say.

Copies of the audit report are prepared for each participant in the windup meeting. During the meeting, appropriate line managers state their response to each audit point, and these comments must be added to the body of the report in the appropriate place. **TIP:** *To facilitate this insertion, the original typing can provide spacing after each audit point so that management comments can be added.*

When the meeting is concluded, and all comments finalized and inserted, operating management signs the report to acknowledge that management replies, as recorded, are proper and correct.

Some audit staffs prepare and circulate audit reports that do not include audited management's comments, though they sometimes attach a letter from line management stating their thinking relative to the audit comments. Some of these reports include the auditor's version of the explanations they received from local supervisors.

Line management's comments usually represent the thinking of local management and that of upper levels of management that were present at the windup meeting. However, the reply may not represent the feeling of top level management of the activity. **NOTE:** *Higher level management may take exception to management comments contained in an audit report.* When this occurs, a copy of their letter of exception is attached to each copy of the audit report when it is distributed. This gives each reader the full thinking of all management concerned.

Who Should Participate in the Windup Meeting

The windup meeting is intended to accomplish several objectives:

- It should ensure that everything stated in the final report is accurate and completely understood by all parties.
- It apprises local management of audit findings, including those items which are not mentioned in the final report. And finally,
- It gives line management an opportunity to reply to audit comments.

KEY POINT: *The contents of the audit report plays a major part in deciding who should sit in on the report review.* If there are no important items, it would be a waste of time to have a number of executives visit a location for an audit windup meeting.

Audit management advises all potential participants. All managers who have an interest in the audited activity are notified of a forthcoming windup meeting, and they make their own decision as to attendance. *All executives should be advised in advance if the audit manager believes that controversial items will be discussed.* If there are important or controversial items, on the agenda, or if high level operating executives are to attend, then it is likely that the audit manager or the assistant audit manager will elect to be present.

If an important report centers on one particular operation, the manager in charge of that type of operation, as well as the local manager and supervisors should sit in on the meetings. Financial supervisors responsible for controls and reporting at the location should also participate.

A problem arises if an audit point concerns more than one department. In rare instances an executive of an operating department may be invited to attend an audit windup of a different department.

For example, a sales vice-president may be invited to attend a production plant audit windup; but an audit manager who gave such an invitation would have to have strong reasons for the action and would first clear it with the vice-president of production. It is more common to invite service department executives to windup meetings of operating departments when the policy or procedure directives of such service departments have created some reported problems.

KEY POINT: *Significant audit findings should be covered at the level of management that is in a position to take corrective action.*

If opposition to audit recommendations are anticipated at that level, the audit manager may elect to invite executives at a higher level who are in a better position to judge the merits of suggestions.

Important audit findings are discussed in advance with the audit manager, who determines the staff or operating executives to be invited. The level of audit management present at the meeting should match the level of operating management invited to attend. When financial management is concerned with audit findings, the organizational level of their participants should match the rank of operating and auditing management attending.

In all events, local operational and office managers are usually expected to attend the audit windup meeting. The audit supervisor may elect to invite specific line supervisors or accounting personnel for some sections of the discussions. After certain items have been discussed, some of the meeting participants may be excused to return to their normal duties. When people are brought in *to participate in a certain part of the discussion,* they are not usually given a complete copy of the audit report, but they are merely read the specific audit point that concerns them.

When and Where to Hold the Meeting

Audit windup meetings should be scheduled for a convenient time and place that conserves audit resources. If the meeting concerns an outlying company location, the ideal meeting place is at the location and the ideal time is the day the audit is completed. If this can be arranged, the audit team is still at the location and can follow-up on any questions raised at the meeting.

If the audited activity is at the office where the audit staff is based, the meeting can be scheduled to fit the desire of operating management, *but should be held close to the completion date so that the audit findings are still applicable.*

In extenuating circumstances an audit review may be held away from the audited office. These "away" meetings can be burdensome, since all working papers must be carted to the meeting place to be at hand if needed, and local records are not available for reference. There is also the problem of pulling staff auditors or supervisors away from current assignments to attend the meeting. **TIP:** *Windup meetings at places away from the audited location should be avoided when possible.*

Illness or emergency may make it necessary for the audit team to leave a location before the windup meeting can be held. In such cases, the meeting is scheduled for an opportune time, preferably one that is scheduled soon after the completion of the audit. Usually the selected meeting site is the audited office.

The location of a windup meeting can be set for any place that is mutually agreeable, preferably a location that is convenient for the majority of participants so as to reduce travel time and costs. It may be held at any mutually agreeable time, but should be held as soon after completion of the audit as possible.

Format for the Windup Meeting

The atmosphere of an audit windup meeting should be relaxed, yet it should be conducted in a formal manner. Every full-time participant is given a copy of the audit report to read and follow along as the audit supervisor reads every statement aloud. This sets the pace for reading and comprehending the meaning of each audit point. It encourages participants to ask questions about the meaning or accuracy of any item, and it provides an opportunity for the auditor to elaborate on any comment that requires further explanation. *It is also the time and place to establish the accuracy of any contested audit statement by producing and displaying the supporting audit documentation.*

The reading of each item in the report is intended to establish the exact meaning of every audit point, and the ensuing discussion clears up any misunderstanding or misinterpretation by displaying documented examples of cited discrepancies.

There may be several interrelated audit points that are separately covered by audit comments. When this occurs, the meeting moderator points out that there are several related items, and suggests that all of them be read first, and then each one will be discussed separately.

Management's reply may also cover more than a single audit point, and in such cases the reply would so state.

Selecting the Audit Points

Business organizations hold line management responsible for controlling all activities in their area of operations. This means that top management has told all lower levels of management that they must know what is happening in their operations and that they must correct any known problems or deficiencies. This attitude encourages auditors to emphasize their recommendations aimed at improving the effectiveness of monitoring and control procedures.

Sometimes auditors counsel with management in setting up operational controls, but in any case, their audits are designed to note and inform management of any weaknesses. The final audit report presents management with the findings of these periodic reviews.

KEY POINT: *An audit staff must be completely objective and impartial and not become too friendly with employees that they will audit.* The audit report should be accurate and factual and be written in a businesslike manner. But in any writings, the subjectivity of the author is interjected through either the selection of subject matter or the choice of language and the way that it is presented. Every internal audit report reflects the philosophic approach of the audit manager.

Some short-sighted audit managers do not recognize any potential value in having the audit staff attempt to improve line operations by actively participating and cooperating with local line management. These managers may not permit their supervisors or staff people to discuss, with operating management, the deficiencies disclosed during the audit. In such cases, operating management first becomes aware of audit findings during the windup meeting. This approach can be very embarrassing to line management and may result in creating a strong antagonism toward the internal auditing function.

The adversary approach is usually designed to make the top executives feel that the internal audit staff is providing a vital service. This is often at the expense of line management.

This adversary technique might result in increasing the prestige of the audit manager, at the upper executive level, but it seriously hampers the efforts of the working staff at the operational level. They would be disliked as spies and outsiders.

Professional internal audit managers recognize that their first obligation is to the welfare of their company, even at the expense of personal prestige. Their audit groups work as cooperative arms of management, and they assist supervisors at all levels. This means that the auditors work to improve an operation by informing line management of the oversights or deficiencies that may be hurting the operation or causing losses to the company. **NOTE:** *Auditors recognize that the sooner these items are brought to management's attention and corrected, the better off the company will be.*

Under a cooperative philosophy, noted oversights are immediately brought to supervisory attention. Even though an audit comment may appear in the final report, it will state that the deficiency has been corrected. More enlightened audit managers may even delete references to some of the minor items from the formal report. Instead of specifically mentioning each item, the formal report may state the following:

> "Other discrepancies noted during the audit review were satisfactorily corrected by local management."

When major deficiencies are noted that show incompetence or an inability to manage, these facts must be brought out into the open and appropriate management be persuaded to take corrective action.

Audit reports must also stress areas that were mentioned previously but where no improvements have been made since the last audit or where conditions are worsening. However, the audit group should work cooperatively with well-intentioned managers who, because of the pressures of work loads, have ignored or neglected some instructions they did not consider important. Perhaps the items are really not important, or maybe management did not understand the full import of the procedure or work which they had been overlooking.

The auditors must evaluate all factors before deciding on the best approach. Obviously, if an oversight is in an unimportant area where the risk factor is very low, there would be no advantage in stressing the delinquency. If a location has been neglecting to perform a specific procedure, the auditor must examine the consequences of such oversight. It may be that the procedure itself is unnecessary or requires modification. Perhaps the procedure was installed many years before, when the operation was different. If the auditor finds that such is the case, the procedure should be referred to the appropriate manager for revision or elimination.

KEY POINT: *If the neglected procedure covers an important internal control, the auditor must examine the consequences of the oversight and should carefully study all pertinent information to see if a loss to the company has occurred.* The auditor must also determine if the oversight was deliberate or unintentional, and whether supervisors understand the full import and meaning of the neglected control.

After completing the analysis, the audit group determines what items to include in the audit report, and how to word them. The language used in the report will greatly influence any decision as to appropriate action. Audit reports may result in the following:

- Location management being reprimanded and instructed to carefully follow the procedure in the future.
- Some employees being demoted, transferred or terminated as a result of the reported findings.
- The discovery and reporting of an employee defalcation.

Whatever the final result of the audit, appropriate corrective action must be taken, and the audit report serves as the stimulus.

After all audit points have been screened and the final ones chosen, the language is finalized and the report is organized and made ready for discussion at the windup meeting.

Management Replies to Audit Points

When all participants are completely aware of the meaning and intent of an audit point, line management is given an opportunity to respond. They may merely agree with the point and accept the audit recommendation. Or they may take exception to a point and disagree with or refute its accuracy. **NOTE:** *At that time the audit representative shows proof to support the statement.*

After management voices its collective thoughts, they agree on a response to be inserted in the audit report. This response is written and read to the group, and the response is amended until complete agreement is reached. During these discussions the auditors may present additional information to clarify management's thinking. When an appropriate response is agreed upon, the meeting moves on to the next audit point.

When all audit comments have been discussed and all management replies agreed upon, the preliminary copy of the report is amended to include all language changes in the auditor's comments and all of management's replies. The final audit report is signed by the ranking management member and auditor, and it becomes the official audit report. The master copy of the report can now be duplicated and distributed.

When a word processor is used for the preparation of audit reports, the procedure for duplicating copies is slightly different. After management's replies have been agreed upon, they are entered into the appropriate spaces in the word processor format and a copy is printed. After review by both audit and line management, the copy is approved and sufficient copies are printed to satisfy distribution needs. Both the designated audit and line managers sign all copies, which are then available for distribution.

If higher level operating management disagrees with management's comments printed on the report, they have the prerogative of changing the reply. Since the management reply section of the audit report is truly just that, the report should be changed before distribution is made. If copies have already been distributed, all recipients should be sent amended pages with a covering letter of explanation.

Examples of Audit Reports

Audit reports are frequently bound in an identifying fashion, such as a blue-back report in which a sheet of heavy blue paper is used as a backing for the report.

The blue backing stands out and makes such a report immediately noticeable.

Standard opening paragraphs are common with a few blank spaces filled in to identify activity audited and dates of audit and records reviewed. An example of a standard opening paragraph follows:

> XYZ CORPORATION
> INTERNAL AUDITING DEPARTMENT
>
> Mssrs: P. R. Sedent
> C. M. Troller
>
> The Internal Auditing Department has completed a review of ____________ located at ________________________. Our review, completed on ____________________, covered an examination of selected records and reports for the period from ______________ to ______________. Significant items are contained in the following report; items of lesser importance were discussed and corrected locally.

After the opening paragraph, the body of the report follows in a normal letter sequence. Following is an example of a *summary approach* that is sometimes used:

> For your convenience we have extracted the major items that require your immediate attention. The details of the findings and local management's responses are included in the attached report.
>
> A. Cash
> 1. Checks received in the mail are accumulated until the Accounts Receivable clerk finds time to review and process them. Many checks are not deposited until several weeks after receipt. This delay in processing exposes the checks to potential loss or misappropriation. It also delays the posting to individual accounts, distorts the A/R and Cash month-ending balances, and costs XYZ the lost-interest value of the funds lying idle. We recommend that all incoming checks be immediately deposited, and that only the remittance advice be given to the A/R clerk.
>
> Management responded as follows: We would have to add at least one employee to conform to auditor's suggestion. The A/R clerk must frequently view the check, since it alone may contain the information necessary to apply the collection to the proper account.
>
> D. Purchasing
> 1. The branch was not using the national form that combines the Requisition, Purchase Order and Receiving Report. The same employee ordered all requirements, received all deliveries and approved all bills for payment. There is no internal control over the purchasing of supplies for this location. We recommend that the national form be used, and that the requisitioner sign the appropriate form to show the need, that the orderer sign to indicate that an order has been placed, and that the items

be received in the warehouse and the receiving report be signed by the employee who actually counted and examined the product brought into the premises.

Management responded as follows: We order only office supplies and don't need an involved form and procedures to handle these small purchases. The office manager calls the supplier who brings our requirements to the office where it is checked. The supplier drops off a bill and we approve it and send it to Accounts Payable for payment.

The auditing department believes that the above mentioned items should be immediately corrected and audit recommendations followed. The final full audit report is attached for your information.

Following is an example of a *portion of an audit report* that was written at the completion of a review of a sales branch operation. After the normal salutation and standard opening paragraph, the *adversary* report reads as follows:

The following comments are offered for management's consideration. All these points have been discussed with local management and their comments have been inserted after the appropriate suggestion.

A. Clerical Procedures

1. Branch files were not kept up to company standards. Even the accounting manual is not up-to-date. Though all revisions and additions were placed in the binder, they had not been properly filed. Auditors experienced some difficulty in locating specific documents and correspondence. Some of these papers were not in their proper place in the files, and audit time was wasted in tracking them down.

   We recommend that branch files immediately be brought up to date and that personnel be assigned to keep files current.
2. The office manager spends much of his time performing office clerical work when office clerks are absent or away from their desks. Though the auditors did not find any irregularities, such activities could lead to a breakdown in internal controls.

   We recommend that the office manager spend his time managing the office and that office clerks perform the clerical work.
3. Office personnel did not have regularly scheduled lunch periods or coffee break times. They appear to take breaks whenever they wish and go to lunch anytime they choose. Such coming and going disrupts the work in an office.

   We recommend that all employees adhere to established lunch periods and scheduled coffee break times.

   Management comments follow:

   Our reply applies to the first three audit observations. As a result of our recent cost-control program, the branch was requested to cut operating costs and we accordingly cut our office staff by two employees. This reduction has made it difficult to keep up with all the clerical work. We have been forced to shift people around to attend to necessary duties since we must cover the telephone order desk, the warehouse sales desk and the cashier's desk at all operating hours. We accomplish this by staggering breaks and lunch periods. It may appear disorderly to auditors, but all employee comings and goings are known and authorized.

Filing of miscellaneous materials is falling behind. We only get to it when one of our employees has free time. We must stay abreast of important daily operations, and we do tend to put aside the lesser important tasks. If management believes it to be of prime importance that all of our files be kept current, we would have to add a file clerk to our staff. We believe that the branch office is being run properly and economically with the present staff, and we feel that the items commented on by the auditors do not justify the addition of another clerical employee.

The above is an example of a poorly written audit report. The location had cooperated in a companywide effort to reduce operating costs, and because of this they were criticized for some oversights. *The report would have better served the audit cause by simply saying:*

Auditors reviewed the office operation and found no important discrepancies. There was some tardiness in filing relatively unimportant documents.

While we did not observe any breakdowns in internal controls, the recent reduction in clerical staff, resulting from the companywide cost-control program, presents the possibility that some weaknesses may develop over time. To minimize this possibility, auditors suggest that an additional clerk be added to the office force.

Such an audit report would not have antagonized local management or employees, and it would still have conveyed the auditor's message. Local management would have reacted to this type of approach in a much more conciliatory manner.

Following is an example of an *adversary* report written by an audit staff whose manager will not let staff people discuss audit findings with local management until the final windup meeting. At that time, all audit findings are thrown at local management, catching them by surprise without time to research or consider actions or answers.

This approach inundates management with the many problems that the auditors encountered during the review and is *really intended to show top management the importance of the audit activity,* and how poorly line management performs its job. It can result in an audit report that is inaccurate or one that shows incomplete audit research.

The body of this audit report contained the following comments:

> We have completed an audit review of the Insurance Department and offer the following comments for management's consideration. We noted many instances of errors and oversights by department management and clerical employees. Some of these are listed as examples:
>
> 1. The reserve set up for fire insurance for the month of July was underestimated by $1,723.
> 2. The charge-off for auto accident costs not covered by insurance was understated by $741 for the month of May.
> 3. The July monthly insurance premium paid to the AQE Insurance Co. was $260 in excess of what it should have been. The department had failed to note the closing of a company location.
> 4. Two new company locations were not covered by insurance from the day that they became operational. The locations were opened during the third week of November, but were not listed as operating locations until December 1st.
>
> Auditors recommend the above items be corrected and that the department adopt a system of cross checking clerical work.
>
> The following internal control problems were also brought to department management's attention:
>
> A. Payments for insurance claims were being sent directly to the Insurance Department instead of to the cashier. Auditors recommend that all insurance companies be instructed to send their payments for insurance claims directly to the company cashier.
>
> B. Department procedure write-ups do not include instructions for handling adjusted claims. Auditors recommend that a proper procedure for adjusting filed insurance claims be adopted and made a part of the insurance procedure manual.
>
> The above points were discussed with department management and their replies to the audit findings were as follows:
>
> "I shall have to look into the matters noted by the auditors, since I was not apprised of any of the audit points prior to the meeting. I do know that the comment concerning claims is misleading. We send copies of every claim we make to the accounting department. Every month they send us a list of open claims, which we follow-up. Should a claim check be lost, the accounting department would let us know. We have never lost a check or ever canceled a claim in the three years that I've been here.
>
> As far as item B is concerned, we have never issued instructions for handling adjustments to claims because we research and make certain that a claim is legitimate, proper and accurate before we file it. We

have never had to adjust a claim, and therefore didn't even think of issuing instructions to cover such eventuality. We could write books of instructions to cover hundreds of actions that will never occur in our operation."

The above demonstrates an adversary condition, where the audit staff is used to further the audit manager's interest instead of being used as an aide to management. **KEY POINT:** *Any audit points that are worth mentioning in an audit report should be discussed, starting with the lowest level of supervision, at the earliest opportunity.* If internal auditors work as members of the management team, there should be no surprises at the formal review. Every item will have been brought to the attention of the operation's responsible supervisor, and the auditors will have a good idea of how management will respond.

Passing Audit Comments on to Concerned Parties

Some audit observations at a particular activity may directly, or indirectly, affect other departments or operations within the company. These duly recorded audit points are included in an audit report, and local management replies become a matter of record. When the report is studied by audit management, a wider application of the observation is noted, and a decision made as to further action. If the decision is to call the matter to the attention of other concerned departments, the audit manager writes a letter containing excerpts of the report.

> **EXAMPLE:** Let's assume that during the audit of a sales branch the auditors noted that deliverypeople were being held personally responsible for all products loaded onto their trucks and for all collections that they had been assigned to make. The final audit report reads as follows:
>
> The location is not following the customary company practice in one aspect of delivery procedure. At this branch all deliverypeople are held personally responsible for their product and collections. If they turn up short on any delivery, they are charged for the product. If funds turned in do not equal amounts that should have been collected, drivers are charged for the shortage.
>
> Deliverypeople are offered the opportunity to check all products being loaded into their trucks, but few elect to do so. The speed with which the product is moved into the trucks makes it almost impossible to check the load. Under this system the driver must pay for any mistakes the loaders make and for any product that may be stolen off the trucks during delivery. Drivers also are charged with the dollar variance of mistakes that may occur while making collections from accounts.
>
> This system is not only inequitable, but it encourages drivers to

> make up known shortages or thefts from vehicle by short delivering unsuspecting customers. Auditors suggest that the branch follow normal company procedures.
>
> Local management responded to these comments as follows:
>
> We initiated this procedure because of experiencing substantial delivery and cash collection shortages. Since introducing this system, our losses have been significantly reduced. We are being fair to our employees since they are allowed to check their loads as they are placed on their trucks. If loaders move too fast, the driver has the right to tell the loader to slow down so that the product can be checked. This procedure will be altered to permit drivers to count their loads on the staging dock before it is moved into their trucks. We would like to continue our present system of holding all drivers responsible.

After reviewing the report, the audit manager sent an excerpt of the above information with a covering letter to the Comptroller, the Director of Human Resources (Personnel Department), and the head of the Legal Department. The covering letter stated:

> Attached is an excerpt from a sales branch audit report. We are calling this matter to your attention for your information and for whatever action you deem appropriate. If there is no objection to this new procedure, it may possibly be adopted companywide.

Replies received by the audit manager will decide future action in this matter. If there is no objection from any department, the audit manager will so advise the Vice-Presidents of the Sales and the Distribution Departments. If they concur, the procedure may be adopted throughout the company. The Comptroller, working with the Audit Department, would then issue policy and procedure directives that would allow the program to be expanded under controlled conditions.

If any concerned department voiced serious objections to the practice, the objections would be passed on to all parties concerned. If there was disagreement among the executives, the matter would be brought to the attention of the Executive Vice-President or the Corporate President for final decision.

All audit reports are studied by audit administration to note items that might have universal application throughout the company.

KEY POINT: *If an audit recommendation might benefit another location or two, it will be referred to those locations for consideration. The audit department does not make decisions in such matters; it merely acts as a clearing house for distributing important information.* In this way the audit department serves as a useful communication channel between all levels of management and all operations within a company.

If an audit report contains a recommendation that audit management thinks has far-reaching application, the idea is conveyed to other executives in a position to judge and act on the suggestion. As an illustration, let's consider the handling of the following audit observation:

> Auditors noted that the production plant has only two time clocks for employees to use as they punch in and out, causing a long lineup before starting time and at quitting time. When clock punching is permitted, it can take up to twenty minutes for an employee to complete the procedure.
>
> In many cases employees arrive in ample time to start work but when the clock is made available to employees, they are unable to punch in before the expiration of the seven minute grace period allowed before workers are considered to be late. Line foremen initial these cards so that workers are not penalized for punching in late.
>
> At check out time, many employees cannot reach the clock until eight to twenty minutes after quitting time. Employees are paid overtime in quarter-hour intervals for clocking out over seven minutes after shift change. To reduce overtime payments, several line supervisors permit their people to leave the production line ten minutes early so that they will be in the front of the line and not earn overtime. This, in effect, shuts down the line ten minutes early and reduces the line efficiency.
>
> Inconvenience to employees, as well as costs to the company, can be reduced by adding several additional time clocks at strategic points in the plant. At most the addition of four time clocks near the locker rooms would relieve the congestion and pay for the cost of the clocks in a short time.

Local plant management accepted the audit suggestion, and the audit manager recognized that the recommendation would also apply to other company locations. An excerpt was prepared and included in a letter written to the executives in charge of production and distribution and to all other large departments that used time clocks to record working hours. The covering letter simply read, "An audit observation may have application to some of your operations. Attached is an excerpt containing the observation and the audit recommendation. This information is forwarded to you for your consideration and action where you deem appropriate."

In addition to the above distribution, the excerpt is placed in the audit follow-up file for specific locations that might have similar problems. This area will be examined during forthcoming routine internal audits at those locations.

Circulating the Report

After the windup meeting is completed, and management comments are agreed upon and included in the final report, the responsible audit and management representatives sign the report and it becomes official. Copies of the report are given to the audited activity, to the outside auditors, retained in the internal auditing department and all or portions of the report are distributed to all authorized and concerned executives. Most internal audit reports are sent to the chief financial officer and those containing significant findings may be routed to top operating and staff executives.

Summaries of audit findings are prepared at regular intervals by audit management and circulated to the corporate president, executive vice-president, chief financial officer and, depending on the contents of the summary, to other executives who are interested and concerned.

Comments, instructions or directives forthcoming as a result of the audit work are received by audit administration and appropriately acted upon. **NOTE:** *Comments from department executives are reviewed and circulated within the auditing department and frequently form the basis for amending audit working programs or schedules.*

Supervisor's Report to Audit Manager

At the completion of each audit, the supervising auditor may be expected to submit a report to the audit manager. The letter covers personal comments on the caliber of audit work performed, briefly evaluates the audit staff members who participated in the review and mentions general observations that were not included in the report.

This report also contains some *other important items that need to be considered after every audit.* Any comments or suggestions relating to the audit program and associated instructions must be spelled out in detail. Required revisions are identified, and reasons for suggested changes are explained. Finally, the audit supervisor is expected to suggest a proper time interval before the next audit. *If the review had been rushed, the next audit might be scheduled in the near future.*

If the operation had been unusually good, a longer interval might be suggested. The final decision rests with the audit manager, but a good deal of weight is given to the audit supervisor's suggestions.

Follow-Up on Management's Responses

If the audit staff has done a professional job, the most common response to an audit point will be, "We agree with the audit suggestion and will put it into effect immediately." The auditor's responsibility now becomes vague because the answer presents four distinct possibilities:

1. The suggested action is taken and solves the problem.
2. The suggested action is taken, but the action doesn't solve the problem.

3. Management takes action, but had misunderstood the audit suggestion.
4. Management fails to take the action they agreed upon.

If the first possibility occurs, the auditing department has no further interest. If number 2 or number 3 occurs, the audit department believes that the problem has been corrected and may not learn of the failure until the next audit visit. If local management is alert and notices that the problem has not been resolved, auditing may be called back to make a further study.

Auditing departments are plagued by the fourth possibility. If management fails to take the action they agreed to take, the audit manager is placed in a difficult position. When the failure is disclosed, usually at the next audit, the auditing department must report the oversight and its consequences. If it is a significant failure, the audit report will emphasize that management reneged on their commitment after the last audit, and the report will point out the consequences of the failure. If it is a minor matter, the auditors will merely repeat the item of the last report and state that action was agreed upon in the previous report but that no action was taken.

Realizing that the audit department is not equipped to monitor all operations on a continuing basis, the audit manager must seek help in discharging a responsibility for insuring that corrective action is taken on audit findings. This help is usually found in the offices of controllers responsible for controlling and reporting the operating results of the various activities.

The XYZ Corporation's Internal Auditing Staff is specifically required to insure that appropriate corrective action is taken on all audit recommendations. The audit manager elects to discharge this obligation through a system of reports that are processed through responsible control personnel.

In an attempt to solicit help from concerned executives, the audit manager of the XYZ Corporation distributed the following letter to all financial executives and personnel responsible for controlling the various corporate activities.

Subject: AUDIT REPORTS

Each of you has received the corporate policy statement on internal auditing distributed by the Chairman of the Board. An important paragraph dealt with the responsibility of management at the audited location, to take corrective action on all audit recommendations. In order to monitor this requirement, we have adopted a policy that requires a follow-up report from each audited location.

The report must document the action taken, or planned, for each specific recommendation in the audit report. This report is due in this office within sixty days of the audit review. This policy also applies to the external auditor's memos on accounting procedures and internal controls.

> It is extremely important that prompt corrective action be immediately initiated, and that we all follow-up to insure that agreed action is taken. Your continued cooperation in this area is required and appreciated.

The above approach attempts to put the responsibility for monitoring corrective action where it rightfully belongs.

Part 3

Internal Auditing Programs

INTRODUCTION TO PART III

All of the chapters in this section of the manual contain working programs designed to apply to specific areas of corporate activities. Our fictional XYZ Corporation's Internal Audit Program is divided into three sections which immediately follow the presentation of introductory background material.

The first contains the *Audit Instructions* that explain audit procedures and policies. XYZ Corporation uses an audit manual that has a large section of audit instructions. These audit instructions must be carefully read and understood before an audit review is started; but auditors who have already worked with the program will only read these instructions when and as required. In the following sample programs, the portions of instructions that deal with chapter subjects have been extracted and presented separately.

Next is the *Audit Program,* a checklist of audit steps normally required to perform a comprehensive review of itemized transactions. Like a pilot's preflight checklist, it directs attention to specific high risk areas that relate to the activity.

The third section is the *Internal Control Questionnaire* which asks the auditor specific questions relating to operating internal controls. Auditors answer the questions based on personal observations, and then they draw a conclusion as to the adequacy of the controls. Auditor evaluation of internal controls is an essential part of the review.

The last sections of these chapters list some critical points that are based on actual audit experiences. Some may seem remote, but they all are commonplace in the average work environment.

The following information is normally provided in the Instruction section of each program:

1. The audit program is divided into three parts: the introduction, the audit steps or procedures and the internal control questionnaire.

A. In the introduction, the audit objectives are spelled out, and a brief description of a normal operation is provided. It is rare that an operation will not change, so you must alter your approach to meet any unique condition encountered.
B. Audit procedures are listed in concise language, and are intended as a checklist, rather than as the detailed instructions you need to perform the audit work. More detailed information is contained in the Instruction section.
C. Each audit point is followed by two spaces for you to fill in the requested information. The first space is to be noted with the period covered by your review. This column is headed *"Per. Cov."* The second column is headed *"Audit By,"* and provides space for the initials of the auditor who performed the work. Only place your initials after you have completed the work required for a specific audit point. If several staff auditors work on a particular item, then all will place their initials in the *"Audit By"* column.
D. At the end of the program, space has been provided for the signature of the audit supervisor who reviewed audit work papers and determined that all work was done properly. The supervisor will note the date that the review was completed.
E. The internal control questionnaire is self-explanatory. Check off the applicable *Yes* or *No* block in response to the question.

    Any reference to work papers should identify the supporting documentation, and any qualification to an answer must be explained in the "Remarks" column. Space is provided at the end of the form for the names of the auditors who answered the questions and for the signature of the supervisor who reviewed the answers.

2. During your reviews, you will use several different audit programs that are designed to apply to specialized types of activities. These programs appear in other sections of your audit manual. Follow the directions given in a specific audit program, which will direct you to the applicable sections in the manual. When using these specialized programs, limit your study to audit points that apply to the operation. **KEY POINT:** *Note DNA opposite each point that Does Not Apply.*

    EXAMPLE:

    A. Your program may call for an examination of vouchers issued to pay for items purchased for the department and to reimburse for expense reports. The detailed audit program for such a review appears in your audit manual under the heading, Auditing Payables.
    B. The audit program may call for verification of payroll records as they relate to employees in the department being audited. If that payroll has not been recently audited, use your program titled, Auditing Payroll.

3. If any activity has been *recently audited* by our staff or our outside auditors, note the date of such review and the staff that conducted it, and you may omit that portion of your audit.
4. In any audit review, you will find it necessary to prepare for the assignment by performing the following:
   A. Read the applicable Policy and Procedure Manuals and any operational manuals used in the department.
   B. Review previous audit working papers, and any external and internal audit reports. Bring the CAF up to date as the audit progresses.
   C. Review the general and the follow-up audit files. Resolve any open items.
   D. Interview department managers to determine their goals and operating philosophies.

Chapter 11

Internal Auditing of Cash Transactions

Cash represents the life blood of any organization. It is the asset that has a great potential for loss and therefore demands much audit time. This chapter covers the receiving, handling and recording of cash. Pay outs of petty cash type transactions are also covered, but major cash disbursements are detailed in other chapters.

As an internal auditor, you are concerned with the proper handling of all facets of cash operations. Some auditors establish absolute requirements that must be followed under any conditions. But, as a practical matter, cash handling, and all other functional operations, must meet the unique needs of an entity even if some control features are not met. Naturally you must review any variation from established rules to insure that adequate control is in force, but *bear in mind that no rule is absolute for all circumstances.* We will discuss the following:

- Recording and handling of cash receipts,
- Physical safeguarding of the asset,
- Processing of paper work,
- Preparation of bank deposits and the comparison to bank reported receipts,
- Transporting funds to banks,
- Reconciliation of bank accounts, and the
- Tie in to appropriate ledgers.

We will also review petty cash and the expenditures made out of the fund. Though frowned upon, petty cash funds are often reimbursed through cash receipts and this presents problems to the internal auditor. Audit time will also be required to examine receipts from vending machines, miscellaneous sales, and other unusual situations where cash can be diverted if not closely controlled. Stamp funds, change funds and the receipts from sales of scrap, salvage or idle equipment all present unique problems for audit examination.

Conducting a surprise count of cash register contents offers another type of audit challenge. There are many different types of registers that utilize a variety of computer applications, and internal auditors must vary their approach to gain the full audit benefit from these computerized registers. Credit card tickets may be considered as cash or as receivables, but they must be taken into account during an audit of a cashier's register. In this chapter we will consider these tickets to be the equivalent of cash.

Background Information

The sample audit program that follows this introduction is designed to apply to cash activities found in normal operations. The amount of audit time spent on an item depends upon the effectiveness of internal controls and the extent of the potential risk. Some organizations centralize the control of all cash transactions within the treasury department; others give line managers the responsibility for cash receipts but centralize their control over banking.

KEY POINT: *Cashiers may report elsewhere but the Treasurer assumes full responsibility for all cash that reaches the depository.* This is the organizational set up used by the mythical XYZ Corporation in the sample program.

The approach to an audit of cash transactions is determined by the organization and assignment of responsibilities. Many companies use a program of direct depositing, under which customers send remittances direct to a lockbox at the payee's bank. The bank extracts and deposits the payments and forwards the envelope with all transmittal data to the addressee. This procedure eliminates some handling of cash by an organization's personnel and reduces the exposure risk and the volume of paperwork. When this procedure is fully operational, handling of cash by company employees is limited to petty cash funds, local cash sales and receipts from sales of miscellaneous items. The sample XYZ audit program assumes that regular customers send their payments directly to the lockbox at the bank.

The XYZ Corporation also receives cash collected by sales representatives and deliverypeople. These employees prepare their own deposits and either place them in a drop safe or turn them in to a cashier. They prepare collection reports itemizing the source of their collections, but they seal their cash deposit envelopes, which are only to be opened at the bank by authorized bank personnel. If the bank spots any errors in listings or moneys, they are immediately called to the attention of the office manager.

XYZ Corporation's cashier operates in a special room with a safeguarded window. The cashier, who reports to the office manager, receives all mail-in cash items directly from the mail department or from individual employees who received them in personal envelopes. Other cashier duties include cashing employee checks, handling cash for travel advances and the main office petty cash transactions.

There are several cash funds located in various departments of the office and a cafeteria and a store where company products are sold. Each of these operations prepares its own bank deposit which is sealed in an envelope and turned in to the cashier. The cashier writes up a receipt for the stated amount of the envelope and includes these separate deposit envelopes in the main deposit bag which is picked up by an armored car service. The service also picks up any deposits which have been placed in the drop safe located in the Distribution and Sales section of the building.

A separate receipt is given for each item received by the cashier. Receipts are a three part carbonless form, held in a metal locked box. Originals are given to individuals turning items in to the cashier. Second copies are retained by the cashier and attached to supporting documents. The audit copy remains in the locked box. Alterations are not permitted, if the cashier spoils any receipt both exterior copies of that form are removed, stamped "VOID," and placed in a voided receipt file. The total of all cashier's receipts issued during a period should agree with the amount of the deposit for that period.

XYZ's Treasurer is the official contact with all banks. All bank statements of the company are received and reconciled by employees of the Treasurer's department.

With the above as background material, let's look at the sample Internal Audit Program for a review of Cash Receipts and Cash Funds.

INTERNAL AUDIT INSTRUCTIONS, CASH RECEIPTS AND CASH FUNDS

INTERNAL AUDIT PROGRAM—INSTRUCTIONS

Form # CI 001 XYZ CORPORATION

AUDIT INSTRUCTIONS FOR CASH RECEIPTS AND CASH FUNDS

A. Audit Caution:

Take the time to become familiar with these instructions, the Cash Internal Audit Program, Form # CP 001, and the Cash Internal Control Questionnaire before you start your assignment. Refer to information contained in the Introduction to the Program's section. All audit instructions should be understood before you officially enter the premises. You should know exactly what must be done, and be able to do it without delay. **REMEMBER:** *Cash audits require immediate attention and prompt action so as not to seriously hamper normal operations.*

If an audit of Accounts Receivable is scheduled to coincide with your cash audit, cooperate fully with the in-charge A/R auditor. Make your audit listing of cash receipts available upon request.

This portion of the audit program deals with cash receipts. You are expected to review disbursements made out of cash funds; however, the detailed instructions relating to accounts payable and the major disbursement activities are covered in other programs.

B. *Audit Objectives* are to determine the following:
1. That all cash items are deposited intact. All reported receipts are deposited, accurately recorded, and promptly transferred to disbursement accounts.
2. That handling by bank is appropriate and proper.
3. That cash is adequately safeguarded and accounted for.
4. Whether any funds have been misappropriated or manipulated since the last audit of these activities.
5. If improperly dated documents have been used to cover extractions.
6. If postdated checks have been used to cover cash borrowings.
7. If fictitious vouchers were used to cover extractions.
8. That all cash payments are proper, legitimate, accurate, timely, well controlled, and properly authorized.
9. That all involved employees are aware of and following company policies, systems and operating procedures.

C. *Audit Procedures:*
1. Upon arrival, arrange with appropriate management for auditor control of all mail received during audit period. Deviations from normal operating procedures could cause delays in normal operations, so use your good judgement to dictate the degree of control required and the time period for strong enforcement. **KEEP IN MIND:** *The purpose of your cash control is to determine that location controls insure all cash receipts are properly safeguarded and processed.*

   Good audit control requires an auditor to personally pick up mail at the post office or directly from the mail carrier at the location. You will deliver unopened personal mail to the addressee and request the employee to open letters in your presence to insure that no checks or other pertinent company data is included. Terminate control of mail when you are convinced that incoming remittances are handled properly, and you no longer require them for receivable verifications.
2. Upon arrival, arrange to have salespeople's collection reports, driver's trip reports and any other receipts, together with cash, sales tickets or correspondence turned over to auditors before they have been handled by local office employees. From these papers make a complete list of all first-party checks that will later be used to verify accounts when they are in exact payment of oldest open items.

   Total all checks and cash processed by auditors and tie-in to collection reports and/or deposit slips. Compare each check on the auditor's list against the checks listed on each salesman's and driver's daily report. Examine all second-party checks for proper endorsement; they should be endorsed by customers who were scheduled for call on that day. Receipts of an unusual nature should be thoroughly investigated; check with appropriate company operation or location, or contact payer directly, if necessary.
3. For verification purposes, establish contact with the bank that handles our depository account and arrange to phone a specific bank employee to

obtain necessary information relating to first party checks received in the bank lockbox. You will use this contact to obtain complete deposit information during the early stage of the audit and to get selected data during the remainder of your visit. You may accept bank listings of checks as correct for audit verification purposes, but arrange for the bank to send all supporting data directly to you.

4. For the first few days of your audit, schedule all receipts by individual deliveryman, salesman, cashier, employee sales store, warehouse sales and any other source of cash receipts so that each collection report can be verified, and all reports can be totaled and tied into daily cash receipt summaries. Your schedule must list the individual checks as well as total cash turned in by each individual and activity. Company procedure permits out-of-town employees to reimburse their legitimate company expenses out of cash collections, but they are not permitted to cash personal checks to obtain funds.

   IMPORTANT: *Though no audit steps are spelled out in the program, you should be on the lookout for any evidence indicating that any employee is able to cash checks made out to the company.* An employee who is well known at a local bank may persuade a bank official to ignore banking policies and cash such a check. **CAUTION:** *If you learn of any such occurrences, notify the Manager of Internal Audits at once.*

   Your check listings and cash turn-ins should be compared to the copies of deposit slips. See that employees are properly keying all checks to the remitting account and noting on the deposit slip whether checks are first or second party. When practical, examine second-party checks to see that they are properly endorsed by a scheduled customer, and that an excessive number of checks has not been received from any customer. *We are not in the banking business.*

   Compare first-party checks to the invoices they purportedly pay, taking credit memos into consideration, and note any discrepancies. If the amount of the first-party check or the data on the remittance advice does not tie into our records, it may point out an instance where an employee has given a customer an invoice that differs from the alleged copy turned into the company. Since payment is based on the invoice in the customer's possession, the first-party check will be for an amount that differs from our open charge. **CAUTION:** *Since this presents the possibility of employee manipulation, it requires audit follow-up and explanation.* You should immediately contact the customer to determine exactly what the check was intended to cover.

   KEY POINT: *Be very discreet, do NOT make any accusations or inferences of dishonesty, no matter what information is received.* Your standard explanation is that the audit inquiry is aimed at locating missing or misfiled information and in helping the auditors reconcile accounts. Where appropriate, you should request the customer to supply invoice numbers, dates and amounts of tickets covered by the first party check. You may also request copies of important invoices.

If you learn that a customer has an invoice which is not in our files or which differs from our copy, *DO NOT discuss the problem with local personnel* until you have brought the matter to the attention of the Manager of Internal Audits. **CAUTION:** *You probably are looking at potential evidence of fraud, which must be handled promptly and carefully.* If you are assigned to investigate, you will receive instructions as to the proper procedure.

5. Direct deposit envelopes, to be placed into the location's drop safe, should not be opened by auditors; instead, you should prepare your collection schedule from the duplicate deposit slip attached to the collections reports. Later, verify listed checks with the bank.
6. As soon after arrival as possible, count all cash on hand from cash sales and cash funds. When you start your count of the funds in a cashier's cage, close the window and place the appropriate sign to show that an audit is in progress. **CAUTION:** *Don't rush your audit, but try to complete your count rapidly so as to reduce the inconvenience caused by closing of the cage.*

   Schedule and trace all checks found in any fund into a subsequent bank deposit. Your audit sheets listing the cash fund counts should include a brief description of each item making up the total. These sheets are to be submitted to appropriate management for examination, after which the manager should sign the sheet as evidence that it has been seen and approved. If any fund contains evidence of an advance to an employee, obtain the written approval of the employee's supervisor and confirmation from the employee.
7. When counting cash funds, be certain the custodian is present and observing the count during the entire period of auditor control of the fund. If the custodian is called away during the count, the auditor should stop and move back from the counting area, before witnesses, until the custodian returns to take part in the count. At completion, the audit count sheet should be noted as follows. "Above (identify) fund was counted in my presence and returned to me intact as listed above at (time) on (date)." **IMPORTANT:** *Have this receipt signed by the custodian as proof that the fund was returned intact.*
8. If a discrepancy is noted during your cash count, call your audit supervisor immediately. Your supervisor will confirm the problem and contact the cashier's supervisor and state the facts. **IMPORTANT:** *Do not make any accusations! Merely state the facts!* If appropriate action is not taken, immediately contact the home office.
9. From accounting records and discussions with local management, determine if other funds exist at the location. Be alert for stamp or change funds, employee activity funds and vending machine funds.

   Follow the same audit approach that you use for petty cash funds. Cash fund audit steps call your attention to disbursement items flowing through these funds. **NOTE:** *You must determine that all pay outs are proper, accurate and legitimate and that they have been approved by autho-*

rized management. You must also make certain that all cash funds are authorized, recorded and properly used.

10. When auditing vending machine receipts, your audit approach will differ depending on ownership and pricing policies. If an outside company owns the machines and we receive a share of the profits, you should accompany the individual who removes the coins from machines. Witness the count and compare observed receipts to previous reports from the same machines to judge their reliability.

    If the machines are owned by the company, product is priced at cost and if there are only small periodic expenses, you need not count the proceeds. If we permit outsiders to place machines on our premises merely for the convenience of employees and do not share in costs or profits, then you may ignore these machines. If we receive a share of the profits, this money is to go to the location's employee fund. You should trace profits into the applicable employee activity fund.
11. Some minor funds do not use bank accounts, but replenish the fund as expenditures are made. A change fund, for example, always has the amount of the fund, while a stamp fund will contain cash, stamps and records of stamp purchases and issuances that make up the total fund.

    Employee activity funds are often large enough to be deposited in a bank account, usually in joint names of two designated employees with the company relationship spelled out. When you require bank cutoff statements, process your request through one of the custodians.
12. In locations where employee credit unions are operating under the aegis of the company, you should offer your professional services to the president of the credit union. If requested, you may perform an audit of the credit union books concentrating on cash, receivables, other assets, payables, payroll and equity accounts. **REMEMBER:** *Credit unions operate as separate and independent entities, even though we may provide space, utilities, office equipment and perhaps part-time manpower.* Though the Credit Union operations are not responsibilities of the company, we want to protect our employees from potential financial abuse and your review can help accomplish this.

    Your audit is primarily aimed at determining that adequate internal controls exist and are effectively operating. The assigned auditor should prepare an appropriate audit program, using audit steps from the applicable sections of XYZ's Internal Audit Programs.
13. Operations receive periodic miscellaneous payments for out of the ordinary transactions. These may be for the sale of scrap, salvage or distressed product; refunds from utilities; payment from accounts that have declared bankruptcy; payments from accounts which have been written off or from accounts with disputed balances. **KEY POINT:** *Be on the lookout for any such items during the period you control the mail and cash receipts.* Evaluate the systems and control procedures that apply to the physical receiving and handling of such remittances.
14. Company policies and procedures are designed to reduce the amount of

cash flowing through our location offices. Every effort should be made to encourage customers to remit directly to our bank lockbox.

Arrangements have been made at our depository accounts for bank employees to remove the contents of these boxes and give immediate credit to our account. This saves at least a day in putting these funds to work. Location invoices should show the mailing address of the appropriate lockbox. Audit steps are designed to assist in your evaluation of the procedures and the results of our efforts.

15. You review the armored car pickup service to determine that the pickup of deposits is adequately controlled and receipted. Location personnel must make certain that the person picking up our deposit is as represented, and that he or she possesses the pickup service's key to the safe. If the total deposit is placed in one master bag, it should be bound and sealed and the pick up service should prepare only one receipt which states the seal number.

    When a drop safe is used and there are several envelopes collected, the receipt should show the total number of envelopes picked up and should identify them by name or route number. Control procedures state that *both* armored service *and* local management be present to open the safe. One cannot open the safe without the other being present.
16. Bank account cutoff statements should be received directly from the bank so that all accounts can be properly reconciled. Contact the bank and request a cutoff statement for the account. Set the cutoff date for the Sunday after you started your audit. Instruct the bank to return all canceled checks, even if the normal practice is for the bank to retain them. If a bank account is in the name of an individual as custodian, request the custodian to call the bank, in your presence, and issue the instructions. When audit work is completed, place a copy of the statement in the audit file, and return the original to the custodian.

    Your bank reconciliation work is designed to insure that the bank has not made errors in processing and reporting deposits. We must also insure that company records are accurate and reflect actual deposits sent to the bank. **REMEMBER:** *Differences could result from actions of the courier service.* From your reconciliation you can determine the time lapse between receipt, deposit and use of funds. You should also note NSF checks, and applicable bank charges.
17. The security section of the audit program deals with protecting and safekeeping cash receipts and funds. **KEY POINT:** *Keys can be easily duplicated, so they should NOT be hung on wall boards or be kept in unlocked desk drawers.* Many thefts are instigated by former employees who are familiar with company procedures and may have been in possession of keys and/or combinations to safes.
18. A description of the proper procedure for working with this internal audit program appears in the Introduction to the Audit Programs section of your manual. Read this information carefully.

Form # CP 001

XYZ CORPORATION
INTERNAL AUDIT PROGRAM

I. CASH RECEIPTS AND CASH FUNDS

The XYZ Corporation's General Audit Instructions, Form # CI 001, must be reviewed before attempting to follow this program.

A. *Cash Handling Procedures:*
   1. All cash is deposited into a restricted bank account.
   2. All cash received at the office is deposited intact, daily.
   3. Salespeople and deliverypeople place their deposits in the drop safe.
   4. Many remittances are mailed directly to the lockbox at the bank.
   5. Receipts are transferred daily to disbursement accounts.
   6. Bank statements are mailed directly to Treasurer by the bank.

B. *Audit Objectives* are to determine the following:
   1. Internal controls are adequate.
   2. Company procedures are followed by all personnel.
   3. Collections are properly handled, safeguarded and recorded.
   4. All cash on hand is properly handled and safeguarded.

C. *Audit Procedures:* *Per. Cov.* *Audit By*

As soon as practical after arrival, arrange with management for auditor control of all mail receipts during the audit. *Auditors must use good judgement in deciding what degree of control to exercise and the time period for mail control.* Auditors will personally pick up mail at the post office or receive it direct from the mail carrier at the office. *Audit controls should not seriously delay normal operations.* ____ ____

1. Review policy statements, flow charts and written procedures; discuss cash procedures with management. ____ ____
2. As soon as practical, control and test cash receipts. ____ ____
   a. Count, schedule and balance to relevant records all cash on hand from all sources. ____ ____
      1) Compare the amount of checks, cash and vouchers to the total of cash register and/or cash receipts issued to determine that fund is in balance. ____ ____
      2) Check audit copies in receipt machine, account for each number. Review the voided receipt file. ____ ____
   b. Observe deliverypeople and salespeople as they prepare collection and trip reports, their drop-safe procedures and movement of funds. ____ ____
      1) Determine whether any office employees have access to any cash turn-in before placement in drop-safe. If control is not foolproof, *be aware that cash shortages may result from the actions of others.* ____ ____
      2) Check sampling of deliverypeople's and salespeople's reports to supporting detail. ____ ____
      3) Examine driver reports of C.O.D. deliveries and

C. Audit Procedures	*Per. Cov.*	*Audit By*
determine that over or short reports are accurate.	____	____
Review earlier reports to see if there is a pattern of shorts for specific drivers. Discuss such cases with appropriate supervisors.	____	____
c. Obtain duplicate list of mail receipts, from person opening and listing mail, and tie-in to deposit slips. Keep the duplicate list for subsequent control.	____	____
d. Review master control sheet to see that salespeople and deliverypeople all submit daily reports.	____	____
e. Trace total cash received to Daily Summary of Cash Receipts and to subsequent bank transfer check.	____	____
1) For one month, tie-in Daily Summaries to deposits, and to computer summaries of reported receipts.	____	____
f. Trace to authenticated deposit slips, all daily receipts for your period of audit test.	____	____
g. Observe armored service pickup of day's drop-safe collections. Review normal receipt procedures.	____	____
h. Test receipts from vending machines as to amounts, proper handling and good internal controls.	____	____
1) # of machines owned by company? __; By company employees (personally)? __; By outsiders? __; By company employee clubs? __ Determine that all installations have been properly authorized.	____	____
i. Sample postings to A/R. Test should cover amounts received: by mail; directly by bank; and collection reports of salespeople and deliverypeople.	____	____
j. Investigate and explain any differences or oddities.	____	____
3. Review number and amounts of checks received by mail; find out why all checks aren't sent to bank lockbox.	____	____
a. Evaluate cost of lockbox banking versus interest gain in banking transfers, and the improved controls.	____	____
4. Compare statistics of receipts and sales, per monthly summaries for sample periods since last audit, to your audit period figures. Investigate unusual variations.	____	____
5. Examine cash journal entries for the period in which you controlled cash receipts.	____	____
a. Examine adjusting entries for poorly substantiated or vague or improper entries.	____	____
6. Obtain copy of current bank depository statement and copy of prior bank reconciliations. Look for oddities.	____	____
7. Daily deposits and transfers on bank statements should be traced to summaries of cash receipts, sales and statistics. Any differences between book figures, deposits and transfers should be investigated.	____	____
8. Trace opening statement balance to the ending balance on		

C. Audit Procedures	*Per. Cov.*	*Audit By*
the prior reconciliation. Trace deposits in transit on prior reconciliation to deposits on the current statement.	____	____
9. Bank statements should also be reviewed for the following:		
a. Returned customer's checks and miscellaneous adjustments. Standard procedures should insure that these items are properly handled.	____	____
b. Time lapse between date cash is deposited and the date cash is transferred to the disbursement account.	____	____
10. Reconcile bank statements and tie-in to General Ledger.	____	____
a. Trace movement of cash from depository accounts, through transfers to disbursement, investment or other accounts.	____	____

Audit work reviewed by ________________________ Date ____________

II. PETTY CASH AND OTHER CASH FUNDS

A. Company Procedures:

1. A specific employee is designated as custodian of any cash fund.
2. Imprest cash funds, in excess of $500 are deposited in checking accounts. A minor amount of cash is held to meet emergencies.
3. All disbursements from funds must be approved by management.
4. Only purchases totaling less than $50 are paid for out of fund.
5. Reimbursements are made as required, but must be requested at the close of each accounting period.
6. Bank statements and cancelled checks are mailed by bank directly to the Treasurer. After examination they are sent to custodian.

B. Audit Objectives are to determine the following:

1. Fund is intact and is adequate to cover allowable disbursements.
2. Systems and procedures are adequate and followed by all personnel involved. Internal controls are operating satisfactorily.
3. Fund custodians are safeguarding and using fund disbursements.
4. There is proper account distribution of fund disbursements.
5. There is proper compliance with IRS requirements and company policy with respect to reporting employee travel expenses.

C. Audit Procedures:	*Per. Cov.*	*Audit By*
1. As soon as practical count and reconcile cash funds in the presence of the custodian. (Follow procedures outlined in the audit instructions.)	____	____
a. Schedule all cash, checks and vouchers in fund.	____	____
b. Examine all disbursements for proper approval.	____	____
c. Determine that all checks and vouchers are current.	____	____
d. Review register's recording of receipts of cash and reconcile to contents on hand.	____	____

C. Audit Procedures	*Per. Cov.*	*Audit By*
e. Have custodian recount fund and sign the receipt for return of the intact fund.	____	____
2. Discuss with fund custodian, the specific procedures for preparing the applicable accounting records.	____	____
3. Determine from frequency of reimbursement that amount of the imprest balance is adequate, but not excessive.	____	____
4. When a bank account is involved:		
a. Obtain a cutoff statement directly from the bank.	____	____
b. Obtain copy of latest reconciliation and verify the accuracy of all items contained therein.	____	____
c. Trace the ending balance of the reconciliation to the opening balance of the cutoff statement.	____	____
d. Trace deposits in transit, and note the time lag between date of reported deposit and bank credit.	____	____
e. Examine items returned with cutoff statement for proper endorsements and conformance to fund records.	____	____
f. Obtain explanations for any unusual items.	____	____
5. Obtain copies of several recent reimbursement vouchers for review. Perform the following:	____	____
a. For deliverypeople and salespeople, review the supporting papers for compliance with IRS requirements.	____	____
b. Examine disbursements for reasonableness, proper handling and cancellation of documents.	____	____
c. Tie-in reimbursement amounts to accounting records to learn if fund is using cash receipts.	____	____
6. Vending machine and other funds. Perform the following:		
a. Determine if company is incurring expenses for the activity. If so, examine the authority and approval.	____	____
b. Count cash (same as petty cash) and reconcile to appropriate records. If records are not auditable, suggest changes that will enable future audits.	____	____
c. Determine that custodian is properly safeguarding, controlling and reporting funds and related records.	____	____

Audit work approved by ______________________ Date ____________

III. INTERNAL CONTROL QUESTIONNAIRE—CASH RECEIPTS

The following internal control questions should be answered as you perform your audit work. In section B insert names of employees who perform the listed function and write in any conflicting duties.

A. Following are listed practices that indicate good internal control:

1. Employee that handles cash receipts does *not* have authority to sign

checks, does *not* reconcile bank accounts and does *not* have access to non-cash accounting records.

2. Cash receipts are deposited intact, and without delay.
3. Lockbox banking is used where practical.
4. Drop-safe, and armored car pickup is used to safeguard local collections and local cash sales transactions.
5. Receipts given for cash turn-ins are effectively controlled by registers or similar devices.

B. Following lists functions performed by named employees:

Function:	*Name/Position*	*Conflicting Duties*
1. Opens mail	______	______
2. Delivers mail	______	______
3. Receives cash	______	______
4. Prepares bank deposit	______	______
5. Prepares cash receipt report	______	______
6. Reconciles bank accounts	______	______
7. Prepares transfer checks	______	______
8. Maintains Accounts Receivable	______	______

C. Internal Control Questions:	*Yes*	*No*	*Remarks*
1. Are all mail-in remittances generally directed to the bank lockbox?	____	____	______
2. Does clerk opening mail immediately stamp endorsement data on all checks?	____	____	______
3. Does A/R bookkeeper have access to cash receipts?			
a. Does bookkeeper originate C/M's?	____	____	______
4. Does the location promptly bank all remittances they receive?	____	____	______
5. Are cash receipts properly safeguarded *before* and *after* deposit is prepared?	____	____	______
6. Are remittance advices separated from checks by mail room?	____	____	______
a. Are checks and advices delivered directly to department concerned?	____	____	______
b. *Is transfer of cash from mail room to cashier adequately controlled?*	____	____	______
7. Does a disinterested party periodically compare in-house copies of deposit slips to the bank returned copies for cashier, salespeople, drivers, cafeteria, etc.	____	____	______

C. Internal Control Questions	*Yes*	*No*	*Remarks*
8. Does office properly use an adequate collection checkoff chart?	____	____	____________
9. Do salespeople and deliverypeople use their restrictive endorsement stamp on all checks they receive?	____	____	____________
10. Are drivers and salespeople's collections deposited intact?	____	____	____________
a. Are personal checks cashed out of collection? If yes:	____	____	____________
b. Was procedure properly approved?	____	____	____________
11. Are *both* names and amounts of driver and salespeople's checks matched to their applicable reports and deposit slips?	____	____	____________
a. Are they keyed to the account that submitted check?	____	____	____________
b. Are all oddities investigated?	____	____	____________
12. Are drivers and salespeople expense reports approved first by immediate superior?	____	____	____________
13. Does office verify items "scratched short" on C.O.D. tickets?	____	____	____________
a. Is check 100%? Periodical? Never?	____	____	____________
14. Are both armored car AND our local personnel needed to open drop safe?	____	____	____________
a. Who knows the combination? (list)	____	____	____________
b. How many persons have key to safe?	____	____	____________
c. Should safe combinations be changed?	____	____	____________
15. Is control adequate over all keys to building, files and safes.	____	____	____________
a. Are critical locks and combinations changed when employees leave jobs?	____	____	____________
16. Do armored car personnel accept contents without opening any bag or envelope?	____	____	____________

C. Internal Control Questions	*Yes*	*No*	*Remarks*
a. Do they sign for the monies taken?	____	____	____________
17. Are monies received from accounts that were previously written off, handled exactly like regular remittances?	____	____	____________
a. *Is control adequate?*	____	____	____________
18. Is control adequate over checks that are postdated or have been returned?	____	____	____________
a. Are returned checks immediately charged back to receivables?	____	____	____________
b. Are employee payroll checks cashed in violation of policy?	____	____	____________
19. Are remittances received from accounts that apply to other locations? If yes:	____	____	____________
a. Is check deposited locally?	____	____	____________
b. Is check sent to correct location?	____	____	____________
c. Is control adequate?	____	____	____________
20. *Are walk-in receipts handled properly?*	____	____	____________
a. Does cashier ring up all sales?	____	____	____________
b. Is a proper receipt given for all cash sales?	____	____	____________
21. Does a supervisor periodically tie-in total of control copies of receipts issued by cashier to deposits?	____	____	____________
a. Are all receipts accounted for?	____	____	____________
22. Are collection reports of Employee sales and whse. sales prepared daily?	____	____	____________
a. Does a third party compare whse. sales slips to cash sales reports?	____	____	____________
b. Is control adequate to insure that employee does *not* have access to all records on both ends of transaction?	____	____	____________

C. Internal Control Questions

	Yes	*No*	*Remarks*
23. Is control adequate over processing sales of miscellaneous items?	____	____	____________
24. Is cash transfer to disbursement bank account handled properly and promptly?	____	____	____________
a. Are personal checks, cashed for employees, deposited promptly?	____	____	____________
25. Does the same person always reconcile the cash depository account?	____	____	____________
a. Does this person have access to cash or checks?	____	____	____________
b. Is the reconciliation ever reviewed by an independent employee?	____	____	____________
26. Is control adequate over cash redemption of coupons and their destruction?	____	____	____________
27. Do any company employees act as a collection agent for outsiders?	____	____	____________
28. Are handlers of cash required to replace all their cash shortages?	____	____	____________
a. Is the system fair?	____	____	____________
29. Do you believe there is good internal control over the receipt of cash?	____	____	____________

Questions answered by ______________________ Date ____________
Questionnaire approved by ______________________ Date ____________

IV. INTERNAL CONTROL QUESTIONNAIRE—CASH FUNDS

A. Prepare a separate questionnaire for each fund reviewed.

B. Following are listed practices that indicate good internal control

1. Different employees approve disbursements, prepare checks and reconcile bank account.
2. All disbursements are properly authorized and controlled.
3. Disbursement checks are not signed until all papers are approved.
4. Bank reconciliations are prepared monthly by disinterested party.
5. Fund is on an imprest basis and is often checked by a supervisor.
6. Where applicable, incoming funds are verified and recorded by an independent party..

C. Name and location of fund? ______________________

D. *Following list of functions performed by named employees.*

Functions	*Name and Position*	*Conflicting Duties*
1. Custodian.	______	______
2. Approves pay out vouchers.	______	______
3. Signs checks (if bank used).	______	______
4. Reconciles bank account.	______	______
5. Reviews expense distribution.	______	______
6. Verifies funds received.	______	______

E. *Internal Control Questions:*

	Yes	*No*	*Remarks*
1. Is only one person assigned as custodian?	___	___	______
2. Is amount of fund proper for its purpose?	___	___	______
3. Are funds safeguarded at all times?	___	___	______
4. Are any items paid out of funds that should have been processed through A/P?	___	___	______
a. Is there a dollar limit for payment of items out of the fund?	___	___	______
5. Are personal checks, cashed out of fund, promptly deposited?	___	___	______
a. Are any employee payroll checks cashed in violation of policy?	___	___	______
6. Are disbursement vouchers:			
a. Prepared for each pay out of funds?	___	___	______
b. Written in ink or typewritten, and dated?	___	___	______
c. Properly supported and approved?	___	___	______
d. Receipted by person receiving cash?	___	___	______
e. *Properly voided to prevent reuse?*	___	___	______
7. Are reimbursing checks:			
a. Written to custodian as the payee?	___	___	______
b. Endorsed by fund custodian if drawn to "cash"?	___	___	______
8. Are funds periodically checked and reconciled by custodian's supervisor?	___	___	______
9. Are all custodians properly bonded?	___	___	______

E. Internal Control Questions	*Yes*	*No*	*Remarks*
10. Based on your review, do you believe that there is adequate internal control over these funds?	____	____	__________

Questions answered by ____________________ Date __________
Questionnaire approved by ____________________ Date __________

CRITICAL POINTS

An audit of cash activities is fraught with potentially explosive situations. The author has spearheaded hundreds of investigations where employees have stolen cash and have attempted to hide their thefts. There are many critical areas in the handling of cash, where it is most likely to be misappropriated, or where loose handling can lead to added expenses or touchy situations. Some of these critical points are enumerated in the hope that you, the reader, will be particularly alert when you recognize the signs.

THIRTEEN CRITICAL AREAS TO CONSIDER

1. The greatest potential for the misappropriation of cash is in the handling of accounts receivable payments. Withholding of cash that pays an open receivable balance is a common occurrence. When such withholding takes place the account must be adjusted to cover the extraction. **TIP:** *Adjustments are usually credits to the account that wipe out invoices in the amount of cash withheld.*

   In locations where a loose leaf accounts receivable system is used, the withholding is covered by simply removing the invoice in question and destroying it.

   Naturally the receipt of money is never reported. This type of manipulation is often uncovered through the audit routine of comparing first-party checks to items they purportedly pay. Accounts receivable verification procedures are also designed to unearth such activities.

2. Another area of potential misappropriation occurs when payments are received from accounts that declared bankruptcy or carried long overdue disputed balances. Conservative accounting principles require that such doubtful accounts be written off the books. When they are written off, the charges are removed from the active files and placed in other files that require special handling.

   When cash payments are received that settle disputed items or close out a bankrupt account, the person receiving the payment may merely remove the correspondence and take the cash. An employee can then cash such checks or post them to accounts from which the employee can easily obtain cash. Auditors must review current files and previous audit papers for the names of bankrupt or disputed accounts. Current audit lists of accounts written off can be compared with prior list and all differences investigated. Sales people usually keep a copy of all correspondence relating to disputed and bankrupt accounts. Auditors should locate these files and compare names to the audit listing to discover other accounts which may not have been properly handled.

Indications of such manipulations may be detected during audit control of incoming mail. **TIP:** *Strict application of the requirement that the mail department immediately apply a restrictive endorsement stamp to all incoming items can make such checks difficult to cash.* If the check arrives in an envelope addressed to an individual, it is almost impossible for the mail room to identify contents.

Misapplication of such checks is a common occurrence which is more difficult to detect. An audit review of the comparison of application of first-party checks to proper accounts may reveal such defalcations.

3. Cashiers working directly with the public, who use cash registers to record sales and cash receipts, frequently skip recording specific sales but place the cash into the register until it can be removed at an opportune time. The register balances at settlement, and the only evidence is an inventory shortage at month end.

   Such practices usually occur in the retail trade when a customer adds a last minute item to previous purchases. If the original items had been rung up but the change not yet given to the customer, the cashier adjusts the amount of change given, but does not ring up the additional purchase. **NOTE:** *This practice is difficult to detect, but a cash OVERAGE noted during a surprise cash count is an indication that it may be occurring.* Another sign is an inventory shortage.

   Some companies employ shopping services in an attempt to detect this type of cash manipulation. These shopping services check all, or certain specified, cashier stations and give the cashier an opportunity to engage in illegal activity, while surreptitiously paying close attention to the employee's handling of the transaction.

4. Sometimes a cash register is left open when a cashier is busy, and tickets are rung up after the rush clears. A cashier can then merely tear up the tickets and extract offsetting cash.

   If tickets are prepared by sales clerks, a check of the numerical sequence of tickets processed may disclose missing invoices. These could be tickets that the cashier had destroyed. Several methods are used to attempt to thwart such activities. One is to print a star on an occasional register receipt and post a notice advising customers that a starred receipt entitles the customer to a prize or discount. Another frequently used method offers a prize to anyone paying a bill that does not receive a cash register receipt. These methods are designed to induce customers to look for, or demand, a cash register receipt for their purchase.

5. Custodians of cash, particularly in small offices, sometimes get careless in safeguarding their funds. Often, during a break period, change boxes are left on desk tops or in unlocked drawers. When shortages in such funds are noted, the custodian immediately becomes the prime suspect. If a cash envelope disappears from a safe, any person knowing the combination, or possessing a key, becomes a suspect. Many innocent people have thus been falsely accused.

   KEY POINT: *Auditors should be careful not to accuse anyone of anything when confronted with a case of mysterious disappearance.* In such cases a voluntary polygraph approach can be helpful in clearing the innocent employees. Before the polygraph machine is used there should be complete agreement as to which employees will be offered the test. If police officials are called in, they will make the final decisions.

   Company control of such tests enables management to select the best polygraph operator available, and to confine the questions to the issue at hand. It also removes the natural apprehension that many people are apt to feel when questioned by policemen. **CAUTION:** *Such reactions can affect the results of a polygraph test.*

6. Borrowing from a petty cash fund is not an unusual occurrence. Such borrowings are usually covered by the insertion of a fictitious petty cash voucher or an undated check. If the petty cash fund has an undated check or voucher, or one dated prior to the last report for reimbursement, the auditor should consider the item as questionable and act accordingly.

7. Vending machine receipt funds should be considered vulnerable to manipulation. To estimate vending machine receipts of prior periods the auditor should accompany the responsible individual while receipts from the machines are removed and counted. Comparison of audit cash counts to prior reports will disclose major differences.

   Any noted discrepancy should be discussed with the responsible manager and a plan of action adopted. The plan may be designed to find out what happened in the past, or merely to make changes that will close up loopholes in existing controls.

8. Change funds and miscellaneous activity funds make cash available to certain employees. Usually there is a minimum of control over these funds and record keeping is poor. This situation can present a temptation to custodians or other individuals who have access to the funds. Although amounts involved are relatively small, auditors must review the handling and control of these funds. Surprise counts and careful review of disbursement records often disclose manipulations.

9. Stamp funds are frequently used by some employees for personal purposes. When these funds are misused, the first sign is often the rising

postage costs. Audit review of mail volume and costs should be initiated when irregularities are suspected. Your comparison of audited postage costs to prior period costs may raise questions.

To reduce the risk, companies obtain postage meters and exercise strong control over the refilling of these meters. **CAUTION:** *There are cases where postage meter receipts have been altered, so auditors must be alert to this possibility.* Such abuse can be reduced by using a company check, made out to the postmaster, to pay for meter refills.

10. The practice of permitting employees to reimburse their company expenses out of cash receipts presents a special problem. Fictitious or inflated receipts may be used to obtain extra money.

    To minimize this type of manipulation, many companies have adopted a credit card system that requires employees to pay all expenses with their company credit card, and to deposit collections intact. Under this system the company sets up, and requires employees to use, specific vendors for gasoline, motels, restaurants and repairs. Vendors agree to accept specific credit cards in payment for goods or services rendered to employees.

    This system still carries the danger that company employees may induce vendor employees to stretch the rules of the agreement and to bill for amounts in excess of actual purchases or to give the employee cash and add the amount to the ticket total.

    Inflated prices or excessive quantities are frequently a sign of collusion and may indicate a split of the overcharge. Audit review of driver's and salesperson's expenses may reveal charges for goods or services that exceed the going rates, or that bill for quantities in excess of probable usage. Contact with such vendors may be necessary. Discussions with management of vendors often reveal that they are unaware of the illegal practices and want to correct the unauthorized actions of their employees.

    In situations where cash transactions take place, receipts submitted by employees may be fictitious or inflated, and the document itself may have been stolen or actually printed by the employee involved. **TIP:** *If receipts are in continuous numerical sequence, or if they appear odd, a call to the supplier can frequently disclose such illegal actions.*

11. Cash is a commodity and should be treated as such. Frequently its earning power is not considered, and excessive amounts of cash may be left in checking accounts that do not pay interest. Auditors must be alert to delays in using cash to produce revenue or reduce expenses.

    KEY POINT: *Company systems and procedures should require immediate deposit of receipts and prompt transfers of excess funds to the investment department.* A bank prepared analysis of the company's bank account activity, which is usually available in the treasurer's department, should be reviewed. This analysis shows the interest earned and the charges for activity levied against the account. **TIP:** *Balances should be sufficient to cover activity charges, but surplus funds should be put to work.*

12. Outlying operations in small towns may present an unusual type of banking problem. In small communities a manager of a large company's operation is usually well-respected and believed to have the final word on any question involving the company. Local managers frequently suggest the bank to be used, and often serve as the contact with the bank. It is only natural that local bankers should not wish to upset this local tycoon.

    Checks for salvage or scrap sales that are received locally are deposited in the local transfer account. **CAUTION:** *There have been occasions where a location manager has used his position to induce a local banker to cash a check made out to the manager's company.* In such instances, checks for small amounts are cashed when the home office is shut down and the local operation requires ready cash for a specific legitimate purpose. The local manager convinces a local banker to cash the company's check, and there are no repercussions. The local banker unwittingly has established a precedent that could lead to later abuse. **TIP:** *Audit review that discloses a reduction in scrap or salvage receipts could indicate that something of this type may be occurring.*

    Auditors sometimes request their treasurer to send a letter to all or selected banks in a particular area, cautioning them to adhere to the requirement that all checks made out to the company be deposited to the proper account. Banks are reminded that these checks are not to be cashed for anyone. Some letters ask the bank to inform the company of any violations of this restriction.

13. Customers often submit NSF checks in payment of their accounts so that they can order more merchandise. These checks may be for amounts in excess of their bank account balance or to nonexistent accounts. Writing checks on nonexisting accounts is a criminal act and should be treated as such; but an insufficient fund check may result from mistakes or miscalculation of the time required to clear transfers.

    When NSF checks are returned, the established procedure should require immediate redeposit, notification to the sales department and contact with the customer. If a second return occurs, the check should be returned to the customer in exchange for cash or a cashier's check. The sales department must decide whether to continue to do business with the customer.

    Auditors should insure that the system reopens the charge to the appropriate account receivable, and that close control is kept over the possession and handling of all returned checks. **TIP:** *When returned checks are given to salespeople for collection, a receipt should be prepared and signed by the salesperson as evidence of the physical transfer of the check.*

Chapter 12

Auditing Receivable Transactions

Credit turns the wheels of commerce and industry. Everybody uses it, knowingly or unknowingly. Paper money is but a negotiable instrument of credit issued by the federal government and accepted by the general population. It has no intrinsic value, but is readily accepted in exchange for goods and services.

Aside from government, all other enterprises must earn the right to have their paper accepted in the market place. Enterprises and individuals gain a reputation for honesty, integrity and good faith through their timely actions. As long as we meet our obligations and keep our promises, we enjoy a good credit rating. There is no place in the cashless society for anyone who does not keep the faith by promptly paying their bills. Thus credit cards have made debtors of us all.

The Two Sides of Credit Transactions

There are two accounting sides to every credit transaction; to the grantor it's a receivable, while to the recipient it's a payable. This chapter is devoted to the receivable end of such transactions, and will consider accounts, notes and sundry receivables. We will not be concerned with the time element or the type of negotiable instrument used, though these factors differentiate accounts on the balance sheet. The internal audit approach remains basically the same regardless of the accounting distinction.

Receivables are a major item of many organizations, frequently being the largest single asset on the balance sheet. Next to cash and perhaps inventory, receivables are the most vulnerable to manipulation or error. Because of the significance and vulnerability, a great deal of internal and external audit time is directed toward this important activity. Auditors are vitally interested in determining that the account is fairly represented in the books of an entity.

In this chapter we will consider the originating transaction that created the receivable, the processing of paper work necessary to record the transaction, any adjustments to accounting records and the receipt of payment or credit that wipes out the receivable.

Much effort is directed toward reviewing operating internal controls and verifying that the open accounts are accurate and current. Auditors seek to verify open accounts directly with the customer, and this attempt can take up a lot of audit time. An audit manager must determine that his staff is using the most efficient and least costly method of verifying account balances.

TYPES OF VERIFICATION

Auditor verifications can be accomplished in many ways: by letter to an outsider that requests information, by phone call, by personal visit and by examining payments received. During a routine audit all of these methods are used. The most common is a verification letter to customers that contains a summary of the open account.

Verification Letters

A letter gives the customer time to research and determine the accuracy of the data before being required to give an answer. A single phone verification takes time to locate the right employee, explain what is needed and then wait while the customers records are studied. A personal visit requires all of the above plus the time it takes to travel to and from the customer's place of business.

The least costly method of verification is an examination of a customer's first-party check that exactly pays the amount of open invoices. The timing of an audit visit may rule out this alternative. Auditors may be in and out of an operation before the "sale to payment" cycle is normally completed. Payment verification is used for many accounts, but since auditors can't know which checks will be received while they are at the location, the safest procedure is to mail a confirmation letter to selected customers.

There are several different approaches to a confirmation letter. Following is a short description of two different methods.

Positive Verifications

Positive verification means that a customer is asked to positively state that an open balance of an account is correct and requires that the auditor make every effort to prove that balance. Audit statements to selected accounts request that they respond to the audit inquiry. If they fail to respond to the first request, the auditor sends a second request and may even resort to phone calls or a personal visit to an account. The positive approach is tempered by a review of incoming cash payments. Auditors compare cash receipts against open items to spot exact matches that are considered confirmations by payment.

KEY POINT: *Only first-party checks are accepted as proof.* Money orders or cash are not acceptable since the salesperson responsible for the account may have remitted such sums in order to cover a withholding.

Negative Verifications

Negative verification is a less costly and less time consuming approach to the verification problem, since the *auditor assumes that no response is a good one.* Customers receiving an erroneous statement will make an effort to correct the misinformation. Recipients are told that no action is required if all of the information is correct. If any discrepancy exists, they are asked to give certain information for items questioned. Even in a negative approach, a return envelope or post card is enclosed to facilitate the customer's response.

Auditors know that any substantial error will be disclosed by the party responsible for the account, but in a negative approach, an auditor can never be certain that the addressee received the request. A clerk may have discarded it without taking the time required to check out the information. Nor can the auditor be certain that all mailed replies were received, since mail might be misdirected.

Verification statements are prepared by, or for, the auditor who mails them directly to customers. **KEY POINT:** *Regardless of approach used, the verification request must be brief and clear.* It should require a minimum amount of time to read and interpret. The cutoff date should be shown and the recipient advised that the statement only covers transactions through that date and does not include items in transit.

Sample Confirmation Forms

Audit verification statements are created when and as required by the internal audit staff. There are no set rules governing the form or content of verification requests. Auditors must consider printing and mailing costs involved in verifying information, as well as the audit time required to process the requests and the replies. Following are a number of sample verification requests used by internal auditors. These demonstrate the general structure and language of such requests.

When receivables are in the EDP data base, and auditors can control the computer output, normal billing statements are run off and then controlled by the audit group. Selected statements are inserted in window envelopes with an audit verification letter and a self-addressed envelope. The letter, which may be machine generated, asks the customer to examine the statement and inform the auditor if it contains any errors. The letter reads somewhat as follows:

Dear Customer:

Our internal audit staff is conducting a routine audit of our receivable records to ensure that they agree with those of our customers. Please examine the enclosed statement which shows your balance as of the close of business on __________. This balance does not include items received or processed after that date.

If the statement is in order, you do not need to act on this request.

If there are any errors in this statement, please inform the auditors by filling in the bottom section of this letter and returning it in the enclosed self-addressed envelope.

Your cooperation is appreciated.

(The bottom portion of the verification letter reads):

XYZ Auditing Department: Request #_____ (Inserted by Auditor)

The statement dated ______________, contained the following errors:

____

Signed: ____ Date: ____________

A common method of verification is to overprint a notation on the customer's copy of the monthly statement. The notation might read:

> Our records are being audited to insure that customer accounts are accurate. Please note that the information on this statement reflects your balance on the printed date, and does not include payments, credits or charges received after that date. You need do nothing if the statement is correct. We have enclosed a self-addressed post card for your convenience in calling our attention to any errors contained in the statement. Your prompt reply will help us make necessary corrections.

The enclosed reply card is addressed to the company at a specific post office box used solely by the audit staff. The reply section of the card is based on a *negative* verification approach and reads:

(Reply Card)

XYZ CORPORATION No: __ (Inserted by auditor)

YOUR PROMPT REPLY WILL BE APPRECIATED

My monthly statement is *incorrect.*

1. The statement contains the following charges which I paid prior to the cut off date:

   Invoice _______ Date paid _______ By cash ___ By check ___

   Invoice _______ Date paid _______ By cash ___ By check ___

2. I have no record of the following invoice(s):

   ____

   OTHER REMARKS: ____

   ____

   Form # RVR 101 SIGNED ______________________ Date: _________

Some audit staffs prefer to use distinctive audit confirmation statements instead of the usual monthly statement that the customer is accustomed to seeing. They believe that customers will pay more attention to an audit form. Following is a positive reply accounts receivable audit verification form that is individually prepared by the internal auditors. The format is positioned so that the address will fit into a window envelope. Each form is numbered by a stamped sequential numbering device.

The sample *positive* approach audit verification form follows:

Form #1 RV 110 No. ___ (Inserted by auditor)

XYZ CORPORATION

(Address of Company Location)
THIS IS NOT A REQUEST FOR PAYMENT
To Be Used For Auditor's Information Only
PLEASE USE ENCLOSED POSTCARD FOR YOUR REPLY

Name ______________________
Street ______________________
City ______________ State ______ ZIP ______

Dear customer: Our records are being audited in conformance with our desire to keep our customer accounts accurate. We show the following items as open and unpaid on DATE ____________

Inv. Date	**Inv. No.**	**Amount**	**Inv. Date**	**Inv. No.**	**Amount**
				TOTAL	

This may not be your present balance. It does not include any charges, credits or payments which we may have received after the above date. Please determine if our records are correct or wrong, and fill in the enclosed reply card. Your prompt action will be appreciated. Please do not discuss this matter with anyone but the auditor.

XYZ CORPORATION

A reply card similar to the Form # RVR 101, printed above, is mailed with each statement. These *positive* approach reply cards contain slightly different wording, since they request a reply from all customers. The reply card reads as follows:

(Reply Card)
XYZ CORPORATION
YOUR PROMPT REPLY WILL BE APPRECIATED
No: ___ (Inserted by auditor)

The balance as shown on the enclosed statement corresponds with my records as checked below:

1. *Correct* and unpaid as of statement date. _____
2. *Incorrect—paid before* date shown _____
   The statement contains the following charges which I paid prior to the cut off date:
   Invoice ________ Date paid ________ By cash ___ By check ___
   Invoice ________ Date paid ________ By cash ___ By check ___
3. I have *no record* of the following invoice(s):
   ____
   OTHER REMARKS: ________________________________
   Form # RVR 102 Signed ____________________ Date: ________

Notes Receivable Verification Form

Verification forms for notes receivable are designed to fit particular needs and audit approaches. They are sometimes useful as legal proof of outstanding obligation. The following *positive* approach to the verification of notes receivable requires that two copies of the form be sent and that one signed copy be returned to the auditor. The request takes the form of a letter.

XYZ CORPORATION
(Address of Company Location) Date ________

____
____

Dear ____________________

In accordance with our desire to keep our notes receivable records accurate, our corporate audit department periodically verifies our outstanding notes receivable.

They are currently conducting their examination and would appreciate your confirmation of the following note of which you are the maker.

Date of note: ____________________ Original amount of note: $________
Agreed interest: _______% _____ Agreed settlement date: ____________
This note is secured by the following: ______________________________
Outstanding balance due on this note: $________ as of ______________.

Please indicate in the space provided below for your reply, whether the above information is correct. If a difference is reported, please give our auditors any information which may assist them in reconciling the matter.

Please sign and date your reply and mail the original copy directly to the XYZ Audit Department. A stamped, self addressed envelope is enclosed for your convenience.

Yours truly,
XYZ CORPORATION

. . . .

The information concerning the above note dated ____________ in the amount of $____________ is correct. My current balance as of ________________ is $________________.

Signed ________________ Date ________

The above information is incorrect and the following exceptions are noted: ____

Signed ________________ Date ________

Four Special Verifications

Special verifications can sometimes be more subtly accomplished than by using a standard form audit verification statement.

EXAMPLE 1: A bank auditor, reviewing small inactive accounts, writes a letter directly to each account calling attention to the lack of activity and asking if the depositor desires to close out the account. The account may take action as a result of the letter, proving that it was handled properly. If something is wrong with the balance, the depositor will enquire as to the reason.

EXAMPLE 2: An insurance auditor, wishing to verify that a policyholder who receives a monthly annuity check is still alive, can examine endorsements on canceled checks or use a private investigator. Or the auditor may use a legitimate sales offer which requires each recipient to sign the letter as proof of receiving the offer.

EXAMPLE 3: Some staffs successfully utilize a consumer questionnaire to elicit important information. This approach can combine the needs of several different departments in an organization. Questions that help marketing or quality control can be combined with those that interest the internal auditor. The replies are sent to a P.O. Box that is controlled by the audit department.

EXAMPLE 4: Letters which appear to be individually written are frequently sent to people who purchased unusual items not ordinarily sold in the normal course of the firm's business. For example, an auditor may want to verify the purchaser and price paid for a company motor vehicle that had been sold. The letters of inquiry spell out the known facts and then ask simple quality and service questions that the buyer is willing to answer. The answers establish the identity of the buyer, and somewhere in the body of the letter is the important "price paid" question. Postage paid reply envelopes are addressed to a post office box to avoid identifying a department.

SAMPLE INTERNAL AUDIT PROGRAM

Here is a sample audit program of the XYZ Corporation, which is designed to direct the auditor to important areas of the recording and controlling of receivable activities.

Background Information

1. Our mythical XYZ Corporation is a large international company with many operating locations throughout the world. Accounts receivable are computerized, using a unique, custom-designed software program to feed data from strategically located computer terminals into a central data base. Each major sales office enters sales and collection data each day, and their printers immediately provide a hard copy of the data they entered into the system. The hard copy is attached to supporting documentation and retained in local files.
2. Central control of A/R rests in the receivable section of the home office financial department. This A/R group handles all receivable transactions at the home office location, which include a major distribution operation, a large sales branch and the company's central sales section which handles sales to major accounts.
3. The A/R computer system is a real time operation. All scheduled reports are processed and printed during the off hours. Each location enters all daily transactions before an office shuts down for the day. Some credit sales at small sales branches and plant offices, where no terminals are available, are entered into the system at the division office responsible for the operation. These small offices prepare a daily summary of Cash Receipts and Daily Sales which accompanies their daily input forms that they mail to the division offices, and which usually enter the EDP system several days late. The sales branches use a loose leaf ticket control system for their local A/R, even though every transaction is entered into the data base. Aging schedules are computer-generated and distributed to all locations.
4. The head office A/R section, and the cashier are separated physically and organizationally, but all related work is done in the Financial Department. The supervisors of both activities report to the same controller in the Financial Department.
5. The Manager of Internal Auditing reports directly to the Financial Vice-President. A specialized section of the audit staff is devoted to data processing work. This section created a program for use by auditors which is designed to select accounts for verification, and to print out statements from the open receivable files. The selection process uses a combination

of random and stratum samples and has the capability of adjusting samples to achieve a desired percentage of assurance. The audit staff also has the capability of selecting specific accounts to be added to the list for circularization.

6. Notes and sundry receivables are routinely handled in the same financial department section that controls accounts receivable, but different personnel are involved in the handling of those items.
7. A description of the proper procedure for working with this internal audit program appears in the Introduction to the Audit Programs section of your manual. Read this information carefully.

Now let's look at the sample audit instructions for reviewing receivables at the XYZ Corporation.

FORM # RI 002 XYZ CORPORATION
INTERNAL AUDIT INSTRUCTIONS

I. ALL RECEIVABLES

A. *Audit Caution:*

Before starting an audit of Receivables:

1. Determine what action was taken on any unresolved issues contained in the last audit report. You may want to repeat an audit remark, and be certain to mention that it had been brought up at an earlier audit.
2. Read and understand (Form # RP 001) Internal Audit Program, the Internal Control Questionnaire and these Audit Instructions. If you have any questions, discuss them with your audit supervisor.
3. Review the user's manual of the A/R Computer Control System. Discuss that system and your audit plans with the supervisor of the EDP audit group so that you will receive the necessary computer generated information when and as required. The audit group will run a complete listing of open accounts receivable as of the date you select and will also provide appropriate aging schedules. The computer will also prepare your customer confirmation requests, which will be the most current open balances printed on an audit request form. The program selects accounts at random and adds stratum of accounts as designated. **NOTE:** *You may add individual or groups of accounts as you decide.*

   You may accept this computer generated information as accurate, but you remain responsible for errors. Conduct routine audit checks, as spelled out in the program, to determine that the computer output is accurate and current. **TIP:** *Much information is processed daily, and mistakes can easily occur; your audit checks should detect such errors.*
4. Read Cash Receipts Audit Program Form # CP 001 and the associated Instruction Form # CI 002. Pay particular attention to the points dealing with control of incoming mail, the recording of checks as received and the action to be taken when any questionable transaction is discovered. You must be aware of all of these instructions.

B. *Audit Objectives* are to determine the following:
   1. That all transactions that should flow through receivables do so.
   2. That receivable balances truly reflect amounts owing to the firm.
   3. That all open balances are accurate and collectible.
   4. That payments have been promptly, accurately and properly applied.

C. *Audit Procedures:*
   1. We try to plan audits of Receivables to occur at the same time as audits of Cash Receipts, to eliminate overlap of responsibilities and/or duties. **IMPORTANT:** *Lead auditors coordinate this work; however, if cash receipts are not audited at the time that your work is scheduled, you will be responsible for controlling incoming mail and listing checks received as outlined in the Cash Receipts audit program.*

      When two audit teams work together, you may accept the cash listing as being correct, and you are responsible for matching receipts to the open accounts and following up on discrepancies. Checks that relate to other locations, or that cover transactions not flowing through receivables, will be audited by the cash audit group. **KEY POINT:** *Your work should be coordinated so that nothing falls through the cracks.*
   2. As part of the unique computer selection process, entire subgroups are selected for verification. Code numbers enable identification of the subgroup selected. Be certain, before you mail to customers, that you foot each statement and add all totals. Check your independent grand total against the computer-generated subgroup total. They should coincide, which means that the correct files were used to prepare the audit verification statements.
   3. For your customer confirms, you will receive three-part statements from the EDP audit group. First copies are for customers, and may be inserted into window envelopes, along with a self-addressed reply postcard. The second copy has the words, SECOND REQUEST overprinted on the face of the statement. This is mailed if there has been no reply to the first request AND if you have not seen a first-party check which exactly pays outstanding invoices. Third copies are for audit control; they contain spaces for audit confirmation data.

      These requests are serially numbered and should be retained in numerical sequence to facilitate ready reference. Each statement bears a unique code number, under the serial number, which readily identifies the group and subgroup where the account is filed.
   4. Reply postcards, which you include with each confirm you mail, are addressed to the audit department's post office box. Arrange to have these reply cards picked up daily.
   5. Statements should be mailed out as soon as possible after the cutoff date. You must closely control mail-in payments and receive them directly from the mail service so that you will have an audit record of checks that were in transit at cutoff date.

      These first-party checks can be used to verify customer's open balances. Many of these payments will be the subject of questions by customers who mailed their checks prior to cutoff date but don't know the date we received it. **KEY POINT:** *Your control and record of cash receipts will reduce follow-up time, since you may have already posted their payments to the verification statement.* It's not necessary to inform customers that their payments have come in, since their next statement will give them that information. However, if a reported payment is not received then, you must follow up with the customer to settle the matter.

If you cannot locate evidence of a reported payment, request the customer to send you a copy of both sides of the check. Note the date and endorsement on the check. If endorsed "For Deposit to XYZ," it must have cleared our account. Check the dates of clearance, and recheck our deposit records. If you still cannot locate the deposit, contact the proper bank official to resolve the matter. **IMPORTANT:** *If the check is written to XYZ, but bears a different endorsement which the bank accepted, we have problems.* Call the Manager of Internal Auditing for specific instructions.

Any account which does not cooperate in your verification work should be considered a potential problem. Five working days after you mail your second requests, follow up on any account which is not confirmed. Your first follow-up should consist of a phone call to the customer's Accounts Payable bookkeeper to learn if they had received the confirmation requests.

If not, arrange to give the clerk the pertinent information so that he or she can verify the balance. If they have received the confirm and are working on it, we can wait for their reply. **WARNING:** *If the account refuses to cooperate, it may be a danger signal.* It may mean that the account is not legitimate, is reluctant to give out information or may be shielding one of our employees. *Be careful* of the language you use in discussions with such people. Make a routine request, *do not use threatening or vulgar language,* and *do not state or infer that any illegal act has, or may have, occurred.*

Some people are reluctant to give information over the phone. If a face-to-face meeting can help resolve the matter, set it up. When you arrange such a meeting, request the sales department to assign a sales supervisor to accompany you. This representative will be a witness, but he or she should be cautioned to permit you to control the conversation.

Before attending such a meeting, review all documents relating to the sales and shipments, and be certain that there is legal proof of receipt of product by the customer. **CAUTION:** *If you anticipate problems,* request instructions from the Manager of Internal Auditing, who will determine if legal counsel is required. *Sales people will decide whether we will continue to do business with the account.*

6. From your review of aging schedules, select all large accounts for a study of the credit information on file. If there is any doubt about the solvency of an account, obtain a current credit report. To be safe, call the credit information company to find out if a credit alert notice has been issued on the company.

KEY POINT: *If an account is far behind in their payments, make certain that the sales department has taken appropriate action.* Usually these accounts are cut off from further credit. Some accounts may not be permitted to order product, while others may be shipped product on a C.O.D. basis while they work at reducing their open balance. Shipping Orders to such accounts should clearly state that only cash or cashiers checks must be received before product is delivered to the customer.

7. Notes receivable should be audited using the same basic approach we apply to open A/R. Copy the list of open notes from the previous audit which will be the starting point for the new review. Use our standard Note Receivable Confirmation letter form, and use normal audit routines in handling these verifications.

   KEY POINT: *Every note must be confirmed, even if it requires a personal visit.*

   To reduce travel expenses, you may use a private investigator located in the vicinity to visit the maker of the note. Or you may use a staff auditor if one is working in the area where the note maker resides. Discuss the matter with our staff administrator.
8. Sundry receivables will be made up mostly of amounts due from employees. Each open account must be confirmed; use personal letters rather than confirmation forms. *Personal visits and/or phone calls are permissible, but they must be affirmed by a written confirmation from the employee.*

   Copy the list of open items from the previous audit and confirm all other sundry items by using routine audit confirmation methods.

   That completes our audit instructions. We will now look at a sample internal audit program, used by the XYZ audit staff to review their Receivable transactions.

SAMPLE INTERNAL AUDIT PROGRAM

Form # RP 001 XYZ CORPORATION

INTERNAL AUDIT PROGRAM—RECEIVABLES

This program provides a review of systems, procedures and records used to control all receivables owing to the company. Before starting an audit of the receivable section, carefully review audit instructions for this activity, Form # RI 002. Also be sure that you are fully conversant with the Accounts Receivable computer program.

I. ACCOUNTS RECEIVABLE

Start your audit by becoming acquainted with the condition of the records and the personnel staffing. Discuss, with the EDP audit group, the selection of the date you will use for your cutoff. Minimize audit tie-up of receivable personnel and records, but do not rush through the program.

A. Standard Procedures:

1. All transactions affecting accounts receivable are entered into a computer data base, which tracks sales, adjustments and payments of all trade accounts.

2. The computer program prepares regular and special aging reports that are used to keep our accounts current.
3. Sales branches and other locations are responsible for accounts receivable that they service. These locations hold receivable records in open invoice files by routes or accounts. All local transactions are entered into the computer data base.
4. General ledger controls tie-in to the account balance in the computer. Local offices maintain subcontrols, which they balance daily and reconcile to the computer control at month-end.
5. Local offices periodically verify a selection of A/R's.
6. Offices that service an account check the credit of all new customers as well as those who alter their buying patterns.

B. *Audit Objectives,* are to determine the following:
1. Company policies, procedures and internal controls are adequate and are understood and followed by all employees.
2. All shipments of product are properly billed, and all billings are properly collected.
3. Customer pricing is correct and in conformity with company price lists and with FTC regulations.
4. Write-offs of accounts conform to company policies and good business practices, and are properly authorized and controlled.
5. All open accounts are bona fide. Their balances are correct, provable and collectible.
6. Adjustments to accounts are proper, controlled and approved.

C. *Audit Procedures:*

	Per. Cov.	*Audit By*
1. Immediately upon starting audit arrange for an auditor review, in the mail room, of all incoming mail and an audit listing of all first-party checks received in payment of accounts receivable.	____	____
2. Discuss A/R policies and accounting procedures with responsible supervisors and clerks doing the work.	____	____
3. Review Policy and Procedure manuals as they relate to accounts receivable. Review the A/R computer program user's manual.	____	____
4. Arrange to audit the month-end reporting of A/R detail. Tie-in to the subcontrols and follow through to the General Ledger control.	____	____
a. Observe procedures used by section personnel to verify accuracy of computer printouts.	____	____
b. Investigate adjustments and reconciling items.	____	____
c. Verify accuracy of subcontrol figures for selected outlying locations. Use phone, letters or contact audit groups working in the field.	____	____
d. Foot subcontrols and tie-in to final total.	____	____
e. Test check random subcontrols by running totals of all open account balances in those sections.	____	____

C. Audit Procedures	*Per. Cov.*	*Audit By*
f. *Test-check specific balances of selected accounts* by running adding machine tapes of each individual open item in the account. Verify adjustments.	____	____
5. Work with the EDP audit group to obtain verification statements for statistically selected accounts. Add to selection all past due accounts from aging reports and any accounts that appeared unusual during your original observations and balancing.	____	____
a. Use positive verification approach, and mail the first copy of confirm statements to customers.	____	____
b. Examine replies and resolve discrepancies. Post results to your control for audit statistics.	____	____
c. From your audit examination of first-party checks received, post payment to audit copy of individual account confirmation statements.	____	____
d. After seven working days, send second request to the accounts not already confirmed. (Mail or payment).	____	____
e. Perform alternate procedures on non-replies; phone, write or visit accounts as a last resort.	____	____
f. Summarize circularization results. Be certain that every exception is investigated and resolved.	____	____
6. From the EDP audit group, obtain most current aging schedules. After verifying mathematical accuracy of report, perform the following:	____	____
a. Test accuracy of aging schedule by tracing selected past due accounts from receivable files to schedule.	____	____
Also check sampling of past dues as reported on the computer printout to current files of receivables.	____	____
b. Investigate outstanding old account balances that exceed ten percent of established credit limits.	____	____
c. Review support for credit limits on random selection of accounts.	____	____
d. Determine what controls exist to ensure that credit limits are not exceeded.	____	____
7. Review files of accounts written off, and of very old accounts and those with disputed balances.	____	____
a. For those accounts not already circularized, obtain and mail positive audit verification statements.	____	____
b. Send second requests to accounts who have not paid and have not replied.	____	____
c. Make every effort to contact any non-reply account.	____	____
8. Review accounts receivable write-off procedure with the A/R supervisor and the chief financial manager.	____	____

C. Audit Procedures	*Per. Cov.*	*Audit By*
a. Obtain list of accounts written off since last audit; review support for charges and authority for W/O.	____	____
b. Examine customer files to see if any sales were made to accounts after write-offs.	____	____
c. *Contact collection agencies used and determine the recoveries since the last audit.*	____	____
d. Trace recoveries(8.c) to cash receipts and reserves.	____	____

Audit work reviewed by ______________________________ Date __________

II. NOTES RECEIVABLE

Before you start your audit, review the balance sheet account to determine the dollar value of notes receivable and list the open notes. If the previous audit report made any comments regarding notes, discuss with audit manager the current status, and follow up on these items.

A. Standard Procedures:

1. All notes are under the control of the custodian in the Office of the Secretary.
2. Custodian handles all necessary paperwork and is responsible for notifying appropriate personnel when any action is required.
3. Custodian maintains a log for recording all notes and contracts.
4. Original documents are filed, by maker, in the fireproof vault.
5. A copy of each document is numbered and filed numerically in the fireproof safe in the Secretary's area.

B. Audit Objectives, are to determine the following:

1. All notes are properly drawn and legally supported.
2. Notes are legitimate and still open.
3. Documents are properly recorded, safeguarded and administered.
4. General Ledger account accurately reflects the open balances.

C. Audit Procedures:	*Per. Cov.*	*Audit By*
1. Discuss processing, recording, reporting and filing of Notes Receivable with the Secretary and the custodian of documents.	____	____
2. Critically examine original document storage area to ensure that notes are adequately protected and not available to unauthorized personnel.	____	____
3. Examine working file area to see that document copies are protected from fire, theft and unauthorized use.	____	____
4. The list you copied from the previous audit files, should be compared to the current log of open notes.	____	____
a. Add to list, all notes written since last audit.	____	____
b. Examine supporting documents for all notes in file.	____	____

C. Audit Procedures *Per. Cov.* *Audit By*

c. Determine that notes were properly recorded, when applicable, with proper public officials. ____ ____
d. *Review disposition of any notes shown as open on your audit list but not in the current open file.* ____ ____
e. Trace pay off of notes through cash to the G/L. ____ ____

5. From your updated list of open notes receivable, prepare verification requests for all open notes. ____ ____
   a. Mail out first requests. ____ ____
   b. After seven days, mail second requests to all makers of unconfirmed notes. ____ ____
   c. Use alternate means to confirm 100% of open notes. ____ ____
6. Working from your updated schedule of notes, verify that interest payments have been received as due. ____ ____
   a. *For notes paid off since the last audit, verify that all interest due was received, properly processed and recorded.* ____ ____
7. Review procedures for notifying local management of necessary actions on notes and other contract matters. ____ ____

Audit work reviewed by ______________________ Date ________

III. SUNDRY RECEIVABLES

The bulk of sundry receivables is made up of permanent advances to traveling employees. Other transactions are infrequent and irregular. Review the account and the subsidiaries and cover the areas of risk.

A. Company Procedures:

1. Receivables from employees are controlled in accounting.
2. Employee loans, supported by a note, are filed by the Secretary.
3. Royalties, brokerage and commissions due, and other sundry items are controlled by the concerned operating department.

B. Audit Objectives, are to determine the following:

1. All sundry receivables are documented and properly valued.
2. All sundry items are legitimate, still open and collectible.
3. The General Ledger figure for Sundry Receivables is correct.
4. Company policy governing this area is understood and followed.

C. Audit Procedures: *Per. Cov.* *Audit By*

1. Discuss procedures used for handling and recording transactions with responsible personnel. ____ ____
2. Working with the copy of the schedule taken from the previous working papers, bring your schedule of Sundry Receivables up to date. ____ ____
   a. For new items since last audit, examine supporting documentation. ____ ____

C. Audit Procedures	*Per. Cov.*	*Audit By*
b. For items settled or adjusted since last audit, examine documents for propriety and proper approval.	____	____
c. *Any items paid off since last audit should be traced through to the General Ledger.*	____	____
3. From your updated schedule of open sundry receivables, prepare verification statements for all open items.	____	____
a. Mail first requests to all accounts.	____	____
b. After seven days phone any employees who have not responded to your first request. Mail second requests to all other non-replies.	____	____
c. Use alternate means to positively verify 100% of open items.	____	____
4. Where applicable, determine that interest payments have been received, properly processed and recorded.	____	____
5. Determine that all permanent advances are necessary and proper and that they conform to company directives.	____	____
a. Would credit cards obviate necessity for advances?	____	____
b. Are any advances really interest free loans?	____	____
6. Determine that adequate procedures exist to record, control and follow up on these sundry items.	____	____
7. Discuss with your audit supervisor, any areas not covered by this program.	____	____

Audit work reviewed by ______________________ DATE ________

Audit reports of Receivable must contain the following analysis:

SUMMARY OF AUDIT VERIFICATION STATISTICS:	NUMBER	DOLLAR VALUE
TOTAL A/R SELECTED FOR VERIFICATION?	______	__________
TOTAL VERIFIED?	______	__________
PERCENT VERIFIED?	______	__________
TOTAL QUESTIONABLE ACCOUNTS	______	__________

(Be certain to schedule the above statistics in your audit report.)

IV. INTERNAL CONTROL QUESTIONNAIRE—ACCOUNTS RECEIVABLE

The following internal control questions should be answered as you perform the audit checks outlined in the audit program. **IMPORTANT:** *Be certain to list the names of employees who perform the functions listed in part B and write in all conflicting duties of these employees.*

A. Following practices indicate satisfactory internal controls.

1. Policies and procedures are understood and followed.
2. Controls insure that all shipments are recorded and billed.

3. There is adequate evidence to support all billings.
4. Sales at special prices are properly approved before shipment.
5. All credit memos are properly supported and approved.
6. A/R detail records are regularly balanced to control accounts.
7. Detail records are periodically balanced to controls by another, or supervisory employee.
8. All non-cash adjustments to the General Ledger control account are properly supported and approved.
9. Independent separate employees perform the inventory, invoicing, receivables and cash accounting functions.

B. *The following lists the functions performed by named employees.*

Functions:	*Name/Position*	*Conflicting Duties*
1. Approves credit limits	________	________
2. Writes up sales tickets	________	________
3. Authorizes shipments	________	________
4. Initiates billings	________	________
5. Posts Accounts Receivable	________	________
6. Receives collections	________	________
7. Works on inventory records	________	________
8. Initiates credit memos	________	________
9. Approves credit memos	________	________
10. Authorizes bad debt write-off	________	________
11. Approves non-cash adjustments	________	________
12. Balances detail receivable records to control accounts	________	________

C. *Internal Control questions:*	*Yes*	*No*	*Remarks*
1. Are control copies of shipping records adequately controlled and safeguarded?	____	____	________
a. Do unauthorized personnel have access to these documents?	____	____	________
2. Do controls insure the following:			
a. All orders and shipping notices are transmitted to data processing?	____	____	________
b. Billings are subsequently issued?	____	____	________
c. Bookkeeping copies are received, and billings entered into A/R control?	____	____	________
d. Accounts receivable bookkeeper does not have access to cash receipts?	____	____	________
e. Accounts receivable files are properly safeguarded at all times.	____	____	________

C. Internal Control questions	*Yes*	*No*	*Remarks*
f. *No delays exist between transmission of data and actual billing?*	____	____	____
3. Are transmittal slips used to control documents forwarded to data processing?	____	____	____
a. Are they consecutively numbered?	____	____	____
b. Are all numbers accounted for?	____	____	____
c. Are hash total controls utilized?	____	____	____
4. Is a register maintained of shipment data sent to the computer for billing?	____	____	____
a. Is it followed up daily?	____	____	____
5. Are invoices promptly prepared?	____	____	____
a. Are delays in billing investigated?	____	____	____
6. Any errors spotted on computer invoices?	____	____	____
a. *Is procedure adequate to spot errors?*	____	____	____
b. To correct errors?	____	____	____
7. Do procedures require salesmen to route all orders directly to date entry?	____	____	____
a. Are substitute trained data phone operators available?	____	____	____
1) Do they have conflicting duties?	____	____	____
b. Are shippers checked to computer invoices by other than data operators?	____	____	____
c. Are orders promptly shipped from distribution points?	____	____	____
d. Are procedures adequate to insure that shipments and billings will follow?	____	____	____
8. Is a hard copy retained of all data transmitted to the computer?	____	____	____
a. Is the retention period appropriate?	____	____	____
9. Are control copies of shipping manifests removed in office be-			

C. Internal Control questions	*Yes*	*No*	*Remarks*
fore loading?	___	___	___
a. If not, are copies of cover sheets retained in office as ticket control?	___	___	___
10. *Are delivery documents signed by the customer and properly safeguarded?*	___	___	___
11. Does someone, other than bookkeeper, reconcile A/R detail to G/L balance?	___	___	___
12. Does supervisor periodically receive, control and mail out customer statements?	___	___	___
13. Are credits granted to customers properly supported, approved and controlled?	___	___	___
a. If cash credits appear excessive, do supervisors call customers to verify that they actually received credit?	___	___	___
b. Do immediate supervisors promptly receive copies of all C/M's issued?	___	___	___
14. Do managers approve all sample tickets?	___	___	___
15. Does office employee spot check weight and/or quantities on billings to see if the correct bracket price was used?	___	___	___
a. Is a price check made of billings for special price distressed shipments?	___	___	___
b. Are extensions checked for accuracy?	___	___	___
c. Are customers notified of C.O.D. invoice errors by postcard?	___	___	___
1) Are customer signatures obtained for all refunds?	___	___	___
16. *Are returned customer checks immediately charged back to the proper account?*	___	___	___
a. Is sales promptly notified?	___	___	___
17. Do office managers have authority to stop credit to poor risk accounts?	___	___	___

C. Internal Control questions:	*Yes*	*No*	*Remarks*
a. If not, is sales department promptly advised of adverse credit information?	____	____	____________
b. Are salesmen informed of "skips" or bankrupts to forestall future credit?	____	____	____________
18. *Does sales management review credit information before granting credit to new accounts?*	____	____	____________
19. Is weekly aging schedule prepared and circulated to all personnel concerned?	____	____	____________
20. Is effort made to collect before a W/O?	____	____	____________
a. Do all concerned parties give prior approval to all account write-offs?	____	____	____________
21. Based on your review, do we have a good system of internal control over A/R?	____	____	____________

Questions answered by ______________________ Date __________
Answers approved by ______________________ Date __________

V. INTERNAL CONTROL QUESTIONNAIRE—NOTES RECEIVABLE

A. Following are listed practices that indicate good internal control.

1. Notes are negotiated by an operating department.
2. Notes are drawn up by the legal department.
3. Notes from outsiders are registered with proper authority.
4. Original copy is received and filed by the Office of Secretary.

B. Internal Control questions:	*Yes*	*No*	*Remarks*
1. Are all notes properly documented and signature notarized?	____	____	____________
2. Have all notes been properly registered?	____	____	____________
3. When paid, are the originals returned to the maker?	____	____	____________
4. *Does custodian see proof of payment before releasing an original?*	____	____	____________
5. Are originals ever accessible to unauthorized personnel?	____	____	____________
6. Does system insure that custodian keeps up on due dates, and notifies employees concerned on a timely basis?	____	____	____________

Questions answered by ______________________ Date __________
Answers approved by ______________________ Date __________

VI. INTERNAL CONTROL QUESTIONNAIRE—SUNDRY RECEIVABLES

A. *Following are listed practices that indicate good internal control.*

1. Separation of duties between the department that initiates the transaction and those that keep and control the records.
2. Monthly notices mailed, advising accounts of current status.
3. Evidences of obligation and all supporting documentation are filed by document custodian and are not available to other employees.
4. A separate schedule is maintained of all open obligations.

B. *Internal Control questions:*	*Yes*	*No*	*Remarks*
1. Are evidences of debt and associated records adequately protected?	____	____	____________
2. For employee permanent advances:			
a. Does custodian check for proper job classification and approval?	____	____	____________
b. Is system adequate to notify custodian of job change or employee termination?	____	____	____________
3. Does custodian see proof of payment before releasing documents?	____	____	____________
a. Does custodian retain evidence of payment in the "closed" file?	____	____	____________
4. Does independent supervisor periodically verify schedule of open items with individuals or operating departments?	____	____	____________
a. Does supervisor run tape of open items and tie-in to ledger balance?	____	____	____________
b. Are all adjustments to this account carefully scrutinized?	____	____	____________

Questions answered by ______________________ Date __________
Answers reviewed by ______________________ Date __________

CRITICAL POINTS

A large number of employee defalcations are concerned with the handling and reporting of sales and collections. These peculations frequently escape detection because an internal auditor overlooked some "inconsequential" discrepancy. The following list contains brief descriptions of some of the most frequently used methods of manipulating receivables. If you encounter some of these danger signals, be on the alert.

EIGHT DANGER SIGNALS TO WATCH OUT FOR

1. There are many cases of withholdings of cash by salespeople who are authorized to make collections. It is a common practice for salespeople to "borrow" company funds and lap their accounts to cover the action. They apply collections against older balances and juggle accounts so that office people will not become suspicious. Usually the borrowing continues until the amount is too large to hide, and credit limits are exceeded and many accounts become past due.

   Routine circularization of accounts is designed to detect such manipulations. Also, the audit comparison of incoming first-party checks to open account balances should disclose such withholdings.

2. Many salespeople develop a special relationship with some of their customers and gain their complete trust over a period of time. Some salespeople take advantage of this trust to cheat the customer.

   There are many cases on record of a salesperson either altering or substituting an invoice in the customer's open payable files so that more money could be collected than was actually due. The salesperson regularly referred to the last open invoice for prior order data, to help write up a new order. During the preparation of a new order the old open invoice is altered or exchanged for one that had already been prepared. The customer pays the newly inflated invoice amount and the salesperson turns in the old correct amount and pockets the difference. **NOTE:** *If the customer pays by first party check, these manipulations are routinely spotted during an audit comparison of first party checks to open charges.* If the customer pays by cash, this type of manipulation is very difficult to detect. A sales supervisor riding a route to observe a salesperson's job performance may notice an unusual procedure that arouses suspicion. Contact with the customer and comparison of invoice numbers and amounts will disclose any fraudulent action.

   Sometimes the audit circularization of open balances brings the correct amount due to the customer's attention. The customer's natural curiosity and queries of the auditor should lead to disclosure.

3. There have been cases where accounts receivable bookkeepers have extracted unpaid invoices out of an open invoice file system and have offered the invoices to customers for a percentage of the amount due. **KEY POINT:** *Accounts that cooperate in such schemes commit criminal conspiracy and remain liable for the original debt.* This type of manipulation is difficult to detect if the bookkeeper can enter adjustments to the control account. If adjustments are not made, the detail will not tie in to the controls, and the discrepancy becomes apparent during a routine internal audit.

Once the discrepancy is noted, the major problem is to locate the missing invoices. Auditor ingenuity and hard work can usually locate a copy of the missing invoices by comparing the shipping copies to the paid copies supporting cash receipts and relief of receivables. Good numerical control of documents is an invaluable tool in these cases.

If adjustments have been made to cover the extraction of invoices, the auditor can detect such acts through a review of adjustments. **TIP:** *If an adjustment was made merely to bring the detail into balance with the control, the amounts involved become important.*

It is a long and costly job to recheck all transactions for a period of time, unless the operations are computerized. Before reaching a final decision, other periods should be examined to see how often these adjustments were permitted in the past and how much money was involved. Reconstruction of the accounts will disclose the names of customers whose invoices were involved. **CAUTION:** *When questioned, these customers will give excuses for their actions;* but they will usually cooperate fully in the investigation if they are certain that they will not be prosecuted.

4. In a variation of the above practice, when accounts receivable bookkeepers have access to cash receipts, they may misappropriate cash and prepare an adjusting journal entry to cover the withholding. They merely remove and destroy the related invoice. This throws their detail out of balance with the control figure.

   The bookkeeper prepares a journal entry to correct the condition, and if the amount is not large the entry will often be approved to correct an alleged minor error and save clerical time. **NOTE:** *This type of manipulation usually starts on a small scale, but early successes lead to more frequent and greater withholdings.*

   Audit review of adjusting entries might disclose such problems. Upon noting this type of adjustment, a study of earlier periods is made to see if there is a pattern. If one exists, all accounts are reconstructed from the shipping records through to the paid invoices to identify missing invoices. If shipping, billing, receivable and cash functions are computerized, such a review can be programmed and performed by the computer. A manual review of this type can be time consuming. However, once the missing tickets have been reconstructed, auditor contact with customers will usually reveal the manipulation.

5. Credit memos provide a common device for hiding the withholding of collections. The credit memo is prepared, but never given to the customer. It is for the amount of cash that the culprit withheld, and the memo plus the reported collection totals the invoice that has been paid. These memos may be written by deliverypeople, salespeople, clerks, cashiers or

even supervisors when they collect money from accounts. **TIP:** *Internal audit technique of comparing first party checks to open charges may uncover this type of manipulation,* as the customer pays for the full charge even though the C/M relieves the account of a portion of the amount due. Contacting the customer will usually establish that the buyer is not aware that a C/M has been issued.

The major element of control is operational. **KEY POINT:** *A supervisor must see evidence of justification for issuance of a credit and should not approve until satisfied that adjustments are proper.* If credits cover returned product, evidence of product receipt should support the C/M.

6. A method frequently used to manipulate accounts receivable is to run a cash transaction through as a charge sale. The cash collected is borrowed by the culprit, who usually fully intends to return the money. If unable to repay such withholdings, adjustments or credit memos are used to balance the accounts. This type of manipulation is detected during audit verification of open accounts or through the audit review of credits and adjustments.
7. Cases of credit abuse are frequently reported. **CAUTION:** *A sham company may rent a storage location and open for business. They establish credit at a moderate limit, and pay their bills promptly for several months.*

   When they consider that the time is right, they hand out very large orders to their recently established suppliers. When it is necessary, they explain that they are about to launch a major sales campaign and want to be able to supply their customers' demands. They may give a reluctant supplier a check in advance of shipment, which will later bounce.

   When all of the ordered product is delivered, the culprits load it up and haul it away, and the unhappy suppliers are left with worthless accounts on their books.

   KEY POINT: *These scams are more likely to occur when orders are taken by telephone, and salespeople or sales supervisors do not make personal calls on telephone accounts.*

   The internal review of the controls over credit to customers leads the auditor into a study of credit files to determine adherence to established credit limits. If these limits are exceeded or if they appear to be high for unknown accounts, the auditor should try to persuade sales management to visit the customer and reappraise the credit limit. **CAUTION:** *If phone customers place unusually large orders, these should be viewed with suspicion.*
8. Custodians of notes and sundry receivables sometimes become involved with debtors, and have been known to destroy documents so as to hide the indebtedness. Auditors must carefully reconstruct the action in these accounts, starting from the schedule in the previous audit working papers

and tracing item by item through the general ledger account. Sometimes, such an audit review will induce the custodian to discover a document which had been "mislaid." **WARNING:** *Auditors should be particularly careful when permanent advances to employees are involved.* When close friendships develop between the custodian and a debtor, such items are sometimes improperly "adjusted" to reduce or eliminate the amount owing.

Chapter 13

Auditing Inventory Transactions

Not everything that is sold in business is treated in the same manner by accountants. Some people sell words or ideas, some sell money, some sell personal services—all of these "products" are not listed as inventory in current accounting practice. Enterprises that offer a physical product that is readily identifiable and that is stored until sold, carry the costs of these products in a balance sheet account labeled Finished Goods Inventory. The account represents an important asset and is the income producing element in the business life of many entities. One company's finished product is often another's raw materials. Inventory is produced, purchased, stored, sold and delivered in the hope of producing a profit.

In this chapter we will be concerned with all types of inventory items that have been produced or purchased and then stored until used or sold and shipped. Product can be stolen or misappropriated at any point in production, storage or shipment. Internal auditors have developed sophisticated procedures to track and account for inventory items during periods of storage and shipment to the ultimate consumer.

This chapter deals with the timely recording of receipt of product or materials, the storage in the warehouse and in-house movements, shipments to customers and the proper billings for all products moved. We'll consider the internal controls and accounting for all of these activities with particular attention to adjusting entries that could hide the theft of product. And we'll close with some examples of conversions relating to the handling of inventories and records.

Background for Audit Program

We will use as a sample inventory audit program, one that applies to the mythical XYZ Corporation, which produces, buys, stores and distributes products throughout the world. Located in the main office of XYZ is the Finished Goods Inventory control section. The section supervisor reports to a Financial Department Controller and is responsible for accurate and timely reporting of all U.S. inventory transactions and for the control of the balance sheet account.

The inventory control section is not responsible for inventory variances at any specific location but works with local people in their attempt to locate and resolve these discrepancies. The section receives copies of all finished goods inventory records produced in the corporate computer department. Every inventory location is responsible for controlling, safeguarding and reporting their own products; but every inventory transaction is run through the computer.

The computer receives a record of all materials or products that enter a building, tracks these items through the production line; it adds all purchases and follows their movement until written off or billed to a customer. The inventory system interacts with other programs that do the following:

- Control production and compute standard costs;
- Schedule deliveries, prepare shipping documents and the covering billings;
- Generate orders for product to be delivered to sales and distribution locations; and
- Report to every location holding inventory, the quantity of each item that they should have in stock at the beginning of each day.

It is a real-time system that enables any location with a terminal to access their current book inventory at any time during the day. Full daily stock status reports are only printed each morning.

Scheduled reports, run after all pertinent daily entries are entered into the system, are printed at the computer center and immediately delivered to the inventory control section. Location reports are printed at each location every morning. *Special reports are printed on request and delivered the morning following the request.*

Adjustments to inventory accounts are entered into the computer at each inventory location where built-in security systems insure that a data terminal can only enter inventory transactions affecting its location. When two locations are involved in an adjustment, both must enter their respective end of the transaction, and the computer reports on related entries that don't jibe. Adjustments, which must be entered locally, may be instigated by the main office inventory control section, but this section can only enter adjustments for inventories in the public warehouses that it controls.

Standard inventory reports are printed on a scheduled basis and distributed to concerned departments. **NOTE:** *Special reports are available to personnel authorized to receive such information.* Requests for special reports are routed through the inventory control section which disseminates inventory information. Copies of special reports are retained in the central inventory control files.

Except for shipments to and from public warehouses, the inventory control section does not have any authority to order the movement of product. This section and the cost department have the authority to instruct locations to make adjusting entries, but a location would refuse to make an adjustment that it knew to be wrong. Adjustments are authorized by administrative messages, and a copy is retained as support at any location that enters an adjustment into the system.

A by-product of the inventory system is an In-Transit Report. The computer tracks every shipment of product entered into the system until it is acknowledged as received. An In-Transit report is printed daily at both the shipping location and the destination. The central inventory control section receives a daily report of all shipments in transit, and follows up on any shipment that is overdue.

Another feature of the computer system is the recording of overages and shortages reported on every receipt. Shipments of product are made by pallet load, and XYZ assumes responsibility for the accuracy of the pallet count. To increase productivity of the loading crews, product is loaded onto trailers and the doors closed and sealed before the tractor arrives to pull the load. The carrier is thus relieved of any count errors, unless there is evidence of tampering with the door seals. If a seal is broken or there are signs of tampering, the carrier is deemed responsible for shortages, and a claim is filed for any loss.

The basic Finished Goods Inventory system is designed to report in case lots. All reports show cases, though dollar values are often displayed. Much of the necessary inventory information input is computer generated. Computerized Production Reporting and Standard Cost systems input the standard costs and total quantities of items produced or purchased. An EDP Order Entry system provides data on all intercompany movements and a Sales and Invoicing system processes all shipments to customers.

All inventory adjustments are classified, summarized and reported by type of adjustment and location. At the close of each accounting period every location counts and enters their physical inventory and the computer calculates and prints an inventory variance report of the difference between the actual and book inventories. These reports are distributed to central inventory control, the cost department and the locations concerned. Headquarters office inventory control section reviews all pertinent reports and works with local personnel to help locate and resolve variances. It also advises the audit department of inventory disappearance problems that are developing at any location.

In order to audit all phases of the inventory control operation, the audit group conducts simultaneous audits of the central inventory control section, the cost department and all other operations which carry inventories in the headquarters building of the XYZ Corporation. These include a distribution center and a sales branch, both having a warehouse of finished goods inventory under their respective control. Each operation has unique features, and the audit program is designed to direct the auditor into these areas. The building also houses a plant which produces a product that, when packaged at the end of the production line, becomes the responsibility of the distribution center.

Branch salespeople periodically pick up product from the branch, for special delivery to specific customers, for sampling purposes or to have a supply of certain items available in their cars. This car stock inventory usually consists of new products or promotional items.

The plant and the distribution center are housed at one end of the building. All vehicles entering or leaving the area pass a security gate, where a truck scale is located. Each truck is weighed when it enters or leaves. The difference between the entering and leaving weight should equal the weight of product loaded on or dropped off.

The distribution center receives product from various company production plants and suppliers and stores the items until needed. It assembles large truck or railcar orders for branches or customers and ships the product to the designated delivery point. All shipments out of the distribution center are full truckload or carload quantities; lesser quantities are shipped from nearby sales branches. Product movement from the distribution center to the sales branch is controlled in the same manner as shipments to outsiders.

The local plant transfers the finished product to the distribution center as it leaves the production line and therefore carries no finished goods inventory. If outside storage space is required to store finished product, the distribution center makes the arrangement.

The sample internal audit program is divided for separate use in the audit review of the following:

1. *Centralized inventory control section;*
2. *Sales Branch's* and *Distribution Center's* finished goods inventory transactions; and
3. *Plant's* inventory responsibilities.

An audit of the Cost Department's inventory responsibilities is covered in Chapter 21 of this manual. Audit steps required to review an individual location's inventory transactions are described in special audit programs, designed for use in specific types of locations. These special programs appear in other chapters of this manual.

Audit findings during the review of the central inventory control section, or the cost department, frequently lead to surprise audit visits to specific locations that are experiencing discrepancies in their inventory transactions. The internal auditing function receives a monthly report which summarizes inventory variances for all company locations, and this report is used when preparing the audit schedule.

The sample program used for an audit of XYZ's inventory transactions follows.

FORM # II 006 INTERNAL AUDIT INSTRUCTIONS

A. Audit Caution.

Before starting an audit of inventory transactions, read carefully these instructions as well as the Inventory Audit Program Form # IP 005. When using the Inventory Audit Program, be certain to perform all the audit steps spelled out at the beginning of the Audit Procedures under the section titled, "FOR ALL INVENTORY LOCATIONS." Then use the particular section that applies to your assignment. **IMPORTANT:** *Schedule your audit so that you begin a few days before the end of the accounting period.* You will then be in a position to control the physical inventory count to be taken at the close of business on the last day of the accounting period.

Consider the supervisor of the EDP audit group as a member of your team, and use that office for requesting special inventory reports when and as required. Review variance reports of finished goods, raw materials, goods in process, ingredients and supplies. For the larger variances prepare a schedule by product group, of dollar values and quantities, both monthly and cumulative. From this schedule determine the items or product groups that require your major audit emphasis.

B. Audit Objectives are to determine the following:

1. Company policies and procedures are understood and followed.
2. Information entered into the computer data base is authentic, timely and accurate.
3. Computer-generated reports are complete and accurate.
4. National inventory figures as reported are accurate and represent saleable current product that is properly valued.
5. All product shipped is properly billed.
6. All product received is accurately counted, tested, reported and properly paid for.
7. All significant discrepancies are investigated and followed up.
8. All in-transit shipments of product are carefully monitored.
9. All adjustments to inventory are reviewed by authorized managers.

I. ALL INVENTORIES

C. Audit Procedures:

1. On the first day of your visit meet with managers responsible for the periodic count of inventories. Arrange for audit control of the physical count of all merchandise, materials and supplies on hand and in outside storage. Request that you be notified when storage areas have been cleaned and product arranged in an orderly manner.

   At least two independent counts should be made of each selected item. Assign auditors to be part of several count teams.
2. Counting inventories can be a dirty job. Auditors should bring coveralls, or other suitable clothing, to the job on count days. Also bring appropriate shoes as these counts entail much walking and some climbing. Discuss with the warehouse foremen the special clothing they may have available for the auditor's use.

3. Draw up a map of the area to be counted and prepare a schedule showing the numbers on the pallet cards which you will assign to specific rooms. Be sure that counts include part cases and any items set aside for any reason.
4. Confirm inventories stored or consigned in outside locations. Where feasible, confirmation should be by physical audit count. If visits are made, note the condition of the warehouse and the care given to our products. Also attempt to determine if the outside storage location is necessary, advantageous and economical. **NOTE:** *Distances of outside storage from locations being audited, and value of product stored, may not justify a visit.* If so a direct written confirmation from the warehouse will suffice. Submit a list of outside locations not visited to the audit manager, who may elect to schedule a visit at a later date when auditors are in the area.
5. Public warehouses are legally responsible for product under their control; and movements are evidenced by warehouse receipts. These warehouses are very careful to obtain properly authorized paper work. **KEY POINT:** *Any discrepancies at these locations, which are contested by the warehouse, should be followed up by an audit visit.* You should review all pertinent documentation and give the warehouse an opportunity to tell you of their problems in dealing with us.
6. The computerized Standard Cost system establishes the final cost at which materials and finished goods will be transferred in the coming month. Actual costs incurred during the current month are used as the basis for setting the new month's transfer prices.

   Final costs are not official until all costs have been entered into the computer system, usually by the close of the third working day. A preliminary cost report is run on the last day of the month, and this is used to value the first inventory reports. A revised dollar value report is run when the final costs have been computed. *This revised dollar value report is the one that you should work with when tying inventory values into the General Ledger figure.*
7. To prepare for a physical count of inventories, before the count starts, thumb tack the three-part inventory count card to the top pallet of each row of product. The first tear off part will be taken by the first team to reach the merchandise. The second tear off part is removed by the second team, and the top stub of the card will remain on the pallet until all counts have been reconciled. The in-charge auditor will personally remove the stubs, accounting for each number which was assigned to each area. **IMPORTANT:** *Make certain that you have the same number of count cards as stubs.*
8. Before tacking the count card to the pallets, write in the space provided the product number and description of merchandise to be counted. If a storage line contains several products, use a separate count card for each pallet of product. The counters will merely write the product number and their count on the cards as they work the area. **KEY POINT:** *At comple-*

tion, while reconciling counts, be certain to verify that both count cards report the same product number and that it conforms to the number on your stubs.

9. If computerized counting devices are used, the count report will be listed in product number sequence. Compare the two listings by sight, if necessary, or by computer printout for differences. Conduct an audit recount of the product where differences exist. If this recount agrees with either original count, accept the majority decision. **NOTE:** *If all three counts differ, the in-charge auditor and the warehouse manager will count and agree on the proper figure.*
10. Counting of product in freezers presents a special problem. You must wear the protective outer clothing required whenever you enter the freezer area. Freezer gloves make it difficult to write. Your stay in freezers should be limited to fifteen minute periods.

    If you do not use computer entry devices, use your microrecorder to record your counts. When you take your breaks, play back and note the counts that you recorded and be certain that data is correct. If tape is not perfectly clear, recount items in question during the next trip into the cooler. Play back your recordings frequently to ensure that the recorder is working properly.
11. Be certain that your count includes all product in the warehouse. Receipts, delivery returns and put-up orders should be clearly marked as *before* or *after* inventory to reduce confusion, if you later need to recount any product having a large variance. Follow through on these items to see that they were recorded in the proper period.
12. *Your inventory audit work is not complete until you verify that the inventory you counted was correctly valued and included in the national computer report that you tied-in to the General Ledger.*
13. All inventory data is entered into the central computer data base through remote terminals located at or near all inventory locations. Employee work schedules are arranged so that all transactions are entered into the computer before the location shuts down for the night. Some employees are scheduled to arrive early to separate and distribute the daily and special inventory reports that are run off on the location's printer. These reports are ready for review and action when the location starts its morning operations.
14. A description of the proper procedure for working with this internal audit program appears in the Introduction to the Audit Programs section of your manual. Read this information carefully.

II. RAW MATERIALS AND GOODS-IN-PROCESS INVENTORIES

C. *Audit Procedures:*

1. Much of our raw materials are stored in public storages, and it at times is difficult to identify. You must be particularly alert when verifying fungible goods in an outsider's storage facilities.

KEY POINT: *Be reasonable and prudent in your verification work, but be certain to perform at least the minimum checks necessary to assure you that the correct quantity and quality of our materials are on hand.*

The mere presence of a tank does not insure that it contains the quantity and quality of product that we placed there. Visual audit confirmation of quantity is required, and lab tests of samples of contents are necessary to assure that product has not been adulterated or substituted. **CAUTION:** *The addition of water to liquid materials is often difficult to detect with the naked eye.*

Visual verification of these materials can be risky. You may need to climb to a storage tank's top to view the upper level of materials stored therein. When making audit counts under adverse conditions, be sure to use your microrecorder to note calibrations, product color, estimated density and other significant data.

2. Goods-in-process inventories are generally estimates as to the stage of production. Lab tests will establish the percentages of the various materials contained. These ratios when applied to estimated quantity will give you a good total of various materials in process.

   Many of our operations don't shut down for the night until they have completed manufacturing all the raw materials that have been taken into the processing area. Permit these departments to complete their day's operations before taking your inventory count.

III. FINISHED GOODS INVENTORIES

C. *Audit Procedures:*

1. Freezer items are stored in bins that are stacked to the ceiling and difficult to reach. Product is moved by mechanized conveyers that are computer controlled. Perpetual inventory records are real time and can be viewed on the terminal screen in the freezer control room. Your count of frozen products can normally be made in the control room.

   Test-check a sampling of product against the perpetual record. If you select product that has a small quantity, you will speed up your count; however, select at least three items from bins that are full. Instruct the control operator as to which bins to order out, and observe that products from the selected bins are moved.

   When the product arrives at the exit from the freezer, count the stock and immediately return it to storage. Keep product under observation until it is returned to freezer storage. Observe that perpetual records accurately reflect the outward movement and the subsequent return to stock.

   When you order test product out of a bin, if quantities do not correspond to the perpetual record, something has gone wrong. **IMPORTANT:** *You are probably witnessing a serious breach in operations.* Do not leave the control room until the local manager or the assistant manager arrives. *If you are not satisfied with corrective actions taken, call the Manager of Internal Auditing for instructions.*

2. Daily stock status reports are printed every morning at each sales branch and distribution center. These reports show available finished product and the projected movement, in and out, based on orders entered into the computer. This report enables locations to estimate the product cuts on orders that they will be forced to make during the day, and to allocate scarce product among their customers. All locations also receive a computer-generated preliminary order for finished products to be shipped to their locations. They review the report, make any changes that they believe necessary and release it to the computer for preparation of official shipping orders.
3. All locations also receive a daily in-transit report which lists all incoming shipments intended for their operation which have not been reported as received. They also get a report of all outbound shipments they have made which have not as yet been reported as received. Any unusual delays are followed up by locations involved.
4. The computer inventory system automatically writes off small finished goods variances. The system operates on full cases, and small variances usually result from breaking cases open and selling part cases. Broken case variances frequently offset from month to month.

   The computer accumulates and reports on all variance adjustments. Locations study these reports carefully to ensure they are not losing product that gets buried in the automatic write-off feature.
5. When Salespeople pick up car-stock merchandise, or when consignment inventories are sent out to customers, the product movement must be authorized by a standard order form. When the shipment is made or product picked up, the billing document shows the salesperson involved. Consignments also show the name of the customer to whom product is shipped, and the invoice notes that it is a consignment.

   A salesperson who sells car-stock inventory, prepares an invoice and notes that it was filled from car-stock. The salesperson is relieved of the product and the customer is billed. When a salesperson checks consignment inventory, the customer is billed for product sold and the invoice notes that consignment inventory is involved. Records are adjusted to show the sale. Branches maintain a separate record for every salesperson's car-stock and for consignment locations.
6. Salespeople are given a book of disbursement drafts that they use to reimburse some of their "cash" accounts for product or coupons picked up by the salesperson. The top part of the form is the draft itself, and the lower part itemizes the product or coupons picked up by the salesperson. Product that salespeople pick up is returned to the warehouse, where it is taken into stock as saleable merchandise, examined and appropriately reclassified, if not saleable, into dumps or unsaleables.

   The branch office makes certain that they see evidence that the product was returned to the warehouse for all drafts issued by salespeople for product pickup. Coupons, which the salespeople redeem by issuing a disbursement draft to our customer, are returned to the branch office where they are reconciled to the drafts issued.

Form # IP 005 XYZ CORPORATION

INTERNAL AUDIT PROGRAM—INVENTORIES

I. FINISHED GOODS INVENTORY

An internal audit of finished goods inventory transactions encompasses everything from cased production or receipt of finished goods to its shipments and subsequent billings. For our purposes we will consider by-products as finished products and make no distinction, though in the program for auditing the Cost Department, we review cost considerations that apply to by-product production valuations.

A. *Company Procedure:*

1. Complete counts of month-ending physical inventories are taken at designated inventory locations. Some operations are only required to count their inventory once or twice a year.
2. Computer-generated inventory reconciliation report compares book figure to reported case count and shows all variations in cases.
3. Pricing of inventory items is calculated by computer which uses the National Standard Cost program.
4. Location inventories are controlled by local office managers using the National Finished Goods Inventory Control computer program.
5. Special inventory reports are used to follow-up on in-transit shipments and reported overs and shorts on deliveries.
6. Computer programs track all inventories at all locations and value national inventories which tie-in to the General Ledger.

B. *Audit Objectives,* are to determine the following:

1. Computer reports are accurate, complete and timely.
2. Physical counts of product are taken in the prescribed manner and accurately entered into the computer data base.
3. Procedures insure that all adjustments to inventory are timely, legitimate, properly approved and entered into the system.
4. Inventory reports, both scheduled and special, are used for their intended purpose by the appropriate personnel.

C. *Audit Procedures:*	*Per. Cov.*	*Audit By*
1. *FOR ALL INVENTORY LOCATIONS*		
a. Carefully study Inventory Instructions, Form # II 006, and the Finished Goods Inventory Control System's Users Manual. Review this Program and the associated Internal Control Questionnaire.	____	____
b. Review departmental written procedures, listing of personnel assignments and standard work flow charts.	____	____
c. Check accuracy of latest computer inventory summaries and tie figures into the General Ledger.	____	____
1) Trace selected items of opening inventory to the previous months reported closing inventory. Follow up on any differences.	____	____
2) For selected test items, compile quantity of receipts from all receiving reports and compare to summary.	____	____
d. For selected items, compare closing inventory to		

C. Audit Procedures *Per. Cov.* *Audit By*

monthly sales to evaluate inventory levels. ____ ____
e. Review freight bills and bills of lading and match to receiving reports to determine that product was received and recorded in the proper period. ____ ____
f. *Check procedures for determining that incoming truck or rail car seals have not been broken or replaced.* ____ ____
g. Spot check to determine that computer reports are arithmetically correct. Look for massive errors. ____ ____
h. Review documentation and controls over product stored in outside locations. (Including consignments.) ____ ____
   1) Warehouse receipts and signed consignment invoices should be safeguarded, and in total they should equal inventory reports of goods in such storage. ____ ____
   2) Shipments out of public warehouses should only be made on authorized written instructions. ____ ____
   3) Items should not be stored for excessive periods. ____ ____
   4) Review procedure for charging consignee for product sold and public warehouses for product shortages. See that such cash receipts are promptly reported. ____ ____
   5) *Determine that storage dates are considered when deciding which lots to withdraw from warehouse.* ____ ____
   6) Determine that company supervisors periodically count product in outside storage and tie-in to our records. ____ ____
   7) Arrange to make an audit verification count at selected warehouses that carry large stocks. ____ ____
i. When counting freezer stock, select several test bins and have product mechanically moved out of freezer. ____ ____
   1) Record perpetual balance in bin before outward move. ____ ____
   2) Stop product at exit from freezer and count; quantity should match perpetual record. If not: ____ ____
      a) *Have product held until top management arrives.* (Follow procedures outlined in instructions.) ____ ____
   3) Examine terminal screen and note that perpetual record now shows bin as empty. Authorize return of product. ____ ____
   4) Examine screen to determine that the perpetual figure now accurately reflects the return of product. ____ ____

2. *CENTRAL INVENTORY CONTROL SECTION*
   a. Spot check standard cost prices used for the computer inventory settlement against standard costs on record in the Cost department for the same time period. ____ ____

C. Audit Procedures	*Per. Cov.*	*Audit By*
b. Review all adjustments initiated by the section for legitimacy, proper documentation and approval.	____	____
c. Obtain from EDP audit group a list of inventory reports that were printed for the previous month and compare to reports on file in the Inventory Control Section.	____	____
1) *Determine that ENDING balances on previous reports were identical to BEGINNING balances on new ones.*	____	____
2) Were all reports on file? Determine if they serve a useful purpose, or are unnecessary.	____	____
3) Discuss costs of special and routine reports with supervisor and *stress exception reporting features.*	____	____
d. Review administrative messages and correspondence that deal with the section's work in resolving variances.	____	____
1) Determine that variances in warehouses, controlled by the section, are promptly investigated and resolved.	____	____
2) Observe and review the way the section handles variance follow-up with responsible local personnel.	____	____
e. Review the section's actions relative to freight claims.	____	____
f. Review correspondence and other evidence of actions taken on in-transit shipments that were delayed.	____	____
g. At close of period in which auditors verified physical counts, obtain the period-end inventory reports.	____	____
1) Determine that the dollar value of ending inventory is reasonably close to previous comparable periods.	____	____
2) Compare total dollar value of inventory shown on the computer report to the General Ledger F/G balance.	____	____
3) If different, investigate and reconcile difference.	____	____
4) Examine all F/G monthly inventory J/E's for accuracy, appropriateness, legitimacy, and proper approvals.	____	____
5) Discuss with appropriate management *any journal entry that writes off a F/G inventory variances that does not relate to a computer reported variance.*	____	____
h. Observe section's procedures for teaching or informing local personnel in proper use of the computer system.	____	____
3. SALES BRANCH AND DISTRIBUTION CENTERS		
a. Tour warehouse area, docks, storage areas and prepare a layout to use to control your physical count.	____	____
b. Review company and the location's operating procedures with the warehouse manager. Discuss the technique for ordering stocks. Is the computer order used, as is?	____	____

C. Audit Procedures *Per. Cov.* *Audit By*

c. Observe warehouse workers' building orders, loading trucks and checking quantities. Discuss procedures with foremen. ____ ____

d. Check procedure used for sealing full F/G truck or rail shipments before they leave the warehouse. ____ ____

   1) *Determine that guard at gate verifies that seal number is same as noted on B/L and that it's intact.* ____ ____

e. Determine that warehouse manager periodically compares tickets turned in to dispatcher's schedule of weights for the load, to determine efficient use of trucks. ____ ____

f. Arrange to control and participate in the period ending count of physical inventories. ____ ____

   1) Place count cards on front pallets of lines of product after area is prepared, and final movement of stock has been accomplished. ____ ____
   2) Be certain that shipping and product return areas have been clearly separated for proper cutoff. ____ ____
   3) If product is received during count, see that items are properly segregated and marked as to inclusion. ____ ____
   4) If sales are made or items shipped during count, see that records are correct and properly noted. ____ ____
   5) Be certain that last transactions are clearly marked "before inventory" to insure proper allocation. ____ ____
   6) Observe all count teams in action, and determine that they make their counts in a conscientious manner. ____ ____
   7) Make independent audit counts and compare to count teams reports. Recount any differences. ____ ____
   8) Control count cards as they are turned in by both count teams. ____ ____
   9) Arrange cards in numerical sequence and compare counts. Have an auditor participate as a member of each recount team and determine correct count. ____ ____
   10) Determine that areas that should have been counted are included in totals. ____ ____
   11) Note if any damaged or unsalable goods are in the warehouse. Discuss with manager whether or not such items should be excluded. If so, list for subsequent tie-in to inventory adjustments. ____ ____
   12) During count make note of product that is near or past code date. Determine that items have been

C. Audit Procedures *Per. Cov.* *Audit By*

reported to the sales department for action. ____ ____

g. Review consolidation of inventory count cards in the location's office. ____ ____
   1) Obtain copy of recap sheet for audit files. ____ ____
   2) Determine that all count cards have been included. ____ ____
   3) Test footings and cross footings of recap sheet. ____ ____
h. If salespeople carry car-stocks make certain that the items are counted and included in reported inventory. (If not picked up as sales and reported as receivables.) ____ ____
   1) Follow same procedure for goods on consignment. ____ ____
i. When location's inventory reconciliation report is run obtain copy before location personnel can review it. ____ ____
   1) Verify shipments and sales figures to billings. ____ ____
   2) On a test basis tie-in counts shown on the inventory recap sheet to reported counts in the computer run. ____ ____
   3) Review the automatic write-offs of inventory items. ____ ____
   4) Review all adjustments and examine the location's supporting documentation. ____ ____
      a) *For product lost in transit, examine evidence and determine that appropriate freight claim is filed.* ____ ____
      b) For warehouse dumps verify quantities recorded, reasons, and proper approval. Determine that supervisors witness destruction of product. ____ ____
      c) Determine that all samples are approved by manager before product is released, and that recipient signs for product received. ____ ____
      d) Cutting losses, shrinkage and dumps at customers warehouses should be reasonable and supported. ____ ____
      e) Determine that computer billings support all transfers of product between locations, and that code line transfers are explained and approved. ____ ____
      f) *Carefully examine any unanalyzed adjustments.* ____ ____
   5) Study the reported variances and compare to previous reports to see if a pattern of loss is occurring. ____ ____
j. Review inventory reconciliation report with office and warehouse managers, and request that they investigate large loss items. Note their comments. ____ ____
   1) Where required, note that proper inventory adjustment is made in the following accounting period. ____ ____
k. Determine that the computer generated Overs and

C. Audit Procedures	*Per. Cov.*	*Audit By*
Shorts report is properly used.	____	____
1) *Review procedures for insuring that carriers return undelivered, refused or product overages to our warehouse.*	____	____
2) Determine that our procedures ensure that sales offices are promptly notified and that they bill customers for all overages accepted by the account.	____	____
3) Determine that shortages on delivery are properly accounted for and that accurate, approved C/M's are promptly issued to customers.	____	____
l. Review records of loading audits performed by warehouse supervisors and the follow-up work, if any, performed by the office.	____	____
m. Obtain copies of "product cut lists" for the previous month and determine reasons for consistent cuts.	____	____
n. Review procedure for handling warehouse cash sales.	____	____
1) Test-check to determine that all tickets are numerically accounted for.	____	____
2) *Select a sampling of tickets and trace them through warehouse collection reports for the period.*	____	____
3) Determine that all cash sales are promptly and accurately entered into the inventory system.	____	____
o. Determine that product sold at distressed prices are marked in a special way so that they cannot be returned for full price credit or replacement.	____	____
p. *Review methods used to destroy products, so they may not be removed from dumpsters and sold in open air markets.*	____	____
q. Determine that there is a designated area in the warehouse set aside for holding faulty manufactured product, which was received from an outside supplier.	____	____
1) See that product is controlled until returned.	____	____
2) Follow-up to determine that adequate credit was received from supplier and properly processed.	____	____

Audit work reviewed by ______________________ Date ____________

II. RAW MATERIALS AND GOODS-IN-PROCESS INVENTORIES

Sometimes it is difficult to differentiate between raw materials and finished goods, since the finished goods of one operation may be readily used as the raw material of another. Also, it is sometimes necessary to arbitrarily decide what materials are raw and what materials are goods-in-process. So long as distinctions are logical and are consistently applied, the differentiation may be accepted.

However, the values assigned must be reasonable and the quantities must be accurately reported at each stage of the production process.

A. *Company Procedures:*

1. Raw materials are ordered for delivery by plant material managers against blanket purchase orders placed by corporate buyers in the headquarters office.
2. Materials are received by trained receiving personnel at the special raw materials receiving docks.
3. Rail cars and trucks delivering raw materials are weighed as they enter and leave the company's property.
4. Quality control samples are taken and tests completed before any materials are officially received.
5. Raw materials are stored in designated specially prepared areas.
6. At the close of each accounting period, materials and goods-in-process are calculated and reported to plant inventory control.
7. The Standard Cost computer system calculates raw material costs as well as usage. It computes quantities of goods-in-process and reports all variances in quantities and/or dollar values.
8. Computer cost reports are printed locally and at computer center.

B. *Audit Objectives,* to determine the following:

1. Materials are tested and measured on receipt, before movement to storage area; and accurate records are prepared and processed.
2. Raw materials and goods-in-process are safeguarded and protected from contamination.
3. Receiving personnel are aware of, and follow, correct procedures.
4. Timely and accurate reports of raw material usage are prepared.
5. Month-end inventories are accurately counted and reported.
6. Lab tests are made in conformance with quality control specs.
7. Payments for materials conform to quantity and quality of goods actually received.

C. *Audit Procedures:*

	Per. Cov.	*Audit By*
1. Read the Standard Cost computer program's user manual, all of this program and the Internal Control Questionnaire before you start your audit.	____	____
2. Read Internal Audit Instructions Form # II 006. Follow the applicable steps listed in the Audit Instructions under Section I ALL INVENTORIES, Part C Audit Procedures, when you prepare to make your inventory count.	____	____
3. Discuss with the raw materials foreman and the plant materials manager the procedures used to order, receive, use and control the raw materials required by the plant.	____	____
4. Observe first hand the receipt of major raw materials, noting particularly the procedures used to test quality and determine correct quantity.	____	____

C. Audit Procedures	*Per. Cov.*	*Audit By*
a) *Follow quality control samples to lab and observe testing procedures.* What is done is sample does not meet minimum standards? Is product retested?	____	____
b) Observe weighing or measuring of receipts to determine that methods are accurate and germane. *Arrange for test of scales, dip sticks, and flow meters that have not been recently checked by outside agencies.*	____	____
c) Determine that system is adequate to detect and adjust for any quantity of materials that remain in rail or truck tankers. *Make certain that our receivings do not include the weight of water used to wash out the contents of tankers.*	____	____
d) Determine that door seals are checked on incoming delivery vehicles and compared to B/L notations, before the driver is permitted to break the seal.	____	____
5. Determine that materials are not used until quality and quantity have been agreed upon.	____	____
6. Critically examine raw materials storage areas for cleanliness, orderliness and accessibility of product.	____	____
a) Determine that security measures protect against unauthorized personnel in the storage area and against unreported withdrawal of product.	____	____
b) Observe system and controls over material withdrawals. Goods should only be moved on proper authorization.	____	____
7. Arrange with plant manager to control the period-ending count of in-plant materials. This includes materials which may be stored in outside warehouses, silos, bins or tank farms.	____	____
a) Auditors are to count and/or measure all materials and goods-in-process and compare their figures to those reported by the plant count teams. Any differences should be recounted and reconciled.	____	____
b) For upright tanks, auditor will carefully climb to the top of tank and observe the upper level of stored product.	____	____
1) The upper level of product should be established by dip stick or eyeballed against the calibrated scale imprinted on the inside of the tank.	____	____
2) Samples of tank contents should be *drawn from the spigot at the bottom of the tank.* Agitate contents, if appropriate. Samples should be taken to the lab and the *testing observed.*	____	____

C. Audit Procedures	*Per. Cov.*	*Audit By*
3) Results of tests of samples should conform to reported contents of each tank.	____	____
c) For product stored in facilities owned by outsiders, schedule by storage location the product description, quantity and specifications.	____	____
1) Assign auditors to visit all locations that store a significant quantity or dollar value of product. Visits should not be scheduled, but a prior phone call should be made to insure access to buildings.	____	____
2) Where product is stored in a separate building, or section of a building, see that area is clearly marked and that access is controlled.	____	____
3) Note conditions of storage of product. Measure or count product and compare to warehouse's record.	____	____
4) If our product is mixed with others, determine the quantities stored for others and then see that the total quantity in warehouse is *sufficient to cover all reported storage quantities for ALL clients.*	____	____
5) For fungible goods, fill a known receptacle with product and weigh it. Then apply the weight per volume to the total volume of the storage area to compute the total weight of product stored.	____	____
6) When calculating weight of product be certain to allow for the percentage of millage or waste. This factor should be available from official tests.	____	____
7) *If you have any doubts or suspicions,* take a sample of the stored product and arrange for a test to determine product, moisture, millage and waste.	____	____
8) Review system for releasing our product, noting whether they make certain that requisitions or shipping orders are properly authorized.	____	____
9) *If you encounter opposition to your audit steps, or notice discrepancies or suspicious records or actions, immediately contact audit administration.*	____	____
8. For goods-in-process and major raw materials, prepare a manual settlement starting with previous reported ending inventory, add purchases, deduct issues		

C. *Audit Procedures*	*Per. Cov.*	*Audit By*
and apply all adjustments to arrive at new book inventories. Compare to physicals that you counted and compute variances.	____	____
a) Compare your computed variances to those reported by the Standard Cost program and reconcile differences.	____	____
b) Explore the possibility that production employees are using an *outdated formula,* or one that differs from the formula used in the computer program.	____	____
c) Study all of the materials reported by the computer that you did not settle. If any items have large cumulative losses, discuss possible causes with inventory and production managers.	____	____
d) Check mathematical accuracy of computer generated raw material inventory and usage reports.	____	____
9. Review procedures and personnel used to move materials from storage to production or elsewhere.	____	____
a) Determine that all movements are properly authorized and promptly and accurately reported.	____	____
b) Determine that raw materials and goods-in-process are adequately protected against theft and contamination.	____	____
10. For goods-in-process, samples should be regularly taken by quality control and tested in the lab.	____	____
a) Ascertain that all test results are recorded as tests are made, and that they conform to expectations.	____	____
b) Discuss with lab foreman the retest policy, and *what is done if test results are beyond prescribed limits.*	____	____
11. Carefully review all adjustments made to inventories.	____	____
a) Determine that documentation adequately and completely explains the adjustment.	____	____
b) Determine that all adjustments are legitimate, properly authorized and approved.	____	____
c) Compare and tie-in adjustments which you examined to the computer reported adjustments.	____	____
12. Schedule and summarize all of the period's raw material receipts as reported by the receiving department.	____	____
a) Compare your summary of receivings to that reported by the Standard Cost computer program.	____	____
1) Check computer generated reports for accuracy.	____	____
2) Reconcile any differences.	____	____
b) Arrange to have your summary of receivings com-		

C. Audit Procedures	*Per. Cov.*	*Audit By*
pared to Accounts Payable reports of disbursements to suppliers of materials. Follow up on differences.	____	____
13. Verify that your dollar value of inventories jibes with values reported in the Standard Cost reports.	____	____
14. *For any sales of scrap from the production process, see that accounting and cash handling was proper.*	____	____

Audit work reviewed by ______________________ Date ____________

III. INGREDIENTS AND SUPPLIES INVENTORIES

In the production process various ingredients may be added to raw materials or used up while producing a finished product. The final result is often placed in a specially designed package to identify the item. Supplies, other than packaging, that are incidental to the production process are of no concern to us at this time. Audits of supplies used by the garage, janitors or offices are covered in other audit programs. Our concern here is with manufacturing supplies and ingredients that are necessary for producing a product.

A. *Company Procedures:*

1. Packaging and manufacturing supplies and ingredients are ordered out by the plant materials manager against corporate blanket P/O's.
2. Items are received at the general receiving dock and are later inspected for quantity and quality.
3. Items are stored in specifically designated areas.
4. Items are counted at each month-end and quantities are entered into the data base of the National Standard Cost computer program.

B. *Audit Objectives,* are to determine that:

1. All receipts are accurately reported, promptly tested and moved to designated storage areas.
2. Stocks are safeguarded and moved only on authority of properly approved requisitions, and all movements are accurately reported.
3. Stocks are accurately counted, reported and valued at month-end.
4. Billings for items received conform to quality, quantity and price of product ordered.

C. *Audit Procedures:*	*Per. Cov.*	*Audit By*
1. Carefully read *Internal Audit Instructions* Form # II 006 covering inventory transactions. Review this program and the related internal control questionnaire.	____	____
2. Arrange with plant manager to control month-ending inventory count of ingredients, manufacturing supplies and packaging supplies.	____	____
a) Perform independent audit count of selected valuable supply items and reconcile to plant's count.	____	____

C. Audit Procedures	*Per. Cov.*	*Audit By*
b) Supervise summarization of physical count, and retain a copy of the summary for your work papers.	____	____
c) Compare your count as shown on the summary to the computer generated Standard Cost reports. Reconcile any differences and study resulting variances.	____	____
1) Follow dollar values of inventories you counted through the cost reports into the General Ledger.	____	____
2) Investigate and reconcile any differences.	____	____
3) Examine all monthly journal entries for accuracy, reasonableness and proper approvals.	____	____
4) Discuss with appropriate management any large and consistent variances.	____	____
5) *Explore possibility that variances could be caused by production formulas being different from those used in the computer program.*	____	____
6) Check arithmetic accuracy of the computer reports.	____	____
3. Review procedures for insuring that oldest stock is drawn and used first. (FIFO basis.)	____	____
4. Review procedures for locating and disposing of obsolete packaging supplies.	____	____
5. If ingredients are date marked for use, determine that procedures insure that *NO ITEMS are used in production that have passed the code date.*	____	____
a) Evaluate controls over this important area.	____	____
6. Determine that packaging supplies, having free product offers imprinted, are kept under lock and key.	____	____
a) When such supplies are discarded, determine that plant uses procedures that insure that incineration or shredding is witnessed by a responsible supervisor.	____	____

Audit points reviewed by ______________________ Date ____________

INTERNAL CONTROL QUESTIONNAIRE

I. ALL INVENTORIES

A. The following procedures indicate satisfactory internal controls.

1. Computerized records that follow activities and transactions.
2. Comprehensive policy statements and procedures that are known to all employees and diligently followed.
3. Complete documentation of receipts and shipments supporting all entries into the computer system.

4. Periodic physical counts of inventories by responsible employees.

B. Performance of functions	*Name/Position*	*Conflicting Duties*
1. Order materials for stock.	______	______
2. Receive incoming shipments.	______	______
3. Move items from stock.	______	______
4. Authorizes movement of items.	______	______
5. Supervises physical counts.	______	______

C. Internal Control Questions	*Yes*	*No*	*Remarks*
1. Orders and Receivings:			
a. Does operation use national purchasing forms and procedures?	____	____	________
b. Are orders for product approved by supervision before officially released?	____	____	________
c. Do receiving personnel know of incoming shipments in advance?	____	____	________
d. Is *quantity* and *quality* of received goods verified *before* B/L is signed?	____	____	________
e. Do receiving personnel prepare their receiving reports without reference to order documents? (Blind receipt.)	____	____	________
f. Does someone other than receiver compare the blind receiving document to a copy of the shipping manifest before goods are moved from the receiving dock?	____	____	________
g. Are received items immediately moved to their designated storage area?	____	____	________
h. Is shipping area completely separated from receiving operations?	____	____	________
i. Are all receipts entered into computer?	____	____	________
j. Are full tank car receipts weighed or measured, at least on a test basis?	____	____	________
2. Stores:			
a. Are stocks stored so that oldest are drawn out first?	____	____	________
b. Are stocks adequately protected?	____	____	________
c. Are spoiled or obsolete stocks pulled and authorized for disposition?	____	____	________

C. Internal Control Questions	*Yes*	*No*	*Remarks*
d. Are all disposals properly reported?	____	____	____________
e. *Are discarded items mutilated so that they cannot be reused?*	____	____	____________
f. Are packaging supplies that offer free goods safeguarded as cash?	____	____	____________
3. Withdrawals and shipments:			
a. Are properly approved requisitions required for all withdrawals of stock?	____	____	____________
b. Are outside shipments only made on basis of properly authorized documents?	____	____	____________
c. Are quantities of products shipped verified against shipping documents?	____	____	____________
d. *Is care taken to insure that oldest stock is shipped first?*	____	____	____________
e. Are withdrawals and shipments promptly and properly input into the computer?	____	____	____________
4. Physical inventory counts:			
a. Do all sections have written inventory procedures, and are they followed?	____	____	____________
b. Are inventory cutoffs effective?	____	____	____________
c. Are two independent counts taken and compared and differences reconciled?	____	____	____________
d. Are differences between Production and Distribution counts reconciled?	____	____	____________
e. Are warehousing and storage areas neat, and is product stacked uniformly to facilitate moving and counting?	____	____	____________
f. Do office personnel periodically assist in taking physical counts?	____	____	____________
1) Do they participate in resolving variances of count from book?	____	____	____________
g. Is any product on hand ever excluded from the inventory count?	____	____	____________
h. Do supervisors check to insure			

C. Internal Control Questions	*Yes*	*No*	*Remarks*
that protective outer clothing is worn by everyone entering the cooler or freezer?	____	____	____________
i. Are physical counts made at frequencies dictated by the home office?	____	____	____________
j. *Do location personnel count inventories in outside warehouses?*	____	____	____________
k. Are outside warehouse inventory reports reconciled to our records?	____	____	____________
5. Miscellaneous:			
a. Are items that are slow moving, obsolete or overstocked reported to management?	____	____	____________
b. Are inventory areas accessible only to authorized personnel?	____	____	____________
c. Is there adequate control over goods that are dumped in our premises.	____	____	____________
d. Are outside storages selected according to policy and with home office approval?	____	____	____________
1) Do storage rates appear reasonable?	____	____	____________
e. Do outside storages only release goods on the basis of a written release order?	____	____	____________
1) Are invoices immediately processed for product covered by release orders?	____	____	____________

II. SALES BRANCH AND DISTRIBUTION CENTER INVENTORIES

C. Internal Control Questions	*Yes*	*No*	*Remarks*
1. Order and delivery:			
a. Is it possible for any F/G to be shipped without proper records being prepared, retained and promptly processed?	____	____	____________
b. Is there adequate checking and control of all merchandise shipped?	____	____	____________
c. Is any finished product held in the warehouse for any period after billing?	____	____	____________
d. Do loaders know in advance			

C. Internal Control Questions	*Yes*	*No*	*Remarks*
which driver will take the truck they are loading?	____	____	____________
e. *Do drivers have access to merchandise in the warehouse?*	____	____	____________
f. Are drivers rotated to various routes?	____	____	____________
g. Are truck returns (after inventory) added back to inventory count?	____	____	____________
1) Are they physically verified?	____	____	____________
2. Sales Operations:			
a. Are salesmen permitted to carry same car stock products for an extended period?	____	____	____________
1) *Is product periodically verified?*	____	____	____________
b. Do salesmen submit monthly inventories of stocks out on consignment?	____	____	____________
1) Are these compared to local records?	____	____	____________
2) *Are invoices immediately prepared for product that disappeared?*	____	____	____________
3) Are consignment stocks properly reported for inventory?	____	____	____________

Questions answered by ________________________ Date ____________
Answers reviewed by ________________________ Date ____________

CRITICAL POINTS

Anything that has intrinsic value or is convertible to cash is subject to misappropriation. Any item that can be packaged and stored can be stolen. The physical theft of product can occur at any time, and may be perpetrated by anyone inside or outside a company.

Effective physical safeguarding of inventories is a good determent to theft, and timely and accurate inventory reports can help reduce extensive losses by providing an early warning signal that thefts are occurring. **KEY POINT:** *No internal audit or internal security group can prevent thefts of inventory, but an alert auditor can spot loss signals and recommend appropriate action to reduce such thefts.*

Not all losses are caused by theft. Carelessness, inefficiency, failure to follow prescribed procedures and simple inertia account for many dollars of losses.

TEN DANGER SIGNALS TO WATCH OUT FOR

Following are some danger signals that might be noticed during an audit assignment. If any of these strike a responsive chord during your reviews, you will be well-advised to be on your guard.

A. RAW MATERIALS AND GOODS-IN-PROCESS

1. Though cases of abuse by public warehouses are rare, they do occur. There are records of tank farms that were filled with water instead of vegetable oil; allegedly full tanks that were partly or completely empty; warehouse intake tests that were patently false and empty warehouses that were supposed to be full.

   Even though it is an uncomfortable and dirty task, auditors must personally eyeball and determine the weight of stored product, and obtain representative samples of product. **IMPORTANT:** *Auditors must be present in the lab when the samples are tested by impartial experts, so that they can be assured that the materials are as represented.*
2. Faulty materials are frequently accepted at receiving docks, and their defects are not discovered until these materials are later taken into the production process. Their presence shows up in quality tests and the product is discarded. *The problem is at the receiving dock.*

   Internal auditors must carefully observe receiving procedures practiced during all operating hours. Samples of all incoming items must be taken and impartially tested in the lab. Since many problems are caused by careless or improper testing, auditors must observe the testing procedures and insure that tests are appropriate and accurate. If retests are needed, they should be observed to make certain that the correct results are recorded.

   KEY POINT: *If materials do not test satisfactorily, management should be informed and auditor should observe that appropriate action is taken.* Normally, the correct action is to refuse to accept delivery of the product. The driver should be permitted to call the company to inform them of the refusal and to receive instructions. Refused product should not be permitted to remain on the premises.
3. Research and development laboratories frequently devise new and cheaper ways of producing a product. New formulas are drawn up, and new production procedures are printed and distributed. Often the new instruction is simply mailed out with the notation that it is a revised procedure, without spelling out the important changes. Office and supervisory production people receive copies of the revisions, but sometimes the communication chain ends there.

Employees working on production lines or mixing batches of raw materials may not have been informed of the changes, and they continue using the established formulas or procedures. The notepaper of instructions that they have pasted to a nearby wall is not changed, and all the research work goes for naught. Unless a diligent lab technician, a questioning accountant, or an observant internal auditor notices that the new formula is not being followed.

Aware of the potential oversight, some companies draw attention to changes by printing the revisions in *bold* type. They describe the revisions in an accompanying letter, and frequently they require that meetings be held with all employees concerned.

KEY POINT: *Internal audit staffs should include a step in their production plant audit program that requires a review of the system for communicating revisions to line workers.* Auditors should check for proper handling of changes in formulas and production procedures.

B. FINISHED GOODS

4. A frequent method of theft of finished goods is to overload outgoing trucks. Order pullers bring excessive quantities of product to the shipping dock. If the checker is in on the deal, the overage is overlooked and the product is allowed to go into the trailer. The driver, who is also involved, drops off the overage at a prearranged spot and makes a normal run with the remaining product.

   Often a complete pallet load of unordered merchandise is pulled onto a trailer that has some available space and is not being watched. Too, there are many reports of entire truck loads of merchandise stolen or hijacked. Any of these activities are difficult to carry off alone, and usually involve two or more people. **NOTE:** *When a conspiracy is involved, the quantity or value of each theft must bring in enough revenue to distribute among all conspirators.* Such large thefts are brought to light by inventory variance reports. If losses continue at a given location there is a high probability of major theft. Professional security experts might help to discover the culprits and control the problem.

   If you encounter a major theft case, there are several good suggestions that you can make that, if followed, may reduce or prevent these organized thefts. The following suggestions have been effective when used under specific types of conditions:

   - An effective control over large thefts, is the installation and use of truck scales at controlled gates to an operation. Trucks are weighed as they enter the premises and again as they leave and the weight difference should equal the computed weight of the load.

It is essential that the gate guard does not allow any truck to leave the premises that appears to be overloaded. **TIP:** *Good control requires intelligent and diligent enforcement.* A drawback is that the weighing process is time-consuming and can materially slow down the movements of trucks during rush periods.

- Complete or spot checks of setup loads by supervisory personnel, *on a surprise basis,* can be an effective deterrent. **TIP:** *Checks must be made after the load has been approved for shipment.* The count may occur before product is moved into the trailer or by pulling back a loaded vehicle and checking the product. The latter check is more effective, but is also more time and labor-consuming.
- Where practical, separating loads on the docks can be helpful in preventing the unauthorized movement of product from one load to another. When there is at least one empty aisle between loads, such improper transfers might readily be observed.
- Installation of surveillance cameras and continual monitoring by security personnel can be a strong deterrent. The film can be played back when thefts are suspected or known to have occurred.
- Placement of an undercover investigator in a suspect area may disclose the employees engaged in the illegal activity. Such services should be obtained from a private investigating agency. Some states require that undercover operators be licensed private investigators.

  Your help will be required to see that the operator is hired without attracting suspicion. This is sometimes difficult to accomplish. **TIP:** *Janitorial or temporary vacation help usually offers the best opportunity for placement.*
- A good approach is to place under professional surveillance a location that is experiencing losses of product. Watching usually starts after operations have ceased for the day. After-hour thefts are frequently detected, and the thieves caught in the act.
- Using a computer program to process inventory data on a daily basis can provide early warning of a theft condition. When losses begin to occur, alerted local management can frequently stop thefts at an early stage, before the thieves can get fully organized.
- Many theft cases are exposed by an investigation that starts at the selling end of the caper. **TIP:** *A sales force alerted to thefts of product often spot stolen items in the market place.*

  In these cases outside security agencies or police forces may offer the safest approach to resolving the problem. Working backward from the buyer frequently exposes the identity of all links in the chain of distribution, including the employees who initiated the thefts.

- Where practical, a relatively cheap and easy control is to keep dock personnel in the dark as to the load's destination and assigned driver. Trailers and load sheets are simply identified by a unique number. Order pickers and checkers have no knowledge of destination or driver assignment.

  Drivers are confined to a building section that includes vending machines and a rest room. The area is off-limits to shipping personnel. Company truck jockeys pick up empty trailers and drive them to the loading docks where they exchange empties for full trailers which are dropped off at a closely monitored area. Over-the-road drivers are given shipping papers and told the trailer number that they are to haul. They drive their tractor to the staging area, show their papers to the security guard and hook on to the designated trailer number. **KEY POINT:** *Under this type of system, when a substantial delivery OVERAGE is reported, it is a good indication that collusive theft had been attempted and failed.*

  A loader or checker had taken a chance that a deliberate overload would be assigned to a specific truck driver who would be on the lookout for the extra product. Though that attempt went awry, you can be sure it will be tried again. But at least you've learned the identity of an honest driver.

5. Products in storage can often be easily misappropriated. Despite strong physical security measures, product can be illegally removed from any location, though a conspiracy is often necessary to carry off the product. *Deliberate, or accidental, overloading of a truck is seldom detected if the overage is only a small percentage of the total load.* Sometimes a few cases of product are tossed into the trailer, after the loading has been completed but before the trailer is pulled away from the dock and its doors closed and sealed. Or a few cases may be tossed into the cab of the tractor that is pulling the trailer. The "toss-on" may be made by the driver of the tractor, or the loader or checker on the dock. Stolen product is divided among the culprits, or sold at a fraction of its value and the proceeds divided among the conspirators.

   Many deterrents have been tried to reduce this type of activity. One of the best is the installation of surveillance cameras on the shipping docks as previously mentioned. Some unions will fight such installations, contending that they are really tools to monitor the employees' pace of work.

   This deterrent requires that guards constantly watch a number of TV screens at the same time. Playbacks of the tapes, when it becomes necessary, can be a time-consuming task.

   The practice of tossing product into tractor cabs can be deterred by systematic examinations of cabs by security personnel at the gate. **CAU-**

TION: *Such examinations take time and are too frequently ignored during inclement weather, during the night shifts and when the driver of the vehicle is someone that the security guard knows and trusts.*

6. When multiple units of product are packaged in a single case, thieves routinely remove some of the units, and leave the remainder in the carton. Upon delivery to customers or consumers the shortage is noted and reported. This part-case theft usually occurs at a storage point, rather than en route. If thefts are extensive and growing, you should consult with security experts. Traps can be set that could discover the identity of employees who are involved. **TIP:** *If losses are consistently reported by one customer, but not others, then the problem might well be located in the customer's warehouse.* The customer should be advised and might appreciate your cooperation in eradicating the problem.

   This type of theft is usually confined to items that can be easily carried or concealed on one's person. Because of the small units, a weight control system is usually not effective. An examination by shaking containers, and looking for signs that a box had been opened, may help you discover that thefts are occurring in your operation.

   Petty thefts are often detected during lunch pail or tool box searches at quitting time. Some companies, as an employment condition, obtain employee's advance agreement to such searches. Auto and locker searches are also conducted on a surprise basis. It is not unusual to find small quantities of stolen product hidden in lockers or in cars.

7. Products that manufacturers throw away frequently appear in swap meets, farmers markets or other types of open air sales gatherings. These products are frequently extracted from the manufacturer's plant dumpsters or garbage cans. Sometimes products are retrieved from garbage dump sites where they have been taken by the collection trucks. These products are cleaned up and offered for sale with no indication of their past. *If someone is injured through the use of the product, it might be difficult to learn that the product had in fact been dumped by the manufacturer.*

   KEY POINT: *To protect your company from such abuse and potential suit, it is necessary that all dumped product be mutilated beyond recognition.*

   There are good methods of mutilation: shredding, incineration, or pouring dyes over the product may do the job. No matter which method is used, it relies on the diligent action of an individual and is usually an onerous job. The assigned employee may elect to take an easy way out and your company's products may find their way to an open air market.

   Many professional investigating agencies offer a shoppers' service. They send agents into open air markets in selected areas to look for major manufacturer's product being offered for sale. They also spot counterfeit product bearing a brand name or a designer label that has been placed on an inferior product and is offered at an attractive price.

8. Costly items are frequently stolen "on order." Truck drivers, warehouse workers or clerks may take orders from relatives, friends, neighbors or total strangers for items that are much in demand. They offer to deliver at a price well below the prevailing rate. If asked where the goods will come from, they often profess to know a company that is going out of business.

   These people, usually conspiring with other workers, use picking slips and shipping papers that are either counterfeit or stolen from the back of packages of the forms. They arrive in their truck, pick up the product and deliver it to the ordering customer. The paper work, which they used to fool honest warehouse employees, is removed from the files by conspirators and destroyed.

   A study of the logs of incoming and outgoing vehicles, at the guard gate, can unearth this activity. *If the log contains a description, a license number and driver's name, a comparison to dispatch records will disclose the vehicles that had no business on the premises.*

C. GENERAL POINTS

9. Employees who control the actual movements of inventories are frequently not privy to information relating to variances between book and physical count figures. They are oblivious to losses or potential problems. **TIP:** *They could be helpful in preventing losses, if their help were solicited.*

   Some companies conduct periodic meetings of all personnel involved in inventory handling and record keeping. At these meetings inventory variances and other inventory problems are openly discussed. The time spent in such sessions is recovered by making employees more conscientious in their work habits.

   Internal auditors play a part in emphasizing the importance of employee participation in resolving inventory problems. By discussing variances, dumps, distressed sales, obsolescence and close-dated products with the various levels of employees concerned, auditors emphasize the importance of controlling inventories.

10. **KEY POINT:** *It is essential that inventory control personnel take immediate action regarding any unusual inventory transaction.* The great mass of data that is generated by inventory movements can easily hide evidence of major thefts. Such thefts may continue for a long time, unless internal controls and supervisory review procedures are closely followed.

    A late-in-transit shipment could mean that a truckload of product has been stolen. In some instances, federal investigators have spotted trucks selling national brand name items by the side of a highway, but the manufacturer was unable to quickly determine whether the product had actually been stolen. If an inventory control section of a company is not promptly advised of a delayed receipt, the product may be sold and the driver gone before any action can be taken.

Chapter 14

Auditing Property Transactions and Other Assets

INTERNAL AUDIT OF PROPERTY TRANSACTIONS

Almost all commercial enterprises use property items in the normal course of business. Some operations, such as traveling salesmen, may use only an automobile, while an insurance agent may only require a desk, chair and phone; but most operations require a large variety of property items. Physical property is defined as an asset that is expected to provide useful service for an extended period of time.

Auditors analyze property transactions for a variety of reasons.

1. It is an asset that is recorded, traced, valued and reported on the firms balance sheet. The auditor must ensure that it is reported and valued correctly.
2. A company is permitted to write off, as an expense, the original cost of the asset over its useful life. Allowable depletion and depreciation rates vary according to the asset's construction and use and the existing tax laws.
3. Property is valuable, and much of it is susceptible to conversion. Auditors are interested in ensuring that all property items are adequately safeguarded against theft or loss.

Internal auditors examine property records in the same manner that they approach an audit of any other asset. The value of an asset is an important element in deciding the amount of audit time allotted to the review. Each organization is unique, and an internal audit staff must develop an individual approach to an audit of a firm's property.

Some companies use a separate group of property auditors who are responsible for setting up property records for new installations and for reviewing and revising property records of existing operations. These property auditors may be a part of the internal audit staff, may report to the property department or may report to some other department such as production or engineering. If they are a part of the internal audit function, their work may be accepted without review by any other section of the internal audit staff. If they report to any other department, their work is subject to internal audit review.

Audits of property records may require specialized knowledge, particularly in highly technical or research-oriented companies. In such an environment an audit staff that must verify the existence of property might consider supplementing the staff with experts who know and can recognize the equipment that is described in the property records. These experts may come from within the company or from outside, but their work should be supervised by internal auditors.

Leased property must be confirmed in the same manner as owned property. Some companies treat long term leases as obligations, which in fact they are, but the contract conditions of many long term leases clearly show that the property is not leased, but is merely used as security for a loan. These contracts merely lock in rental charges.

Many large companies construct buildings or major pieces of equipment and then enter into a sell-leaseback arrangement, whereby the property is sold to a financial institution and then leased back for an extended period of time. Under this lease arrangement, the lessee maintains the property, pays insurance and taxes, pays a rental charge that is designed to pay off the principal amount over the agreed period and pays the going interest rate for the use of the funds. At the end of the lease, the property may revert to the company that built it.

In this chapter we will present an audit program used for the following:

- Verifying that the property asset account is correctly valued.
- Determining that allowable depreciation has been correctly handled.
- Verifying that property location records are accurate and timely.
- Determining that all property is adequately safeguarded.
- Determining that idle or obsolete property is brought to the attention of management for prompt action.

It is customary to tag items of property so that they can be specifically identified and cataloged. Tags may be of metal with embossed numbers or they may be plastic, or the identifying numbers may be etched or engraved onto the surface of the property item. The identification mark usually contains letters and numerals. The letters may designate a specific department or operation, or may signify a special depreciation class of equipment. The associated number then designates a particular piece of equipment.

KEY POINT: *Where identity tags are used, they must be closely controlled and accounted for.* When an item is sold or junked, the tag must be removed or defaced. Proof of the action taken must be submitted to, and kept on file in, the property department.

Background Information

We will be working with a sample internal audit program designed for a review of the corporate Property Department of the mythical XYZ Corporation. In this company, all property records are maintained by the property department at the corporation's headquarters office.

Since property records are not referred to regularly or frequently they have not been computerized. All postings are made manually. An individual property card is set up for every single item of property that originally cost more than one hundred dollars. Items costing less than that amount are written off to expense when purchased.

The section maintains records for all corporate property in the home country. Invoices for property items are first routed through Property for their review and accounting distribution. The property section is responsible for computing and reporting property additions, deletions, adjustments, depreciation, valuation for tax purposes and for other property information or reports. Individual locations do not keep any property records in their local files.

Property cards are filed by the location that houses the property. Within each location, the cards are filed by property class. Property classes are used to group property items together that are treated alike for tax depreciation purposes.

When property is transferred within the company, the property card is moved to the new location file and the property values at both affected locations are adjusted. Property cards, relating to items that are sold or junked, are removed from the location file and filed in an appropriate disposition file.

The following internal audit program covers the review of the property record-keeping system, and does not include the program that deals with the physical check of property items that are conducted at each location audited. Physical verification of property items is covered in the audit programs for individual locations. **TIP:** *Internal auditors who plan to conduct a location audit that includes a property check, should obtain a list of all property charged to that location.* After the audit is completed, the property section is advised of all changes, and the location's property records are adjusted accordingly. Though the section is advised of all property transactions, it has no approval responsibilities nor can it authorize movement of any item.

OTHER ASSETS

Deferred charges, prepaid items and intangibles make up the bulk of the minor assets that appear on a corporation's balance sheet. These other items, often comparatively insignificant, must be reviewed by internal auditors, who must attest that the assets exist and that they are fairly valued. This section deals with the verification of these assets and the determination that they are properly safeguarded and handled in conformance with company policies and procedures.

Asset values are sometimes set up for *consumable items* that are not used up in the normal accounting period. The remaining residual value is reflected in the reports. Some companies ignore these fine points of accounting procedures and charge the total cost of these items to expense at time of purchase. They reason that these insignificant charges will even out over time.

Prepayments are another matter. These transactions require attention and accurate records, since they represent advance payments for goods or services to be received at a later date. One of the most costly of these items is the purchase of insurance.

Every major business activity purchases insurance to cover their risks of doing business. Coverage is usually placed by an insurance department, which may consist of one or many individuals. The audit objectives in reviewing an insurance department are to determine the following:

- All risks are covered and all policies are current;
- Consideration is given to self-insurance coverage;
- Coverage is adequate, but not excessive, for the risk involved;
- All policies, and conditions, are understood by management.
- Premiums paid are reasonable, accurate and timely;
- All insurance claims are filed on a timely and correct basis;
- All claims filed have received proper handling and disposition;
- All proceeds from claims are promptly and correctly deposited.

CAUTION: *The high original cost of insurance, and the handling of values and claims, requires careful audit attention.*

Intangible assets present a different audit problem. Where the intangible represents something that has been purchased, the price paid for the item may be used for accounting purposes, regardless of its true worth. Sometimes an intangible is valued at a specific sum to make up for the difference between the book value of a purchased business and the paying price. This difference, labeled "goodwill," is set up as an asset to be written off in subsequent years.

If internal auditors are involved in acquisition studies they have an opportunity to evaluate the worth of items of that nature. In such instances, the auditor is in a position to point out how much is being paid for goodwill and may venture an opinion as to its probable value. **NOTE:** *Auditors can at least verify that intangibles such as copyrights, patents and royalty rights exist and are good and valid.* Basically the internal audit review establishes that the valuation is based on acceptable accounting practice, is properly handled and controlled and is written off the books in accordance with existing tax laws and good accounting practice.

A section is devoted to an internal audit examination of the other assets listed in the usual balance sheet. These other assets consist of prepayments, deferred charges, deposits for services, investments, patents, copyrights and goodwill.

The sample audit program contains audit steps designed to apply to an entity that consists of a headquarters office, division and subsidiary offices and various field production and sales operations. Division offices are responsible for all accounting within their division, and the head office combines all division reports and adds the headquarters' information. All contracts are processed, approved, controlled and filed in the headquarters office.

Insurance operations are the responsibility of the Financial Department, but most insurance policies are procured through a wholly owned insurance company that is regularly audited by the CPA firm that certifies the corporate statements.

XYZ carries the following intangible items on their books:

1. Goodwill, created through the purchase of subsidiaries.
2. Patents, which consists of experimental and developmental costs and legal fees paid for obtaining the patents.
3. Royalties, coming out of agreements to allow others to use patents.
4. Copyrights, made up of cost of creating and registering trademarks.

With that as background, we are now ready to examine the internal audit programs for a review of these headquarter's operations.

INTERNAL AUDIT PROGRAM—INSTRUCTIONS

IA PI002 XYZ CORPORATION

INTERNAL AUDIT INSTRUCTIONS

All Sections

1. Before starting your audit, review the XYZ Accounting Manual and the Financial Department's Policy and Procedures directives relating to property and

other assets. Compare the work actually performed in the department to these directives and comment on any differences.

2. A description of the proper procedure for working with this internal audit program appears in the Introduction to the Audit Programs section of your manual. Read this information carefully.

Property Section

1. *Coordinate your review of this department with the field audit groups.* Send the field auditor teams a current listing of all property reported at locations they are auditing. Have them check and return the list showing any additions, deletions or corrections.
2. When an audit team conducts a property recheck they should make certain that every item on the property list is being used at the location, paying particular attention and reporting on any equipment that is idle or that may have been recently transferred into or out of the location. If the location has many property items and numerous transfers, it might be best to have it visited by the property recheck auditors, rather than take up the time of the internal audit staff.
3. When our staff conducts a property recheck, be certain that the records that we use are current and that we pay particular attention to expensive portable items. *If any of these items are assigned to, and in the possession of, individuals,* these employees should be sent a letter describing the equipment and requesting confirmation that the equipment is in good condition. Their signature on this letter will serve to prove that they have possession of the property item.
4. When our staff completes a property recheck, a copy of the list of items should be left with the location manager, one copy sent to the property department and a copy kept in the audit working papers.
5. Pay particular attention to the disposition of equipment. Bear in mind that the property department is merely a recording operation and does not make decisions as to acquisition or disposal of property. **IMPORTANT:** *If you note unusual or questionable transactions that have occurred at a company location, consider taking the following actions:*
   a. If the location is being audited, or an audit group is within one hundred miles of the location in question, send the information to the audit group to have it checked out. But before doing so advise the audit administrator of your intentions.
   b. If there are no auditors working in the area, make a copy of your note describing the questionable transaction and send it to the audit administrator. Audit management will review the data and may decide to refer it to a team scheduled to pass the location.
   c. **KEY POINT:** *If there are several questionable transactions, all involving one particular location, contact the manager of internal audits immediately. The manager will probably assign an auditor to visit the location at once.*
6. Use the following standard form letter when you circularize the disposition of

selected property items. Fill in the blank spaces on the form, and send all copies that require signatures to the audit manager. They will be appropriately signed and mailed.

XYZ CORPORATION

Request number ________ Date ____________

____

____

Dear customer:

Records of the XYZ Corporation indicate that the following property was sold to you from XYZ Corporation located at ______________________________

DESCRIPTION	PRICE
______________________________	__________
______________________________	__________
______________________________	__________

Please advise the undersigned if the above is *not correct* regarding price, equipment or location of sale.
Your cooperation is appreciated.

Sincerely yours,

Internal Audit Manager

____

If you are verifying automotive transactions, use the following format for your verification letter. Fill in the blank spaces on the top half of the form, and send all copies to the audit manager for review, signature and mailing.

XYZ CORPORATION

Phone ____________
Date ____________

____

____

Dear ______
At present we are conducting a routine examination of the disposal of XYZ Corporation's automotive equipment. The records show that you purchased a ______________________________. We are interested in verifying the details of this transaction. We will sincerely appreciate your cooperation in enabling us to determine that our company policies have been followed.
Will you please give us the information requested below and return the original copy in the self-addressed, stamped envelope enclosed.
Sincerely yours,

Manager of Internal Audits

. . . .

Date purchased ____________________ Amount Paid $____________________
Payment by: Personal Check ________ Money Order ________ Cash ________
Was equipment picked up at an XYZ location? Yes _____ No _____
Salesperson's name? ________________________
Were any commissions or additional fees paid? Yes _____ No _____
If yes, how much? $__________ To Whom? ____________________

Remarks: ____

Signed: ________________________________ Date ______________

Make every effort to get 100% of selected transactions verified. If buyers have moved, attempt to trace and contact them. If this is not possible, at least determine that such an address existed and that the purchaser lived at that address at the time of the transaction.

It may be necessary to employ outside investigative agencies to study the problem for you. Check with the audit administrator before making a commitment with any agency.

Select transactions in which the paying price appears to be below the value of the item transferred. Also look for repetitive purchases. If any party has made a number of purchases, make every effort to check out these transactions and communicate with the individual involved.

OTHER ASSETS

Before starting your review of prepayments, deferred charges and intangible assets, read these instructions and review the audit steps checkoff program and internal control questionnaire.

1. From the general ledger and a review of the supporting detail schedules, list the minor assets by account number and amount.
2. Using the above list, select assets with significant value to verify. Use your audit time wisely; don't waste time on minor items.

   When verifying asset valuations, accept the value placed on the asset at acquisition after you establish that it represents the sum actually agreed for the asset. If the asset has a determinable value, then make an effort to verify that the balance sheet value conforms to the formula for determining the asset value.
3. When determining the legitimacy of an asset such as a copyright or a patent, simply send a letter of verification to our lawyers and to our outside patent attorney and request a written reply. The letters of reply will be placed in your audit working papers.
4. If royalties are due from outside companies, verify that proper royalty payments are received. If oil reserves are reported on our statements, review reports that establish the value of such reserves.
5. For insurance prepayments, be certain to examine all major policies for timeliness and amounts of coverage. Most of XYZ's needs are covered by our inhouse agency, and you may skim over these areas. But do examine the

retrospective rating schedules for *indications of poor safety rules or carelessness* at locations with poor experience.

6. All deposits for utilities or other services are to be verified. *Though the amounts may be small, this type of transaction is open to manipulation.* Prepayments, such as rent, should also be verified.
7. Transactions involving pension funds and taxes may be ignored, since these items are closely monitored by our outside auditors.

INTERNAL AUDIT PROGRAM—PROPERTY

IA PP 007 XYZ CORPORATION—INTERNAL AUDIT PROGRAM PROPERTY TRANSACTIONS

This program is designed to lead you through an internal audit review of the headquarter's Property Department. Before starting your work on this program, read audit Instructions, form # IA PI002.

A. Company Procedures

1. All property records, general and detailed, are maintained at headquarters and balanced at least once per year.
2. All property acquisitions conform to the approved capital budgets.
3. Property additions and retirements at company locations are all approved by headquarter's operating department management.
4. Property items are periodically inventoried and reconciled to property records.
5. Property items are procured and disposed of on the basis of competitive bids.
6. All official reporting of property transactions, valuations and depreciation is handled by the central property section.

B. Audit Objectives are to determine the following:

1. Corporate policies and procedures for handling property transactions are understood and followed by all employees.
2. The property asset account valuation is correctly reflected in the General Ledger.
3. Property records for individual locations are current and accurate.
4. Adjustment to property records are timely and properly approved.
5. Obsolete or idle items of property are promptly reported to appropriate management.
6. Depreciation, and depletion, is correctly computed and taken.
7. Property items are properly safeguarded.

C. Audit Procedures	*Per. Cov.*	*Audit By*
1. General		
a. Discuss with section supervisor, corporate policies and procedures relating to property transactions.	____	____
b. Observe procedures followed by property clerks and discuss their individual assignments.	____	____
c. Determine if any clerical operations could be computerized at a savings.	____	____

C. Audit Procedures — *Per. Cov.* | *Audit By*

2. *Property Additions*
   a. Select a sampling of appropriation requests and review for proper handling and approvals. ____ ____
      1) Examine justifications for accuracy and completeness. ____ ____
   b. Review procedures for ensuring that property additions have been listed in the approved budget before the Property section approves invoices for payment. ____ ____
      1) For items not included in the budget, are procedures adequate to inform concerned executives of purchase? ____ ____
      2) Review sections's procedures for initiating and getting approvals for supplemental budget requests. ____ ____
   c. Determine that property cards are immediately prepared for all additions. ____ ____
   d. Review the section's procedure for preparing the monthly Property Additions Schedule. ____ ____
   e. Check the latest monthly Additions Schedule against all disbursements charged to property accounts. ____ ____
      1) Verify that total on schedule ties-in to total of property additions on computer A/P payment summary. ____ ____
      2) Review each disbursement listed and compare to property records prepared in the section. ____ ____
   f. Select, by class and type, a number of items to be price verified. ____ ____
      1) Schedule information from the microfiche records of property cards. ____ ____
         a) See purchase data from A/P and section's files. ____ ____
         b) Test-check to determine that all information on the microfiche card is accurate. ____ ____
      2) Examine catalog prices for each item; take discount structure into consideration. ____ ____
         a) Determine that costs of comparable items are reasonably close. ____ ____
         b) Review Purchasing files for those items whose costs appear excessive. ____ ____
      3) Examine Purchasing Department bid files to determine that truly competitive bids were received. ____ ____
         a) If lowest bid was not accepted, review documents for justification and proper approvals. ____ ____
         b) Discuss exceptions with the Purchasing Agent that handled the transaction. ____ ____
3. *Property Dispositions*
   a. Determine that the section's personnel are aware of

C. Audit Procedures	*Per. Cov.*	*Audit By*
company policies that relate to property dispositions.	____	____
1) Examine file of competitive bids that accompany Equipment Disposition Reports. (EDR's)	____	____
2) If highest bid was not accepted, review explanation and approval for accepting a lower bid.	____	____
b. Verify accuracy of last six months disposition reports.	____	____
1) Examine all EDR's for legitimacy and proper approval.	____	____
a) Review items sold out of headquarter's office and determine what the signature of approval means.	____	____
2) Send confirmation letters to selected purchasers of XYZ equipment. *Circularize all cash transactions.*	____	____
3) Follow through to determine that all cash received was properly handled and reported.	____	____
c. Determine that accounting was properly handled for profit or loss on disposition of property items.	____	____
d. Determine that dispositions were properly posted to individual cards and were correctly reported.	____	____
e. Select, from property section's files, a sampling of requests for authorization to dispose of equipment.	____	____
1) Note locations that dispose of many items.	____	____
2) *Note if any single purchaser has bought a number of items that were disposed of.*	____	____
a) Obtain credit reports on frequent purchasers and compare information to the authorization requests.	____	____
b) *Compare prices received from frequent purchasers, to prices from others for comparable equipment.*	____	____
4. *Reporting of Idle Equipment*		
a. Review accounting manual procedures for proper reports and handling of temporary or permanent idle equipment.	____	____
1) Determine that transfers are made from temporary to use, or to permanent idle, on a timely basis.	____	____
b. Review idle equipment records and reports.	____	____
1) Determine that all idle properties are listed.	____	____
c. Follow one month's dispositions of idle equipment through property records to the general ledger.	____	____
d. Review requests for transfers of idle equipment for prompt and proper handling and reporting.	____	____
e. Review procedures for decisions to junk idle equipment.	____	____
1) Determine that *classified equipment is cannibalized or destroyed,* rather than sold, even as junk.	____	____

C. Audit Procedures	*Per. Cov.*	*Audit By*
2) Ascertain if the system provides for recovery of potential spare parts from equipment to be junked.	____	____
5. *Miscellaneous*		
a. Review the section's procedures for computing monthly depreciation and depletion charges.	____	____
1) Determine that depreciation accounting was handled accurately for property items that were disposed of.	____	____
a) Determine that locations are promptly relieved of depreciation charges when properly approved idle equipment reports are received in Property section.	____	____
b) Determine that depreciation for idle equipment is taken by XYZ until items are disposed of.	____	____
2) Determine that section employees follow the Tax Department's directions in depreciation matters.	____	____
b. Determine that tags are returned to property section.	____	____
c. Review payroll records and personnel files.	____	____
1) Distribute payroll checks to verify employees.	____	____
a) Compare to payroll register.	____	____
2) Determine that all earned vacations were taken.	____	____

Audit program reviewed by ______________________ Date ____________

INTERNAL AUDIT PROGRAM—OTHER ASSETS

A. Audit Purpose is to determine the following:

1. All accounting for assets is properly handled and is in accord with acceptable accounting practices.
2. Ownership of all assets are confirmable and protected.
3. A good basis was used to establish valuations.

B. Audit Procedures *Other Assets*	*Per. Cov.*	*Audit By*
1. List all miscellaneous assets that were on hand at the completion of the last internal audit.	____	____
a. Schedule all miscellaneous assets listed on the corporate books as of the close of last month.	____	____
b. Reconcile and prove current listing against list from previous audit working papers.	____	____
1) *Bring any discrepancies to audit manager's attention.*	____	____
2. Verify existence and ownership of intangible assets.	____	____
a. Obtain written verification from company's legal firm as to copyrights, royalty rights and patent rights.	____	____
1) Examine registrations and patent files.	____	____
a) See that registrations are in company name.	____	____

B. Audit Procedures	*Per. Cov.*	*Audit By*
b) Determine that they are still valid.	____	____
2) Determine that rights are not close to expiration, and that renewal rights are being policed.	____	____
b. Through the legal department, determine the following:		
1) Documents in file are valid and up to date.	____	____
2) No transfers of ownership have taken place.	____	____
3) No violations of rights have occurred.	____	____
3. Review procedures used to insure that rights have not been infringed upon.	____	____
4. Verify valuation of intangible assets. If the asset was purchased, examine purchase agreement.	____	____
a. For patents, examine costs of experimental work and legal work to obtain patents.	____	____
b. For copyrights, examine developmental and legal costs.	____	____
c. For goodwill, examine purchase agreements.	____	____
d. Establish that intangible assets still have a value.	____	____
5. Examine and verify the write-off of each intangible asset.	____	____
a. Determine that W/O accords with good accounting.	____	____
b. Determine that W/O conforms with statutory tax laws.	____	____
6. Review all royalty records and determine that royalty income is accurate and timely.	____	____
a. Send confirmation letter to companies paying royalties.	____	____
1) Request support for royalty computations.	____	____
a) Verify this information in any way possible.	____	____
b. If contract gives us the right to audit their records, request permission to review the pertinent records.	____	____
1) If company's records are audited by CPA firm, review the audit papers and accept findings if work is OK.	____	____
c. If no audit rights exist on contract, suggest we *arrange to modify contract if licensee refuses to allow examination of supporting documents.*	____	____
7. Prepare a list of prepayments and deferred charges from latest General Ledger.	____	____
a. Verify balances in the selected accounts.	____	____
1) Examine disbursement supporting papers.	____	____
2) Inventory items as required.	____	____
b. Send confirmation letters to verify all prepayments.	____	____
1) Follow up to insure that any XYZ money being held on deposit is verified.	____	____
c. Send confirm letters to verify that our ledger truly represents advanced royalty payments we have made.	____	____
8. Write up audit suggestions for future reviews.	____	____

Audit work reviewed by ______________________ Date ____________

INTERNAL AUDIT PROGRAM—INTERNAL CONTROL QUESTIONNAIRE

The following internal control questions are intended to direct your attention to the high risk areas of this operation. Some of these points are covered in the audit program and are included here to insure that they receive adequate attention.

Answer these control questions as your audit progresses. In section B you are to write in the names and job titles of the various employees who perform the listed functions. Be certain to note any conflicting duties that could jeopardize internal control.

I. The following are indicative of satisfactory internal controls:

1. There is an effective system of authorization and approval with respect to capital expenditures.
2. Accurate records are kept of all acquisitions, transfers and dispositions of capital assets.
3. Competitive bids are usually required for all purchases.
4. All capital assets are tagged for ready identification.
5. All property items are periodically verified.
6. Effective procedures are used to control the authorization for, and the handling of, property disposals.

II. Performance of Function:

Function	*Name/Position*	*Conflicting Duties*
1. Reviews bids.	______	______
2. Compares purchase price paid, to budgeted amount.	______	______
3. Prepares property cards.	______	______
4. Monitors dispositions.	______	______
5. Controls miscellaneous assets.	______	______
6. Controls receipts from assets.	______	______

III. Control Questions	*Yes*	*No*	*Remarks*
A. Are all section's employees well versed in company policies and procedures?	____	____	______
B. Are exceptions to policy brought to the attention of proper executives?	____	____	______
C. Are all section's records complete and readily available for examination?	____	____	______
1. Are records accurate and legible?	____	____	______
2. Are they balanced at regular intervals?	____	____	______
D. Do property employees approve requisitions *after* verifying item on the approved budget?	____	____	______
1. Is purchase price verified as reasonable and within budget allowance?	____	____	______

III. Control Questions	*Yes*	*No*	*Remarks*
E. Are property cards prepared promptly?	____	____	____________
1. Are they double checked for accuracy?	____	____	____________
F. Is property addition schedule checked by section supervisor before publication?	____	____	____________
1. To insure that all purchases are included?	____	____	____________
2. To insure that dollar values are correct?	____	____	____________
3. To insure arithmetic accuracy of report?	____	____	____________
G. Do custodians promptly report all changes?	____	____	____________
H. Is a physical inventory of property taken periodically and compared to property cards?	____	____	____________
1. Are resulting adjustments approved by operating executives as well as Financial?	____	____	____________
2. Does section supervisor examine and approve adjustments to section's records?	____	____	____________
I. Do locations promptly report idle equipment?	____	____	____________
1. Are idle equipment lists promptly circulated to concerned executives?	____	____	____________
2. Are idle equipment reports circulated to all subsidiaries and international divisions?	____	____	____________
a) Is there ample time for these outlying locations to claim equipment?	____	____	____________
J. Are all property sales properly approved?	____	____	____________
1. Is the 3 competitive bid rule enforced?	____	____	____________
a) Does approval signature attest to this?	____	____	____________
2. Do procedures insure that the agreed sales price was received and properly deposited?	____	____	____________

III. Control Questions	*Yes*	*No*	*Remarks*
K. Are controls adequate over royalties due?	____	____	____________
1. Are amounts verified and sums deposited?	____	____	____________
L. Have we satisfactory proof of all deposits?	____	____	____________
M. Are you satisfied that all property is adequately safeguarded?	____	____	____________
N. Are you satisfied with the internal control over these areas of operations?	____	____	____________

Questions answered by ______________________ Date __________
Answers reviewed by ______________________ Date __________

CRITICAL POINTS

Many irregularities occur in the handling of business property. Items of property are frequently stolen, or perhaps they are sold and not so reported. Additional property-related losses occur when idle equipment is disposed of and not reported. In these instances the property records continue to reflect the value of the disposed items, and the locations concerned continues to be charged for their depreciation. In addition, insurance premiums continue, and they are based on the book value of such property. Taxes, also based on property values, are not reduced by the disposition of these items.

Following are some critical areas to watch when reviewing property transactions and some matters relating to other assets. You should be continually on the alert for possible misappropriations.

EIGHT CRITICAL POINTS TO CONSIDER

1. Sometimes company secrets are given away when a specially designed machine is replaced by a newer, faster model. The old machine may be sold for salvage value. The buyer might be a representative of a competitor who recognizes the opportunity to buy the equipment at a low price and learn how the machine operates. **CAUTION:** *Your internal audit program should have a point about checking on disposition of secret or confidential machinery. Such items should be broken up and sold as junk, not as used equipment.*
2. Very expensive pieces of photographic equipment may be assigned to supervisory personnel for use in sales presentations. These items are

frequently kept in the employee's home. **CAUTION:** *When the person terminates employment or is transferred to another location or job, these items may be overlooked and not recovered.*

If during a recheck of property it is determined that certain items have been taken by former employees, the auditor can usually recover the property by simply writing to the ex-employee and requesting that the items be returned.

3. There are many instances where company property is sold to an outsider, and the sale is either not reported, or reported to have been made at a price well below the actual transfer price.

   These transactions are uncovered during an internal audit through audit confirmation of equipment dispositions. If items are reported as junked, the audit trail is frequently lost at point of junking.

   KEY POINT: *It therefore becomes imperative that any property to be junked be examined by a supervisor, independent of the requester, to verify that the equipment is actually junk and not a usable piece of property.* The item may then be sold for junk or salvage value.

   The auditor's job is then to determine that the cash from the junk sale is properly handled and reported.

4. Any item sold for cash is highly suspect and should be verified. It sometimes is revealed that such sales were made contrary to company policy or to buyers who would not be approved by the company.

   TIP: *If a first-party company check is received for a purchase, the maker of the check and the amount should correspond with the name of the purchaser and the amount of the sale as shown on the invoice.*

   When verifying selected cash transactions, the audit confirmation letters should provide space for a description of the article and for the purchaser to report the actual price paid for the property. Try to locate all buyers, and verify the details of the selected transactions.

5. Another frequent ploy is to sell an item of equipment and identify it as in poor condition, when it actually may be new or nearly new. These transactions most often occur when items are sold to employees and the office service supervisors are friendly with the purchaser. *Such transactions frequently involve executives who purchase used company equipment for their personal use.* When preparing a disposition request, office services describe the item in a way that enables the sale to be justified at a very low price.

   Auditors may detect this type of manipulation during a property audit if they carefully look at each piece of equipment to see that it actually corresponds with *all* of the information on the property card—*particularly the serial number (if applicable), the purchase price and the date the property was originally purchased.*

In these cases it is not unusual for office service people to exchange identification tags. They place the sold item's tags on old equipment and throw away the tags that were originally on the old equipment. This exchange enables them to report the older equipment as sold, and the better or newer items as still in the warehouse.

The manipulation becomes readily apparent when an auditor examines an older piece of equipment which bears a tag of a new purchase. The audit problem then is reduced to finding out the buyer to whom the newly purchased item was sold. This information can usually be obtained from those office service employees who did not willingly participate in the manipulation.

6. Such items as goodwill, patents, copyrights or other intangibles may be set up on the books to show a stronger balance sheet than should be reported. These items should be conservatively valued, not used to prop up a bad operation. **CAUTION:** *A large goodwill figure, resulting from an acquisition, may be an indication of impropriety in the negotiations.* An unjustifiably large goodwill figure indicates that there was a substantial difference between the acquired asset values and the amount paid for the business.

   An auditor who is a member of an acquisition team should carefully examine all intangible assets appearing on a balance sheet. Every effort should be made to trace these items back to their origin.
   KEY POINT: *It may be that these values were recently set up to increase the seller's book value in anticipation of the sale of the business.*

7. You should be alert to some critical areas in an Insurance Department examination. One of these areas concerns the handling of payments of claims. Since the receipt of insurance payments are out of the normal course of business, they may not be closely controlled. **TIP:** *Auditors should carefully study claim settlements as it is not uncommon for this type of cash receipt to be diverted.*

   Another concern is related to the amount of insurance coverage. Frequently an insurance policy is written and forgotten until a loss occurs. Risks may be altered by the passage of time.

   Many insurance policies are kept in force for operations that have been discontinued or for disposed property. Values of property at risk can change and the amount of coverage might not reflect those changes.
   KEY POINT: *Every insurance department should have an effective review program that periodically evaluates all risk areas and potential losses.* The audit staff should review all open policies, as well as canceled policies, to evaluate the effectiveness of the Insurance section.

8. Another area of risk in an insurance audit deserves mention. In a loosely controlled insurance operation, employee's invoices for insurance cover-

age of their personal property may slip into the processing and be paid by the company.

It is possible that the use of an employee's personal property for company business may justify this handling. Auditors must be on the lookout for such payments, and must be certain that they have been properly approved by the appropriate executives.

Chapter 15

Auditing of Payable Transactions

Every organization uses an accounts payable system that has been conceived and designed to fit its unique operation. But all payable activities have several things in common. In this chapter we will address some of the more common features of a payable operation, and will present an example of an internal auditing program and the associated instructions used to review these operations.

The bulk of this chapter is devoted to accounts payable, but it also covers the internal audit of other payable operations. We will be concerned with *establishing the authenticity, appropriateness and accuracy of all disbursements of company funds.* This requires the verification that all pay outs are properly approved, processed and reported and that all personnel understand and follow company policies and procedures relating to cash disbursements.

Most of an organization's routine payouts of funds are handled by the Accounts Payable Department. Even petty cash disbursements find their way through A/P via the reimbursement request. Notable exceptions are dividends and bond interest payments that are often handled by agent banks, and the processing of paychecks which are usually handled by the Payroll Department.

Accounts Payable

All accounts payable operations assume responsibility for paying outside suppliers for goods and services received by the organization. A/P is charged with ensuring that such payments are made on a timely basis, for legitimate purchases, which are billed at agreed rates and terms. A/P is usually responsible for determining the period-ending outstanding liability for goods and services received but not yet paid; and for setting up the liability at that point in time.

In normal processing, the A/P department receives notification of all purchase commitments that are made by authorized personnel. The department also is informed of all goods and services received in the company. Records of commitments and receipts are matched and held until the covering invoices are submitted by suppliers. At that time the invoice is compared to ordering and receiving documents and processed for payment. The actual writing of the check may be handled in A/P or be printed by computer in the data processing center.

After checks are issued, the requests for payment, together with supporting documentation, are usually filed in the A/P department. These files are arranged so that any specific disbursement record can be readily located and examined when required.

Manually written disbursement drafts are prepared on multi-part forms which may be distributed as follows:

1. Sent to vendor,
2. Filed alphabetically by vendor,
3. Filed numerically with supporting documentation attached,
4. Filed numerically in a binder for use as an accounting copy to support the monthly journal entry.

The files of voucher copies and supporting papers are so arranged that a search for a specific voucher can be made alphabetically by vendor or numerically by voucher number—or sometimes, as in freight bills or advertising bills, by the type of disbursement.

Even if the check is written in data processing, the A/P department is the custodian of supporting documents which are usually filed together by daily batches. The daily disbursement register, prepared by the computer, individually lists each payment and reports the significant information concerning each item. A copy of this register is also filed in the A/P department.

Under an EDP system, batch files contain all the supporting documentation. Invoices are numerically mixed together in the batch files. In order to have some semblance of order, specific types of payments are gathered together daily and batched. This means that several batches are entered each day, such as one batch for expense reports, one for advertising payments, one for freight bills and perhaps another for utility bills. All heavy volume types of transactions are batched together, and this reduces the search time required to locate the supporting documentation for any particular payment.

Serial numbers on the computer batch reports makes it simple to locate a batch. The numbers identify supporting documentation when it becomes necessary to examine and verify the propriety and accuracy of any batch, or any single transaction within the batch.

Accounts Payable records contain a storehouse of information which may contain evidence of every type of error and misappropriation imaginable. *Overcharges, missed discounts, arithmetic errors, inflated expense reports, fictitious invoices, charges to the company for items purchased for personal use or charges for higher quality items than were actually delivered can be found in abundance in many of these files.* Auditors are expected to review this mountain of paperwork and cull out improper payments. This is a formidable task. One helpful approach is to organize the information so that it can be analyzed and reviewed to provide leads to possible areas of manipulation. **TIP:** *This is an operation in which a computer is very useful as an audit tool.*

EDP accounts payable systems can provide detailed information about all the transactions entered into the computer data base. If all pertinent data is required to be entered into the system, the computer can be programmed to provide specific reports that summarize any information in the data base. The computer can easily and speedily sort and compare data and print out a list of defined discrepancies.

However when misapplication or fraud has occurred, the computer generated information does not in itself constitute proof that will stand up in a court of law. An auditor must examine the original supporting documents for legal proof. Such things as erasures, forged documents, changed figures and unauthorized signatures are not readily apparent when examining computer reports. **KEY POINT:** *Critical analytical work and the physical review of each supporting document must be performed by an internal auditor.* Every bit of information and scrap of paper must be studied, and every person who might have knowledge must be interviewed to learn what had actually transpired.

Certain reasonability checks can be built into a computer system, and any transaction that exceeds these limits may be refused by the system, or it may only be reentered after coded approval by a designated, closely controlled, authority. The computer will quickly detect clerical arithmetic errors, and it will compare P/O's, R/R's and billing documents to insure that they are all in agreement. These are all useful tasks that would routinely be performed by the accounts payable auditor and would selectively be checked by the internal auditor. The amount of internal audit time required to review an accounts payable computer system should be much less than the time required to audit a manual system, if there is no fraud involved.

Computer generated reports can supply much of the information that the internal auditor requires to make an analysis of the contents of accounts payable files. Reports can be obtained which list all payments to specific suppliers or individuals or total payments for specific types of purchases. The computer can provide a variety of other types of useful data, *but it cannot audit this information beyond a certain point.*

The computer can also be useful for investigating defalcations, but only if properly programmed. The auditor must still look at every document. Data search problems can be reduced if a company uses an Optical Character Recognition device (OCR), or a microfiche to record both sides of every document. The file search time can be reduced, but in large operations, the preparation of a microfiche for hundreds of thousands of papers can be very expensive. The system is not usually economically justifiable unless the bulk of the information is frequently used.

Whatever system your company uses, you should become thoroughly familiar with the procedures and controls associated with the operation. Such a study must be made before you start any audit of payable activities. *The direction and scope of your audit will be affected by the systems and procedures that are used in the operation.*

Background Information for Accounts Payable

Our sample program is based on an accounts payable system that requires A/P to perform all associated and necessary activities up to the actual writing of checks. After receiving suppliers invoices and verifying the proper ordering and receipt of product and the accuracy of the billing, A/P enters the invoice into a data terminal, which is set up to list the payments that are to be made. *Covering drafts are then written by data processing under strict physical security and strong internal controls.* The written drafts are directly under the control of the mailing department, and supporting documentations are retained by A/P. Original drafts are never returned to A/P, but the department does receive a copy of the Daily Disbursement Register which lists every payment made by the computer program.

The sample XYZ Corporation's audit program was designed to apply to a recently converted accounts payable computerized system. Under this system, supporting documents are kept together by controlled batches, which are used as the basis for data entry. Our sample program covers the manual part of the operation as well as the off-line EDP system.

Accounts payable activities are conducted by a section of the Financial Department, with the supervisor reporting to one of the controllers. It is basically a data gathering and entering operation. The section does not originate or approve payments, but merely processes disbursement requests received from authorized employees.

XYZ's ordering process begins when an authorized employee prepares a multi-part combined requisition, purchase order, receiving report form. The requisitioner prepares the form, obtains proper approvals, keeps one copy and forwards the form to the Purchasing Department.

Purchasing places the order and sends the purchase order copy of the form to the supplier, after adding the necessary vendor and price information. One of the remaining copies of the form is sent to A/P and filed in an open purchase order file to await evidence of receipt of the ordered items. It is at this point that the transaction is entered into the computer system, when pertinent P/O information is initiated into the A/P data base as an open purchase order.

Two receiving copies of the P/O are sent to the point of receipt, and when an item arrives, the receiver notes necessary receiving information, retains one copy for files and sends one receiving report to A/P. There the receiving data is entered into the computer and the purchase becomes a legal and accounting obligation which is classified as "awaiting billing." The form itself is matched in A/P to the P/O copy and held in a separate file waiting for the covering invoice.

When the invoice is received in A/P, it is compared to the data in the files and if the arithmetic is correct and all else agrees, the billing information is entered into the data base. The system matches the invoice to the P/O and receiver and classifies the transaction as "awaiting payment," where it remains until the draft is issued.

Disbursement drafts are printed periodically to meet the payment conditions specified in billing documents. The drafts, under close security, are printed in duplicate. Original copies are mailed to the payee and duplicate copies are sent to A/P for a numerical sequence file. Distribution is controlled by the Mailing Department.

Regularly scheduled or special reports are printed, summarizing selected information in the data base. Computer reports of drafts issued, receipts "awaiting billings" and billings "awaiting payment" dates are issued each day. At the end of a month all transactions are summarized by the computer, and the necessary information for the A/P journal entry is calculated. The Accounts Payable Department prepares the journal entry which is supported by the computer reports.

All the documents that had served as the basis for information fed into the computer are retained in accounts payable.

Background Information for Other Payables

In the sample program, other payables are handled differently than A/P. Notes payable are not issued in great numbers, though the dollar amounts are substantial. Most notes originate in the section of the Treasury Department that handles commercial paper. The notes are few in number and the operation is handled manually. This operation is covered in the program for auditing the Treasurer's Department.

Sundry payables include such items as dividends, interest, taxes, commissions, royalties and brokerage payable. Each of these sundry payable categories requires careful study. Dividends payable are set up when declared by the Board, but the payments are handled through a special dividend account. Bond interest payments are handled by an agent bank. XYZ issues a covering check to the bank on the day before the bank is to issue interest payments to bondholders. The audit review of any of these sundry payable activities basically follows the same audit routines established for the review of A/P. An audit of the Employee Payroll is covered in Chapter 17.

Internal auditing must evaluate the reliability and adequacy of internal controls that operate within the payable operations and also the controls that operate over purchasing, receiving and data processing.

With that as background, we are now ready to examine the audit program instructions for the review of Payable operations.

IA PI350 XYZ CORPORATION

INTERNAL AUDIT PROGRAM—INSTRUCTIONS

All Payables

Before starting an audit of payables, read these instructions, the audit program check off chart (Form # IA PP360), and the internal control questionnaire. Review policies and procedures manuals so that you will be familiar with XYZ's approach to this function.

The following program will lead you through the audit steps required for your review of this payable activity. Schedule your work to start at the latter part of an accounting period so that you will have the opportunity to review the month-ending accounting reports that contain summaries of much of the work that you studied.

A. Timing is an important consideration in all payable activities; direct your attention to this factor, particularly when reviewing taxes and commercial notes payable.
B. A description of the proper procedure for working with this internal audit program appears in the Introduction to the Audit Programs section of your manual. Read this information carefully.

Accounts Payable

A. Study the user's manual for the computerized Accounts Payable system. Work closely with the EDP audit group when you review the system's effectiveness in the A/P area.
B. You will be working with many reports generated by the computer. Remember that the computer only reports on the basis of information fed into it. You must determine that the reports are accurate and timely. **CAUTION:** *You must also determine that the computer programs have adequate built-in controls.* You will use the EDP audit group to help your team audit this phase of computer operations.
C. The computer printing area is in a separate controlled room adjoining the processing room, so that the final output of printed matter is beyond the reach or control of the computer operators. Output of important papers, once printed, are controlled by the mailing department. Checks and drafts must be safeguarded during printing, and stuffing in envelopes and delivery to the post office.

   This physical separation of computing and printing activities was designed so that collusion would be required between a computer operator and a mail handler in order to remove any paperwork before its distribution. Collusion is not necessary if the printed matter is properly addressed for mailing purposes. *However, a proper address creates an audit trail.* If fictitious payroll checks or disbursement drafts are printed, a good security system will ensure that these documents are delivered to the P. O. to be mailed to the addressee.

D. Bear in mind that the preparation of a requisition does not in and of itself constitute an obligation of the company. Every requisition must be examined, approved and then acted upon by Purchasing before an obligation is created. (Review program titled Audit of Purchasing.)

The P/O obligation means that a specified sum must be paid if and when the supplier delivers the goods or services ordered. To the time of receipt, there is a potential obligation that becomes actual upon satisfactory delivery. Then the company must make payment and has a legal obligation which must be recorded and reported at month end.

E. There is a contingent liability for purchase orders issued, where goods or services have not as yet been received. Since some of these orders may have been partially received, there is a problem of reviewing each outstanding P/O to determine whether any goods or services have already been received. If so, the value of such items must be established as well as the remaining contingent liability.

Every item that is set up in an unaudited bills account is reversed at the beginning of the next month. These items should be cleared in the early part of each month, and *any item that remains in the account for more than a month must be thoroughly investigated.*

At the close of an accounting period, the A/P department enters into the computer system all transactions that apply to the month but have not yet been input into the system. The computer is programmed to print a list of the items making up the unaudited bills account, and a review of these printouts provides a historical picture of the movement into and out of the account. **CAUTION:** *You should investigate any item that appears on this list two months in succession.*

F. During your review, make certain that an auditor interviews every member of the A/P department, including the department auditor. Ask each employee if they have noticed any unusual transaction or event that occurred relating to the computer processing operation. **NOTE:** *If any employee volunteers information that may indicate a problem, be certain that it is investigated during your visit.*

G. Bear in mind that additional drafts could be issued by the computer operation and perhaps be omitted from the printed summary reports. These possibilities are explored during an audit of computer operation, but you should be alert during your review of A/P for any indication that such manipulations may be occurring. **IMPORTANT:** *Be aware that fractional pennies can be accumulated to a substantial sum of money and be siphoned off by knowledgeable and dishonest computer experts.*

As part of your audit of A/P you will include a review of the draft handling operation in the computer center. **KEY POINT:** *Remember that A/P is your responsibility,* so be sure that one of your team auditors personally reviews the physical handling of these drafts rather than relying on the EDP audit group to conduct this check.

H. When scheduling disbursements for an audit analysis, use fourteen column analysis paper. Leave enough space on the right-hand side for notations of the results of follow-up work on discrepancies. It is not necessary to list each document that you examine, but if a cursory review raises questions, the document should be listed. **KEY POINT:** *All listed items should be completely audited and all questions answered.*

For those listed disbursements that contain discrepancies, your work papers should note all explanations and who presented them. If an explanation is offered by a clerical employee, write it down, and then review the write-up with the supervisor and note the response.

KEY POINT: *If inflated or fictitious payments have been made, prepare a separate work paper outlining the details.* Your work paper should indicate the results of your conversations with the employee and the supervisor involved. **IMPORTANT:** *Such cases must be immediately called to the attention of the internal audit manager.*

I. If you encounter a situation that raises a question about the authenticity of a disbursement draft, call the Treasurer's Office and ask that the draft in question be extracted for your examination. Be certain to examine the endorsement on the original draft document, and *if it contains evidence of misapplication, make a photocopy of both sides of the draft.* Give the photocopy to the Treasurer, but keep the original for audit use. Keep the audit manager informed; you will be advised as to when the original document may be returned.

J. If your review indicates an error or overpayment that appears to be the result of an unintentional mistake, route your note through normal channels for corrective action. Your audit working paper should note the names of the employees who were informed, when and what action was taken and the results. If the action or the response is not satisfactory, discuss the problem with the audit manager.

K. In some situations the discrepancies that you note may be of such a nature that it becomes advisable for the Auditing Department to take action to correct a problem. **TIP:** *Sometimes outsiders respond quicker and more favorably to letters written by the Auditing Department rather than those written by the Accounts Payable Department.* In these cases, you will draft a letter for the signature of the Audit Manager and discuss the problem and your suggested approach.

IA PP360

XYZ CORPORATION

INTERNAL AUDIT PROGRAM—PAYABLES

This audit program is designed to cover the high risk areas of the payable operations. The program emphasizes Accounts Payable since this is the major operation for disbursing corporate funds.

I. Company Procedures

A. All disbursements for goods and services are processed through our payable sections. Bond interest services are handled by our agent bank, but all other payouts are company controlled.

B. There are effective, well thought out internal controls over all payouts of company funds.
C. Disbursement, payroll and dividend checks are written by the corporate data processing department and distributed by the company mailing department.
D. Complete and timely records of all disbursement checks issued are prepared by the computer at the completion of every run.
E. All supporting documents are closely examined by payment control personnel before any data is entered into the computer data base.

II. Audit Objectives are to determine the following:

A. Company policies and procedures are understood and followed.
B. All disbursements are reviewed and approved before payments are processed.
C. Computer programs used for payable operations are protected and contain built-in security safeguards that protect against abuse.
D. Computer reports are complete, accurate and timely.
E. Returned disbursement drafts and checks are adequately controlled.

III. Audit Procedures *All Payables*	*Per.* *Cov.*	*Audit* *By*
A. Test-check footings of all disbursement records. This checking in some cases may be limited to registers.	____	____
B. Have all disbursement checks and drafts issued during a one month period sorted into numerical order to be subjected to a complete detailed audit.	____	____
1. Run adding-machine tape of all disbursements and reconcile total with the disbursement register for the month being checked. Allow for outstanding items.	____	____
a. Tie disbursement registers into the General Ledger.	____	____
2. Account for all check or draft numbers, allowing for those outstanding.	____	____
3. Retain instruments until you have completed your audit of them, which includes a review of supporting papers.	____	____
C. Carefully audit all disbursement instruments. On the face:		
1. Determine if there are any signs of alterations.	____	____
2. Determine that a proper signature has been applied.	____	____
3. See that amounts do not exceed printed restrictions.	____	____
4. Note that date shown corresponds with date issued.	____	____
5. Determine that all instruments payable to banks state, on the payee line, how the bank is to use the funds.	____	____
D. Carefully audit all disbursement instruments. On the back:		
1. Determine that all instruments have been endorsed.	____	____
2. Compare endorsement to payee named.	____	____
3. Compare bank processing date stamp to date of issuance.	____	____
E. For outstanding items, near the close of your audit, look at items that have cleared as provided in C and D above.	____	____
1. Ascertain whether handling and controls are adequate for items written off.	____	____

III. Audit Procedures *All Payables*	*Per. Cov.*	*Audit By*
2. Examine records for items written off which are later presented for payment. Make a test-check of items.	____	____
F. Investigate possibility of miscarriage of funds which seem to be transfers from depositories to Treasurer's account.	____	____
G. Prove Balances in the Payable accounts at the end of one month. Investigate all adjustments.	____	____
H. Audit all support for checks and drafts listed in B above:		
1. Compare payee's name on each instrument with the name on the supporting documents.	____	____
2. Check for proper amounts and approvals.	____	____
3. Check for presence of all necessary supporting papers.	____	____
4. Check for arithmetic accuracy of disbursement.	____	____
5. Determine that all discounts and allowances were taken.	____	____
6. Evaluate procedures to prevent duplicate payments.	____	____
a. Spot check for duplicate payments by requesting a list of all payments to selected vendors and reviewing all payments to them.	____	____
b. If you noted any payments supported by "copies" of invoices, check for later payment of the original.	____	____
7. Look for purchase of personal items charged to XYZ.	____	____
8. Evaluate procurements for general propriety of the expenditures for the type of business conducted.	____	____
9. Look for large renewal items of property to be sure that they are capitalized, rather than expensed.	____	____
10. Notice if items are purchased locally that should have been procured by head office Purchasing.	____	____
11. A sampling of rental payments should be checked to leases or letters of authorization from head office. Comment on any exceptions noted.	____	____
I. For a test period, compare outbound freight bills to XYZ invoices covering shipments, and compare inbound bills to our receiving reports. You may check all bills from a few carriers, rather than all bills for a shorter period.	____	____
J. Determine that all supporting documents are properly canceled to prevent reuse.	____	____
K. Review system for removing supporting documentation from files. Determine which employees are authorized to remove items, and if adequate records exist.	____	____
L. Evaluate the normal departmental auditing of disbursements, and the internal handling of documents.	____	____
M. Audit the department's payroll. Determine that they are following Personnel policies and procedures.		
1. Verify employees on payroll by distributing paychecks.	____	____
2. Refer to audit program titled Auditing of Payroll.	____	____

Accounts Payable	*Per. Cov.*	*Audit By*
A. Work with EDP audit group to have a member of your team in the computer area when they run disbursement drafts.	____	____
1. Determine that computer program has adequate built-in controls, and review these with the EDP audit group.	____	____
2. Determine that the computer processing is monitored and physically safeguarded so that computer generated reports and drafts are properly prepared and handled.	____	____
3. Determine that built-in security measures prevent access to unauthorized parties or terminals.	____	____
a. Determine if unauthorized instructions or data can be introduced into the system.	____	____
b. Attempt to learn if the computer program has been altered in any way since its original acceptance.	____	____
4. See that computer personnel cannot gain access to checks printed in the room that is controlled by Mailing.	____	____
a. Observe to determine if disbursement drafts are printed under close security conditions.	____	____
1) Follow drafts through complete cycle, from print shop to U.S. Post Office and observe security.	____	____
B. Review procedure for handling rejected and returned goods to ensure that payment is not made for such items.	____	____
C. Satisfy yourself that adequate controls exist at local level for proper authentication of bills, which prevents duplicate payments and assures that product has been received as per the covering invoice.	____	____
D. Select a group of checks issued in payment of employee expenses. Don't bother with departments that are in the process of, or are approaching the scheduled date for, audit.	____	____
a. Check for adequate supporting documentation.	____	____
b. Check for propriety and reasonableness of charge.	____	____
c. Examine for proper approvals.	____	____
E. Examine credit memos in file, and evidence of returned merchandise to see that they are adequately controlled and promptly and properly processed.	____	____
F. Review all disbursements to advertising agencies for a test period, and make a thorough audit of documentation.	____	____
1. Follow procedures outlined in the audit manual for program titled Auditing Advertising Expenditures.	____	____
2. Be certain to look for possible duplicate payments.	____	____
3. Determine that *all discounts are earned and taken.*	____	____
4. Determine that we do not pay out funds until due date.	____	____
5. Evaluate control systems used by A/P for determining that agency bills are fair and accurate.		
Sundry Payables		
A. Examine the most current month-ending General Ledger.		

Sundry Payables

	Per. Cov.	*Audit By*
List all sundry payable accounts.		
1. From the previous audit report, copy the list of payables at the completion of the last audit.	____	____
a. Reconcile previous list to current list.	____	____
2. Tie-in subsidiary ledgers to current General Ledger.	____	____
3. Audit a sampling of entries to subsidiary accounts.	____	____
a. Carefully review any adjustments.	____	____
1) Check for proper arithmetic and proper approval.	____	____
2) Check for propriety and legitimacy.	____	____
B. Examine terms and conditions of items under A above.	____	____
1. Determine their timeliness, legitimacy and accuracy.	____	____
2. Determine that internal controls are adequate to insure proper handling.	____	____
C. Examine supporting documentation for proof of obligation and the accuracy of supporting calculations.	____	____
D. Determine that payouts are made promptly and in accordance with the instruments of obligation.	____	____
1. Determine that interest costs on commercial papers are correctly calculated, paid and reported.	____	____
a. Determine that interest earned from the use of funds is correctly computed, received and recorded.	____	____
E. Determine that operating reports correctly reflect the revenues and costs of the commercial paper operation.	____	____
F. Determine that Dividend Payable account is correct.	____	____
1. Examine minutes of Board of Directors and note the declared dividend rate and date ex-dividend.	____	____
2. Examine list of stockholders and verify outstanding.	____	____
3. Determine that calculations are correct and that setup and pay out are accurately handled and recorded.	____	____
G. Determine that Interest Payable Account is accurate.	____	____
1. Follow some procedure as in F above, for Bonds.	____	____
a. Be certain to consider sinking fund repurchases.	____	____
H. Determine that Royalties Payable account is accurate.	____	____
1. Tie-in the amount setup to production records representing the covered machinery.	____	____
a. Verify calculations of units times rate.	____	____
I. Determine that Commissions Payable account is accurate.	____	____
1. Tie-in amount set up to sales figures of products covered.	____	____
a. Verify calculations of units times rates.	____	____
b. Determine that sales returns are correctly handled.	____	____
J. Audit pension fund transactions. Schedule all activity since the previous audit.	____	____
1. Reconcile account balances to current reports.	____	____
2. Determine that the payable account truly reflects deduc-		

Sundry Payables

	Per. Cov.	*Audit By*
tions made from employee's salaries that have not as yet been deposited to the fund.	____	____
3. Examine the CPA report of pension fund management.	____	____
a. Follow up on any questionable items which were not resolved by our outside auditors.	____	____
4. Make a list of all investments of the fund.	____	____
a. Make a copy of the investments listed in the previous audit report and reconcile to present list.	____	____
1) Verify ownership of assets.	____	____
2) Verify costs for acquisition of investments, and the current market value of all holdings.	____	____
5. Review investments written off.	____	____
a. Determine reason for selection, who authorized investment and what approval was obtained.	____	____
b. Ascertain sources of information used by managers.	____	____
6. Perform the same steps as in 5 above for investments that produced a loss when sold.	____	____
a. *Check market reports to verify reported price paid at purchase and price received at sale.*	____	____
7. Verify administration costs and fees.	____	____
a. *Look for churning of investments to increase brokerage fees.*	____	____
b. Review brokerage fees paid for transactions. Inquire if managers consider using discount brokers.	____	____
c. Explore possibility of kickbacks from brokers to fund managers.	____	____
K. Review processing of retired employee pension payments.	____	____
1. Test-check to determine that amounts of payments correctly conform to established formula.	____	____
2. Determine that retirement checks are mailed promptly.	____	____
3. Review handling of withholdings from pension checks for accident and medical insurance.	____	____
a. Select a group to test-check, and verify that deductions are correct and handled properly.	____	____
L. Write memos expanding on items noted above or on items that should be added to the audit program.	____	____

Audit program approved by ____________________ Date ____________

INTERNAL AUDIT PROGRAM—INTERNAL CONTROL QUESTIONNAIRE

The following internal control questions are intended to direct your attention to the high risk areas of this operation. Some of these points are covered in the audit program and are included here to insure that they receive adequate attention.

Answer these control questions as your audit progresses. In section B, you are to write in the names and job titles of the various employees who perform the listed functions. Be certain to note any conflicting duties that could jeopardize internal control.

A. Following are listed practices that indicate good internal control

1. All disbursements are approved prior to submission for payment.
2. All disbursement documents are audited before payment.
3. Checks and drafts are distributed by the mailing department.
4. Supporting documents are canceled after payment to prevent reuse.

B. Following lists functions performed by named employees.

Function:	*Name/Position*	*Conflicting Duties*
1. Controls mail from EDP center.	______	______
2. Writes adjusting entries.	______	______
3. Approves adjusting entries.	______	______
4. Cancels supporting documents.	______	______

C. Control Questions	*Yes*	*No*	*Remarks*
1. Does A/P check prices and arithmetic on vendor's bills?	____	____	______
2. Are all invoices that differ with P/O on price, terms or related charges routed to Purchasing for approval prior to payment?	____	____	______
3. Does computer system spot duplicates?	____	____	______
a. Are all disbursement documents given a unique identifying number?	____	____	______
1) Are numbers entered into the system?	____	____	______
b. Is the computer report of questionable payments followed up immediately?	____	____	______
c. Does A/P prepare a manual list of all duplicate invoices cleared for payment?	____	____	______
1) If so, is periodic check made to see if original comes at a later date?	____	____	______
4. Are field location's supporting documents properly supported and approved?	____	____	______
5. Does control over movement of drafts and checks insure that they are actually mailed to addressee?	____	____	______
6. Are monies paid out as close to the last due date as possible?	____	____	______
7. Is sufficient data received to process and approve freight bills?	____	____	______
8. Do we act on suggestions from the			

C. *Control Questions*	*Yes*	*No*	*Remarks*
outside audit agency concerning our utility bills?	____	____	____________
9. Are adequate approvals required by A/P to process ad agency bills for payment?	____	____	____________
a. Are supporting documents sufficient to justify payments?	____	____	____________
10. Does document review system preclude the possibility of someone altering a R/R to cause an excessive payment to a vendor?	____	____	____________
11. Are bank fees for handling stock and bond transfers reviewed before payment?	____	____	____________
a. Are they properly approved?	____	____	____________
b. Does our CPA firm audit the accuracy of the billing?	____	____	____________
12. Do our controls insure accurate recording of timing of commercial paper we issue?	____	____	____________
a. Do procedures insure that accurate and timely interest payments are made to holders of our commercial paper?	____	____	____________
b. Are commercial paper items accurately and properly reported and posted to correct accounts?	____	____	____________
c. *Is revenue from commercial paper sales promptly deposited and put to work?*	____	____	____________
d. Is an independent reconciliation made of receipts from commercial paper to deposits in banks?	____	____	____________
13. Are sundry disbursement items closely controlled?	____	____	____________
a. Are they all properly approved.	____	____	____________
b. Are they adequately supported and paid on a timely basis?	____	____	____________
14. Are A/P checks, returned by the Post Office as undeliverable, adequately controlled?	____	____	____________
a. Is every effort made to locate Payee?	____	____	____________
b. *Does A/P supervision follow up to*			

C. Control Questions	*Yes*	*No*	*Remarks*
determine if payment was legitimate?	____	____	____
c. Is check voided and our bank account promptly and appropriately adjusted?	____	____	____
15. Are dividend checks, returned by the P.O. as undeliverable, adequately controlled?	____	____	____
a. Do we attempt to locate stockholder?	____	____	____
b. Is check voided, and retained until holder or heir is located?	____	____	____
c. When replacement check is issued, do procedures insure proper handling?	____	____	____
16. Do we adjust our bank account for old outstanding dividend and interest checks?	____	____	____

Questions answered by ______________________ Date ____________
Answers reviewed by ______________________ Date ____________

CRITICAL POINTS

Company disbursements present a fertile field for potential manipulations. So much money is involved, and so many transactions processed daily, that it becomes very difficult to control. Any knowledgeable and persistent employee can illegally obtain company funds; but if the internal controls are sound and the internal auditing effective, the manipulation stands a good chance of being detected. Presented here are but a few of the many ways that disbursements of company funds can be abused. These merely illustrate the type of frauds or defalcations that may occur.

SEVEN POINTS TO CONSIDER

1. A very common method of defrauding a company is through the conspiratorial act of an employee working in collusion with an outside company. The outsider submits invoices that are completely fictitious or that bill for more than was actually shipped or that charge for a higher quality product than was actually delivered.

   The outside company works with a purchasing agent, a receiving clerk or a personal service supervisor. All documentation supports the billing, so there is no basis for A/P to question the payment. These types of manipulations are difficult to detect. **CAUTION:** *Continuous reports of variances can indicate fictitious or short shipments; but quality distinctions are frequently a matter of personal opinion.* Depending on the product involved, it might require an expert to detect a quality substitution scam.

One action, which might reduce the possibility of collusion between an employee and an outsider, is to insist that all purchases and service contracts be awarded on the basis of competitive bids. Most conspiracies are discovered when the conspirators have a falling out, and introducing competition might lead to misunderstandings between the conspirators.

If you encounter antagonism when recommending competitive bids, there's a good chance that an unhealthy relationship exists between the dissenting employee and the company presently handling the business. **TIP:** *You would be wise to insist that competition be introduced or that another supplier be used at least for some orders.*

2. A problem similar to the one just cited occurs when a vendor's invoice accidentally, or intentionally, charges for more product than was received. The supporting papers usually match the invoice. This type of error occurs when the P/O is ambiguous as to the ordered quantity and applicable price; or when the P/O price does not correspond to the normal packaging of the product.

EXAMPLE: The quantity on the P/O may read 12. The product is packed 12 units to a case. One case is received, and the receiver opens the cases sees twelve units and assumes that the 12 on the P/O means one case of twelve units, and writes a 12 on the receiver.

The price stated on the P/O is "open," meaning that the billing price is to be the current price at time of shipment.

The supplier bills for 12, but the price on the invoice is a case price. The invoice is processed and paid and the vendor receives twelve times the amount that should have been paid.

If the error is spotted in A/P by an observant employee who knows the product, the quantities usually ordered and the method of packaging, the vendor issues a credit for the "oversight." If not detected, the vendor has received a substantial overpayment.

KEY POINT: *Careful internal auditing of "open" priced P/O's with ambiguous quantities, can detect these types of errors.* Once spotted a review of previous payments to the same supplier will disclose if a pattern had been established.

The supplier should be billed for the overcharges and be cut off from future business. Unless, of course, the vendor can prove that it was also an innocent victim of a dishonest employee.

3. Disbursement instruments are frequently stolen out of a mail room and altered and cashed. The theft may go undetected until a supplier complains of not having been paid, and most suppliers are loathe to make such complaints on a timely basis.

   In such cases the responsibility for loss rests with the party that cashed the altered document, since the alteration is usually evident. If the document is a draft, the alteration should be detected before the draft is accepted. When "protection" paper is used to print the drafts, any erasure becomes very noticeable. If normal paper has been used, the change may be overlooked by clerks who handle vast numbers of drafts each day. **NOTE:** *Altered checks can easily pass through the mountain of paper processed daily.*

   No matter the circumstances, the net result is a delay in paying a just debt and a loss to the third party who cashed the instrument. Sometimes these third parties are accessories since they cash such items knowing full well that they have been altered.

   One possible way to reduce this practice is to require that all checks or drafts be placed in a sealed mail bag by the employees who process the instruments. In addition, all employees handling both incoming and outgoing mail should be under close supervision at all times when working in the area.

   Once the theft has been accomplished, it will be detected in the normal course of business if a legitimate payment has been extracted, because the intended recipient will soon complain of non-receipt. **KEY POINT:** *During audits of A/P, the normal routine of examining both sides of checks and drafts should disclose those items that were stolen during the period selected for the audit test-check.* If someone succeeds in stealing, without being detected, their success usually encourages them to repeat the thefts regularly until they are caught.

4. As an internal auditor, you are expected to challenge everything that is questionable. This extends to authorization signatures. **KEY POINT:** *The fact that a disbursement document contains an authorized signature does not, of itself, mean that the payment request is legitimate and proper.* Signatures and distinctive initials can easily be forged. Some people develop the ability to copy initials so perfectly that even the person who owns the initials cannot detect the forgery.

   There are many instances of payments of fictitious invoices on the strength of approvals that had been improperly obtained or applied. Executives, who must sign hundreds of documents each day, soon break down and buy a signature stamp. After a period of time, they grow careless and leave the stamp in an unlocked drawer in their desk.

When they are attending conferences or executive meetings they are out of their offices for several hours, and the stamp is available to anyone that knows or suspects where it might be.

KEY POINT: *Sometimes, such a signature stamp permits an obvious manipulation to be processed, simply because no one will question the executive.* That's where you come in. Executives know the auditor's responsibility, and will cooperate completely if they find that their signature has been misused. No executive will be offended if asked to verify that the signature on a questionable document is genuine.

5. Expense reports can be touchy and dangerous, particularly for the higher executive levels. There are cases where executives trust their private secretaries to the point where they give their personal expense receipts to the secretary to prepare the expense report. The secretary obtains the executive's signature and the supervisor's approval and then takes the report to the cashier for reimbursement.

   Along the way, after the executive knows the amount of submitted receipts, a dishonest secretary may increase one of the expenses or add an item that does not require a receipt. Total expenses are increased and the secretary receives the total cash and retains the amount that had been added. The unknowing executive receives the correct amount.

   This scam can occur even if cash isn't used to reimburse expenses. The reimbursement check, for the inflated amount, is returned to the secretary who handles the executive's bank account. At the bank, the dishonest secretary prepares a deposit slip listing the correct amount of the check, and then reduces the total deposit to the amount of actual expenses by obtaining cash for the executive's "pocket money."

   This cash is retained by the secretary as payment for a job well done. The executive's bank statement merely lists the amount of the deposit and doesn't report on the cash given to the depositor.

   Alterations of this type are difficult to detect but there are some procedural safeguards which may discourage such practices. If the cashier is permitted to pay out cash, and it is not feasible to require every expense reporter to draw their own reimbursement, the cashier should place the funds in a special envelope and write the amount on the face of the envelope. All executives should be informed of the procedure and requested to personally check their envelopes.

   Another safeguard is to control the expense report by requiring the superior that approves the expenses to send the report directly for payment instead of returning it to the reporter. **NOTE:** *This is not a guaranteed safeguard because the report may have been inflated before it was passed on for higher approval and the superior may assume that all items are legitimate expenses.*

   One other procedure that discourages this type of manipulation consists of a report issued monthly to each executive, which itemizes the executives expense reports by type of expenses, total of each report and the total payments for the month. Executives review their report, sign it and return it to their superior. **CAUTION:** *When auditing expense reports, you must be alert to all changes and to any expenses that are not supported by receipts.* Gather a group of expense reports for selected executives and look for any variation in writing or signature or for any consistent oddity. Your polite, direct questioning of an executive, by pointing out oddities and requesting that the report be reexamined, will be well received.

6. Some unethical companies send a solicitation for business in a form that appears to be an invoice. In a common approach, the bill states that your company's name will be printed in a local publication when the bill is paid. These solicitations are understandably taken as billings and treated as such. **NOTE:** *The individual requests are for such small sums that they often fall into a category that bypasses normal operating controls.* They usually are received from an area where the company has several operations, and accounts payable personnel assume that they have been sent in by a location manager who elected to be listed in the local publication.

   A/P personnel should be alerted to be on the lookout for these solicitation invoices, and they should route them to local management for their approval. The document should be accompanied by a note indicating the nature of the solicitation. **TIP:** *Some companies authorize their accounts payable section to destroy these solicitations when received.*

7. Another frequent scam occurs when a con artist phones a major supply house and places a large order in the name of a well-known company. The order is for customary items, and the supplier is told that a P/O will be mailed, but that shipment must be expedited. In some cases a phony purchase order number is given to the supplier.

   The caller directs delivery to an address that turns out to be an empty home, office or warehouse. When the product is delivered, the caller is there to accept the items. If questioned, a plausible story is invented to satisfy the delivering agent.

   The supplier believes that product, as ordered by a legitimate customer, has been delivered and expects to be paid. The supplier who does not have a legitimate P/O is the victim of the scam, providing the supplier's improper billing is spotted in A/P before payment.

   KEY POINT: *This type of improper billing can be detected through rigid enforcement of the requirement for matching each invoice against a legitimate P/O and R/R before paying a bill.* The supply house can protect itself and detect this type of scam by adopting a practice of verifying all call-in orders before making a shipment.

Chapter 16

Auditing Taxes, Debt and Equity Accounts

The previous chapter discussed the internal audit procedure for reviewing payables, the short term debt items that have come due. A short term debt is defined as an obligation which is to be paid off within a year period. Agreements that stipulate a payoff period that is longer than a year are considered to be long term debts which we will consider in this chapter. We will also look at all of the other operations that usually fall under the Corporate Treasurer and the Secretary. Our review will center on real estate, taxes, debentures, short term borrowing in the commercial money market, short term investments and equity accounts.

This chapter is devoted to some of the various types of audit assignments that an internal staff is called upon to perform. Some of these reviews are in areas that are closely watched by the external auditors and are, therefore, used as fill-in jobs, since they only require a small amount of internal audit time to complete and can be performed at almost any time. They offer flexibility in planning an audit schedule. For the sake of brevity, we have combined many of the above mentioned areas into one all-inclusive audit program.

Taxes

Taxes present a variety of problems. Tax laws, at all levels of government, are complicated and contain so many concessions to special interests that it takes more than the full time of a tax expert to stay abreast of even a small area of tax laws. Any in-house tax department could understandably overlook potential tax breaks that were written into law to benefit a particular company. This is an area where an outside tax consulting service can be useful.

At the lowest level, cities and counties attempt to induce businesses to locate in their community by offering tax incentives or tax forgiveness for a period of time. A corporation's study of economic justification includes tax benefits in the calculations that shape their decisions; it is important that the entity takes full advantage of these concessions for the stipulated period.

At the next higher level of government, some states use their income and other taxes to encourage, or to discourage, economic activity. These taxes can have an affect on how a company conducts its business. For example, some states have taxed a corporation on total operations, no matter where the corporation was chartered or did business.

This action caused a reaction that lead to the formation of subsidiary corporations that operated solely within the geographic confines of a state, and they paid taxes based only on property and operations within that state. Tax laws also lead to wholesale movements of property just before the effective tax date. It is important that these laws be understood and followed, but at the same time an entity should not pay more than its fair share of the tax load.

Federal tax laws are replete with special interest incentives and tax breaks passed into law to induce citizens to use, or to produce, specific types of products. These tax breaks can make a substantial difference in operating results of affected companies. Federal tax laws can encourage or discourage corporate actions including mergers and acquisitions or a corporation's organization and administration.

KEY POINT: *Internal auditing of the corporate tax department requires a detailed study of all tax laws affecting a company.* Some larger audit staffs may employ a full-time tax expert as a staff member, but most utilize tax consultants when and as required. Tax consultants are usually provided by the firm's public accounting staff.

Corporate Bonds

A review of corporate bonds can be accomplished rapidly, if everything has been handled properly. External auditors concentrate on determining that the corporate books accurately reflect the extent of outstanding obligations, and that payments into the sinking fund and for bond interest assure that there is no default of the bond agreement. Internal auditors share those concerns.

Normally the administration of corporate bonds is handled by a trustee bank, under a formal agreement. When an outside bank is used, auditors must review all agreements and determine that all parties conform. They must also see that sinking funds are used properly, and that the bonds called in for redemption are selected in a fair and impartial manner that does not benefit any special bondholder.

Commercial Paper and Other Notes

Many large organizations issue short term commercial paper as a means of obtaining operating cash at reasonable interest rates. These short term obligations are usually handled within the Treasurer's Department by a section that devotes its full time to this activity. Corporate commercial paper is sold on the open market and redeemed as required by the terms of the note.

The section closely watches the money markets and acts to reduce the corporate interest costs. Commercial paper carries an interest rate that is determined by market conditions at the time the note is issued. The interest rate varies with the credit rating of the issuer, but for the blue chip companies it is usually well below the going prime rate. Volume of trading in commercial paper is somewhat limited because of the large sums of money involved in each transaction. **NOTE:** *A review of these transactions is best performed by an auditor who has a good knowledge of banking, money markets and interest rates.*

Other notes, issued in the normal course of business, cover purchases of equipment or property. Some evidence of indebtedness is used when banks or major stockholders advance funds to companies that need additional cash to meet current obligations. Each transaction carries variable terms and conditions, and the loan document spells out all the pertinent factors.

IMPORTANT: Internal auditors must determine that the following conditions are met:

- All notes are proper legal documents.
- All conditions are followed by all parties.
- Applicable interest payments are made when due; are recorded properly and accurately; and truly reflect interest costs.
- Company records fairly present the extent of the obligations.
- The notes resulted from legitimate, arms-length negotiations.
- The stipulated conditions are fair and reasonable.

Equity Accounts

Internal auditors have a responsibility to protect the interest of the owners of an enterprise. This protection extends to the review of equity accounts to determine that owner's interests are not watered down. In a corporation, ownership interests, as evidenced by stock certificates, are traded on stock exchanges and are easily transferred.

Corporate stocks are divided into different classes with different voting and/or dividend rights. Preferred stock gives the holder some sort of preference over an owner of common stock. The most common preference calls for a set dividend to be paid to the preferred holder before any dividend can be paid on the common stock.

The Corporate Board of Directors authorizes the issuance of stock and defines its rights, privileges and obligations. The minutes of the director's meetings spell out the guidelines controlling all evidence of equity interests in the corporation. These minutes provide the basis for an internal audit review of equity accounts. The *major areas of concern* to the internal, and external, auditor are the following:

1. The issuance of stock and subsequent transfers.
2. The voting of stock, either by proxy or in person.
3. The payment of dividends to the proper holder.

An internal audit of Capital Stock transactions concentrates on the three items listed above and also determines that SEC regulations are followed. Auditors must determine the following:

- All recordings of stock trading are timely and accurate.
- Shareholder lists are accurately and properly updated as required.
- All dividend payments are legitimate, timely and proper.
- All owners receive the same operating reports and notices of shareholder meetings.
- Each owner is given a fair opportunity to exercise voting rights.

These stock transfers are under the jurisdiction of the Corporate Secretary and may be handled in house, but are usually contracted out to the stock transfer department of a bank. Transfer agents receive certificates from sellers, cancel the item and then reissue the same number of shares to the purchasing party. Transfer agents issue periodic reports of the names and stock ownership of all stockholders.

Dividend disbursing agents are usually the same company that handles stock transfers, since these transfers must be coordinated with stock ownership so that dividends are paid to the appropriate holder of the corporation's stock. Some companies elect to pay dividends directly, and they use their in-house payable facilities for these disbursements.

BACKGROUND INFORMATION

Our mythical XYZ Corporation has separate departments for the Secretary and the Treasurer of the corporation. The Secretary is responsible for the issuance and recording of all stock transactions, and for all activities involving stockholders. The Secretary plans the annual meetings, handles proxies, issues the quarterly, annual and special reports and acts as custodian of all official records.

The Secretary of XYZ Corporation has an agreement with a commercial bank which acts as a stock transfer agent. This agency issues new certificates, and cancels the old certificates that have traded hands. The agency keeps an up-to-date list of share owners and the number of shares issued and outstanding in their name.

The Treasurer is responsible for the control and use of cash funds. The department opens and closes bank accounts, transfers funds from depository to disbursement accounts, prepares short and long term cash forecasts, obtains working funds as required, and selects the various financial institutions used by the company. The Treasurer negotiates for the issuance of funded debt and for the issuance of short term commercial paper, and the treasurer decides where to invest available excess funds. The Treasurer is also responsible for the disbursement of dividend checks and interest payments to the proper parties.

XYZ has outstanding bonds that require an annual contribution to a sinking fund that is used to retire a percentage of the outstanding bonds each year. The sinking fund is controlled by the treasury. The corporation uses the short term money market to obtain working funds at a rate well below the prevailing prime rate. Excess funds are used in the short term money market, where interest is earned on funds that would be idle over short periods, such as weekends.

The Treasurer's Department also contains a section that handles taxes and real estate. The director of this section reports directly to the Treasurer. The section is separated into taxes and real estate operations, both of which are headed up by managers.

The company has many locations throughout the United States and has organized the tax department to handle all U.S. locations' taxes. The head office maintains separate files for each U.S. operation and handles all tax matters for those locations.

Records and procedures are designed so that each location receives and approves all tax bills for their operation, and then sends them in to the central tax department for review and payment. Local approval merely means that the tax bill is legitimate, but it does not mean that the amount is correct. A local manager may question the amount of a tax bill in a separate letter to the tax department, but all official challenges are initiated by headquarter's tax department. The tax department has an extensive library containing pertinent tax laws and codes for each operating location. Tax experts study each bill and decide whether to pay it as submitted or to take appropriate action to contest the tax bill or its amount.

If approved by the tax department, the bill is forwarded to accounts payable for processing and payment. A copy of each tax bill is retained in the location's tax file, and a copy which is used to support the disbursement is filed in the A/P files.

We are now ready to examine the internal audit program for a review of taxes and real estate, funded debt, commercial paper transactions, investments and equity accounts.

INTERNAL AUDIT PROGRAM—INSTRUCTIONS

IA MAI700

XYZ CORPORATION
AUDIT INSTRUCTIONS—MISCELLANEOUS
BALANCE SHEET ACCOUNTS

All Operations

A. Read all pertinent accounting manual sections, the Secretary's handbook and the Treasurer's Department Guide before starting your review. Discuss with the EDP audit group the services and reports that are provided to management in this area. Read User's manuals for any computer programs that may be in operation at this time.

B. Enter the department unannounced, and soon after your preliminary meeting with the department head, start your audit work by taking possession of vital records. Copy or schedule important information immediately, so that the records can be returned to the proper party.

C. These balance sheet accounts are studied by our external auditors, and we must coordinate our reviews to reduce duplication of effort. Arrange to meet with our CPA's audit partner that handles our account, and discuss your audit plans. Delete from your program any areas that our external auditors have recently reviewed or are planning to audit in the very near future. **NOTE:** *Some duplication is unavoidable, so be certain that you explore any area that raises a question in your mind.*

Our public accountants are vitally concerned that these accounts are properly handled, controlled and reported. We are also concerned that these activities are handled efficiently and economically and that XYZ's financial interests are wisely and prudently protected. **IMPORTANT:** *We must be certain that any question or evidence of fraud or manipulation is thoroughly investigated.*

Taxes and Real Estate

A. For your review of the tax department, you must become familiar with XYZ's policies and procedures for handling tax matters. Read all of the material relating to taxes in the Accounting Manual, particularly those sections dealing with tax handling of construction costs and equipment purchases.

B. Review the tax department's organization chart and their procedural directives. At the start of your audit, discuss the federal income tax reports with the department manager and determine the identity of the tax consultant that they use. If a situation arises where you think a consultant would be helpful, be sure to clear your request through the audit manager's office before you arrange a meeting. Fees are charged by consultants, and the information you seek may be readily available in our office.

C. From our Locations Register schedule all company locations by city, county, state and country. Compare this list to the individual location tax records that are maintained in the section. Your purpose is to determine that all location's tax assessments and payments are properly recorded, and that the tax department *does not continue to approve the payment of taxes on locations that have been sold.*

D. Review prior tax payment records, from the A/P files. Work with the EDP audit group to obtain a computer printout of tax payments for the period that you select. A study of this listing will give you an idea of the type and amount of taxes paid by specific locations.

Compare amounts of tax bills from comparable locations; if you note any wide discrepancies, discuss them with the tax section manager.

E. Select a small random sample of location cards and use the data in the tax library to confirm that reports and valuations are properly prepared for the locations studied. Discuss these items with tax personnel to determine that they are using a proper approach.

F. **CAUTION:** *Be particularly careful not to misfile, or lose, any reports or correspondence in the tax operation.* Although there are copies of tax bills in A/P, they are filed under the name of the payee, a local tax official, and might therefore be difficult to locate.

G. When reviewing the tax department's operations, bear in mind that XYZ carries a considerable tax load. We want to pay our fair share of the tax burden, but not more than we are legally required to pay. Tax loopholes are deliberately written into the codes and XYZ desires to take advantage of any tax benefit to which it is legally entitled. **IMPORTANT:** *We will not tolerate deliberate undervaluation, or any attempt to illegally reduce our tax liability.* A gift or gratuity to an assessor is contrary to our company policy and, if discovered, is cause for termination of any employee involved. Occasional lunch meetings are acceptable, when the time factor justifies this approach.

H. The Real Estate section is responsible for locating desirable land when required as a potential construction site. It also locates available rental property when and as required. The section also negotiates the terms of lease or purchase, and upon gaining the approval of the Executive Committee, formally completes the contract.

I. You will trace selected land transactions to insure that company real estate people do not profit from their advance knowledge of impending decisions to purchase specific parcels of land. **NOTE:** *Any possibly excessive purchase price or rental rate must be studied.* Take into account the type of land or rental facility involved and the specific area in which it is located.

1. Carefully review the real estate acquisition files. Schedule any purchases or rentals that have been consummated since the last internal audit. Working from a copy of the property schedule in the previous audit working papers, identify and concentrate on those locations which have been added.

   List the additions, and note the dates on original memos or correspondence that first mentioned the location that was finally selected. Examine the Acquisition Committee's minutes and note on your schedule the date that a location is first mentioned. Also note the date the committee approved the location.

2. *Attempt to determine if anyone associated with XYZ profited from knowledge of our intention to obtain the proposed property.* Work with the audit administrator, who will know if an audit team is in the area in question and may

decide to request them to study the matter. Or we may decide to use an outside agency.

A title search is made in the office of the county assessor or recorder. The title transfer search should start at a date *three months before* the first mention of the location in our files. All transfers should be documented up to the date that XYZ acquired the property. This applies to rental as well as purchased property. **KEY POINT:** *Note particularly any transfer that occurred immediately before or after the Acquisition Committee approved the location.*

3. The search information should include the dates, parties involved and price reported as paid. Also have a study made of the transfer price of similar property in the same area at that time. If the price seems to be inflated, if you note any names that could be related to XYZ employees, or if there were businesses involved in these transfers, discuss the matter with the internal audit manager. **IMPORTANT:** *If a business or a familiar name had been involved in the purchase of the property during this period, we may employ an outside agency to determine the identity and background of all interested parties.*
4. It is preferable to have these searches made by staff members, but it may be less costly to use an outside agency located in the area. Any agency hired to gather information should be closely supervised and used merely to obtain specific information. *Don't express an opinion on information gathered by the agency.*

J. Examine the file of leases, and review any leases entered into since the previous audit. Determine, in the manner just described, that the owners of the leased property have no relationship to any XYZ employee. Also satisfy yourself, through examination of the files and discussions with personnel, that leases were entered into after legitimate arms-length negotiations.

Determine that the rental rates charged to XYZ Corporation conform to prevailing rates, for similar quarters in the area at the time that the lease was negotiated. **IMPORTANT:** *If there are any relationships between the owners and XYZ, note if they were disclosed before negotiations began.*

Commercial Paper and Other Notes

A. All of our commercial paper transactions are handled through financial institutions. Each day the responsible section receives a report of short term interest rates offered by leading companies. Our company's offer is included in the list. The interest that we are willing to pay is set by the section's manager after discussions with several financial institutions and approval by the Treasurer.

Our interest rate is affected by our needs for funds, the interest rate offered by our competitors and the prevailing rate in the banking business. In the opposite direction, any periodic excess funds that we have available are put to work overnight, on weekends or for specific periods of time. We attempt to earn a fair return on excess funds, and we strive to obtain required funds at the lowest interest rate possible. **IMPORTANT:** *XYZ does* not *speculate in the money market.*

B. When a sale is made of XYZ's commercial paper, the financial agent notifies our Treasurer of the name of the buyer and the terms of the agreement. The commercial paper section prepares a note naming the buyer and containing the variable information provided by the agent.

The financial institution deducts their fee and remits the balance to our account. Their confirmation notice contains all variable data pertinent to the transaction.

Equity Accounts

A. Arrange through the Corporate Secretary to visit our stock transfer agency. Be polite and open in your discussion with supervisory people at the bank and confine your questions to the handling of our account. Pay close attention to the dates of transactions that are being handled during your visit, so that you can evaluate the timeliness of the agency's handling of our account.

B. All of our surplus accounts are carefully and minutely audited by our public accountants. Our internal audit staff spends very little time in this area. We do not include any audit points in our check-off program and do not expect you to audit this area. However, if any information is noted *which raises a question* as to the accuracy or the handling of any of the surplus accounts, you are to bring the facts to the immediate attention of the audit manager.

C. The Treasury Stock account reports the value of XYZ stock that is held by the company to meet the needs of our employee stock option plan. The Corporate Secretary is responsible for administering this program. That office keeps a record of all options granted, by name of employee, and notifies an employee when certain grants may be exercised. The Secretary also orders purchases of company stock in the open market to meet the needs of the plan. You are expected to review these transactions to insure that proper procedures are followed.

D. The Secretary is responsible for handling all stockholder matters. A major task is the annual meeting of stockholders. The Secretary's office sends out notices of the meeting stating the place, date and time of the scheduled session. The notice includes a proxy statement which may be used by stockholders who do not plan to attend. The proxies are returned to the secretary's office where the results are tabulated. You should determine that stockholders voting rights are fully protected and that proxy counts are accurate.

E. The Secretary is also responsible for insuring that the minutes of the Board of Directors meetings are approved and accepted and that the wishes of the Board are implemented. **IMPORTANT:** *The Secretary must insure that operating or staff departments are informed of the Board's directives, and that they take appropriate action.*

You will review the minutes of the Board meetings and determine that the follow-up work by the Secretary's staff is appropriate and adequate. You should coordinate this work with other audit teams that are reviewing other operations which may be affected.

F. Directors are paid a stipend for each Board meeting that they attend. Necessary paper work is prepared by the secretary's office, and you should verify that payments conform to attendance records.

G. A separate section of the Secretary's office files and controls all important documents. The originals must be carefully guarded, and are held in the fireproof, burglar-proof vault. Copies of all important documents are periodically sent to our attorney's office for filing in their safe. You will evaluate the procedures for handling and safeguarding these documents.

This section is also responsible for informing management of upcoming decisions that must be made in reference to leases or contracts or other legal matters that are about to expire. **KEY POINT:** *You must determine that management is notified in ample time so that an intelligent decision can be reached without undue pressure.*

H. A description of the proper procedure for working with this internal audit program appears in the Introduction to the Audit Programs section of your manual. Read this information carefully.

INTERNAL AUDIT PROGRAM

IA TSP500 XYZ CORPORATION

OFFICES OF THE TREASURER AND THE SECRETARY

The following internal audit program is designed to lead you through the high risk areas of the operations conducted by the corporate offices of the Treasurer and the Secretary. This program is a check list and reminder which you are to modify to meet current conditions.

I. Company Procedures

A. The Treasurer's office handles all financial matters affecting the company.

B. An outside financial agency is used for the issuance, registration and transfer of all corporate bonds.

C. The Secretary's office handles all stockholder matters.

D. An outside transfer agent is used to handle the recording of capital stock movements. The agent issues and cancels stock certificates as required, and keeps up-to-date records of ownership.

E. Dividend and bond interest checks are written in the EDP center and are controlled and distributed by the mailing department.

II. Audit Objectives are to determine the following:

A. Corporate policies and procedures are followed in these operations.

B. The balance sheet accurately reflects funded and short term debt and the equity accounts.

C. All payments of dividends and interest are properly made to the correct parties.

D. Commercial paper transactions and short term loans are promptly processed and properly reported.

E. All valuable papers are properly recorded and safeguarded.

III. Audit Procedures *ALL Operations*	*Per. Cov.*	*Audit By*
A. Review directives, policy statements, procedure manuals and bulletins that relate to the Secretary and the Treasurer.	____	____

III. Audit Procedures	*Per.*	*Audit*
ALL Operations	*Cov.*	*By*
B. Review the outside auditor's bluebacks for items relating to the Secretary and Treasurer operations.	____	____
1. Determine that proper corrective action was taken.	____	____
C. Discuss the operating criteria for their department's activities with the Treasurer and the Secretary.	____	____
1. Note that department personnel follow company policies.	____	____
D. Verify department's payroll by distributing paychecks.	____	____
1. Audit payroll records; follow audit program in the section of your manual titled Auditing Payroll.	____	____
E. Audit disbursements authorized by departments, using the section of your manual titled Auditing Payables.	____	____
F. Audit contracts entered into by departments. Refer to the section of your manual titled Auditing Purchasing.	____	____
G. Review internal operating procedures to determine their necessity and efficiency. See if there are any clerical areas that could be computerized at a savings to XYZ.	____	____
H. Forward any suggestions for improvement of this program.	____	____
Treasury Department		
A. Audit the movement of funds controlled by the Treasurer. Refer to audit program titled Auditing Cash Transactions.	____	____
1. Check the reconciliation of all bank accounts.	____	____
a. Carefully review adjustments made to any account.	____	____
1) *Bring any unusual, or suspicious items to the immediate attention of the internal audit manager.*	____	____
b. Note minimum balances remaining in the accounts.	____	____
1) Study analyses reports received from banks.	____	____
2. Review department's handling of cash receipts.	____	____
a. Determine that all locations collecting funds send a daily message advising treasury of amount deposited.	____	____
b. Tie-in administrative messages of deposits to local depository account records for a test period.	____	____
1) Determine that department performs a daily tie-in.	____	____
c. Tie-in monthly cash receipts reported by locations, to the depository bank statements.	____	____
1) Determine that department does this monthly.	____	____
B. Carefully review all bank transfers. Check timing of in and out movements of funds for timeliness.	____	____
1. Review all bank charges. Study the unusual ones.	____	____
2. *Determine that funds do not lie idle in any bank.*	____	____
C. Review all large pay outs authorized by the treasury.	____	____
1. Tie-in dividend disbursements to stock outstanding.	____	____

III. Audit Procedures *Treasury Department*	*Per. Cov.*	*Audit By*
2. Tie-in interest payments to registration of bonds.	____	____
3. Determine that transfers to the general disbursement account tie-in to the EDP reports of moneys paid out.	____	____
4. Tie-in interest payments to the commercial paper section's report of interest costs.	____	____
a. Tie-in transactions with financial institutions to section's report of short term investments or loans.	____	____
D. Prove the General Ledger figures. Tie-in figures used in your detailed audit to general ledger accounts.	____	____
E. Review correspondence files from banks soliciting business from XYZ. Compare proposed service charges to those that we actually pay for such services.	____	____
1. If lower proposals are in file, discuss with Treasurer the reasons that lower proposals were not accepted.	____	____
2. *If you are not completely satisfied with explanation, discuss the facts with the internal audit manager.*	____	____
F. Review the Treasurer's appointment calendar. Note if any bank representative has a standing luncheon date with a treasury employee. If any do, discuss with employee the frequency of the meetings to learn the purpose.	____	____
Tax Section		
A. Compare your schedule of company locations, which lists all owned or rented locations to the individual location cards and files in the tax section.	____	____
1. Determine that all dispositions of real property are promptly reported to the tax department.	____	____
B. Determine that the section receives monthly reports of values of inventories in outside storage.	____	____
1. Determine that the tax section is advised of all changes in the use of outside warehouses.	____	____
C. Determine that operating systems promptly report all obsolete or spoiled items of personal property.	____	____
1. See that these items are promptly written off the asset values, so that we do not pay taxes, or insurance, on inflated values of personal property.	____	____
D. Obtain computer list of tax payments for selected period.	____	____
1. Tie-in the list to property cards in the section.	____	____
a. *Carefully follow up on any questionable payments.*	____	____
b. See that amounts paid are posted to proper account.	____	____
c. See that payments are charged to correct locations.	____	____
2. Determine that taxes are timely paid to avoid penalties.	____	____
a. See that payments are not made before time required.	____	____
E. Review procedures to insure that tax department takes		

III. Audit Procedures	*Per. Cov.*	*Audit By*
Tax Section		
advantage of every legal means to minimize taxes.	____	____
1. Ascertain that department can support all deductions.	____	____
Real Estate Section		
A. Using the above tax schedule (Tax Section A), check this list against location cards in the Real Estate Section.	____	____
1. Determine that there are deeds or rental agreements for all property listed on your schedule.	____	____
2. Ask the EDP audit group for a computer printout of all rental payments for the past twelve months.	____	____
a. Compare this list to your schedule of locations.	____	____
1) Follow up on any discrepancies. (XYZ may properly pay rent for an office for a broker or sales rep.)	____	____
3. Determine that rental payments conform to agreements.	____	____
B. Study files relating to property purchases and rentals.	____	____
1. Review all acquisitions since last internal audit.	____	____
a. Examine information presented to the Executive Committee when they approved the acquisition.	____	____
1) Determine that information was accurate, complete and that it included known derogatory information.	____	____
2. Select newly acquired and newly rental property for an in-depth study of previous ownership.	____	____
a. Determine that deals were at arms length, between independent parties and that XYZ paid a fair price.	____	____
1) Ascertain whether any XYZ employee was involved as a seller. (Owner, partner or shareholder.)	____	____
a) *If so, report information to audit manager.*	____	____
C. Determine that property taxes conform to agreements made with local taxing bodies *prior* to construction.	____	____
Bond Section		
A. Review the files supporting all outstanding bond issues.	____	____
1. Determine that all actions were approved by the Board.	____	____
2. Confirm that bond issuance decisions were approved.	____	____
a. Were competitive proposals solicited? If not, why not?	____	____
B. Review the list of registered bonds and determine that the value of outstanding ties-in to XYZ's general ledger.	____	____
1. Schedule bonds by specific interest rates.	____	____
a. See that total bond interest payment is correct.	____	____

III. Audit Procedures *Bond Section*	*Per.* *Cov.*	*Audit* *By*
C. Audit sinking fund transactions.	____	____
1. Determine that retired bonds are accurately recorded and properly handled.	____	____
a. Ensure that no interest is paid after retirement.	____	____
2. Determine that any bonds recalled are selected in a random manner that is fair and equitable.	____	____
3. Discuss with the Treasurer the practice of buying sinking fund requirements in the open market.	____	____
D. Review the billings from the transfer agency.	____	____
1. Ascertain what verification of activity is made before the bill is approved for payment.	____	____
2. Note if Treasurer verifies charges before personally approving the bill for payment.	____	____
E. Have Treasurer arrange for auditor visit to the office of the bank trustee.	____	____
1. Review operating procedures relating to our account.	____	____
2. Evaluate controls over transfers and cancellations.	____	____
3. Determine that work is accomplished on a timely basis.	____	____
4. Test check endorsements on bonds turned in against the registered holder's name.	____	____
a. Follow up on all exceptions.	____	____
5. Review complaints relating to handling XYZ's account.	____	____
a. Determine that prompt action is taken on complaints.	____	____
6. Review controls and safeguarding of blank certificates and canceled certificates.	____	____
a. For a test period tie-in cancellations to reports.	____	____
b. For a test period tie-in issuances to reports.	____	____
7. Reconcile total number of certificates to the billing from the company that printed the certificates.	____	____
F. Determine if the Treasurer's department has a program for evaluating the interest market with the thought of calling in the outstanding high interest bonds.	____	____
1. Do they consider issuing a new debenture?	____	____
2. Do they consider exchanges?	____	____
a. Are the costs of redemption and new issuance or exchanges considered in the equations?	____	____
G. Review procedures used for preparing all cash forecasts.	____	____
1. Are figures accumulated from operating departments, or do treasury personnel make independent calculations.	____	____
2. Determine that forecasts are reviewed by Financial before they are presented to the Operating Committee.		

III. Audit Procedures	*Per. Cov.*	*Audit By*
Commercial Paper Section		
A. Carefully review all procedures and controls relating to the issuance of short term commercial papers.	____	____
1. For test period, schedule all confirms of paper sales.	____	____
a. Compare notes written during period to the schedule.	____	____
b. Tie-in totals on schedules to the entries made to the appropriate accounts.	____	____
c. Determine that receipts are promptly deposited.	____	____
2. Note that interest rates conform to day's offerings.	____	____
a. Compare rates actually paid to the sheet listing of daily offerings, for the day issued.	____	____
b. Compare interest rates paid, to published rates in financial papers for the appropriate period.	____	____
B. Determine that issued notes were paid as per agreement.	____	____
C. Determine that fees paid to financial agencies conform to agreements and tie-in to reported transactions.	____	____
D. Review in detail all of this section's loan transactions.	____	____
1. Carefully check the timeliness of dating and recording transactions. *A few hours difference can amount to much money.* Review all overnight and weekend transactions.	____	____
a. Determine that department procedures insure accurate and timely recordings of transactions.	____	____
b. Determine that section obtains legal confirmation of every loan made, which states all conditions.	____	____
c. Determine that interest rates are appropriate.	____	____
1) *Determine that all interest earned is received.*	____	____
d. Determine that all loans are collected and that funds are accurately recorded and promptly deposited.	____	____
E. Determine that there are *NO speculative transactions.*	____	____
Office of the Secretary		
A. Audit stockholders records. Obtain a complete list of stockholders of record as of a specified date.	____	____
1. Specified date should be the last date of record of the last declared dividend.	____	____
a. Tie this listing in to Secretary's control listing of outstandings received from our transfer agent.	____	____
2. Request a two month listing of all stock transfers.	____	____
(One month before and after quarter earnings are reported.)		
a. Review this list for large trades which might be an indication of insider trading. Determine if any employees were involved in large trades.	____	____

III. Audit Procedures *Office of the Secretary*	*Per. Cov.*	*Audit By*
1) *Possibility of XYZ employee involvement in insider trading should be reported to the audit manager.*	____	____
B. Audit the billing from the transfer agent.	____	____
C. *Review procedure for handling uncashed dividend checks.*	____	____
1. Determine that every effort is made to locate stockholders whose checks are returned by the U.S. mail.	____	____
2. Determine that uncashed checks are written off after six months, but still retained in our records.	____	____
D. Review procedures and controls for safeguarding and filing important documents.	____	____
1. Update the previous audit listing of the important documents on file in the Secretary's office.	____	____
a. Reconcile old listing to new. Follow through on retirements or additions for proper handling.	____	____
1) *Trace interest transactions through to Ledger.*	____	____
2) *Trace royalty or commissions through to Ledger.*	____	____
b. Refer to program in manual Auditing Receivable Transactions, and use applicable audit steps.	____	____
c. Refer to program titled Auditing Property and Other Assets, and use applicable audit steps.	____	____
2. Determine that an adequate system exists for notifying concerned personnel of termination dates of leases.	____	____
a. See that system provides ample time for looking for new quarters or renegotiating existing leases.	____	____
3. Determine that all notes and contracts are filed in a fireproof, burglar proof safe or vault.	____	____
a. See that copies of these important documents are filed at a second location. (Lawyer's office.)	____	____
E. Review the minutes of the Board of Directors meetings.	____	____
1. Schedule all decisions that were of a directive nature. See that appropriate action was taken on all matters.	____	____
a. Review follow-up procedures used by the Secretary.	____	____
b. Report to audit manager on any items still pending.	____	____

Audit papers reviewed by ______________________ Date ____________

OFFICES OF THE CORPORATE SECRETARY AND TREASURER

INTERNAL CONTROL QUESTIONNAIRE

The following internal control questions are intended to direct your attention to the high risk areas of this operation. Some of these points are covered in the audit program and are included here to insure that they receive adequate attention.

Answer these control questions as your audit progresses. In section B you are to write in the names and job titles of the various employees who perform the listed functions. Be certain to note any conflicting duties that could jeopardize internal control.

I. The following indicates satisfactory internal control procedures.

A. Important Treasury actions receive Executive Committee approval.
B. Written confirmations are received for all loan transactions.
C. Outside agencies handle all stock and bond transfers.
D. Outside auditors carefully review Surplus and Equity accounts.
E. All real estate transactions are approved by Acquisition Committee.

II. Listed functions are performed by:

Function:	*Name/Position*	*Conflicting Duties:*
A. Agrees to sell notes.	______	______
1. Approves transactions.	______	______
2. Records transactions.	______	______
B. Tabulates proxy votes.	______	______
C. Controls stockholder list.	______	______
D. Controls bondholder list.	______	______
E. Custodian of records.	______	______
F. Negotiates leases.	______	______
G. Approves tax bills.	______	______

III. Control Questions	*Yes*	*No*	*Remarks*
A. Are land purchase intentions held in strictest confidence?	___	___	______
1. Is a real estate company name used in negotiations, rather than XYZ Corp.?	___	___	______
2. Is there any evidence of impropriety in purchase or rental negotiations?	___	___	______
3. Are all commissions and fees adequately supported and properly approved?	___	___	______
4. Are all transactions properly reported and approved by the Executive Committee before agreements are signed?	___	___	______
B. Are controls over processing of taxes adequate to prevent payment of duplicate or personal or fictitious tax bills?	___	___	______
1. Have we taken advantage of all tax concessions offered by local officials?	___	___	______
2. Do controls insure that all property dispositions are promptly reported and property tax records adjusted?	___	___	______

III. Control Questions	*Yes*	*No*	*Remarks*
C. Are tax department employee expense reports closely scrutinized before approval?	____	____	____________
D. Do controls insure that payments of bond interest is timely and accurate?	____	____	____________
1. Could a name be added for bond interest payments even if no bond was issued?	____	____	____________
2. *Are interest checks returned by P.O. handled properly and promptly?*	____	____	____________
3. Are outstanding checks that have not been cashed in six months written off?	____	____	____________
E. Are trustee fees for handling bond matters reviewed by Treasurer before approval?	____	____	____________
1. Do charges conform to agreement?	____	____	____________
F. Is there a double-check to insure the accuracy of bond holder identification?	____	____	____________
1. Are all certificates accounted for?	____	____	____________
2. Are numbers tied-in to printer's bill?	____	____	____________
G. Does Treasurer consider calling in bond issue when interest rate falls well below our interest rate on outstanding bonds?	____	____	____________
1. Are bank fees considered?	____	____	____________
2. Are bonds bought in the open market when bond prices fall well below par value?	____	____	____________
H. Are equity accounts correctly stated on the Balance Sheet?	____	____	____________
1. Are these accounts closely audited by our outside auditors?	____	____	____________
2. Are stockholders lists complete, accurate and kept up to date?	____	____	____________
a. *Can a fictitious name be added to list to receive dividends?*	____	____	____________
b. Is there a double check to insure the accuracy of holder's identification?	____	____	____________
I. Are dividend payments adequately controlled?	____	____	____________

III. Control Questions	*Yes*	*No*	*Remarks*
1. *Are checks "Return to Sender" handled properly and promptly?*	____	____	____________
a. Do supervisors determine reason for not having a proper address?	____	____	____________
2. Are uncashed items written off after an appropriate period of time?	____	____	____________
3. *Do we use drafts* for dividend, and interest payments, *rather than checks?*	____	____	____________
J. Does Secretary purchase treasury stock to insure supply for stock options?	____	____	____________
1. Is stock for options purchased when market falls below option price?	____	____	____________
K. Does the Secretary prepare a list of large transfers of stock that involve employees?	____	____	____________
1. Is it reviewed by top executives?	____	____	____________
L. Are transfer agent's bills examined by Secretary before approval?	____	____	____________
M. *Are supplies of blank stock and bond certificates closely safeguarded?*	____	____	____________
1. Are controls adequate to determine if any certificates are stolen?	____	____	____________
N. Are all reports and public statements cleared in advance with Legal?	____	____	____________
O. Do payments to Directors conform to the attendance records of the Board?	____	____	____________

Questions answered by ____________________ Date __________

Answers reviewed by ____________________ Date __________

CRITICAL POINTS

The following cautions are described to alert internal auditors to some of the pitfalls which may lay hidden in the operations of the Corporate Secretary and the Corporate Treasurer.

ELEVEN CRITICAL POINTS TO CONSIDER

1. Many communities only pay their tax assessor a token salary. Assessors, in these areas, must find other sources of income. Sometimes they accept gifts from grateful taxpayers whose tax base is less than what it should be. Some of these taxpayers are businesses who find it easier to drop a fifty or a one hundred dollar bill at a lunch table, than to go through the cost and bother of legal action to get a fair tax assessment.
   KEY POINT: *Public corporations cannot afford to permit such activities.* Even though the legal method is much more time consuming and expensive, it is the only ethical and safe approach. A precedent can be established if a company allows any of their employees to engage in payoffs of any type, even though the employees may believe that what they are doing is best for the company.

   Such payments, when made, are in cash, and are often charged to the company on the personal expense report of the tax department employee. Auditors should review expense reports that cover trips to locations where assessments are being prepared. If county assessors are listed as being entertained, look for unsupported expenses. If any are noted, a brief conversation with the employee who submitted the report should bring out all pertinent facts.

   It is not uncommon, nor improper, to hold business discussions over a lunch table. Picking up the lunch tab cannot be faulted, but your company policy should forbid excessive entertainment or payments to officials to gain favorable rulings. **REMEMBER:** *It is much wiser to encourage the use of legal counsel for tax negotiations or litigation.*
2. If a taxing body unfairly assesses company property, sometimes the most economical long term action is to move the property out of the jurisdiction of the taxing body. Some companies have resorted to forming new corporations that handle all activities within a given area to avoid being taxed on the full corporate activity and results.
3. Potential tax savings start in the design stage of construction, and tax experts should be consulted during that period. **NOTE:** *The distinction of real or personal property can rest on the method of attachment and the use of the property.*

   Taxable classifications affect the size of the tax bill. Advance planning and considering all the tax factors can result in a design and a plan for construction which may materially reduce the tax load.
4. Property valuations may include allocated charges that should not be taxable. Valuations, particularly of personal property, may include obsolete materials or items which have been disposed of but not properly reported

or adjusted. Point of sale materials, or packaging supplies can become useless, but through oversight are not discarded. **CAUTION:** *These items may be carried on your books at cost, even though they may not even have a salvage value.*

5. A company's tax department may inadvertently or deliberately approve the personal tax bill of a company employee. Sometimes the distinction can be fuzzy, such as when an executive's personal property is often used for company business. Tax bills frequently identify property by parcel and lot number or some other technical way that is not readily apparent to an A/P clerk. If the bill is approved by the tax department, it is usually paid without question.

   KEY POINT: *During an audit of the tax department, auditors must carefully study every tax bill paid to be certain that it covers property that is owned or used by the company.* All facts should be made known and the handling should be approved by appropriate management.

   When personal tax bills are improperly paid by company funds, the employee involved may claim that the bill was approved in error. **TIP:** *An audit of previous period payments may disclose similar errors.*

6. Payroll tax computations, calculated and recorded by data processing equipment, are capable of being manipulated. **CAUTION:** *Fractional cents, when all are rounded and accumulated, can amount to a substantial sum of money in a large payroll.* Improper accumulations has been found to have been added to a particular paycheck, or used to create a separate paycheck that is taken by a computer employee.

   Auditors must verify that tax computations are exactly correct, and that reports of tax withholdings exactly match payroll records.

7. Many people earn fortunes by speculating in real estate. In some instances there is no risk involved, since the investors know in advance that the property is being sought by a government agency or a major corporation. Rezoning and putting blocks of property holdings together, can turn cheap farm land into expensive commercial property. A little advance knowledge in this area can be worth a lot of money.

   Some companies form real estate firms that are basically created to procure property for the organization without revealing the name of the prospective buyer. This approach can be effective if used sparingly. But so long as individuals are involved, there is always the danger of a leak of information in a critical situation.

   Once the contract is signed, the price is fixed. If the property value skyrocketed just before purchase, someone profited, perhaps illegally. If the profiteer is a company employee, legal action may possibly recover some of the profit. If no relationship can be established, there is nothing that the company can do.

TIP: *To guard against such possibilities, a firm can obtain a title search before reaching final agreement on a price.* By procuring an option on the property, the potential purchaser buys time to consider all data and search out previous ownership and recent transfer prices. With this information in hand, an intelligent, well informed decision can be reached.

8. Any activity that involves large sums of money carries with it the potential for loss through ignorance, carelessness, manipulation or fraud. Corporate bond or stock issuances are activities of this nature, and the agencies that handle these transactions receive a high fee for the service. **CAUTION:** *These agents are willing to pay a substantial commission for the business. Some of this commission can find its way back to the individual who selects the agency to be used.*

   In the handling of various funds, the fund managers and the stock brokers may engage in the illegal activity of rebating part of the brokerage to the fund manager in return for selecting the broker. **TIP:** *If assets of the fund are actively churned, the broker earns more commissions which means a greater return to the fund manager.*

   In floating new stocks or bonds, the financial institution that is selected stands to make a tidy, risk free profit. The fee paid by the client may include a commission for the employee that awarded the business. Auditors often learn of such arrangements through accident or because of a falling out among the parties.

   When faced with this type of activity, you should attempt to at least determine that an element of competition was present in the selection of the successful firm. **TIP:** *Open and fair competition is the best protection against illegal commissions.* The agreed fee should be close to fees paid to other agencies for similar offerings.

   One important control over these offerings is to require that a committee of executives consider the proposals, rather than placing the matter solely in the hands of the Treasurer. Such a committee should be composed of independent and concerned executives who have no possible interest in any company that is soliciting the business.

9. Any bank executive would be very grateful for the opportunity of servicing a major corporate account. These people may show their gratitude for new or continuing business by showering the employee responsible for these decisions with lavish gifts, entertainment, vacations or cash payments.

   This expression of gratitude is very difficult to detect, particularly since it is quite common for bankers to entertain corporate officials. **KEY POINT:** *Auditors must at least determine that bank service charges and fees are reasonable and that they are not greater than the prevailing rates in the area for similar services.*

You should review the Treasurer's department files of solicitations from other banks, taking note of proposed service charges, fees and free services offered. You may find it interesting to discuss some of these proposals with bankers who failed to get any business.

KEY POINT: *If your company pays more for services than the proposals suggest, you have adequate reason to question the Treasurer as to why your company is overpaying for banking services.*

Proposals offering lower charges may be destroyed by an employee who receives kickbacks from the current bank. To find if this type of deception has occurred, you should study the Treasurer's department appointment calendar and determine that a proposal is in the file from every bank that has sent a representative to call. **TIP:** *If there is no correspondence in files from a visiting banker, you may wish to call the banker to ask if a proposal has been submitted.*

10. If your company uses an outside financial agency to issue dividend and interest checks, you should consider suggesting that drafts be used instead of checks. You need not deposit funds to cover drafts until they are presented for payment. Several days could elapse before the bulk of the drafts are presented, thus saving interest.

    KEY POINT: *In addition, the use of drafts eliminates the need for your company to provide funds to cover checks issued to recipients who do not rush to cash their checks.* Your company can be using these funds rather than allowing the bank to use them.

11. There are frequent reports in the daily papers of incidents of counterfeiting and theft of corporate bonds or stock certificates. You should be alert to weaknesses in the physical security over these important documents.

    CAUTION: *Remember that the risk factor starts at the print shop.*

Chapter 17

Auditing Personnel and Payroll Departments

This chapter covers the internal audit of both a Personnel and a Payroll Department. Internal auditors review these departments to insure that all employees are aware of, and follow, company policies and procedures. They examine both the open and closed files to determine that Personnel and Payroll Departments are adhering to all labor laws.

Locating, interviewing and selecting new employees can be a difficult and sometimes costly undertaking. The method of advertising for a needed employee can vary from advertising in newspapers to working with available public employment agencies, private agencies, and/or high priced "headhunters."

Hiring costs, nil when using public employment agencies, may be as high as one year's salary when using a high priced agency. The selection of publications to carry help wanted ads can vary from a few dollars up to thousands of dollars. **NOTE:** *Advertising and hiring costs are areas that the internal auditor must carefully review.*

Personnel departments play a major role in staffing an organization; through this service they help determine the future of the company. Unless given explicit instructions to the contrary, people who conduct original interviews automatically reject a great many prospects. Without thinking, personnel people may establish criteria for height, build, color, weight, age, sex, religion or nationality factors in their screening process.

There are certain fair labor standard acts that require large organizations to avoid discrimination, but these laws are difficult to enforce. Sometimes it is hard to tell whether a company has conformed to the rules or has violated them. Generally, the fact that a company employs a percentage of people of different sexes, races, religions, nationalities and ages will be accepted as proof that the company is at least trying to comply with the law.

The use of temporary help is another area of operations that must be studied by internal auditors. Personnel selects the companies that supply temporary help and negotiates the price to be paid. At times a company may elect to hire new permanent employees, but they place them on the temporary agency's payroll for a period of time.

This type of handling is useful if there is doubt about the prospect fitting into an organization, but it is more common in government agencies operating under a tight budget restriction that prevents adding new permanent employees but allows temporary help. These employees are used until the next budget period permits the adding of more employees. During this transition period the operation is paying much more for the worker than would have been necessary had they hired the individual directly.

Personnel departments also play an important role in establishing pay scales for company employees. In order to obtain salary, and similar types of information, the personnel department subscribes to publications that print salary surveys by professions, trades and lines of business. These surveys are useful in evaluating existing pay scales and fringe benefits.

Once an employee is hired and compensation agreed to, payment for services rendered becomes the responsibility of the Payroll Department. Payroll works closely with Personnel, and handles all matters relating to employees paychecks. Payroll costs represent a major controllable expense in most businesses, and is potentially subject to manipulation or fraud.

KEY POINT: *Padded payrolls may be charged off to expense indefinitely unless and until they are disclosed during an internal audit or by some other unforeseen event.*

The payroll department handles deductions for taxes and special withholdings as authorized by employees. These withheld sums are then accumulated and paid out to appropriate parties. Payroll must make certain that proper authorizations are obtained for all withholdings.

Internal auditors are interested in the manner in which company funds are used to advertise for prospective employees and to pay outside employment agencies for services rendered. They are concerned that employees are paid their agreed salaries and that all deductions are handled accurately and promptly. They must insure that retirement and termination payments are properly computed and handled.

In short, the audit examination follows through from the point that a requisition for a new employee is received in Personnel until the final payment is made to a terminating employee. The auditor ensures that company interests are protected in the following:

- The advertising, interviewing and selecting of employees.
- Wage negotiations and the payments of wages to all employees.
- The final payments to all retiring or terminating employees.

IMPORTANT: *Where the payroll operation is computerized, the auditor must become fully conversant with the computer program and must audit the computer generated information.*

Background Information

Our sample program is designed for XYZ Corporation's Personnel and Payroll operations. These are two separate and distinct functions in the company. The Personnel Department of XYZ is under the control of a Director of Human Resources and the Director reports to the President of the company. The Personnel department has managers of various sections, such as Placement, Benefits, Wage Classifications, and Administration.

Headquarter's staff establishes personnel policies and procedures for the entire company. All major operating locations have a local personnel department that reports to the top executive of the location but has a dotted line responsibility to the headquarters staff.

The Supervisor of the *Payroll Department* reports to a financial controller. XYZ processes its payroll on a computer, using a custom designed payroll program. The central payroll staff is located in the headquarters office, but all locations employ a payroll clerk who handles local payroll problems in conformance with established policy, forms and procedures. The clerk reports to the local office manager.

There are three separate and distinct entities that auditors must examine in this audit: the Personnel Department, the Payroll Department and the Computer operation that processes employee paychecks.

The hiring process starts in the Personnel Department that locates the prospective employee and conducts the preliminary interview. This interview is intended to determine whether the prospect has attained the degree of proficiency and/or education that the job requires, and that the prospect's application form contains all the necessary information.

After the application is checked for accuracy and completeness, Personnel schedules an interview with the supervisor who requested a new hire and who makes the final decision. If the decision is made to hire, the prospect is returned to the Personnel Department for salary negotiations. When an agreement is reached, Personnel prepares a payroll notice.

Once hired, the Payroll Department receives the payroll notice and creates the employee's job file. Authorizations for all withholdings are filed in the employee's payroll jacket, and all necessary information is entered into the payroll data base so that the computer can issue the proper payroll checks. Although the computer writes the checks and summarizes the information, the Payroll Department is responsible for maintaining the employees' file of payroll records.

Payroll checks are written by the Computer Department in conformance with data entered into the system by Payroll clerks. This data includes the number of hours to be paid, the applicable rates, and any overtime or premium bonuses earned by the individual. Records of all disbursements are retained in the data base.

The computer generates a periodic payroll report each time the payroll is processed. This report lists all pertinent information relating to each individual paycheck.

Paychecks are printed in a room that is separated from the computer processing center. They are printed under tight security and under the control of the mailing department.

With that as background, we can now examine the sample internal audit program for a review of operations conducted by the Personnel and Payroll departments.

IA PPI009 XYZ CORPORATION

INTERNAL AUDIT PROGRAM—PERSONNEL AND PAYROLL DEPARTMENTS

INTERNAL AUDIT INSTRUCTIONS

This program is designed to cover Personnel Department activities in locating, selecting and hiring new employees; and Payroll Department operations involved in the issuance of paychecks and the discharging of Payroll's responsibility for all related functions.

Before starting your audit, review these instructions, the audit checkoff program (IA PPP008) and the internal control questionnaire. Use this program as a guide to be revised when or as appropriate.

I. Both Departments

A. You must become familiar with all policies, directives and operating procedures relating to personnel and payroll matters. Read the Employee Benefits Manual, the Personnel Policies Manual and the Accounting Manual pages covering personnel and payroll activities.

B. You must also read and fully understand the information in the User's Manual for the Computer Payroll System. Consult with the Manager of EDP Auditing and discuss the payroll program. Arrange to obtain pertinent regular and special computer reports as required.

C. Remember that you are responsible for the audit of these two departments. **CAUTION:** *Even though reports are prepared by computer, you must verify their accuracy.* Not only will you verify that all rates and deductions are accurate, *but also that the computer calculations are accurate.*

Fractional pennies, when added up, can amount to a lot of money. You must select samples of payments that involve fractional cents for gross pay and for deductions from payroll. The computer program must be designed to increase by one cent when the third figure to the right of the decimal is a 5 or over, and to drop the third figure when it is a 4 or under. **IMPORTANT:** *If you determine that this is not the way the computer is handling these fractions, so inform the audit manager.*

D. A description of the proper procedure for working with this internal audit program appears in the Introduction to the Audit Programs section of your manual. Read this information carefully.

II. Personnel Department

A. Personnel policies and procedures are conceived and written by the Personnel Department, but they are frequently prompted by action of the Executive Committee. Directives issued by the Executive Committee are frequently assigned to Personnel to implement. During your audit you will review the minutes of the Executive Committee meetings to ascertain that decisions made at these meetings are correctly interpreted and implemented by Personnel.

B. Your review of Personnel screening procedures is intended as an evaluation of their instructions and guidelines. Your main concern is to determine that these directives encourage adherence to the laws that relate to hiring practices.

C. The Personnel Department participates in all labor union contract negotiations. The negotiating team also includes a member of XYZ's outside legal consultants.

You should be certain to include in your review of department authorized disbursements, an audit of the expense reports for all members of the negotiating team. *Scrutinize any large outlays.*

D. Personnel should have a file for all current and former employees. The file should contain the application form, all payroll notices and work evaluation reports. The file should also contain all reprimands or commendations which the employee received.

Any enquiries concerning former employees are to be answered by merely stating the dates of employment and the job titles of positions held while employed by XYZ.

E. Unclaimed paychecks for terminated employees are usually turned over to the personnel department. These occur when an employee suddenly leaves the company without waiting for a termination check. **CAUTION:** These checks are an invitation to steal, *particularly since there are currency exchanges that offer to cash any check presented.*

III. Payroll Department

A. Payroll jackets must contain all information concerning current employees. Records of former employees must also be retained for fifteen years after they leave the company. These files should contain copies of payroll information found in the Personnel files, plus signed authorization forms supporting all payroll deductions and a record of all payments made to an employee.

B. Payroll is the only department with authority to instruct the computer to increase salaries, make adjustments or to delete or add names to the payroll. **KEY POINT:** *With this thought in mind, be particularly careful when you review adjustments to payroll records.*

C. Computer terminal operators are assigned a specific entry code that permits them to gain access to the payroll data base. The code is tied-in to the specific computer terminal that the operator uses. These codes must be kept confidential and only used by the rightful employee. Operators should sign off when leaving their station and sign in when they return. **CAUTION:** *Once a terminal is admitted to a data base, anyone can input data.*

You should observe operators just before breaks or lunch periods to see if they sign off or leave the terminal open while they leave their station.

Observe whether the section supervisor takes breaks with the operators or remains in the area during the absence of the operators.

D. To further protect against unauthorized data entry to the payroll program, a daily report of Payroll Base Changes is printed in the computer center and delivered daily to the Manager of Payroll. The manager is responsible for insuring that all changes entered were accurate and authorized.

E. A report of all payroll information input through remote terminals is printed daily and delivered to the Manager of Payroll. Any unusual entries that the manager notes are brought to the attention of the appropriate line executive of the operations concerned. The payroll manager cannot change this data, since any corrections or alterations must be entered by the location that entered the original data. Line executives, in headquarters, order local managers to make necessary changes and give a copy of their directive to the payroll manager who ensures that changes are correctly and promptly entered.

F. The computer prints payroll transfer checks to banks, which lists employees, their account numbers and their net pay. *Each transfer check is for the total of all net pays listed.* The computer program will not issue other checks to employees listed on a transfer check.

G. If you note an employee's name that appears on our payroll records for just a short time, review all pertinent records carefully. Compare the paycheck endorsement against employment application records and other correspondence in the files. Also compare the check endorsements to the signature of applicable supervisors and department heads. **KEY POINT:** *If a similarity of signature arouses suspicion, bring the matter to the attention of the manager of internal audits.* A handwriting expert may be employed to compare the writings.

H. Pay particular attention to verifying any employee whose record indicates termination on or about the time that you started your audit of payroll. **CAUTION:** *Your payroll audit should be a surprise visit, but it could cause a miscreant to terminate a nonexisting employee in order to avoid detection when you pass out the paychecks.*

Bear in mind that many payroll frauds begin when a production line employee terminates, but the line supervisor neglects to inform payroll and a paycheck is sent to the supervisor. **NOTE:** *The foreman can continue to receive the paycheck by merely filling out or punching and approving a time card bearing the terminated employee's name.*

I. Paychecks may be mailed directly to an employee's bank or may be sent to supervisors for distribution to employees. During your audit you will select a sampling of departments to verify the payroll, and will personally distribute or mail all paychecks. **KEY POINT:** *Your verification should include all employees of the Personnel and Payroll departments.*

Before you mail out any checks, speak to the employee whose check is mailed, to verify the individual and the job.

In selecting departments to verify payroll, favor the departments that don't have many employees. Larger departments are all audited by our department and the payroll is verified at that time. If audits of headquarter's departments are being conducted while you are auditing payroll, work closely with the other audit teams so that we do not duplicate our efforts.

J. Except for checks for Payroll Department employees, valid paychecks are not supposed to be returned to the payroll department. Unclaimed paychecks are to be returned to the Personnel Department so that they can locate the proper parties and release the checks.
KEY POINT: *Carefully review this area, because some of these checks may be fraudulent.* Even though Personnel and Payroll perform their jobs properly, there may still be fraudulent paychecks issued. These may be written for people who have left the company or who never existed.

INTERNAL AUDIT PROGRAM

IA PPP008

XYZ CORPORATION
INTERNAL AUDIT PROGRAM—PERSONNEL AND PAYROLL DEPARTMENTS

This audit program is designed to lead you through a routine audit of the Personnel and Payroll departments. Use this program as a guide to be altered to meet any unusual conditions encountered. Bring to your audit supervisor's attention any changes that appear necessary.

I. Company Procedures

A. All transactions affecting employees are authorized by a properly approved payroll notice.
B. All employees, below the executive level, prepare a weekly time report or punch a daily time card which supports payments.
C. Company wide personnel policies are approved in advance by the corporate Executive Committee.
D. Paychecks are computer generated and printed and then mechanically inserted in envelopes to be directly distributed by Mailing Dept.
E. Accounting data is prepared by the computer, which summarizes all paycheck information, and all deductions made from the payroll.
F. Personnel establishes and monitors all employee benefit programs.

II. Audit Objectives are to determine the following:

A. Company procedures and internal controls are adequate and are being followed by all department personnel.
B. Personnel additions, terminations, and adjustments are handled accurately, properly and promptly.
C. Computer programs are operating efficiently, effectively, properly and correctly.
D. Company benefit programs are adequately controlled, and all funds are properly handled and reported.
E. Hiring practices, working hours and conditions meet all legal requirements.
F. Outside agency contracts, and contacts, are well controlled.

	Per. Cov.	Audit By
III. Audit Procedures		
Both Departments		
A. Read all directives and manuals covering these operations.	____	____
1. Read sections of the Accounting Manual that relate to Payroll and Personnel responsibilities and activities.	____	____
2. Read the Personnel Policy Manual and the Payroll Procedures Manual. (Read until you understand those parts that are not familiar to you.)	____	____
3. Study the Users Manual for the computerized Payroll control system, and any other computer system used by the Payroll or Personnel department.	____	____
a. Discuss audit plans with the supervisor of the EDP audit group.	____	____
1) Ask that they inform you, well in advance, when the computer operation is about to process any Personnel or Payroll data.	____	____
a) Arrange for one of your team members to be in printing room when paychecks are run.	____	____
B. Update organization charts and enumerate duties and responsibilities of employees.	____	____
1. Note if duties and responsibilities are clearly defined and properly delegated and followed.	____	____
2. Note if there are any overlapping or duplication of functions or responsibilities.	____	____
C. Review the coordination and cooperation existing between the Personnel and the Payroll departments.	____	____
1. Determine that an independent attitude is displayed by the Payroll department.	____	____
a. Determine that payroll demands and receives proper documentation and approval *before taking action.*	____	____
D. Discuss policies and procedures with department employees to insure that their interpretations are correct.	____	____
E. Verify department payroll by taking possession of paychecks, as they are printed, and personally distributing them to all Payroll and Personnel department employees.	____	____
1. *Carefully follow up on any unclaimed paychecks, or checks that have been returned by the post office.*	____	____
F. Review purchases made by or for the departments. (Refer to audit pıogram titled Audit of Purchasing.)	____	____
1. Determine that controls over ordering of services, such as want-ad placements, or merchandise are adequate.	____	____
2. Determine that approval controls are adequate.	____	____
G. Determine that controls are adequate over the receiving of goods and services. (Refer to audit program titled Auditing of Payables.)	____	____

	Per. Cov.	Audit By
III. Audit Procedures		
Both Departments		
1. Determine that supplier's bills are carefully reviewed before approval.	____	____
H. Carefully review termination reports for a selected period since the last internal audit.	____	____
1. *Pay particular attention to additions right after the last audit was completed and to terminations close to the starting date of your current review.*	____	____
a. Review payroll jacket for legitimacy of employment.	____	____
b. Examine paychecks, look closely at endorsements.	____	____
1) Review paychecks of applicable supervisors, see if there is a similarity of endorsements.	____	____
a) If deposited, check out bank account number.	____	____
c. If practical, talk to employees who worked with or near questionable name. Ask if they knew the person.	____	____
I. Determine from discussions and written directives how unclaimed payroll checks are handled.	____	____
1. Determine that these checks are adequately protected and properly recorded and handled.	____	____
J. Determine that record retention program is being followed.	____	____
Personnel Department		
A. Review the department's general philosophy and approach with the Director of Personnel. (Human Resources)	____	____
B. Review minutes of the Executive Committee meetings and determine that Personnel has complied with all directives.	____	____
1. Ascertain that the Executive Committee has approved of all significant policies initiated by Personnel.	____	____
C. Review instructions as to hiring policies and procedures.	____	____
1. Determine that all applicants are treated identically and fairly.	____	____
2. Review file of rejected applicants and note reasons.	____	____
a. Determine if pattern exists for rejections.	____	____
b. Determine whether decision to reject was made by the requesting department or by Personnel.	____	____
c. See if there is a pattern of rejections because of race, national origin, religion, sex or age.	____	____
D. Determine that all Personnel policies and procedures are followed without fear or favor by the department.	____	____
E. Review use of outside employment agencies.	____	____
1 Determine that we use more than one agency.	____	____
2. Review contract arrangements with agencies.	____	____
3. Establish that we show no favoritism to any agency.	____	____
a. Obtain reports on management of agencies used		

III. Audit Procedures *Personnel Department*	*Per. Cov.*	*Audit By*
and note the principals who own or operate the agencies.	____	____
1) *Note if there are any obvious relationships between agencies used and XYZ employees.*	____	____
4. Audit payments to agencies for a three-month period.	____	____
a. Obtain a computer printout of payments to selected agencies. Include frequently used companies.	____	____
b. Schedule all payments made to individual agencies.	____	____
1) List names of employees that we paid fees for.	____	____
a) Compare these names to payroll jackets.	____	____
2) If some employees only worked a short time, see if the payment to the agency was fair.	____	____
a) Determine reasons for termination.	____	____
b) Audit paychecks issued to these people to determine if they were legitimate employees.	____	____
c. Select several names listed in b.1 above and talk to them about how they came to work for XYZ.	____	____
1) Determine if agency initiated the original contact.	____	____
F. Audit all employee activity funds, using the Cash Funds portion of the audit program titled Auditing Cash Transactions. Use audit points pertinent to this audit.	____	____
G. Determine that Personnel handles employee training sessions efficiently and economically.	____	____
1. Determine that information is presented in concise fashion to reduce time of sessions.	____	____
H. Determine if there are any departments that prefer to bypass Personnel in the hiring of new employees. If so:	____	____
1. Discuss with department the reason for such bypass.	____	____
2. Consider the reasons and take appropriate action.	____	____
Payroll Department		
A. Review payroll distribution summaries. For a selected period make the following checks:	____	____
1. Test-check for arithmetic accuracy of reports.	____	____
2. Test-check for proper accounting distribution.	____	____
3. Tie summary figures into subsidiary accounts.	____	____
4. Verify accuracy of subsidiary accounts.	____	____
5. Tie subsidiaries into general ledger control accounts.	____	____
B. Determine that supervisors review hard copy of all data input into the computer from outlying locations.	____	____
1. See that changes are compared to approved notices.	____	____
2. See that all questionable entries are referred to appropriate executives and followed-up properly.	____	____
C. Test representative employees for the following:	____	____

III. Audit Procedures *Payroll Department*	*Per. Cov.*	*Audit By*
1. Check time cards/reports for extensions and footings.	____	____
2. Trace pay rates to union contracts or latest approved payroll change notice.	____	____
3. Tie figures into payroll register reports.	____	____
4. Verify that employees are legitimate.	____	____
D. Conform the arithmetic accuracy of the payroll register.	____	____
1. Select a sampling of employees and check the arithmetic of the calculations for gross pay, and all deductions.	____	____
a. Insure that fractional cents are accurately and consistently handled.	____	____
1) Refer to audit instructions for details.	____	____
E. Determine that terminal operators make certain that all information is *properly approved BEFORE* they enter data.	____	____
F. Carefully check the sign-in procedure for entering the payroll data base.	____	____
1. Determine that sign-in code is known only to authorized operators.	____	____
a. Note whether supervisor signs on for temporary workers that may have to be used in the section.	____	____
b. *Ensure that the code is not written at or near the terminal where anyone might see it.*	____	____
c. Observe procedures during break periods.	____	____
G. Determine that hard copy of payroll input data is carefully controlled by payroll manager.	____	____
1. Hard copies should be reviewed by payroll supervisors.	____	____
H. Observe or distribute one payroll payoff, accounting for all employees in the departments selected for test. *Be certain to verify employees whose checks are mailed.*	____	____
1. If actual physical identification is not practical, trace to organization charts, physical exam records, reports or letters written by employee, etc.	____	____
a. If employee is absent, follow up upon return.	____	____
2. Ascertain that individual who distributes paychecks is certain that all issued checks, have been received. (Employees receive stubs, if checks are sent to bank.)	____	____
I. Carefully audit all payroll transfer checks issued to banks during a selected three-month period.	____	____
1. Check names of employees listed on the transfer checks to insure that they are all bona fide XYZ employees.	____	____
2. Verify the net pay for all listed employees.	____	____

III. Audit Procedures *Payroll Department*	*Per. Cov.*	*Audit By*
3. Determine that all listed employees receive their pay summary directly from the payroll department.	____	____
4. *Determine that none of the listed employees have been issued an additional individual paycheck.*	____	____
J. Test to determine that deductions from employee paychecks are fully supported by properly signed authorizations.	____	____
1. Tie-in deductions from payroll into the ledger accounts.	____	____
a. Review withholdings for odd items, such as deposits to the credit union and contributions.	____	____
1) Request credit union to verify several of these deductions to insure posting to correct employee.	____	____
K. Review last three-months adjustments to payroll account.	____	____
1. Review data supporting each adjustment, and verify the authenticity and accuracy of supporting documentation.	____	____
L. Schedule all adjustments to the computer payroll data base for a selected several month period.	____	____
1. Tie each adjustment back to a payroll notice in the specific payroll jacket.	____	____
a. Verify authenticity of payroll notice.	____	____
b. Verify existence of every new employee added to payroll during the period.	____	____
1) *Pay close attention to employees who were added to payroll for a short period and then terminated.*	____	____
a) Study endorsements of these employee's paychecks. Compare signatures to time cards or reports.	____	____
M. Review procedures for processing taxable earnings reports.	____	____
1. See that department ties-in total of those issued.	____	____
2. *Review procedure for handling returned tax reports.*	____	____
N. Determine that fringe benefits conform to policy.	____	____
1. Test-check termination and retirement pay awards.	____	____
O. Check for conformance to legal requirements.	____	____
1. Test-check to determine conformity with provisions for maximum hours, minimum wages and overtime payments.	____	____
2. Test-check for status of exempt and nonexempt workers.	____	____

Audit work reviewed by ____________________ Date ____________

INTERNAL AUDIT PROGRAM—INTERNAL CONTROL QUESTIONNAIRE

The following internal control questions are intended to direct your attention to the high risk areas of these operations. Some of these points are covered in the audit program and they are included here to insure that they receive adequate attention.

Answer these control questions as your audit progresses. In section B, you are to write in the names and job titles of the various employees who perform the listed functions. Be certain to note any conflicting duties that could jeopardize internal control.

I. The following are indicative of good internal control.

1. All major Personnel policies are approved by Executive Committee.
2. Personnel policies apply to all employees.
3. Records and reports are accurately maintained.
4. Written authorizations support all wage payments and deductions.
5. Preparation and approvals of time summaries, paycheck printing and distribution are all separate and independent operations.

II. Following lists functions performed by named employees.

Function:	*Name/Position*	*Conflicting Duties*
1. Maintains Personnel files.	______	______
2. Final payroll notice approval.	______	______
3. Distributes paychecks.	______	______
4. Enters time summaries.	______	______
5. Custodian of activity fund.	______	______
6. Approves agency contracts.	______	______
7. Approves agency bills.	______	______

III. Internal Control Questions:	*Yes*	*No*	*Remarks*
A. Are all national Personnel Policies approved by the Executive Committee?	___	___	______
1. Are Committee actions promptly implemented?	___	___	______
B. Are provisions of the Federal Wage and Hours Act being followed? As to the following:	___	___	______
1. Max. hours, min. wages and overtime pay?	___	___	______
2. Adequate records on covered employees?	___	___	______
3. Classification of exempt employees?	___	___	______
C. Do Personnel directives governing hiring practices conform to legal requirements?	___	___	______
1. Are provisions of Fair Employment Act being closely followed?	___	___	______

III. Internal Control Questions	*Yes*	*No*	*Remarks*
a. Is there any evidence of discrimination?	___	___	___
D. Does Personnel periodically review salary ranges and fringe benefits?	___	___	___
E. Is a representative of Personnel available for any employee that wants to complain?	___	___	___
1. Does Personnel provide a counseling service for disgruntled employees?	___	___	___
F. Does Personnel cooperate fully with Auditing in handling cases of employee defalcations?	___	___	___
G. Does Personnel get prior clearance from Auditing for all policies and procedures that affect internal control or security?	___	___	___
H. Does Personnel see that proper approvals exist before processing new hires, salary adjustments or terminations?	___	___	___
1. Does Personnel have a good program for interviewing terminating employees?	___	___	___
a. Are important findings conveyed to the proper executives?	___	___	___
I. Are working hour regulations enforced in the headquarters building?	___	___	___
1. Any complaints about the flex hour system?	___	___	___
J. Are internal controls adequate over the handling of employee activity funds?	___	___	___
1. Are all expenditures properly approved?	___	___	___
2. Are funds used solely for purpose stated?	___	___	___
K. Does Personnel keep "hands off" attitude toward employee credit union activities?	___	___	___
L. Do controls insure that payroll clerks cannot make unauthorized entries into the system?	___	___	___
1. Is it possible for clerks to destroy			

III. Internal Control Questions:	*Yes*	*No*	*Remarks*
the hard copy printout of payroll changes?	____	____	____________
M. Is access to payroll program limited to authorized employees?	____	____	____________
1. Are terminals within view of supervisors?	____	____	____________
2. Do supervisors insure that terminals are not used by unauthorized personnel?	____	____	____________
3. Are terminal operators required to sign off when they leave a station, and sign back on upon return?	____	____	____________
4. Are terminals unused for long periods?	____	____	____________
5. Is it possible for payroll changes to be made by telephone?	____	____	____________
N. Are all returned Federal reports followed up?	____	____	____________
O. Are all changes to the payroll data base reviewed by supervisory personnel?	____	____	____________
1. Are these changes verified against approved payroll notices?	____	____	____________
a. Are discrepancies promptly and properly followed up?	____	____	____________
P. Are all payroll bank transfer checks mailed directly to the banks?	____	____	____________

Questions answered by ______________________ Date __________
Answers reviewed by ______________________ Date __________

CRITICAL POINTS

Disbursements of payroll funds offer multiple opportunities for manipulation and fraud. Be extremely wary while performing audit work; there are many possible dangers that you can encounter in these operations. Some examples of the more frequent abuses follow:

TWELVE CRITICAL POINTS TO CONSIDER

1. There is a classic computer payroll fraud case in which the computer program was designed to manipulate the third decimal place in each payroll computation. These figures were dropped from individual paychecks, but

were accumulated and moved into a special account. A regular paycheck, to a fictitious employee, was written for the amounts thus accumulated.

A large payroll was involved and these fractional pennies added up to thousands of dollars over a year period. The scam was discovered because no withholding tax was deducted from the paychecks issued, and the report to the federal government was not matched by a tax return.

This type of defalcation could have been detected by an auditor who manually test checked the calculations of gross pay and deductions to the fourth decimal point and noted that some of the pennies were not handled correctly. This case induced many audit staffs to adopt a practice of spot checking all payroll calculations to the fourth decimal point for proper treatment.

TIP: *Another useful audit approach is to require EDP auditors to dump critical programs and verify that they conform to specifications and that they properly handle all computations.*

Control over the printing of federal tax information forms, and insuring that the total of these forms equals the payroll cost for the year, can also be an effective audit step. A study of all individual reports should spot any that are obviously above the salary expected for the employee's position. If the accumulated figures were added to an employee's check, the tax report would stand out like a sore thumb.

2. Paychecks may inadvertently be issued for employees who have left the company. These checks are usually routed to the department supervisor or manager for distribution. Some of these supervisors take advantage of the opportunity, and continue to report the ex-employee as still with the company. Thus, they continue to receive and cash the paychecks. In large operations the dollar amount of such salaries might not be noticed in the expense analysis reports.

   This type of manipulation frequently occurs where many temporary or part-time employees are used. In these situations, the supervisors may also have an opportunity to short stop the distribution of Federal Income Tax withholdings forms, thereby reducing the risk of detection if the ex-employee received the form. If fictitious employees are added to the payroll, the miscreant must give an address where any form or notice mailed to that name can be intercepted. **TIP:** *This address provides an audit trail that is useful during an investigation.*

   Rigid adherence to the payroll audit program and tracking down every discrepancy will usually disclose these manipulations.

   KEY POINT: *Long time employees of a department can be a good source of information for identifying people who actually worked in an operation.*

3. Payroll padding is an old custom that is still in everyday use. Some of this doctoring is difficult to detect, depending on who does it and how it is

done. Several of the most notorious methods of payroll padding are listed for your information.

- Sometimes a supervisor adds a family member or close friend to the payroll, although the individual rarely shows up at the job location. Regular paychecks are prepared and distributed or sent to a bank account for these individuals. A good portion of wage payments are kicked back to the supervisor, after taking into consideration the tax liability incurred and a nominal payment for the risk and cooperation.
- An easy method of payroll padding is to increase the reported work hours of selected hourly paid employees. In some cases an identical result, overpayment of wages, is achieved when the foreman authorizes payment for overtime even though all work was performed during regular hours. In all of the above, the foreman receives a kickback for all, or a large portion, of the padded payments. The employee is told to go along or lose the job.

  Another modification, is for a foreman to hire an employee at an agreed salary, but report a higher starting salary on the payroll notice. The excess is kicked back by the new employee to the individual who authorized the hiring.
- A very common method is to place a fictitious name on the payroll. The checks are endorsed with the fictitious name and cashed at a currency exchange. This system does not require the cooperation of a fellow conspirator. The perpetrator is usually a supervisor who distributes the paychecks.

In some cases the perpetrator creates a dummy person, opens a bank account in the fictitious name and deposits the check in the account. Some careful individuals even pay income tax on the salary received by the fictitious person.

In still other cases, paper work is prepared that indicates that withholdings are unnecessary, and in some of these instances there were no reports issued by the payroll department. This indicates either a complete breakdown of internal control over payroll operations or that a payroll supervisor was involved.

When wage payments are made in cash instead of checks, the possibilities of irregularities are multiplied. **NOTE:** *Tracing of payments becomes very difficult, since a signature on a wage pay out list can easily be forged or written in an illegible manner.* Forged signatures do not leave a positive audit trail, but the paymaster may be able to identify the culprit.

All of the aforementioned manipulations of payroll records present difficult audit problems. To insure that employees exist, you should hand out paychecks preferably while employees are performing their jobs. If you can observe all employees at work, there is a good possibility that all names on the payroll are valid.

In most audits this complete visual verification will not occur, so you must concentrate on those employees who have come in merely to pick up their paychecks and on any paychecks mailed to an employee or a bank. Due diligence can assure you that all employees are legitimate.

Kickbacks between conspirators are more difficult to detect. One method that may produce results is to have an auditor spend time in the rest area or lunch room. This can give employees an opportunity to meet and talk to a member of the audit staff. An interested observer or a reluctant conspirator may take such an opportunity to give some indication that something is awry.

An important precaution against payroll manipulation is to prohibit any payment of cash wages. This might not always be possible, particularly where casual or temporary workers are common. Casual wage payments should be examined carefully, and if possible, the basis for payments should be verified against independent records, such as sign in and out sheets.

KEY POINT: *You should carefully review the basis for all wage payments by verifying the hours actually worked and judging that the wage rate is fair and reasonable for the type of work performed.* Extensions of hours times rate must be checked and all deductions proven to ensure that the payment is exactly what it should be.

You must then verify that gross wages and the net amount of all pay outs tie-in to general ledger postings. Finally, all deductions must be audited for accuracy and to verify that the withholdings were paid out to the proper parties.

4. Key employees in the Personnel or Payroll departments may give themselves wage increases that are not authorized, or they may process increases that exceed the amount that their supervisor had approved. Such people have been known to prepare payroll notices that appear to be genuine but in which they have closely forged the approval signature. The notice sent to payroll authorizes an inflated amount, and it is correct in all other details except for the forged signature. In some cases the payroll notice retained in the Personnel file shows the correct salary, and a comparison discloses the forgery. **IMPORTANT:** *Pay particular attention to salaries paid to employees in key positions in the Personnel and Payroll departments.* Payroll data should be reviewed with particular attention to payroll increases and adjustments. If rate of increase to any of these people appears out of line with increases to other department employees, you may want to take the payroll notice and discuss it with the approving supervisor.

The manager will remember the good reason for the higher increase or will spot any unauthorized adjustment that was made.

During your audit a comparison of the total department payroll to previous periods, after adjusting for blanket salary increases and any change in number of department employees, may indicate an irregularity.

If not already in effect, you may want to suggest that a quarterly report of all employees be run and circulated for approval. The report should list all Department employees with a separate page containing each section's employees. The full report is routed to the department executive for examination. It is then separated, and each section's report is sent to the section supervisor for examination and approval. Any irregularity in payroll will probably come to light during such an approval procedure. **TIP:** *If your company has such a system, the audit staff must insure that the circulated reports match the actual payroll that is used in the computer processing.*

5. A particularly vulnerable part of the payroll procedure lies in bonus payments that are frequently given out at year end. It is relatively easy for key personnel or Payroll Department employees to increase the bonus paid to selected employees. A figure of 50 can be increased to 150, or 500, with the stroke of a pen, depending on the method used to prepare the bonus authorization list.

   Some companies have the bonus checks printed and then given to supervisors for distribution. The supervisor examines and then hands the checks out to employees. If an amount has been altered, the supervisor would be certain to notice the change. This control might not be practical in some instances, as when checks are written by computer and mailed directly to employees or banks. *In such cases a print out of bonus amounts can be directed to supervisory personnel.*

   Internal auditors can only examine the record of bonus payments made and determine that they conform to the formula dictated by company directive. **TIP:** *If any payment is out of line with the formula, or with payments made to employees in similar jobs, an auditor should ask the supervisor to explain why that employee was favored.*

6. Vacation pay is another area where alterations may be made and passed through the system without being detected. Many vacation payments are based on average earnings over a set period of time, which includes overtime earnings. As a result the vacation paycheck may properly be for an amount greater than the normal base salary. **TIP:** *Under these conditions you should review previous pay records to verify that they justify the amount of the vacation check.*

7. Termination pay is another area that should be examined. There are times when termination pay does not conform to the established formula; it may

be a negotiated amount and may be used as an inducement to persuade certain employees to leave the company.

All termination checks should be audited, and those that do not conform to standard should be compared to a written agreement. **CAUTION:** *Don't overlook the possibility that a termination check may be written for a fictitious employee.* You must also verify the date of termination to make certain that paychecks were not issued to cover periods after the employee had actually terminated.

8. Another potential danger area relates to retirement payments that are handled by the payroll department. If these amounts are adjusted from time to time, the clerks making the adjustments may not treat all retirees the same. Payments to some may be increased in excess of the authorized amounts, perhaps at the expense of other retirees if total payments are controlled. You should review the justification for all changes and then verify that they were properly made.

   There are many cases on record where a retiree has died, but the company is not informed of the death. In such cases the annuity check continues to be mailed to the ex-employee's home or bank. If the bank is aware of the death, they are obligated to inform the company.

   Auditors for employer companies, or insurance companies, should adopt some method of annually checking payments to retired employees to see if there is evidence of death.

   TIPS:

   - Endorsements on checks mailed to homes may be examined for any signs of change.
   - Some type of audit verification may be periodically used, or an exchange of letters may be helpful.
   - If there are any questions raised, the auditor may decide to employ an outside investigative agency to determine if the retiree has died.

9. Some payments made to Personnel agencies may be excessive or may not have been earned. Agreements with outside personnel agencies stipulate terms under which services are supplied. Many companies pay fees for any employee that the agency locates. For higher level jobs, fees may call for a month to a year's salary payment to the agency.

   When collusion occurs between an outside agency and a company Personnel employee, the billing for services rendered may exceed the agreement amount. Or an agency may bill for new hires that didn't come through the agency. In some cases the names of prospects that were not hired may be listed, and an amount requested.

   When auditing this phase of the Personnel Department's activities you should carefully review the agreement documents and determine that they have been properly approved and that billings conform to the agreements. **KEY POINT:** *Most important, you must be alert to the possibility that a new hire was not brought in by an agency, but was sent to the agency after a member of the Personnel Department learned that the prospect was wanted in the company.*

People looking for employment send their resumes to Personnel departments of various companies. If the prospect looks good, the personnel interviewer may state that all hires are made through a particular employment agency and send the prospect to the agency. The agency then receives the commission and either gives the personnel employee a percentage of the fee or other gifts.

This type of manipulation can be readily discovered through a routine audit form letter asking each new employee how they first heard about the company, and when and to whom they made their first contact. **TIP:** *This form of verification is particularly helpful when it is known and authorized by the Director of Personnel.* The approach can obtain additional information that can be very useful for the Personnel Department.

10. Large companies frequently need temporary help for vacation or holiday relief, sick relief or to help during temporary peaks of activity. The selection by a major corporation can be of great value to the supplier of temporary employees.

    You should be alert to the possibility of kickbacks or gifts in this area of personnel operations. Bills submitted by such agencies should be carefully checked and the supervisors that used the temporary help should be interviewed to learn all the related facts of the transactions and to verify that they approved the billing.

11. At times an employee may be hired by the Personnel Department and placed on the payroll of an outside temporary service agency. This may occur as a probationary period or because a department's budget prevents the hiring of a permanent employee but allows the use of temporaries. These employees understand that they have been selected, and that they will be paid by the service agency for a short time until they can be placed on the permanent payroll.

    The outside agency is paid an amount in excess of the employee's salary to cover the costs of administering the salary payments with its attendant fringe costs. The agency understands and agrees that it is being used as a go between, perhaps assisting in bypassing a foolish regulation, and is paid a fee for its assistance. **NOTE:** *This procedure might also be used to improperly increase payments to an agency.*

    If you suspect that this type of unusual activity is occurring in your company, the audit trail is quite clear. Review billings from temporary help agencies to learn the names of people they have sent into your company. If you find the names of current employees on the billings, a short interview with the employee will quickly establish the facts. **NOTE:** *The employees have nothing to hide since they acted in good faith and were not a willing party to the deception.*

Most temporary agencies have rules that prohibit their employees from accepting positions with the agency's clients. The people we are discussing did not consider themselves as agency employees even though that company issued their salary checks.

12. Your Personnel Department may, perhaps unwittingly, be violating federal laws. Sometimes the perimeter security guards report to local personnel management and they may perform a pre-screening service for Personnel. Guards at the gates may be given possession of application blanks with specific instructions for handing them out to prospective employees. The intent is to aid Personnel in efficiently running their department.

    Under such a system the applicant is given a blank at the gate, to fill out at leisure and then bring in to the office prepared to discuss the information requested. If there are no job openings in their particular field, they need not waste their time and the time of the interviewer by making a useless application.

    Perimeter security guards may take it upon themselves to screen out individuals that they consider undesirable. They merely state that there are no job openings even when a plant is desperately seeking workers. Applications may only be given to certain types of people. **CAUTION:** *This practice violates Federal Equal Opportunity laws, if the guards intentionally, or unconsciously, discriminate against certain races, ages, sexes, religions or national origins.* **TIP:** *If one of your large operations is ethnically homogeneous, there is a chance that some type of illegal screening is occurring.*

Chapter 18

Auditing a Purchasing Department

In a manufacturing or a retailing company, purchasing activities play a vital role in the day-to-day operations and the profitability of the firm. Purchasing is a service department that at one time or another is used by every other department in a company. The purchasing operation is important in any major company, but its relative significance may not be as great in a middleman or brokerage operation where selling is the prime activity.

This chapter reviews the internal audit of a Purchasing Department in a major consumer goods manufacturing company. The same basic approach, applies to purchasing operations wherever conducted.

Starting with the requisition for materials by an authorized employee we will follow it to Purchasing where it is converted into a formal order. The receiving and paying functions are merely mentioned here, since these subjects are more fully covered in chapters on Payables and on audits of certain operating locations.

Purchasing is strictly a service operation set up to procure items required, or desired, by other departments. It is charged with the responsibility of obtaining these requirements at the most favorable price and terms available in the market. Information relating to any product that has been requisitioned, is sought out by Purchasing and relayed to the requesting party who usually makes the final decision as to what to buy. Purchasing negotiates the final price and terms and writes the formal order.

In this chapter we'll consider the internal workings of a Purchasing Department and review the value analysis work that is performed. We'll also include portions of an operational audit program that may be useful in studying purchasing operations.

Background Information

The sample audit program was designed to review the purchasing operations in the XYZ Corporation. XYZ is a large consumer products manufacturing company with hundreds of company locations throughout the country. The Purchasing Department is headed by a Director of Purchasing who reports to the President of the company. Headquartered in the main office, its staff consists of purchasing agents, buyers and an administrative section.

Each of the company's subsidiary offices has a Purchasing Agent who follows the guidelines, procedures and policies established by the headquarters staff. These purchasing agents report to the president of their division, but they have a dotted line responsibility to the Director of Purchasing. Local purchasing employees are hired by the subsidiary presidents, subject to the approval of the main office. Many of these division purchasing agents had been transferred from the central Purchasing Department and there is a close working arrangement between all purchasing offices.

Purchasing negotiates national contracts whereby vendors make and hold supplies that are drawn out by operating plants throughout the country. Each withdrawal is priced at the national contract price. Make and hold contracts are used for all packaging supplies, office forms and supplies and raw materials required in the corporation.

The department administrator polices the clerical operations of the department and establishes guidelines that govern the actions and reports prepared by purchasing personnel. The administrator is responsible for insuring that all corporate policies and procedures are followed in the purchasing operation.

The Purchasing Department administrator controls and safeguards incoming proposals from suppliers and participates in the bid opening of major purchases. Bids are recorded on a spread sheet which lists the bidders and the various elements of their bids.

The administrator acts as the Purchasing Department representative on the Construction Control Committee. This committee, permanently composed of managers from Engineering, Financial, and Purchasing and augmented as required by operating managers, decides on all matters relating to the control over construction projects.

With that as background, let's examine the internal audit program used to review XYZ's Purchasing Department.

INTERNAL AUDIT PROGRAM—INSTRUCTIONS

IA BPI9090 XYZ CORPORATION

INTERNAL AUDIT PROGRAM—PURCHASING DEPARTMENT

1. Read the Purchasing Policies and Procedures Manual, and the Plant Materials Management Manual and become familiar with all headquarters purchasing policies and the procedures used in production plants.
2. Up date or prepare flow charts of internal controls operating over requisitioning, ordering, receiving merchandise, processing supporting papers, matching invoices with supporting documents and processing the voucher. Any noted weaknesses should be mentioned in your report.
3. The Purchasing Department has established a sophisticated and successful

program that requires competitive bids for all *major* purchases. Carefully review the written procedures, and then determine that all sections of the department follow prescribed procedures.

Note any evidence of a supplier being permitted to submit a phone-in bid. It is against company policy to accept verbal bids.

4. Be alert for any indication that bidding suppliers have conspired to establish a going price for goods or services to XYZ. Collusion among companies in the same business is not uncommon. **TIP:** *If many bids are submitted at the same price, it is a good indication that there is collusion among the bidders.* Under such conditions the best way to get a fair bid is to throw out all of the original bidders and select a new group of potential suppliers. **KEY POINT:** *None of the original bidders should be permitted to bid again.*
5. Collusion among suppliers is common, particularly where there is a strong trade association. In some trades there is a reluctance for a potential supplier to bid against a long-standing supplier of a company. We must make it known that XYZ is not bound to any vendor, and that we will accept any honest bid for a product that meets our specifications. Our criteria are that the product must meet specs, be delivered on a timely basis and that the price must be fair.

   You may find evidence of price fixing in areas where we use several suppliers and divide up the business. If we use three suppliers and the bids received show three companies at the same low price, and all the other bidders well above the low bidders, *then you can safely assume that you are NOT looking at honest bids.* Probably the high bids were from companies who had submitted courtesy bids to protect the price bid by the favored suppliers.

   If you suspect collusion, we have the capability of an in-house estimate of what it costs to produce almost anything we use. We should know the material costs and have a good idea of the labor cost. For large purchases, we should have prepared an advance estimate of what a fair bid price should be, which can indicate if the bids have been rigged. If the bids are not truly competitive, there are a number of options open to us. XYZ can elect to do one of the following:

   - Enter into a cost plus contract with a company that has a good reputation in the field, but whom we have not used as a supplier.
     + Negotiate a fair price with the company, taking advantage of our cooperation in scheduling large production runs.
   - Produce the item at one of our plants, or convert an operation into a production facility for the item.
   - Buy a small company in the business of producing the item.

   Any of the above alternatives represent drastic action, that requires due consideration and executive committee approval.

   KEY POINT: *We need irrefutable evidence that prices are rigged and that we cannot procure our needs at a fair price in the open market.*
6. A raw material buyer makes carload purchases on the futures and the spot

market of the Board of Trade, using a special direct wire phone for these transactions. The phone is wired into a recording device located in the purchasing administrator's office. Calls are recorded with an automatic voice insertion of the time that each call is made.

The buyer notes every transaction in a trade log, using separate pages for futures and for spot orders. At the close of each business day, the buyer gives a copy of the log to the purchasing administrator.

On Friday afternoon, after the market closes, the raw materials buyer summarizes weekly transactions and gives one copy to the administrator who compares it to the tape recordings of calls to the broker. If everything checks out, a new disk is inserted for the coming week. The recordings are retained for a six month period, and then erased and the disk is used again.

When you enter the department to start your purchasing audit, you will ask the administrator to remove the disk from the recorder, give it to you, and insert a new disk. **IMPORTANT:** *Safeguard the removed disk until you make your comparisons called for in the audit program.*

Remember that this operation is responsible for assuring that XYZ has an adequate supply of raw materials when required. *We do not speculate in the market.* Order quantities should conform, within set tolerances, to our estimated requirements as calculated by production planning. XYZ prefers to order in the futures market to try to keep the materials price constant, but when estimates are wrong we may be forced to deal in the spot market. XYZ does not normally sell, except in those instances where we have grossly over estimated our production needs. **CAUTION:** *Any sales transaction should be closely examined.*

7. Purchasing has developed a value analysis program that is used for all substantial purchases. You will be expected to review the logic of the approach, and the accuracy of the computations. You should also be prepared to evaluate the recommendations that result.

   In any of these studies, the approach does not take personal preference into account. When you review decisions that do not appear to have been in the best economic interest of the company, be certain to discuss the reasons for the action with the marketing, production or engineering manager that made the final decision.

   Value analysis studies can be most meaningful in areas that do not relate to product ingredients. Any ingredient change may materially affect the marketability and consumer acceptance of a product. If you feel that a valid study is being ignored, discuss the matter with the audit manager before taking a position for the audit department.

   KEY POINT: *We must be very cautious when it comes to product ingredients or anything that directly touches a product.* Such changes require long periods of shelf testing and research evaluations. Adequate channels exist for these considerations, though we might help move tests along.

8. You should participate in several bid opening sessions to enable you to judge the adequacy of control over this important activity. Bids are held in the department safe, under the administrator's control until the set bid opening

time. These bids may not be opened until it is determined that all bids submitted have been received.

At bid opening time, if proposals are not on hand from companies who stated that they would bid, a phone call is made to the company to determine whether they have changed their mind. If the bid is not yet on its way, the supplier is told that it is too late, and the proposals on hand are opened. If the vendor states that the bid has been sent, bid opening is delayed until the en route message arrives. *Once the bids are opened, the bidding process is completed.* No bid is considered that is received after bid opening. Any late proposal is torn up and thrown away without opening or viewing the contents. **KEY POINT:** *Any serious irregularity in any bid is justification for discarding the proposal.* Minor irregularities must be immediately corrected by contacting the vendor and clarifying the matter. These conversations, as well as the calls asking vendors if their bids are on the way, are taped with the knowledge and consent of the supplier. The vendor is requested to follow up with a letter acknowledging the clarification covered in the phone conversation. Any phone call to a vendor is made after all bids have been opened, and such calls are usually confined to the group of low bidders. These calls are of a conference type in which the administrator, the buyer and perhaps a member of the requesting department all participate.

9. Good salespeople develop a rapport with purchasing agents. They strive to get the buyer to consider them as personal friends so that if their product gives trouble, they will be contacted and given an opportunity to correct the situation. If not quickly corrected, the irritation level may rise to the point where a product is thrown out and will not again be purchased by the company. **KEY POINT:** *To foster this friendly relationship, vendors frequently shower purchasing people with gifts and with dinner and luncheon invitations.*

   XYZ has adopted strict policies relating to entertainment by vendors and to the acceptance by our employees of gifts or gratuities from suppliers. **NOTE** *Read these policies very carefully and be on the alert for any indications of violations of these restrictions.*

10. During your discussions with the Director of Purchasing, suggest that the time might be appropriate to send the survey letter to XYZ's suppliers. This questionnaire, signed by the Director of Purchasing has been successful in past audits. It is sent with a covering letter from the Director to the President of the supplier company requesting the vendor's cooperation and candid responses.

    The questionnaire provides adequate space for vendor's comments, and asks the following questions:

    A. Payments for materials and services are prompt___ slow___?
    B. Policy on rejected material is reasonable___ arbitrary at times___?
    C. Purchase specifications and other data suppliers have been adequate___ incomplete or inaccurate___?
    D. Have visits by our employees been too frequent___ too large a group___ generally timely and helpful___?
    E. Have Purchasing personnel conducted themselves in a manner which

reflects credit to XYZ and fairness to your representative: consistently___ not always___ seldom___?

F. Have relations ever been complicated by request for entertainment or special favors___ solicitation of gifts, loans or commissions___?
G. Do you believe that the awarding of our business is generally accomplished on a basis of price, quality and delivery: Yes___ No___?
H. Do you believe we have an acceptable procedure for establishing qualified and approved suppliers: Yes___ No___?
I. Are you aware of any unusual or improper practices involving our employees and your competitors: Yes___ Rumor___ No___?

Arrange with the Director to have the return envelopes addressed to the department administrator. You should be permitted to receive and open the replies, and then discuss them with the Director.

11. A major problem in the purchasing area is caused by so-called friends of top executives who try to use their influence to induce buyers to place orders with a particular firm. Purchasing should be aware that friendship has no place in business transactions. These relationships may induce a buyer to allow a company to submit a bid, but only after a careful screening finds that the firm is sound, and that it is capable of meeting the specifications and delivery date. **KEY POINT:** *If you note a situation in which an outsider is attempting to exert undue influence on a buyer, notify the audit manager at once.*
12. Your program calls for an examination of vouchers issued to pay for items purchased for the department and to reimburse for expense reports. The detailed audit program for such a review is contained in your audit manual under the heading Auditing Payables.
13. Purchasing participation in construction projects is covered in detail in the audit program titled Auditing Construction Projects.
14. The audit program calls for verification of payroll records as they relate to Purchasing employees. If Purchasing's payroll has not been recently audited, use your program titled Auditing Payroll.
15. A description of the proper procedure for working with this internal audit program appears in the Introduction to the Audit Programs section of your manual. Read this information carefully.

INTERNAL AUDIT PROGRAM

IA BPP9100 XYZ CORPORATION

INTERNAL AUDIT PROGRAM—PURCHASING DEPARTMENT

The following program is designed to lead you into important areas in Purchasing Department operations. This program is intended as a guide, and is not all inclusive. You are expected to revise this program as necessary, but be certain to inform the audit administrator of all changes that you make.

I. Company Procedures

A. Purchasing is responsible for all company commitments, except for advertising agreements and small local requirements.

B. All major purchases are contracted for by central Purchasing.
C. Local operations draw against make and hold contracts that are negotiated by central Purchasing.
D. All major requirements are purchased through competitive bids.
E. All forms and procedures used in the purchasing function are designed and controlled by central purchasing.

II. Audit Objectives are to determine the following:

A. Company policies and procedures are followed by all employees.
B. All purchasing commitments are in the best interests of XYZ.
C. The department is operating efficiently and is well controlled.
D. All vendors are treated fairly and considerately.
E. Value analysis studies are properly used in buying decisions.

III. Audit Procedures	*Per. Cov.*	*Audit By*
A. Read this audit program, the associated instructions (BPI9090) and the Internal Control Questionnaire before starting your work so that you are aware of Purchasing activities and our audit approach.	____	____
B. Review responsibilities of all Purchasing employees. Be certain to include the following:		
1. Review the specific tasks performed.	____	____
a. Determine that authorizing signatures on requisitions are examined and verified.	____	____
b. Review method of selecting vendors.	____	____
c. Note recent changes in suppliers and check reasons.	____	____
1) Determine that a company is checked out before any orders are issued to the firm.	____	____
d. Examine P/Os issued to major suppliers.	____	____
1) Determine if supplier is designated by requester.	____	____
2) Determine if recommended supplier is used.	____	____
a) If so, determine that other bids are obtained.	____	____
e. Note the procedures for processing orders.	____	____
1) How are prices and terms arrived at?	____	____
2) When are "Advise Price" P/Os used?	____	____
a) Are these followed up for acceptable price?	____	____
2. Review forms used in the department. Determine their purpose and chart their flow.	____	____
a. Are all forms necessary and processed efficiently?	____	____
1) Note if a complete file of all P/Os written is maintained in numerical sequence.	____	____
2) Determine that commodity records show quantity purchased and price paid to specific suppliers.	____	____
a) Refer to these records when checking prices.	____	____

III. Audit Procedures	*Per. Cov.*	*Audit By*
b. Determine that confidential information is confined to proper parties and is adequately safeguarded.	____	____
c. Review handling of acknowledgment copies of P/Os.	____	____
d. Determine that there is no unnecessary use of P/Os.	____	____
1) Review distribution of P/O copies.	____	____
3. Study the method used to solicit all types of bids, whether written or verbal.	____	____
a. Determine that verbal bids are confirmed in writing.	____	____
b. Determine that economic order quantities are used as the basis for quantities listed on proposals.	____	____
c. Review system for analyzing proposals.	____	____
d. Review procedure for selecting successful bidder.	____	____
e. See that copy of bids are kept for proper period.	____	____
4. Review procedures and controls for the receipt, protection and recording of vendor's bids.	____	____
a. Determine that bids are safeguarded at all times.	____	____
b. Determine that a bid opening time is set and kept.	____	____
c. Determine that procedures insure that no bids have been opened and resealed.	____	____
d. Determine that procedures are adequate for opening proposal envelopes and recording bids.	____	____
5. Review procedures and controls for discussions with bidding suppliers to resolve questionable items.	____	____
a. See that minutes of meeting are made and signed.	____	____
6. Examine all perpetual inventory records, quantity requirements, and controls over make and hold orders.	____	____
a. Check for contingent liability on make and hold items.	____	____
b. See if procedures and controls are adequate to prevent over or out of stock.	____	____
c. See how overruns are handled on printed materials.	____	____
1) Do we pay for all overruns or is there a limit?	____	____
a) If we pay, determine that price is fair.	____	____
b) Determine if price is same rate as normal run.	____	____
d. Determine how obsolete items are handled.	____	____
1) Determine that dispositions are properly handled.	____	____
C. Review types of agreements used for making purchase commitments, and evaluate the associated records.	____	____
1. Determine whether there are any serious problems.	____	____
2. See that disagreements are equitably resolved.	____	____

III. Audit Procedures	*Per. Cov.*	*Audit By*
3. Determine how frequently requisitions are made up after orders are placed or bills received.	____	____
4. Review a selection of cost-plus P/Os.	____	____
a. Note if they stipulate a maximum price.	____	____
b. Note that all conditions and costs are spelled out.	____	____
c. Determine that they contain an audit clause.	____	____
1) Determine if adequate audits have been performed.	____	____
2) Perform your own audits where necessary. (See audit steps under D following.)	____	____
5. Examine support for trade discounts and quantity rebates.	____	____
a. Review the evidence of such agreements.	____	____
b. Determine that these agreements can be readily audited and that they are known to all concerned.	____	____
D. Review procedures and controls over cost-plus work that is performed for XYZ by the various machine shops.	____	____
1. Review our standard audit clause, and conform to the provisions. Audit all time records.	____	____
a. Study all time cards and job time cards and tie the total hours paid for to the total hours charged to all the jobs. (If the shop uses two separate cards.)	____	____
1) Confirm that allocation of total man hours to all open projects are correct.	____	____
2) *Determine the reasons for any discrepancies.*	____	____
3) Carefully review catchall projects for idle time and see that allocations conform to contract.	____	____
2. Review the firm's contract file. Schedule all jobs in progress for the period our job was in their shop.	____	____
a. Determine that all jobs were charged for some labor during this period.	____	____
b. Compare shop's estimate of labor required per job, to time charged to the job. Prove hours charged against job ticket allocations.	____	____
c. Review shop's delivery record for period and schedule deliveries to other clients.	____	____
1) Determine that any job delivered was charged for man hours during period. (At least for crating.)	____	____
a) For jobs with no labor charges, learn if job was completed before your audit period.	____	____
3. Check material prices against invoices and see that all discounts are passed on to XYZ.	____	____
a. For the more costly items, have XYZ buyers check		

III. Audit Procedures — *Per. Cov.* / *Audit By*

material prices to prove reasonability. ____ ____

4. See that add-on percentages were correctly applied to the proper figures *in the proper sequence.* ____ ____
5. If glaring errors are evident, discuss procedures with foremen and workers. Relate discussions to billings. ____ ____
   a. Carefully study any erasures or alteration of records. Discuss changes with employee involved. ____ ____
   b. *Any questionable items should be brought to the attention of the Manager of Internal Auditing.* ____ ____

E. Check procedures and controls over buying of raw material. ____ ____

1. Play back the tape removed from the administrator's office. Prepare a schedule of each transaction noting date and time of order, quantity, delivery date, point of delivery and agreed price. Include one month's prior transactions from daily logs. ____ ____
   a. Compare listing with brokerage confirmations. ____ ____
      1) *Carefully follow up on any discrepancies.* ____ ____
   b. Trace these transactions through payables or receivables as the case may be. ____ ____
2. From Office Services, obtain the phone bill which lists outgoing calls. Use a three-month period immediately preceding the start of your audit. ____ ____
   a. Look for any calls, other than the tie-line, to the commodity brokers. If any were made, note the day, time and phone number of the calling phone. ____ ____
      1) Ascertain location of the phone that was used. ____ ____
         a) If owner made calls, ascertain reason. If not, try to find out who may have used phone. ____ ____
   b. Determine if any XYZ transaction occurred close to time of unknown phone call. ____ ____
      1) If any occurred, carefully check all details of the transactions. (Discuss with audit manager.) ____ ____
3. Check prices XYZ paid against market price report for the days of the transactions. ____ ____
   a. If any price we paid was outside the reported range, discuss with buyer and department administrator. ____ ____
      1) *If answers are not satisfactory, bring the information to the audit manager's attention.* ____ ____

F. Check ordering and withdrawals of packaging supplies. ____ ____

1. See that proper commitment records are maintained. ____ ____
2. Review procedures for determining quantities to order. ____ ____
   a. Determine that bids covered varying quantities. ____ ____

III. Audit Procedures	*Per. Cov.*	*Audit By*
1) Determine that economic order quantity was used.	____	____
3. Determine that using locations are informed of orders.	____	____
4. Determine that items are closely checked at receipt.	____	____
G. Review procedures and controls over automotive equipment.	____	____
1. Review method for determining type of equipment needed.	____	____
a. Determine that costs are considered in decision.	____	____
b. Determine that acceptable accessories are specified.	____	____
1) Check to see that list is followed.	____	____
2. Check for vendor favorite at local or national level.	____	____
3. Review pricing arrangements with vendors, and examine competitive proposals.	____	____
4. Review procedures and controls over dispositions.	____	____
a. See that mileage and/or year basis is followed.	____	____
b. Examine the competitive bids to determine validity.	____	____
c. Determine that trade-in values are fair.	____	____
d. For cars sold to employees, check condition reports and amounts paid to see that prices were fair.	____	____
H. Review procedures and controls over purchases made in conformance with a capital appropriation.		
1. Review Purchasing's participation on the Construction Control Committee. (Detailed audit steps are listed in the manual program titled, Auditing Construction.)	____	____
2. Determine that a P/O was issued for all purchases for an appropriation that required a formal order.	____	____
a. See that P/Os are issued when contracts are signed.	____	____
3. Determine that Purchasing checks to be certain that an appropriation is approved before ordering materials.	____	____
4. Determine that affected locations are informed of all purchases made against their appropriations.	____	____
I. Review specific purchases through an examination of paid vouchers and supporting papers. Refer to audit manual program titled Auditing Payables.	____	____
1. Limit your review to a selected time period, and study all vouchers for purchases during that period.	____	____
a. Note that good purchasing procedures were used.	____	____
b. See that P/O was issued in advance of commitment.	____	____
c. Review confirmation P/Os to determine purchasing actions by other departments.	____	____

III. Audit Procedures — *Per. Cov.* | *Audit By*

2. In addition, study six-months vouchers paying specific vendors whose prices are questionable or who appear to be selected on the basis of favoritism. ____ ____
3. Cross-check this review to your examination of purchase orders. (B.2.a.1 and B.2.a.2.) ____ ____
   a. Determine if any P/Os have been used that were not issued by Purchasing. *(If so, notify audit mgr.)* ____ ____
   b. Determine if any P/Os have been improperly used. ____ ____

J. Review Purchasing relationships with other departments. ____ ____
1. Review Production actions on value analysis studies. ____ ____
2. Examine Marketing reactions to value analysis reports. ____ ____
3. Study rejected value analysis suggestions. Evaluate logic and computations. Determine if there are any that should be brought up to a higher level. ____ ____
4. See that Advertising uses Purchasing where appropriate. ____ ____
   a. Does Advertising use Purchasing to check on items bought by the advertising agencies? ____ ____
5. Review cooperation with Engineering & Research. ____ ____
6. Review problems with A/P department. ____ ____
   a. Determine that A/P refers all "advise price" billings to purchasing for approval. ____ ____
   b. Determine that A/P refers all differences between P/O and billing prices or terms to buyer. ____ ____
7. Determine Purchasing's role in disposition of salvage materials, scrap, capital assets and obsolete supplies. ____ ____
   a. Note if all operations use the same salvage firm. ____ ____
   b. Determine if competitive bids are obtained. ____ ____

K. Review the relationship between central purchasing and divisional and local purchasing personnel. ____ ____
1. Examine release orders for conformity to instructions. ____ ____
2. Check dollar limits for local petty cash purchases. ____ ____
3. Determine that groups work together in disposing of excess supplies and idle equipment. ____ ____
4. Review files for complaints concerning any central purchases or contract commitments. ____ ____
   a. Determine how such complaints are handled. ____ ____

L. Determine that products of new suppliers are tested. ____ ____
1. Evaluate the test reports that are prepared and determine that they are distributed to all concerned. ____ ____

M. Review the Purchasing Department payroll. Use applicable program in your manual titled Auditing Payroll. ____ ____

N. Select a sampling of department disbursements, made on the approval of Purchasing employees, and audit as indi-

III. Audit Procedures	*Per. Cov.*	*Audit By*
cated in item I. (Manual program titled Auditing Payables.)	____	____
O. Arrange through audit administrator to send staff auditors into all locations that have a division purchasing agent.	____	____
1. Lead these auditors through a review of these local purchasing operations.	____	____
2. See that national purchasing policies are followed.	____	____
P. Forward all comments and suggestions for improving this audit program to the Manager of Internal Auditing.	____	____

Audit work reviewed by ______________________ Date ____________

INTERNAL CONTROL QUESTIONNAIRE

The following internal control questions are intended to direct your attention to the high risk areas of this operation. Some of these points are covered in the audit program and are included here to ensure that they receive adequate attention.

Answer these control questions as your audit progresses. In section B, you are to write in the names and job titles of the various employees who perform the listed functions. Be certain to note any conflicting duties that could jeopardize internal control.

A. The following are indicative of good internal control.

1. All national purchasing policies are approved by the President.
2. All major purchases are based on competitive bids.
3. Value analysis studies are made to aid purchasing decisions.
4. XYZ has strict policies that forbid acceptance of gratuities.
5. Purchasing administrator closely observes department activities.

B. Following lists functions performed by named employees.

Function:	*Name/Position*	*Conflicting Duties*
1. Approves differences in P/O and invoice.	________	________
2. Controls incoming bids.	________	________
3. Opens competitive bids.	________	________
4. Records and analyzes bids.	________	________
5. Approves P/Os or contracts.	________	________

C. Internal Control Questions:	*Yes*	*No*	*Remarks*
1. Are all national purchasing policies approved by the Corporation President?	____	____	________
a. Are all department employees aware of, and do they follow these policies?	____	____	________
b. Is the Purchasing manual up to date?	____	____	________

C. Internal Control Questions	*Yes*	*No*	*Remarks*
2. Have all standard agreement forms been approved by the Legal Department?	____	____	____________
a. Is any XYZ equipment being used by an outsider, covered by detailed agreement?	____	____	____________
3. Are P/Os written for all equipment rented or borrowed by XYZ?	____	____	____________
a. If not, is Purchasing aware of, and in agreement with, all formal arrangements?	____	____	____________
b. Does Purchasing write or approve service and equipment rental agreements?	____	____	____________
4. Are all major purchases made on the basis of competitive bids?	____	____	____________
a. Are these bids truly competitive?	____	____	____________
1) Are early bids properly safeguarded?	____	____	____________
2) Are all bids opened at the same time?	____	____	____________
3) Are late bids rejected?	____	____	____________
4) Are call-in bids accepted?	____	____	____________
a) Before other bids are opened?	____	____	____________
b) After other bids are opened?	____	____	____________
b. Were any large companies or other logical sources overlooked?	____	____	____________
c. Are there bids from all who agreed to bid?	____	____	____________
1) Are bids recorded and kept on file?	____	____	____________
d. Is the lowest bidder always used?	____	____	____________
1) If not, do files contain adequate justification for exceptions?	____	____	____________
2) Do all purchasing personnel keep bid prices confidential?	____	____	____________
a) Are unsuccessful bidders told the accepted price?	____	____	____________
e. Are clarifications of bid questions confirmed in writing?	____	____	____________
f. Are all agreed changes to bid documents covered in the P/O?	____	____	____________

C. Internal Control Questions	*Yes*	*No*	*Remarks*
5. Do P/Os always state quantity, price, FOB point, delivery instructions and terms?	____	____	____________
a. If not, are exceptions justified?	____	____	____________
b. Are routings on P/Os checked with Traffic to insure cheapest transportation costs.	____	____	____________
1) Are invoices with shipping charges routed to traffic for approval?	____	____	____________
a) Does Traffic get the freight bill when XYZ pays the freight?	____	____	____________
c. Is any cost-plus work exempt from audit?	____	____	____________
6. Are unfilled P/Os periodically brought to the attention of proper parties?	____	____	____________
a. Are unmatched R/R checked to determine that XYZ's debts are promptly paid?	____	____	____________
b. Is A/P promptly told of all P/O changes?	____	____	____________
1) Are P/O Change Order forms always used?	____	____	____________
a) Are they properly distributed?	____	____	____________
7. Are canceled P/Os brought to A/P attention and removed from files to prevent payment?	____	____	____________
8. Do Purchasing Personnel check all approvals before releasing a P/O?	____	____	____________
a. Are requisition approvals closely checked?	____	____	____________
1) Is there a current and correct list of personnel authorized to approve?	____	____	____________
a) Does it contain sample signatures?	____	____	____________
b. Are properly approved requisitions received to support all awards by Purchasing?	____	____	____________
9. Is the combination form used? (Req., P/O, R/R)	____	____	____________
a. Does it result in minimum clerical effort?	____	____	____________

C. Internal Control Questions	*Yes*	*No*	*Remarks*
b. Is internal control adequate?	____	____	________
10. Are lists of approved signers for P/Os and R/Rs on hand in the A/P department?	____	____	________
a. Does A/P have a list of all suppliers who grant trade or cash discounts and quantity rebates not shown on their invoice?	____	____	________
b. Does Purchasing follow up to insure that XYZ receives all quantity discounts due?	____	____	________
11. Are invoices for small items that don't need P/Os, sent to Purchasing for approval?	____	____	________
a. Are petty cash purchases periodically reviewed by Purchasing?	____	____	________
b. Are local purchases on monthly statements periodically reviewed by Purchasing?	____	____	________
12. Are purchases made by advertising agencies reviewed by the Purchasing Department?	____	____	________
a. Should certain types of items be bought by XYZ's Purchasing Department?	____	____	________
b. Does Purchasing work with advertising agencies in the selection of suppliers?	____	____	________
13. Are any items bought that XYZ can or does produce in our own printing plant or shops?	____	____	________
14. Are purchases of ingredients and supplies adequately controlled for quality and price?	____	____	________
a. Is the local program of releasing against national orders working effectively?	____	____	________
b. Are perpetual inventories maintained in Purchasing the same as those kept in Cost?	____	____	________
1) If so, is such duplication necessary?	____	____	________
15. Does Purchasing fully participate in controlling construction jobs?	____	____	________
16. Is Purchasing Manual current and followed?	____	____	________

C. Internal Control Questions	*Yes*	*No*	*Remarks*
17. Is record retention schedule followed?	____	____	____________

Questions answered by ______________________ Date ____________
Answers reviewed by ______________________ Date ____________

CRITICAL POINTS

Purchasing decisions made by the buyers of major corporations can affect the economic well-being of a supplying company. The buyer in many cases may not be a purchasing agent. Even though a purchasing employee writes the order, the buying decision may be made by the employee that writes the specification or the purchase requisition. These documents can frequently lock the order into a company selected by a technical employee.

Many of these decisions are justified and proper; but many are not. In an audit of the purchasing function, the path is booby trapped with many different types of land mines that an auditor may trip over.

Here are a few examples of the various types of manipulations that have occurred, or could occur, in a large purchasing operation.

FOUR POINTS TO CONSIDER

1. One of the major problems in purchasing operations is the danger of kickbacks from suppliers. These illegal payments are not confined to the buyer who writes the P/O, since the kickback is always given to the employee that really makes the purchasing decision. Two examples demonstrate the point.

> An acquaintance of the author, whom we will call Mr. X, was employed as a Vice-President of a major corporation. His job required extensive traveling, and he was within three years of retirement. The Director of Purchasing of his company died, and Mr. X was offered and accepted the job. His salary was to remain the same, and he would no longer be required to travel.
>
> On the second day at his new job, he was paid a visit by the Sales Manager of one of his company's large suppliers. Mr. X was happy to meet the representative of a company whose products had always performed satisfactorily, and they had a pleasant introductory meeting. As the session came to a close, the sales manager led into the problem that was the main reason for the meeting by asking Mr. X:

"Shall we continue the arrangement we had with your predecessor?"

Mr. X replied, "Of course, no reason why we shouldn't."

The supplier asked, "How do you want your five percent?"

Mr. X, surprised, asked, "What do you mean?"

"We give you five percent of your gross billings. Do you want it in cash, or shall we open a bank account for you? Or do you have some other preference?"

When relating the experience to me that night, Mr. X admitted that he did some fast mental arithmetic and arrived at a yearly figure that was several times his annual salary. He also admitted that the major reason he made a fast decision was that he had only a few years to go before retirement.

He refused the offer and immediately ordered the product put out for competitive bid. He also specified that the present supplier be taken off the list of acceptable suppliers. He reported the matter to the corporate internal audit staff.

Another incident demonstrates the other end of a kickback transaction. A friend, whom we will call Mr. Y, joined a medium sized company that was managed by its President and sole owner. After several months, Mr. Y had earned the trust of the company President, and was given the title of Sales Manager. One day the President gave Mr. Y a small brown paper sack to deliver to the buyer of a large corporation. Curious, Mr. Y looked into the bag and saw a large number of one hundred dollar bills.

He left the company a short time later after realizing that delivering payoffs was to be his main assignment. Mr. Y died of a stroke a few months later. The trauma of being drawn into those illegal activities no doubt played a part in his early death.

The above two examples demonstrate a type of problem that faces an internal audit staff. In both of the cases, the employer could have purchased materials at a lower price than was paid to the supplier. Had the purchasing agents performed properly, the price paid would not have provided a margin for kickback. **TIP:** *You can, therefore assume that one way to discourage kickbacks is to insure that your company requires honest competitive bids on any major purchase in the hope of buying product at the lowest possible price.*

2. It is sometimes difficult to convince executives of the merits of competitive bidding. Particularly since your company probably sells something to others and doesn't relish being on the other end of a bid system. Sometimes, if competitive bidding is dictated when buying materials, a purchasing agent may unwillingly follow directives.

- A purchasing agent that is opposed to competitive bidding procedures may permit vendors who cannot possibly meet the stringent requirements to bid. These small firms bid low and are awarded the job, but are unable to perform when faced with insurmountable production and delivery problems. The firm is then thrown out for failure to deliver, and the order is given to the former supplier on an emergency basis. The standby supplier receives a premium price, and this episode is used to discredit the entire competitive bidding concept—at least in that area of operations.
  KEY POINT: *The failure is not in the policy, but in the prescreening process which permitted a vendor to be placed on the bidders' list who was not qualified to handle the business.* All prospective bidders should be studied to be sure that they can supply the quality and quantity of products being ordered and that they have a record of meeting their delivery commitments.
- Another ploy used to discourage competitive bidding is to insist that supplier responsibility is eroded when more than one company is used to supply multiple goods or services. **NOTE:** *It IS important that one company assume responsibility for getting a complete job done properly and on time.* If more than one company is involved and a problem develops, each will try to blame the other.

Buying of goods or services must clearly state exactly what is expected of each supplier, and at times it is advisable to assign a purchase commitment entered into with one company, to another firm who is given the responsibility to coordinate delivery and hookup. The coordinating company receives a fee, spelled out in the bid documents, and in return assumes full responsibility for the final results. **TIP:** *In this manner all products and services can be competitively bid.*

3. Sometimes, a supplier may be an unwilling partner to a kickback. I once had a call from a supplier who requested a personal meeting. The supplier contended that his firm was forced to kick back to a buyer in order to retain the business. The vendor had received our company's Statement of Policy letter, but wasn't certain that it was sincere. The firm was forced to bid competitively and to meet the lowest bid, and as a result the firm actually lost money on some of the jobs.

   My caller had complained to the buyer, who threatened not only to rescind a large order, but to throw the firm off the acceptable bidders' list. This threat had lead the firm to decide to test the sincerity of our policy. They produced adequate proof of many of the payoffs that they had made to the buyer.

   The buyer's excuse was that the employer was not injured, since the supplier was forced to accept a job at the lowest bid received from competitive companies. Anything that the buyer personally received was out of the supplier's pocket, not the employer. The bad faith act of passing information to a favored supplier was brushed aside by the buyer, who felt that the bidding process had not been affected even though almost all the jobs were awarded to the same firm.

Though the company that had blown the whistle was permitted to remain on the bidders' list, the termination of the errant buyer did have the effect of encouraging other companies to bid. Prices seemed to be better, and other firms received portions of the business.

KEY POINT: *In order to receive full benefit, there must be free and open competition among qualified bidders without any restraints.* Internal auditors can point out areas where competition is not being solicited and could possibly be effective.

If you have any reason to suspect that kickbacks are occurring in any area of your company you should consider hiring an investigative agency that has some expertise in the field. There are some strong preventive measures that you might suggest to top management, such as the following:

- Issue a strong policy statement concerning gifts or gratuities which forbids soliciting or receiving such items. The formal policy should require immediate dismissal of *any* employee guilty of violating the word or spirit of the directive.

  A strong statement will make any employee pause to consider, and it may frighten others from engaging in such practices. **TIP:** *It could be interesting to see if any buying practices change after such an announcement.*
- Another possible, though extreme, measure to discourage kickbacks is to require all employees who determine suppliers of significant materials to agree to take a polygraph test when requested. Even if they are never requested to take the test, the possibility will encourage employees to follow company policies.
- An effective method of breaking up a kickback relationship is to find some way to force a purchase to be made from someone other than the normal supplier. This is also an effective way of disturbing a price-fixing cartel. Awarding a good-sized contract to a higher bidder may lead to a falling out among conspirators.

  KEY POINT: *What is lost on one order may be gained a hundred times over on future orders.*
- You may be able to learn what other companies are paying for the same product from other suppliers. This should give you an indication of whether there might be an irregularity in the procurement of the materials.

Another approach is to give the specs of a product to a reliable company that has never solicited the business, and ask them for their price. You may discover that they are willing to supply the product at a lower price. This does not, of itself, prove that a kickback arrangement has been operating, but it can at least result in a savings to your company.

4. In some kickback arrangements, the company paying off is an unwilling partner. In such cases, discussions with the top people of the company can lead to full disclosure. One partner of a firm called in to report pressure from a buyer who was soliciting a kickback. The anonymous caller, though refusing names, gave enough information to identify the category of the products that were involved and narrowed the field to the probable buyer. One of the main buyers in that section was a long-term employee with an excellent reputation.

   An audit was started in that area of Purchasing, and the senior buyer recognized the audit concentration. Having been through many audits, the buyer had developed a friendly acquaintance with the author and requested a meeting. When informed that we had received reports of kickbacks in that area of Purchasing, the buyer stated that such reports were lies.

   During the discussion, the buyer was informed of our offer to provide a polygraph test, upon request, when it could help to establish the innocence of any employee who had been placed under a cloud of suspicion. These tests were not used to prove guilt.

   The buyer asked, "Should I take a polygraph test?"

   I replied, "I'm not certain whether you have received any kickbacks; but if I were in your position I'd demand a polygraph. Unless I had received kickbacks; if so, I'd hand in my resignation and get out of here fast."

   The buyer left the office, stating that it was likely that a test would be requested. Twenty minutes later the irate Director of Purchasing called to ask what right I had to fire a purchasing agent. After hearing a summary of the conversation, the Purchasing Director agreed that the matter was closed and the buyer was permitted to resign.

   The audit results confirmed that the anonymous caller was correct and appropriate action was taken against the buyer.

Chapter 19

Auditing an Engineering and a Research Department

Many companies spend large sums of money to improve or discover products. All companies need to repair existing facilities or to construct new buildings and equipment for production, research and distribution operations. Both of these operations, Research and Engineering, employ professional specialists who earn their salaries through creative thinking. Though these experts are only a small segment of the total staff, they make it difficult to enforce routine rules and regulations. This situation mandates that auditors have knowledge of problems relating to engineering and research work.

This chapter is devoted to an internal audit of both the Engineering and the Research Departments. Some companies combine these functions into a single department because their work is so closely intertwined. In other companies, research may be the dominating field, and in others there may be little or no research work performed in-house. Here, we will consider these as two equally important functions and plan our audit accordingly.

An engineering audit reviews the policies and procedures that an Engineering Department uses to develop project concepts for management approval, and then to design and construct the necessary building, machinery and/or equipment to implement the plan. **NOTE:** *Auditors are concerned with operating and cost controls that are used within the Engineering Department, and with the selection of materials and the procedures for contract letting used for construction projects.* Auditing also is concerned that costly concepts are properly approved.

Research operations present a similar problem to the internal auditor. Because of the nature of research work, and the type of experts that are most successful in research and development projects, the operating controls tend to be looser than in any other area of a company. Even though less than ten percent of the number of employees may be truly gifted, their success rubs off onto the entire research operation and cloaks the department in an aura of untouchability. An auditor must evaluate controls, but must do it with tact and finesse and must accomplish the task without antagonizing any of the geniuses.

Background Information

We will use a consumer products manufacturing company, the XYZ Corporation, to illustrate an approach to an internal audit of both an Engineering and a Research Department. In XYZ, these two operations are separate and distinct functions, each headed by a vice-president, who reports directly to the Corporate President.

The Engineering Department is charged with the responsibility for planning and constructing all new facilities and for repairing or enlarging the existing ones. The department also is responsible for developing new production processes or machinery. XYZ has a machine shop, under Engineering control, where prototypes of new production machines are built and tested.

The department has a company Architect who designs the new structures and supervises their construction. A small group in this section is responsible for the design and specifications for the construction of all buildings and building services. The Architect's section supervises the on-site construction work to ensure that all work is performed in conformance with plans and specifications.

A separate section of Engineering designs production-line layouts for heating, ventilating and electrical services required by production lines. This mechanical section is also responsible for developing and constructing production machinery and equipment.

The Engineering Department has an administrative section that is responsible for an engineering library, a special file room and all the clerical work required in the department. The administrator acts as the chairman of the Construction Control Committee which oversees all construction and major repair work performed in the company.

Research operations are conducted in a separate building, which houses the entire research staff and also contains a miniature production plant where prototype equipment is used to test product and materials under actual production conditions.

The Research Department is divided into three sections:

- Administration contains the department administrator who acts as the controller of the operation.
- Production research is devoted to line-production testing, and it is here that the miniature plant is controlled. Research performs some product testing on special request, but normally the quality control aspect of product testing is handled by the production department.
- Product research is concerned with improving existing products. But in

addition, this section contains scientists who work on pure research in the fields that XYZ has some concern.

Many companies spend considerable sums on research and development activities. This phase of operations is very difficult to evaluate and to control. Time and motion studies are impossible in the field of true research, and even the experts themselves find it hard to judge whether satisfactory progress is being achieved on any specific project. But experience shows that one successful project or original idea can pay back the total cost of years of research work.

In an attempt to get a handle on controlling research costs, XYZ has formed a Research Control Committee composed of the top executives of the company. The Director of Research acts as chairman of the committee, and all possible or potential projects are run through the group to determine interest and potential benefit that could be realized if a project were successful.

The committee formulates and approves an annual operating budget and then approves each specific project. Monthly progress reports are prepared which list each active project and the progress achieved during the month. The report is sent to all committee members and other top company executives.

An internal audit of Research is concerned with the operations of a large department. Most of the department's employees are clerical or maintenance workers and the technical employees are individuals that have agreed to work for and to obey the rules and regulations of the company that pays their salary. Auditors determine that hourly paid, administrative, and clerical employees are working at proscribed jobs, and that expenditures are properly authorized, approved and controlled.

Auditors must also determine that all records and reports are accurate, timely and complete. **NOTE:** *An auditor, who might not be an expert in evaluating progress, can still determine that projects being worked on are properly reported and that assigned personnel actually appear to be working on authorized assignments.* **KEY POINT:** *The auditor is also interested in the legal aspects of the projects, particularly the filing of patents and the confidentiality of the work and results.*

XYZ's Research Department is self-contained and handles most of its everyday needs. The department is housed apart from the head office building and has its own accounting and administrative staff. The corporate Computer, Payroll, Purchasing and Engineering service departments are used by Research as required. The Controller of the department reports to the Vice-President, Research, but the Controller has a dotted line responsibility to the Comptroller of the corporation. The department has a purchasing agent and an engineer who report to the V.P. Research but have a dotted line responsibility to their counterparts in the headquarters office.

The internal audit approach, taking all of these factors into account, emphasizes an evaluation of internal controls and an in-depth review of procedures and approvals associated with the formulation and presentation of progress reports and requests for project approvals.

With that as background, here is the sample internal audit program for a review of operations that are conducted by the XYZ Engineering and Research Departments.

IA ERI2001

XYZ CORPORATION
ENGINEERING AND RESEARCH DEPARTMENTS

INTERNAL AUDIT PROGRAM—INSTRUCTIONS

A. *Both Departments*

1. You must become familiar with all policies, directives and operating procedures relating to engineering and research matters. Review the Engineering and Research Administrative Manuals and compare the information contained therein to the Accounting Manual pages covering engineering and research activities. Make certain that there are no conflicts between these directives.
2. Carefully review these instructions, the audit program (Form # IA ERP2002) and the internal control questionnaire before starting your audit so that you will be aware of the full scope of your examination.
3. During your review be certain to have conversations with all supervisory personnel in the departments so that they will be able to discuss any matters they may believe to be of interest to the auditors.
4. As your work progresses, carefully observe operating systems and procedures to determine their efficiency, accuracy and timeliness. Determine if a computer application could result in improvements and discuss your observations with the supervisor of the EDP auditors.
5. Review all reports prepared in the departments and evaluate their necessity, accuracy and cost of preparation. Determine if the need justifies the cost.
6. Review the capital budget, and all files relating to active and closed projects. List, for audit review, all major projects and a sampling of the smaller projects.
7. You will review several activities that are detailed in different sections of your audit manual. Use the program referred to and use the audit checks that apply. Your program calls for an examination of the following:

    - Vouchers issued to pay for items purchased by the department and to reimburse for department employees' expense reports. The detailed audit program for such a review is contained in your audit manual under the title Auditing Payables.
    - Payroll records as they relate to Engineering and Research employees, covered in the program titled Auditing Payroll.
    - Purchases made directly by employees in these departments. Outlined in the program titled Auditing A Purchasing Department.

- Inventories of materials, and perhaps products, in the engineering machine shop and the research prototype plant. Use the audit program titled Auditing Inventory Transactions.

- Although the cash funds in these departments are minor, there are some cash sales made in the Research operation and in the Engineering machine shop. Use the audit program titled Auditing Cash Transactions to review these operations.

- Both the Engineering Department machine shop and the Research Department's production plant contain expensive items of property, much of which may be attractive to some of the employees in those operations. Unless the property has been checked recently, you should perform a complete property recheck, using the audit program in your manual titled, Auditing Property Transactions.

8. A description of the proper procedure for working with this internal audit program appears in the Introduction to the Audit Programs section of your manual. Read this information carefully.

B. Engineering Department

1. Read and fully understand the information in the User's Manual for the Engineering Project Control System. Consult with the supervisor of EDP Auditing and discuss this computer program, which is used extensively by the Construction Audit group.
2. Discuss your current assignment with the supervisor of the construction audit group. You may skim over those projects that the group has supervised or is currently working on. Concentrate your effort on those projects that the construction group does not review. Engineering participation in construction projects is covered in detail in the audit program titled Auditing a Construction Project.
3. Although the Engineering Department has a staff of designers and draftsmen, there are times when outside engineering design services must be used. Service people may work in our office under the direct supervision of XYZ Engineering personnel, or the work may be performed in the outside service company's office under their supervision. In this latter case, an XYZ supervisor periodically visits their office to check on the job's progress and to answer any pertinent questions.

   When work is performed in the agency's office, they should follow a rigid time allocation system. Each specialist records the project number and the exact time that work is begun on the job. The card should contain a brief description of the work assignment. The agency employee is supposed to record the exact time and reason that work is interrupted or when an assignment is terminated.

   If you need to audit an outside agency's services, you should make a surprise visit and examine the time reports of all employees working on our projects. Compare their job cards to the plans or specs they are working on. **IMPORTANT:** *If any are working on jobs for other clients,* *but their cards indicate that they are assigned to XYZ work, immediately call one of the agency's principals to the work stations and point out the discrepancies.* Inform the engineering administrator of your findings, and cover the matter with the internal audit manager.

4. Review the minutes of the Construction Control Committee for the period following the previous audit. Meet with the three permanent members of the committee, and discuss your current assignment. Note and follow up on areas that they suggest for an in-depth review.
5. Engineering requires that all contractors, who have agreed to submit bids for a project, deposit a sum of money that covers the cost of duplicating the plans and specifications. This deposit is returned when the contractor returns the plans and specs. The deposit has the effect of discouraging contractors from agreeing to bid if they are really not interested; and it encourages the losers to return the bid documents which can then be used as extra sets where required.
6. Prepare a list of open projects taken from the previous audit work papers. Add new projects and note completed ones. This is the list that will serve as the starting point for your current review.
7. The engineering machine shop is to be reviewed using the same audit approach that we use to study any machine shop. **KEY POINT:** *Be particularly alert for purchases of materials or project work that is for an employee's personal use but is charged to company expense.*

   The machine shop may perform personal work, when the work schedule is light, but these must all be approved in advance and clearly labeled as personal work. Billings are to be prepared that *completely reimburse XYZ for the total cost of all such work.* The standard shop labor rate is to be used, and materials are to be billed at actual invoice cost. No markups are to be applied to these jobs.

C. *Research Department*

1. Carefully review the minutes of the Research Control Committee's meetings since the last internal audit. Starting with the list of open research projects taken from the previous audit working papers, add all new approved projects to the list, and note the projects that have been reported as completed. This new list of active projects will be the base for your project review.
2. The research prototype plant, merely duplicates our in-plant machinery. **NOTE:** *The operation does* not *utilize the normal internal control over receiving, transfers and shipments that prevail in our operating production plants.* You must therefore carefully review these areas of activities to determine whether controls are adequate.
3. Project requests may originate from any source, but some sources are more likely to receive attention than others. Review the file of open requests and the file of rejected requests to see if there are any that have not received the attention they deserve. **NOTE:** *Discuss any requests that you believe to have merit with the manager of internal auditing before mentioning them to research personnel.*

INTERNAL AUDIT PROGRAM

IA ERP2002

XYZ CORPORATION
INTERNAL AUDIT PROGRAM—ENGINEERING AND RESEARCH DEPARTMENTS

This audit program is designed to lead you through a routine audit of the Engineering and Research departments. Use this program as a guide to be altered to meet any unusual conditions encountered. Bring to the audit supervisor's attention any changes that appear necessary.

A. *Company Procedures*

1. All engineering and research projects are authorized in advance.
2. All department expenditures are charged to applicable projects.
3. Progress and costs of projects are reported monthly.
4. Department administrators exercise close control over clerical records, procedures and reports.
5. All construction projects are competitively bid.

B. *Audit Objectives* are to determine the following:

1. All employees are aware of and adhere to company policies and procedures.
2. Records and reports are accurate, complete and timely.
3. Department employees use good judgment and efficient systems in conducting their day to day activities.
4. Bidding procedures insure active competition and are carefully controlled.
5. The executive control committees are informed of all department projects and act to control these operations.

C. *Audit Procedures* — *Per. Cov.* | *Audit By*

I. Both Departments

1. Study the audit instructions (form # IA ERI2001), this program and the internal control questionnaire before starting your audit. _____ _____
2. Interview every supervisor, and a sampling of every job classification in these departments so that you are familiar with all department activities. _____ _____
   a. Obtain a sample of every form originated in the department and estimate the cost to prepare each form. _____ _____
      1) Discuss with the EDP audit group the advisability of computerizing any of this work. _____ _____
   b. Determine that an adequate method is used to decide work assignments and work force requirements. _____ _____
      1) Determine that work loads are periodically reviewed and adjustments are made when necessary. _____ _____
      2) Review controls over employees assigned to work at a location out of the main office. _____ _____
   c. Determine that departments are using standardization in all areas where feasible. _____ _____
      1) Where standards are available, determine that they

C. Audit Procedures	*Per.*	*Audit*
I. Both Departments	*Cov.*	*By*
are properly used in-house and by outside agencies.	____	____
d. Review filing system for efficiency and security.	____	____
1) See that latest methods of reproduction are used.	____	____
2) See that record retention schedule is followed.	____	____
3. Review the annual budget and add to your list from the previous audit all the costly newer projects.	____	____
a. Review all files relating to these projects. Pay particular attention to economic justifications.	____	____
1) See that all projects have been properly approved.	____	____
b. Examine all charges against these projects.	____	____
1) See that all charges conform to work authorized.	____	____
4. Review procedures for initiating, approving and setting up controls over appropriations.	____	____
a. Determine that all major expenditures are covered by a properly authorized appropriation, and that they are in conformance with the authorization.	____	____
b. See that appropriations are closed at completion.	____	____
5. Check procedure for requesting and obtaining supplemental appropriations and the handling of over-expenditures.	____	____
a. Spot check to see if large expenditures are broken up so that they can be charged to blanket appropriations.	____	____
1) See if any charges are shifted to completed projects that had funds left over.	____	____
6. Review procedures for initiating and approving the establishment of an experimental or research project.	____	____
a. Review procedures for establishing priority ratings for new projects.	____	____
1) Determine that priorities are regularly reviewed.	____	____
b. Determine that all departments concerned are given an opportunity to review and to input into the concept.	____	____
c. See that all charges are authentic and proper.	____	____
1) Verify charges by examining materials or items bought, and evaluate control over writing the R/Rs.	____	____
d. Review procedures for closing out these projects.	____	____
7. Evaluate system for charging project costs to department or location that requested project.	____	____
a. If charges are divided among several users, determine that allocations are fair.	____	____
8. Determine that travel expenses are adequately reviewed, approved, and controlled.	____	____
9. Audit both departments' originated purchases using the audit program titled Auditing a Purchasing Department.	____	____
a. Determine channels of communication and contacts		

	Per. Cov.	Audit By
C. Audit Procedures		
I. Both Departments		
between department personnel and outside suppliers.	____	____
1) Verify that such channels are known to Purchasing.	____	____
2) Determine that employees are careful not to rule out negotiations by purchasing agents.	____	____
b. See that suppliers are authentic, and controls insure that goods or services are received prior to payment.	____	____
1) See that accounting work is accurate and proper.	____	____
10. Audit both departments' payroll costs using program titled Auditing Payroll.	____	____
a. Review control over work performed and time reported by outside agency people.	____	____
b. Check the necessity for employing outside help.	____	____
c. Verify existence and work assignments of outside help being presently employed in XYZ's office.	____	____
1) If any help is kept on for an extended period would it be more economical to increase permanent staff?	____	____
11. Audit all cash receipts or cash funds. Use audit program titled Auditing Cash Transactions.	____	____
12. Audit disbursements authorized by department personnel using program titled Auditing Payables.	____	____
13. Where applicable, audit inventories of supplies or products using the program titled Auditing Inventories.	____	____
14. Verify property items used in the departments using the audit program titled Auditing Property.	____	____
15. Audit operations at prototype plant and machine shop by using the audit program titled Auditing Production.	____	____
16. Verify billings from outside agencies that supply specialists to work in our buildings.	____	____
a. Schedule these employees sign in and sign out times, from guard register, for past three months.	____	____
1) Compare schedule to billings from agencies.	____	____
2) *Follow up on any discrepancies.*	____	____
17. Review procedures for evaluating project leaders.	____	____
a. Review method of measuring efficiency of technicians.	____	____
18. Review formal periodic status schedule of all projects.	____	____
a. Determine that schedules list all open projects.	____	____
b. Determine that all projects were properly approved.	____	____
II. Engineering Department		
1. Review Engineering's internal controls, processing procedures and departmental records for disbursements.	____	____
a. Verify charges for outside services supplied to Engineering such as blueprints, drawings and typing.	____	____
2. Audit a selection of the projects that you have listed.	____	____
a. For construction projects refer to the program in your manual titled Auditing a Construction Project.	____	____

	Per. Cov.	Audit By
C. Audit Procedures		
II. Engineering Department		
3. Review costs and advisability of practice of bringing prints "up-to-date" at completion of a project.	____	____
4. Review agreements with outside professional firms.	____	____
a. Determine that responsibilities are clearly stated.	____	____
b. Determine that agreement itemizes the basis of charges; ownership of drawings; and contains provisions for termination of the agreement.	____	____
5. Visit the offices of engineering agencies that we frequently use to assist in project work.	____	____
a. Clarify how time of principals are applied to jobs.	____	____
1) Principals time should be covered in hourly rate.	____	____
b. Discuss work being performed on our projects with the specialists doing the work.	____	____
c. Determine procedure for recording the starting and stopping times on assigned jobs.	____	____
1) Evaluate their internal controls that ensure time spent on a specific project is accurately recorded.	____	____
2) Compare time cards to project records for accuracy.	____	____
d. Arrive at agency office early, before work day begins. Observe that employees assigned to XYZ projects record the time started and record the proper project number.	____	____
1) See that job time cards accurately reflect the projects you noted that they were working on.	____	____
2) *Ensure that we are not charged for time that was actually worked on another account.*	____	____
6. For those engineering service agencies that perform a large percentage of their work for XYZ, perform the following checks, in addition to those of 5 above:		
a. Schedule total monthly sales for past twelve months.	____	____
1) Verify total billings to XYZ.	____	____
2) From billing records note amount billed to others.	____	____
b. Relate percentages from a. above to percentage of work you observed being performed for XYZ.	____	____
c. Any evidence of padding hours, or of shifting costs from one job to another should be discussed with agency supervisor and also with employees involved.	____	____
1) *If there is any evidence of manipulation, or if any suspicion remains, contact the audit manager.*	____	____
7. Use the same procedure as described in 5 and 6 above to audit any machine shop doing cost plus work for XYZ.	____	____
a. Material costs should be audited as covered in your audit program titled Auditing Purchasing.	____	____
8. Review charges for equipment rental at our machine shop. See that rental is necessary and properly approved.	____	____

	Per. Cov.	Audit By
C. Audit Procedures		
II. Engineering Department		
1) Note frequency and period of rental and determine if it would be more economical to purchase item.	____	____
2) Determine that rented item is returned promptly.	____	____
3) Determine if any equipment is being purchased on a rental purchase agreement. If so:	____	____
a) Check for proper authorization and approval.	____	____
III. Research Department		
1. Determine that research prepares and maintains adequate records to prove development for patent application.	____	____
a. Determine that records describe the work done and the pertinent dates involved.	____	____
2. Verify that all research and testing is corroborated by independent scientists and supervisors.	____	____
3. Determine that records relating to research projects are held in a secure fireproof, burglarproof vault.	____	____
a. See that access is limited to authorized personnel.	____	____
b. Determine that the circulated project status reports do not contain detailed confidential information.	____	____
c. Verify that accurate records name all people present at any meeting in which secret research work is discussed.	____	____
d. Determine that a good system of visitor control is rigidly enforced and that no visitors are permitted in any restricted areas.	____	____
4. Determine if any research equipment is being used by research personnel in their personal homes.	____	____
a. Check for proper approval, and evaluate reasons.	____	____
b. Determine that supervisors monitor all product or equipment taken out of the research facility.	____	____
5. Study the records of production runs in prototype plant.	____	____
a. Determine if plant is a wise economic investment.	____	____
b. Consider possibility of experimental runs in normal operating plant when lines are shut down for night.	____	____
c. Review procedures for control of items produced.	____	____
1) Trace records for disposition of items produced.	____	____
6. Select projects from your updated list and carefully audit all charges. Refer to the following audit programs in your manual: Auditing Payables; Auditing a Purchasing Department; and Auditing a Construction Project.	____	____
7. Determine whether projects are worked on in-house, to keep staff busy, that might better be farmed out to a specialized research lab or a university.	____	____
a. Observe work pace of employees performing routine tasks. Determine if operation is over-staffed.	____	____

C. Audit Procedures *III. Research Department*	*Per. Cov.*	*Audit By*
8. Carefully review charges to catchall jobs that are used to pick up charges not related to specific projects.	____	____
a. *See if these projects are used to bury personal items.*	____	____
9. Determine that Research works closely with Purchasing in their value analysis studies.	____	____

Audit work reviewed by ______________________ Date ____________

INTERNAL AUDIT PROGRAM—INTERNAL CONTROL QUESTIONNAIRE

The following internal control questions are intended to direct your attention to the high risk areas of these operations. Some of these points are covered in the audit program and they are included here to ensure that they receive adequate attention.

Answer these control questions as your audit progresses. In section B, you are to write in the names and job titles of the various employees who perform the listed functions. Be certain to note any conflicting duties that could jeopardize internal control.

A. The following are indicative of good internal control.

1. All Engineering and Research projects are approved and monitored by Committees of executives.
2. All company policies are followed by all employees.
3. Records and reports are accurately maintained.
4. Complete and detailed plans and specs are prepared for every major engineering project.
5. All construction projects and major equipment purchases are competitively bid.

B. Following lists functions performed by named employees.

Function:	*Name/Position*	*Conflicting Duties*
1. Approves plans and specs.	__________	__________
2. Negotiates contracts.	__________	__________
3. Approves bills for payment.	__________	__________
4. Approves research projects.	__________	__________
5. Acts as cashier.	__________	__________
6. Approves change orders.	__________	__________
7. Acts as receiving clerk.	__________	__________

C. Control Questions:	*Yes*	*No*	*Remarks*
1. Do all projects receive executive approval before any work is started?	____	____	__________
a. Do all projects clear the committee after preliminary study, before additional work?	____	____	__________
2. Are all legal requirements being met, and are all policies and proce-			

C. Control Questions	*Yes*	*No*	*Remarks*
dures being followed by all employees in both departments?	___	___	___
a. Have all signed inventions agreements?	___	___	___
b. Are all expense reports properly supported and approved?	___	___	___
3. Does the Construction Control Committee meet regularly to discuss project problems?	___	___	___
4. Are all bidding documents carefully checked by the architect before being sent out?	___	___	___
a. Are they also reviewed by Auditing?	___	___	___
5. Do specs provide for at least two competitive products for every requirement?	___	___	___
a. If not, is there provision for an "or equal" proposal?	___	___	___
6. Does Engineering administrator participate in the opening of bids for all projects?	___	___	___
a. Does administrator receive approval from Legal before making any changes in the standard form contract?	___	___	___
7. Are all construction contracts covered by a properly authorized purchase order?	___	___	___
a. Are Waivers of Lien required before any payments are made to contractors?	___	___	___
b. Are all contract change orders properly controlled and approved?	___	___	___
1) Are they submitted promptly, before the work is performed?	___	___	___
8. Is retention taken out of every payment?	___	___	___
a. Is inspection made of work before final acceptance and release of retainer?	___	___	___
b. Is walk-through list carefully controlled and followed up till all work is accepted?	___	___	___

C. Control Questions	*Yes*	*No*	*Remarks*
9. Does engineering administrator work closely with construction auditor to control project?	___	___	___
a. With Property in preparing property cards?	___	___	___
10. Are funds received as deposits for bid sets properly recorded, handled and returned?	___	___	___
11. Does Engineering have a method of evaluating materials and machinery used on our projects?	___	___	___
a. Do such evaluations play an important part in writing new specifications?	___	___	___
12. Is there a good system for testing an item before it, or the project, is accepted?	___	___	___
13. Do supervisors approve all billings from outside agencies for work they performed?	___	___	___
a. Do these firms adequately support their billings for time and other charges?	___	___	___
b. Are all outside agency people required to sign in and out at lobby guard desk?	___	___	___
14. *Are there adequate controls to insure that items are not procured for personal use?*	___	___	___
15. Does Research Control Committee regularly meet to discuss research projects?	___	___	___
a. Is all work stopped immediately if control committee decides to terminate a project?	___	___	___
16. Are research personnel cost conscious in their ordering of materials?	___	___	___
a. In their work habits?	___	___	___
b. Are charges to projects fully controlled?	___	___	___
c. Are costs an important element in deciding what items to specify for a project?	___	___	___
17. Are all materials delivered to Research, received by an independent receiving clerk?	___	___	___

C. Control Questions	*Yes*	*No*	*Remarks*
a. Are all billings approved by supervision prior to payment?	___	___	___
18. Are research tests thoroughly checked by supervisors as work progresses?	___	___	___
a. Are results verified and certified?	___	___	___
b. Are project reports complete and accurate?	___	___	___
1) Are accurate records kept of employee time worked on specific projects?	___	___	___
c. Are research reports reviewed by Director before they are officially offered?	___	___	___
19. Are Engineering experimental projects closely coordinated with the Research Department?	___	___	___
a. Are formal estimates of costs prepared?	___	___	___
20. Are numbers of prints, specs, etc. carefully computed and reproduced at a minimum level?	___	___	___
a. Is record retention program followed?	___	___	___
21. *Does Research Quality Testing put items on hold immediately if questions are raised?*	___	___	___
a. Are "held" items only released after extensive testing clears product?	___	___	___
b. *Is all faulty product promptly destroyed?*	___	___	___
c. Are all tests accurately recorded?	___	___	___
d. Are results reviewed by supervisors?	___	___	___
22. Do both departments enforce the package pass system for items leaving their buildings?	___	___	___

Questions answered by ____________________ Date __________
Answers reviewed by ____________________ Date __________

CRITICAL POINTS

The highly technical nature of Engineering and Research operations present a formidable hiding place for manipulation and fraud. **CAUTION:** *You must be meticulous and wary as you perform your audit in these areas.* Allow your common sense to lead you through the possible pitfalls that you'll encounter. Following are a few brief comments concerning some of the more frequent abuses that occur in these areas.

ELEVEN CRITICAL POINTS TO CONSIDER

1. Tolerances on machine-made items can materially affect the cost of these products. Specs may call for a very tight tolerance, that carries with it a very high cost. **KEY POINT:** *The operation may not really require such a tolerance,* and an outside company in collusion with the spec writer, is aware of the situation. Price is based on the specs, but the delivered product conforms to a much looser tolerance.

   EXAMPLE: In one such instance, a machined key, that would normally sell at ten cents apiece, was purchased at over ten dollars each because of a tight spec that normally would cause a manufacturer to discard fifty keys before one met the specs. Satisfactory keys checked out on a micrometer to a normal tolerance rather than the stringent one. It was determined that the supplier had actually purchased standard keys at less than ten cents per, and delivered them at a fantastic markup. Several thousand keys were purchased.

   This type of manipulation can be exposed by testing the high precision of the items called for, to see if they actually conform to specs. **KEY POINT:** *If they do not, and the items are working satisfactorily, then you know that something is wrong!* A quick check with Purchasing should disclose the going price for the items actually delivered.

   You have a claim for the overpayment and for potential losses. The supplier's legal position is poor, which means that you will receive full cooperation in your investigation to find the culprit.
2. Specifications are frequently written in such a way that only one manufacturer can qualify, and, of course, that company is aware of the situation. It is impossible to get competitive bids under these conditions. Employees responsible for writing specs often use a restrictive approach to insure that the business goes to a specific supplier. Naturally, the supplier is expected to be grateful.

   Where no courtesy bidding is involved, other companies are quick to point out the closed area. **CAUTION:** *If collusion is present, the facts may not become known unless the plans and specs are checked by an auditor or an outside expert.* Once the closed area is located and pointed out management should cooperate in opening up the specs. Sometimes there is ample justification for the spec as written, and your company must pay the price.

TIP: *In other cases, the problem is solved by merely adding the phrase, "or equal" to the specs.*

If a supplier suggests an alternate, the product may be tested to see if it will qualify. Deficiencies are pointed out, as is the price differential, and management can make an informed decision. **TIP:** *The mere act of considering an "as equal" product, often has the effect of bringing the price of the desired product into line.*

3. A major area of concern lies in the costs of engineering work required to perform a project. Each construction job carries its own individual problems, and there are various ways of approaching each project. The type and magnitude of engineering work prepared depends on the basic approach and organization of your company's Engineering Department. Your company may decide to design and construct required facilities, or may elect to contract for a building of specific dimensions and/or usage. Dollars saved at one point may be lost in repairs, changes or additions at a later date.

   There is an element of potential savings in engineering costs if your company constructs many similar items. **MONEY SAVING SUGGESTION:** *A standard set of specification paragraphs, standard detail drawings and standard contract conditions can reduce duplication of effort.* Engineering time can be spent reviewing existing standards and selecting the appropriate one, instead of completely analyzing each situation and working out a new economic solution.

4. In both Engineering and Research there is the ever present danger that an employee who is working on a confidential project may decide to move to another company. Some employees attempt to take drawings and specifications with them when they leave. They believe that they have the right to this information since in many cases they actually created the work. Here are some control suggestions:

   - A good control system at the library and file room will disclose what information the departing employee has taken from those sources. Restricted materials should normally only be released to authorized employees, and a record should be kept of all movements. The duplicating section should also have a record of all materials that have been copied. **TIP:** *A study of these records will disclose the exact information that any employee withdrew or copied.*
   - All personnel in Engineering and Research should be required to sign an "Inventions Agreement" when they are hired. This agreement stipulates that anything the individual develops while on the company payroll becomes the property of the firm.
   - Employees, at termination interviews, should be directly asked if

they have any confidential information in their personal possession. They should be reminded of the inventions agreement and questioned as to the whereabouts of any restricted information they have taken.

- A polite request from the individual's immediate superior usually produces the material in question. A reminder that the information is confidential and that it belongs to the company, will usually forestall any improper use of the materials.

5. When outside engineering agencies are used to design work required for a project, the basis for charge is often a cost-plus contract. Cost of labor may be charged at a standard rate per type of service, which charge usually covers salary, fringe, overhead and profit. It is not unusual for an audit to disclose that all the employees of a small firm have been charged to the project. **CAUTION:** *Sometimes, the total hours charged exceed the total labor hours paid by the agency for the period that the job was in their office.*

   When this type of discrepancy is pointed out to the principals of the agency, they will respond with some type of explanation. Some may state that they personally spent many unrecorded overtime hours working on the project and that the excess hours are to reimburse them for their personal overtime.

   To reduce the possibility of this actually occurring, your contract with such agencies should spell out what is chargeable and what is not. **TIP:** *It should also clearly spell out whether the time of the firm's principals is a chargeable item.* If so, the rate should be itemized and the nature of supporting records should be stated.

   Normally, the time of principals is covered in the overhead and profit factors built into the technicians' rates, but there may be justification for agreeing to pay for time of a particular manager.

   The agreement should list the names and job titles of all employees, who are to be assigned to the project, and their applicable rates. It should also state what charges are to be made for clerical work, for outside services and for extra copies of materials that are required by the owner. **CAUTION:** *It should also clearly define responsibilities and identify ownership of the work upon completion.*
6. The preparation of bid documents and the duplication of plans and specs can be expensive. Some of the work may be done in-house, but it is frequently necessary to use an outside company to reproduce the information. Copies of blueprints can be expensive, and available copy companies are limited. It is not uncommon for such a company to pay a commission to engineers or purchasing agents that steer business to their firms. Busi-

ness can be directed to a supplier by stating that the company has better quality and service than any of the competitors.

One method of discouraging a kickback arrangement, is to competitively negotiate a scale rate and a quantity rebate arrangement with an acceptable house, and all the work is then automatically directed to that firm. Another system that is frequently used is to divide the business among two or three acceptable firms. This keeps all the suppliers alert and gives your company the flexibility to use any available firm when the others are busy.

7. Another area of potential kickback lies in the employment of outside services or experts that provide professional expertise. It is often difficult to evaluate the contribution by these outside experts, and the charges can sometimes be exorbitant.

   When substantial payments are made to an outside company, the auditor must insure that something is received for the expenditure. This requires an examination of the report and an evaluation of the suggestions contained therein. Such review insures that there was work done on the project and that something of value was received.

   Your company should at least require competitive proposals from outside companies that outline the background of the experts they intend to assign to the project. The proposal should state the fee to be paid and how any additional charges are to be computed. It should also state what the firm intends to do to earn the fee.

   All proposals should be evaluated by a group of executives who then agree on the acceptance of a particular firm. Auditors should ensure that all billings conform to the terms of the proposals.

8. A touchy area in both Engineering and Research operations is the use of department labor to perform personal work on company time. The professional expertise of many of these department specialists can be much in demand by other employees. The ease of obtaining materials in these departments is an added attraction.

   Sometimes, engineers design personal homes or additions for themselves or friends, or perhaps as a sideline business. Personal drawings are frequently found on drawing boards, usually between company drawings where they can be worked on at opportune times, such as lunch periods or coffee breaks. In some cases personal work has been cloaked under a drawing identification that appears to be for an assigned project.

   Control over this type of abuse lies with first line supervision, who should know what work has been assigned to designers and draftsmen. **KEY POINT:** *Supervisors should frequently check to insure that the work being performed is progressing satisfactorily and that it relates to active company projects.* An auditor would be well-advised to finger through the paper work being performed by technicians to review the type of problems being considered.

9. Some research labs perform regular tests on finished products. After testing is completed the product is either destroyed, returned for reprocessing or moved into sales channels. **CAUTION:** *Research personnel can easily report that items were junked when in fact they were taken for personal use, or sold or given away.*

   Sometimes items from research labs are donated to charity or used as prizes in company activities.

   Good operating controls require that all products be identified and recorded as they enter Research. The record should identify the item, show time of receipt, describe the tests performed and state the disposition of the products. These records should be examined and approved by supervisors and reviewed by the department administrator.

   Problems are more complicated if items are removed by supervisory personnel. One method of protecting against such extractions is to control everything that leaves the building. *A strict package pass system can be an effective control.* Under this system an employee carrying any object, must show a properly approved authorization to remove the item. Package passes are examined by the guard at the exit, to insure that the description applies and that the approval signature is genuine. Guards have the authority to open any package that appears suspicious to ensure that it conforms to the pass description, and they contact the approving supervisor if anything appears to be wrong.

   NOTE: *The mere introduction of such a system will materially reduce the quantity of items taken from a laboratory.*

10. Expense reports for Engineering and Research personnel are a potential danger area. Examination of these reports may disclose payoffs to public officials for a variety of reasons. **CAUTION:** *A common payoff occurs in connection with construction projects, to expedite building permits or required inspections of work as the job progresses.*

    Your company should have a firm policy prohibiting such payoffs. But this is a difficult area to police, and presents a problem to employees charged with the responsibility for getting a job done.

    Building inspectors have the authority to condemn work, and can cause work to be pulled out and redone. The approval of satisfactory work can also be manipulated to cause a contractor or an owner to suffer financial loss through deliberate delays in conducting inspections. Crews of high-priced workers may sit around for hours or days waiting for an inspector to approve the work, so that they can get on with the project or leave the job site.

    Under this type of condition the payment of an inducement to an inspector to perform the check quickly, appears to be an economic decision. These payoffs are frequently made at the lunch table, and the official visits the job site immediately after lunch to perform the inspection. **KEY POINT:** *Evidence of payoffs to any government worker should be turned over to the proper police authorities for investigation and prosecution.*

11. When a corporate research lab is in a separate building, there may be a desire to relax security and internal control measures. In a relaxed, creative atmosphere it is relatively simple to order products that are for personal use. The items are received by the employee and charged to an active research project. Materials needed for personal construction projects may be charged to building maintenance.

    A careful audit review of project expenditures may disclose payments for materials that obviously cannot be used for the project to which they are charged. A good control system requires that all deliveries to the research facility be made to the receiving dock, and that a receiving clerk prepare and sign a receiving report. An audit trail of materials charged to research should originate at the dock.

    KEY POINT: *This means that everything received should be specifically noted as to the project or purpose intended.*

    Materials delivered anyplace other than the research building must be carefully investigated. **TIP:** *If receiving clerks are forced to sign documents to show receipt of materials that were delivered elsewhere, they become reluctant conspirators and are usually anxious to discuss the situation with an auditor.*

Chapter 20

Auditing a Construction Project

Construction work, because of its nonrepetitive nature and inherent opportunity for deception, requires a careful audit approach. The approach evaluates the legitimacy of payments and the honesty of the employees involved in the operation.

This chapter covers the internal audit of a construction project. It starts at the inception of the project and follows through to the final acceptance and release of amounts retained. It assumes that your company has decided to build a major installation and has given the internal audit department the responsibility for auditing the project as the work progresses.

To properly audit a construction project, the auditing department should start its participation at the first stage of the project and stay with it until completion. Most companies perform audits of construction expenditures, but only a few authorize their audit staff to actively participate in managing a project. If the audit staff has a special section that specializes in construction projects, that section's supervisor should personally get involved in decisions affecting the internal controls. This means that an internal auditor attends all important meetings that conceive and control the project. In this chapter we will assume that the audit department is involved in all phases of the undertaking.

Most projects start with a study of needs then, after obtaining budget approval, follow through to selection of a site. For budget approval, Engineering prepares sketchy preliminary plans and a ball park estimate of the cost of the project. These projected costs are usually square footage estimates that vary to suit their purpose. The estimate is low if there is concern about getting approval, and it is high if approval is certain and the engineer wishes to provide an ample cushion for contingencies.

After budget approval, the Engineering Department proceeds to work on the plans and specifications for the building and grounds. These documents describe and define the project. It is at this point that the Auditing Department should become actively involved.

When a company requires a new facility it considers all of the options available at the time. It may elect to do one of the following:

- Buy a building, already built, and modify it as required.
- Use a contractor, who promises to construct a facility meeting certain general requirements, and then turn it over to the owner.
- Plan the facility to exactly meet its requirements, and then supervise the construction to insure that the building meets all plans and specifications.

Let's consider each of the above options. But first, remember that usually about one half of the cost of a building is buried underground or under a coat of paint, behind plaster or above ceiling tile. In these buried areas, large quantities of inferior quality products may lie, swiftly deteriorating, and waiting to cause trouble. Thousands of dollars may be saved during construction by using second rate materials but these savings will, in later years, haunt the owner.

A preventive building maintenance program begins at the inception of construction. A company that occupies many buildings must consider the repair and upkeep problems that will occur in the future if they scrimp on building materials today. If a company allows an outsider to construct a building for them, there is a good chance that they will later learn that cheap materials were used in construction.

How to Deal with the Three Options

1. Under the first option, the building is already built, and it is difficult to exactly determine what went into the construction. If construction appears sound and inspections by experts do not disclose any serious flaws, if the dimensions are pretty close, if the layout is efficient for use as is, if the location is acceptable and if the price is low enough, then this could well be the best option.

   Even though some modifications are bound to be required, these may only take a few months to accomplish, which would make the facility available for use at an earlier date than building from scratch.
2. The second option also has some potentially desirable features. The contractor performs all of the architectural, engineering, construction supervision, administrative and clerical work necessary to complete the building. Naturally the fee will cover all work performed, though there may be a good deal of scrimping on any or all of these necessary services. The total price may be well below the cost that would be incurred by using an inhouse Engineering Department to handle the project.

   Under this option the owner doesn't really know much about the building that has been constructed, unless all plans and specs are reviewed and approved prior to bid letting. Even then, there is a degree of uncertainty since plans and specs are usually vague, relying heavily on the custom of the trade and local building codes. The owner may gain some protection by assigning a company Engineering representative as an observer on the construction site.

3. The third option may, or may not, be the most expensive in the short term. Under this system the owner decides what materials to use for every part of the building and how everything will be constructed.

   All bidding contractors or suppliers know exactly what their bids should cover, and they do not have to include amounts for contingency or to provide for interest charges in the event their invoices are not promptly paid. Their bids, if submitted directly to a major company, should be lower than if submitted to an unknown general contractor. Handled properly, the comparable cost for *exactly the same work* should be lower than would occur under the second option described above.

   For our purposes we will assume that the third option is the one that is being used, and our audit program is based on this assumption. Even if one of the other options were used, much of the following information could be helpful in controlling the project.

Background Information

The sample audit program is used by the XYZ Corporation to control construction costs. In this company the Internal Audit staff serves as a member of management in actively controlling a construction project. The Construction Audit staff acts as the Financial Department representative, working closely in coordination with the Engineering and Purchasing Departments to insure that XYZ's interests are protected. A construction auditor is assigned full time to the job site of every major construction project, and periodically visits the job site of the medium sized jobs. For smaller jobs, the staff reviews project records after the work has been completed.

The audit program was designed to assist a construction auditor in the performance of assigned responsibilities. In the XYZ Corporation the internal audit department reports to the Financial Vice-President. Supervision of construction projects rests with Engineering which is headed by a Vice-President of Engineering.

The technical portion of the construction project lies completely within the Engineering Department. An engineering superintendent is assigned to see that the company gets exactly what was specified and that the construction work conforms with the plans and specifications.

The Financial Department, responsible for protecting the financial interests of the company, assigns an auditor who is charged with the responsibility of assisting in the control of construction costs.

KEY POINT: *A project auditor is responsible for seeing that the company gets what it pays for and does not pay for something it doesn't get.*

These two independent representatives must cooperate on the job site to protect the interests of the company.

In the everyday work world individual lines of responsibility can sometimes become blurred. Internal auditors may get involved in a question of interpretation of plans or specs, particularly where costs are at issue. Auditors may also suggest changes in materials that can reduce project costs without affecting quality. These ideas are given to the Engineering Department for evaluation and final decision.

The auditor's thinking is not restricted by written plans and specs, but the project engineering representative has the prime responsibility to see that the plans and specs are followed to the letter. When obvious savings are available without reducing quality, the project engineer and the auditor frequently combine forces to point out ways that a job can be done more economically than is contained in the formal documents. **NOTE:** *Final decision rests with the Architect and the Vice-President of Engineering.*

The XYZ audit staff has a group of construction specialists. On major projects a full-time auditor is assigned to the job site, while for the giant projects a team of auditors may be assigned at different stages of the construction work. Audit assignments are affected by the type of construction contracts that have been written.

For the smaller construction jobs, the internal audit staff uses roving auditors who travel these sites and spend as much time as necessary at any location. Auditors plan their visits so that they are at specific sites when certain types of work are scheduled to be performed. Smaller jobs might never be visited during the construction period, but the auditor reviews the records after the fact.

XYZ Corporation uses a Construction Control Committee to control all administrative and financial matters relating to construction projects. The committee also establishes companywide policies and procedures relative to construction work. The committee chairman is the Engineering administrator, and its other permanent members are the administrator of the Purchasing Department and a representative of Financial. It is augmented with an appropriate representative of the operating department that is involved in a major project. When a decision is not unanimous, the matter is referred to the VP's of the departments involved, and if necessary carried to the President.

The supervisor of the construction audit group usually serves as the Financial representative at the control meetings. The audit supervisor works very closely with the administrators of Purchasing and Engineering who represent their departments. Committee members meet frequently when a major project is being let, or whenever the chairman believes it necessary to convene the group.

Construction auditors, assigned to a major project, are usually brought aboard at the concept stage of the work, and remain until the project is completed. The auditor reviews the work of the designers, draftsmen, spec writers and contract technicians. If an outside engineering firm is hired to help in any part of the job, the auditor reviews the work of the outside group as the job moves along.

The following sample audit program is designed for use by the construction audit staff of the XYZ Corporation. It is divided into two sections. The first contains audit information that explains audit procedures and policies.

The second section is the audit program. It contains a checklist of audit considerations that have important consequences in monitoring construction work. It is intended to remind the auditor of procedures or controls that may be of use when working in specific areas. The program is organized to enable the auditor to separate the specific section that applies to a particular type of problem.

The sample audit program that follows is designed for use on major construction projects. Applicable portions of it can be used to audit smaller construction jobs.

INTERNAL AUDIT INSTRUCTIONS

IA CAI550 XYZ CORPORATION
INTERNAL AUDIT PROGRAM—CONSTRUCTION JOB AUDITOR
AUDIT INSTRUCTIONS

These instructions should be read and understood before starting your assignment. If anything in this audit program is not completely clear to you, discuss the matter with the supervisor of the construction audit staff. There is no assurance that every possibility is considered in this program, and there is no substitute for common sense. Evaluate each audit instruction and use those that apply.

I. General

A. Review these instructions, the audit program (Form # IA CAP555), the Engineering Manual, the Purchasing Manual and the Construction Control Manual before starting a construction auditing assignment.
   1. Also discuss with the EDP audit staff supervisor, the various computer reports that will be useful during this assignment. Be certain to read the user's manual for the Construction Progress Control System, so that you may obtain computer prepared progress charts to aid in planning the progress of the on-site work.
   2. The Construction audit program refers to several specific programs that are contained in your audit manual. Read all the information in advance so that you will better understand XYZ's company policies, systems and procedures. Examine the following; pay particular attention to the portions that may relate to your construction project.
      a. Carefully review the internal audit program in your manual titled Auditing an Engineering Department. This should give you a good insight into the inner workings of the department.

b. The program titled Auditing a Purchasing Department will point out acceptable purchasing practices.
c. Auditing Payables will give you an insight into the information that is available in this area.
d. Auditing Computers should alert you to some of the possible problems that may arise relative to using computer data.
e. You will follow much of the audit program titled Auditing Inventory Transactions if you are called upon to audit any cost-plus work that entails the use of materials.
f. If a phase of your project calls for use of cost-plus labor, you will find help in the program titled Auditing Payroll.
g. A construction project means that property items will be added at the site. Use the program titled Auditing Property Transactions to review this phase of your work.

B. Meet with the members of the Construction Control Committee and discuss the particular project and any unusual features that apply or that might be troublesome.
1. Also meet with the Architect and the Engineering Project leader and discuss items that are of interest to these managers.

II. Bidding Phase

A. If the plans and specifications are in the process of being drawn up, meet with the engineering personnel working on the project and review the work they have completed. Pay particular attention to any spec or drawing that can reduce or eliminate competitive bidding.

You have no authority to demand, or even suggest, that certain pieces of equipment or specific companies be used on the project. If you note that the bid documents lock-in a specific company or a specific identifiable make of equipment, then you should call this restriction to the attention of the Construction Control Committee.

In some instances a particular piece of equipment, or a particular company, may be so outstanding that there is justification for writing the item or company into the specs. **NOTE:** *In such cases, advance notice to Purchasing will enable that department to negotiate a fair price.* At that time they may elect to take competitive bids so that engineers may judge whether the price spread is justified.

After Purchasing negotiates a satisfactory price, a P/O is written to the supplier and XYZ later assigns the P/O to the successful bidder for that phase of the project. All assignments are spelled out in the bid documents, and the bidders are asked to indicate the fee they desire for taking over the P/Os and *assuming full responsibility for coordination and assuring that everything will be done properly.*

B. You should sit in on the project meetings that define the building layout and its positioning on the property. Our department has some concerns which you should address. **KEY POINT:** *You will want to ensure that there is adequate storage space and physical security over materials and equipment delivered to be stored on the job site during the construction period.*

Be certain that there is good control over entry and egress from the property. There should be good perimeter protection, and traffic should be routed so that every vehicle entering the property must pass a location where it can be seen and checked. This enables a verification of everything entering or leaving the site.

Our department is concerned with the interior layout. We will express an opinion regarding office work flow and the security provided for vital assets and information. We are concerned with provisions for the external security of the complex, and where applicable, that there is a well-planned weigh scale near the truck gate.

We also are interested in such things as the size and location of guard shacks, separation of truck and auto traffic, access control, and obstacles designed to prevent casual entry to the property.

Your participation in these concept meetings will give you an insight into the project's purpose and importance; why certain decisions are made; what special items are to be included; who requested them and how much they think these items will cost.

C. The next stage in a project is the preparation of the plans and specifications. You must carefully review these documents while they are being prepared. The main consideration is to locate items that are locked in without any challenge from competitors. **IMPORTANT:** *Work closely with Purchasing to ensure competition in all areas.*

   You should also be on the lookout for ambiguities that will likely result in change orders. **TIP:** *Almost any change during construction will wind up costing XYZ money.* Substitutions, and sometimes even deletions, will cause a contractor to request more money.

D. As the plans and specs are developed, Purchasing starts to prepare a bidders list. Working with Engineering, and with our construction auditors, a list of competent contractors is drawn up. These firms are asked to bid our project and upon agreement are added to the list.

   If the list contains any firms of dubious ethics or companies that have performed badly on other jobs, you should object to their inclusion. **IMPORTANT:** *State your objections,* and if you are overruled and have not changed your mind, bring your objection to the attention of the Construction Control Committee for decision.

E. *Be alert to the ever present danger that a specific building or mechanical trade may believe that a particular contractor is locked in to our business.* This can occur if the same contractor or supplier consistently wins our contracts. When such a relationship is believed to exist, other companies are loathe to waste their time and money in bidding for a contract that they "know" they cannot get. Instead they may talk to the locked-in contractor and submit a courtesy bid at a figure suggested by the favored contractor.

   If you learn, or feel, that we are overpaying for work in a particular field and that we are not actually receiving competitive bids for that trade, bring the matter to the attention of Purchasing.

   Purchasing should add new bidders to our list, after assuring them that if their bid is low they will receive the contract. Discuss the problem with your supervisor, *if your evidence is sufficient we may persuade the Construction Control Committee to bar certain firms from bidding on our jobs.* Once a strangle hold is broken, we can expect to realize substantial savings.

F. When the list of bidders is finalized, you should participate in the distribution of documents to insure that all bidders receive identical sets, and follow through to see that all firms are treated equally during the bidding stage.

During the bidding period keep aware of the questions being asked of Engineering and Purchasing by contractors, and review the answers they are given. All questions are to be received by Purchasing where a question is written up exactly as asked. These are forwarded to the proper parties in Engineering and the Operating department, and you should also receive a copy.

After making certain that a question is understood, the purchasing agent obtains a written answer from the appropriate party and periodically issues a letter to all contractors, listing all questions received and the answers given. **IMPORTANT:** *These letters become a part of the bid documents, and the final bid price includes all factors affected by these questions.* This procedure helps ensure that all contractors are bidding on an identical and equal basis.

You are not expected to guarantee that all questions are handled properly. But, since all records are included in the contract, you will be able to note any deviations during the construction period. And a contractor cannot claim verbal authorization for a deviation.

G. After all questions have been answered, a final date is set for receiving and opening the bids. All proposals are scheduled to arrive at a specified time in a specially marked proposal envelope. All bids received in advance of the scheduled opening are placed in a vault until the proper time. They are marked in such a way that the envelope could not be opened without the fact becoming noticeable.

At the appointed time all bids are examined by the Construction Control Committee, to verify that envelopes have not been previously opened. Contractors often hand deliver their proposals at the last minute to enable them to include last minute price reductions. Out of town bidders may send agents to deliver bids and wait for results.

If all bids have not been received at opening time, Purchasing telephones contractors whose bids have not been received to find out what has happened to their proposals. If they've decided not to bid, the purchasing agent attempts to learn what prompted their decision.

If they contend that their bid is on the way, the Committee may elect to wait for its arrival. If a delay appears justified, all bidders are notified of the new bid opening time.

H. When the bids are opened each member of the committee verifies that it has not been tampered with, and they then initial each bid. Proposal prices are recorded on a spread sheet. You will be asked to participate with the engineering contract technician in the analysis of the bids. As soon as the analysis is completed, the committee meets to determine the low group of contractors.

I. You will be invited to participate in the discussions with the low bidders. The low bidders are scheduled in for discussions as soon as practical. Discussions are chaired by the engineering administrator, with representatives of Purchasing and Financial in attendance. At the completion of these meetings a decision is reached and the successful contractor is notified of our intent to award a contract. Other contractors are informed that their bids have been rejected.

III. Writing the Contract

A. Minutes are kept of all meetings with contractors, and all questions and answers that occurred during the bidding stage are summarized and reduced to writing. **NOTE:** *Meeting minutes as well as all additions, deletions, clarifications, or modifications are written down, reviewed by all parties and signed by the contractor and XYZ.* All of these notations become a part of the construction contract.

B. A standard form contract is used as the basis for drawing up the project contract. After agreement and signature, a P/O is written which uses the signed contract, bid documents, minutes of meetings and letters of clarification as supplementary documents defining the P/O.

C. Be certain that you completely understand all of the contract clauses, because you will be responsible for insuring that all parties conform to this contract. You will keep a copy of the P/O and all of the attached supporting documents, including the formal contract, at the job site to refer to when necessary.

D. The contract spells out the procedures for processing a change order. **IMPORTANT:** *Remember that change orders are supposed to be prepared and approved BEFORE work is started on the change.* There are provisions for emergency changes, but be certain that a true emergency exists before you allow this procedure.

IV. Job Site Procedures

A. Many of the procedures that you will be expected to execute on the job site are spelled out in various programs in your audit manual.

In almost every project there will be some work that is performed on a cost-plus basis. On a firm price job, this will probably be work related to change orders. You will be expected to verify labor hours and rates, material quantities and prices and costs of contractor owned or rented equipment. Also keep close records on the time periods that construction equipment is actually used on a cost-plus change order.

There are publications, issued by associations or by estimators, that may be useful to you. These cover such things as wage rates, average time required for specific types of work and rental rates for construction equipment. Check with the contractor's job site clerk, and then discuss the matter with your supervisor.

B. On large projects we may assign an audit team so that at least one auditor is in the control shack at all times. You may be authorized to hire a job site clerk to assist you in your audit duties. If so, you must carefully check all work performed by the clerk. **NOTE:** *If audit work is performed by the engineering rep during your absence, verify the accuracy of such reports at your earliest opportunity.*

C. The contract spells out in detail the provisions relating to the use of subcontractors. Subcontract work must be audited carefully. Before such work begins the general contractor and each of the subs must be made to understand that only one markup will be permitted on subcontract work. *We do not pay markup on markup ad infinitum.*

D. Waivers of Lien must be obtained from everyone working on a construction site. Our contract provides that we only make payments after we receive proper waivers. If a contractor needs financial help we may pay for work actually accomplished and wait for contractor to pay subs and receives a valid waiver. We must receive these waivers before we make any additional payments.

E. A description of the proper procedure for working with this internal audit program appears in the Introduction to the Audit Programs section of your manual. Read this information carefully.

IA CAP555 XYZ CORPORATION

INTERNAL AUDIT PROGRAM—CONSTRUCTION PROJECTS

This program is intended for use by members of the construction audit staff when reviewing construction expenditures or acting as a job site auditor on a construction project. The program is by no means all-inclusive, but should be used as a minimum review guide.

Note appropriate dates in the space labeled Date comp.

I. General

A. Read the audit instructions (Form IA CAI550) and this program carefully before you start your assignment. Become familiar with all manuals and programs listed in the instructions. Date comp. ____________

1. Meet with the Architect, the engineers directly involved in this project, the members of the Construction Control Committee and the executives in the operating department that are directly concerned. Establish lines of communication with these employees, and learn of their concerns.

Date comp. ____________

B. Be aware that our basic philosophy and primary approach is that we do not want to take advantage of any outside company, nor do we want them to take advantage of us. We expect to pay a fair price which allows a fair profit for all work performed for XYZ, but we do not want to pay for materials not received or inferior to that ordered, nor do we want to pay for labor that was not of benefit. We expect all construction work to be performed professionally and conscientiously, and we do not expect to pay for mistakes made deliberately or not. When poor workmanship is evident to our engineering superintendent, we expect that the contractor will make corrections without charge to us.

As a job site auditor, if you note instances of poor workmanship, it is your duty to inform the superintendent so that corrective action will be taken without cost to XYZ. *If you are not satisfied with action taken, discuss the matter with the engineering administrator and if still not satisfied, with your supervisor.* Date comp. ____________

C. Study the engineering files of the project that you are assigned to audit. Consult with the designers, draftsmen and specification writers working on the project. Determine that any closed specs are called to the attention of appropriate parties. Date comp. ______________
   1. Refer to Purchasing, any locked-in pieces of machinery or equipment or materials. Date comp. ______________
   2. Refer to Construction Control Committee any indication that a particular contractor is being favored. Date comp. ______________

D. Determine that all interested departments have had an opportunity to review and input into the project. Date comp. ______________
   1. See that Budget dept. has been consulted. Date comp. ______________
   2. Traffic should see that adequate space is planned for railroad sidings, truck maneuvering space and docks. Date comp. ______________
   3. Insurance Department should examine for decisions on location of sprinklers and conformance to fire regulations. Date comp. ______________

E. Review the bidding procedure. *Determine that internal controls are adequate to ensure that price information cannot leak out before bids are opened and contract negotiated.* Date comp. ______________
   1. Review procedure for selecting and contacting prospective bidders. Determine that system insures a geographical separation of bidders, and gives all departments concerned an opportunity to suggest prospective contractors. Date comp. ______________
   2. Determine that system requires contact with firms who said they would bid, but whose bid is not received. Date comp. ______________
   3. Review procedures for opening and recording the bids and for analyzing proposals in a methodical manner. Date comp. ______________
      a. *Determine that bids are accepted that best serve the interests of XYZ Corp.* Date comp. ______________
      b. *Determine that any changes to the original bid price are legitimate and proper.* Date comp. ______________
   4. Review procedures for contacting low group of bidders and for negotiating to resolve questions. Date comp. ______________
      a. Review procedures for selecting alternate materials or construction methods for the job. Date comp. ______________
   5. Review procedures for final selection of firm, and determine that all departments concerned have an opportunity to agree on the successful bidder. Date comp. ______________
   6. Review procedures for notifying successful bidder of the award and also notifying losing bidders. Date comp. ______________

F. Review forms used for construction contract commitments. Determine that standard forms are used. Date comp. ______________
   1. Determine that contract form covers all variable factors, and has obtained Legal approval. Date comp. ______________
   2. For your project, determine that all conditions of the contract were diligently discharged by all parties. Date comp. ______________
      a. Review open commitments to determine what liabilities may still exist

and what rights or privileges have not as yet been determined or realized. *Prepare a written report on all such items that warrant management's attention.* Date comp. ____________

G. IMPORTANT: *Journeymen guarantee their work.* Corrections required by poor workmanship should not be charged to XYZ.
Date comp. ____________

H. Ensure that your audit work papers, especially when on a job site, are kept under lock and key at all times. *Be certain to take critical papers with you when you leave a site.* Date comp. ____________
   1. Your system should ensure that no papers can be put into a file that could lead to approving fictitious charges. Date comp. ____________
   2. Before approving, carefully compare monthly billings against paperwork that you have verified. Date comp. ____________
      a. Keep one copy for your files, and forward other copies to engineering administrator for processing. Date comp. ____________
         1) Be certain that engineering superintendent approves the contractor's billing before you forward it. Date comp. ____________
      b. *Personally mail invoices to Engineering.* Date comp. ____________
   3. Make certain that invoices clearly show the amounts that are to be retained by owner until acceptance of work. Date comp. ____________
      a. When job is complete and accepted, the retention will be released to contractor, unless there is a good reason not to. *If you know of any reason, contact the Engineering administrator and discuss the problem.*
      Date comp. ____________

I. Our system requires receipt of a contractor's waiver of lien for all work performed, before we make a payment. This means that the contractor may have to use large sums of money for a period of time. To reduce a contractor's interest costs we may elect to permit the firm to obtain waivers immediately after we make payment. They then submit waivers as soon as they make payments, so that all waivers are received before the next billing is submitted.
Date comp. ____________

J. Work through our EDP audit group to set up the computer to run a periodic Progress Control chart of the project. Post chart in construction office so that contractors and engineering supervisor can benefit. Keep chart current, at least weekly. Date comp. ____________

K. You will assist in aiding the Property Department in setting up property cards for all new installations. On major jobs, a property department specialist will be assigned at the closing phase of the project. Help identify pieces of equipment, and help prepare property cards, and also help affix property tags. On smaller jobs, you will be responsible for all phases of this work.
Date comp. ____________

II. Cost-Plus Work

A. The following common questions should be resolved *before* a cost-plus contract is signed:
   1. Shall overtime work be permitted. If so, does owner have right of granting prior approval in writing? Date comp. ____________

2. If it is a long job, who will bear the costs of vacations and illnesses of workers and supervisors? Date comp. ____________
3. What conditions justify payment for workers living expenses and travel time? Date comp. ____________
   a. If such payments are necessary, is the contractor to receive overhead and profit on these payments? Date comp. ____________
4. Has owner the right to approve all purchase orders before they are released by the contractor? Date comp. ____________
5. How is the necessity for and the rates for rental equipment to be decided upon and controlled? Date comp. ____________
6. On owner supplied materials, is contractor entitled to markup on the cost of these items? Date comp. ____________
7. If construction error is made by contractor, who pays for correcting error, and how are costs computed? Date comp. ____________

B. Review and understand all of the contract clauses that relate to cost-plus work. Date comp. ____________
   1. A definite distinction should be understood between items that make up cost and items covered by markup. Date comp. ____________
      a. Cost is the figure *after* all rebates and cash and other discounts have been taken. Date comp. ____________
      b. *Office supplies are overhead whether purchased at the home office or at the job site.* Date comp. ____________

C. Set up controls that ensure an accurate count of all materials used on cost-plus work. Date comp. ____________
   1. Where possible control materials entering or leaving the area where cost-plus work is being performed. Date comp. ____________
   2. Ensure that accurate receiving reports are prepared for all materials taken in, and shipping papers are prepared for all items that are removed from the area. Date comp. ____________
      a. Formalize understanding with contractor as to responsibility for safekeeping materials taken into a cost-plus area. *If XYZ is responsible, set up adequate security.* Date comp. ____________
   3. Make an accurate takeoff of materials that should have been used for the job and compare to quantities actually disappeared. If takeoff shows that too much material was used, find out why. If contractor is responsible for safekeeping materials, negotiate for proper credit for excess materials. Date comp. ____________
   4. *Be certain that we obtain proper and adequate credit for all materials that we return to suppliers.* Date comp. ____________
      a. See that proper credit is received for all surplus materials taken over by a contractor. Date comp. ____________
      b. If surplus materials, equipment or tools are designated to remain for use of the facility, inventory the items and ensure that they are stored in a secured locked area. Date comp. ____________

D. Review prices paid for materials. Refer to audit program titled Audit of Purchasing and use pertinent points. Consult with purchasing agent who handles types of materials involved. Date comp. ____________

1. Be certain that price is after all trade and quantity discounts. *See that contractor passes all discounts on to us.* Date comp. ____________
   a. Be on the alert for evidence of secret rebates that are granted to contractor by supplier. Date comp. ____________
   b. See that there's a clear understanding as to what the price covers—i.e., delivery to site, unloading costs, loading costs, delivery to work area, stacking costs, etc. Date comp. ____________

E. Audit labor costs for direct labor use on job. Refer to audit program titled, Auditing Payroll and use the applicable audit points. Contractor is obligated to supply payroll records. Date comp. ____________

1. If possible, use a time clock to control labor in and out of cost-plus area. Be certain that auditor observes punching of time. Good control dictates that each worker wear a numbered button for identification, which ties in to number on card. Date comp. ____________
2. If no time clock, auditor should visit work area several times each day. First thing in morning, just before quitting, and at other odd times. *Conduct an obvious labor check, so that all workers are aware that check is being made.* Date comp. ____________
3. Reconcile time observed by auditors to time that is charged by the contractor. Date comp. ____________
   a. Insure that all time cards are retained.
   Date comp. ____________
4. Determine that labor rates charged conform to labor rates in the district, and are as actually paid to workers. Date comp. ____________
   a. Verify charges for insurance, taxes and welfare funds. Some contracts state a fixed % to cover these items. Date comp. ____________
   b. Determine that markups are added only to applicable items. (Markups should be lower on overtime labor.) Date comp. ____________
5. Determine that only the required number of foremen are carried on the payroll. Date comp. ____________
   a. Determine that administrative salaries are not charged as direct labor. (They're covered in overhead.) Date comp. ____________
6. *No overtime payments should be made unless authorized in writing in ADVANCE of work.* Normally there would be none.
   Date comp. ____________

F. Verify the costs of small tools that are charged to the job. Tradesmen supply their own small tools, and though we don't want to supply them with new tools, we expect to pay for small tools that are used up on the job. Tools that we buy are ours. Date comp. ____________

G. Review all subcontract work and charges. Date comp. ____________

1. Verify all materials and labor in same fashion as general contractor's charges. Date comp. ____________
2. For work performed off site, use audit program titled, Auditing an Engineering Department for approach to machine shop review. P/O to sub must allow for audit of records. Date comp. ____________
3. Be certain that *we only pay overhead and profit factors to one other contrac-*

tor. We pay for sub who performed the work, and then allow one other markup. Date comp. ____________

H. Schedule all chargeable construction equipment as it arrives and when it leaves the job site. Keep a record of the time that such equipment is actually used on a job. Date comp. ____________
   1. Be alert to contractor's equipment moved to job. *Verify we are only billed for time it is NEEDED and USED.* Date comp. ____________
      a. We should not pay more than rental rate available locally for similar equipment from rental company. Date comp. ____________
      b. Insure that we are not charged for overhaul of contractor's, or rental agency's equipment. Date comp. ____________
   2. Examine rental agreements. See that charges are for economical periods: either hour, day, week or month. Date comp. ____________
      a. On major jobs it may be most economical to purchase, or set a fee for use and return of construction equipment. Discuss with Purchasing. In any event, be certain to spell out how repair costs to equipment are to be handled. Date comp. ____________

I. Review all expense reports submitted by authorized construction workers. *Be alert for purchases of small items, which may also be billed by supplier; and for cash payment of wages.* Date comp. ____________
   a. Determine that charges are authentic, properly supported and adequately approved. (Refer to A/P program.) Date comp. ____________

J. Review all other charges for legitimacy and propriety. See that they are chargeable, and markups properly applied. Date comp. ____________

K. Observe all trucks leaving the site to see if they are improperly carrying off any equipment, tools or materials. Date comp. ____________

III. Firm Price Work

A. Examine the bidding documents, and carefully study any differences between the bid and contract price. Date comp. ____________

B. Be certain that the contract covers the following:
   1. Identification of all drawing and specs. Date comp. ____________
   2. The general conditions of the contract. Date comp. ____________
      a. These should include provisions for licenses; insurance; taxes; acceptance of work; misinterpretations, disagreements, or errors; and other controversial items. Date comp. ____________
   3. The specified completion date. There should also be a penalty clause for not completing the job on time. Date comp. ____________
   4. Provision for retaining. We should hold an agreed percentage of monthly bills until satisfactory completion. Date comp. ____________
   5. Our right to approve all subcontractors and suppliers to insure that reliable firms are employed. Date comp. ____________
      a. The profit and overhead percentages that we are to pay for subcontract work should be stated. Date comp. ____________
   6. An auditing clause that permits examination of the contractor's records when deemed necessary. Date comp. ____________
   7. A listing of methods of pricing change orders.
      Date comp. ____________

C. For any changes made to firm price work, refer to the contract for the various ways these changes can be priced. Date comp. ____________
   1. Determine that change is necessary and that it actually is a chargeable change based on contract documents. Date comp. ____________
   2. If unit prices used, verify number of units. Date comp. ____________
   3. If lump sum is used, verify fairness, and necessity. See that engineering approves, and verify that work is done. Date comp. ____________
      a. Determine that change is properly approved and authorized before any work is started. Date comp. ____________
         1) Method of pricing any change should be determined before work is begun, except in emergency. Date comp. ____________
   4. For changes priced on a cost-plus basis, refer to the above section (II) dealing with this type of work. Date comp. ____________
      a. Bear in mind that cost-plus changes on a firm price job can cause problems. Work being done on the firm price job may be charged to the cost-plus change. Avoid authorizing cost-plus changes in an area close to firm price work. If change cannot be avoided, watch workers and materials closely. Date comp. ____________

D. Work closely with the engineering superintendent to assure that the quality of equipment and materials delivered to the site conform with the specifications. Insure that all receiving reports describe materials received exactly. Date comp. ____________

E. Carefully examine all progress billings. Date comp. ____________
   1. Consult with engineering superintendent to determine percentage of completion of the firm price work as at billing date. Take into consideration the inventory of materials on the job site. See that billing accurately matches job site condition. Date comp. ____________
   2. Insure that proper retention is held back. Date comp. ____________

F. Cooperate with engineering rep in walk through inspections. See that all improper or incomplete work is accurately described in writing to contractor. Date comp. ____________
   1. Determine that all items are corrected. Date comp. ____________
   2. Determine that all waivers are received. Date comp. ____________
   3. After completing F.1 and 2 above, authorize payment of sums retained from previous billings. Date comp. ____________

G. Gather all job site engineering records, cross reference them, place them into appropriate binders and turn them over to the engineering administrator. Date comp. ____________
   1. Gather all auditing records and place them in appropriate files. File them in our audit files. Date comp. ____________

H. Write an audit report covering the project. Date comp. ____________

Audit work performed by ____________ Date completed ____________

Project number ____________ Location ____________

Project audit work reviewed by ____________ Date ____________

CRITICAL POINTS

In auditing construction work there are two main areas of concern that auditors must watch carefully. One is the possibility that there is collusion between company employees and outside contractors or suppliers. The other is the attempt by a contractor to charge a company for more money than is rightfully due.

If truly competitive bids have been received and accepted, the contractor must perform efficiently in order to make a profit on the project. If work efficiency is below standard, if weather has caused unforeseen delays, or if material prices have risen, the contractor may see the profit percentage erode and may face the possibility of losing money on the job. Under such conditions the contractor will search for ways to increase margins and reduce losses. This means scrimping on the job or finding ways of getting more money out of the owner.

The following cautions relate to these possibilities.

SIX CRITICAL POINTS TO CONSIDER

1. A contractor's continued existence depends upon success in winning contracts. Associations of contractors provide an excellent meeting ground for business people to get together and discuss mutual problems. They may also illegally discuss particular projects and the advantage of cooperation rather than cutthroat competition. In building trades there are usually some contractors who will cooperate with one another.

   If a contractor is known to be favored by a particular company, other contractors hesitate to attempt to disturb such a condition. Preparing a bid proposal can be a costly task, and good businesspeople will not waste time and money in bidding a major project if they believe that one of their competitors already has the job "sewed up."

   Costs of bidding a job are usually not reimbursed and can only be recovered by winning a contract. Contractors are loathe to bid a job unless they feel that there is a good chance of winning the award, and they know that bidding against a favored supplier is a waste of money.

   But many contractors will oblige if the favored firm asks them to submit a courtesy bid. They are given a minimum figure and told that their bid should exceed that amount. The starting figure for courtesy bids is usually well above the competitive value of the job. The favored contractor's bid may be twenty to thirty percent below this figure, which makes the favored contractor look very good.

For example if all other bids exceed five million dollars and the favorite's bid is only four million, the company believes they have saved a million. If the job is only worth three million, the favored firm makes an additional million and everyone is happy. This farce has not cost the courtesy bidders anything, and they are happy that they did not waste money estimating a job that they could not have won anyway. In addition these "bidders" have won a favor due from the favored contractor when they need a courtesy bid.

KEY POINT: *One method of detecting bid rigging, is to obtain, in advance, an independent, honest estimate.* There are professional estimating companies who offer this service, and in some situations hiring them is money well spent. These estimating services offer their product to owners and/or contractors. The takeoffs break down the job and provide a list of materials and labor hours required to construct the building as per plans and specs. Estimates may also show prevailing wage rates in the area and an allowance for breakage and loss normally experienced.

Estimates may be purchased that present a complete package cost of the project. They use prevailing wage rates in the area and standard experience data to estimate the hours required for installations. Their takeoffs apply customary overhead and profit factors, so that an owner has a final price that can be used for budget purposes and to evaluate the bids received. **IMPORTANT:** *If bids are not reasonably close to these estimates, an owner is justified in throwing out all bids and bidders and rebidding the project.* In some countries these quantity surveys are used as the basis for competitively bidding a construction job. The bidders are given copies of the quantity survey and they actually bid unit prices, which are applied to the quantity survey to arrive at the estimated cost of the project. The professional quantity surveyors assume responsibility for the accuracy of their estimates. They supervise the job and vouch for conformance. This system assures that all bidding contractors use identical quantities in their bids. It reduces the likelihood of a large bidding error which could become a major problem.

KEY POINT: *The quantity survey approach reduces the variables, but it does not eliminate all of them.* There is still the matter of pricing the materials and estimating the labor hours and rates required to construct the project. There is also the matter of markups for fringe costs, other overhead costs and profit.

Here's a way to detect a major problem before a contract is signed:

- Have owner invite low bidders to contract discussions to which they bring in their estimates.
- Owner has an independently prepared quantity takeoff which is com-

pared to the contractor's estimate. This ensures that all items have been included and that quantities essentially agree.

- Any large variances are discussed, studied and reconciled.

2. When bid rigging is present and the low bid is substantially above the owner's estimate, there are several options available. However, the elapsed time taken by the bidding process can create a timing problem that may rule out some alternatives.

  - The *first,* and *best* option, is to *throw out all bids and select a new list of bidding contractors.* None of the original bidders should be on the new list.

An important consideration in a contractor's bid is the number and size of jobs currently in-house, their state of completion and the number and size of jobs that are sure to be won. Contractors want to keep their better workers continuously employed, and they try to avoid lulls in their schedules. A contractor who has a full schedule for the foreseeable future may not want to take on additional work unless the return is so attractive that it justifies increasing the work force and training new supervisors. Any bid submitted by such a contractor will be very high. It will be much lower if current jobs are nearing completion and there is no place to put the crews.

Throwing all bids out and soliciting new proposals changes the time frame of the project, and might affect the price. Geographic weather considerations can also be a factor. The act of rebidding a job sends a message to the trades that no one has a lock on the work, and that it is open to anyone that wants to submit a reasonable bid.

  - When time is of the essence and it is not practical to rebid, a company may elect to award the work on a cost-plus basis and use the low bid as a guaranteed maximum price.

If the bids have been rigged, this might not be a good idea. **CAUTION:** *The low bidding contractor will waste much money on the job, so that the original bid will not appear too far out of line.*

Let's consider a case study example of this type of problem.

EXAMPLE: On a major project the low bid of one of the important trades was almost double the amount of the owner's estimate. The contractor, who had been used on almost all major jobs of the company, admitted that a sum had been included to provide for inflation.

Time was of the essence and top management decided that the project must not be delayed. A cost-plus contract was negotiated that established the contractor's bid as a guaranteed maximum price.

A job site auditor was assigned to keep close watch of the project. Work went along at a good pace for several months, and the *OWNER'S original estimate appeared to be accurate.*

Then the work pace of the trade in question slowed dramatically. The on-site auditor was powerless to cope with the problem. The contractor was called in and explained that the tradespeople had learned that they were working on a cost-plus job and had decided to take full advantage of the situation. Any changes in work force would not help the situation since all tradespeople came out of the same hall, and there was an area shortage. The contractor stated that the only possible solution was to change the contract to a firm price job.

After some negotiations the contract was altered to a firm price that was three quarters of a million dollars less than the original bid. The work pace returned to normal, and the job site auditor kept accurate records of expenditures. Total job costs were almost one million dollars below the *adjusted* firm price. Had the job progressed at a normal pace, the total cost would have been about two million dollars less than the guaranteed maximum.

The contractor, early in the job, realized what was happening, and in order to save the firm's reputation succeeded in slowing down the work. They won the battle but lost the war. The contractor was taken off the bidders' list and was never again given an opportunity to bid on that company's projects.

3. Sometimes a major subcontractor can decide who the general contractor will be. A major sub who is known to be favored by a firm, can set any price for its services. When general contractors come to this sub for bids, the price can vary depending on the personal whim of the sub. The best price to a cooperative general will be well below any price given to competitors. If the price spread is large enough, the sub may effectively select the general contractor.

KEY POINT: *One possible method of fighting this practice is to require the generals to break down their bid by trades and to show the name and price of the subs that the general intends to use.* If it is clear that a major sub has given different prices to different generals there are ways to correct the situation.

A sub who is called in and asked to explain the wide variance in bids will usually contend that (1) they had trouble with some of the generals before; (2) they are not familiar with a particular company; or (3) some of the generals are slow payers; and so on.

In these cases the sub believes that they have a lock on the job and bid accordingly.

When the otherwise low general contractors are called in to discuss their bids and are told that they are free to use a sub of their choice, they usually turn up with another sub at a much better price. These generals communicate with tradespeople that have been used on other jobs and word gets around that the "favored" sub is out.

4. Favored contractors learn how to deal with company representatives; that is why they are favored. *They know what is expected and what is acceptable.* They know how to short cut and how to save on materials, no matter what the plans and specs may spell out. They study specs to learn what other companies would have to charge for the job, and then bid accordingly; but on the job they cut corners wherever possible.

   To combat this condition, many company assign an engineering representative to the job site to ensure that everything is done according to plans and specs. On site auditors are used by some companies who have extensive building programs. Auditors are not engineers but in a short time they gain enough experience to recognize when something is not done correctly. **KEY POINT:** *When they notice a deficiency, they act to compel the contractor to make corrections.*

   Another approach to breaking the stranglehold of a "favored" contractor is to *solicit bids in other parts of the country.* Posting the job in national contractor's publications can result in enquiries from contractors who are not familiar with a situation. If a bidders' list can be kept confidential, some surprising bids might be received.

5. In theory, all construction materials used on a job should be approved by the owner's representative. If the rep is conscientious, knowledgable and acting in the firm's best interest, it would be difficult for a contractor to use inferior materials. However, even in such cases, a contractor might obtain approval for substitutions by pleading that specified items are not close at hand, but that other satisfactory materials are readily available. Even if a credit were given, it is unlikely that the full savings would be passed on.

   Inferior materials are generally used in areas where the possibility of detection is limited. Underground work is particularly susceptible to substitution. The piping or wiring laid in walls, floors or ceilings and even paint can provide a source of additional revenue to a chiseling contractor.

   The only protection against this type of practice, is an on-site representative of the owner. The mere presence of an owner's rep may reduce the possibility. **CAUTION:** *Unless the rep is knowledgeable in many fields, there is a good chance that not all of the attempts to make substitutions will be identified.*

6. A major area for fraud on a firm price job lies in the change orders that are

made to the contract. **TIP:** *Incomplete or ambiguous plans or specs lead to job site interpretations that cause changes.* Changes mean additional charges to the owner. In the atmosphere of an active construction job, decisions are often made on the spot without much time to consider all of the factors. Sometimes these are verbal decisions and the responsible parties forget to confirm them in writing. *Change orders, written well after the fact, are subject to suspicion and may be fraudulent.* Consider the following case study.

> **EXAMPLE:** Near the completion of a large project, a change order was processed that charged many thousands of dollars for extending the building foundation from four to six feet. The contractor explained that they had encountered poor soil conditions at four foot levels and had been forced to excavate to six feet before finding bedrock. The condition had been called to the attention of the owner's rep at the time and the contractor had been verbally authorized to "go as deep as you have to."
>
> The contractor had forgotten to process a change order, had noticed the oversight only when final job cost records were being analyzed, and the quantity of concrete purchased greatly exceeded the original estimates. The change order was duly approved and paid.
>
> An internal auditor later reviewed the cost records and doubted the validity of the extent of the change. Soil tests had been used as the basis for the original foundation depth. It was unlikely that these tests would be wrong over the entire area. When asked, the contractor supplied invoices for cement that proved usage as per the change order claim. But the auditor was still not satisfied.
>
> At the humorous suggestion of the company Architect, the auditor visited the site and had the ground removed at various points around the edge of the building. The foundation had been generally laid close to a four foot level, but at many points was closer to three feet than four. There had been no extension of the foundation, in fact there should have been a credit for the runs that were less than the four foot specified.
>
> Other change orders were then examined in detail which disclosed many other fictitious and overpriced changes. A considerable sum was recovered and the contractor was barred from any further contracts with the company.

There are some audit techniques that may detect this type of practice, but the nature of the construction business is such that the problem is ever present. Your audit examination of change orders should at least determine the following:

- Whether they actually constitute changes or additions from the contractual plans and specifications.
- That such changes or additions have been approved by authorized executives and that they achieve their stated intended purpose.
- That the change was actually accomplished as instructed.
- That the amount charged for the change is fair and equitable, and conforms to contract terms.

KEY POINT: *Most important, you should insist that all changes be approved in writing BEFORE permitting the work to begin.*

Chapter 21

Auditing Production Operations and Cost Accounting

In companies that manufacture products, the production operations and the associated costs are of vital importance. Production departments are concerned with the area of the country in which the facility will be located; where plant workers will live and what the wage ranges will be; what the sales projections and production quantities will be; where to best locate the plant in a given area and how to best lay out the plant facilities.

Cost accounting is not a glamorous activity, but in a production oriented company it plays an important part in determining what will be produced and how it will be produced. The allocation of costs to a product, or group of products, can determine success or failure.

In this chapter we will discuss an audit of cost accounting and of a Production Department. These two operations are interrelated in a production oriented company, though they are separated for reasons of internal control. **KEY POINT:** *These operations should be audited simultaneously.* The same approach to an audit of a Cost Department would apply whether the company produced its own product for sale or purchased items on the outside for resale.

The sample program for a Production audit concentrates on the following:

- Production formulas and processes;
- Quality control and product testing;
- Handling of goods in process; and
- Control over finished goods.

We will consider inventory problems and the purchasing functions relating to production operations, however, these are covered in detail in separate chapters so they will not be minutely examined here. The sample audit program directs attention, when appropriate, to the specific program that applies to a particular phase of activities.

In the internal audit of the Cost Department, we are interested in the sources, timeliness and accuracy of cost information. We must also look at the conversion of such information into product costs as well as the accounting for by-products and the allocation of plant and office overhead costs to product groupings and individual products. We are also concerned with the dissemination of cost information and the timeliness of giving cost changes to the marketing department.

BACKGROUND INFORMATION

I. Production Operations

Our mythical XYZ Corporation produces and sells consumer products. Production is a major department, headed by a Vice-President who reports to the President of the company. The department has the responsibility for the production of all company manufactured products. The Production Department selects the location of all production plants, plans the placement of the building on the site and the plant layout of facilities and equipment.

Control over production activities is divided geographically into regions with a regional manager coordinating all operations within a given area. All regional managers are also plant managers of major processing plants. They serve in a dual capacity, as plant manager and as a supervisor of all the other plants in the region.

The central production department creates national policies and procedures that are used by all production operations. In addition it directs and instructs all production locations on quality control and laboratory testing methods and procedures that plants are to use. There is a central laboratory in the headquarter's office that routinely tests products randomly selected from production lines and sent in to the main office.

Preventive maintenance plays an important part in any high speed sophisticated production operation. Any mechanized product, no matter how well built, will eventually fail. When it does, line efficiency suffers since line workers stand around idle until the machine is repaired, and the line restored to operational status.

XYZ has studied the cost comparison of a preventive maintenance program as opposed to the option of waiting for a machine to fail before repairing or replacing it. Detailed records were kept that showed what maintenance work was performed on each critical machine, when it was performed, and the resulting down time and associated costs. After a few years, these records proved to be a good basis for predicting machine failures. The corporation has determined that a well-designed and administered preventive maintenance program is cost effective, and it has installed the program in all of its major plants.

Under this program every major production plant has a machine shop and a tool room to hold the special tools and materials that are needed to perform necessary repairs. Required maintenance work is performed during the time that a machine is idle. If a machine runs continuously, the maintenance program is made to fit into the production schedule.

The shops present a control problem because the tools and materials stocked can be useful to plant mechanics in performing personal work. **NOTE:** *In some operations the mechanics are permitted to borrow the tools, usually over weekends, because local management believes that it is better to permit borrowing then to tempt theft.*

II. Cost Accounting

XYZ's Cost Accounting operation is a section of the Financial Department. The cost accounting manager works very closely with Production Department management, but reports to a controller.

A computer program is used to calculate local and national costs. User control of the National Standard Cost computer program rests with the manager of the cost accounting section. The program processes all production and cost information into a data base and calculates a national cost for each item produced. Preliminary costs are computed at month-end, and the final monthly cost report is printed five days later. This final report recomputes costs based on month-end costs of materials, supplies, labor and overhead. This final computed cost is used as the transfer price for all product moved in the current month.

The standard cost program is used to value F/G inventories. It is used by the Marketing Department as a guide in determining selling prices. The information is also used by Production to review controllable costs, and by purchasing agents who are responsible for buying raw materials, condiments and packaging supplies.

The cost program interfaces with the Accounts Payable computer program, and it extracts all pertinent cost information from that data base. It picks up labor costs from the computerized Payroll program. Each producing plant inputs their daily production, by shift, line and product. Adjustments to production figures are input solely by the concerned location, and the computer prints out a daily exception report containing all adjustments, which is routed to the cost accounting manager. The cost accounting section may suggest that a location enter an adjustment to a reported figure, but the adjustment is only accepted by the computer if entered at the affected plant.

With that as background, we are now ready to examine the sample internal audit program for a review of Production Operations and the Cost Accounting function at the XYZ Corporation.

INTERNAL AUDIT PROGRAM—INSTRUCTIONS

IA POCI770

XYZ CORPORATION
INTERNAL AUDIT PROGRAM
PRODUCTION OPERATIONS DEPARTMENT AND
THE COST ACCOUNTING SECTION

This program will lead you through an internal audit of the Headquarters Production Department and of the Accounting Department's Cost Accounting Section. Cost Accounting works very closely with the Production Department, but is organizationally separated for internal control purposes. The following instructional section is designed to introduce the audit program (POCP771) and to clarify some items that might otherwise be troublesome.

I. Both Operations

A. Read the Production Operations Manual, and the Cost Accounting section of the Accounting Manual. Also read all Controller's Bulletins relating to these operations.

B. Discuss with the supervisor of the EDP audit group, the project that you are undertaking. Arrange to have applicable computer reports run off at your request. You will be working with several computer reports during this review. **IMPORTANT:** *Remember that you alone are responsible for this audit and for the accuracy of all records used.*

You must test-check to verify the accuracy of computer-generated reports that you use for this audit. Check for arithmetical accuracy and also be certain that the information you receive applies to the dates that you are studying.

C. As your work progresses carefully, observe operating systems and procedures to determine their efficiency, accuracy and timeliness. Determine if a computer application could result in improvements, and discuss your observations with the EDP audit supervisor.

D. Review operating policies and department procedures with management of these operations. Ask these managers if there are any particular areas that they would like the staff to examine in-depth. *Make notes of all suggestions and follow up as soon as practical.*

E. Carefully examine the handling and accounting of items produced that are classified as by-products. Review quantities produced and sold to evaluate whether classification is correct. **NOTE:** *Discuss any high volume by-products with the marketing manager concerned, and determine who is responsible for product designation.*

See that overhead allocation and cost of product is fairly and equitably computed and applied to the proper product. Treating a main line item as a by-product may result in reporting inflated profits on these items. This could produce profit bonuses that are greater than what was truly earned.

F. You will be working with highly confidential information; treat it accordingly. **IMPORTANT:** *Only allow supervisors or audit seniors to review formulas or experimental production projects.*

G. Some production inventories are stored in locations owned by outsiders. You are expected to verify all such products.

H. A description of the proper procedure for working with this internal audit program appears in the Introduction to the Audit Programs section of your manual. Read this information carefully.

II. Production Operations Department

A. Product is sent in to Headquarter's Production for quality tests. Samples of these products are also tested in the plant where they are produced. This duplication of testing is brought about by the desire to insure that a plant does not shirk its testing duties. All costs relating to this operation are duplication of effort. Add to this the cost of shipping and handling and the risk of product loss.

KEY POINT: *You should examine this operation carefully to evaluate the necessity, or to determine if there is a better way to reduce costs without jeopardizing product quality.* Also study the procedures and policies that control disposition of products after they are tested.

B. Review policy statements regarding assignment of company automotive and in-house carts to company employees. Use of these carts can appreciable speed up movement of supervisors working in our major plants, but these may be a waste of money in smaller plants. **NOTE:** *Merely because an employee has a title of manager does not of itself justify supplying a company car or in-plant cart.* The floor space area to be covered in a plant should be a critical factor.

C. You will be directed to review the production planning process. This is a Production Department responsibility but much of the basic information is derived from computer reports and Marketing Department projections. Computer sales reports and inventory reports are the basis for these projections. Discuss these reports with the EDP audit supervisor, and arrange for the most current reports when required.

D. Scrap sales are reviewed when we audit individual manufacturing locations; however, you should be alert for any signs that indicate that smaller plants send their scrap receipts into the headquarters office. If this procedure is noted, refer to the audit program in your manual titled Auditing Cash Transactions.

E. Your audit will include an appraisal of the preventive maintenance program that is in effect in all of our major plants. These plants submit regular reports of machine down time. **KEY POINT:** *Under this program there should be a minimum of reported down time.*

Review the study made before the introduction of the system, and compare it to current downtime reports. The decision to adopt the new system considered the added costs of the preventive maintenance program as against the costs of machine failures and resulting down time. The program asks you to compare the projected added costs to the actual cost increase. Allow for general increases in wages, as well as any other inflationary elements. At least confirm that the program is monitored by Production Operations.

F. Production should cooperate closely with Purchasing in preparing value analysis studies. They should provide facilities for *prompt testing* of materials that offer opportunities for cost savings.

Production should seriously consider every cost savings suggestion and must have a valid reason for rejecting any of these substitutions.

G. Production should also cooperate closely with both Research and Engineering Departments in the development of new formulations, new production processes or new production equipment. An open-minded cooperative spirit should be apparent.

III. Cost Accounting Section

A. Become familiar with the National Standard Cost computer system. Read the User's Manual and discuss the program with the supervisor of the EDP audit group. There is a preliminary report, followed five days later by the final monthly cost report. Be certain that you are using the correct report when performing your work. Also remember that much of this information is used by the National Inventory System, and that errors in this report can affect many other areas.

Remember that this information is used by our Marketing Department as an important factor in the pricing of our finished products. *Any errors in costing could affect our product pricing, sales and profits.*

B. The Cost section deals with outside companies who hold our materials and supplies in their plants. Cost approves handling and shipping charges from these firms. You should arrange to spot check inventories of items we've paid for in these locations and to verify the accuracy and legitimacy of the handling and shipping charges. **CAUTION:** *Some of these companies might bill in advance, reporting items as ready for shipment, when they have not actually been produced.* They then get the use of our funds and produce as we order. This usually causes delays in our receiving these materials. Decide on the best and most economical method of verifying these inventories. *Discuss your problems and intended solutions with the audit administrator.*

C. Although the Cost section receives records and prepares reports of various inventories in the hands of outside companies, this activity is one of record keeping rather than control or supervision. Cost does not decide where or when to ship materials; they merely determine that the vendor's records accurately reflect the balance of inventory owing to XYZ. Actual orders for new materials are processed by Purchasing, while all outgoing shipments originate at the production locations. There is no authority, nor should there be any attempt by Cost to initiate the movement of any materials out of any location. Cost designates lot numbers, but merely serves as the record keeper.

D. Records of costs of individual products must be kept current. The section uses vendor's invoice prices to help establish product costs.

All billings that contain charges for any items relating to costs of product are routed to Cost by A/P. Cost retains a copy of these invoices and uses them to verify the cost calculations resulting from processing the A/P computer program. This program feeds data relating to payments for materials, ingredients and supplies into the National Standard Cost computer program.

You will verify that these invoices are legitimate and correct, and were properly used in the calculation of product costs. These invoices, and associated hard copy of computer input, are retained for one full year in addition to the current year, so there are adequate records that you can use to verify the accuracy of data input.

KEY POINT: *A serious understatement of costs could result in our selling of product at a loss without realizing it.* This has happened before, and can happen again. Any unusually large sales of a finished product could be the result of low pricing caused by cost errors. Your audit program directs you to examine sales reports to spot items which have unusually large sales, as against comparable periods. **CAUTION:** *Make certain that such activity is the result of Marketing actions rather than that of low pricing based on cost errors.*

IA POCP771 XYZ CORPORATION
INTERNAL AUDIT PROGRAM

This audit program is designed to lead you through a routine audit of the Production Operations Department and the Cost Accounting section of the Financial Department. Use this program as a guide, and alter it to meet any unusual conditions encountered. Bring any necessary changes to the attention of the audit supervisor.

I. Company Procedures

1. Production is responsible for all production operations. It decides what machinery will be placed at every production location and what products will be produced.
2. Production Scheduling works closely with Marketing in determining the quantity of products to be produced. A computer program is used to assist in scheduling production at all plant locations.
3. Production Planning works closely with the long and short range planning sections of Financial in establishing need for and location of new production facilities.
4. Production establishes quality control standards and procedures.
5. The Cost section uses a National Standard Cost computer program to calculate the cost of every item that XYZ carries. All daily production activities are entered into this program.
6. The National Standard Cost program interacts with several other computer programs in processing and supplying information.

II. Audit Objectives are to determine the following:

1. Employees are aware of and follow company policies and procedures.
2. Department employees use good judgment and efficient systems in conducting their day to day activities.
3. Records and reports are accurate, complete and timely.
4. National Standard Cost computer program is working satisfactorily and the User's Manual is up-to-date and understood.
5. Cost information is timely and accurate, is computed correctly, and is distributed to all concerned employees on a timely basis.

	Per. Cov.	Audit By
III. Audit Procedures		
A. Both Departments		
1. Study the audit instructions (Form # IA POCI770), this program and the internal control questionnaire.	____	____
2. Discuss with department executives their goals and their approach to department problems.	____	____
3. Interview every supervisor, and a sampling of every job classification in these departments, so that you are familiar with all department activities.	____	____
a. Obtain a sample of every form originated in the department, and estimate the cost to prepare major forms.	____	____
1) Discuss with EDP audit group the advisability of computerizing any of this work.	____	____
b. Review filing system for efficiency and security.	____	____
1) See that latest methods of reproduction are used.	____	____
2) See that record retention schedule is followed.	____	____
4. Determine that departments are operating efficiently and utilizing their resources to the best advantage.	____	____
a. Review some of the special studies conducted by these departments for efficiency, accuracy and objectivity.	____	____
1) Determine that results are circulated to all departments concerned.	____	____
5. Review the prior six-months department expense analyses reports, and obtain explanations for any items that seem out of line or that are exceeding budget.	____	____
6. Where applicable, audit inventories of materials or supplies using the program titled Auditing Inventories.	____	____
a. *Remember to check items held by vendors for XYZ.*	____	____
7. Audit both departments' originated purchases using the audit program titled Audit of Purchasing.	____	____
a. See that suppliers are authentic, and controls insure that goods or services are received prior to payment.	____	____
1) See that accounting work is accurate and proper.	____	____
8. Audit disbursements authorized by department personnel using program titled Auditing Payables.	____	____
a. Be certain to include review of handling and shipping charges billed by suppliers holding our materials.	____	____
9. Audit both departments' payroll costs using program titled Auditing Payroll.	____	____
B. Production Operations Department		
1. Review Production Manual, pay particular attention to the quality control standards and procedures.	____	____

	Per. Cov.	Audit By
III. Audit Procedures		
B. Production Operations Department		
a. Review procedures for policing quality standards.	____	____
1) If periodic reports are received, examine files and question irregularities to determine what follow-up is usually performed by department personnel.	____	____
b. Review files of inspections made by quality control supervisors, and evaluate the results obtained from their observations and recommendations.	____	____
2. Review procedures and controls used in the production planning section to insure that plant production orders are followed by all locations.		
a. See that inventory records support planning orders.	____	____
b. Compare production reports to planning orders.	____	____
3. Review procedures designed to *ensure that new processes, or changes in formula, are properly carried out in the production plants.*	____	____
4. Review the Capital Additions Budget and discuss the items listed for Production with the responsible supervisors.	____	____
5. Determine that a member of Production management sits in on meetings of the Construction Control Committee when they are considering production projects.	____	____
a. Determine that production department agrees before Engineering specifies a particular make of machinery.	____	____
1) See if Production tries to encourage competition.	____	____
2) Determine if Production is aware of the potential cost of not considering a competitive product.	____	____
3) Determine that Production has an open door policy toward all vendors so that competitive products are given a fair hearing.	____	____
6. Through a sampling review of the National Finished Goods Inventory reports and the National Standard Cost reports, see if there is a relationship in inventory variances between a plant and the associated distribution center.	____	____
a. Determine that Production policy requires plant personnel to independently count all production.	____	____
1) *See that policy requires plant office to check out major, or recurring variances.*	____	____
a) Determine that letters of explanation are		

III. Audit Procedures *B. Production Operations Department*	*Per. Cov.*	*Audit By*
sent by local office, and reviewed in headquarters.	____	____
b. Determine that Production has issued detailed procedures for the proper counting of inventories.	____	____
1) Do instructions adequately define goods-in-process relative to raw materials or finished goods?	____	____
7. Review procedures for disposing of scrap in the plants.	____	____
a. *Determine that controls are adequate over handling of cash receipts and accounting for transactions.*	____	____
8. Note whether production cooperates closely with Research and Engineering in developing new formulations and processes and in designing experimental equipment.	____	____
a. Review department's procedures for putting new ideas into operation in the producing plants.	____	____
1) For new processes, determine that there is an adequate system for insuring that all production personnel are well trained.	____	____
a) *Evaluate system that insures new formulations are followed by line production personnel.*	____	____
9. Determine that Production works closely with Purchasing in value analyses studies.	____	____
a. Ascertain that Production provides facilities and conducts fair tests of new materials that offer opportunity for cost savings.	____	____
1) Follow through to determine disposition of any analyses studies that looked promising.	____	____
2) *Report to audit manager on any value analyses studies that offered savings but were not accepted.*	____	____
10. Review the procedures and controls established over the in-plant machine shops.	____	____
a. Review controls before items are issued to mechanics.	____	____
1) See that approval levels are appropriate for value of items requisitioned.	____	____
b. Determine that job order forms are required to be initiated and approved for all maintenance jobs.	____	____
c. Determine that inventory control cards are required for all items costing over a minimum amount.	____	____
1) See that inventory settlements are required.	____	____

	Per. Cov.	Audit By
III. Audit Procedures		
B. Production Operations Department		
11. Review the preventive maintenance program.	____	____
a. See if the use of the program is still cost effective.	____	____
1) Compare original estimate of added maintenance costs to actual added costs resulting from program.	____	____
2) Compare preprogram downtime to current results.	____	____
C. Cost Accounting Section		
1. Study the Standard Cost Program User's Manual, so that you fully understand the system.	____	____
a. Determine that the manual is up-to-date, is understood by personnel using the system and that correct procedures are being followed.	____	____
b. Observe procedures for entering cost information into the computer system.	____	____
2. Thoroughly audit the formulations used in the costing of products to determine their accuracy and completeness. (*An audit supervisor should perform all of the audit steps under this section of the program.*)	____	____
a. Work with the EDP audit supervisor to obtain a printout of the formulations of selected products.	____	____
1) Determine that these printouts conform to formulas on file in Cost Accounting.	____	____
2) Using the unit costs of materials and supplies, manually confirm some computer calculated costs.	____	____
a) *Any discrepancies should be brought to the attention of the audit manager.*	____	____
b. Compare the computer formulations to those on file in the production department.	____	____
1) Reconcile formulation to the detailed Production Processing descriptions in Plant Operations Manual.	____	____
2) Compare to the quality testing formulations.	____	____
3) Discuss any variations with the production manager.	____	____
c. Compare computer formulation with formulas on file in the research laboratory.	____	____
1) Discuss any variations with the Research manager.	____	____
d. *Determine that product formulas are treated as confidential information, and properly safeguarded.*	____	____
1) Review disposition of superseded copies.	____	____
3. Determine that the section analyzes and summarizes		

III. Audit Procedures — *Per. Cov.* / *Audit By*

C. Cost Accounting Section

plant efficiency reports for Production review and action. ____ ____
   a. Determine that there is proper follow-up by Cost to encourage action by Production supervisors. ____ ____
4. Determine that the section works closely with the Marketing managers who set selling prices. ____ ____
   a. Determine that Marketing is advised of any significant changes in costs. ____ ____
5. If section controls any inventories, ascertain that they are handled properly and efficiently. ____ ____
   a. See that dates of storage charges and handling costs are considered when deciding on lots to be shipped. ____ ____
   b. Determine that storage charges are added to costs. ____ ____
6. Determine that all disbursements made by accounts payable for production costs clear through cost accounting, before entry into the computer data base. ____ ____
   a. Spot check to determine that the computer program accurately allocates costs to appropriate accounts. ____ ____
   b. Check procedure for follow-up on reported exceptions. ____ ____
7. Review system for noting accounting coding on invoices that contain charges allocated to product costs. ____ ____
   a. Evaluate Cost's procedures for ensuring that charges are correctly classified before entry into system. ____ ____
      1) Analyze method of determining if a miscellaneous charge is cost, or a different type of expense. ____ ____
         a) Is freight charged to cost of product? If so, determine how it is distributed among the various items in a shipment. ____ ____
         b) Review allocation procedures when shipment contains both finished goods and raw materials. ____ ____
         c) Allocation should be appropriate and equitable. ____ ____
   b. Review freight costs for items carried on XYZ trucks. ____ ____
      1) See that charges are based on competitive rates. ____ ____
      2) Evaluate system for passing back truck operat-

III. Audit Procedures — *Per. Cov.* / *Audit By*

C. Cost Accounting Section

ing profits to materials or products carried. ____ ____

a) Determine that basis for pass-back is equitable. ____ ____

c. Review procedures for costing finished products purchased from outside suppliers. ____ ____

1) Review allocations of freight and handling costs. ____ ____

8. Review sales analysis reports for the past six months. List products that had unusual sales spurts. List prices and compare activity to selling prices for the period. ____ ____
   a. Discuss these products with the responsible marketing manager, and note reactions and comments. ____ ____
   b. Review cost records for these items for the period. ____ ____
      1) *See that costs are accurate, and below sales price.* ____ ____
   c. Determine if any by-products have sales volumes that justify reclassification to main line products. ____ ____
9. Review procedures and controls over classifying and accounting for by-products. ____ ____
   a. Determine that there is a regular periodic review of by-products to see if classification is appropriate. ____ ____
      1) Determine if there are any by-products that have become mainliners since last audit. ____ ____
         a) Determine that these items are costed properly. ____ ____
10. Evaluate method of allocating location overhead costs. ____ ____
    a. See that allocation to individual products is reasonable, equitable and proper. ____ ____
    b. See if there are any product, or groups of products, that receive unfair benefit from the allocation. ____ ____
11. Repeat steps in 10 above for allocation of costs from headquarters and regional offices. ____ ____
    a. Evaluate logic in costing of products that were discontinued because of low return on investment. ____ ____
       1) Would any of these products have been profitable if the allocation of overhead had been different? ____ ____
12. Review Cost's procedures for entering month-ending costs that result in the final costs for month-end closings. ____ ____
    a. Determine that final costs are checked before entry. ____ ____
       1) Sample to verify that costs are latest pay outs. ____ ____
13. Determine that cost systems and procedures used in the section result in fairly reflecting costs of products. ____ ____

III. Audit Procedures *C. Cost Accounting Section*	*Per. Cov.*	*Audit By*
a. Test-check several groups of items to see if there are any gross errors in costing products.	____	____
b. Comment in audit report on any items that should be costed differently.	____	____

Work reviewed by ______________________ Date __________

INTERNAL AUDIT PROGRAM—INTERNAL CONTROL QUESTIONNAIRE

The following internal control questions are intended to direct your attention to the high risk areas of these operations. Some of these points are covered in the audit program. They are included here to insure that they receive adequate attention.

Answer these control questions as your audit progresses. In section B, you are to write in the names and job titles of the various employees who perform the listed functions. Be certain to note any conflicting duties that could jeopardize internal control.

A. The following are indicative of good internal control.

1. All company policies are followed by all employees.
2. Records and reports are accurate and current.
3. All production locations are closely monitored by headquarters.
4. There is close working cooperation between operating departments.

B. Following lists functions performed by named employees.

Function:	*Name/Position*	*Conflicting Duties*
1. Keeps records of inventories.	________	________
2. Approves adjustments.	________	________
3. Assigns acctg. distribution.	________	________
4. Approves bills for payment.	________	________

C. Control Questions:	*Yes*	*No*	*Remarks*
1. Do all production projects have executive approval before construction work is begun?	____	____	________
a. Does Production always name at least two manufacturers to introduce competition?	____	____	________
b. If competition is impossible, is item bought by XYZ and supplied to contractor?	____	____	________
1) Do specs spell out the fact that the item will be supplied by owner?	____	____	________
2. Does Production Quality Control put items on hold immediately if questions are raised?	____	____	________
a. Are "held" items only released after extensive testing clears product?	____	____	________

C. Control Questions:	*Yes*	*No*	*Remarks*
b. *Is all faulty product promptly destroyed?*	___	___	___
c. Are all tests accurately recorded?	___	___	___
d. Are results reviewed by supervisors?	___	___	___
e. *Are tested products adequately controlled and all movements reported?*	___	___	___
3. Has plant preventive maintenance program reduced downtime for production lines?	___	___	___
a. Is preventive maintenance cost effective?	___	___	___
4. Does Production Planning do an efficient job of keeping product available for Marketing?	___	___	___
a. Is it effective in controlling inventory?	___	___	___
b. Are change orders promptly implemented?	___	___	___
1) Does section follow through to ensure that changes are received and obeyed?	___	___	___
5. Does Production keep plant management advised of pending changes in formulas or packaging?	___	___	___
a. Is the PMM advised, to forestall over-order of materials that are to be discontinued?	___	___	___
6. Are all plant managers aware of policy that prohibits giving employees free products?	___	___	___
7. Does Production have an adequate system for monitoring night production at plants?	___	___	___
a. *Does plant staffing require adequate supervision on the night shifts?*	___	___	___
8. Can the Cost Accounting section enter any adjustments to local cost reports? If so:	___	___	___
a. Would they appear as adjustments on the computer generated exception reports?	___	___	___
1) Would this be reported to location?	___	___	___

C. Control Questions:	*Yes*	*No*	*Remarks*
9. Does Cost regularly review individual items to see if there are any obvious gross errors?	____	____	____________
a. Is Marketing immediately informed of cost changes, especially increases?	____	____	____________
b. *Is Financial management advised when costs of product nears or exceeds selling price?*	____	____	____________
10. Are controls adequate to insure that Cost cannot order shipments of products?	____	____	____________
a. Does Cost control the designation of lots to be shipped from public warehouses?	____	____	____________
1) *Do they insure that lots approaching shipping dates are ordered out first?*	____	____	____________
11. Does Cost work with Marketing in deciding whether products are main or by-products?	____	____	____________

Questions answered by ______________________ Date ____________
Answers reviewed by ______________________ Date ____________

CRITICAL POINTS

Production Operations and Cost Accounting are *not* fertile areas for employee defalcations or frauds. However there are the customary problems associated with employee expense reports and purchases of personal items that are charged to company expense. Losses to a company resulting from production and cost activities are usually caused by errors or carelessness.

Following are a few brief comments concerning some of the types of errors or oversights that frequently occur in these areas.

ELEVEN ERRORS TO WATCH OUT FOR

1. Errors in costing can have serious consequences, particularly when they indicate that the production cost of an item in much less than is actually the case. A misplaced decimal point can often lead to this type of situation. Customers are usually fully aware of the value of a product that they normally use, and when they spot a low price they buy up as much as they can afford and can handle.

Identical products that are sold in different-sized or -shaped packages should have prices that are proportional to the product contents. If one item is very much under-priced, it is a sign that a pricing error is likely to have occurred. Under-pricing might result from misinterpretations, but it is more likely due to costing error.

An effective audit technique to spot this type of error is to study the selling prices of comparable items. **TIP:** *If one product is out of line with others in the group, it stands out during such an examination.* However a cost error in raw materials would not be detected since all products would be identically affected.

Raw material errors may be detected by reviewing several periods of sales statistics. **TIP:** *If a product group suddenly experiences a sales spurt that the Marketing manager cannot explain, it is probably the result of under-pricing.* An audit comparison of vendor's billings to cost data should determine if a raw material cost error was made.

If a cost error is in direct or indirect labor or in other production costs or allocations, it would require more audit time to track down. **TIP:** *A percentage analyses of the various individual cost factors to the total sometimes helps locate errors.*

2. Another common area of waste in production operations is caused by failure to coordinate packaging supplies or raw materials inventories to production requirements, for products that are reformulated. Sometimes local plant personnel are not informed of impending changes in packages or formulas, and they may order large quantities of supplies that arrive just a short time before the changeover is announced. *The supplies must then be junked, and the raw materials returned, if possible, usually at a substantial loss.*

   One possible method to reduce such losses is to require local plant materials managers to check with the head office before they order production quantities of materials. **NOTE:** *If a change is pending, they are so notified and instructed to adjust the order to minimal quantities that will last until changeover.*

3. Many production losses occur during night shifts, usually because of insufficient or poor quality supervision. Most top executives prefer to work during daylight hours, and they rarely visit operations during the night hours. A case in point follows:

   EXAMPLE: A major plant was experiencing large variances, and an auditor was assigned to find the reason. Daytime operations were reviewed without detecting anything amiss.

   The auditor walked into the plant at two o'clock in the morning. The approach of the auditor was spotted, and numerous card games in progress in the cafeteria broke up, and the players scattered back to their jobs of supervising the production lines.

In a discussion with the night superintendent, the auditor was startled when told that no top manager had ever before visited the operation at night. When asked, "Aren't you a representative of top management?" the superintendent was surprised, apparently never having considered a manager of night operations as a member of top management.

The total problem was traced to a lack of supervision during the night shifts. Several new supervisors were named, made aware of their importance, and the situation was corrected.

4. Another major loss problem occurs in the production planning area. When a product, or group of products, is overstocked, the delicate balance between inventory, sales and production is disrupted. Production planning issues orders to stop producing an item, but the change order may not reach some line foremen, and they continue to produce as originally planned. **CAUTION:** *This often occurs on a night shift when the night foreman fails to notice a note left on the desk that instructs the change.*

   The oversight not only increases the overstocked condition, but fails to help alleviate a different product shortage that production planning tried to correct.

   Some plants improve communication between shifts by scheduling a daily meeting of supervisors, attended by both the departing and the incoming supervisors. They get together about thirty minutes before the normal changeover time and discuss current schedules and problems.

5. Some production departments permit local managers to contribute product to local civic or charitable organizations. Other companies strictly forbid the practice; instead, they have all such requests come to a central point for decision. Centralized Contribution Committees are sometimes created because of abuses by local management.

   A plant manager, in a company that tightly controls its contributions, may start out by giving a small item to a local civic affair. Over time the size of contributions usually increases. The plant shows a cost variance, because the local manager chooses not to remove the items from inventory, but instead has them taken from the end of the line before they are recorded as production. By using this method, the manager avoids questions about contributions or finished goods inventory shortages. *If the practice becomes known to many employees, it may lead to removal of product for personal use or sale.*

   When tracking down variances, if you note a ratio of missing raw materials and packaging supplies that match the formulation of any items of finished products, direct your audit effort toward the method of recording production. **TIP:** *See if the system can be easily bypassed. If so, discuss the problem with line supervisors to learn if they are aware of any such actions. Their answers might be surprising.*

6. An area of potential product loss for a company that produces consumable items is to allow employees to help themselves to product. This practice, which is common in small companies, can get out of hand and lead to significant losses in a large operation. The following case study illustrates the point:

    EXAMPLE: A small plant that purchased milk from local dairy farmers had a work force of six employees. The plant owner allowed employees to take milk for their personal use. The plant was purchased by a large company, and the owner was retained as the local manager. The plant was significantly enlarged and the work force increased twentyfold.

    During an audit of Production and Cost Accounting, auditors noted that the plant had raw material variances which were several times larger than comparable plants. Tracing back, auditors saw that large losses began shortly after the completion of the major addition. Headquarters personnel could not explain the reason for the variances.

    An audit of the plant was immediately scheduled, and one of the auditors chanced to be entering the plant during shift changeover. The auditor noticed that all of the departing employees carried gallon jugs filled with milk. Discussion with the plant manager immediately disclosed the free milk practice. The goodwill gesture, made when only six employees were involved, had mushroomed to the point where over a hundred employees were taking gallons of milk for themselves and their neighbors. The plant manager had never even suspected that this practice could be creating the raw material variance that everyone was trying to explain.

    The practice was stopped, and so was the variance.

7. Major losses of materials, supplies or product can occur if cost clerks are permitted to order shipments from warehouses. If the clerk conspires with a trucker, they can arrange to pick up loads and drop them off where ever they choose. Through adjustments of cost records, the thefts can be hidden for a long time, particularly if the dollar value is held to a moderate amount.

    The cost clerk may be able to make charges to plants for items that were never received and to cause plants to report variances that they did not create. By changing formulations, or costs, the variance can be made to disappear. The only hard evidence that may be easily found is the signature on the release order and on the bill of lading.

Auditors may spot irregularities between standards and actual formulations used by production lines. Following up on such discrepancies may disclose the cover up actions. **KEY POINT:** *The audit comparison of formulas used in production to those used by cost accounting may reveal such manipulations.*

Internal controls that prohibit any cost accounting employee from authorizing the movement of any product, are the best safeguards against a manipulation of this kind.

8. A frequent action which wastes money can occur when a cost clerk orders shipments out of public storage without paying attention to the dates that items were moved into storage. Storage charges are usually assessed for a full month, and paid in advance each month. There is less paper work involved in shipping out a lot that matches an order, than in preparing papers for shipping out of several lots.

   An order may direct the shipment of a lot that has many days of paid-up storage remaining, while other lots of identical product are permitted to remain in storage, even though they had only a day or two until billing date. Such practices, which increase storage costs, are readily noted during an audit of in and out movements of products in public warehouses. **TIP:** *Some improvement can be achieved by prominently stamping the IN DATE on each lot card.*

9. A major area of concern in the Production Department is identical to that mentioned in several other operations. That is the decision by a Production Department executive that a specific manufacturer's item is absolutely necessary in a production process and that there is no other product that can possibly take its place. Such a decision by a high ranking production executive locks in that particular product and makes the price nonnegotiable.

   A pay off of some type to the production executive in such situations is a good possibility. **TIP:** *You might suggest that Research study competitive products that are available at a better price.*

10. The quality control operation that conducts tests of finished products offers a high risk that products may be misappropriated after testing is completed. You should be able to trace finished products that are sent in for testing. Test records should show the results and the disposition of the products. **CAUTION:** *You should verify that subsequent handling is proper and that items are turned over to distribution or are returned to production for reprocessing.*

11. Errors in costing can lead to serious losses. Some of the more common type of errors follow:

A. Failure to allocate certain handling charges to cost of product can understate the actual product cost.
B. Failure to change cost allocations affecting a by-product, which has suddenly developed a high value and a great demand. Treatment as a full line product might materially raise the selling price and reduce the demand.
C. Failure to detect gross errors in standard costs of individual, or groups of, products.
D. Erroneously passing on wrong cost information to the Marketing Department. This often occurs when information is sought via telephone which places the cost clerk under pressure to give a quick answer. When looking at a long line of little figures, it often happens that the eye may go up or down a line and lead to stopping at a wrong figure.
E. Failure to credit waste recovery funds to the production process. In some operations the waste recovery expenses may be greater than revenues; but in other operations revenues from waste or trim can be substantial and should be applied to reduce the cost of the product involved.

Chapter 22

Auditing Marketing: Sales Operations and Couponing

AUDITING A MARKETING DEPARTMENT

Marketing is the heart of an industrial organization, and it can either make or break a company. The best product imaginable will not sell if not marketed properly.

In a business entity, the marketing department takes a product from its original conception through design, production, packaging and into the distribution channels to the ultimate consumer. Marketing experts decide how a product is to be packaged, what the package will look like, how it is presented to potential customers, how it will be advertised, and what the sales price will be. Marketing includes advertising, collateral literature and public relations matters.

This chapter deals with the internal audit of a Marketing Department. It covers the fields of product planning, packaging, sales and sales promotion, sales training, trade shows and all such associated activities.

Background Information

XYZ is a large manufacturer and distributor of consumer products. Its Marketing Department is in charge of all products and determines all product features that affect positioning in the consumer market. The department makes final decisions on products and product lines and the manner in which products are packaged and cased. It determines packaging specifications, and it sets the price at which products are offered for sale. Marketing prepares point of sale materials and product instructional materials; it decides what trade shows or conferences to participate in and what materials will be presented. It is also responsible for all advertising and public relations work.

A major section of Marketing is the Sales Department, which decides how many salespeople are required and how they will be compensated. Sales originates sales contests, promotions and sales incentives. It decides how to run sales contests and how winners will be selected. It establishes sales training classes, selects curricula, and trains the instructors. It also develops sales promotional programs.

Other major sections of Marketing are advertising, packaging, point of sale advertising, photography, product testing and administration.

For our purposes we will consider advertising as a separate audit, since the expenditures in this area are so large. If you find it necessary to review any advertising expenditures, use the program in your manual titled Auditing Advertising.

XYZ's Marketing Department is headed up by a Vice-President who reports to the President of the corporation. The sections within the department are headed up by managers who report to the Marketing VP.

An administrative section of the Marketing Department handles all of the financial and administrative duties of the function. Since many of the transactions affecting marketing operations are of a technical nature, and because there are such large sums of money involved, XYZ decided to set up a separate staff of employees to handle the department's needs.

All specialized purchases are made by members of the Marketing Department, rather than by the corporate Purchasing Department. Purchasing is not involved in procuring these items, though it does buy such standard items as office supplies and equipment.

Accounts Payable and Payroll activities are completely handled within the Marketing administrative section. Administration transmits the necessary data directly to the Computer Department and receives related reports and documents from EDP in exactly the same manner as the A/P department and the Payroll Department.

The following sample audit program used by the XYZ internal audit staff includes several distinct parts that apply to the various sections of the Marketing Department.

Because the total area to be reviewed constitutes a major audit assignment, the full review may be divided into three or four separate audit visits, and the program is designed to enable this type of audit approach.

INTERNAL AUDIT PROGRAM—INSTRUCTIONS

IA MI101 XYZ CORPORATION

MARKETING OPERATIONS

The Marketing Department is solely responsible for all marketing activities including sales, advertising, public relations and all of the related operations. The department is divided into major sections with a manager responsible for each distinct operation. Much of your work will be processed through the Marketing Administration section, who should cooperate in your review.

I. General

A. Read the Marketing and the Sales manuals and the portions of the Accounting Manual that apply to this operation.

B. Read the User's Manual for the Sales Analysis computer program. Meet with the supervisor of the EDP audit group and discuss your current assignment. Arrange to receive computer reports upon request.

C. Some of your audit work will involve questioning some activities and decisions made by marketing employees. **CAUTION:** *Be certain to have respect for the integrity and ability of the individuals that you interview.* Do not give the impression that you doubt any answer that you receive, even if it seems improbable.

D. Be extremely careful when questioning expenses for meetings, personal travel, procurement of artistic supplies and services and other areas where personal judgment is involved. Your job is to determine that the appropriate supervisor is aware of all the facts concerning such expenditures and has approved the item as a proper disbursement of company funds. **IMPORTANT:** *We do not question matters of personal judgment, providing they are made objectively, with full knowledge of all the facts and in the normal course of authorized business activities.* If you have doubts about an expenditure after discussions with first line supervisors, discuss the matter with the next higher level of management. If you are *still not satisfied, bring the matter to the attention of the Manager of Internal Auditing.*

II. Coupons and Rebates

Your audit review will center on the major risk areas of coupon promotions and offers of rebates. Bear in mind that we spend millions of dollars annually in this area. Internal controls and adequate safeguards are vital in all handling of these items, because they are treated as and exchanged for cash. There are four key activities that require close audit attention.

1. *Production* of the piece, either a cents-off coupon or a rebate request. They may be produced by a company selected printer, or they may be printed by a newspaper or magazine. **NOTE:** *They may also be counterfeited and printed and redeemed in large quantities.*
2. *Distribution* of the coupons or rebate slips. If printed in a magazine or newspaper, the publication handles distribution. If printing is controlled by the company, distribution may be handled by mailing, by attaching the item to the product, or by passing offer slips out at the location where the sale is made.
3. *Redemption* of the coupon or rebate request. Local coupons are sometimes exchanged for cash at the location of sale by a company sales representative. Most offers are sent in to a redemption center or sent directly to the company for payment.
4. *Destruction* of the coupon or rebate slip, so that they cannot be resubmitted for payment. Destruction is usually by incineration or shredding. In some cases the slips may be immersed in a dye. Your audit program will lead you through these critical areas, but **CAUTION:** *you must be alert to any unusual conditions that may negate any of the normal audit routines.*

A. Prior to auditing a specific coupon or rebate offer or premium promotion, read the offer carefully, and be certain that you understand all of the ramifications before you visit a redemption center. During your visits determine that the center's employees, who work on our projects, fully understand the conditions of our offer.

B. If redemptions are processed through an optical scanner, test to insure that the equipment is accurate. Examine internal controls that prevent the *same documents from being processed more than once.*

As you work in this area bear the following dangers in mind:

- In printing an offer, the printer's employees may illegally obtain large quantities of the documents and sell them to businesses that are able to redeem them without purchasing the items involved.
- The document may be counterfeited and redeemed at our expense.
- Redemption center employees are usually paid by the number of pieces they process; it is not to their advantage to reject any requests for reimbursement. In their haste to process the work, they may fail to spot obvious counterfeiting or mass redemptions of uncirculated papers.

CAUTION: *Despite all outward appearances, submissions of large groups of cents-off coupons that do not appear to have been handled MAY be legitimate.* The purpose of couponing is to move product to the consumer, and the coupon may take the place of a price reduction.

Some retailers attract customers by lowering the product price by the amount of the coupon, and they then submit mint condition or gang cut coupons for the quantity of product actually sold. This action has the affect of offering the coupon to everyone, even those who did not receive the mailings or see the coupon in the newspaper. It accomplishes what marketing had in mind, and is not a fraudulent use of coupons. **NOTE:** *However, the redemptions should not exceed the quantity of product that we actually sold to the outlet.*

C. When evidence of abuse is strong, you should consider the advisability of turning the information over to the Postal Inspectors for their study and action. In most couponing and rebate offers, the U.S. mails are used to transport the offers and the redemptions.

Using the mails to defraud is a federal offense. Postal inspectors may have information from other companies that relates to a specific activity that you have also encountered, and they will welcome any information that we can provide. *However, be certain to consult with audit management before discussing the problem with the Post Office.*

D. Production costs can be sizeable if a high quality multicolored coupon is printed and individually mailed to potential users. Cost of the paper and of the engravings can be reduced by any of the following:
1. Using a lower grade of paper,
2. Reducing the size of the coupon,
3. Reducing the number of colors used,
4. Using a print media coupon.

E. Distribution costs can be reduced by any of the following:
   1. Using print media for the coupon or rebate offer,
   2. Distributing the offer forms in the sales establishment,
   3. Multiple or cooperative mailings where different coupons are included in one envelope, thus dividing the mailing costs.

F. Final redemption of coupons or rebate offerings are accomplished through a redemption center selected by Marketing. Customers mail their rebate requests to a special P.O. Box that is controlled by the redemption agency. The agency examines each coupon, sorts it by product, summarizes the redemptions, and then prepares a billing to the issuer. Consult with marketing administration to *set up an audit visit* to selected agencies redeeming our coupons or rebate requests.

G. When you are satisfied that all charges for redemption are proper, you may authorize the destruction of the coupons or rebate slips.
   KEY POINT: *An auditor should personally supervise destruction, and remain with the bags to be destroyed until the job is completed.*

   Make certain that all the pieces are destroyed before you prepare the Certificate of Destruction. The Certificate shows the date, place, quantity, names of witnesses and manner of destruction. A copy is sent to Marketing, one is retained by the redemption center, and another is held in our work papers for all destructions witnessed by auditors.

H. Premium promotions are usually planned as break-even offers. The price charged for the premium covers the product cost and the expenses of mailing and handling. Some of these offers are company subsidized to make the offer more attractive. **NOTE:** *These subsidized offers should be audited in the same manner as a rebate offer.*

I. A description of the proper procedure for working with all of the internal audit program appears in the Introduction to the Audit Programs section of your manual. Read this information carefully.

IA MP100 XYZ CORPORATION

INTERNAL AUDIT PROGRAM—MARKETING DEPARTMENT

The following program is designed to lead you into important areas in Marketing Department operations. This program is intended as a guide; it is not all inclusive. You are expected to revise this program as necessary, but be certain to inform the audit administrator of all changes that you make.

I. Company Procedures

A. All decisions relating to packaging, advertising, selling, sales training, trade shows and public relations rests with Marketing.

B. All specialized marketing requirements are contracted for by the Marketing department.

C. All other requirements are procured by the Purchasing department.

D. Marketing administration handles all financial and internal control responsibilities.

II. Audit Scope. The internal audit is intended to determine the following:

A. All company policies and procedures are followed.

B. No laws or governmental regulations are violated.
C. All employees are competent, diligent, and fully informed as to their respective duties.
D. The department is operating effectively and economically.
E. All records and reports accurately reflect the department's operations.

III. Audit Procedures	*Per.*	*Audit*
General	*Cov.*	*By*
A. Interview department management to determine goals and operating philosophy.	_____	_____
B. Read the Marketing and the Sales Manuals.	_____	_____
C. Interview each employee to determine responsibilities and assigned duties. Gauge their effectiveness.	_____	_____
D. List major records and reports prepared by the department.	_____	_____
1. Estimate for each listed item, the preparation time.	_____	_____
2. Estimate time spent reviewing each item.	_____	_____
3. Estimate handling and filing time.	_____	_____
4. Compute cost and then the necessity of each item.	_____	_____
E. On a sample basis, examine the significant reports. Determine that records are accurate and timely.	_____	_____
1. Determine that information is wisely distributed.	_____	_____
F. Determine that there are accurate, complete and timely records maintained of all company equipment that is being used personally by department personnel.	_____	_____
1. Determine that our policy regarding *acceptance of gratuities* is rigidly followed.	_____	_____
2. Determine that all marketing personnel are adhering to company policy regarding *entertainment expenses*.	_____	_____
G. Review the system for processing contribution requests.	_____	_____
H. Review department purchasing procedures. Follow audit program titled Auditing A Purchasing Department.	_____	_____
I. Review advertising expenditures using the audit program titled Auditing Advertising Expenditures.	_____	_____
J. Review A/P procedures using the Payables' audit program.	_____	_____
K. Review expense reports submitted by department employees.	_____	_____
1. See that reports are properly supported and approved.	_____	_____
2. Check reports for accuracy and legitimacy.	_____	_____
3. Spot check expense reports against trip records to see purpose of trip and evaluate cost vs results.	_____	_____
L. Examine payroll procedures. Follow audit program titled Auditing Personnel and Payroll.	_____	_____
Sales Operations		
A. Examine the Sales Training program.	_____	_____
1. See that the plan considers all related costs.	_____	_____

III. Audit Procedures *Sales Operations*	*Per. Cov.*	*Audit By*
2. Determine that training materials are well planned and prepared.	____	____
3. Determine that costs are considered in selection of training site and class participants.	____	____
B. Review the records relating to periodic sales meetings.	____	____
1. Evaluate basis of selectivity for determining sites, time of meetings and list of guests.	____	____
2. Determine that there is top executive approval for all plans *before* commitments are made.	____	____
3. If awards are given out, evaluate the basis for determining winners.	____	____
a. Determine that basis is fair and equitable.	____	____
4. If prizes are awarded, determine that proper approvals were obtained.	____	____
a. Determine that *prizes were fairly earned.*	____	____
b. Check back over several meetings, see if there is a consistent pattern of winners. If so, review criteria for selecting winner. If due to unique market condition, suggest change from \$ to % basis.	____	____
C. Review pricing policies.		
1. Determine that selling prices of all products are reviewed systematically and regularly.	____	____
2. Determine that marketing managers are *promptly advised* of *significant changes* in the cost of an item.	____	____
3. See if there are any "loss leaders" in a product line.	____	____
a. If so, evaluate reasons and determine the cost.	____	____
b. Review approvals to insure that top management is *aware and agrees* that action is proper.	____	____
4. Determine that product cost and revenue information is properly supplied to marketing managers.	____	____
a. Select a group of products and check cost data for timeliness and accuracy.	____	____
b. Determine that cost information is current. Note time lag between cost change and notice to manager.	____	____
c. Determine *lag* between the time managers get word of change and time that selling price is changed.	____	____
d. See if there is any way of speeding up word of cost increases to marketing managers.	____	____
D. Review procedure for calculating, preparing and issuing sales price lists.	____	____
1. Determine that sales price lists are reviewed at regular intervals and revised when necessary.	____	____
2. Review the impact on prices of distribution costs. De-		

III. Audit Procedures *Sales Operations*	*Per. Cov.*	*Audit By*
termine that these costs are a consideration.	____	____
3. Determine that "introductory" or any other special prices are properly evaluated and approved.	____	____
4. *Select a sampling of products, and determine that selling price returns a fair rate on investment.*	____	____
5. Examine procedure for printing retail, jobber and institutional price lists. Check for competitive bids. Pay particular attention to extra charges.	____	____
E. Review the systems and procedures used to test products, and assure that quality is up to expectations.	____	____
1. Determine that these operations are well controlled, efficient and cost conscious.	____	____
F. Determine that the sales reports received from sales branches are used to good advantage.	____	____
G. Examine the Sales Manual to see if it kept current.	____	____
Packaging		
A. Review packaging specs for the high volume items.	____	____
1. Determine if specified items are standard or custom made. For custom made items:	____	____
a. Determine price differential.	____	____
b. Discuss potential savings with marketing manager.	____	____
2. Review system for obtaining artwork.	____	____
a. Audit a sampling of jobs to determine that the billings for art conform to contract agreement.	____	____
b. Review system for determining numbers of duplicate artwork required for the various printers.	____	____
c. Discuss the possibility of doing layout, lettering and simple artwork in the Marketing Department.	____	____
3. Review procedure for obtaining legal approval for packaging copy.	____	____
4. Examine the art library, evaluate the safeguarding of art pieces and the conditions of storage.	____	____
a. Determine that adequate records are kept of the movement of all artwork.	____	____
5. Review adequacy of controls over engravings.	____	____
B. Review the in-house photo shop. Determine that photo equipment and supplies are adequately controlled.	____	____
1. Determine that an accurate record is kept of all activities and assignments of photo personnel.	____	____
Point of Sale		
A. Schedule all point of sale promotion items produced during a selected period of time.	____	____
1. Note description of the piece, listing the code number, quantity produced and the dollar value.	____	____

III. Audit Procedures *Point of Sale*	*Per. Cov.*	*Audit By*
2. Study your schedule and select a sampling of items to be reviewed.	____	____
B. For the items selected in A.2, determine if bids were obtained for the item or group of items.	____	____
1. Review all bids received. (Refer to bid procedures described in the Purchasing audit program.)	____	____
2. If bids were not obtained, enquire as to reasons for not soliciting competitive quotations.	____	____
a. If possible, attempt to obtain an estimate of the market value of items purchased. (Use Purchasing Department to assist in the valuation.)	____	____
b. Compute probable loss through lack of competition and discuss with appropriate sales management.	____	____
C. Arrange to take a physical count of all items being held by outside suppliers and in our own warehouse.	____	____
D. Schedule all point of sale material shipments to company locations for the test items selected in A.2.	____	____
1. Determine whether shipments were based on orders from individual locations or were allocations made by the sales section of the Marketing department.	____	____
2. Contact locations that received large shipments and have them report their current inventory of the items.	____	____
a. Ask local managers for their opinion of the method of allocating point of sales supplies.	____	____
E. Reconcile inventory on hand to purchases less shipments.	____	____
1. *Investigate any variances. All important variances should be listed in your audit report.*	____	____
2. If satisfactory explanation is not received for shortages in printer held stock, *Suggest that supplier be rebilled for unexplained disappearance.*	____	____
F. Investigate large supplies on hand at our warehouse or supplier's plant.	____	____
1. Find out why supplies ordered were not promptly used.	____	____
2. Determine if appropriate controls exist to prevent over-ordering of pieces. Would advance orders, from locations using the items, reduce the problem?	____	____
G. Review overruns by the supplier.	____	____
1. Are they consistent for any particular supplier? If so, determine the reasons.	____	____
2. If a % overrun is standard in the industry, discuss idea of reducing order quantity by calculated probable over-run. Thus obtaining the quantity needed.	____	____
H. Discuss with department employees responsible for order-		

III. Audit Procedures *Point of Sale*	*Per. Cov.*	*Audit By*
ing these items whether there is a better way, such as in-house printing or acquiring a captive supplier.	____	____
1. Talk to knowledgeable purchasing agents to hear their views on the subject.	____	____
I. Examine gimmicks, display materials and miscellaneous equipment for excessive or obsolete items. Note storage condition and protection of items.	____	____
J. Write memos expanding on significant points noted above or on items that should be added to the audit program.	____	____

Audit work approved by ____________________ Date ____________

INTERNAL CONTROL QUESTIONNAIRE—MARKETING OPERATIONS

Internal control questions that appear below should be answered during your review of the Marketing Department. Be alert to spot any weaknesses in internal controls. The control questions follow the general organization of the audit program.

Internal Control Questions	*Yes*	*No*	*Remarks*
A. Are company policies and procedures followed by the Marketing Administrative section?	____	____	____________
1. Are records posted promptly and properly?	____	____	____________
2. Are budget figures current and accurate?	____	____	____________
a. Are they frequently reviewed by supervisors?	____	____	____________
b. Are expenditures compared to budget estimates?	____	____	____________
c. Are potential overruns immediately called to the attention of marketing manager concerned?	____	____	____________
3. Are all agreements and contracts reviewed by Legal before they are officially signed?	____	____	____________
B. Are sales training plans cost effective?	____	____	____________
1. Is the size of the sales force reviewed?	____	____	____________
2. Are sales approaches and territories reviewed?	____	____	____________
3. Are salesmen salaries and commissions reviewed?	____	____	____________
C. Are all products test marketed be-			

Internal Control Questions	*Yes*	*No*	*Remarks*
fore final marketing decisions are made?	___	___	___
1. Are market tests reviewed for pertinence?	___	___	___
2. Is basic approach approved in advance?	___	___	___
3. Is proper disposition made of items prepared or tested in the quality assurance section?	___	___	___
D. Does the copy on packaging supplies meet all Federal requirements?	___	___	___
1. Does copy have Legal approval before printing?	___	___	___
E. Does Marketing consider all value analysis reports prepared by Purchasing before making a final decision on packaging specifications?	___	___	___
1. Does Marketing coordinate with Purchasing to avoid placing orders when copy is to be changed?	___	___	___
F. Are photo supplies ordered through Purchasing?	___	___	___
1. Are all loan-outs of photo equipment recorded?	___	___	___
2. *Is the use of photo equipment and personnel confined to company business?*	___	___	___
G. Are point of sales pieces received and counted by an independent employee?	___	___	___
1. Is this count used as the basis for payment?	___	___	___
2. Is all artwork assigned a unique code number?	___	___	___
3. Are all engravings coded to prove ownership?	___	___	___
a. Do we have records showing where these engravings are stored?	___	___	___
4. Do we transfer and reuse engravings, rather than purchase new ones when we change printers?	___	___	___
H. Are billings for Public Relations services all examined and approved by Marketing management?	___	___	___

Internal Control Questions	*Yes*	*No*	*Remarks*
1. Are all out-of-pocket expenses supported by proper receipts.	____	____	____________
2. Is there proper prior approval for all assignments given to Public Relations?	____	____	____________
I. Does the department have any cash funds?	____	____	____________
1. If yes, are they adequately controlled?	____	____	____________

Questions answered by ____________________ Date __________
Answers reviewed by ____________________ Date __________

INTERNAL AUDIT PROGRAM—COUPONS AND REBATES

Cents-off coupons and purchaser rebates are tried and true methods of increasing consumer product sales. These techniques enable a manufacturer to reduce the price that a consumer pays for a product. A reduction in selling price to retailers does not ensure a reduction to the consumer, since the retailer may merely use the price reduction as a means of increasing their markup.

During periods of inflation, marketing managers typically will not hesitate to increase prices for their products, even though they know that any price increase will meet consumer resistance. However, they are much slower at reducing prices when a deflationary period sets in, because they cannot be certain when the price spiral will reverse. Deflation is frequently considered to be a short term adjustment, and Marketing is reluctant to reduce prices and then be forced to increase them again in the near future. To avoid such gyrations, a cents-off coupon promotion, or a consumer rebate offer is authorized.

This has the effect of lowering the tab to a price conscious purchaser, without changing the price paid by buyers who are not concerned. The use of these devices to reduce prices for consumers, leads to numerous problems for internal auditors.

We will present a sample audit program used by the XYZ audit staff to review couponing and rebate programs. First let's consider the manner in which XYZ handles such promotions.

Background Information

All coupons, premium offerings and rebate programs are conceived, put into effect and controlled by the Marketing Department. Marketing works with advertising agencies in the planning and design stages, and usually employs an outside clearinghouse for handling the redemption of the coupons, premiums and rebate requests. Redemption houses are selected by marketing administration, who monitor the operations.

Honored coupons, premium and rebate requests are retained by the redemption house until they are examined by representatives of XYZ. One of the conditions of the contract with a redemption center gives XYZ the right to audit the agencies operations as they affect the handling of XYZ's coupons, premiums or rebate offers.

Auditors, or marketing administration personnel, periodically visit the redemption houses to review their operations. On a random sampling basis, they tie-in reports of redemptions to the requests being held, and then supervise the incineration or shredding of the redeemed documents.

Rebate and premium requests are processed by outside companies, selected by marketing administration, and these agencies are audited in exactly the same manner as the coupon redemption centers.

Local coupon promotions are redeemed at the local sales branches, and these redemptions are controlled by the sales office. Some items are redeemed by salespeople, while others are mailed into the branch office. *Destructions of redeemed coupons at sales branches are supervised and attested to by the office and warehouse managers.*

Regular monthly reports are prepared by marketing administration, showing redemptions and total costs by individual promotions. These reports are carefully monitored by the marketing managers.

Audit techniques differ slightly if a redemption operation is performed by company employees rather than an outside company. An in-house examination includes the normal payroll and personnel audits, which are not a part of an outside review. Audit of coupons at local sales branches is covered in the Sales Branch audit program.

In our sample program for auditing a coupon redemption center, we are assuming that an outside agency provides the services. The redemption center receives requests and examines all documents before honoring them. Any questionable items are referred to the XYZ's Marketing Department for decision. The agency prepares weekly reports of redemptions which support their billings to XYZ.

Following is the sample audit program used by the XYZ audit staff to review the handling of cents-off coupons and consumer premium and rebate requests.

IA MCR300 XYZ CORPORATION

INTERNAL AUDIT PROGRAM—COUPONS AND REBATE REQUESTS

I. Preparatory work

A. Carefully read the contract or Purchase Order that spells out the agreement between XYZ and the outside redemption center. If the agreement appears weak in any respect, make notes and determine if an amendment is required.

1. Work through marketing administration to set a convenient time for an audit visit to all redemption locations.
   a. If a member of the marketing administration's staff has reviewed any of the centers within the last three months, you *may elect* to exclude those locations from your visits.

B. Review all reports and correspondence relative to our business relationship with the redemption center.
   1. Follow-up on any open items during your visits.
   2. Schedule payments over the past six months.
   3. Examine certificates of destruction for previous six months.
   4. Study legal correspondence relative to wording of coupon.

C. Study the purchasing agreements with the companies that print our coupons, *pay particular attention to the sections dealing with in-plant security over printed materials.*

II. Scope of Audit. The purpose of your audit is to determine the following:

A. There is adequate control over the printing, distribution, redemption, and destruction of (1) cents-off coupons, (2) labels or packages that which can be redeemed for premiums, and (3) rebate offer certificates.

B. Charges for services are legitimate and proper.

C. Improper and counterfeit submissions are detected and rejected.

D. Proper approvals are obtained for all promotion activities.

E. Competition for all printing and redemption work is open to all qualified bidders.

III. Audit Procedures *Coupons and Rebates*	*Per. Cov.*	*Audit By*
A. Discuss with marketing managers their approach to the various types of direct-to-customer promotions.	_____	_____
1. Determine that a market analysis is obtained before a final commitment is made.	_____	_____
2. See if the costs of handling and redemption are taken into account as well as the costs of the estimated rebates, premiums or coupons to be redeemed.	_____	_____
3. Determine that accurate estimates are used for the costs of printing and distributing the offers.	_____	_____
4. Review previous promotions to see if timing of delivery or publications of offers tie-in to sales promotions at consumer level.	_____	_____
B. Review handling of negotiations and contracts with printers of packages, coupons and rebate offers.	_____	_____
1. Determine that competitive bids are received and properly handled.	_____	_____
2. Determine that lowest bidder was awarded the job.	_____	_____
a. If not, study reasons for actions. (Companies that are not acceptable should not be permitted to bid; and the low bidder should get the contract.)	_____	_____

III. Audit Procedures *Coupons and Rebates*	*Per. Cov.*	*Audit By*
b. Determine that all bids are in writing and all bids are received before any are opened.	____	____
3. Determine that all suppliers are made aware of our special requirements for security over production processes and our right to audit their conformance.	____	____
C. Select a sampling of large contracts, and arrange to have an audit visit to the supplier's production plant.	____	____
1. During visit to printers, observe their disposition of make up sheets, rejects and overruns.	____	____
a. Evaluate safekeeping of our engravings.	____	____
b. Evaluate controls over quantities run, delivered and billed. *If supplies of our items are held in storage observe security and storage conditions.*	____	____
1) Are records of quantities in storage accurate?	____	____
2) Determine if we pay on delivery or at printing.	____	____
2. Determine who decides on timing and means of shipping materials to proper users.	____	____
3. See what action is taken in event of loss in transit.	____	____
D. Review procedure for obtaining approval of copy.	____	____
E. Review the system for determining the methods and costs for distributing coupons or rebate requests.	____	____
1. Determine if Marketing considers combining several coupons into one mailing to reduce mailing costs.	____	____
2. Determine if Marketing considers combining coupon and advertising with noncompetitive companies.	____	____
3. Determine if managers consider national and regional publications for running coupons.	____	____
a. If cooperative advertising and mailing of coupons is used, determine that there is close control and accurate accounting over shared costs.	____	____
1) Determine that intra-company billings are proper, timely and accurate.	____	____
F. Determine that redemptions are carefully reviewed for adherence to conditions printed on the forms.	____	____
1. Visit major redemption centers and review their operating controls and billing procedures.	____	____
2. *Review system for spotting fraudulent requests.*	____	____
3. Review procedures for returning large groups of mint condition and gang cut coupons to our sales branches.	____	____
a. Contact office managers at locations that have received coupons and ask for their procedures.	____	____
b. Determine that salesmen visit offending accounts and that branch compares our *total product* sales to the account against *total coupons* submitted.	____	____

III. Audit Procedures *Coupons and Rebates*	*Per. Cov.*	*Audit By*
4. For a test period, compare reports of redemptions against the requests on file for those periods.	____	____
a. Determine that reports are accurate.	____	____
b. Test-check several days business at random. If everything checks, authorize destruction.	____	____
5. If errors are detected in processing requests or in the billings for services, determine cause.	____	____
a. *If not accidental, notify audit manager at once.*	____	____
G. Select several major agencies handling rebates and premiums and set up an audit visit.	____	____
1. Have auditors perform audit steps listed above in F.1, F.2, F.4, and F.5.	____	____
2. If there is a revolving cash fund, reconcile account.	____	____
3. Review procedures for spotting multiple requests from same party or address.	____	____
4. Insure that mail processers are on the alert to spot counterfeit documents, or fraudulent requests.	____	____
5. Insure that money and premiums are safeguarded.	____	____
6. *See what happens to contents of envelopes returned.*	____	____
a. Review files to see how long envelopes are held.	____	____

Audit work reviewed by ______________________ Date ____________

INTERNAL CONTROL QUESTIONNAIRE—COUPONS AND REBATES

The following internal control questions are concerned with Marketing Department's handling of consumer cents-off coupons, consumer premium offers and consumer rebate requests. These questions should be answered during the routine audit of these activities.

Internal Control Questions	*Yes*	*No*	*Remarks*
A. Does Marketing keep close control over the following:			
1. Printing of cents-off coupons and rebate slips?	____	____	____________
2. Distribution of coupons and rebate requests?	____	____	____________
3. Redemption of consumer requests?	____	____	____________
4. Payments for redemption services?	____	____	____________
5. Destruction of coupons and consumer requests?	____	____	____________
B. Are adequate records kept of supplies of coupons being held by printers in their plants?	____	____	____________

Internal Control Questions	*Yes*	*No*	*Remarks*
C. Are adequate records kept of premium packaging supplies and of premiums held by distributors?	____	____	____________
1. Are premium items priced to break-even?	____	____	____________
D. Are bills from redemption centers carefully checked before payment.	____	____	____________
E. Are plants alerted when plans are made to use a packaging supply to offer a premium?	____	____	____________
F. *Does Marketing alert sales branches when they discover that certain customers are submitting fraudulent redemptions.*	____	____	____________
G. Do contracts with all of our rebate houses provide that we only reimburse after rebates are mailed?	____	____	____________
H. Do contracts with premium houses provide that the agency purchase the premiums and that we have no responsibility if requests don't meet estimates?	____	____	____________
I. If we subsidize a premium offering, is a careful audit made to insure that all mailings are honest?	____	____	____________
J. Do we attempt to keep all of our premium offerings to a break-even point?	____	____	____________
K. Do we use drafts when paying out rebate money?	____	____	____________
1. Do we avoid handling cash whenever possible?	____	____	____________
L. *Are non-receipt complaints handled promptly and properly?*	____	____	____________
1. Is a prompt comparison made to mail returns?	____	____	____________
M. Is the handling of mail returns proper?	____	____	____________
1. Is an accurate accounting made of these items?	____	____	____________
N. When we pay, is there a careful tie-in made of mailing costs to the number of requests handled?	____	____	____________
O. Is a proper P.O. box used that minimizes costs?	____	____	____________

Internal Control Questions	*Yes*	*No*	*Remarks*
P. Is outgoing mail sorted to minimize postage?	____	____	____________
Q. Are charges for carting documents to destruction points tied-in to destruction certificates?	____	____	____________

Questions answered by ______________________ Date ____________
Answered reviewed by______________________ Date ____________

CRITICAL POINTS

Marketing employees, as in any other service operation that spends large sums of money, are subjected to high pressure sales techniques designed to win business. Some of these sales practices are illegal, but the practices prevail and ensnare some of the less sophisticated employees, who succumb and accept kickbacks from suppliers.

Perhaps a greater loss danger to a consumer products company lies in the handling of coupons. Billions of dollars change hands each year through promotional programs that are designed to move products. Consumer-oriented company's place major emphasis on coupons and rebates. Billions of dollars in redemption money are paid out annually. Millions of these dollars go to those people who illegally obtain and redeem these documents. The purpose of these promotions is to sell products, and the vast bulk of the offerings are properly used, but the misuse can be costly.

Following are some common examples of abuse in the marketing area.

SIX COMMON MARKETING ABUSES

1. Some Marketing people, like all other business people, may tend to direct business to friends or companies that they favor. Favoritism may be based on excellence in work or in service. But at times the preference is created by the fact that the preferred company gives nice gifts or even a percentage of the billings as a kickback.

   If a person placing business is reluctant to use competitive bidding it may be a sign that there is an undisclosed reason for the opposition to competition. An auditor should try to *determine the real reasons for shunning competition.* If the reasons are valid then the auditor should seek some method of allowing the buyer to continue the relationship within a system that controls costs.

   One method is to work out a cost-plus agreement with the desired supplier; another is to acquire the company and use it as an in-house supplier. **CAUTION:** *If both of these suggestions receive an antagonistic* *reception by the buyer, an auditor should be on the lookout for kickbacks.*

In such circumstances, the auditor should insist that Purchasing be brought into the act and that bids be obtained at least on a trial basis for some of the items. If the test bidding resulted in the favored supplier underbidding the competition, then the cost of that job should be carefully compared to similar jobs in which there was no competition. **TIP:** *This comparison should disclose whether rebates might have been involved in the past.*

Sometimes under these conditions, an auditor's visit to the supplier's manager may disclose that the supplier is a competent and aboveboard contractor who is being forced to kickback in order to hold the business. These disclosures may exonerate the supplier and lead to changes in the vendor's company staff.

In reverse, if it is discovered that kickbacks have been given and the supplier is a willing partner who increases the bill by twenty percent and kicks back ten to the buyer, then the supplier should be banned from doing any further business with the company.

2. There are many cases on record where personal purchases of goods or services have been made by company credit cards, with the billing going directly to the company for payment. Where a company does not require employees to cover all disbursements by expense report, an employee could explain that the charge was personal but the employee planned to pay the bill when submitted.

   Some employees use their company credit card to obtain cash or items other than what is recorded on the receipt. Such transactions can only be proven through conversations with the issuing vendor. **NOTE:** *When charges appear to be ridiculously high, an auditor should contact the supplier involved and discuss the items purchased and the normal rate that applied at the time of the transaction.*

3. Inflated charges for artwork, engravings and printing are common in the Marketing field. Much of this work is valued subjectively, and a purchaser can choose to be very critical. It is important for a supplier to stay in the good graces of the important buyer. Frequently this means some heavy entertainment or valuable gifts. The supplier recovers the investment through inflating the bills submitted for services.

   Auditors may discover these transactions by placing a price tag on every purchase and evaluating costs. Competitive bids are possible in some areas and reliable cost estimates for engravings and printing may be obtained from competent honest suppliers.

4. Cents-off coupons present an opportunity for abuse at the point of original redemption. Some retailers improve their profits by obtaining coupons

through improper channels and submitting them for collection even though they have not sold the products covered by the offer.

Coupon counterfeiters, or people who buy up newspapers and gang cut all offerings, may attempt to sell their wares to retailers at a fraction of the redemption value. A merchant who buys these items sends them in to a redemption center and receives payment which includes a handling charge in addition to the value of the coupon. A dishonest retailer can receive a large profit on a small investment. If caught there is the risk of a fine and imprisonment, but *few are caught, and fewer prosecuted.*

Following are some observations that may be useful:

A. As a protection against such abuse, conditions for redemption are printed on the offer and an expiration date is frequently stated. Some stated conditions for redemption protect the issuer against serious abuse. For example the offer may be limited to one rebate or coupon to a customer or to an address. **IMPORTANT:** *The expiration date encourages prompt use and enables marketing management to evaluate the success of a program in a timely fashion.*

To further protect the issuer, a manufacturer may stipulate that a retail outlet cannot submit more coupons for a product than it had sold during the promotion. This provides a degree of protection against retailers making bulk purchases of coupons.

B. Improper coupons, detected at the redemption centers, may be returned to the salesperson handling the submitting account to show to the customer and point out the stated conditions. The manufacturer then refuses to honor some of the obviously fraudulent redemptions—at least those that are in excess of the quantity of product actually purchased by the customer and no longer on the shelves.

C. Many fraudulent claims are detected at the redemption center, when a retailer submits large quantities of "mint condition," or "gang cut" coupons. **NOTE:** *The term "mint condition" refers to submissions which show little wear and tear, and have obviously had very little handling.* A legitimate coupon must be handled by the recipient, carried in a purse or holder, then handed to a cashier who stuffs it into a register and then handles it again when checking out. They are then handled again when preparing for redemption and by that time exhibit noticeable signs of wear and tear.

Gang cut coupons also show little signs of wear and tear and in addition they are uniformly cut, from newspapers or magazines, and the cut signs appear at the identical spots on the coupon edges. This occurs because the people doing the cutting don't take the time to cut each one individually. They batch them together and use a paper cutter to cut many at one stroke. **NOTE:** *Some people buy, or steal, all the papers they can get that were printed on a large coupon day. They then form a production line to* *cut the offers out of the publication.* There are many cases on record where retail stores have employed many people and set up production lines to cut coupons.

D. Redemption center employees examine submissions and extract those that are potentially fraudulent. These are banded together and referred to the issuer for instructions. *The issuer decides whether to withhold payment and assumes full responsibility for the action.*

If an issuer decides to redeem its own coupons or rebate requests, the company examines all submissions for compliance and authenticity. The company then assumes full responsibility for any refusal to honor such requests.

E. Major problems sometimes start at the printing plant where the coupon, rebate or premium offer is printed. Proof sheets and spoils are thrown into a wastebasket, and these may be *retrieved and used by some of the printing plant employees or garbage collectors.* Overruns, not accepted by the manufacturer, may also fall into dishonest hands.

These may be spotted in the manner described above, since they are sent in for redemption in mint condition. The condition of the coupon frequently indicates the source, and an audit visit to the printing plant may lead to the disclosure of the source of supply.

KEY POINT: *Strict security instructions to print shops may forestall such occurrences.*

5. Manufacturers may print their universal product code symbol on coupons that they distribute. When these coupons are redeemed, they are run through optical scanners that are programmed to prepare reports showing redemption quantities by individual product. These reports are very useful to Marketing personnel. When the scanning is performed on coupons which have been screened through a redemption center, the reports are reliable since the totals can be tied back to the redemption center reports.

   If optical scanning is performed at a redemption center, auditors must carefully review procedures to ensure that fraudulent coupons are extracted before they are run through the scanning process. **TIP:** *Procedures must also prevent rerunning coupons through the scanners.*

   Audit procedures should determine that redemption centers are only charging for the coupons actually redeemed. An audit count of redeemed coupons, even on a sample basis, is time-consuming. Using a weight verification system can produce fairly accurate results in a minimum of audit time. Under this system a sampling of identical coupons are extracted, counted and weighed, and a per ounce value is established. The total quantity of coupons is then weighed, and the per ounce value applied. If results are within an allowable percentage, the reports are accepted and redeemed coupons destroyed.

   If there is a *large discrepancy, the auditor may decide to make several more test-checks* or may even decide to hire some temporary help to physically count all of the coupons that have been redeemed.

6. Your company may pay substantially more for custom-made items than they would be charged for items that are standard in the industry. And in many instances the standard item is completely acceptable. Many manufacturing standards have ranges within which a set price will apply, but if someone orders something that is beyond the range, it becomes a custom transaction and the price rises dramatically.

Cost Savings Suggestions

EXAMPLE 1: By paring 1⁄32 of an inch off the size of a package, a customized item might fall into the standard range.

EXAMPLE 2: Four-color artwork and printing is customarily used for point of sale and advertising brochures. If an artistic individual desires to obtain a distinctive shade that requires five or six colors, you can be certain that the price of the artistic endeavor will reflect the additional color requirements.

As an internal auditor, you can point out to the individual and to the responsible supervisor, the additional costs incurred by such requests, but the final decision rests with the experts.

Chapter 23

Auditing Advertising Expenditures

INTERNAL AUDITING—ADVERTISING GENERAL

It pays to advertise, but it costs as well. A large portion of an aggressive sales company's budget is frequently spent on advertising. An internal auditor must have some knowledge of the types of media and placements that are available and their associated costs.

KEY POINT: *Auditors are generally not qualified to place a dollar value on a specific ad or campaign, but they do have the responsibility to determine that full value is received for company payouts.* To discharge this responsibility auditors must determine that advertising funds are not misdirected, misappropriated or wasted.

Major advertising expenditures are processed through agencies that prepare the copy and work with the media to present the ads to the public. Media charges are designed to include the ad agencies costs of producing the advertisements. The client pays the bill. The media pays the stipulated percentage of the total billing to the ad agency.

Ad agencies purchase either time or space for their clients, and prepare the copy necessary to create an advertisement. They may also work with creative agencies in preparing shows which are aired over local or network stations. For all work, other than production of ads which are paid by the media out of time and space charges, agencies work on a set fee for a specific service or on a cost-plus basis.

Under a cost-plus arrangement, the agency charges the client for all costs and then adds a fee to cover the agencies administrative expenses and hopefully provides a margin for profit. **NOTE:** *The internal auditor must review the agency's cost records to insure that only legitimate, authorized costs are passed on to the client.*

Advertising time and space costs are reported in published rate schedules which can be studied in the "Standard Rate and Data Service" manual which lists major publications, network radio and TV stations.

Some large companies produce their own shows which are nationally aired on cable or national networks. The associated production costs for such shows are harder to judge and verify. Talent costs can be verified by examination of contracts or payroll records and the miscellaneous charges are usually supported by paid receipts.

Magazine or newspaper ads can be examined either as a tear sheet or in an "advertiser's copy" of the publication. The ad itself shows clear evidence supporting charges for photography, engravings, art and quantity of space occupied.

If the radio or TV time is a network program, the successful presentation of the advertising is generally known. However, most ads on radio and TV time slots are spot announcements. These announcements can only be verified by listening at the stipulated time to the station carrying the ad. It is obviously impractical for advertising agencies to listen to all of their spot announcements, so the agencies accept a "certificate of performance" as sufficient proof for making payments. These certificates, periodically prepared by each station, list the company and product advertised and show the time used for each spot. They further contain a notarized statement that such advertisement was accomplished as per contract.

This chapter describes various methods for auditing radio and television time charges, periodicals and billboard space charges, ad agencies associated disbursements that are charged to clients and the general purchases of an advertising section of a marketing function.

The internal auditor's approach to a review of an Advertising Department's activities follows.

I. Background Information

XYZ Corporation is a large consumer products company whose advertising operation is controlled by the marketing department. The advertising manager reports to the VP of Marketing, and is responsible for all contractual agreements with the agencies.

Marketing managers work directly with agency personnel when and as required. They need not clear through the advertising manager so long as the work is on a project that has been included in the budget and an advertising project estimate has been properly approved.

All media time and space advertising is placed through an agency. XYZ uses several different agencies to insure that an agency does not handle a competitive product. All agency work is performed and billed in conformance with contracts that spell out the basis of charging for services rendered. XYZ has some in-house art services, such as a photo studio and a small print shop, but much of the artwork required for national ads is purchased on the outside by the agencies. Public relations work is obtained as required from the various ad agencies.

Here is a sample internal audit program used for a review of an Advertising section of a Marketing Department.

INSTRUCTIONS—ADVERTISING AUDIT

IA ADI 300 XYZ CORPORATION

INTERNAL AUDIT PROGRAM—ADVERTISING DEPARTMENT

1. This instruction section relates to the check-off audit program, (Form # IA ADP 400). Carefully review that program and the associated internal control questionnaire before starting this audit.
2. At the start of your examination, meet with management personnel of the advertising function and discuss your audit approach. Assure them that you will not question advertising decisions made in good faith. **KEY POINT:** *Your prime purpose is to determine that all company policies and procedures are followed, and your review is designed to improve the section's operations.*
3. Request the EDP audit supervisor to obtain for you a list of all payments made to all advertising agencies during the last six months. You will select several of these disbursements to test check, but will check *all payments* made to one or more agencies at your selection.
4. Work with the Marketing Department administrator in scheduling audit visits to all agencies. Prepare a short audit program before visiting an agency. Make your extractions of audit points to be performed from this audit program, concentrating on applicable items at a particular agency. You may need several different programs, one for print ads, one for media, another for billboards, and one for public relations.
5. There are many things to keep in mind when visiting an advertising agency. The vast majority of agencies are scrupulously honest, and will not tolerate any questionable act. Just like our own company, some of their employees may succumb to temptation. Be continually alert, but not obviously so. If you note an irregularity, first assume that it is an honest mistake and act accordingly. **IMPORTANT:** *If your evidence convinces you that it is not a mistake, call the Manager of Internal Audits for instructions.*
6. When reviewing spot commercials, remember that there are several different rate schedules that could be applicable. There is the:

   - "Standard Rate and Data Service," sometimes referred to as the national rate.
   - "Network Standard Rate and Data Service" that quotes network prices which are frequently higher than the national rates.
   - "Local" schedule of rates which are set by each individual station. These rates do not appear in any national publication, but may be obtained by local advertisers.

   Although we audit to published rates, *be aware that there are times when a network, or an individual station, grants special discounts to specific adver-*

tisers. Perhaps as a lure to induce a large advertiser to switch networks. Be alert to such possibilities.

Local rates are much lower than national or network, but our company is not granted such a rate even if only advertising in a local market where we are testing a product. **NOTE:** *These local rates usually apply to ads that do not go through an advertising agency, and all of our ads are placed by outside agency personnel.*

7. We generally use spot announcements which means that the ad takes less than a few minutes to run. Most of our ads are recorded or filmed and run in a fifteen-second, thirty-second or one-minute period. The ad agency rarely monitors to see if the ad appeared. However, by regulation, all radio stations are required to make recordings of all radio transmissions, and all TV stations are required to make recordings of the audio portion of their programs. These recordings are available at the station and are subject to inspection by F.C.C. representatives. A station that charged for an ad that was not aired would lose its license if discovered.

   Each station submits a Certificate of Performance with their bill to an ad agency. The certificate, prepared by the station either weekly or monthly, lists the company and product advertised and the time used for each spot. They contain a notarized statement that such advertisement was accomplished as per contract. **CAUTION:** *The fact that we receive many unexpected credits, because of the interruption of the ad or because of a station breakdown, indicates the weakness in controls over such payments.* Many of these credits are not received until months after the original payment. *But this also demonstrates the honesty of the stations involved.*

8. The rate cards, published by each station, set out the charge for ads classed by length of announcement and the time of day that it is to be aired. Announcements are classified alphabetically with A or AA being the most desirable and highest priced time. Within each time class, the station offers quantity discounts.

   Advertisers are billed for the portion of time used in any class; and all classes of time may be combined to obtain quantity discount rates, which are retroactive to all ads placed with the station. Some stations charge the same amount for a twenty-second station break as for a one minute film announcement, though the available spots for one minute ads may not be at desirable times. Only a few spots are available between network shows.

   For every time-purchase, an advertising agency prepares a standard written contract which states the advertiser's name, description of time-purchased, rate to be paid and general contract conditions relating to the purchase. *A copy of each contract is supposed to be sent to our major advertising agency.* This is done to enable us to place ads which will obtain the full discounts earned by our total advertising business.

9. The pricing structure for space publications is similar to the described time purchases. Tear sheets and advertiser's copies are available as proof that the ad appeared as scheduled. **NOTE:** *Your review should ascertain that these purchases took advantage of all available discounts.*

10. This audit program is an integral part of a comprehensive audit of the Marketing Department, which includes the Advertising function. You should review the Marketing Department audit program, and become familiar with the audit points contained therein.

    If, for any reason, this program is used for a separate audit of the Advertising function, you will select and use pertinent points in the Marketing Department audit program. This will naturally lead you into a review of several other audit programs in this manual.
11. A description of the proper procedure to use when working with this internal audit program, appears in the Introduction to the Audit Programs section of your manual. Read this information carefully.

INTERNAL AUDIT PROGRAM

IA ADP 400 XYZ CORPORATION

AUDIT PROGRAM—ADVERTISING

This program will lead you through an operational review of the Advertising section of the Marketing Department and an internal audit of the expenditures made on our behalf by our advertising agencies. We schedule this audit in conjunction with an internal audit of the Marketing Department, and you will coordinate your work with the team performing that review.

Your initial contacts with any advertising agency will be arranged by the Marketing Administrator at your request. Visits to suppliers or media companies used by our agencies should be arranged by the agency. For your first visit to an outside company used by our agency you should be accompanied by an agency representative.

Before visiting any of our advertising agencies, carefully read the contract between XYZ and the agency. Also review agency billings for the past six months so that you will be acquainted with the type of work that the agency performs for us.

I. Company Procedures

1. The advertising section of the Marketing Department selects and works with the advertising agencies in the placement of ads.
2. All advertisements appearing in newspapers, magazines, on TV or radio are placed by advertising agencies selected by the company.
3. The rate we pay to the media company includes a commission which is retained by the agency to cover creative costs of the ad.
4. XYZ pays for excessive changes in art work and for the costs of plates or special work on the part of the printer. We pay the agency a markup on all work chargeable to XYZ.
5. The agency reviews all media billings, and then prepares a summary billing to XYZ each week for bills received the previous week. The bills include a separate listing of agency services provided.
6. Public relation services are provided as required and are paid on a basis stipulated by a separate contract. These bills are submitted separately from the agency advertising bills.

II. Audit Scope is to determine the following:

1. The advertising section operates efficiently and economically.
2. Procedures are adequate for auditing and approving agency billings.
3. Agency billings are properly supported and conform to contracts.
4. Agency purchases of goods or services for XYZ are fairly priced and are received as billed.
5. Billings by media companies are accurate and truly represent time or space purchases required for our ads.
6. Rates charged by media companies correspond to published rates and give us the advantage of all offered discounts.
7. All XYZ agencies cooperate in obtaining earned discounts.

III. Audit Procedures	*Per. Cov.*	*Audit By*
A. General		
1. Read audit instructions (ADI 300), this audit program and internal control questionnaire before starting audit.	____	____
2. Discuss with advertising managers their policies and procedures and their general approach to advertising.	____	____
a. Determine the responsibilities of all personnel.	____	____
b. Review procedures for devising initial advertising plans and for working up to the final agreement.	____	____
1) Insure that Marketing managers are consulted.	____	____
B. Budgetary Processes		
1. Review procedures for establishing the annual budget.	____	____
a. Review procedures for determining funds required.	____	____
1) Note whether funds are allocated before or after all estimates are received and processed.	____	____
b. Note responsibilities and objectives of personnel.	____	____
1) Determine that executive committee approves any changes from original accepted budget.	____	____
2. Review procedures for the preparation and control of advertising estimates.	____	____
a. Determine that priorities are established.	____	____
b. Determine that estimates conform to Standard Rate manuals and are used to earn quantity discounts.	____	____
c. Review procedure for approval of all estimates.	____	____
d. Determine that approved estimates are well controlled and used as basis for approval of bills.	____	____
1) See that agency uses estimates to control costs.	____	____
3. Review procedures for deciding amounts to be charged to products to set up reserve for advertising costs.	____	____
a. Review procedures for summarizing estimated costs by product group and sub-detailed by type of media.	____	____
b. Discuss any recommendations for improving the budget procedures, with the marketing administrator.	____	____
4. Review procedures for accumulating and recording ad		

III. Audit Procedures *Per. Cov.* *Audit By*

B. Budgetary Processes

costs for comparison to budgeted amounts. ____ ____

5. Spot check the summarization of costs by ledger sub accounts and tie subs into the general ledger. ____ ____
6. Study all statistical reports prepared by Budget Control. ____ ____
   a. Determine that reports are accurate and timely. ____ ____
   b. List reports prepared showing all distribution. ____ ____
      1) Determine from users how report is used. ____ ____
      2) Evaluate necessity of each report, and determine whether information is available elsewhere. ____ ____
      3) Consult with EDP audit group to determine whether information is available from A/P EDP program. ____ ____

C. Relations With Advertising Agencies

1. Study contracts and agreements between XYZ and agencies. ____ ____
   a. Check procedure for preparing and approving contracts. ____ ____
   b. Check filing and control of agreements and contracts. ____ ____
   c. Review procedure for analyzing and recording data to determine that agreed conditions are followed. ____ ____
2. Check procedures and controls for processing billings. ____ ____
   a. Determine that responsibilities are clearly defined. ____ ____
   b. Determine that personnel are efficient, thorough and objective in evaluating these agency billings. ____ ____
   c. Spot check the distribution of advertising costs. ____ ____
3. Review all disbursement vouchers issued by XYZ to ad agencies for a test period. Thoroughly audit as follows: ____ ____
   a. Check for proper purchase order and proof of receipt. ____ ____
   b. Check for proper approvals and account distribution. ____ ____
   c. Spot check for accuracy of extensions and footings. ____ ____
   d. Determine that all cash discounts earned are received. ____ ____
4. Arrange for visits to all agencies, preferably at the same time. Clear the visits through Marketing administration. ____ ____
5. Before visiting agency, study billings for the past months and schedule discrepancies and other items for follow-up. ____ ____
   a. Prepare a list of questions that you will want an-

III. Audit Procedures *C. Relations With Advertising Agencies*	*Per. Cov.*	*Audit By*
swered by the agency's office controller.	_____	_____
b. Ascertain whether agency bills at actual cost to which they add their agreed percentage markup.	_____	_____
1) Note whether agency computes commission on gross amount of bill or on net after discounts.	_____	_____
2) *Determine if commission is paid on overtime penalty charges which were caused by agency actions.*	_____	_____
3) Determine that agency commissions are added to credits or rebates from suppliers.	_____	_____
c. Check for duplicate payments by agency.	_____	_____
6. Examine list of suppliers of goods and services.	_____	_____
a. Check prices closely on those used repeatedly.	_____	_____
b. *Look for agency favoritism in planning work and selecting suppliers* for XYZ's requirements.	_____	_____
c. *Determine that all discounts earned were passed on.*	_____	_____
7. Determine extent of competitive bidding and the basis for selection of suppliers.	_____	_____
a. Spot check vendor invoices not yet attached to agency billings to clients, to see *whether supplier offers better terms, or competitive bids,* to other companies.	_____	_____
8. Determine that "due dates" are shown on agency bills.	_____	_____
a. Test-check some due dates on invoices for space and time against payment terms in standard rate manuals.	_____	_____
b. Determine that our payments are made on basis of date.	_____	_____
1) Satisfy yourself that XYZ funds are not released to agency before they are required.	_____	_____
9. Evaluate the relationship between the agency and our A/P and Purchasing departments.	_____	_____
a. Determine what controls are exercised by A/P.	_____	_____
1) Evaluate adequacy of approvals to make payments.	_____	_____
2) See that A/P requires adequate supporting documentation before making payment to agency.	_____	_____
b. Determine if Purchasing exercises any control over agency expenditures on XYZ's behalf.	_____	_____
1) Determine if Purchasing reviews agency purchases.	_____	_____
a) If not, are there some items, or suppliers, that Purchasing should handle or at least be consulted?	_____	_____

	Per. Cov.	Audit By
III. Audit Procedures		
C. Relations With Advertising Agencies		
10. Examine "No charge" services offered to XYZ.	____	____
a. Examine complimentary art work to determine that XYZ does not pay some other source for this work.	____	____
b. *See that XYZ is not billed for work that should be covered by the commission in standard rates.*	____	____
c. Determine if agency bills XYZ for clerical work that has no direct bearing on ad material or media buys.	____	____
11. Examine nature of, and support for, other misc. bills that are charged to XYZ.	____	____
12. *Check controls, distribution and safekeeping of items of value that were purchased for XYZ's account.*	____	____
a. Determine that advertising plans and ads are adequately protected from competitors or theft.	____	____
D. Visit to Agency Suppliers		
1. Prepare a tentative list of suppliers used by the agency that you will want to visit.	____	____
a. If possible, have an agency rep accompany the auditor on the first visit to a supplier.	____	____
2. Evaluate method used by supplier to price services.	____	____
a. Spot check vendor invoices not yet attached to agency billings to clients.	____	____
1) Note whether supplier submits bids to any clients.	____	____
3. Examine agency purchase orders issued to supplier.	____	____
4. Examine billings submitted by supplier to agency for work performed for the account of XYZ.	____	____
a. On a spot check basis, examine canceled checks that the agency issued covering services for XYZ.	____	____
1) Tie back to the billings to XYZ for the work.	____	____
b. Look for unusual charges in the billings.	____	____
1) Review for *excessive or unnecessary changes.*	____	____
c. Determine that all available discounts were taken by the supplier and passed on to the agency.	____	____
E. Audit of Media Placements	____	____
1. Study a sampling of billings for spot announcements and purchases of space in national and regional magazines. Review the standard rate manuals in the agency office.	____	____
a. Select several suppliers for your examination, pay particular attention to frequently used companies.	____	____
2. Determine that we received the lowest price that our placements earned. *Could we have received a greater discount by ordering just a few more ads?*	____	____
a. Determine that we get the discount earned by the		

	Per. Cov.	Audit By
III. Audit Procedures		
E. Audit of Media Placements		
total placement of *all XYZ corporate business.*	____	____
1) Obtain schedule of ads placed by subsidiary companies, and combine with ours for your study.	____	____
2) Determine whether agency receives a copy of the ad schedules prepared by our subsidiaries.	____	____
3. Verify that the agency paid out to suppliers the amounts that they billed to XYZ for the advertisements.	____	____
a. Examine contracts, original invoices, canceled checks and other supporting records of disbursements.	____	____
1) Tie Certificates of Performance for spots and tear sheets, or advertiser copies for space, to billings.	____	____
2) If possible, note if other companies receive better prices or higher discounts for their placements.	____	____
3) Determine that payments were made on "due dates."	____	____
4. Review the agency files of credits received from radio or TV stations for lost or interrupted service.	____	____
a. List credits received by agency that apply to XYZ and determine that they were all *promptly* passed on to us.	____	____
b. Ascertain whether our sales force reports to agency on any failure to appear or interruption of our ads.	____	____
5. Examine the procedure for handling "repeat ads." Do we pay the same agency commissions for such ads?	____	____
a. *Determine that we do not pay any production costs for ads that are repeated.*	____	____
6. When using inserts for trade publications, see that quantities sent out relate to circulation of publication.	____	____
7. Carefully review the cost records for production of our advertisements that appear in publications.	____	____
a. Review basis for selection of photographer, and prices charged for services. Are bids sometimes obtained?	____	____
1) Is our company photographer used whenever possible?	____	____
2) When agency decides the type of photo to use, do they consider the related engraving and retouching costs?	____	____

III. Audit Procedures | *Per. Cov.* | *Audit By*

E. Audit of Media Placements

b. Determine that we get all credits due for "positives." ____ ____

c. Review all engraving costs for a test period. See how many different engravers were used and how selected. ____ ____

1) Ascertain if engraving charges are based on the association's recommended rates. ____ ____

2) If another basis is used, determine that it is fair. ____ ____

3) Note if number of proofs furnished are excessive. ____ ____

a) Is the price charged per proof fair? ____ ____

b) Do we require all the proofs that are ordered? ____ ____

4) Test-check penalty charges to determine that amounts are assessed only on the penalty area. ____ ____

a) Determine that the type of photo, on which the penalty was based, was actually used. ____ ____

d. Review method for determining whether letterpress or gravure is to be used. Is cost considered? ____ ____

e. Review all costs for electrotypes for a test period. ____ ____

f. Review all costs for typography for a test period. ____ ____

1) If numerous "alterations" are noted, study jobs and determine the reasons for the changes. ____ ____

2) Review charges for prints; are these all necessary? ____ ____

g. Review all costs for "art" for a test period. ____ ____

h. Review all other miscellaneous production costs for a test period. Determine correctness and fairness. ____ ____

8. Try to compare production costs for similar XYZ ads placed in the same magazine by different ad agencies. ____ ____

a. Compare approaches and the associated costs. If there are noticeable variances in costs, track down the reasons for the differences. ____ ____

b. Evaluate procedures used by several agencies for comparative ads and placements. ____ ____

c. Discuss with advertising executives noted differences in procedures and point out related costs. ____ ____

1) Suggest that they consider discussions with the higher cost agency to reduce costs to XYZ. ____ ____

9. Ascertain whether the contracts with agencies contain a cancellation clause. ____ ____

a. The clause should give us the right to cancel any item or program before work is started. ____ ____

	Per. Cov.	Audit By
III. Audit Procedures		
E. Audit of Media Placements		
b. We should be permitted to cancel anything by just paying all incurred costs up to cancellation notice.	____	____
10. Examine all aspects of television package shows. Study the contracts for such shows and insure that they are being adhered to by all parties.	____	____
a. Carefully review all payments relating to talent costs.	____	____
b. Review technical costs. Are all technicians necessary?	____	____
c. Review approach and costs of filming commercials.	____	____
1) Could commercials be purchased as a group so as to obtain quantity discounts from producers?	____	____
2) Determine if consideration is given to using sections of old commercials in current productions to eliminate duplications and reduce costs.	____	____
11. Review all outdoor advertising costs for a test period.	____	____
a. Note agencies used and the basis for their selection.	____	____
b. Examine and analyze space charges.	____	____
c. Examine procedure for determining and approving the locations of boards to be used.	____	____
d. Examine proof of advertising for a selected period.	____	____
e. Check production costs for a selected group of ads.	____	____
f. Check for appropriate maintenance contracts.	____	____
F. Public Relations		
1. Examine contracts for public relations work.	____	____
2. Review all agency charges for public relations activities. Schedule these payments for a representative period.	____	____
a. If agency is on a fee basis, determine how computed, and what activities and personnel are included.	____	____
1) Check to see if we received all services we paid for. Examine any existing proof of performance.	____	____
2) Verify number of people working on our account and that we receive number of hours that we pay for.	____	____
b. For a test period, schedule all expenses paid to PR people and thoroughly analyze these disbursements.	____	____
1) Note if more than one employee travels to the same city at the same time. Is the second person necessary?	____	____
2) If the expense reports submitted to XYZ are only copies, check the originals at the agency.	____	____

	Per. Cov.	Audit By
III. Audit Procedures		
F. Public Relations		
3) Determine that expense reports are properly approved and properly supported with receipts.	____	____
4) Examine large charges for entertainment and note that the names of those entertained are listed.	____	____
c. Schedule for a test period all "out-of-pocket" expenses charged by agency. (Other than those already checked.)	____	____
1) Determine that these expenses are essential, are economically procured and are properly controlled.	____	____
d. Review all specialized work performed, such as sales training films and youth educational activities.	____	____
1) Determine that expenditures are properly controlled.	____	____
3. Evaluate costs of activities versus services received.	____	____
4. Review the work of the in-house public relations staff. (Use same audit steps as for 2. b. and 2. c above.)	____	____
a. Determine if this group overlaps with the agencies.	____	____
G. Miscellaneous Items		
1. Determine that agency advertising campaign proposals are reviewed and approved by the Executive Committee *before* they are formally accepted and contracted for.	____	____
2. Review procedures that are aimed at detecting duplicate payments for bills submitted by agencies.	____	____
a. For a test period, check every item listed of payments made of duplicate bills, and insure that the originals were not paid at a later date.	____	____
b. For a test period, compare all bills paid to the list of duplicate bills as scheduled in a. above.	____	____
1) Follow up on any discrepancies.	____	____
3. Determine that advances made to agencies are carefully recorded and monitored to insure that XYZ receives all the goods/services that the advance was intended to cover.	____	____
4. Determine that all agreements with suppliers clearly *establish our ownership rights in all artistic endeavors that were created for and paid for by XYZ.*	____	____
5. Determine that all contracts with agencies, and all contracts by agencies written on our behalf, contain a cancellation clause that permits XYZ to cancel any advertisement or associated work at any time we wish.	____	____

III. Audit Procedures *G. Miscellaneous Items*	*Per. Cov.*	*Audit By*
6. Review all charges relating to the publication of employee and trade magazines.	____	____
7. Review the contracts, and value, of consumer panel reports. Determine that contracts are followed.	____	____
8. Review payments made for the Press Bureau services.	____	____
9. Review supporting data for payments made for special surveys in connection with XYZ products.	____	____
10. Review cooperative advertising agreements with customers.	____	____
11. Review expense reports of Advertising personnel.	____	____

Audit work reviewed by ______________________ Date ____________

INTERNAL CONTROL QUESTIONNAIRE—ADVERTISING

The following internal control questions should be answered as you perform your audit work. Be on the alert for any violations of internal controls. In part B, insert the names of employees who perform the listed functions and write in any conflicting duties.

A. Following are listed practices that indicate good internal control

1. Employees that process agency bills do not have direct contact with agency representatives.
2. All bills are supported and checked to estimates before payment.
3. The section's paperwork is controlled by the Marketing department's administrator who is independent of advertising control.

B. Following lists functions performed by named employees

Function:	*Name/Position*	*Conflicting Duties*
1. Approves billings from agency.	________	________
2. Keeps budget records.	________	________
3. Compares bills to estimates.	________	________
4. Approves expense reports.	________	________

C. Internal Control Questions	*Yes*	*No*	*Remarks*
1. Is the advertising budget obtaining the results desired?	____	____	________
a. Is it useful as a control mechanism?	____	____	________
1) Is it a good method of holding down advertising costs without dampening creativity of agency professionals?	____	____	________
b. Are accounting procedures followed in accumulating advertising reserves?	____	____	________

C. Internal Control Questions	*Yes*	*No*	*Remarks*
1) Any deviations from those prescribed?	____	____	____________
c. Does our advertising section request funds based on their calculated needs?	____	____	____________
1) Or do they plan to spend any funds that are allotted to them?	____	____	____________
2. *Are items of value, such as engravings, artwork and photos returned to us and safeguarded and properly filed.*	____	____	____________
a. Is artwork that has proved successful, reused to reduce creating new pieces?	____	____	____________
b. Is proper use made of various mats when the same ad is to appear in different publications and sizes?	____	____	____________
3. Do we require that all publishers return our engravings so that we may reuse them?	____	____	____________
a. If same ad runs in different magazines, do we circulate engravings?	____	____	____________
4. Except for creative work, does agency use competition to buy layouts and lettering?	____	____	____________
a. If not, is some sort of contractual arrangement made to control costs?	____	____	____________
5. Are bids obtained for filmed commercials?	____	____	____________
6. On items that agencies bid out, does XYZ advertising sometimes also obtain bids?	____	____	____________
7. Are employees at all concerned cities informed of all billboards in their area?	____	____	____________
a. Are local people told before postings?	____	____	____________
1) Do they check scheduled locations?	____	____	____________
b. Do procedures insure that XYZ			

C. Internal Control Questions	*Yes*	*No*	*Remarks*
receives all discounts earned?	___	___	___
8. Are inventory records kept in Advertising?	___	___	___
a. Are they needed and achieving purpose?	___	___	___
b. Do they provide desired controls?	___	___	___
9. Do internal agency procedures prevent sending a duplicate billing to XYZ?	___	___	___
10. Do our internal procedures insure that any duplicate billing would be detected?	___	___	___
a. *Would we detect a duplicate bill among a group submitted by the agency?*	___	___	___
11. Do agency internal controls insure that we are not charged for complimentary work?	___	___	___
12. Are all unusual items billed by agencies, properly approved before payment by XYZ?	___	___	___
13. Should we establish an in-house agency?	___	___	___
14. Are agencies effectively controlled?	___	___	___

Questions answered by ______________________ Date ________
Answers reviewed by ______________________ Date ________

CRITICAL POINTS

Audit of advertising expenditures is a difficult assignment. First there is the magnitude of the job, the tremendous amount of money that is directed toward inducing the public to buy the product.

Then there is the special nature of advertising expenditures, a business operation in an environment typically unsympathetic to artistic perspective. There is the often difficult task of getting timely proof of performance, and finally, the problem of subjectivity which is involved in accepting and evaluating artistic works.

This latter situation is most difficult to comprehend when a piece of art that would sell for a price of less than a hundred dollars, even if offered in an attractive frame, might cost a national advertiser several thousand dollars when purchased for a national ad.

There was an actual situation in which artwork submitted for a national ad was refused until the artist adjusted the asking price upward by many times the amount originally requested. The artist's written explanation to the ad agency stated that his billing clerk had misplaced the decimal point. The artist had no employees and had prepared the original bill. The replacement bill was offered when the artist learned that the agency buyer was shocked at the low value the artist had placed on the rendering.

This is not an isolated case, and artists soon learn to value their products at a going rate.

However, there are areas of advertising expenditures that are capable of close measurement, and in these areas the auditor is on familiar ground. Here the auditor must be alert to possible errors or oversights that may, and do, occur.

EIGHT CRITICAL POINTS TO CONSIDER

1. National ads, placed on network radio and TV and in national publications, are valued at a scale of prices that are spelled out in various standard rate and data publications. The rates vary according to time of ad and number of appearances for airtime, and on size and number of ads placed in particular publications over a specified period of time. The standard rates apply to all ads placed by a single corporate entity, and this is sometimes a problem.

   Large corporations may control a number of companies that are permitted to operate under their original names and who do not publicize their new ownership. When these companies within a company advertise they are entitled to the combined ad frequency discount that the total corporation earns. Unless the media company carrying the ads is aware of the affiliations, they charge the rate based on the assumption that they are dealing with a single company. This same condition applies across division or product lines in smaller firms.

   An audit analysis of all ads placed by all the corporate divisions and products may disclose that the rate charged for individual ads did not reflect the discounts that should have been earned. In some instances a higher discount may have been earned by the placement of another ad or two. **KEY POINT:** *Since the discount applies to all ads placed, the additional ads might actually result in a credit due the company over and above the cost of the ads required.*

   This type of situation can be avoided by making all advertising agencies aware of all the other agencies that provide services to the corporation. A central clearance agency should be selected to police the placement of ads and insure that the company gets all discounts earned. All advertising managers should be apprised of opportunities to obtain additional advertising time or space at a low price. To accomplish this, each agency must send a copy of every media contract to the central clearing agency for their information and action.

2. Local stations on a network occasionally have interruptions in their broadcasts, and if an ad is being aired, the problem disrupts the airing. In such cases the advertiser is entitled to a refund for the air time lost. These credits are usually slow in finding their way back to the advertiser. Credits are passed to the ad agency by the local stations when an audit of air time is completed.

    An agency's credits, received from a single station, may include hundreds of items belonging to many accounts. The agency holds these credits until they can analyze them, identify the accounts involved and then issue credit to the advertiser. A delay of a year or more is not uncommon between the date of payment for an ad and receipt of credit from the ad agency. Some agencies may overlook these items, since they usually involve many advertisers and the individual amounts are small. **KEY POINT:** *As a control over this type of oversight, auditors should visit their ad agencies periodically and review these credits issued by the stations to determine that they have received all credits due.* Such visits will encourage ad agencies diligently to pursue and distribute credits that resulted from interrupted service.

    A possible method of getting notice of interrupted service is to request your sales force to inform the home office of all problems that they observe. The sales force is usually informed, well in advance, of ads that are to appear during the coming months so that they can use this information in tying the ads into planned promotions. If a planned ad is not aired in a market, the sales reps in that area soon learn of the oversight and they should send a complaint to Marketing.

3. Another frequent occurrence that wastes corporate advertising money is the repeated airing of an ad during a short period of time. A viewer may see and/or hear the same ad four or more times within an hour or two. Such repetition can antagonize and produce the opposite effect from that desired. Repetitive showing usually occurs on local stations that are airing local ads in support of local promotions.

    When an advertiser contracts for thirteen slots, and pays for this discount bracket airing, the station is obligated to air the ad that many times during the contract period. The rate paid determines the time of day that the ad will be aired. When the contract period comes to a close, and the station finds that they owe the client several airings, the station fits the ads into every available space until the contract terms are met. Ads may be inserted at ten to fifteen minute intervals if necessary.

If auditors note while reviewing certificates of performance that a particular station has bunched their ads, they should apprise the advertising department of the occurrence so that the ad agency can be informed and alerted to prevent a reoccurrence of this practice.

4. Engravings for national print advertising can be a very expensive purchase. The cost of engravings, and other artistic services, can be materially increased by making changes in the copy. Excess changes are charged to the advertiser. If there is collusion between the art buyer and the engraver the buyer can order numerous unnecessary changes that add several thousand dollars to the cost. Changes may cancel out, leaving the end product pretty much like the original submission.

   Auditors can detect this type of manipulation by reviewing each proof sheet submitted, in sequence, and reviewing the requested changes noted on the proof sheet. **TIP:** *Where such changes are trivial and frequent, they should be brought to the attention of Advertising management for explanations and corrective action.*

5. Any cost an advertising agency incurs for a client is passed along together with a handling fee that varies from twelve to twenty percent. The more of their client's money that the agency spends, the more money they make. It is not to their advantage to procure artistic work at a low cost. The only controls that an advertiser can use are a tight budget and captive or contractual art facilities. These protections can help control art costs and reduce changes that add to costs.

   In addition to the above mentioned controls, the auditors should verify that any artistic charges assessed against the advertiser, were really paid out by the agency. This can be verified by examining the agency pay outs to art suppliers. **KEY POINT:** *Auditors should be alert to any adjustments that may occur after a pay out has been made.* Such adjustments could be overcharges, duplicate charges or kickbacks.

6. Some advertising people like to entertain, particularly at the expense of their clients. The client not only pays for entertainment but in addition pays the agency their customary percentage markup. There is therefore *no incentive* for an ad agency to draw in the reins on the entertainment phase of advertising. The three, four or five martini lunch appears to be a fixture in the industry.

   Some companies attempt to control entertainment expenses by requiring a detailed report of all meetings and entertainment that result in entertainment charges to their company. The report must list all people present and identify the companies they represent. The report must disclose the purpose of the meeting, what was accomplished and who paid the bill. **NOTE:** *This type of reporting program does not eliminate improper entertainment, but it must give the free spenders some moments of doubt.*

   An internal auditor who reviews these entertainment expenses and reports may note some charges that seem out of line. **NOTE:** *Upon checking with suppliers, the auditor may learn that certain of the charges are for items, such as cash, which are not shown on the expense report submitted by the individual who paid the bill.* These matters need to be resolved with the individual's boss.

When examining advertising department and agency expense reports, the auditor may find that the agency has billed for entertaining a company executive, and the executive has also submitted an expense report for entertaining the ad agency employee. Duplicate reporting comes to light when an auditor schedules all incidental expenses paid to agencies and then schedules personal expense reports of Advertising and Marketing Department managers for the same period of time.

Frequently one of the principals involved in cases of duplicate reimbursements explains that the actual check was split between the two parties. The explanation seems doubtful if the ticket number and the dollar value are exactly the same. **TIP:** *A check with the supplier should disclose the total amount of the bill and show how it was paid.*

If questioning brings forth the explanation of a split bill, the auditor should consider calling the ad agency employee on the phone from the company employee's office and ask the agency rep how the payment for the affair was handled. Unless there has been some disclosure of the audit investigation, the agency representative should have no reason to misstate the facts.

7. There are instances where executives pay a large entertainment bill and then collect a portion of the charge from each employee present, explaining to subordinates that the allocation will eliminate any questions being asked about the affair. The exec then expenses the complete bill, and each employee submits an expense report for the amount of money given to the exec plus incidental expenses incurred in connection with the meeting. These types of manipulations are difficult to detect without a full scale investigation because the individual employee's expense report would only show their cash apportionment plus transportation and tips. If any employee noted on an expense report that cash had been given to the executive, an audit trail would be established.
8. Quantity and other types of special discounts and rebates are offered by suppliers of goods and services. These periodic payments, are based on total business during the period, and the agencies sometimes feel that they are not obligated to pass these savings on to accounts. Some suppliers offer rebates after receiving a specified dollar value of business, and in these cases an advertiser who can establish that their billings exceeded the required amount should be entitled to the portion of the rebate earned by their billings.

KEY POINT: *Contracts between agency and advertiser should spell out that the advertiser is entitled to all discounts and rebates that their business enabled the agency to earn and receive from suppliers.* The details will vary with agency and advertiser.

Chapter 24

Auditing Distribution Operations: Traffic and Export

Distribution functions are concerned with the movement of materials, supplies, finished products and personnel. To efficiently accomplish these movements, a Distribution Department must work closely with Production, Sales, Procurement and Planning Departments.

Distribution must be kept informed of what, when and where materials and supplies will be coming from, and in what quantities. They must also know the quantity, destination and timing of movements of all finished products if they are expected to provide for the economical movements of products and supplies.

The department needs to know of plans to build new branches or plants and of changes in anticipated volumes of product movements. And Distribution must keep abreast of the best and most economical carriers for employees to use while traveling on company business.

When all significant information is known, Distribution can determine the size, type and number of vehicles that are required to accomplish the desired movements. They can then decide whether to use common or contract carriers, or carry part or all shipments on company equipment. If company equipment is used, Distribution must develop a plan to operate and maintain the equipment.

This chapter reviews Distribution activities as they are found in a consumer products company which manufactures many of the products it sells. Following is a list of activities that describe separate sections of a Distribution Operations Department:

1. Supervision of Distribution Centers. This section is the backbone of the department; all Distribution Center activities report here. It decides how many centers are needed and where they should be located. It decides if and where new centers are to be built, and which locations to close down. The manager of this section selects and monitors the performance of the individual managers of all the distribution centers. Department operating policies and procedures originate in this section, which also provides necessary counsel or assistance.

2. Traffic. Traffic activities center around the negotiations and procurement of common carrier or contract carrier services. Traffic selects acceptable carriers, negotiates rates and surcharges and determines routings. It selects specific carriers for each shipment and schedules the loads. The section also verifies and approves all freight bills. A separate group within the traffic operation is responsible for the filing and collection, or cancellation, of all claims against carriers. These employees must be familiar with all tariffs and carrier contracts in order to know if a legitimate claim exists. They prepare, negotiate and process claims for in-transit product losses, or for carrier overcharges.

3. Export. This section is concerned with any movement of company property outside the continental boundaries of the United States. It is actually concerned with both import and export shipments. Export personnel are specialists in the legal aspects of international shipments and they determine the best routes, carriers and manner of shipment. They decide how to pack and mark the materials, and if containerized shipments are advisable.

4. Fleet Management and Garage Operations. This group is concerned with all automotive, rail, air or marine equipment that is owned and operated by the enterprise. They determine the type, specifications and numbers of pieces of equipment required, and schedule the runs of this equipment. They specify preventive maintenance programs, and determine the time period that individual pieces of equipment are to remain in service.

Supervision of the garages establishes policies and procedures governing the operations of garages and workshops for servicing fleet equipment. It determines the number of garages required, where to best locate them and the number of mechanics needed at each operation. The fleet management supervisor selects garage managers for all locations and then monitors their performances.

5. Long and Short-Range Planning. The Distribution supervisor of this section must work closely with Production and Marketing in developing short and long-range plans. Corporate planning is conducted in several departments, but is brought together for the entire company in the Corporate Planning Department.

Major operational departments assign knowledgeable employees to gather information and prepare plans for future activities and needs. Distribution plans depend upon the projections of the Sales and Production operations, since it is responsible for the movement of raw materials, supplies and finished goods.

6. Employee Travel Reservations. This group is concerned with the movements of company personnel. It is a service operation, that assists new employees or transferred employee in moving household goods, and obtains reservations for employees who need to travel. It also makes necessary travel arrangements for groups who are to attend meetings or conferences. This section usually controls the company limousines and airplanes.

7. Administration. This section is responsible for ensuring that company and departmental policies and procedures are followed by all Distribution employees. The department administrator, who works very closely with Financial, develops necessary forms and records that are used in the department, and ensures that adequate internal controls are built into all clerical operations.

The sample audit program contains separate sections for Traffic and Export, but all of the other areas are also covered in the section of this audit program that is labeled Distribution Operations.

Background Information

The XYZ Corporation, a large consumer products manufacturer and wholesaler, has a Distribution Operations Department that contains all of the sections enumerated above. The department supervises fifteen distribution centers: some are free standing, some located at the end of the production line of major plants, and the rest located in giant complexes that house a variety of company activities.

The Supervisor of Distribution Centers is directly responsible for operations at all company distribution centers. There is daily communication between the supervisor and individual center managers.

All computer-generated inventory and production control reports are printed daily at each distribution center and production plant. Several exception-type reports are printed each night and delivered to the supervisor in headquarters the following morning. Operational data and efficiency reports for Distribution Centers are printed weekly and delivered to the supervisor on Monday mornings.

XYZ's Traffic Section does not directly handle product. They negotiate rates with carriers and instruct company locations as to the carrier and the routing to use for specific movements.

The Traffic Section approves all freight bills for payment, after auditing the bills to insure that all charges are correct and proper.

The Export Section is involved indirectly in the sale of product. Export selling is accomplished through brokers and agents who operate as independent contractors and make sales to customers throughout the world. XYZ's Export Section actually sells product to the sales agencies, but ships the related products wherever directed.

Export instructs a Distribution Center to make shipments and directs the carrier and routing to be used for shipments outside the borders of the country. Specialized export forwarding companies are used for certain shipments, while others are made from an XYZ center.

An internal audit of a Distribution Operations Department verifies that the department is intelligently and diligently striving to move company materials, products and personnel in the most efficient and economical manner. And also that the department conforms to company policies and does not violate public laws or regulations.

Auditors are also interested in determining the following:

- Company property is protected and traced during movements,
- Records are accurate and timely,
- Service charges are legitimate and reasonable,
- Claims are filed where appropriate,
- Transportation tickets are only for company personnel traveling on company business.

For internal audit purposes the Distribution Operations Department is considered a separate audit and is so treated in the sample audit program that follows. A detailed internal audit program for a Distribution Center is covered in a separate chapter.

IA DOI321 XYZ CORPORATION

INTERNAL AUDIT PROGRAM—INSTRUCTIONS

DISTRIBUTION OPERATIONS DEPARTMENT

These audit instructions are used in conjunction with the check-off program (IA DOP320) and the associated internal control questionnaire, to conduct a review of the Distribution Operations Department. If you believe that any changes should be made in this internal audit program, discuss the matter with the audit supervisor.

A. Read the Distribution Manual, the Traffic Operations Manual, the Export Operations Manual and the Daily Stock Status User's Manual before you officially begin your audit, so that you are familiar with the information contained in these publications.
    1. Discuss your current assignment with the EDP audit supervisor and arrange to receive computer generated reports when required. **IMPORTANT:** *You will refer to various finished goods inventory reports during this review,* so that you become acquainted with all of the information that is available in the inventory data base.

B. During your review, meet every supervisor in the operation and discuss procedures and controls in their sections. Also interview every other employee in the department and determine their job assignment and their understanding of their responsibilities.

C. One of the major problems faced by distribution center management concerns the integrity of shipments. Policies and procedures spell out the requirements that are imposed on the shipping and receiving functions at distribution centers, but even if these are followed to the letter there remains a strong possibility of thefts from shipments.

    Distribution management will always consider any suggestions for better ways to control shipments, but the controls must not cost more than the value of product lost under our present system. The Finished Goods Inventory program produces accurate reports of product losses and pinpoints the carriers or XYZ trucks involved in the shipments.

    KEY POINT: *You should study these exception reports to see if there is an obvious pattern that should be investigated.*

    The carrier door sealing program can help reduce in-transit thefts, but only if it is diligently employed and intelligently checked. **IMPORTANT:** *Any change of a car seal indicates that the old seal was removed, which probably occurred when the door was opened and product removed illegally.* If the seal number is not checked before it is removed at the receiving location, all of our prescribed controls go down the drain. If a seal has been cut open and then glued together, a careful check of the entire seal, before opening, will disclose the tampering. Written instructions spell out proper procedures and emphasize their importance.

    Study the security portion of the audit program in your manual titled Auditing Production Plants, Distribution Centers and Branches. Pay particular attention to the internal audit steps relating to the security over outgoing and incoming shipments. *If you note any actions by security personnel that are in conflict with any national policy or procedure directive, notify the Manager of Internal Audits at once.*

D. The National Finished Goods Inventory system produces a daily stock status report for each inventory location. **NOTE:** *It is capable of producing an exception report listing any location's product inventory that exceeds a prescribed range.* This exception version should be used by the Supervisor of Distribution Centers to stabilize inventory levels and to stay abreast of local problems, so that transfers of product between centers can be ordered when necessary.

E. Movement of product is a major cost factor. Product is generally moved in one of four types of carriers.
    1. *Truck* movement is widely employed for small shipments, local deliveries and for long hauls to locations that are not situated on rail lines.
    2. *Railroad* movement is universally employed, usually for large shipments traveling long distances. Sometimes railroads are used to piggyback trucks over long distances.
    3. *Air* transport is generally limited to items that must be moved rapidly. It is the most costly form of product movement, when the shipment is not subsidized, and is therefore used sparingly.
    4. The fourth method is transportation by *ship*. This is usually the slowest

form of movement, and is used in conjunction with one or more of the other forms. Various combinations of these four movements are used in an effort to keep costs to a minimum.

Each type of carrier requires some differences in audit approach. But no matter the carrier used, the audit approach to traffic decisions is basically the same. You must consider the following elements:

- Product must be prepared and properly placed for movement,
- It must be loaded onto a vehicle and transported to a destination,
- There it must be unloaded and officially received.

Each of these activities requires a contractual agreement and knowledgeable handling.

F. The Traffic Section selects the carriers, negotiates rates for movement and for all special handling, and frequently participates in the writing and interpretation of tariffs. The section is active in the formulation and acceptance of tariffs covering movement of XYZ products. Traffic employs experts who argue our cases before the rate commissions when such agencies establish the tariffs.

The section also directs the selection of carriers for specific movements, and it reviews and approves all carrier billings.

G. *Traffic administration* processes the department's accounts payable work. Routine purchases are approved and related paper work is sent to A/P for handling. The department keeps a copy of every freight bill. The originals are audited and approved and are sent to the central A/P department for processing, paying and filing.

KEY POINT: *Paid freight bills are accumulated in the Traffic Department and are sent out at regular intervals to be audited by an outside freight audit agency.* These independent agencies receive a percentage of any recovered overcharges that they discover during their audit.

H. The *Planning Section* obtains and uses information from Production and Marketing, and then coordinates plans with Corporate Planning.

I. *Fleet operations* has the responsibility for controlling a large XYZ trucking operation which is used to transport company products. This section decides the number and types of trucks that XYZ requires. They write the specifications for the trucks and trailers, but the actual buying is done by the Purchasing Department.

There are several strategically located garages that perform routine maintenance and repairs on this equipment. **NOTE:** *We normally audit these garage operations at the same time that we review the Distribution Center that is located on the complex.*

J. Each *export* order is accompanied by a Bill of Exchange in payment for the product ordered. Export obtains proper licenses, prepares necessary papers and determines carriers and routing.

Our sales agency accepts the Bill of Exchange when product arrives and funds are remitted to our Export Section through a bank designated by the Treasurer's office. The Export Section controls the receivable.

K. Export has stocks of goods that are specially produced for export. This inventory is stored at Distribution Centers or at forwarding companies. When product is shipped to an outside forwarding company, or moved into a segregated area of a distribution center, the product is charged to the Export operation, and is added to their inventory. **NOTE:** *You are expected to confirm this asset.*

L. A description of the proper procedure for working with this internal audit program appears in the Introduction to the Audit Programs section of your manual. Read this information carefully.

INTERNAL AUDIT PROGRAM

IA DOP320 XYZ CORPORATION

INTERNAL AUDIT PROGRAM

DISTRIBUTION OPERATIONS DEPARTMENT

The following checklist program is designed to lead you through an internal audit of the Distribution Operations Department. Read this program, the Audit Instructions (IA DOI321), and the attached Internal Control Questionnaire before you start your audit.

I. Company Procedures

A. Distribution Operations is responsible for policies and procedures governing the activity of all company Distribution personnel.

B. The department is responsible for planning the movement of all materials and products under XYZ control.

C. Distribution selects carriers and negotiates rates for movements.

D. The department is responsible for determining that rates charged by carriers are accurate and conform to agreements.

E. The department determines the number and types of equipment to be owned and operated by XYZ.

F. Distribution manages the company fleet and determines its use.

G. The department manages shipments entering or leaving the country.

H. Distribution controls reservation services used by XYZ personnel.

II. Audit Objectives are to determine the following:

A. All company policies and procedures are followed and there are no violations of any laws or regulations.

B. Systems and procedures are adequate and insure that all payments for freight charges are accurate and proper.

C. Security systems ensure the integrity of products being carried.

D. Records and reports are accurate, adequate, complete and timely.

E. Claims are handled promptly and correctly.

III. Audit Procedures — *Per. Cov.* | *Audit By*

All Sections

A. Meet with department executives and supervisors to discuss their operations. Ask if there are any areas that they would like auditors to closely check. *Make notes of these comments and follow through during audit.* ____ ____

B. Review all reports generated in the department for necessity, efficiency and accuracy. ____ ____

   1. Determine that pertinent information is disseminated to all employees concerned. ____ ____

C. Determine that all department policies and procedures are compatible with and conform to national directives. ____ ____

D. Review short- and long-range planning activities. ____ ____

   1. Determine that all pertinent information is sent to the planning section on a timely basis. ____ ____
   2. Review the section's access security clearance to information in the computer data base. ____ ____

E. Verify the department's payroll, using the program in your audit manual titled Auditing Payroll. ____ ____

F. Audit purchases that originate in the department, refer to program in your manual titled Auditing Purchasing. ____ ____

   1. Be sure to review the selection of carriers. ____ ____
   2. *Consider the specifications for truck equipment.* ____ ____
   3. Review the selection of freight bill audit agencies. ____ ____

G. Audit disbursements for goods or services received in the department using the program titled Auditing Payables. ____ ____

   1. Pay particular attention to checking expense reports. ____ ____
      a. Determine that the department requires expense reports of outlying managers to be sent in for headquarter's approval, prior to payment. ____ ____

Distribution Operations

A. Review methods used to analyze and appraise local management's performance at Distribution Centers. ____ ____

   1. Determine that data used for comparative analyses is pertinent, accurate and timely. ____ ____
      a. Determine that method does not induce managers to cause losses in an unreported area in order to avoid reportable losses. ____ ____
      b. Determine that local managers do not instruct vendors to send in two small bills instead of one big one that would require headquarter's approval. ____ ____

B. Review the comparative analyses reports of distribution centers' operations. List those centers performing far

III. Audit Procedures *Per. Cov.* *Audit By*
Distribution Operations

below average, and send list to audit administrator to review and place in follow-up file. ____ ____

C. Review the section's special studies to determine type of equipment to use and the frequency of replacement. ____ ____
   1. Determine that specs are not closed, so that some competition is obtainable. ____ ____
   2. Determine that cost is an important consideration. ____ ____
   3. Verify accuracy of studies that decide number, size and type of trucks needed to make local deliveries. ____ ____

D. Review rules and regulations established to control truck operations, and driver work periods and conditions. ____ ____
   1. See that reports and rules conform to ICC regulations. ____ ____
   2. Determine that violations are reported and explained. ____ ____
      a. Determine that main office action is appropriate. ____ ____

E. Review scheduling of fleet operations and determine that equipment is fully and intelligently used. ____ ____
   1. Determine that movements by common carrier are all monitored by the section to judge whether additional equipment should be added. ____ ____
   2. Determine that XYZ owned trucks are used in a fashion that eliminates, or at least reduces deadheading. ____ ____
      a. Determine that our trucks are used to pick up our manufacturing supplies instead of returning empty (deadheading) to a Distribution Center. ____ ____
      b. Determine that section *regularly studies other alternatives to owning fleet equipment.* ____ ____
   3. Determine that studies consider possibility of offering pickup allowances to customers which might reduce the required size of the XYZ fleet. ____ ____

F. Review the analyses studies of the garage operations. ____ ____
   1. Determine that there are strict and adequate internal controls mandated for these operations. ____ ____
   2. Note that garage reports are studied and verified. ____ ____
   3. Discuss with audit administrator, *any garages that are experiencing regular supply losses* or have comparatively poor operating statistics. ____ ____

Traffic Section

A. Review the procedures and systems that are used to process and plead tariff cases. ____ ____
   1. Determine that use of outside consultants are monitored, controlled and used only when necessary. ____ ____

B. Determine that method of filing tariffs insures that they are readily available when needed. ____ ____
   1. Check to see that filings are current so that rate clerks

III. Audit Procedures *Traffic Section*	*Per. Cov.*	*Audit By*
and routers refer to accurate rates.	____	____
C. Review procedures for meeting with carrier agents and for selecting freight lines and routes to use.	____	____
1. If carrier is selected for a route on the basis of service, check to see whether more economical carriers have had poor service records.	____	____
a. For a test period, compute the additional cost of using the higher priced carrier.	____	____
D. Review the section that audits freight bills.	____	____
1. Evaluate system for making first audit in-house; then sending bills to outside agencies for further audits.	____	____
a. Analyze merits of elimination or reducing section.	____	____
1) Your analysis should compare costs of in-house freight bill auditing to amounts recovered.	____	____
a) *Also consider only auditing bills that are above a set dollar limit; based on analyses.*	____	____
E. Review billing from outside freight bill audit agencies.	____	____
1. Ensure that claims prepared by outside agencies are analyzed to determine reason error passed first audit.	____	____
a. *Determine that rate clerks are notified of oversights so that they do not repeat mistakes.*	____	____
F. Review procedures and controls for handling claims.	____	____
1. Make copies of claims for previous three months.	____	____
a. Trace quantities on claims to computer reports.	____	____
2. Review office procedure for processing claims.	____	____
3. Determine that all claims are checked by supervisor before they are officially filed.	____	____
a. *Determine that significant claims are called to the attention of all the other rate clerks.*	____	____
4. Review all adjustments to claims.	____	____
a. Ensure that adjustments are valid, accurate, reasonable and justified.	____	____
5. Select major dollar claims and verify open amount and status directly with carrier involved. (Refer to your audit program titled Auditing Receivables.)	____	____
G. Review the computer generated Finished Goods Inventory exception reports that show delivery shorts by carrier.	____	____
1. Relate reports of shortages to comparative hauling rates of carriers and the number of loads carried.	____	____
a. Explore possibility that drivers are compensating for low hauling rates by stealing product.	____	____
2. Discuss obvious trouble carriers with administrator.	____	____
a. *Participate in the discussions with carriers.*	____	____
H. Review all charges for the company limousine operation.	____	____

III. Audit Procedures	*Per. Cov.*	*Audit By*
Traffic Section		
1. Compute per mile cost of using company owned limos.	_____	_____
2. Compare costs to hiring limos when needed.	_____	_____
a. See if adequate service is available locally and how long a wait between call and service.	_____	_____
3. Compare cost of owning versus leasing limousines.	_____	_____
4. Send a copy of your analyses sheets to audit manager.	_____	_____
I. Review the Reservations Section's operations.	_____	_____
1. Audit one full month of purchases of airline tickets. Tie totals into the billings from airline companies.	_____	_____
2. Verify postings to ledgers.	_____	_____
3. See that all tickets issued are charged to employees.	_____	_____
a. Examine expense reports and follow through to see that charges are cleared out.	_____	_____
1) See that all charges agree on amounts and that all trips were on company business.	_____	_____
b. *Determine that all personal ticket purchases are approved in advance and are properly noted.*	_____	_____
c. Study all tickets purchased in last three months. List all transactions that might be personal trips.	_____	_____
1) Follow through to see that all personal items were charged to employee's account.	_____	_____
a) Verify that all charges were paid and that money was properly and promptly deposited.	_____	_____
2. Determine that section purchases tickets as requested by traveler, at lowest available fare.	_____	_____
J. Audit all charges against the company airplane operation.	_____	_____
1. Check airport fees and hanger rental fees.	_____	_____
a. Determine that fees coincide with company trips.	_____	_____
2. Audit expenditures for fuel to determine that all gas paid for was used by the company plane.	_____	_____
a. Analyze miles traveled and normal fuel consumption rate and compare to quantity of fuel purchased.	_____	_____
3. Compare the cost of using company plane to the use of first class commercial air travel.	_____	_____
a. Use the airplane operating costs and divide by the miles traveled to arrive at per mile cost.	_____	_____
4. Compare present costs to costs of charter flights.	_____	_____
5. Send a copy of your analyses sheets to audit manager.	_____	_____
Export Section		
A. Analyze the section's operating cost statements.	_____	_____
1. Review the section's internal operations for economy, necessity and efficiency of effort.	_____	_____
a. Check time taken to personally deliver documents.	_____	_____
1) Consider use of delivery service.	_____	_____

III. Audit Procedures *Export Section*	*Per. Cov.*	*Audit By*
B. Audit receivables in the Export Section. Refer to audit program in your manual titled Auditing Receivables.	____	____
C. Audit cash items in the section, using the program titled Auditing Cash Transactions.	____	____
D. Audit the inventories that are charged to the section. Use program titled Auditing Inventory Transactions.	____	____
1. If audit teams are in areas where inventory is stored, work with audit administrator to have them verify the accuracy of inventory records.	____	____
E. Write memos expanding on items noted above or on items that should be added to the audit program.	____	____

Audit program approved by ______________________ Date ______________

INTERNAL AUDIT PROGRAM—INTERNAL CONTROL QUESTIONNAIRE

The following internal control questions are intended to direct your attention to the high-risk areas of Distribution Department's operations. Many of these points are covered in the audit program, but they are listed here to ensure that they receive adequate attention.

Answer these internal control questions as your audit progresses. In section B, you are to write in the names and job titles of the employees who perform the listed functions. Be certain to note any conflicting duties that could jeopardize internal controls.

A. Following are listed practices that indicate good internal control

1. Comparative analyses reports are acted upon as required.
2. Selection of routings are suggested by routing clerks and decided by supervisors.
3. Claims are prepared by rate clerks and approved by supervisors.
4. Freight bills are sent to outside audit agencies to pick up any claims that rate clerks missed.
5. Adjusting or canceling a claim requires supervisory approval.

B. Following lists functions performed by named employees

Functions	*Employee names*	*Conflicting duties*
1. Approves standard routings.	____________	____________
2. Approves freight claims.	____________	____________
3. Authorizes adjustments to claims.	____________	____________
4. Writes travel tickets.	____________	____________
5. Assigns accounting distribution.	____________	____________
6. Approves the selection of freight forwarding companies.	____________	____________
7. Receives and keeps records of foreign bills of exchange.	____________	____________

C. Internal Control Questions	*Yes*	*No*	*Remarks*
1. Does Distribution administration act as an effective control over operations?	____	____	____________
a. Are records accurate, current and pertinent?	____	____	____________
1) Is confidential information treated accordingly?	____	____	____________
2) Is all information properly and promptly disseminated?	____	____	____________
b. Are P/O's for all department requirements approved by administrator before issuance?	____	____	____________
c. Are all invoices for department's purchases approved by administrator before payment?	____	____	____________
2. Are inventory shortages and "out-of-stock" conditions at centers promptly followed up?	____	____	____________
3. Are exception reports of inventory daily stock status reviewed and appropriate action taken?	____	____	____________
4. Are confidential planning reports and similar information held under tight security?	____	____	____________
a. Are changes in planning data promptly conveyed to attention of proper planners?	____	____	____________
b. *Are changes in plans immediately brought to the attention of all concerned personnel?*	____	____	____________
5. Is Fleet Management cost conscious in their purchasing and operating procedures?	____	____	____________
a. Are economic delivery quantities computed and used as a basis for shipments?	____	____	____________
b. Do they consider renting, rather than owning, when acquiring or operating their existing equipment?	____	____	____________
c. Do they periodically study the economics of operating their equipment?	____	____	____________
1) Do they update or revise the period that equipment can be used before trade-in?	____	____	____________

C. Internal Control Questions	*Yes*	*No*	*Remarks*
6. Does the supervisor of garage operations study the per-mile costs for parts at XYZ's garages?	____	____	____________
a. Are there any operations well out of line?	____	____	____________
7. Are airline tickets adequately controlled?	____	____	____________
a. Are personal use tickets well controlled?	____	____	____________
1) Are they properly recorded and paid for?	____	____	____________
8. *Is there favoritism in selecting air carriers?*	____	____	____________
9. Is limousine service closely controlled?	____	____	____________
a. *Is service prohibited for personal use?*	____	____	____________
10. Does owning a company plane save money?	____	____	____________
11. Do agreements with carriers require return to XYZ of product over and refused on delivery?	____	____	____________
a. Do delivery receipts note all overages?	____	____	____________
12. Are problems of product loss discussed with the owners of carriers who are responsible?	____	____	____________
13. Are carriers selected on the basis of rates?	____	____	____________
a. *Any obvious favoritism in scheduling loads?*	____	____	____________
14. Are freight bills approved before payment?	____	____	____________
a. Are they checked for proper local approval?	____	____	____________
b. Are copies of freight bills kept in files?	____	____	____________
15. Are freight claims accurately computed and filed promptly and impartially?	____	____	____________
a. *Are they collected promptly?*	____	____	____________
b. Are all adjustments properly approved?	____	____	____________
16. Are shippers notified of carrier changes?	____	____	____________
a. Are they notified when routings			

C. Internal Control Questions	*Yes*	*No*	*Remarks*
are changed?			
17. Does Export use containerized shipments?			
18. In export, is the conversion of national currencies to dollars, closely controlled?			
19. Are Bills of Exchange adequately controlled?			
20. Are all customer credits, issued by Export, reviewed and approved by supervisors?			
21. *Is there any favoritism in selection of forwarders?*			

Questions answered by ______________________ Date ____________
Answers reviewed by ______________________ Date ____________

CRITICAL POINTS

Distribution of materials, products and personnel is a major expense of any large business. Just as in any other service operation, the central decision point is carefully nurtured by outside companies that benefit from operational decisions. Auditors must objectively scrutinize these decisions to insure that all levels of management act in the best interests of the company.

There are many areas of potential defalcations in distribution activities. Following are a few of the different types of frauds or manipulations that frequently occur.

SEVEN COMMON TYPES OF MANIPULATIONS TO WATCH OUT FOR

1. Selection of a common or contract carrier is a vital decision that can affect any carrier. A carrier gains a financial advantage if it is selected by a large organization to transport goods. The competition for this business frequently leads to an attempt to gain the favor of the people responsible for the selection. **KEY POINT:** *Auditors should be aware that, despite its illegality, payoffs are not rare in this area.* Payoffs occur in various forms such as gifts, parties, vacations, payment of outstanding debts, or cash. Payoffs are usually not made by check, since this leaves an audit trail.

   Examination of volume of business given to various carriers will disclose the companies that you should closely audit. A study of comparative rates of competitive carriers for similar runs will show whether your company is overpaying for the service. **TIP:** *A study of sign-in sheets at the headquarter office's guard desk may list frequent visitors from trucking lines.* This could mean free meals or perhaps the delivery of a payoff.

As in any kickback arrangement an effective audit approach is to create dissension and mistrust between the conspirators. **TIP:** *Introducing competing lines, and forcing the granting of some of the business to a competitor can sometimes produce startling results.*

2. Shipping rates charged, or those authorized by tariffs, generally result from negotiations. Once established, these rates become the basis for charges for all covered movements. These agreements are usually complicated and require an expert to analyze and compute.

   Freight bills, when received, are usually approved for payment by a rate clerk, after the details of the shipment have been verified. **CAUTION:** *These rate clerks are aware that freight bills are sent out for further audit and they may become careless,* since the outside audit agency will probably catch any overpayment.

   KEY POINT: *Herein lies the potential danger that requires your alertness.* Outside audit agencies earn their money by discovering billing errors made by the carriers, which are not detected by the shipper's rate clerks.

   Some of these freight bill audit bureaus are owned and operated by rate clerks who audit these bills as a second job. They may work as full-time rate clerks during the day and operate their audit business during nights and weekends. The audit bureaus receive a percentage of all overcharges that are refunded as a result of their work. **CAUTION:** *This example of entrepreneurship is commendable, but it may pose a threat if the audit agency is owned, or if it employs, some of your company's rate clerks.*

   If an audit bureau uses rate audit clerks who review bills paid by their primary employer, it can lead to carelessness or worse during the original routine examination of freight bills. **TIP:** *If a clerk spots an error that can later be corrected at an audit agency for fifty percent of the overcharge, there is a strong reason to neglect to correct the error.* The rate clerk can make a note of the invoice number and approve the bill as is. This oversight, accidental or deliberate, can put money in the rate clerk's pocket at a later date.

   This potential for fraud can be reduced by analyzing errors picked up by the audit agency and noting the rate clerk that approved the invoice. The next step is to determine why the error occurred at the carrier end, and why it was missed when checked before payment. Then find out if the responsible rate clerk also works for the audit agency or has an interest in that company. With this information in your possession, you'll be able to determine appropriate action.

   Another preventive measure is to prohibit your company's rate clerks from holding down a second job at a freight audit bureau. **TIP:** *At* *least insist that the bureau used by your company is not owned by, nor does it employ, any of your company's rate clerks.*

3. Truck carriers conduct their business in a variety of ways. Some own all of their equipment, others own no equipment but merely act as brokers between truckers and shippers, and others own some equipment and use independent truckers as required. Hauling rates and control over driver's actions are affected by the carrier's organization.

   Here is a case in point:

   EXAMPLE: A large shipper was experiencing regular and frequent losses of product carried by a particular freight line. Analyses of the losses pointed to a dozen trucks as the main culprits. Further study showed that the freight rates of the line in question were considerably lower than the nearest competitor, and the carrier therefore received the bulk of the loads.

   Audit counts of product were made and rechecked before cases were loaded on the carrier's trucks and the loading process was carefully observed. All audited loads, upon delivery, reported small losses which were attributed to loading errors.

   The owners of the trucking line were called in and shown the information supporting the accuracy of the loads. Since theft from an interstate shipment is a Federal offense, the owners were told that if the losses did not stop the matter would be reported to the proper authorities and the truck line would no longer be used. The owners promised to take action, and they did. The thefts stopped.

   Several weeks later the carrier's owners returned to discuss the matter with executives of the shipper. They explained that they had called a general meeting of all their drivers. The carrier owned and supplied trailers, but used independent truckers who owned their own tractors. These truckers worked for a certain percentage of the freight charges for the loads they carried, and they were therefore affected by the rates the carrier charged.

   Some of the drivers had complained that they could not continue to drive for the carrier if they were not able to supplement their income by taking small quantities of products from loads. The carrier had forbidden any further thefts, but was now in danger of losing many drivers unless they were granted a rate increase. The owners of the freight line promised to pass on the full increase to the drivers, and a small rate increase was granted.

   In the above case, the action of the shipper to stop thefts of product actually resulted in an increase in shipping costs, but the losses stopped. All drivers benefited, instead of only those who stole product.

4. Company garage operations are particularly susceptible to thefts and fraud. Internal controls may be nonexistent or easily bypassed, since the garage building often stands alone and is frequently isolated. In order to have an economical operation, clerical workers are few in number, with the garage manager often being the only person that performs clerical tasks. In such circumstances the manager orders and receives all supplies, and approves the covering bills for payment. **CAUTION:** *This lack of control may encourage collusion between a garage manager and an automotive supply house.*

   When garage management and a supplier work together, the scam occurs in a variety of ways, usually conforming to one of the following:

   - The supply house bills for more parts than actually shipped.
   - The supplier charges for some items at a price well above the going rate.
   - The supplier presents a completely fictitious billing.

   Some cases combine several of the above methods. There are even instances, in those garages where receipts are closely controlled, where auto parts are properly delivered, received, and are then promptly *carried out of the garage and returned for cash refunds.*

   In the above cases, the overcharges may all be remitted to the garage manager in appreciation of receiving business, or the supply house may retain a portion to pay for their additional work and risk.

   There are several audit approaches to forestalling or disclosing such illegal acts. **KEY POINT:** *The starting point is to require that all work performed by garage mechanics be initiated by an official work order that describes the work to be done.* The order must contain a request date, a description of the vehicle and the odometer reading. It should be signed by the individual that ordered the repairs.

   All parts used should be clearly written, showing part number and quantities, and this includes tires. **IMPORTANT:** *Such records do take a few minutes to prepare, but the system discourages garage employees from "borrowing" company supplies or parts and forgetting to return them.*

   Analysis of these records, compared to disappearance of parts will quickly show if the operation has been paying for items that are never delivered or were stolen. A Purchasing Department check of prices charged for selected high priced and high volume items, should disclose any overpricing. **TIP:** *Armed with information of any type of discrepancy, a routine questioning of garage employees will often disclose if the manager has been acting in a suspicious manner.*

   Some supply houses are reluctant coconspirators. They only retain the correct amount due at their going rate, for items that were actually delivered. They have been coerced into acting as directed by the dishonest employee in order to retain the business, and *they will cooperate in an investigation if they are assured that they will not be barred from any future business.*

Those companies that share in the illegal overcharges, will not cooperate willingly in your investigation. But it may be that an employee of the supply house, who shares in the deception, is not the owner of the business. **TIP:** *In such cases the owner may be cooperative and thankful that the situation was brought to light.*

An effective method of combatting the above described fraud, is to require that all agreements with outside repair or service operations be negotiated by Purchasing, and that these agreements be periodically reviewed and renegotiated. Under these arrangements, Purchasing negotiates the discount structure off of the parts catalog prices, and updated copies of these catalogs are retained in both the Purchasing and Accounts Payable departments.

5. Another common abuse at company garages is the use of the facilities and parts to repair personal auto equipment. Such repairs are often permitted by company management, with certain restrictions, such as doing the work after business hours or on weekends. **CAUTION:** *The danger is that mechanics may use company tires and other expensive items and fail to reimburse the company.* Also, mechanics may take tools and supplies from the garage, since controls over such items are usually very loose.

   Where management permits after-hour use of garage facilities in a closely monitored operation, losses may be minimal. All mechanics may appreciate the value of the perq, and realize that if it is abused they will not only lose their job, but all other employees will suffer because the perq will be withdrawn. This has the effect of using all garage employees to enforce the rules against theft or abuse of the facility. **REMEMBER:** *Peer pressure is a most effective control and it can work in this type of environment.*

6. Reservation clerks can write travel tickets for themselves or friends and charge the cost to company expenses. The charges may be applied to Distribution expenses, or perhaps to an account that a clerk knows will not be questioned. A favorite account usually reflects top executive expenses and is not closely audited. If the improper account allocation is questioned, the reservation clerk checks and acknowledges that an "error" had been made.

   An effective method of reducing the likelihood of improper writing of travel tickets is to insist that all such tickets be charged directly to the employees using them. **IMPORTANT:** *This restriction should apply even when large groups are traveling to a convention and all other meeting expenses are charged directly to a meeting expense account.*

7. As in many other areas of business operations, there is the usual possibility that owners or agents of various companies may kick back a commission to your company's employee who sends business their way. This frequently occurs in the following Distribution Operations areas:

    - Selection of carriers, including freight forwarding companies.
    - Selection of travel agencies,
    - Selection of freight bill audit bureaus,
    - Selection of truck or auto sales agencies,
    - Selection of service stations, repair shops and parts stores.

    Protection or appropriate action against this type of kickback has been described in several earlier chapters, such as Auditing Purchasing and Auditing Engineering.

Chapter 25

Auditing Data Processing Operations and Library

Once upon a time someone invented a lightning fast calculator and gave it a memory. To differentiate it from ordinary calculators, it was given the name *computer.* That was the beginning of a revolution in the elimination of paper shuffling and many associated tasks.

In the beginning the computer was used as a fast adding machine or calculator and was accepted as just another office machine. As speed, capacity and memory increased, this technology improved to the point where it materially changed the world of business.

The computer can remember intricate formulas and apply them at call. It can sort, analyze and compare a mass of information—can make preinstructed decisions and act accordingly. The computer is a competent, reliable and dependable employee. It doesn't retire, take vacations, or even coffee breaks. It follows instructions completely and meticulously and doesn't talk back or gossip, and its morale is generally high.

But, it is *not perfect.* **CAUTION:** *A loss of power or contact with a magnetic field can be a catastrophe.* And the computer cannot think creatively, although some trial and error thinking processes have been designed into some programs. A computer requires finite instructions, refined to the *n*th degree. When errors are generated, they are frequently gigantic. It can only do what it is programmed to do, and it follows orders minutely even if the orders are ridiculous.

When internal auditors first encountered computers, they treated them as they would other business machines. As the computer's usefulness and capabilities improved, auditors began to recognize that they were dealing with a formidable monster. A great debate arose as to the best method of auditing computer output. Half of the profession argued that it was best to audit *around* the computer; another half argued that it was best to audit *through* it; and half of all the befuddled auditors really wanted it both ways. A small group argued that it would be best to audit *with* the computer—that is, by using the computer as an audit tool.

The Computer Department is now one of the most important operations in big business. EDP handles thousands of transactions each day and accumulates the necessary information to prepare periodic analyses and reports. The capability of the computer is limited only by the capability of programmers who apply computer technology.

There are thousands of commercially available computer programs that can be used by companies, but the larger organizations usually design their own computer programs for their special use. These custom programs fit their organizational and philosophic structures.

There are a number of business areas in which computer use has become widely accepted. You will find computers used to automate the following:

- Payroll,
- Accounts Payable,
- Accounts Receivable,
- Shipping records and customer billings,
- Production controls and inventory records,
- Cost accounting and general accounting,
- Some engineering design work,
- Word processing.

This chapter discusses some of the problems encountered in auditing a computer operation and a computer library. Machine accounting and electronic data processing systems present unique problems to the internal auditor. Since computers are normally completely accurate for arithmetic calculations, and since they follow orders exactly, our main attention turns to the controls over input and operations, and only incidentally do we test individual transactions.

The sample program for auditing an EDP operation contains a section devoted to an audit of a computer library. The library is significant because that is where all of the programs and data are stored.

Background Information

The audit program is designed for a review of the XYZ Corporation's computer operations. The Computer Department is a completely independent function which assists all other departments. Computer operations are located in a separate controlled portion of the headquarters building. There is tight security over this area of the building; access to the computers, printers, ancillary equipment and the computer library is limited.

The computer production room is completely enclosed and separated from the systems analysts and programmers and from the printing area. The mainframe computers are housed in the production area, and the computer library adjoins the production room with a window providing space for passage of tapes, disks and records.

Access to the computer library is also strictly limited. The library controls tapes and disks required to run programs, and it also contains master copies of the computer's technical and user manuals.

Many of the computer programs are real-time applications, some are batch processed and the rest are a combination of batch and real time. Batch processing is normally run at night and printed at night so that the reports are ready for review first thing in the morning.

Computer printers, and certain pieces of ancillary equipment, are housed in a separate room adjacent to the production room. The room contains printers, strippers, separators, folders and envelope stuffers. During critical runs, only authorized mail department personnel are permitted entrance to this room. The computer operation has the capability of printing reports in the printing room, at the printers located at the data terminals or at both location's printers.

The rest of the Computer Department's area contains private offices for the department's managers and an open office area where analysts and programmers work. Each specialist has access to a terminal conveniently placed at each working desk. The department's files are close at hand.

Mainframe computers are scheduled and loaded by a computer management program that ensures that the proper disks are loaded on the proper drive at the correct time. The required tapes, or disks, are taken from the library and mounted as needed. When processing is completed, the disks are removed and returned to the library.

Protection of data against a catastrophic loss is achieved through the use of a grandfather, father, son series of data bases. Current records are retained in the computer library until the day's operations have been recorded on the disks. They are then moved to the mail room and placed on a truck bound for storage in a company location far removed from the computer center. Upon receipt at the storage point, the disks that are replaced are loaded on the truck for return to the computer library. There are, therefore, three records of transactions available—one in the computer library, one in transit and the third in storage at an outside location. **KEY POINT:** *In the event of a catastrophe, at least one of the disks should be available for use as a starting point to reconstruct and recover transaction data.*

XYZ Corporation utilizes a Computer Control Board to approve and monitor all EDP projects. The board is composed of executives from the Operating and Service Departments that make use of the computer. The audit manager and the EDP director also serve on the control board.

Task force chairpeople are appointed to head up employee groups that are responsible for designing new computer applications. These chairpeople are operating executives who have an interest in creating a good program at a reasonable cost. Each major task force has an internal auditor assigned to work with the group and with the systems analysts and programmers who work on the project. Task force chairpeople present periodic reports to the Computer Control Board. These reports outline the progress and costs of their projects.

The Auditing Department has a special group of EDP auditors who work with the Data Processing Department in the development of new applications and to ensure that existing programs are being handled properly. Auditor's major concerns that new programs be the following:

- Workable and efficient,
- Properly documented,
- Protected with adequate internal controls to prevent abuse to the operating program and to input and output data.

Auditors are not supposed to be programmers, though many know how to create programs. They are not systems analysts, but many know how to analyze a system. They are not computer production technicians, but they know how to operate the computer.

The EDP audit group works closely with the other audit teams to ensure that the EDP information sent to auditors is accurate and timely. They also design special programs to assist the audit staff in conducting their routine examinations of various operations. The group also obtains information from the corporate data bank for use by the regular audit teams. There is a close working relationship between this small group and the rest of the internal audit staff.

Following is the sample internal audit program used by the XYZ Corporation's audit staff when reviewing the Computer Department and Library.

IA DPI999 XYZ CORPORATION

INTERNAL AUDIT PROGRAM—DATA PROCESSING INSTRUCTIONS

The Data Processing Department is responsible for all computer operations in the company. The department is divided into four sections with a manager responsible for each distinct operation. The sections are: production, design, implementation, and administration. Most of your work will be processed through the administration section and you will work closely with the administrator during your review.

1. Before starting your audit of the EDP operation, prepare for the review by completing the following:
   a. Read the Computer Department's Operations manual.
   b. Read to understand the audit checklist Program (IA DPP998), the Internal Control Questions, and these instructions. For those software applications that you elect to audit, carefully study the user's manual to determine that it is complete, accurate and readily understood.
2. Discuss technical questions relative to EDP operations with the Audit group

supervisor before talking to EDP personnel. This will enable you to receive some basic information and enough background to intelligently discuss the matter with technicians involved.

Become acquainted with the technical manual for the systems that you elect to study. When you review the computer system technical manual, ask your starting questions of the EDP audit group, they should be able to give you much information as to the technical terminology and approach that the computer technician used in preparing the manual.

3. The in-charge auditor will use the EDP audit group as a major segment of the audit team. There must be close coordination between the supervisor of the EDP group and the in-charge auditor. The EDP group should supply most of the technical expertise necessary to perform the audit and will supply technical information when and as required. Use the EDP group to review the technical items in the audit program. **IMPORTANT:** *However, the in-charge auditor is responsible for the audit work and for the results of the EDP audit.*
4. When you select programs to dump and study, choose programs that were not dumped on the previous internal audit. During your entire audit of the data processing operation, make certain that the staff member selected to review a particular program is not the auditor that worked directly on the formulation of the program. **CAUTION:** *An involved auditor may be consulted or questioned about a program but should not be in a position to decide an audit approach or question.*
5. Use the EDP auditors in a manner that makes it clear that their area of responsibility is not being usurped. Bear in mind that the EDP auditors spend most of their time working with systems analysts, designers and programmers. They normally have little time to devote to the auditing examinations that are required for this review.
6. Determine, from observation of the machine schedules, when payroll and disbursement checks are to be run. Perform a surprise audit of these operations by having auditors simultaneously enter the computer production room and the printing room immediately before the checks are to be run. **IMPORTANT:** *It is best to enter the rooms after the disks have been mounted and the data is being processed.* Take possession of the checks after they have been inserted in envelopes and sealed and wait until you receive the computer report listing checks issued before you begin your audit work.
7. When opening disbursement checks on a test basis, be certain that the computer mailing room supervisor is present during the entire time that envelopes are open. When satisfied that the disbursement checks are accurate, supervise the reprocessing through the envelope stuffer and sealer, and then ensure that the mail bags are properly processed.

If there are *any differences* between the printed registers and the checks that you examine, you are looking at a *serious problem.* **IMPORTANT:** *Retain the evidence and notify audit management at once.* Do it as calmly as possible, try not to alert employees to the problem. Continue to work while waiting for the audit manager. *But don't let any papers out of your possession* until audit management arrives.

8. During your interviews in the computer library room, stretch the conversations out so that you will have time to observe the normal routine used by library personnel in issuing and receiving items. Pay particular attention to the care taken in checking identification labels and in recording movements of computer disks and tapes.
9. A description of the proper procedure for working with this internal audit program appears in the Introduction to the Audit Programs section of your manual. Read this information carefully.

INTERNAL AUDIT PROGRAM

IA DPP998 XYZ CORPORATION

INTERNAL AUDIT PROGRAM— DATA PROCESSING DEPARTMENT

The following program is designed to aid in your review of the Data Processing Department. It is by no means all inclusive.

Technology in this field changes rapidly, and part of this program may be obsolete before it is printed. It is your responsibility to modify this program as your work progresses and to inform audit management of necessary changes in any part of this program. You need not give this notification until you have completed your audit.

I. Company Procedures

1. Data Processing is an independent department reporting directly to the President of the Corporation.
2. The department performs data processing work for other departments in the corporation and bills the operations for services rendered.
3. Data processing building area, equipment and input and output data are under close security control.
4. The department purchases all specialized computer products based on its own value analyses studies.
5. All computer projects are approved and controlled by the Computer Control Board composed of executives of all operating departments and the Financial department, the Manager of Internal Audits and the Director of Computer Operations.

II. Audit Scope. The purpose of your audit is to ensure the following:

1. The department is working efficiently and economically.
2. Data is processed under authority and approval of proper executives.
3. Operations, personnel, computer equipment, and the computer library are all adequately controlled, and safeguarded.
4. No computer programs have been compromised and that all programs process information in the manner approved by operating management and the Computer Control Committee.
5. All project work is approved in advance by the Control Committee.
6. There is good control over all information in the computer library.
7. Physical security regulations in the operation are rigidly enforced.
8. There are adequate backup systems for recovery after a catastrophe.
9. Handling of computer problems is efficient, timely and adequate.

III. Audit Procedures

	Per. Cov.	*Audit By*
A. Review the minutes of the Computer Control Committee since the last audit. List all projects approved.	____	____
1. Determine that the costs for all approved work lies within the approved annual budget.	____	____
2. Determine that all projects worked on by the computer department have been approved by the committee.	____	____
3. Determine that status reports to the committee accurately reflect the work done by the department.	____	____
a. If overtime is worked on projects, determine that such overtime is authorized by and reported to the Computer Control Committee.	____	____
B. Review procedures for establishing new applications. Ensure that consideration is given to modifying existing applications or using commercial software.	____	____
1. *See that buying of commercial programs is controlled in the same manner as in-house created projects.*	____	____
a. Review adherence to the project plan.	____	____
b. Determine extent of user involvement in preliminary meetings and in preparation of specifications.	____	____
1) Determine that users are satisfied with procedures.	____	____
2) Review procedures for user approval & sign off.	____	____
c. *Ascertain that purchased software is properly tested before being accepted.*	____	____
d. Determine that implementation is properly controlled.	____	____
C. Review procedures for obtaining any outside services.	____	____
1. Determine that potential vendor's reliability and financial stability has been adequately investigated.	____	____
2. Review some formal agreements to determine that:		
a. Services and prices are spelled out in detail.	____	____
b. *The services were not available in-house.*	____	____
c. If vendor has access to our system ensure that our procedures give adequate security and that any *access* or *authority* is *withdrawn* at completion of work.	____	____
d. Confidentiality and non-disclosure of data is properly addressed and ownership of data identified.	____	____
D. Test review some documentation for operating systems.	____	____
1. Determine that User Manual includes the following:		
a. Review of data elements, and user responsibilities.	____	____
1) Description of menus and access instructions.	____	____
2) Input screens defining sources and entry routines.	____	____
3) Output screens and reports.	____	____

III. Audit Procedures	*Per. Cov.*	*Audit By*
4) Special request routines and data available.	____	____
5) *Correction procedures and controls.*	____	____
b. Description of operating system.	____	____
1) System objectives and how attained.	____	____
2) Data sources and flow charts.	____	____
3) File names, field descriptions and relationships.	____	____
4) Identity of documents used within system.	____	____
5) Built-in controls and audit trails.	____	____
6) Console messages and halt delays with appropriate corrective actions.	____	____
c. Description of production operations.	____	____
1) Production job flow, with sequence of job steps.	____	____
2) Run time and timing, volumes, frequency, storage and peripheral machinery requirements.	____	____
3) Terminal operators' instructions, console messages, language, checks and halt and restart procedures.	____	____
4) Handling of input and output data.	____	____
5) Files, passwords, codes with security description.	____	____
E. Audit the records of project costs, on a test basis, to determine that systems and records are properly controlled, adequate, timely and accurate.	____	____
1. Review method of allocating the department's administrative costs to the individual projects.	____	____
2. Review system for charging departments for computer time used to process their work.	____	____
a. Determine that the system for allocating charges is equitable and based on accurate records.	____	____
3. Determine that the planning schedule contains time slots for testing and debugging programs.	____	____
F. Interview supervisors who are users of major computer projects. Determine whether the service level has been satisfactory, and operational problems resolved.	____	____
1. Review EDP's system for handling complaints.	____	____
2. Review downtime records and performance records.	____	____
a. *Determine the major reasons for down time and evaluate the corrective measures taken.*	____	____
G. Test-check modification procedures. Select a program and do the following:	____	____
1. Verify that proper authorizations exist for each change.	____	____
2. Determine that the change was performed properly.	____	____
3. *If program testing requires using live data, determine*		

III. Audit Procedures — *Per. Cov.* / *Audit By*

that duplicate file is prepared and used as precaution. ____ ____

4. Print out a current program and compare with the file copy. Look for unauthorized changes, and carefully study highly specialized subroutines. ____ ____
5. Determine if programs are maintained by originators. If so, determine that adequate controls exist over changes. ____ ____

H. Review controls over access to software and to related documentation. ____ ____

1. Ensure that documentation is physically secure and that access to it is carefully controlled. ____ ____
2. *Determine that application programmers are not permitted in the production room, and do not operate computers.* ____ ____
    a. In emergencies when entry is necessary, determine that programmer activities are closely supervised. ____ ____
3. Determine that there is adequate control when application programmers use on-line system for developing software. ____ ____
4. Ensure that programs which allow bypassing of normal controls are prohibited. *If emergency bypassing is required, ensure that procedures call for the presence of top EDP supervisory personnel.* ____ ____
5. Ensure that there are no backdoors to system software. ____ ____
6. Determine that written procedures exist for recovery of the data base in event of total or partial destruction. ____ ____
    a. Determine that access to the data base is under tight security and is closely controlled. ____ ____
    b. Determine that periodic reviews are conducted to ensure that no unauthorized changes have been made. ____ ____
7. Review rerun records and determine reasons. Evaluate supervisory follow-up and action. ____ ____
8. Determine that program designers tried to build in a system that encourages special reports of exceptions, rather than full complete voluminous reports that no one will ever read completely. ____ ____
9. Determine that an efficient high level language is used so as to make future changes and portability possible and easy to accomplish. ____ ____

I. Review computer department controls over input data. ____ ____

1. Determine that written directives relating to input controls are understood and followed. ____ ____

III. Audit Procedures *Per. Cov.* *Audit By*

a. Review records of receipt of input data. See that they contain batch totals or document counts. ____ ____
b. Review system for reconciling control information: such as run to run controls, batch controls, and file balances. ____ ____

J. Review computer department controls over output data. ____ ____
1. Examine the schedule of computer generated reports. ____ ____
 a. Review the distribution list for each report. ____ ____
2. Determine that output is reviewed, before distribution, to assure reasonableness of the reported data. ____ ____
3. Determine that specific instructions exist and are followed for program run failures. ____ ____

K. Review procedures for manual intervention in programs. ____ ____
1. *Ensure that operating controls are adequate to prevent abuse or unauthorized alteration of a working program.* ____ ____
2. Ensure that complete records are made of intervention. ____ ____

L. Select several critical programs (not audited recently): ____ ____
1. Review all documentation for completeness and security. ____ ____
2. Evaluate the applicable communications network. ____ ____
3. Dump a program and compare to approved specifications and documentation. ____ ____
4. Evaluate controls over input and output. ____ ____
 a. Review the edit and validation routines. ____ ____
  1) Evaluate built-in logic checks and audit trails. ____ ____
 b. Review error reporting, control and resubmission. ____ ____
5. Ensure that any patching is fully documented and that the work is fully described, justified and approved. ____ ____
 a. *Determine that patching has not compromised the integrity and internal controls in the system.* ____ ____
 b. See whether user's manuals are promptly amended when changes are made in a computer program. ____ ____
6. Review contents of output, and its distribution. ____ ____
 a. Review for necessity, all reported data. ____ ____
 b. Determine whether all personnel on the distribution list need to receive copies. ____ ____
 c. Determine whether exception reporting could suffice. ____ ____
7. Audit data base, and ensure adequate security. ____ ____
 a. Compare *test* data base to live base. ____ ____
 b. Use test data, (prepared by the EDP audit group) to audit processing and output. ____ ____
  1) Upon completion of test, *be certain to delete any*

III. Audit Procedures — *Per. Cov.* | *Audit By*

data which you introduced into the system. ____ ____

8. Review procedures for filing and retaining sources of documents. Can they be easily retrieved if necessary? ____ ____
9. Review backup plans and facilities. ____ ____

M. Review specs and documentation for modems and terminals. ____ ____
   1. Test selected pieces of equipment to determine that they conform to specifications. ____ ____
   2. Determine that phone numbers are changed at regular intervals and provide for electronic identification. ____ ____
   3. *Evaluate error detection and control capabilities.* ____ ____
   4. Determine that central system has flexibility in transmitting data to one or more terminals. ____ ____
   5. See that spare modems have been provided where deemed appropriate. ____ ____
   6. Determine that available data is sufficient to aid in reconstructing total system, if necessary. ____ ____

N. Arrange to have auditors in the production and printing rooms at the following times: ____ ____
   1. Disbursement checks or customer Invoices are printed. ____ ____
      a. Compare payees to the printed disbursement register. ____ ____
      b. *On a test basis, open envelopes and compare the checks to the printed information on the register.* ____ ____
      c. Perform same procedure for customer invoices. ____ ____
   2. Payroll checks or drafts are written. ____ ____
      a. Take possession of the checks and verify that they are written for legitimate employees. ____ ____
      b. Compare payees to the payroll register. ____ ____
   3. *Verify arithmetic, to determine that the third decimal is properly rounded up or down.* ____ ____
   4. Ensure that checks or drafts are properly distributed. ____ ____

O. Audit the computer department's payroll records, using the program in your audit manual titled Auditing Payroll. ____ ____
   1. Visit the computer production and programming sections during the off hours to see if supervision is adequate; if employees are efficiently employed and that *idle time or equipment is not used for personal business.* ____ ____
   2. Review personnel records and discuss with supervisors whether any of their people are engaged in outside activities that conflict with their company duties. ____ ____
   3. Review travel expenses for the previous three months. ____ ____

III. Audit Procedures — *Per. Cov.* | *Audit By*

a. Check for supporting documentation and for trip reports showing the results of the trips.

P. Spot check library records; from the listing of shelf items (that you prepared) to library records and from library records to shelf stock to verify that records are accurate and current.

1. *Follow up to locate missing tapes and disks.*
   a. First determine that disks have not been returned and refiled without a proper record being made.
   b. If still missing, contact computer production manager and request that missing disks be located.
2. Determine that the computer library maintains an accurate record of all computer disks or tapes that are in-transit.
   a. Follow up to ensure that record is accurate and that all in-transit items have been received.
3. Check empty disks and those ready for reuse to ensure that they do not contain any current information.
   a. Verify proper disposition of faulty tapes or disks.

Q. Review the department's purchasing procedures. Use the program in your manual titled Auditing Purchasing.

1. Review the purchasing procedures used for selecting the suppliers of the data terminals, modems and printers used at all locations throughout the company.
2. Review the decision making process that decides on the purchase and use of the input devices for sales representatives throughout the company.
   a. Should Purchasing get involved in these purchases?
3. Check purchase price of tapes and disks to see if competition is used in purchasing these items.
4. Check to see that competitive bids are received on purchases of all paper products.
   a. Determine that paper products are independently received and correct receiving reports prepared.
5. *Determine that economic order quantities are considered when deciding quantities to order.*
6. Review value analyses studies that support important purchases. Ensure that the logic and the figures used are applicable and accurate.

R. Check machine log records and tie back and verify billings for rented equipment. (See item S.1.a.)

1. If equipment is rented, see if terms are competitive and whether outright purchase would save money.
2. *Determine if there is idle computer time, and whether*

III. Audit Procedures	*Per. Cov.*	*Audit By*
some rental equipment could be returned to vendor.	____	____
3. Review machine records for use of owned equipment.	____	____
a. Determine if any personal work is being run.	____	____
S. Audit the property assigned to the department using the program in your manual titled Auditing Property.	____	____
1. Pay particular attention to rented equipment in the department. Schedule all such items.	____	____
a. *Tie your schedule into equipment rental billings.*	____	____
T. Audit disbursements authorized by the department, using the program in your manual titled Auditing Payables.	____	____
1. Determine whether utility bills for the computer section are sent to an outside utility audit agency for review.	____	____
U. If there are any cash funds in the department, audit them using the Cash Audit Program in your manual.	____	____
V. Review the department's method of prioritizing work. Is the basis need? Or position of requester?	____	____
W. Review general security in the department.	____	____
1. Determine that any security breaches are immediately reported to appropriate data processing management.	____	____
2. Review contingency plan for computer operations during periods of prolonged business interruptions.	____	____
3. Determine that backup facilities are tested.	____	____
a. Review contract agreements with outside services.	____	____
4. Review security precautions used during off-shift hours.	____	____
5. Review system for security and accounting for supplies.	____	____
a. Make a physical count of paper, envelopes, ribbons and new disks and tapes.	____	____
1) Obtain reasonable estimate of supply usage.	____	____
2) Use department's record of opening inventory, and prepare settlement of purchases vs usage.	____	____
6. Determine that an adequate sprinkler system exists, and that all fire fighting equipment is regularly checked.	____	____
7. Determine when last inspections were made of fire fighting equipment and of the total security system.	____	____
8. Determine that power backup system is adequate to take over in the event of a power surge or outage.	____	____
9. Determine that security over entry into critical programs is air tight. *See that system for controlling access entry codes prevents entry by unauthorized parties.*	____	____
X. Ascertain whether financial systems have special accounts for audit use; such as dummy A/R or A/P, partial cases		

III. Audit Procedures	*Per. Cov.*	*Audit By*
for inventories, currency conversion balances and inter-company transfers or claims.	____	____
1. Review the use of and control over these accounts.	____	____
Y. Review method of costing the work performed on the various projects.		
1. Pay particular attention to the allocation of the departments' overhead expenses to projects.	____	____
Z. Review training programs conducted by the department for material content and appropriateness of personnel trained.	____	____

Audit work approved by ______________________ Date ____________

INTERNAL CONTROL QUESTIONNAIRE

The following internal control questions are intended to direct your attention to the high-risk areas of the Computer Department operations. Many of these points are covered in the audit program, but are listed here to ensure that they receive adequate attention. Answer these questions as your audit progresses.

In section B, insert the name and the job title of the employee responsible for discharging the listed function. Be certain to list any conflicting activities that might jeopardize internal controls.

Internal Control Questionnaire

A. *Following are listed practices that indicate good internal control:*
1. Employees that run computer programs do not have access to printouts, particularly checks or invoices.
2. Any program designs or changes are approved by Computer Department management and the Internal Audit Staff.
3. Employees who order computer supplies do not receive the items.
4. The operating departments that receive computer printouts and reports, check for accuracy of such information.
5. All operations of the department are monitored by an independent committee of knowledgable executives.

B. *Following lists functions performed by named employees:*

Function:	*Name/Position*	*Conflicting Duties*
1. Schedules production runs.	__________	__________
2. Loads programs.	__________	__________
3. Orders supplies.	__________	__________
4. Receives supplies.	__________	__________
5. Authorizes payments.	__________	__________
6. Removes data from mail room.	__________	__________
7. Prepares bills for services.	__________	__________

C. *Internal Control Questions*	*Yes*	*No*	*Remarks*
1. Do preliminary studies consider, during design:			
a. Transmission requirements?	____	____	__________

C. Internal Control Questions	*Yes*	*No*	*Remarks*
1) Do they consider all factors relating to our complete network?	____	____	____
a) *Is a central site established for reporting all problems encountered?*	____	____	____
b. Suitability of existing computers, modems and terminals?	____	____	____
1) Are both controlled and uncontrolled terminals considered?	____	____	____
c. Data base and software requirements?	____	____	____
1) Do they include directories, all related activities and both periodic and special request reporting?	____	____	____
2) *Is an audit trail created of all changes to the data base?*	____	____	____
d. Adaptability and potential expansion?	____	____	____
1) Is flexibility built-in to enable tie-ins to current or probable future applications?	____	____	____
2. Do the programmers and designers consciously attempt to use all spaces to reduce processing time and paper usage?	____	____	____
a. Are computer terminal formats designed to use data entry screen space efficiently?	____	____	____
1) *Is access to the data base restricted to only authorized terminals?*	____	____	____
2) Are access codes tightly controlled?	____	____	____
3. Is production control program working properly.	____	____	____
a. Are controls adequate to ensure that proper disks are used during computer processing?	____	____	____
4. Does the department promptly correct problems?	____	____	____
a. *Are user complaints handled properly?*	____	____	____
5. Is each modification thoroughly			

C. Internal Control Questions	*Yes*	*No*	*Remarks*
tested before implementation?	___	___	___
a. Are users promptly notified of all changes to a system?	___	___	___
b. Do procedures ensure that backup programs are current?	___	___	___
6. Can system software commands be entered from several sources?	___	___	___
a. Is it possible for a remote terminal to be configured as a master command point?	___	___	___
7. Does Data Control have a schedule listing when data is due from user departments? Do they do the following:	___	___	___
a. Ensure that only authorized data is processed?	___	___	___
b. Reconcile totals received to input totals submitted by users?	___	___	___
8. Are adequate and efficient methods used to assure accuracy of data entered into the computer?	___	___	___
a. *Do the systems acknowledge the successful or unsuccessful receipt of all messages?*	___	___	___
b. Is handling of input data adequate to prevent duplicate processing?	___	___	___
9. Are records retained of EDP errors which were found by Data Control and user departments?	___	___	___
a. *Are all error corrections approved by an independent supervisor?*	___	___	___
10. Does originator receive a listing of inputs in proper form to be easily reviewed and approved?	___	___	___
11. Do procedures ensure that users are promptly notified of delays in processing EDP data?	___	___	___
12. Are tapes, disks and manuals in the computer library well controlled?	___	___	___
a. Is there a complete record made of every movement of all tapes or disks?	___	___	___
b. *Could tapes or disks be copied without the knowledge of computer management?*	___	___	___
13. Are controls adequate to prevent			

C. Internal Control Questions	*Yes*	*No*	*Remarks*
computer operators from removing console control sheets?	____	____	____________
14. Do formal agreements with outside vendors spell out damages in event of their default?	____	____	____________
a. Are there provisions for arbitration?	____	____	____________
b. Can either party cancel the agreement?	____	____	____________
1) Is the notification period appropriate?	____	____	____________
15. Is the purchasing of specialized computer items well-controlled?	____	____	____________
a. Are computer supplies periodically counted?	____	____	____________
b. Are regular inventory reports prepared and used for ordering of supplies?	____	____	____________
16. Is the method of allocating overhead costs to specific projects equitable and accurate?	____	____	____________
17. *Is the principle of exception reporting being used to the fullest extent possible?*	____	____	____________
18. Is disk spacing reviewed to assure efficient use?	____	____	____________
19. *Are computer programs working to properly handle fractions of whole numbers?*	____	____	____________
20. Is security adequate over output reports, files and documents?	____	____	____________
a. Do test data bases exist?	____	____	____________
1) Is the live data base properly separated from any test base created?	____	____	____________
21. Do precautions ensure adequate destruction of all confidential data?	____	____	____________
22. Are passwords randomly and frequently changed?	____	____	____________
23. Are security regulations enforced during the second and third operating shifts?	____	____	____________
a. Does the picture identity card effectively control movements in the computer area?	____	____	____________

C. Internal Control Questions	*Yes*	*No*	*Remarks*
b. *Are employees well prepared for emergencies?*	____	____	____________
c. Is the computer production room kept clean and free of dust and smoke?	____	____	____________

Questions answered by ______________________ Date ____________
Answers reviewed by ______________________ Date ____________

CRITICAL POINTS

The large quantity of transactions, the speed of the calculations, the intricacy of the mechanics and the dearth of the usual hard copy of transaction records makes the life of a data processing auditor very difficult. Computer manipulations and frauds are reported daily, and value of dollars involved and numbers of cases are substantial. All of the danger signals relating to kickbacks and manipulations of expense reporting that we referred to in other chapters also appear in the field of data processing.

However, there are some special types of manipulations that are facilitated by the use of computers. We will mention a few of the more unusual events.

SIX MANIPULATIONS TO WATCH OUT FOR

1. Computers are used to calculate and prepare any type of checks or drafts needed. Computers customarily produce payroll checks for all employees, and also calculate amounts of disbursement checks, dividend and interest checks and other types of pay outs. Many of these calculations involve carrying a decimal point to three or four places. **CAUTION:** *There are several cases on record where fractional cents, that is the figure beyond the second decimal place, have been dropped from the calculation and writing of a check, and instead transferred to a special account known only to the programmer.* The substantial dollars accumulated in this manner was periodically paid out by a check written against this special account.

   One audit technique that can detect this type of manipulation is to perform a manual calculation on a sampling of checks drawn for a specific purpose. The sample must be of calculations that involve fractional pennies. *If all fractional cents are dropped, then you know you have problems.* But if the program is designed to increase the cent if the third position is a five or above, but to drop and accumulate all fractions below five, then you could not be certain.

   The best procedure is to obtain the production run program and dump it. Then have an EDP auditor, an expert designer or a programmer study the program and make certain that there is proper handling of the decimals in the third position and beyond.

2. There are many reported cases where computers have been used to transfer funds from dormant bank accounts to an account from which the funds can be easily withdrawn. Such manipulations, on a manual basis, have been frequently reported, but the use of a computer makes it easier to do and harder to detect. It also facilitates a gradual siphoning rather than a one shot transfer that might attract attention. The siphoning also has the affect of transferring the account out of the dormant class into an active class and makes it easier to manipulate.

   Dormant bank accounts are regularly reported and closely watched by the internal auditors, so there is a risk involved in tapping these accounts. **KEY POINT:** *When a dormant account has any action at all, the internal auditor should investigate and track down the movement of funds and verify that all transactions are legitimate.* At the first withdrawal, an examination should be initiated and followed through even if it means personal contact with the individual in whose name the account was opened.

3. A computer follows directions implicitly and does not conduct a reasonability check unless it has been programmed to do so. Program directions decide how figures must be entered and how computations will be made by the computer.

   If an entry operator skips entering a decimal point, the resulting error can be gigantic. There are many reported cases where the elimination of a decimal point resulted in the computer writing checks for fabulous amounts. Fifty dollars becomes five thousand, and so on.

   It is generally difficult to create internal logic checks that detect an operator's entry error, but a system can require that a decimal point be entered before a figure will be accepted. It is possible, and should be required in every critical program, to build in logic and reasonability checks that question any single computation that falls outside a logical range.

   In order to have a practical operating program, these internal checks must be capable of being overridden, and the *danger is that a reject may be hastily approved even though a gross error has occurred.* Having all rejects spelled out in a daily printed report that goes to the internal audit department might discourage manual overrides from being made without proper investigation.

4. A computer requires electrical power to operate, and it requires a steady, uninterrupted power supply to operate accurately. There are many cases

on record where a temporary loss of power has resulted in the substantial loss of data in computer processing operations. Sometimes, these power surges create situations in which data is lost without any outward signs that a problem has developed. The same situation can be caused by tapes or disks being exposed to magnets.

These problems come to light when someone spots gross errors in reports or other types of computer output. Sometimes the loss of data may go unnoticed until period-ending reports are run. A daily tie-in of all batches of data entered into the system, against processed work, might bring the problem to light the following day.

To prevent this type of computer problem from occurring, emergency generators are held on a standby basis to instantaneously operate at the first indication of a potential loss of power. This power supply is completely independent of the normal sources, and also goes into operation at any interruption of normal power flow. **TIP:** *If your company has such an emergency source of power, determine when the system was last checked.*

5. Sophisticated computers are very expensive and very fast. They have the ability to complete a project in a very short time. Given unlimited access, these machines can be useful to a knowledgeable expert who wants to use them for personal work.

   Night shifts usually have a minimum staff, and security controls are frequently relaxed since so few employees are on the premises. There are cases of night supervisors using computers to perform personal projects, in some instances as a part of a business venture. Total computer running time is usually minimal, but the practice can get out of hand if not detected and stopped at an early stage.

   This practice is particularly difficult to spot if a designer or programmer works at night to debug programs or design new applications. There is usually a period when the technician has free reign with the computer and the printouts. This is an ideal time to run personal work without fear of detection.

   Good supervision, and continuance of security measures at all hours, can discourage these activities. **KEY POINT:** *Surprise visits by managers to the night operations can also help improve controls.*

6. Computer operations are not immune to the more mundane thefts that occur in manufacturing or selling operations. **CAUTION:** *Wherever there is a storage point for inventories, there is a danger of theft.*

   Large computer operations must maintain a large supply of items required in the production of paper work. Most thefts in the computer area are of paper and disks or tapes. There are instances of theft of computer terminals and portable computers. Printing ribbons are another favorite walk-away item.

One way of reducing this type of loss is to make someone responsible for these supplies, and insist that a reconciliation be periodically prepared of usage versus purchases. At least that should give management an idea of the extent of such losses.

Chapter 26

Auditing a Security Department and Related Services

Every organization has some type of a security operation. It may be a major department or it may consist of a small staff. The responsibility may be divided among the operating departments, without having a formal coordinating security department. Some companies use the internal audit staff to handle selective security responsibilities.

An audit of a *separate* Security Department is approached in the same manner as that of any other service activity. The audit must examine the stated responsibilities of the operation, and determine if it is fulfilling its obligation in an efficient and economical manner.

The security function commonly covers many of the following:

1. Security guard force,
2. Visitor control,
3. Emergency assistance,
4. TV surveillance,
5. Package pass and locker inspections,
6. Weigh master,
7. Exit check for products or tools being taken from premises,
8. Building evacuations and fire drills,
9. Handling bomb or extortion threats,
10. Preemployment checks,
11. Apprehending thieves,
12. Conducting interrogations.

It is not possible to foresee and protect against every conceivable security risk. At best the security function should be flexible and intelligently prepared so that immediate action can be taken to hold security losses to a minimum.

A Security Department may employ a staff of security officers; may contract with outside agencies that supply such people, or use a combination of both approaches. Many security functions are headed up by a chief security official who has an office in the headquarters building. The usual organization chart lists an assistant, several supervisors and perhaps a staff of investigators. Each company location may have a designated security officer who operates alone or has a staff of security guards. If an outside guard service is employed, it reports to the local security official.

In this chapter we will deal with the auditing of security operations no matter how they are organized. Certain types of security matters are covered here, but interrogations and thefts are covered in Chapter 29 on Fraud.

Auditors are concerned with the adequacy and nature of physical security over property, personnel, production formulas and processes, and confidential materials. They also review costs, the manner in which the service is procured, and the department's purchases of supplies and necessary services. Finally, they are concerned with the recording and reporting of all security operations.

Communication can be costly. But this type of expense can be controlled. The major communications services are sound and visual transmissions and mailing activities. Both require handling by outsiders, and are watched closely by security personnel.

There are many telephone service options available, and companies use communication analysts to determine the best and most economical telephone systems and equipment which may include computer to computer communications.

Mailing services offer a variety of delivery and rate options. Although the U.S. Postal Service has a monopoly on home carrier letter delivery, many competitors operate to deliver packages and urgent priority messages. The importance and timing of a message, and the cost of transmitting the information to the proper party at the right time, determines the method to be used.

In all communication areas, we are interested in the selection of options, the control of costs and the security given to information transmitted. Auditors also review charges for these services.

The sample audit program is designed for an internal audit of a security operation. It covers a complete review of a formal security department and of mailing and telephone operations. Any part may be used where applicable.

Background Information

The following program is used in the XYZ Corporation, which has a centralized Security Department headquartered in the main office. The department is responsible for the physical security of all company assets, personnel and confidential written matter. The Director of Security, a staff position reporting to the Financial Vice-President, is responsible for all security policies and procedures.

The Director of Security is responsible for the security of the Headquarters building. A staff of company employees perform security guard services at that building. The Director makes the final decision as to the security requirements at any company location.

At some locations, outside guard services are used because they provide a number of advantages over an in-house force, such as:

1. Outside agencies are flexible and can supply required trained guards upon short notice.
2. Rates charged are reasonable and they cover all fringe benefits.
3. Agencies provide continuous supervision of their employees to insure that their guards remain alert and perform their jobs. And,
4. They can quickly bring in guards to cover for illnesses, vacations or terminations.

At other locations, company employees are used as security guards. The advantages of in-house security forces are the following:

- Management can ensure that these people receive training that meets company imposed guidelines.
- Supervisors can monitor job performances.
- Instructions to guards can be changed whenever necessary. And,
- Locations can immediately apprise all guards of procedural changes.

Each major XYZ location has a small security force that reports to the location manager. These groups receive policy and procedure guidance from the Director of Security, and are frequently visited by the Director or the Assistant Director. All changes required in an individual location's staff are discussed with the local manager who orders the changes that are approved by the head office.

The Director of Security works very closely with the Internal Auditing Department, and uses the staff to conduct special studies when such use is appropriate. On the other hand, the audit staff reports certain observations to the security department when they are the appropriate group to take action.

Appearance of security, or perceived security, is sometimes as effective as real security in place. Wrongdoers usually look for soft touches, and will often avoid a location that appears to be well guarded. They seek targets of opportunity, and direct their attention to locations that do not appear to have any security measures.

The Director of Security has issued a Security Manual which is used in all company locations by personnel responsible for security operations. All concerned employees are obligated to follow the procedures outlined in the manual. In addition to this manual, the various operating and staff departments have issued directives on the subject of security as it affects their particular operations. All executives have a responsibility for security over their department's operations, personnel and information.

The XYZ security forces that are concerned with perimeter security at major locations may be in-house employees or outside agency guards. They are supervised by a designated manager at the location. These groups, whether in-house or outside agencies, follow the procedures and policies stated in the security manual. Each manual may include some additional items to meet individual problems or unusual conditions existing at a particular location.

Security uses outside agencies whenever necessary for specific assignments. One common type of usage is to conduct preemployment checks on information shown in applications of prospective employees.

There are several competent agencies that the Security Department turns to for help in this area. Credit bureaus can provide credit information concerning individuals. Other information reported on these applications can be checked out by a variety of investigative agencies who are familiar with all public records and know how to research them with a minimum of effort.

This chapter is concerned with security measures to protect a major complex which contains the headquarters office, a distribution center. a sales branch and a production plant. The audit program encompasses all security considerations at this complex.

The mailing function is a responsibility of the Financial Department. The mailing supervisor reports to a controller in general accounting. There is a central mail room in the headquarters building where all incoming and outgoing letters and packages are processed, separate from the receiving room for products or supplies.

Mail room supervisors are also responsible for controlling the EDP output of checks, invoices and shipping papers. Mail personnel take charge of the computer printing room when critical papers are run. The ancillary equipment in the room strips, separates, inserts into window envelopes and seals the envelopes making them ready for stamping and mailing. The closed envelopes are placed in a bag which is sealed and carted to the mail room for final processing. To take advantage of rate concessions, the mail room sorts some outgoing mail by zip code, and then bags it for specific post offices.

Mailing handles the daily transfer of critical computer disks in the son, father, grandfather sequence of providing back-up security over vital information. This section is also responsible for the postal meters used in the headquarters complex.

The supervisor of telephone services in Corporate Headquarter's building reports to the Office Services Manager in general accounting.

XYZ has several WATTS lines, and has a separate private phone line for every full time employee. All employees are free to use their individual phones as required, but are requested to attempt to use the WATTS lines for long distance calls. Two of the WATTS lines are operator controlled, so that important calls can be prioritized and put through. If all WATTS lines are tied up, rush calls are made on the employee's line using the normal long distance channels.

With the above information in mind, look at a sample internal audit program used to review the headquarter's Security operations and the field operations of any and all security personnel.

INTERNAL AUDIT PROGRAM—INSTRUCTIONS

IA SI26

XYZ CORPORATION
SECURITY DEPARTMENT AND RELATED SERVICES
INTERNAL AUDIT PROGRAM—INSTRUCTIONS

This audit program is designed to lead you through an in-depth review of a Security Department and the related activities of Mailing and Telephonic Services. It applies to XYZ's Headquarter's operation as well as any of the company's field locations or operations.

A. Before starting your audit, carefully review these instructions, the associated check-off program (IA SP25), and the attached Internal Control Questionnaire.
B. Study annual budgets, and last six months operating costs.
C. You will analyze security costs, but these are not broken out in some locations' operating statements. Extract the portion that is directly related to security and estimate the additional costs. Be certain that security is audited at all locations where the cost of the function is well above average.
D. Read the Security Manual, and all bulletins in the Personnel and the Accounting Manuals that relate to security.
E. Read all Accounting Manual directives that are related to communication problems, specifically Mail and Telephone.
F. Meet with the Director of Security and discuss the audit approach. Request the Director to inform security supervisors that auditors have authority to visit any guard post at any time during an audit. This is to insure that a surprise visit does not result in untoward actions.
G. When reviewing case studies, bear in mind that a successful security operation is designed to *prevent* incidences, rather than to catch the culprits. **KEY POINT:** *A location that would be expected to have problems, but has none, shows a successful security program.*
H. When you wish to check the job being performed by security guards at their stations, be certain that, *in advance,* you discuss the matter with the location manager and the chief of security. **CAUTION:** *Be certain that they know what you plan to do, but don't tell them the exact time or day that you plan to do it.*

   You want your visit to be a surprise. **TIP:** *If possible visit the guards during the early morning hours to see if they are alert during the off hours.* On your visits, stop at each guard post, during each shift, so that auditors see every guard that is on the payroll, and so that they will know that someone is interested in their service.

I. When you audit a security function at a location that uses a guard force of XYZ employees you must keep in mind the major drawback of using such a staff. *Guards are often drawn from other positions in the company.* In production plants, long time employees that can no longer perform their customary line functions may be assigned to the guard force. **KEY POINT:** *Such transfers can result in the new guard being friendly with former work mates and, therefore, not challenging their actions even when company rules are being broken.*

J. You should determine that security guards are alertly performing their jobs at all hours of day or night, without being affected by the operating status of the location. Security guards must closely monitor movements into and out of an XYZ complex.

Where guards play a part in the weight control program, you should determine that they are fully aware of, and are properly handling, their responsibilities. **KEY POINT:** *Security guards who serve as weigh masters should be versed in the intricacies and pitfalls inherent in the weighing of large, heavy vehicles.*

A guard who notes a weight discrepancy that exceeds allowable limits, should call a line supervisor and state the difference between the scale and the manifest weight. The guard is instructed to follow the direction of the line supervisor.

During your review, if you note that operating personnel are not paying attention to the weight control operation, and are routinely passing all exceptions through; take possession of the records and discuss the problem with the location manager. **IMPORTANT:** *Unless there is a very good reason for this attitude, the manager should immediately take drastic action to correct the situation.*

From your study of weight reports, note what actions are instructed by the various line supervisors. If any decisions raise a question in your mind, make notes of the most recent cases and discuss them with the line manager that made the decision. If you are not satisfied with the reasoning, discuss the matter with the supervisor's boss. **IMPORTANT:** *If you are not completely satisfied, bring the matter to the immediate attention of the Manager of Internal Auditing.*

K. Become thoroughly familiar with the procedures for test weighing of loads. Some of the instructions appear in the Security Manual, and you will find more detailed audit information in the program in your manual titled Auditing a Plant or Distribution Center.

CAUTION: *Remember that if the vehicle is not positioned on the scale properly, the weight will be considerably off.* Drivers are aware of this and may deliberately rest part of a tire off the scale platform. The guard must check for proper positioning.

To reduce the number of trucks weighed, those that regularly come and go, may be weighed once to establish a standard empty weight. This standard is then used as the empty weight in calculating the weight of a load carried.

During your visit to the weigh master guard station, have the guard weigh selected empty vehicles that have an established empty weight. Choose two or three on each shift when there is no truck movement. **IMPORTANT:** *If your test weights do not correspond to the standard weight used for the vehicle, notify the head of security and the manager. They should arrange to have all trucks reweighed. If you meet any opposition, notify the Manager of Internal Auditing.*

You are not a security expert, but your common sense will spot a gross failure in security. Don't hesitate to ask questions.

L. Each guard is expected to be fully aware of the contents of the book of instructions which is on file at every guard station. This book contains much information; some of the more important items are the following:
   1) Names and telephone numbers of people to notify in emergencies.
   2) Visitor controls, containing restrictions that apply to people who attempt to enter the complex.
   3) Nature of alarms to be given, how and under what conditions.
   4) What degree of force may be used, and how it is to be applied.
   5) What conditions justify shutting down a guard post, and what procedures must be followed.
   6) What reports are to be prepared, how they are to be prepared, and where they should be sent.

   During your visits to the guard posts you should determine that security officers are well-versed in the above instructions. Any who are not should be reported to the chief security official.

M. A security system must provide immediate assistance in the event of an emergency. It must also provide for the relief of a guard and immediate substitution or replacement of a guard at any time. Such emergencies are frequently handled by supervisory personnel.

N. Security personnel must be continually alert to any diversionary act designed to draw their attention away from an area where an illegal act is planned. Guards may be stationed at switchboards or TV monitors where they watch for signs of intrusion. If a suspicious act occurs, a guard must decide whether to investigate or remain at the assigned post and merely record the time and nature of the breach. Communication facilities should enable the guard at the monitor to contact field guards and direct them to the breached areas.

O. You must be alert to the possibility that in their zeal to protect the company, some security people might be tempted to bend the rules. XYZ cannot tolerate such actions. *We do not permit phone tapping, recording of conversations, voice analysis or polygraph testing without the express consent of all parties involved.*

   Any extraordinary action by the Security Department must have the prior approval of the Financial Vice-President. If you note any questionable act by security personnel, discuss the matter with the Director of Security. *If you are still not satisfied, bring the matter to the attention of the Director of Internal Audits.*

P. Security provides a preemployment checking service for Personnel. When the Personnel Department seriously considers adding a new employee, they request that the employment application be checked out. Security usually uses an outside agency for this service.

Q. Mail couriers, or robot carriers, pass each desk at scheduled rounds during the day to deliver incoming and pick up outgoing mail. Mail is sorted in the mail room, stamped, bagged and the bags are sealed ready for shipment. Some are picked up by post office trucks, others are delivered by messengers to the airport or main post office.

R. When the computer is running critical items, the output room is controlled and manned by mail personnel. Mail supervision is present during the entire running period. Documents are printed, processed, bagged and carted directly to the mail room.

S. All outgoing personal mail must be stamped by the sender. The cashier, the mail room and several departments provide a stamp fund for the sale of personal stamps, as a convenience to employees. *Audit these stamp funds, if they have not recently been reviewed.*

T. All mail room personnel wear company supplied uniforms that do not have pockets. They change into their uniforms in the adjoining locker room, before entering the mail processing room. At completion of the shift, after donning street clothes, they do not reenter the mail room.

U. Every permanent XYZ employee is assigned a private telephone, which may be used for personal calls when necessary. Employees are expected to keep personal calls to a minimum, but are not charged for personal local calls. *All employees are expected to pay for all personal long distance calls that they make.*

Phone bills are reviewed by supervisors who see that their people are properly billed, and pay for personal calls. The supervisor notes which calls are personal and the Employee Receivables section prepares the billings so that items are properly charged.

V. The WATTS lines are open to all employees, but they are to be used for company business during working hours. Personal calls are allowed over these lines after the office is closed. Some lines are tied up with incoming and outgoing computer data, but the open lines can be used by employees at no charge.

Two of the WATTS lines are operator controlled, so that important calls can get through quickly. The operator uses a priority listing to assign call sequence. If there is a long line waiting, the operator informs the requester who may then decide to make a direct call.

The other WATTS lines are open on an "as available" basis; an employee dials the line and if open, the call goes through immediately. If all lines are tied up, the caller keeps trying until a line is free.

A monthly report is prepared which lists the originating phone number, the phone number called, the time of day and the number of minutes used for all calls going through the WATTS lines. These reports are viewed by the telephone supervisor as a guide to the adequacy of the private phone line system.

W. The computer also provides a company wide electrical mail system for communications among locations. Each computer terminal has a printer which is used when required for the transmittal of administrative messages. This system must be used with discretion because the message may be read by anyone passing by the terminal.

X. Your audit will encompass all of the financial aspects of these operations. When an audit step requires a routine examination, you will be referred to the appropriate program in your audit manual.

Y. A description of the proper procedure for working with this internal audit program appears in the Introduction to the Audit Programs section of your manual. Read this information carefully.

Z. If you have any doubts or questions about any of the directions or information contained in this instructional write-up, discuss the matter with audit management *before* starting your audit.

INTERNAL AUDIT PROGRAM

IA SP25 XYZ CORPORATION

INTERNAL AUDIT PROGRAM—SECURITY AND RELATED SERVICES

This program is designed to assist in your audit of security responsibilities. Carefully read this program, the associated instructions (IA SI26), and the attached Internal Control Questionnaire before you start your review.

I. Company Procedures

A. The corporate Security Department is responsible for all external security in the company. The Director reports to the Financial Vice-President.

B. The department controls security at the headquarters complex, and it sets policies and procedures for controlling all other locations.

C. The department negotiates contracts with outside security agencies for services required at any company location.

D. The department works closely with mailing and telephone services to insure that their security is not compromised.

II. Audit Scope is to determine the following:

A. The Security Department performs its assigned task while adhering to company policies and ethical standards.

B. Rules, regulations and procedures established by Security, do not unnecessarily hamper business operations.

C. All reports are accurate, timely and complete and conform to all company requirements.

D. The department operates efficiently and economically, and it ensures that employees' legal rights and privacy are not violated.

E. Internal controls are in place and followed by all personnel in the Security, Telephone and Mailing operations.

F. All security officers are well-trained, with adequate instructions to ensure that they conform to the stated scope of the department.

III. Audit Procedures *All Departments*	*Per. Cov.*	*Audit By*
A. Review organization charts, job assignments and job descriptions of all personnel.	____	____
1. Study all forms and reports prepared in departments.	____	____
2. Look for areas of overlapping responsibilities.	____	____

	Per. Cov.	Audit By
III. Audit Procedures		
All Departments		
3. Determine that a designated responsible manager is available at all times during operations.	____	____
4. Determine that all employees are carefully screened before being hired.	____	____
a. Review procedures for selecting personnel for critical positions.	____	____
b. *Check hiring procedures for part-time or temporary employees.*	____	____
B. Review operating budgets for these activities.	____	____
1. Review system for drawing up budget requests.	____	____
2. Evaluate controls over use of budgeted funds.	____	____
C. Determine that the Purchasing Department is involved in the procurement of materials, supplies and services. Refer to the program in your manual titled Auditing Purchasing.	____	____
1. Pay particular attention to the agreements made with outside agencies and consultants.	____	____
a. Determine that departments consider a number of different agencies when awarding contracts.	____	____
b. Determine that contract prices are in line with competitive rates for comparable services in the area.	____	____
D. Review other payments authorized by a department. Refer to your manual audit program titled, Auditing Payables.	____	____
1. Review selected purchases of supplies and services for the adequacy of internal controls.	____	____
E. Verify the payroll of the Mailing, Telephone and Security Departments. Refer to the program in your manual titled Auditing Personnel and Payroll.	____	____
Security Department		
A. Study the XYZ Security Manual, and read security pages in the Accounting and the Personnel Manuals. Determine that the Security Manual is current and is provided to and used by personnel in all security operations.	____	____
1. Review operating expense statements to determine costs of security in total and at the various locations.	____	____
a. Schedule security costs by location. If costs are not shown as separate item, make an estimate.	____	____
b. *Arrange to have an audit of high cost operations.*	____	____
B. Meet with the Director of Security and department supervisors and discuss their approach to security problems, and the concepts used to deal with security challenges.	____	____
1. Determine the Director's attitude toward the use of outside services as opposed to in-house security guards.	____	____
a. Determine security management's attitude toward		

III. Audit Procedures *Per. Cov.* *Audit By*
Security Department

employee's rights to privacy and respectful treatment. ____ ____

2. Review the security files to determine types of reports regularly prepared by security officers. ____ ____
   a. Procedures require that all guards submit a daily report of all unusual events that occurred during shift. ____ ____
      1) Determine if these reports are reviewed by supervisors, and when appropriate, referred to line management and other interested parties. ____ ____
      2) See if distribution of these reports is proper. ____ ____
      3) *See if appropriate corrective action is taken.* ____ ____
3. Review reports of security supervisors. Determine that they report posts visited, time and results of visits. ____ ____
   a. *Any deficiencies should be followed up to learn what corrective action was taken.* ____ ____
4. Determine that every company location has a security program that has been approved by the Director. ____ ____
   a. Determine that the program provides for an emergency evacuation of the premises, if necessary. ____ ____
   b. All visitors should be required to pass a control point and sign a register indicating in and out time. ____ ____
      1) The identification tag system should ensure that all tags are picked up as visitors leave. ____ ____
   c. Specific supervisors in all areas of a building should be designated to question anyone not known by sight. ____ ____
   d. Procedures should require that all extinguishers and fire hoses be clearly marked. Designated employees should know the locations and how to use the equipment. ____ ____
5. Review department's case study reports. See that they are circulated to all managers that might benefit. ____ ____
6. Review gate reports of incoming and exiting vehicles. ____ ____
   a. *See that weight discrepancies are properly handled.* ____ ____
      1) Do reports describe actions taken by management? ____ ____
      2) Determine what action is taken if security guard does not agree with line supervisory decision. ____ ____
   b. If line supervisors' decisions do not appear proper, perform an in-depth study and *take appropriate action.* ____ ____

C. Visit guard posts when the complex is shut down. ____ ____
   1. Determine that guards satisfactorily perform tasks. ____ ____

III. Audit Procedures Security Department	*Per. Cov.*	*Audit By*
2. If any guards carry firearms:		
a. Determine which XYZ executive authorized such use.	_____	_____
b. Determine if guard is licensed to carry a gun.	_____	_____
c. Enquire if guard is proficient in the use.	_____	_____
3. Determine that the guard's rounds are not made at the same time or in the same fashion. Rounds should be varied so that their movements may not be anticipated.		
4. Revisit same posts at a later time to review activity of other security personnel.	_____	_____
5. Travel around perimeter of complex and examine condition of security fencing and underbrush.	_____	_____
a. Determine that all breaches have been reported.	_____	_____
1) See if appropriate action has been initiated.	_____	_____
6. If any activity is noted anywhere on the premises, contact the security supervisor and find out reasons.	_____	_____
7. Determine when gate locks were last changed. How many keys exist, and who controls the keys.	_____	_____
8. If outside contract guard service is used, visit posts during each guards assignment.		
a. Review the book of instructions with each guard.		
1) *Determine that each guard knows the contents.*	_____	_____
D. Review payments made to outside security agencies.	_____	_____
1. Verify that records are adequate to support payments.	_____	_____
2. Review the contracts between the agencies and XYZ.	_____	_____
a. Is language clear and free of ambiguities?	_____	_____
b. Determine that fees are reasonable and in line with fees charged by others in the community.	_____	_____
3. See that XYZ supervisors regularly determine that contract service is provided in a professional manner.	_____	_____
E. Review system used by Security Department to perform preemployment checks on prospective employees?	_____	_____
1. Determine that department checks out routine items with former employers and schools.	_____	_____
2. Determine that reliable, established agencies are used to obtain necessary information as to criminal or civil actions involving prospective employees.	_____	_____
a. Agencies located in area of employee's former residences should be used, to control costs.	_____	_____
F. If location has a TV monitoring system, check to see if a guard watches the screen at all times.	_____	_____
1. If a period is missed, determine if missed period is played back and viewed at first opportunity.	_____	_____
2. *See that camera blind spots are not in critical areas.*	_____	_____
a. Locate all blind spots in TV coverage and ascertain		

III. Audit Procedures *Security Department*	*Per.* *Cov.*	*Audit* *By*
that they do not include areas where doors are located.	____	____
b. Determine what action the guards take when vehicles or individuals move into blind spot areas.	____	____
3. *See if supervisors play back TV tapes for selected periods, as a check on the alertness of the monitors.*	____	____
4. Review procedures for retaining tapes. See that they are not erased until enough time has passed to be certain that any irregularities would have become known.		
G. Where perimeter guards are used to act as weigh masters:		
1. See that guards follow the explicit instructions in the Manual for weighing vehicles entering or departing.	____	____
2. See that no vehicle can pass the gate without being examined and weighed if necessary.	____	____
a. Confirm that guards are consistent in weighing equipment with driver either in, or out of the rig.	____	____
b. *Confirm that guards visually inspect the inside of the cabs, regardless of weather.*	____	____
c. Learn reasons and authority for any exceptions.	____	____
1) Determine that exceptions are proper and necessary.	____	____
2) If standard weights are used, guards should ensure that rig has standard equipment and a full gas load.	____	____
a) Standard weights assume a clean vehicle. Weight can be altered by snow, rain, wind and dust.		
b) Selected standard weight equipment should be reweighed to confirm that weight used is correct.	____	____
3. See that proper records are made of all reconciliations, and that records state the results of each check.	____	____
a. Ascertain what action is taken if the scale weight does not reconcile to the bill of lading weight.	____	____
1) Determine that records show time of day, decision, and the name of the supervisor who made the decision.	____	____
2) Select several of the questionable discrepancies and verify that supervisors' actions were proper.	____	____
a) *If supervisor does not have a valid reason, bring matter to attention of higher management.*	____	____

III. Audit Procedures *Security Department*	*Per. Cov.*	*Audit By*
b) Discuss matter with internal audit management.	____	____
H. Determine that an executive protection plan is in effect.	____	____
1. Does it provide for irregular times and different routes?	____	____
I. Review the bomb threat program.	____	____
1. Determine that protection of employees has priority.	____	____
2. Note if plan provides that all areas be examined and cleared before employees are returned to their stations.	____	____
J. Determine that critical locks and combinations are changed when personnel shifts makes it advisable.	____	____
1. Determine that there is adequate control over keys and combination to the safe, files and building. Controls should prevent unauthorized persons from making copies.	____	____
2. See that department makes certain that employees holding positions of trust take their regular vacations.	____	____
a. During vacations, the critical work should be performed by another employee.	____	____
Telephone Services		
A. Discuss the satellite system and the existing phone system with the supervisor of telephone services.	____	____
1. Determine the date of the last analysis of our telephone system by an outside communication expert.	____	____
a. If time span has been over two years, send a note to this effect to the Manager of Internal Auditing.	____	____
2. Review telephone bills for the last three months.	____	____
a. Verify that all long distance calls are approved.	____	____
b. *Determine that all personal long distance calls are billed to, and paid by, employees concerned.*	____	____
3. Review call records for WATTS lines	____	____
a. Determine whether all lines are necessary, and if they are being properly used.	____	____
4. Review procedures for determining placement of phone answering devices, speakers and other special equipment.	____	____
B. Discuss phone security measures with Director of Security.	____	____
1. Review measures that ensure that phones are not tapped.	____	____
2. Determine what provisions have been made for emergency communication if phone lines are not operative.	____	____
3. Review systems for radio communication between		

III. Audit Procedures	*Per.*	*Audit*
Telephone Services	*Cov.*	*By*
outer perimeter and roving guards and the control panel.	____	____
a. Review TV surveillance systems and evaluate the method used to dispatch guards to point of intrusion.	____	____
C. Review training program for *operators* so that they will react properly in emergency situations.	____	____
1. See that operators have a copy of questionnaire to be used if a bomb threat or coercion call is received.		
2. Determine that they all have been instructed as to the proper executives that are to receive such calls.	____	____
Mailing Department		
A. Discuss mail room operations with the appropriate manager. Study systems used to perform assigned responsibilities.	____	____
1. Pay particular attention to security system used to ensure that there is no tampering with the mail.	____	____
a. See that mail room cannot be improperly entered.		
b. Verify that sales of personal stamps are all handled through the cashier's controlled window.		
c. Audit any stamp funds which have not been recently audited. Refer to program titled, Auditing Cash.	____	____
B. Determine that computer data is properly safeguarded against theft or harm from temperature of magnetism.	____	____
1. Determine that mail supervisor is advised in advance of computer schedule so that the computer printing room can be controlled during designated runs.	____	____
C. *Determine that only trusted employees are assigned to deliver and pick up mail from Post Office or other places.*	____	____
1. Evaluate system and control over postal meter purchases.	____	____
a. Ensure that XYZ disbursement check is used, and that the receipt is carefully checked to meter.	____	____
2. Note if all mail bags are sealed before shipments.	____	____
a. Check to see if P.O. verifies that bags are sealed when they are received at the postal station.	____	____
D. Determine that a supervisor is in the mail room at all times when the mail is being handled.	____	____
1. Evaluate the mail pickup and delivery schedule.	____	____
a. Does schedule minimize time that mail is held in room?	____	____
2. Review procedures for training and control of part time or temporary help in the mail room.	____	____
E. Review control and handling of extra cost mail service.	____	____

III. Audit Procedures *Mailing Department*	*Per. Cov.*	*Audit By*
1. See that extra cost mail service is used wisely.	____	____
a. Pay particular attention to special mail sent out Friday, since our offices are not open until Monday.	____	____
b. *Spot check to see that shipments of packages only use special mail on appropriate occasions.*	____	____
2. Learn from mail supervisors those departments that insist on special services for all shipments.	____	____
a. Discuss problems with concerned administrators.	____	____

Audit work reviewed by ____________________ Date ____________

INTERNAL AUDIT PROGRAM—INTERNAL CONTROL QUESTIONNAIRE

The following internal control questions are intended to direct your attention to the high-risk areas of these operations. Some of these points are covered in the audit program and are included here to ensure that they receive adequate attention.

Answer these control questions as your audit progresses. In section B, you are to write in the names and job titles of the various employees who perform the listed functions. Be certain to note any conflicting duties that could jeopardize internal control.

A. *The following are indicative of good internal control.*
   1. All major security policies are approved by Executive Committee.
   2. Security policies apply to all employees.
   3. Security officers are closely supervised and monitored.

B. *Following lists functions performed by named employees.*

Function:	*Name/Position*	*Conflicting Duties*
1. Final payroll notice approval.	________	________
2. Distributes paychecks.	________	________
3. Approves contracts and purchases.	________	________

C. *Internal Control Questions*	*Yes*	*No*	*Remarks*
1. Has the security section, at all locations, established channels of communication with local police forces?	____	____	________
2. Is there a training program for security personnel, with regular updates?	____	____	________
a. Are guards well trained in first aid procedures?	____	____	________
1) *Is security prepared to deal with any medical emergency in the office?*	____	____	________
2) Are oxygen cylinders periodically checked for contents?	____	____	________

C. Internal Control Questions	*Yes*	*No*	*Remarks*
b. Is fire fighting equipment regularly checked?	____	____	____________
1) Are fire extinguishers full and operable?	____	____	____________
2) Are hoses in good condition and working?	____	____	____________
3) Are fire drills called as a surprise?	____	____	____________
c. Are guards cautioned against getting too friendly with non-security personnel?	____	____	____________
3. Does emergency evacuation program appear to be understood by all employees?	____	____	____________
a. Are lead people thoroughly trained in the proper actions they are to take?	____	____	____________
1) Do they all know the people they are responsible for?	____	____	____________
4. Is there a clear cut program outlining the handling of extortion threats?	____	____	____________
5. Are executive's telephones periodically checked to ensure that they are not bugged?	____	____	____________
6. Are perimeter gate locks properly used?	____	____	____________
a. Are keys adequately controlled?	____	____	____________
b. *Are gates kept locked when not in use?*	____	____	____________
c. Is control over keys and combinations adequate?	____	____	____________
7. Are local security groups given strict operating instructions?	____	____	____________
a. Are they authorized to conduct periodic locker examinations?	____	____	____________
b. Do they periodically check lunch pails and inspect vehicles of departing workers?	____	____	____________
c. *Do supervisors conduct surprise checks of posts to insure that guards are awake and alert.*	____	____	____________

C. Internal Control Questions	*Yes*	*No*	*Remarks*
d. Are video tapes quick scanned before reuse?	____	____	____________
e. Does guard schedule provide relief for each guard at some time during shifts?	____	____	____________
1) Is there always someone at the post?	____	____	____________
a) If not, does departing guard lock up to prevent entry during the absence?	____	____	____________
8. Is the package pass system rigidly enforced?	____	____	____________
a. Do guards have the authority to open all suspicious looking packages?	____	____	____________
9. Is control adequate over incoming packages?	____	____	____________
a. Do guards have the authority to check contents of incoming packages?	____	____	____________
1) Do they check with recipient to learn if the package is expected?	____	____	____________
b. Do they have an established procedure for action, if a package appears suspicious?	____	____	____________
10. Does Mailing cooperate closely with Security?	____	____	____________
a. Are any suspicious items received in the mail room cleared with security before delivery?	____	____	____________
b. Is security informed when mailing is in the computer area processing checks or invoices?	____	____	____________
1) *Is security increased during such periods?*	____	____	____________
c. Is a disbursement check used to replenish the postage meter?	____	____	____________
1) Is meter reading checked before and after it is taken to the Post Office for filling?	____	____	____________

C. Internal Control Questions	*Yes*	*No*	*Remarks*
11. Does Telephone Department work closely with Security?	____	____	____________
a. Have all operators attended the security training class?	____	____	____________
1) Are new operators, part time or temporary people given adequate training before they are permitted to handle the switchboard?	____	____	____________
b. Are all switchboard positions provided a copy of the questionnaire to be used if an unusual call is received?	____	____	____________
1) Do all operators know how to handle calls?	____	____	____________

Questions answered by ______________________ Date ____________
Answers reviewed by ______________________ Date ____________

CRITICAL POINTS

Auditing a Security Department is a sensitive assignment, since internal auditing and security operations have much in common. The very nature of the function reduces the probability that security personnel will become involved in illegal acts. Following are some examples of the types of problems that a Security Department may encounter on a day-to-day basis.

NINE EXAMPLES OF SECURITY THREATS

1. Bomb scares and threats pose a serious problem. If they are legitimate, no time should be lost in clearing the area. The difficult task is to determine whether the threat is real, or merely an attempt to shut down an operation. If someone calls in to warn of a bombing attempt, they should be willing to cooperate if they are *really* interested in warning people to prevent injury. They should be asked who they are and where they got their information. **KEY POINT:** *Many false bomb threats are made to shut down an operation, so that someone can go home early or need not go to work.*

   The Security Department usually has an established approach for handling telephone threats. Phone operators have a questionnaire form close at hand, so that the right questions can be asked, and pertinent observations recorded while the caller is still on the phone.

EXAMPLE: The author recalls an incident in which the Chairman of the Board of a major corporation was faced with the problem of handling a bomb threat. The Treasurer of the company received the threat and rushed into the Chairman's office announcing that a caller had said that a bomb would go off in the office in thirty minutes. The Treasurer asked the Chairman what to do. While walking toward the closet to get his coat, the Chairman replied, "I don't know what *you're* going to do, but *I'm* going to get the hell out of here!"

The story demonstrates the need for a plan of action that is to be followed in an emergency.

For a bomb threat, a practical plan calls for the complete examination of the premises by knowledgeable employees. **IMPORTANT:** *Supervisors, who are familiar with everything in their area, should be designated as area leaders.* These leaders must carefully examine everything in their area, and if they note any unusual object, or building variation, they immediately transmit the information to Security. The decision is then made as to whether to evacuate a part or all of the building, and to call the police bomb disposal squad. If the examination discloses nothing unusual, the threat is ignored.

2. Some innocent, unthinking employees have been injured or killed, because they resisted giving up company funds to an armed robber. They may have been partially motivated by the fear that their boss might not believe that they were actually robbed.

   To forestall this possibility, a company should issue a directive making it a hard and fast rule that employees are not to put up a fight when confronted with an armed robber. **KEY POINT:** *An employee's life is worth much more than any amount of money that may be involved.* The employee can establish the validity of the robbery by requesting a polygraph test if there is any question as to the facts.

3. Some security managers issue a periodic letter that describes security breaches which have occurred during a period. This letter is distributed to concerned employees to inform them of such activities and to alert them to the possibility that such events might happen again in their area of responsibility.

   These letters serve to keep executives informed as to the type of security breaches that are occurring in the company. **NOTE:** *They often generate good ideas from operating management for methods of preventing future security problems.*

4. Thefts of stored product can occur in very unusual ways. The primary problem is to determine when and where the product is stolen. Once that is known, if there is a regular pattern, the security professional can usually find the culprit. The following case is an example:

EXAMPLE: Product was regularly stolen from a production plant, and through a series of isolation measures it was learned that the product was taken after the plant shut down and before it started operations the next day. Night plant security was beefed up, but the thefts continued.

A security expert studied the problem, and quickly found the solution. Dust on the floor, underneath a skylight, gave the clue that the skylight was the means of entry and egress. A light beam barrier was erected on the roof covering all skylights, and the alarm was tied into the local police station.

The next weekend the alarm was tripped, and the police arrested several boys who lived near the plant. The youngsters climbed to the roof and used a crude rope ladder to enable one boy to enter the plant through a skylight. They hauled up several cases of product, took them to a side away from the guard station, lowered the product and themselves, by rope, and then divided the spoils. They watched the exterior guards, from the roof, so there was no danger from that source.

Protective fencing was installed around the skylights, and the plant did not again experience such thefts.

5. Security guards who work when an operation is closed down are in an unusually good position to steal product. **CAUTION:** *It is not uncommon to discover that the very guard who is supposed to protect product is stealing it.* A guard may take available items, place them in a car, and drive off with the stolen product at the end of the shift.

   Competent supervision offers the most practical safeguard against such actions. One measure that has some degree of success is to require that vehicles be parked a minimum of fifty feet from the edge of the building. This distance provides a shield and can discourage an individual from carrying boxes from the building to the vehicle for fear of being seen. The deterrent fails if the stolen item can be carried in a pocket or under a coat.

   If a surveillance camera is used, there is a chance of detecting the theft when the film is later reviewed. Some guards turn off the camera while they carry items to their cars. If shortages occur at a location that uses cameras, check to see if the system has been turned off at anytime during the off-hours shift. **KEY POINT:** *If there is a pattern of turn-offs at a set time, that would be an excellent time to set up a surveillance to see if the guard is stealing product.*

   If no camera is in use, surprise spot checks of guards' vehicles, as they are leaving the premises, may disclose product being taken. **TIP:** *The knowledge that such checks are made will serve as a deterrent to theft.*

6. *Surveillance is a potent security weapon,* but it can be costly and should be used with discretion. Weeks of watching may prove fruitless, and they may waste a lot of money. But sometimes the pay back comes quickly, as in the following case.

 EXAMPLE: An operation in a small town was experiencing large losses of product. Local management was telephonically instructed in the proper procedures to tie down the period that thefts were occurring and to locate the area from which the product was being taken.

 The local manager determined that thefts were occurring nightly while the operation was shut down, and the product was stolen from the shipping area.

 Two private investigators were hired to watch the building, starting at fifteen minutes before quitting time, and to remain until the doors were opened the following morning. One half hour after closing, a shipping department employee returned to the building and entered through a rear door. A piece of cardboard had been inserted at the locking point of the door to keep it from locking. The employee stacked product on the dock, and then called his relative who arrived ten minutes later in a truck. They were apprehended as they prepared to drive away. The total surveillance time was two hours.

7. A building security warning system that ties into a central office can be very effective; *if the console attendant is awake and alert.* The author recalls an event where a building that was fully wired was broken into and items stolen.

 The break-in occurred in the early morning hours, and the security company's console attendant was sound asleep during the intrusion. Although the security company reimbursed for the loss, the case made it clear that *any system is only as good as the people behind the mechanical devices.*
8. Security guards can perform a useful task by checking to ensure that truck door seals have not been removed. **CAUTION:** *There are many instances of product theft that occurred because truckers realized that no one at the receiving end of a shipment checked the integrity of the seal.*

 These dishonest truckers pull their rigs up to the docks, and then they pretend to be removing the door seal which they had earlier broken so that they could remove product. The load is short, and it is assumed to be a loading error. **KEY POINT:** *If all companies carefully checked seals when trucks are entering or departing their gates, the billions of dollars of transport losses could be substantially reduced.* Your company should have a policy that prohibits anyone other than a receiving supervisor from removing, or breaking open, a door seal. The supervisor should *get off the* *platform,* inspect the condition of the seal, verify that the numbers are correct, and then personally remove the seal and immediately order the truck to back into a receiving dock.

Immediate movement of the vehicle protects against transfer of product while waiting for an open dock. *Product is frequently removed from one vehicle and placed in an empty one that is about to depart,* during the time that trucks are parked and waiting for open dock space.

9. There frequently are honest differences of opinion about spending money to improve security. There are no easy or absolute answers to these problems. Here is a case in point:

> **EXAMPLE:** A situation had developed in which an argument, lasting several weeks, resulted from a suggestion that a TV surveillance system be installed in the parking lot of a large administrative office. There were frequent instances of theft and assault in the parking lot, usually in the late afternoon or evening hours. A security guard was always available at the main door, but the guard could not view or control the entire parking area.
>
> A meeting was held to discuss the problem and make a final decision. One of the participants wondered what other companies in the area were doing. I called a friend who worked for a large company that was headquartered in the general vicinity of the location being discussed. To our question of whether they had ever considered a TV surveillance system for their parking lot, my friend replied: "What a coincidence! We have a system in our parking lot, and just this morning we had a meeting and decided to get rid of it."
>
> When asked why that decision was made, my friend replied, "Well, we're looking for ways to save money, and we've had the system for three years and haven't had a single incident in all that time."

Our group immediately decided to install such a system, and it succeeded in eliminating the thefts and assaults from that parking lot. Even sincere, intelligent people can look at the same set of facts and come up with completely opposite conclusions.

Chapter 27

Auditing Administrative Offices and Selected Office Services

Many companies are diversified and have major administrative offices in locations throughout the world. There are regional or division offices, international offices and subsidiary offices.

These major administrative offices generally house the division manager or subsidiary president, and the administrative staff. The office is responsible for all activities and personnel in the total operation. The staff establishes operating forms, procedures and regulations for all activities. All operations must conform to local and national laws and to manufacturing procedures and operating guidelines set up by the corporate office.

Successful corporations expand their operations into other countries because they feel that they have something to offer people anywhere. They broaden their market with the expectation of increasing their profits. The expansion may come about through the acquisition of an existing business or in some other manner. If successful, they build plants and offices and frequently staff them with local personnel managed by an executive from the parent office. No matter the approach, the distance from the home office and language and cultural differences create a number of unusual problems.

Major public accounting firms have offices or correspondents in all of the major cities where multinational corporations operate. They audit companies almost anywhere in the world. Operating mainly with local inhabitants, they do not have a cultural or language problem. Their travel expenses are considerably less than they would be if they sent a team of headquarters auditors around the world. But they are not internal auditors. *They are not familiar with home office attitudes and thinking, and they may not be aware of the operating procedures, policies or activities that interest Headquarter's executives.*

The corporate internal audit staff can work closely with these outside auditors and help them provide the type of services that aid company executives in evaluating the performance of their operations in other countries.

The headquarters audit staff can operate in a variety of ways:

- It can use customary communications channels, or it can send staff members to meet with, review working papers of, or even work with the public accountants on audits of specific locations or operations.
- It can assist in resolving policy misunderstandings and can help to insure that supervisors and employees understand and follow corporate policies and procedures.
- It can evaluate the effectiveness of the operational review work of the outside auditors.

Corporate internal auditors know the true operating organization and the guiding principles and goals of the executives. They audit all company operations, no matter where located, and modify their programs to fit specific operations and conditions. *They perform an objective review, free of fear of reprisal or awe of local executives.*

Some wholly owned subsidiaries are free to operate completely on their own, merely being required to report their operating results to headquarters. Usually the head office issues a chart of accounts that the sub must use in its accounting reporting.

The chart of accounts gives a designation to each account and a description of the type of activities that are to be allocated to each account. This enables the head office to combine all corporate accounting into meaningful consolidated reports.

In this chapter we will describe an internal auditing approach to a review of a completely independent operation, or to one which has a great deal of latitude, with the top executive reporting to the top executive in the corporate office. **TIP:** *The audit approach is affected by the amount of autonomy granted to the activity being reviewed.*

The major distinction between headquarters and a division or regional office is that headquarters handles all corporate financing and reports to stockholders and government agencies. Headquarters obtains cash as needed, and it issues stock or bond certificates as required. Legal matters are handled by corporate headquarters, and the head office houses the top executives of the company.

Outlying administrative offices normally are involved in some or all of the following activities:

1. Sales operations,
2. Production operations,
3. Supervising distribution of product,
4. Engineering services and research work,
5. Purchasing functions,
6. Personnel activities,

7. Traffic operations,
8. a Controller department that handles all accounting functions.

Sometimes a subsidiary, or an international division may perform some or all of the functions, but in all cases the total consolidation of information and formal reporting is handled by headquarters.

We will also cover the office services that are usually provided, including word processing and duplicating, office machinery servicing, and building and office maintenance.

Auditing of mailing and telephone services is covered in the chapter titled Auditing A Security Department And Related Services.

Various office services are found in any administrative office, and these activities are audited at the same time as the other operations. Much of the routine audit work performed in an audit of a service operation is identical to any personal service study.

Audits of outlying administrative offices, generally follow the same pattern as an audit of headquarter's operations. Presented is an internal audit program designed for a review of such an administrative office. It is all inclusive and refers to many of the departmental audit programs printed in this manual. When a specific activity is covered in an individual chapter in this manual, the parts of the program dealing with such operations refer to the applicable chapter.

One minor difference between audits of headquarters and outlying administrative offices is the timing and scope of the audit work. In a review of an administrative office, the auditors usually perform a complete study of all activities in the office during one visit. But an audit at headquarters is often broken up into departmental audits that may be used as fill-in assignments for staff members that have reasons to remain in the geographic area of the home office.

I. Background Information—All Operations

The sample audit program is used by the XYZ Corporation's internal audit staff to review the activities that are conducted in their division, international and subsidiary offices. XYZ has seven division offices in the United States, ten international administrative offices, and fifteen subsidiary companies, each of which has its own main administrative office. The subsidiaries operate under their original corporate name though they are all one hundred percent owned by XYZ.

Each major administrative office has a President who reports to the President of the parent corporation. Basic office organizations are skeleton versions of headquarters office. Local staff executives take orders only from their President, but they work closely with their counterparts in the corporate head office.

Though the selection of an executive in an administrative office is made by the local President, it is subject to approval from the headquarters office. This system assures a close working relationship between the top executives in the administrative offices, and their counterparts in the main office.

All subsidiaries and the international divisions handle their own marketing, distribution, data processing, engineering and advertising.

All home country activities are tied in to the headquarters data processing operations, but the international offices have independent computer centers. All EDP operations use the same basic approach and programs as the corporate operation.

Operations that are responsible for advertising, coordinate their advertising programs and time and space purchases through the major advertising agency used by the headquarters operation.

Other activities are also coordinated with comparable operations in the headquarters office.

All of the administrative offices have a word processing center which services all supervisory personnel. This center also houses the duplicating equipment required by the operation. Each office has a small group of technicians who service and maintain most of the equipment. The offices also have a staff of service people responsible for the appearance and cleanliness of the work areas and of the condition of all office furniture. All of these service operations are under the supervision of the controller of each administrative office.

The corporate internal audit staff is responsible for the internal auditing of all of these activities and operations. Each of the large international, and a few of the subsidiary companies, have a small group of internal auditors that review their individual company's operations. Managers of these staffs report to the top financial officer in their company, but they have a dotted line responsibility to the Director of Internal Auditing in the headquarters office. These local groups receive audit programs and directions from the headquarter's internal audit staff.

Audits of administrative offices are designed to determine the following:

- All main office policies are understood and followed,
- Forms and procedures that are used conform to main office directives,
- The office is being run efficiently,
- All records are current, accurate and prepared efficiently,
- All information is correctly summarized and reported,
- All internal controls are operating satisfactorily,
- Controls insure that all information is consistently handled in a reliable manner.

To achieve these objectives, normal routine audit checks are made of all pertinent paper work in each operation. Auditors also review accounting manuals, controller bulletins, operating directives and letters of instruction. They examine records and supporting detail to verify that all information is correctly accumulated and summarized.

Personnel records are reviewed and any agreements entered into by an office are studied to see that they are in the best interests of the corporation and that they conform to established directives.

Our sample audit program is designed to be used for a complete audit of all described operations, or it can be selectively used to review any of these activities. The general portion applies to all functions, while specific operations are grouped together.

II. Background Information—International

Multinational corporations have several management problems that result from doing business in different countries. Such problems are these:

- Language difference, which limits the free flow of information between company employees,
- Currency variations, tax considerations and legal differences,
- Customs of the people. People differences are a problem since work ethics, society goals, attitude toward business entities, and presence of foreigners can affect the thoughts and actions of employees.

Internal auditing helps management control these international operations. Corporate auditors review all operations where no local internal auditors are used. The corporate group also does selective auditing and provides advice to existing local staffs in divisions in which these staffs operate.

All audit programs used in the international divisions have been designed, or approved, by the headquarters staff. All international audit reports, and follow-up reports of actions taken on audit recommendations, are addressed to the division President with a copy to the corporate Director of Internal Auditing. **IMPORTANT:** *Though the basic philosophy remains unchanged, audits of international divisions must be handled differently than administrative offices in the native country. Language and differences in customs and business practices dictate an individual approach to each operation.*

Accounting may be slightly different, but headquarter's rules and internal control procedures apply to all record keeping and reporting. Some international operations arrange their own local financing, and use banks of their choice, usually with the advice and consent of the corporate Treasurer. Divisions are normally audited by accountants who are correspondents of the CPA that certifies corporate statements.

Accounting procedures, systems, directives or reports may be different than prescribed by headquarters. This occurs when a country in which an international division is operating, requires special reports or has a tax system that results in unusual bookkeeping practices. In these countries the internal auditing approach must give consideration to these different customs or regulations.

Headquarters internal auditing periodically visits each of the international divisions. The audit group works very closely with, and through, the President of the operation, and all audit work is cleared with the top financial officer in the division. The headquarter's staff follows the same basic audit program that they use for a study of any administrative office.

During these visits, the corporate staff works with, and evaluates, the personnel and approach of the local auditors. They attempt to improve the internal audits conducted by staff members, who are usually natives of the country where the operations are housed. Some of these local auditors, usually the managers, are made a part of the headquarter's staff for a period of from three to twelve months. This training broadens their outlook and improves their audit techniques.

Several joint audits of specific operations are conducted during visits to an International Division. The local auditors assigned to these jobs are closely supervised by the headquarters staff, and this process serves as on-the-job training for the local auditors.

The corporate staff may elect to omit auditing certain operations which have been recently visited by local auditors, if they are convinced that an adequate review was performed. A study of audit working papers is frequently sufficient to satisfy the headquarters staff.

The following sample internal audit program was specifically designed for auditing an administrative office and the associated office services.

INTERNAL AUDIT PROGRAM—INSTRUCTIONS

IA AOI821

XYZ CORPORATION
INTERNAL AUDIT PROGRAM
ADMINISTRATIVE OFFICES AND OFFICE SERVICES

INSTRUCTIONS

Before starting your audit of an administrative office, read these instructions, the audit program (IA AOP820), all pertinent accounting manual pages and study both the operating and expense statements of the activity. Become thoroughly familiar with the operation before leaving the home office. Discuss the assignment with headquarters operating executives who are responsible for the administrative office activity.

The following instructions will give you some guidance in your present assignment, but the audit program is not all inclusive. You will probably find it necessary to add sections for activities that are not covered.

Before you add items to this program, read all directives relating to an activity and then prepare flow charts of all procedures and forms that must be reviewed. These charts will enable you to locate the critical points that require audit attention. **IMPORTANT:** *You will encounter unique problems and, when in doubt, call audit management for advice and counsel.*

During this audit assignment you will be referring to many of the programs in your audit manual. IMPORTANT INSTRUCTION: *Before you start your audit of an administrative office, carefully read the two programs titled Auditing Cash Transactions and Auditing Receivables, and follow the pertinent cautions that are listed in the Instruction section of these programs.*

A. Each administrative office is headed by a division President. Before leaving on your assignment, have the Headquarter's VP call the appropriate executive and advise of your coming visit and the date that you will arrive. Immediately upon arrival, you will visit the location's president and introduce yourself and your staff members.
    1. Specifically ask if there are any areas of the operation that the President would like the audit staff to examine. *Make appropriate notes and be certain to at least present a verbal report of your findings at the completion of your audit.*
B. Arrange to meet, individually or in a group, all of the executives of the operation. After preliminary meetings with all supervisors, schedule individual interviews and review their responsibilities and approach to their assignments.
C. Review all local policy and procedures, and compare to National Headquarters directives. If necessary have the writings interpreted, word for word into English so that you can clearly understand the *meaning and the intent* of all significant directives.
D. If the Administrative Office has an audit staff that reports to a local executive, review the work of the group and use these local members to perform routine audit tasks. **IMPORTANT:** *For any significant audit work, be certain that members of your team supervise local auditors and verify that their work is accurate and complete.*

    Do *not* discuss your observations of *significant discrepancies or unusual transactions* with local auditors. You may discuss or question them about local policies or procedures that affect the transactions in question, but the related follow-up investigative work should be done by your staff and *any derogatory results should be treated as confidential material.*

    This requires a great deal of discretion and personal judgment on your part, in deciding the extent of your cooperation with, and trust of, the local audit staff. Do not assume that because they have the job title of internal auditor they are aware of everything that goes on in the operation.
E. Investigate discrepancies using the same approach that you would use in Headquarter's Office. First talk to the employee who made the entry, and then, talk to the supervisor responsible for the transaction. If necessary, move up the chain of command until you are completely satisfied, or until you find that there has been a violation of company policies or procedures. **IMPORTANT:** *Your audit report should contain a listing of all the significant*

deviations and all violations of company policies, ethics, and national or local laws. Under no conditions will we condone any violation of law. If something is done, which would be considered illegal if done in Headquarters, even though it does not violate laws in the country where the office is operating, it should be brought to the attention of the proper executives in Headquarters. We will try to persuade the headquarter's decision makers to order that the practice be stopped, even if we know that our competitors are doing it.

F. XYZ has an open door policy to all employees. This means that the doors to all private offices are kept open unless there is a meeting going on or a confidential phone conversation is in progress.

Any employee should feel free to talk to any supervisor or manager if they have a good reason. If the administrative office has a different policy, discuss the matter with the top executive of the operation. Forward a copy of your notes to the internal audit manager, who will discuss the item with the appropriate headquarters executive.

G. When working in a country that uses a language that you do not understand, you will be assigned an interpreter. The employee may come from the office that you are auditing. **IMPORTANT:** *Let the interpreter know that you want a literal and complete translation, word for word, of everything that is said.* You do not wish to hear an interpretation of what an employee may have said or really meant to say. You must make this clear; otherwise, you will be getting the interpreter's thinking instead of the words spoken by the employee being interviewed.

Problems can occur despite the best intentions, particularly if the interpreter works in the office being audited and is familiar with the system or procedure that is being studied. A reply may be the accurate or prescribed one for the system or procedure being audited, but it may not truly represent what the employee said was really being done.

H. Some of our international divisions elect to use external auditors instead of having an in-house audit staff. They believe that their operations are too small to support a full-time audit staff. This condition usually exists where we have purchased a local business as the starting point for XYZ's entry into that country.

You should work closely with these external auditors, and review their approach and working papers relating to our operations. You may decide to participate in a joint audit of specific locations or operations. **NOTE:** *You should evaluate the effectiveness of the public accountant's approach to our particular problems, and be prepared to suggest whether the present arrangement be continued or changed.*

I. The management of each administrative office determines the office services that are needed for their operation. They then obtain required services at a minimum cost. Once in place these service operations are rarely looked at in a critical fashion. During your review you are expected to examine each service used to determine whether the activity is necessary, whether it is the proper size, and whether it is run efficiently and economically.

J. It is XYZ's policy that these service operations be set up to satisfy the needs of administrative personnel. However, the work load of a specialist may be sporadic and there will be periods when some of them have idle time. XYZ permits these specialists to work on personal equipment of other employees during these idle times; but the employees that benefit must be charged for all materials and for labor at a rate that reimburses XYZ for the specialist's direct labor costs.

All personal work is to be done on the premises. It is contrary to XYZ's policy to permit any employee to leave the building to perform work for any other employee. Carpenters, masons, painters, and other such tradesmen are not permitted to perform personal work for others during working hours. If an emergency arises, an exception may be allowed; but all records and reports should clearly describe the emergency, and the fact that certain employees left the premises to perform personal work. **NOTE:** *Charges should be fair and correct.*

K. Your evaluation of office services should answer these questions:

- Is the service necessary?
- Is it conducted efficiently and economically?
- Is the cost of the service well controlled? And,
- Are all personal services billed at a proper price?

L. Office equipment should only be used for company business, but local management, at their discretion, may allow employees to use their assigned machines for personal work when the office is closed. This is a fringe benefit that costs XYZ very little.

M. A description of the proper procedure for working with this internal audit program appears in the Introduction to the Audit Programs section of your manual. Read this information carefully.

INTERNAL AUDIT PROGRAM

IA AOP820 XYZ CORPORATION
INTERNAL AUDIT PROGRAM

Location: ____________

ADMINISTRATIVE OFFICES AND SELECTED OFFICE SERVICES

The following checklist program is designed to lead you through an internal audit of an Administrative Office. Read the audit Instructions, form # IA AOI821, this program and the associated Internal Control Questionnaire before you start your audit.

Audit Procedures	*Per. Cov.*	*Audit By*
I. General		
A. Study operating reports of the activity, and discuss the operations with headquarters executives concerned.	____	____
1. Arrange for the proper executive to call the activity President and tell of your planned arrival.	____	____

Audit Procedures	*Per. Cov.*	*Audit By*
I. General		
2. Select important reports or statements that you will verify first hand at the proper office.	____	____
3. Gather supplies and take stats of one full year of vital accounting reports sent in by office you are visiting.	____	____
B. Upon arrival, meet with the President of the activity and all staff members and introduce yourself and audit team.	____	____
1. Explain purpose of visit and our method of approach.	____	____
2. Ask if there are specific areas that their staff wishes the audit group to examine.	____	____
a. *Make notes of any requests, and follow up at the earliest opportunity.*	____	____
3. Arrange to meet with each executive separately, and then interview their supervisors and employees.	____	____
4. Arrange, if necessary, to be assigned an interpreter.	____	____
C. Check your trial balance against the General Ledger.	____	____
1. Examine the General Ledger of the previous year. Determine that P&L accounts were properly transferred.	____	____
2. Examine Journal entries and supporting data for an entire month. See that all entries are approved.	____	____
a. Determine that explanations are clear and adequate.	____	____
b. See that supporting papers are appropriate.	____	____
c. Determine that papers are properly headed and filed.	____	____
D. Review all local procedures to see if there are any that are in contradiction of headquarters office directives.	____	____
1. Determine that they all conform to our Code Of Conduct, and to the stated goals of the company.	____	____
2. See that deviations have been disclosed & are approved.	____	____
E. See that vital reports are accurate, complete and timely.	____	____
1. Any unusual accounting practices should be known to and approved by the corporate Comptroller.	____	____
a. Learn if there are separate sets of records for tax purposes. If so see that they conform to laws.	____	____
1) Ensure that system was approved by headquarters.	____	____
2) If system does not conform to local laws, note whether office was instructed to discontinue it.	____	____
II. Assets		
A. As soon as practical, audit all cash transactions:	____	____
1. Count all cash on hand, including collections, cash on hand from cash sales, remittances from outlying locations, petty cash and all cash funds.	____	____
a. Count petty cash again during your visit.	____	____

Audit Procedures *II. Assets*	*Per. Cov.*	*Audit By*
2. Thoroughly audit all cash transactions. Use program in your manual titled Auditing Cash Transactions.	____	____
a. Reconcile cash on hand from cash sales to cash sales records. *If cash sales system is one not readily auditable, suggest changes to make it so.*	____	____
3. Reconcile all bank accounts for month preceding visit.	____	____
a. Obtain bank statements and canceled checks from banks, as of date you counted all cash on hand, and prepare complete reconciliations.	____	____
4. If funds are deposited in Treasurer's account, send deposit list to Treasurer for checking to statement and to explore possibility of miscarriage of funds.	____	____
B. Confirm all receivables. (Use audit manual program titled Auditing Receivables.)	____	____
1. Send out confirmations on miscellaneous A/R and Notes Receivable in the same manner as Trade Accounts.	____	____
a. Returned audit verification statements should be left at the office audited, for future reference.	____	____
2. *If management requests certain items not be confirmed by mail; examine correspondence and payments and discuss account with employees of the activity concerned.*	____	____
3. Test check last aging of A/R that you brought from the head office, against accounts receivable ledger.	____	____
4. Check A/R trial balance to A/R ledgers. Check total of A/R detail to General Ledger Control Account.	____	____
5. Review W/O's of A/R or notes with responsible employee.	____	____
a. Study credit file relating to write-offs. Note references to recoveries and check to Reserves.	____	____
6. Test check credit memos to recaps, footings of recaps, and recaps to totals as posted to ledger.	____	____
a. For a test period completely check each C/M as to the following: Approvals, R/R, correspondence and posting to ledger.	____	____
1) *Investigate thoroughly all C/M's bearing unusual, ambiguous, or incomplete explanations.*	____	____
7. Look for unusual receivables. *If there are any from other than customers, study supporting documentation.*	____	____
a. Be certain to confirm such receivables.	____	____
8. For any transactions with brokers or other middlemen, determine that they are known and approved by headquarters.	____	____
a. Review contractual agreements and determine that all parties live up to their obligations.	____	____

Audit Procedures	*Per. Cov.*	*Audit By*
II. Assets		
C. Audit all inventories, using the program in your manual titled Auditing Inventory Transactions.	____	____
1. Carefully review procedures for control of inventories.	____	____
2. Physically count inventories at convenient locations, and reconcile to book inventory reports.	____	____
3. Test check inventory reports to General Ledger Account.	____	____
4. Test audit XYZ inventories held by outsiders.	____	____
5. Review procedures and controls for disposition of scrap, salvage materials or machinery.	____	____
a. *Test check some receipts from sales of such items.*	____	____
6. Review controls over advertising supplies, point of sale items and trade show equipment and supplies.	____	____
D. Review handling of appropriation files and the property ledger. (Refer to program for auditing Property.)	____	____
1. Tie in Property Ledger to the General Ledger.	____	____
2. Test closings of some appropriations to property cards.	____	____
3. Test-check property listed at selected locations, against inventories at those locations.	____	____
4. Test-check sales or scrapping of property items for legitimacy and proper handling.	____	____
E. Analyze balances in the Prepaid Expenses and Deferred Charges accounts as at the end of month preceding visit.	____	____
III. Liabilities and P&L Accounts	____	____
A. Review A/P items; be certain to look at rent payments. Use audit program in manual titled Auditing Payables.	____	____
B. If operation issues bonds, or short term paper, audit the operation using program titled Auditing Equity Accounts.	____	____
C. Depending on the size of the office, verify employee job assignments and count by distributing payroll checks.	____	____
1. When actual physical identification is not practical, examine organization charts, physical exams, etc.	____	____
2. Audit the payroll and personnel functions using the program titled Auditing Personnel and Payroll.	____	____
D. Audit the purchasing operation using the program in your manual titled Auditing Purchasing.	____	____
E. Audit any engineering or research activities using the program titled Auditing Engineering and Research.	____	____
F. Review production and cost accounting activities, using program titled Production Operations & Cost Accounting.	____	____
G. Review the marketing function using the programs designed for Auditing Marketing and Advertising operations.	____	____
H. Audit the distribution and traffic function using the program titled Auditing Distribution Operations.	____	____

Audit Procedures	*Per.*	*Audit*
III. Liabilities and P&L Accounts	*Cov.*	*By*
I. For an audit of an outlying location use program titled Auditing A Plant, Distribution Center or Sales Branch.	____	____
J. If the office has a data processing department, refer to the program titled Auditing Data Processing.	____	____
IV. Equity and Tax Accounts		
A. If the operation issues stocks or operates as an agency of the Secretary, use program titled Auditing Equity Accounts.	____	____
1. See that everything is cleared through the Secretary.	____	____
V. Selected Office Services		
A. Evaluate method used for allocating costs of services.	____	____
1. For services charged on basis of work performed, examine work orders for test period to verify charges.	____	____
2. For services controlled by one department, examine records to see if rebillings were accurate and fair.	____	____
3. If personal work was performed, see that charges were proper, accurate and timely.	____	____
a. *See that billings were to employees who benefited.*	____	____
b. See that cash payments were properly handled.	____	____
B. Visit the Word Processing center and discuss the operation with the supervisor.	____	____
1. See if size of section is appropriate to work load.	____	____
a. Determine if requests are handled methodically in the sequence received.	____	____
1) *Review the priority system for handling work.*	____	____
a) Determine whether the importance of the work outweighs the job position of the requester.	____	____
b. Review supervisor's method of determining the size of staff required.	____	____
1) Review supervisor's method of evaluating the section's personnel.	____	____
2) Determine if temporary employees are brought in to help handle peak periods.	____	____
3) Determine that controls are adequate over work that is farmed out.	____	____
2. Evaluate the equipment in the section.	____	____
a. Determine that equipment is efficient and adequate.	____	____
3. Be certain that in your reviews of Purchasing and A/P, you have checked purchases of paper, ribbons, etc.	____	____
C. Meet with the supervisor of building services and discuss the methods and procedures used to control this operation.	____	____
1. Evaluate the work requisition system and determine that it complies with headquarter's directives.	____	____

Audit Procedures	*Per.*	*Audit*
V. Selected Office Services	*Cov.*	*By*
a. Review requisitions over a test three month period.	_____	_____
1) Ensure that all work was performed on the premises for the benefit of XYZ.	_____	_____
2. Talk to each employee about their work specialty.	_____	_____
a. Ask if they have performed any work, during business hours, for executives or for any fellow employees.	_____	_____
3. In your review of Purchasing and A/P, be certain to test-check items purchased by this section.	_____	_____
a. Determine that quantities were appropriate for the specific jobs selected for review.	_____	_____
b. *See that materials and supplies purchased by this section were all used for company building repairs.*	_____	_____
4. Be certain that utility bills are audited.	_____	_____
a. Inquire as to whether there is a utility bill audit service available in the community.	_____	_____
D. Talk to the supervisor of office services about the systems and forms used to control this operation.	_____	_____
1. See that office items are ordered by Purchasing	_____	_____
2. Review selected charges from the interior decorators.	_____	_____
a. Determine that charges were for company work that was authorized and performed.	_____	_____
1) Determine that billings were properly approved.	_____	_____
3. If there is a limo or chauffeur service in the office, audit all related activities and costs. (Refer to the program that covers an audit of Traffic operations.)	_____	_____
VI. Miscellaneous		
A. Review auditing work performed in the operation.	_____	_____
1. Arrange for joint audits with local audit staff.	_____	_____
2. Evaluate cost of public auditors.	_____	_____
a. Should operation have an internal audit staff?	_____	_____
B. Locate executive responsible for security in the operation and discuss the approach and methods used.	_____	_____
1. Refer to program titled Auditing Security.	_____	_____
C. Investigate all balances in clearance accounts which should not carry a balance.	_____	_____
1. If an analysis of entries becomes necessary, have this prepared for you by office employees.	_____	_____
2. Have a list prepared for you of items contained in the unaudited bills account.	_____	_____
a. *Determine that this account is not used as a dumping ground for questionable transactions.*	_____	_____
D. Check reconciliations of drafts outstanding. If volume of work so warrants, make only a test check.	_____	_____
E. If office maintains a garage operation, closely check the		

Audit Procedures	*Per. Cov.*	*Audit By*
VI. Miscellaneous		
internal controls over this activity.	____	____
1. Review cost statements and vendor's invoices. (Refer to audit program titled Auditing Payables.)	____	____
2. Determine that controls are tight over garage supplies.	____	____
F. Note whether employees having access to assets and critical records took regular vacations during the past year.	____	____
1. If vacations were not taken, check to see if employee was absent for illness or out-of-town business.	____	____
2. Review employee accounts receivable. Discuss past due items with appropriate management.	____	____
G. Discuss significant findings with appropriate executives.	____	____

Audit work reviewed by ______________________ Date ____________

INTERNAL AUDIT PROGRAM—INTERNAL CONTROL QUESTIONNAIRE

The following internal control questions are intended to direct your attention to the high-risk areas of these operations. Many points are covered in the audit program, but they are listed here to ensure that they receive adequate attention. Answer these internal control questions as your audit progresses.

Internal Control Questions	*Yes*	*No*	*Remarks*
A. Is the office following all of headquarter's policies and procedures?	____	____	__________
1. If no, have all deviations been cleared and approved by headquarters?	____	____	__________
2. *Is it mandatory that ALL employees, regardless of job title, conform to ALL company rules and regulations?*	____	____	__________
B. Are all the reports, sent in to headquarters, accurate, timely and complete?	____	____	__________
1. Are they carefully reviewed by local execs before they are sent in to headquarters?	____	____	__________
a. Are alterations or deletions justified?	____	____	__________
b. *Are you aware of any attempt to send in false information to headquarters?*	____	____	__________
2. In the International Division is English used as at least the second language?	____	____	__________

Internal Control Questions	*Yes*	*No*	*Remarks*
a. Are all reports written in English, or is a translation sent in to headquarters?	____	____	____________
1) Are both the original language report and the translation sent in?	____	____	____________
2) Are reports checked at headquarters for accuracy of translation?	____	____	____________
b. Are government officials treated with respect, but at arms length?	____	____	____________
C. Are company records adequately safeguarded?	____	____	____________
1. *Are corporate formulas, production processes, and confidential machinery safeguarded and not shown to unauthorized persons?*	____	____	____________
2. Is a protectograph machine used to imprint the dollar value on all checks and drafts?	____	____	____________
D. Does control of cash conform to directives from headquarters?	____	____	____________
1. Is locally controlled cash used wisely?	____	____	____________
2. *Are all cash funds promptly deposited?*	____	____	____________
a. Is reporting accurate and prompt?	____	____	____________
b. Have all local banks been approved by the Corporate Treasurer?	____	____	____________
3. In your opinion, are any cash funds inadequate, excessive or unnecessary?	____	____	____________
4. Does local system require employee responsible for cash funds to make up shortages out of their personal funds?	____	____	____________
a. If yes, could such requirement result in overcharging customer to recover shortage?	____	____	____________
5. Did you see any evidence of any loan made to an administrative officer?	____	____	____________

Internal Control Questions	*Yes*	*No*	*Remarks*
a. *If yes, was it approved by Headquarters?*			
6. Did you verify the accuracy of the report of *total* of issued drafts sent to Treasurer?			
E. Do personnel and payroll procedures and policies conform to national directives?			
1. Do employees list time worked on weekly time report or punch a time clock?			
a. Are time cards, absences and sicknesses approved by first level supervisors?			
2. Are all local or national laws followed that concern wages, hours or working conditions?			
a. Do office hours conform to local custom?			
b. Has headquarters been informed of any unusual working arrangements?			
1) Have they approved such arrangements?			
3. Does person preparing payroll time summary distribute the paychecks?			
4. Does an office executive personally know all employees; including out-of-town workers?			
5. Have all supervisors and employees who have access to cash, A/R, merchandise, etc. taken vacations during the last year?			
6. *Are any employees used to perform personal work on property or outside interests of supervisors or executives?*			
F. Does the operation have an open door policy that applies to all employees?			
1. Do employees feel that they can discuss their problems with any executive?			
2. Are communications restricted by customs of the country?			

Internal Control Questions	*Yes*	*No*	*Remarks*
G. Does Office Machinery Repair section only work on company equipment?			
1. If section repairs personal equipment:			
a. Is authorization and control adequate?			
b. *Are employees charged for full amount of repair parts and labor costs?*			
2. Is there a possibility that the shop operates as a private business by repairmen?			
H. Is the Word Processing section operating effectively and efficiently?			
1. Is the facility used by all employees?			
2. Are users satisfied with the service?			
3. Does the section request date deadlines on all work requests received?			
a. If section cannot meet deadline, is employee concerned promptly notified?			
I. Does the supervisor of Building Maintenance exercise close control over the section?			
1. Are controls adequate over work assignments for porters and maintenance engineers?			
a. *Are all workers' services confined to company property and premises?*			
2. Are controls adequate over purchases of materials used by section employees?			
3. Does the section utilize a program for preventive maintenance of the building?			
a. Are building maintenance engineers cost conscious in their activities?			
1) Is an effort made to conserve power?			
J. Does the supervisor of Office Ser-			

Internal Control Questions	*Yes*	*No*	*Remarks*
vices keep close control over the section's operations?	____	____	____________
1. Are there adequate controls over the receipt of office furniture?	____	____	____________
2. Is there good control over the disposition of office furniture?	____	____	____________
a. Is control adequate over furniture sold to office employees?	____	____	____________
1) Are receipts handled properly?	____	____	____________

Questions answered by ______________________ Date ____________
Answers reviewed by ______________________ Date ____________

CRITICAL POINTS

The presence of high ranking executives in an administrative office presents an opportunity for employee manipulation and fraud. There is a natural reluctance to question an order of important executives, since some unlikely transactions could possibly be the product of an executive perq.

You must be continually alert as you audit administrative offices, since you are the outsider that might cause uncomfortable changes.

Following are some examples of the types of abuses that may occur.

EIGHT AREAS OF POTENTIAL ABUSE

1. Every country has its own customs and acceptable business practices. Some of the everyday occurrences may be different than what is permissible in the home country, and this can create problems.

   In some countries a job title automatically entitles the person to certain privileges that may not be available, or acceptable, to an employee in the headquarters office with the same or even a higher position. It is not uncommon for those privileges to continue even though the executive is separated from the company. Here is a case in point:

   EXAMPLE: A founder of a company sold out to a major international corporation, and was kept on as President of the division. The company prospered and expanded, but the president could not handle a large operation, and after a few years, was fired because of incompetence and failure to comply with company rules. The former executive vice-president was promoted and the head office was moved to a larger city.

Corporate internal auditors visited the division a year later, and one of the locations selected for an audit check was the plant and office that had formerly served as the division headquarters. They found that the former president still had an office in the building and received the full benefits, except for pay, that he had enjoyed while serving as the division president.

All of the division executives denied knowing of the arrangement, and the former owner made certain to stay away from the office during any internal audit visit to the location.

The situation was discovered when a headquarter's auditor unexpectedly returned after office hours, to retrieve a brief case that had been left when the team departed earlier in the day. The conference room, where auditors had worked, was next to a private office. The former owner was in the office at that time and asked the auditor what business he had being there.

This unusual arrangement could have been disclosed during a full audit of the location when auditors control all incoming mail. **TIP:** *If there is an abundance of mail addressed to a former executive, it might mean that the individual maintains close contacts at the office.*

Another audit approach to such a situation is to study closely all disbursements charged to miscellaneous administrative accounts.

2. It is not uncommon for corporate executives to receive personal services or goods from suppliers who do business with the company. In some countries it is an accepted practice. Contractors may build houses or other buildings for executives and not even charge the company for the work. Of course, the costs of these projects are buried in the costs of work in progress or yet to come.

   An effective method of disturbing this type of arrangement, is to insist that competitive bids be obtained for any large purchase.
   KEY POINT: *The top executives must be forbidden from interfering with purchasing or engineering departmental operations, unless there is a question about the integrity of one of those employees.*

   If, as a result of competition, the business goes to someone other than the regular supplier, the repercussions may lead to a disclosure of the personal work or goods that have been given to the executive.

3. In some countries, bribes to government employees are an accepted way of life. Some government employees are paid very low salaries and are expected to supplement their earning through gifts from companies they work with. Some countries pay their tax collectors a percentage of all money they collect over the original report of taxes due.

This can create a situation where a tax collector may persuade companies to file tax returns for amounts well below the correct tax owed. The collector looks at their records and determines that they owe additional taxes, perhaps twice as much as originally reported. The collector is happy to share in the recovery; the government is happy because they receive much more than originally filed; and the company is happy because they wind up paying much less taxes than due.

This type of dilemma is difficult to deal with. It can easily arise in connection with the buy-out of a small business. The new owner discovers, too late, that the practice has been going on for years. If the company decides that it will file honest returns, the changeover might create problems for the tax collector if earnings quadrupled in a single year. Since the former company has been a part of the conspiracy and benefited from it, the new owner may decide to gradually correct the situation over a few years. The form of the country's government can be a significant factor in any decision.

4. In some countries the police operate on the principle that an individual is guilty until proven innocent. Police interrogations can be rough and might induce innocent people to agree to anything that will stop the ordeal.

   Such a situation can be very unnerving if you are investigating a mysterious disappearance or theft. If you report the theft to the police, they are likely to be suspicious of everyone that works in the operation. You may therefore decide to conduct your own investigation, so that you can resolve the questions without subjecting innocent employees to rough interrogation. **TIP:** *In such instances, an international detective agency can sometimes be very useful.* Their local office should have the knowledge and experience to help you decide how to handle such a problem.

5. In some countries the scarcity of dock space has led to some creative ideas for overcoming the dock shortage. One interesting concept is the use of steel cages to hold and ship products. The cages are filled in the warehouse, locked and then moved directly onto open body trucks that enter the shipping dock. The receiver, normally an inter-company location, has a key to the cage.

   The actual shipping operation takes from ten to fifteen minutes per truck. It has the advantages of permitting a check on the load before or after it is placed in the cage, controlling the product en route, and reducing the amount of time that a truck ties up a dock.

   But all good things have their offsets. *A major problem here is that a full truckload of product can be easily stolen.* Unauthorized trucks may pull in, load up and be gone in a few minutes, before shipping personnel can discover the true nature of the pickup.

   In some cases a truck driver might work in collusion with an employee on the shipping dock. The unauthorized driver arrives ten to fifteen minutes before the scheduled pickup time, knows what is to be picked up and where it is to go. The load is picked up and the truck gone before the authorized truck arrives. The scheduled truck may even arrive and be waiting at the gate for the dock space to open.

There have been instances where a scheduled truck is sabotaged so that it needs repairs that delay the time of arrival. This enables a substitute truck to pick up the product. Where a system requires identification, the bogus driver calls the shipping office and tells the clerk that the scheduled truck is having problems and that they will send a substitute truck to pick up the load. This approach convinces shipping personnel that everything is in order.

One protection against this type of scam is to require advance notice of the truck identification, license number, truck driver's name and description from the responsible company that is to pick up the load. The shipper must then confirm that all items are correct. If everything does not check out, the shipper, before loading the truck, should check out the driver and the vehicle.

6. Office services that handle the furnishing of private offices may have a warehouse of office furniture under their jurisdiction. The storage may contain expensive pieces of furniture that have come from executive offices that were remodeled.

   Executives spend a good portion of their waking hours in their offices and the Personnel Department recognizes the importance of pleasant surroundings. Executives share a good percentage of reported income with their government, but private offices are theirs alone.

   Top executives who move into new offices frequently want to redecorate to reflect their character and to provide an atmosphere in which they feel comfortable. The furniture removed from a top executive's office may wind up being used by someone down the line or be moved to storage. From storage the furniture may be junked, broken up for repair parts or stored for later use. **NOTE:** *The items stored are sometimes stolen or sold for cash, which may be kept by the seller.*

   Office service managers often decide the disposition of items in storage. Some are given, or sold, to retiring employees who lived with the furniture for years. Others are sold to employees when it is decided that the storehouse is full and the older items should be discarded. Disposition of this equipment presents a control problem.

7. Many office service employees possess marketable skills that may only be used occasionally during the work day. **CAUTION:** *It is not unusual for these employees to use their skill at personal endeavors when they are not busy with company work.* Word gets around and soon the employee may have a service shop going during business hours.

   Some of these people actually take the items and repair them at home using their own time and materials. But others make repairs in the shops that the company provides, and they freely use company materials. These service people may contend, probably correctly, that company work comes first and that they only repair personal items of other employees when they have nothing else to do and then only as a convenience to fellow employees.

This is a difficult area to control. **KEY POINT:** *A work order system is a necessary first step toward eliminating the practice, if management wants it eliminated.* Work orders should show date and time that a job was started, the type of work, the technician assigned, the number of hours spent on the job and a complete list of all parts and supplies used on the project.

NOTE: *This work order system is also appropriate for charging out a section's services to other departments.* It serves as a basis for determining amounts to charge, usually applying a standard hourly wage rate to the number of hours spent on an assignment. Materials are charged at cost and overhead as a set percentage.

When auditing such operations, work orders should be analyzed to determine the full use of personnel and materials. **KEY POINT:** *Your study may disclose purchases of personal items that were charged to the company. It will also enable a tracking of billings and receipts for personal work, if such work is permitted.*

8. Personal work performed by specialists, while on the job, can frequently be found in the following areas:

   - Repairs of small appliances and office equipment of the type that is also used in the home.
   - Repairs of furniture.
   - Preparation of term papers and school assignments, and other types of correspondence or reports prepared in word processing.

   CAUTION: *Although the above items may not of themselves be objectionable, the permitting of such activities, even though fairly charged, makes it difficult to analyze staff size requirements.* If staff is held to a bare bones level and if all company assignments are promptly handled, management frequently permits servicing of employees' personal requests.

Chapter 28

Auditing a Plant, Distribution Center or Sales Branch

We will now consider an internal audit of a production plant, distribution center or sales branch. Though each is a distinct operation, they have much in common. The major audit emphasis lies in the intake or production of product, the sales of such products and the storage and movement of products to customers.

In a *production operation* we are interested in what comes into the building, how it is handled internally, and what goes out of the plant.

Distribution facilities may be located adjacent to a producing plant; often they are housed in the same building. In *distribution operations* we're concerned with what is taken into inventory and what moves out.

Sales branches may be located in the same complex with plants and distribution centers, or they may stand alone. These operations may or may not carry an inventory of products, but their salespeople sell available products, arrange for delivery and are responsible for collecting amounts due. In *sales branch operations,* auditors are interested in the sales transactions, the delivery of product to the customer and the collection and handling of the sales proceeds.

Many companies that engage in all three distinct operations often house them all in one major installation. Each activity may be independent of the others, or there may be various combinations of responsibility, but each function has its unique features. The interrelationships of these activities are such that an internal audit is *most effective when all the activities are reviewed simultaneously.*

However, an internal audit program should be divided into distinct parts. This chapter assumes that all operations are audited at the same time, but it sets out audit points in a way that enables you to review any single function individually. Auditors perform the audit steps listed in "All Operations," and then add the items listed under the particular portion that is to be studied. If all operations are to be reviewed, the staff will perform all of the listed points.

I. Production Plants

Every production facility is unique. Production processes play an important role in the economic life of many large companies. An enterprise that produces a product as an important part of its operation, takes in materials and supplies and provides labor and energy to produce a saleable product. The actual production process usually takes raw materials and supplies, and transforms the materials into finished products. At the end of the process, the products are packaged and labeled and offered for sale.

We will concentrate on a production facility that is designed and used for the production of consumer type products. The sample audit program leads through the total operation, starting at the receiving docks, through storage and requisitioning to the production area. It goes from the processing operations into packaging and casing. Once cased, the product is turned over to an independent distribution function. All of the major plants covered by our sample program are located in a complex that contains a Distribution Center.

The program considers the following elements:

- *Ordering* of raw materials and supplies,
- *Receipt and handling* of goods into and inside the plant,
- The *costing processes* and the *treatment of by-products,*
- *Labor efficiency,*
- *Controls* over inventories and movements of materials and supplies,
- *Materials and supply settlements,*
- *Calculations of variances* for raw materials, labor and supplies,
- The *machine shop* and the *tool room* that contain the special tools and materials needed to perform required repairs, and
- The *miscellaneous activities* that are necessary to provide for the needs of the hundreds of people who work in a production facility.

Since the program envisions a large processing operation, it may contain audit steps that would not be required in a small plant. The internal auditor is expected to omit those steps that do not apply, and to spend minimum time on those that are not of major significance.

II. Distribution Centers

Distribution of product is a major activity, generally requiring a large investment and competent personnel. Product from a variety of sources is gathered under one roof and combined into shipments to customers, sales branches, plants or other distribution centers.

Complex computer programs reduce the time required to manually calculate and print warehouse pull and loading sheets. Computer generated routing and delivery instructions enable orders to be combined to make economic shipments and hold costs to a minimum.

Distribution facilities sometimes occupy over a million square feet of floor space, perhaps fifty feet high, and may contain millions of items. Without computer assistance, product could easily be mislaid or lost for years.

In an audit of a distribution facility you are concerned with the following:

- The *receipt of merchandise* and its *storage and handling,*
- The *pulling of product for shipment,*
- The *checking of product* placed in the staging area,
- The *loading of product* onto delivery vehicles,
- The *accuracy of bills of lading* for product shipped,
- The *official receipts* for products delivered,
- Determining that *notices of shipments* and the *subsequent billings* are handled promptly and properly,
- The *periodic counts* of inventories that may disclose variances or product disappearance; and
- The *physical safeguarding* of products.

The audit program contains specific points designed to lead through an in-depth review of an independent distribution activity housed together with other independently controlled operations. The center is not responsible for a sales force, or a production plant.

III. Sales Branches

In any enterprise the sale of goods or services is vital to the continued existence of the firm. The seller may operate out of a vehicle, over a telephone, in a shop or standing on a street corner. Facilities housing sales operations are appropriate for the type of business conducted therein and can vary from a one person office to a large building housing hundreds of people. Types of sales facilities can even vary within a company, and the auditor must use an approach that suits a particular situation.

An internal auditor must accomplish several important objectives in a review of any sales operation. The audit must verify the following:

- A *legal sale* has taken place,
- *Terms and conditions* conform to stated company sales policy,
- The *price* charged is proper and does not violate company policies or any pricing laws,

- A legally *enforceable document* sets out the conditions of the sale,
- Legal proof is available of the *delivery* of goods or services, and
- *Accounting records* of the sale are complete, accurate and timely.

When goods are involved in transactions, the auditor must verify the following:

- That *products shipped conform to the sales agreement,*
- That *proof of delivery is available,* and
- That the recipient of the product is *promptly and properly billed for all shipments.*

Background Information

The XYZ Corporation is a major consumer products company that has numerous plants, distribution centers and sales branches. These company locations may contain a variety of operations depending on the purpose of the installation. Production plants are responsible for producing products for sale in the consumer market. Sales branch operations house the activities associated with the sales of company products and the related collections. Distribution centers are responsible for the movement of finished goods from the end of the production line to sales branches or directly to large customers. In day-to-day operations, these activities may overlap.

Production Plants

Each plant is managed by a plant manager who operates under instructions from the Headquarter's Production Department. Managers conform to policies and procedures set by the main office though they select staff personnel and are responsible for day to day operations.

The primary purpose of the plant is to manufacture products as required by the organization, and it is the job of plant personnel to receive raw materials and supplies and turn them into finished products. Monthly production schedules are established by the head office, but the plants are free to schedule daily production runs as necessary to achieve the monthly plan.

Local plant managers are responsible for the labor used in their operation, though labor rates are based on union contracts negotiated by headquarters. Materials and supplies are withdrawn from suppliers by the local Plant Materials Managers who order against national contracts written by the headquarter's Purchasing Department.

Production plants may have sales of such things as scrap, salvage, junked equipment or sales of finished products to cafeterias or to employees. **KEY**

POINT: *These operations sometimes create accounts receivable, and the plant may also receive cash from these sales. Some plants may even carry an inventory of finished products.*

Every major plant utilizes a preventive maintenance program which requires a tool room and a machine shop. This operation is similar, from the audit standpoint, to the garage operations that distribution centers or sales branches may have in their area of responsibility.

NOTE: *The maintenance facility presents a control problem* because the stored materials and tools can be useful to mechanics in performing repairs outside the plant. Some plants permit mechanics to borrow the tools during off hours because some local managers believe that such a policy eliminates the temptation to steal the tools.

Production at a major plant is cased and counted and turned over to Distribution at the end of the production line. A dual count is made by Production and Distribution, and when agreed, is entered into a National Production Cost computer system, and a Finished Goods Inventory system. In smaller plants, products are the plant's responsibility until they are picked up by Distribution vehicles.

The Production Cost computer system calculates the standard cost of each product and determines materials, supplies and labor variances. It prints out production reports and feeds data into the Finished Goods Inventory System.

Distribution Centers

Distribution Centers are charged with the responsibility for moving finished goods from production plants to sales branches or directly to customers. In order to economize on shipping costs, almost all of a center's finished product movements are in truckload or carload lots. Local deliveries to customers of less than truckload quantities are handled by delivery trucks out of local sales branches.

These centers are directed by local managers who report to the Distribution Department in headquarters. They operate around the clock during the week, but normally shut down on weekends. Local managers select the working staff, but all are bound to follow the strict systems and procedures that are established by the headquarters office.

Each distribution center receives daily computer reports showing their book inventory by product and projecting their daily activity. All shipping documents are computer prepared with the data being initiated by computer program or the ordering location. The centers enter shipping information as the loads are completed and shipped, and the computer automatically prepares the proper billings.

Distribution does not engage in direct selling of product, and it is not set up to handle cash transactions or accounts receivable. However, product is sold to cafeterias that serve the center's employees, and finished products are sold to company employees as a fringe benefit. In addition, the centers sell distressed product to selected outlets. They also have sales of scrap, junk, and old furniture and equipment. They must control the handling of cash, A/R, and F/G inventories.

A major problem at these centers is controlling the movement of product into and out of the complex. They use a weigh scale, at the truck gate, to weigh selected vehicles that enter and depart the property. The scales are manned by security officers who are also trained to perform the weigh master tasks. Security operations use TV surveillance cameras to observe movements on the premises.

Sales Branches

Sales branches store and then ship product in local delivery vehicles. They use an order and delivery system whereby the salespeople take customers' orders, and the product is delivered two days later. The route salespeople are responsible for the accounts that they service, and they collect funds due from these customers.

Since each location is responsible for both the sale and delivery of product, they require a staff of salespeople and deliverypeople and an efficient office staff. The office force reports the actions of the salespeople and drivers, and it exercises control over the inventory of finished products that move to customers or other company locations.

The top location executive is really a sales manager and is assisted by a warehouse manager and an office manager. Though office managers report to branch managers, they have a dotted line responsibility to a controller in the headquarters office.

The branch warehouse manager is responsible for the storage and control of products in the warehouse, for shipment of goods to local accounts, and for sales to walk-in customers. The warehouse manager cooperates closely with Distribution, and works with the office staff to determine warehouse variances and resolve these differences.

Financial responsibilities at a sales branch rest with the local office manager who enforces the controls and procedures that are laid down by headquarter's financial personnel. Much of the clerical work is performed with the aid of a computer that handles shipping papers, billings to customers, inventory control, payroll and A/P records.

Some sales branches are located adjacent to a distribution center, and in these cases, the branch does not get involved in the delivery function. In such locations, the branch concentrates on selling product, processing receivables and collecting cash.

Major control problems at branch locations include cash handling, accounts receivable and quite frequently, inventories. The branch keeps track of its own route receivables and collects from house customers. Cash is processed through a local depository account. The branch can deposit but cannot withdraw funds from this account. Each branch has a petty cash fund that is used for small local purchases, but major expenditures are handled through the A/P operation in the headquarters office. Invoices from vendors for branch purchases are paid on the basis of submitted disbursement documents that are approved by branch management and sent in to the main office for processing.

In the audit of a sales branch, internal auditors review the following:

- Writing and processing of orders,
- Receipt, storage and shipment of finished product,
- Accounting for receivables,
- Receipt, handling and deposit of cash, and
- Methods for reporting all activities promptly and properly.

Background Information—All Operations

The XYZ Internal Audit program is designed to cover major areas of Plant, Distribution Center, and Sales Branch operations. It draws heavily on other audit programs in the Internal Audit Manual. Some audit points may be very important at one location, and relatively insignificant at another. Auditors must carefully evaluate the risk factor in every operation. If an activity is important, the auditor performs all of the audit steps, while the minor items will be skimmed over and only obvious discrepancies will be given attention.

Each audit staff must design its own unique audit program to fit a particular situation. The sample program is divided into four parts:

1. All operations, which lists audit points that apply equally to Plants, Distribution Centers and Sales Branches.
2. Plant operations, designed for use at a production plant.
3. Distribution Center operations, which primarily deal with receipt and handling of finished goods.
4. Sales Branches, which mainly concentrate on the special problems of controlling a staff of salesmen.

Following is the sample internal audit program used to review an operation containing a production plant, a distribution center and a sales branch.

INTERNAL AUDIT PROGRAM—INSTRUCTIONS

IA PDBI308 XYZ CORPORATION
INTERNAL AUDIT INSTRUCTIONS
PLANTS, DISTRIBUTION CENTERS AND SALES BRANCHES

These internal audit instructions are designed to be used in conjunction with the check-off program (PDBP307), and the internal control questionnaire, when reviewing a plant, distribution center, or sales branch or any combination of these three activities. Use the portion of the program that applies to the operation you are auditing. **IMPORTANT:** *For an audit of an outlying location, you will use the Audit Checkoff Form (IA CO1, sample of form follows), to record your audit work.* Fill in the heading, and give copies of the form to each auditor. Auditors will write in the proper columns: MAJOR DIVISIONS: *All* for All Operations; *Plant* for Production Plant; *Center* for Distribution Center and *Branch* for Sales Branch. For MAJOR SECTIONS: an applicable note, either a capital letter(A) or a number(1). Appropriate SUBSECTION(S) should follow for assigned work.

For the questionnaire section, *Ques* indicates the major question label; *Sub* for sub question; *Yes* or *No* for the answer, and *Remarks* provides space for pertinent comments. All audit points and questions should be precoded on the form, before starting the audit.

Be certain to sign and date the form when work is completed.

IA CO1 **INTERNAL AUDIT CHECK OFF FORM**

Approved by: ____________________ **LOCATION** ______________

PROGRAM

Maj. Div.	Maj. Sec.	Sub. Sec.	Sub. Sec.	Sub. Sec.	Per. Cov.	Aud. By	Maj. Div.	Maj. Sec.	Sub. Sec.	Sub. Sec.	Sub. Sec.	Per. Cov.	Aud. By

QUESTIONNAIRE

Ques	Sub	Sub	Yes	No	Remarks	Ques	Sub	Sub	Yes	No	Remarks

I. All Operations

A. In this audit your general objectives are to do the following:
   1. Check for compliance with Corporate policies and procedures.
   2. Check compliance with Federal regulations and all laws.
   3. Evaluate the adequacy of internal controls and suggest improvements where applicable.
   4. Determine the accuracy and reliability of information furnished to management and make recommendations to improve efficiency.

5. See that company assets are properly reported and safeguarded.

This program is a general guide to assist you in meeting these responsibilities, *it is NOT an ALL-INCLUSIVE checklist.* If during your audit, you determine that certain related policies or procedures no longer apply, write the matter up and send your notes to the audit manager at the completion of your review.

B. Before leaving Headquarter's office, perform the following:
   1. Make copies to take, of current operating and expense reports, and employee outside interest reports.
   2. Plan your timing of the work to be done at the location, and clear the audit with the necessary executives in Headquarters.
   3. Gather together the supplies necessary to perform the audit.
      a. Use our standard form titled Auditor's Requirements For Outlying Locations Audits. (See sample of form, which is shown following these instructions.)

C. Upon arrival at the location you should:
   1. Introduce the audit staff to local management.
   2. Work out arrangements with the office manager to obtain office space, and clerical help when and as required.
   3. Set a time for taking a physical count of inventory.
   4. Review the self-audit program with top location management.
      a. Your review of this self-audit program should point out the areas of potential weakness in internal controls. Be certain that your review emphasizes those areas.
      b. You should determine whether the answers are accurate and adequate. *If there is any evidence that the answers have been deliberately falsified, notify the audit manager at once.*
      c. Where the program accurately indicates effective internal controls, you may de-emphasize or completely eliminate related audit steps. Note reasons for omission on the program.
   5. Review the instructional manuals maintained at the location for completeness and timeliness.

D. Complete the audit statistics form, and compare to operations that are similar. *Concentrate your audit effort in those areas where this location shows up unfavorably.* Pay particular attention to the Cash, A/R, Inventory, Payroll and Operating Costs statistical comparisons.
   1. You may wish to send in your statistics to our administrator, who will have an appropriate comparison made for you.

E. You are responsible for verifying the accuracy of the location's reports of physical inventories. You should control the inventory count, but instruct the location to follow normal counting procedures.

   Auditors should accompany count teams, and in addition you should select a few important items and count and record all pertinent data. Your independent count should be compared to the count of local teams, and all differences reconciled before the count is accepted as final.

IMPORTANT: *Any counts that differ from the computer generated record must be recounted by a team of an auditor and a supervisor.*

You should retain a copy of the counts and the reconciliations for your work papers. The office will provide copies of summaries they prepare, such as samples, unsaleables and line transfers.

If the location is experiencing excessive inventory shortages, take the time to determine whether the problem is caused by clerical errors or product disappearance. *If clerical errors are determined NOT to be the cause, contact the audit manager for instructions.*

F. Your inventory field work presents several problem areas. These include Consignments, Refused and Returned product, Car stocks, and Faulty, Distressed, Seconds, Rejects, or Obsolete products.

For all of these items, perform whatever audit steps are necessary to verify that each transaction was properly handled and reported. Returned product may, or may not, reach the warehouse; and it may, or may not, be saleable. Refused items can also be a challenge since carriers may hold product indefinitely; awaiting disposition instructions.

G. At your earliest opportunity, examine the locally controlled A/R files and determine the cutoff date to use for your statements. Discuss the matter with the office manager so that the A/R clerk can be told to post the accounts through the set date.

When the local posting is completed, take possession of the files and reconcile the detail to the control accounts. Then prepare your verification statements for the accounts you selected to test. Use the standard audit verification statements and reply cards. Mail in a standard window envelope. For replies received after you depart, have your mail forwarded to the audit administrator.

Use phone, letters or personal visits, to follow up on all customer exceptions noted in your detailed examination of cash receipts, as well as those reported on A/R verification statements.

H. Don't hesitate to use local clerical, or supervisory employees to assist you in routine audit tasks. But *be certain that these people work directly under your close personal supervision.* If such help is required, but not available from the XYZ staff, you may elect to hire people from a local temporary office help agency. Be certain to *check with audit management before making a commitment to the agency.*

I. You will be working with many computer generated reports. Discuss your assignment with the supervisor of the EDP audit staff, and rely on that group to supply you with the computer information you need. Become acquainted with the programs that produce the information you will be using, and be sure that you read and understand applicable software documentation. Bear in mind that *you are responsible for assuring that the computer information is accurate and timely.*

J. A description of the procedure for working with this audit program is in the Introduction to the Audit Programs section of your manual.

II. Production Plants

A. Review the Production, Quality Control, and Accounting Manuals dealing with production operations, costing and reporting. Review the User's Manual of the Standard Cost Computer System which processes all production data into the National Finished Goods Inventory System.

B. Each plant must carefully and completely follow the directives issued by the Headquarters Production Department. You should read all Production directives and determine that local executives are aware of and understand and follow these instructions.

C. When performing your inventory reconciliation work, keep in mind that there are *two major reasons that may cause substantial, but erroneous, inventory variances in finished goods inventories.*

1. *Cutoff problems.* You should be alert to movements of product during the period that inventories are being counted. Cutoff errors will usually offset in the next month's settlement.
2. *Proximity of the distribution operation.* Frequently local personnel shortcut national procedures, with a resulting large inventory variance. Procedures require independent counts of production by plant and distribution personnel. Since everything produced is moved to the distribution area, *some local people merely count the product in the storage area and accept that as the quantity produced.*

   Any movement of such product, before final counting, results in an understatement of production. Where no theft is involved, the distribution operation would report an overage that offsets the losses shown in the production operation. When you note a relationship between production shortages in materials, supplies and labor and a finished product overage at the associated center, you will probably be correct in assuming that the fault lies in the failure to make accurate counts of production.

D. All plants follow national personnel and payroll policies, but you may run into exceptions. When you note that a policy, or procedure, is not being followed to the letter, enquire for an acceptable reason. But keep in mind that any exception must be formally requested and be properly approved by an authorized executive. You should see documentation in the files that proves Headquarter's approval.

E. Each location is responsible for security within their perimeter. In a multiple-complex operation, the production department is considered the property landlord, and they must take necessary steps to ensure that items of a confidential nature are protected.

Auditors should not enter a restricted area unless it is necessary to accomplish an audit task. **TIP:** *If you feel required to enter an area containing confidential machinery, clear your intentions with the audit manager, and upon approval, inform the plant manager that you will be entering the area.* The manager may wish to call the audit manager to confirm that you have the authority; encourage such a call.

If you wish to test the security of a restricted area, after you receive approval from the audit manager, you may walk into the area to be tested without informing the plant manager in advance. *But you should spend no longer than a few minutes to establish that your actions were not challenged.*

1. Auditing of formulas is restricted to audit supervisors or long term staff members. **REMEMBER:** *New audit members, or trainees, are not permitted to see product formulas.* If you need to do audit work in a restricted area, it must be performed by supervisors or senior auditors, and not by personnel that are new to XYZ.

F. If it is necessary to make a twenty-four hour settlement of any production process, you should inform the Personnel manager that your staff will be in and out of the building around the clock, so that the security force will be aware of auditor presence.

For such settlements, you should arrive at least one-half hour before the normal plant schedule. Plan to have an auditor present for at least one hour after the operation is scheduled to shut down. Also use your team in shifts, so that there is at least one auditor present at all times (including lunch periods and breaks), during the full settlement period.

G. When large consistent variances occur, locate the problem source and plan a period settlement. For smaller plants, it's best to test the total operation. Select a day when no shipments are scheduled, and audit everything going in and out of the building. Remember to record names and hours of all employees working during the period, and check your labor listing against payroll records for that period.

For the larger plants, you should try to isolate the department(s) that are creating the variance, and concentrate on them. **IMPORTANT:** *Pay close attention to materials that are discarded for any reason.*

Lab samples require close attention; station an auditor in the laboratory for the full settlement period to record every sample that is brought into the lab. Use the sample schedule, and the video tape to ensure that all samples taken from the line, are brought into the lab. Be certain that you take possession of the video recording of product movement at the end of the production line.

KEY POINT: *If your audit production count does not jibe with the plant office records, these tapes can verify the accuracy of the audit count and help isolate the period when the discrepancy occurred.*

H. XYZ's reputation rests on the quality of its products. We have a strict quality control program, which you are required to check out.

TIP: *Pay particular attention to this phase of the operation during the hours when the top plant executives are not in the building.* Visit the lab during these periods and observe that all personnel are alert and performing scheduled tests in the prescribed manner.

I. Formulas, or production procedures, may be changed as a result of work accomplished in our Research department. **CAUTION:** *These changes may get lost in the communication channel from Research to the line operator.*

After you determine that the Formula Books and the Processing Manuals are current, compare formulas and directions to the line postings to ensure that they accurately reflect the most current instructions.

Then observe that those instructions are being followed.

III. Distribution Centers

A. The huge inventory carried in a distribution center creates many operational problems. One of the most serious to XYZ is the rotation of product so that the oldest product gets shipped out first. Though your program does not emphasize this area, *you should be continually alert to the procedures that the Center uses in moving product within the warehouse. When checking inventory, look at the code date on the pallets against the wall, and ensure that they contain newer product.*

B. Trucks will be coming and going at all hours, and perhaps every day of the week. Scheduling of these trucks is a manual job. We have introduced a time saving, and more secure system of moving product.

XYZ owned trailers are loaded and moved to a staging area. When a rig arrives, the driver does not know what the load contains or its destination until given the shipping papers at the staging area. The rig merely hooks on to the trailer and exits the premises without approaching the shipping dock. The shipping papers and the trailer number and door seals are checked by the guard at the exit gate.

C. A major control utilized for truck shipments, is the sealing of truck doors. *If the seal succeeds in barring entry to the load, any loading error is disclosed at point of receipt.* This means that on inter-company loads we do *not* have to incur the additional cost of *double checking.* **IMPORTANT:** *It is imperative that the seals be checked at the GATE for outgoing loads, and at the RECEIVING DOCK for incoming loads.* Loads coming in to our locations are checked by the gate guard, and then checked by the receiving clerk who removes the seal.

These seals are allegedly tamper proof, but there are many cases where a driver has cut the seal, removed product, and then glued the seal together in a professional manner that was almost perfect. Be on the alert for such a practice. Make certain that the removed seals are attached to the B/L, and remain in file for the prescribed period.

For inter-company shipments we use a steel corded seal, that can only be fastened and removed by a special tool. *These tools must be carefully controlled and should only be available to supervisors.*

D. Our major control procedure, designed to detect loading errors, is our weight control system. We weigh all trucks that enter or leave the premises. Before authorizing departure, the guard weigh-master determines that the weight reconciles to the empty weight of the vehicle plus the product involved in the shipment. *If the weight difference exceeds a set tolerance, the vehicle is held while the guard seeks instructions from the appropriate supervisor.*

If an inter-company shipment is involved, in which a steel cord seal is used, the guard automatically passes the shipment. All others are reweighed, and if still at odds, are sent back to the dock, or permitted to pass as determined by the line foreman. **IMPORTANT:** *A complete and detailed record is kept by the guard of every vehicle that passes the gate.* You will examine this record and follow up on any large discrepancies to see what action was taken; and why.

IV. Sales Branches

A. It is our goal to remove any cash handling from our Sales Branch operations. Most of our control problems occur in this area. Our direct banking program is a giant step in this direction, and you will examine the workings of this program to see where it can be improved.

The branch should have an active program to inform customers who remit to the branch, to send their checks directly to our lockbox at the bank. All salespeople and deliverypeople must prepare their deposits, and place them in the safe to be picked up by the courier service. The only cash requirement in the office should be for petty cash, and for the occasional warehouse cash sale. *Warehouse customers should be encouraged to pay by check or money order.*

B. Procedures require that office supervisors periodically review the duplicate deposit slips of drivers and salesmen to ensure that collections are being properly applied. To do this effectively, we must see a copy of the deposit slip that accompanied the deposit. (We have had instances where an employee sent a deposit slip to the bank which correctly listed all checks, but turned in a doctored slip which incorrectly listed deposit detail, though the total was identical.)

The purpose of this review is to see that the amounts on the checks received match exactly the amount of the invoices purportedly paid. *Any difference might indicate employee manipulation.*

C. Our branches are authorized to make consignment sales. Under this arrangement, product is shipped to customers on a memo basis. Product is regularly counted by salesmen, who bill the customer for any sales.

When making your inventory settlement, you must take consignment stock into account. These items should be treated in the same fashion as product in outside warehouses. **NOTE:** *On a selected sampling basis, you should have an auditor verify that such products are on consignment at the locations that are shown on branch records.*

D. Salespeople may carry stocks of merchandise in their cars. This usually occurs when we introduce new products, and sample the trade. Car stocks can come about from an error in product shipped or when an account needs immediate delivery, before the scheduled date. Product may be delivered by a salesman who picks up other merchandise that was delivered in error. Car stock is recorded as branch inventory. When a sale is made, the salesperson writes an invoice noting delivery from car stock, and the inventory records are accordingly posted.

You will selectively verify the accuracy of car stock records. It may be best to examine the stock of salespeople that work out of the local branch, or to wait for a meeting when all the salespeople come in.

SAMPLE FORM

IA R01 Auditor's Requirements For Outlying Location Audits

Enclosed are the pertinent records needed to conduct an audit of:

Location ______________________ Date ____________

	Date or Period of Data	Date Mailed
1. Copy of reported inventories at location.	Last month-end	
a. Inventories of items stored in outside warehouses.	Last month-end	
b. List of reported inventory variances.	Last six months	
2. Latest bank reconciliations.	Latest	
a. Latest petty cash reconciliations.	Latest	
1) Amount of authorized petty cash fund.	Latest	
3. Month end balance of all A/R.	Last month end	
a. List of write-offs and recoveries.	From last audit	
4. Copy of payroll and rates.	Current	
a. List of payroll terminations, showing names and dates.	From last audit	
b. List of Medical claims and list of Sick payments made to local employees.	From last audit	
5. Last two self-audit programs, and related follow-up correspondence.	Per request	
6. Representative sampling of vouchers paid on local approval, for period before audit.	Discretion of administrator	
7. Property list in triplicate.	Current	
8. List of owned or leased locations within approximately a fifty mile radius.		

IA PDBP307 XYZ CORPORATION

INTERNAL AUDIT PROGRAM—PLANT, DISTRIBUTION OR SALES

This program is designed to lead you through a routine audit of a Production Plant, a Distribution Center or a Sales Branch. Read this program, the associated Internal Control Questionnaire and the Instructions (PDBI308) and use them as a guide to be altered to meet any unusual conditions encountered. Bring to your audit supervisor's attention any changes that appear necessary.

Company Procedures

A. All records, reports and activities are under the control of local managers, but must conform to Headquarter's directives.

B. Accurate and timely records are kept by office personnel.

C. Regular periodic reports of pertinent activities are submitted to Headquarters personnel.
D. Internal controls are built into all systems and procedures.

Audit Scope, is to determine the following:

A. Prescribed systems, procedures and internal controls are adequate.
B. Local personnel operate in an efficient manner.
C. Company property is adequately protected and reported.

Audit Procedures—I. All Operations

During the course of your audit be alert to any obvious inefficiencies or waste, or practices which result in additional costs. Keep the following considerations in mind as you perform your work:

- Physical layout, and how it affects flow of work and efficiency.
- Employee morale. Note whether lines of responsibility are clear.
- General condition of equipment, and housekeeping of complex.
- Systems used to bring problems to the attention of management.

TIP: *If any of these items suggest problems, discuss your observations with local management, and cover the subject in a separate letter to the audit manager.*

A. Meet the operation's manager and identify yourself and staff. Have the office manager assign work space, and meet with all supervisory personnel. While you discuss the audit with location management, have your staff take possession of critical records and start the audit.
   1. During your work with section supervisors note their definition of responsibilities and how they discharge the section's duties.
B. *As soon as possible, count ALL cash on hand,* including petty cash, stamp funds, employee funds, and cash receipts. Follow steps in your Audit Manual titled Auditing Cash.
   1. Schedule daily deposits for the full month before your visit. Send copy of schedule to hdqrts for checking to Treasury records.
   2. Verify the accuracy and authenticity of the reconciliation for the last month, which you brought from headquarters.
C. Take possession of receivable records at your earliest opportunity. You may permit local personnel to bring files up to date. Audit these records as set out in the program titled Auditing Receivables.
   1. Prepare confirmation requests for any local accounts that are not listed in detail in the computer data base.
      a. Confirm these accounts in the same fashion as outlined for major account confirmations.
   2. For accounts that check out, you may leave confirmation replies with the local office manager.
   3. Verify employee receivables with each employee concerned.
      a. Determine that accounts are current and handled properly.
      b. Check to see if permanent advances are necessary.
D. Arrange with the local supervisor of warehouse operations to physically count inventories at your request.

1. Vehicles holding product at time of count should be locked and sealed. Retain and audit the control copies of invoices.
2. Select items, and groups of items, to count on a statistical sampling basis. Conduct your verification work conforming to the program in your manual titled Auditing Inventories.
   a. Trace computer reported adjustments to the operation's detail records supporting warehouse dumps, samples, inventory transfers, freight claims, shrinkage and unanalyzed losses.
      1) Determine that adjustments are valid and approved.
3. Determine that the location carefully reviews and follows up on every item listed in their Daily In-Transit Report.
4. Determine that the location verifies the accuracy of the Location's Over & Short On Delivery Report.
5. If the location is charged with inventories that are stored far away, our administrator will assist you to verify these items.
6. Review sales to employees for a selected period. Determine that all sales are for cash and at approved prices.
7. Check procedure for recording and controlling warehouse samples.
   a. Determine that all tickets are properly approved by manager.
   b. See that tickets contain name of recipient, and explanation.
   c. Determine whether quantities of samples are excessive.
   d. Evaluate control over the monthly summaries.

E. Verify property records as they relate to the location. Use the audit program in your manual titled Auditing Property.
   1. Verify selected items on property list taken from headquarters.
   2. Check condition and use of office equipment and files.
      a. Determine that files are regularly reviewed for transfer to storage or for destruction, as per record retention program.
   3. Observe and evaluate the security control of property.
   4. Verify accuracy and timeliness of Idle Equipment Reports.
   5. Visit every nearby leased or owned location. If property is rented to others, see that rent is received and properly processed.
   6. Compare number of vehicles to number of authorized personnel.
      a. *Verify that all spare vehicles have been properly reported.*

F. Have payroll checks sent to you for distribution to employees. Verify payroll; follow steps in program titled Auditing Payroll.
   1. Make a list of all employees you did not verify by sight. Find out where they can be reached, and speak to them over the phone.
      a. *Meet and verify those employees before completing the audit.*
   2. Satisfy yourself that employees are actually working at the job classification for which they are paid.
      a. To comply with regulations, determine that original driver's logs, dispatching records, doctor's certificates, and driver's expense reports are available for all drivers.
         1) Test these records for accuracy and proper maintenance.
   3. Check sickness and accident payments to employees, to determine that they are proper and within allowable limits of company policy.

4. *Determine whether any employees are used to perform personal work on property or an outside interest of a supervisor.*
5. Carefully check out the list of terminated employees that you brought with you from headquarters.
6. Review procedures for handling unclaimed pay checks.
7. *Note if there are employees having access to product, cash, A/R, etc. who have not taken vacations or were never absent.* List all such employees, to be reviewed by audit supervision.

G. Check procedures and controls for processing A/P vouchers sent to headquarters for payment. Use program titled Auditing Payables.
   1. Check procedures for preparing R/R's and their routing to A/P. *See that system prevents altering a R/R to cause a higher pay out.*
   2. Local contracts should be reviewed for necessity, reasonableness of costs and valid proof of receipt of goods or services.
   3. If location has a garage operation, check internal controls.
      a. Evaluate controls over supplies and parts. Analyze daily usage reports for accuracy and reasonableness of parts used.

H. Review controls over data processing terminals and reports.
   1. Determine if unauthorized entries can be made.
   2. Test edit routines and built in parameters that guard against entry errors.
   3. Ensure that appropriate run-to-run controls and balancing routines are properly utilized.
   4. If any terminals exist outside of the accounting offices, carefully review these operations.
      a. Determine that receiving docks only input receipts.
         1) Select good sample of receiving reports and follow through to see that EDP received accurate and timely data which is correctly reported in formal output.
      b. Determine that shipping docks only input shipments.
         1) Perform audit steps as above for shippers. (4.a.1)
      c. Determine that traffic office only enters routing, scheduling and freight bill data.
         1) Select sample of input and perform audit steps as above.
      d. Review procedures and controls over changes in input.
         1) Select sample of changes and perform audit steps as above.

I. Observe safety measures to prevent loss by fire, carelessness or theft of all mail, cash, records, reports and A/R files.
   1. Determine that safe is properly anchored to premises.
      a. Check to see who has custody of keys to the safe.
         1) Note whether keys are kept in a safe place at all times.
   2. See if the safe's combination was changed within the last year.
      a. *If not, change it, or arrange to have it changed.*

J. Review the Self-Audit program with management. Determine that answers are correct and represent current systems and procedures.
   1. Review related correspondence to see if there are any answers or omissions that indicate a policy conflict or poor control.

a. *Identify areas of weak controls, and audit these carefully.* You may skim over areas of good controls.

Audit Procedures—II. Production Plants

A. Review the Production, Quality Control, Plant Processing and Cost Control Manuals. Discuss with management their control concepts.
   1. Become familiar with all documentation that relates to computer programs used by production plants.
B. Use your manual program titled Auditing Production Operations and Cost Accounting for your review of pertinent operations.
   1. Make whatever tests you deem necessary to evaluate the security in restricted areas of the plant.
   2. Determine that security over formulas is adequate.
C. Compare reported production to planned figures.
   1. List significant variances that occurred during recent months.
   2. Analyze and determine reasons for variations.
      a. Note and comments on any of the following causes:
         1) Machinery down time or outright machinery failures.
         2) Lack of necessary raw materials or supplies.
            a) Review procedures for finding Economic Order Quantities.
         3) Labor inefficiency or unavailability of necessary workers.
         4) A natural catastrophe such as a flood, tornado, etc.
         5) Poor coordination between departments or poor management.
   3. Comment on volume of orders that were produced or shipped late due to inventory problems.
      a. Determine the frequency of production order changes that are initiated by the Marketing Department.
      b. Determine the incidence of unnecessary line setups.
      c. Evaluate the effects of deviations, of actual production from planned, on the inventory levels of materials and supplies.
   4. Determine that production planning considers the down time and costs involved in changing over a production line for a new product versus scheduling a slightly modified product.
      a. Review overtime reports. Select significant examples and determine reasons for excessive overtime.
D. Analyze product changeovers on production lines.
   1. Review system for determining line use and scheduling production.
   2. Determine the ratio of planned to total number of actual changes for selected lines for a two month period.
   3. Determine that communications between the various shifts assures prompt and accurate transmission of instructions regarding all changes in any production schedule.
   4. Determine that system includes an economic productin lot as one point to be considered when scheduling changeovers.
   5. Determine the effect on line efficiency reports of the number of product change overs.

E. Study efficiency of physical locations of storerooms relative to applicable production lines.
   1. Evaluate rationale that was used to decide whether to centralize or decentralize each storage point.
      a. Comment on any decisions that appear questionable.
   2. Determine that there is adequate control over movements of items both into and out of storage points.
   3. Determine that Stores personnel have an approved list of signatures with applicable limitations shown.
   4. Review file of approved requisitions for withdrawals.
      a. Select sample and compare dates with the dates that they were reported to the accounting office.
         1) Compare dates received in accounting to dates they appear in formal reports.

F. Review procedures for ensuring that changes in production formulas or processing steps are immediately disseminated to all supervisors concerned, and are followed by workers in the production lines.
   1. *Watch line workers to see that latest instructions are followed.*
      a. Note if meetings with line workers are held to describe new machinery, processes or methods.
      b. See if EDP controlled lines are promptly adjusted for change.

G. Review procedure for handling machinery changes that are issued by the Engineering or the Research department.
   1. See that they are properly approved and controlled.
   2. Determine that all change orders are promptly acted upon.
   3. Review the feedback reporting, by plant, on their experience in implementing changes and on the affect on operating results.
   4. Review procedures for disposing of materials or machinery that are obsoleted by engineering or research changes.

H. Through a sampling review, determine if F/G inventory variances are the result of offsetting items in the associated distribution center.
   1. Determine that representatives of *both* Distribution and Production count product at the end of the production line.
      a. Review procedures for resolving disputes over counts.
   2. Determine that there is adequate control over the accounting for goods-in-process, which has not yet been accepted by Distribution.
      a. See that system checks raw materials and goods-in-process to note whether items were produced but not recorded as production.

I. Determine that a system exists for the prompt issuance of necessary change orders, or cancellation of purchase orders where applicable.
   1. Review extent of judgment permitted to Materials Managers in requisitioning additional materials.

J. Determine that procedures are adequate to identify excess and obsolete items of materials or supplies.
   1. See that such items are isolated and controlled.

2. Determine that the program for disposing of such items of inventory is adequate and is being followed.
3. See that good communications between production supervision and the PMM ensure there is a minimum of materials to be discarded.
4. Study reporting routine over scrap, trim, spoilage and rework.
   a. Review the operations that are main producers of such items.
   b. Evaluate techniques that are implemented to reduce losses.
   c. Determine that proper disposition occurs.
      1) Follow through on any sales to reports of cash receipts.

K. Review procedures used at the receiving dock. *Determine that items remain on the receiving dock until the B/L is verified.*
   1. Verify that *all scales* have been checked within past 3 months.
      a. Any that have not, should be checked by auditors. Use the set of true weights available in all plants.
         1) Be certain that scale reading is correct through the normal range that the scale is used.
   2. See that managers resolve questions before R/R's are signed.
   3. *Determine that R/R's only list items actually received.*

L. Determine that the cost section has a good program for periodic supervisory studies of existing cost standards.
   1. Review procedures used to approve changes in cost standards.
      a. Assure that the headquarters Cost Department is advised and concurs in all changes in standards.
         1) Ensure that changes are entered into the EDP Cost system.

M. Observe cleanup crew in action during night shifts.
   1. Determine that they adhere to quality control standards.
   2. Determine that all areas are cleaned every night.
      a. See that correct cleaning solutions are used.

N. Review the plant's preventive maintenance program. Refer to program titled Auditing Production Operations.
   1. Review budget for maintenance operations, and compare to current cost reports. Determine reasons for variances.
   2. Review systems, procedures and security over tools and materials in the plant machine shop and in the tool room.
   3. Check inventory of expensive items and compare to book records.
      a. If there are wide differences it may be advisable to order a complete count in order to adjust bin cards to actual.

O. *If necessary,* perform a production settlement test. Observe and record activity during test period which should cover a full operating cycle. Most plants work 16 hours and clean up for the next 8, so your test will probably be for the sixteen hour period. The purpose of the test is to determine if production and cost standards are correct, and to spot any obvious problems occurring in the production area.
   1. Select operation to be tested, and seal off area during period.
      a. Arrange for TV cameras to record everything moving in or out.

        1) *Be sure to take possession of tapes at completion of test.*
2. Inventory all materials and supplies in area before starting.
3. Observe all production operations during *full* test period.
   a. Record all receipts of materials and supplies. Note identity of employees bringing items into area, and time of delivery.
      1) *If your record differs with office, the video tape will prove which record is accurate.* The same procedure applies for verification of reports of production.
   b. Keep accurate record, by job title, of names of all workers in the area. Note absences and record total direct man-hours.
   c. Record all production that leaves the area.
      1) Record identity of employees removing product, and time.
      2) Include ALL pickups of lab samples and spoilage.
4. At completion of test, take an inventory of everything in area.
5. Compare your record to office's and reconcile differences. Use video tape if necessary to identify employees moving items.
   a. Compare your record of receipts against office transfers into the production operation.
   b. Compare your record of production against office reports.
   c. Check your record of lab samples and spoils against both the lab office records and the plant office records.
6. Report your usage and production results to the EDP audit group and request a computer variance report for the tested production.
   a. Material and supply usage is the difference between opening inventory, plus receipts, minus closing inventory. (If there were transfers out, reduce usage by amount of transfers.)
   b. Direct labor hours is total working hours of line workers. Supervisory time should be reported separately.
   c. Production is the difference between opening inventory (if any), less ending inventory (if any), plus total product removed from the area. *Be certain to consider lab samples and rejects.*
7. Within 48 hours, you should receive the computer report of the results of your production settlement check. It will be sent to you via the local computer terminal printer. The computer uses standards contained in the cost program. Refer to your manual program titled, Auditing Production Operations and Cost Accounting.
   a. *If results prove that standards are wrong, inform the audit manager at once.* We will arrange to have a team of production analysts restudy the operation to arrive at correct standards. (An auditor should be a member of the recheck team.)
   b. If results confirm accuracy of standards, then *variances that caused your test are occurring through carelessness or theft.* Discuss problem with local manager, and set a course of action. *If carelessness is ruled out, phone audit manager for advice.*
   c. Any sloppy procedures or examples of mishandling noted during settlement, should be written up for your work papers.

III. Distribution Centers

A. Review the Distribution and Traffic Manuals. Discuss the operating systems used for building loads, scheduling trucks and safeguarding and controlling property and personnel.
   1. Follow applicable audit points listed in the program in your manual titled Auditing Distribution and Traffic.

B. Observe warehousemen building orders and loading trucks. Look for:
   1. Efficient flow of products and employee movements.
   2. Movement of product on a FIFO basis. Is code date checked?
   3. Efficient use of equipment. Are trucks fully loaded?
   4. Regular checking of loads by supervisors.
      a. Review time analyses, routing schedules and any other controls used by the warehouse manager, for reasonableness.
      b. *Determine that manager periodically reviews tickets turned in on test load, to dispatcher's schedule of weights for that load.*

C. Check to determine that the distribution center is using the routings and carriers as designated by the Traffic Department.
   1. Determine that carriers and/or routings are *immediately changed* when Traffic so directs.

D. *Carefully review the system used for controlling the accuracy and integrity of loads shipped or received in the Center.*
   1. Obtain copies of "Product Cut List" for the last few weeks and determine if cuts appear excessive.
   2. Review records of loading audits and office follow-up work.
   3. Determine that the steel cord is used to seal truck doors on inter-company shipments.
      a. Find out if the Sales Department is making a concerted effort to expand the steel cord program to our large customers.
   4. Determine that we cooperate fully with pickup customers who want their trucks sealed after loading.

E. See that inventory control clerks are aware of and make full use of all the features of the National Finished Goods Inventory system.
   1. See that it is used to caution those *carriers that are slow in delivery,* as well as those that *report consistent shortages.*
   2. See that *late deliveries*(in-transit), are promptly investigated.

IV. Sales Branches

A. Review the Sales Operations, Sales Branch Operations and Branch Manager's Manuals. Discuss systems, procedures and controls.
   1. Review activities, refer to the applicable audit points in the program titled Auditing Marketing and Sales.

B. Review one month of billings covering all product shipments.
   1. Discuss procedures relating to accounting for sales with office manager and clerk responsible for the assignment.
      a. Carefully review procedures relating to:
         1) Customer pricing policy.
         2) Faulty manufacture, unsaleables and close code dates.

3) Price protection, allowances and incentives.

2. Observe salespeople at end of day as they complete their reports. Note order, shipping and billing dates to see if orders have been accumulated to allow unqualified bracket prices.
   a. *Storage of goods purchased by a customer might be an indirect way of guaranteeing a price.* If price rises, they take delivery of stored product, if price drops items are returned for credit.
3. Check, in detail, all billings for at least one full day during the inventory period. *Check cash invoices for erasures or changes.*
4. Observe deliverypeople at end of day, completing the trip reports. Tickets, returned by drivers, should be tied-in to office control copies for all orders shipped. See that all tickets are returned.
   a. Tickets should be returned by the same driver indicated on office control and at the same time as others in the group.
   b. *Investigate any that are missing, turned in late, or turned in by a driver different than the one noted on office control.*
   c. Review branch procedures for handling overages and shortages.
      1) *For a test period, schedule and analyze all overs and shorts by deliverymen, and investigate consistent shortages.*
         a) If schedule is maintained by branch, test for accuracy and discuss handling with supervisor who reviews schedule.
5. Obtain copy of month end master sales and cash receipt summary; foot and cross foot and review for unusual items.
   a. Compare total of computer reported sales, received from main office, to total sales listed on monthly summary.
      1) *Investigate any material differences.*
   b. Trace house sales summary build up to summaries of drivers, salesmen and warehouse sales.
      1) Randomly test invoices supporting the House Sales Reports.
   c. Schedule invoices that contain items not at standard prices.
      1) Test-check distressed sales and determine that prices charged have management approval.
         a) *Carefully check invoices priced at local branch.*
         b) On test-check basis, compare prices per invoice to standard price list.
         c) *List any exceptions; investigate and explain.*
      2) Allowances or service charges should be checked to price list or branch manager's authorization.
6. Trace local invoices through to A/R, or cash receipts if paid.
7. During sales test, review time lapse between order taking, shipping, and invoice issuance to customer. *Study unusual delays.*
8. For test period, trace any sales adjustments or credits to source documents, noting proper approvals and authorizations.
   a. Trace detail to hard copy of sales adjustments sheets.
      1) Obtain copy for tie-in to EDP controls at head office.

C. Audit cash receipts as per section B. under *I. All Operations.*

1. For current business, confirm C.O.D. sales invoices on a random basis directly with customers. Use positive approach.
    a. *Pay particular attention to C.O.D.s with items cut from the invoice by deliveryperson.* (Short merchandise.)
    b. Use standard postcard form which requests: date delivered, invoice number, date paid, and exceptions of quantity or price.
    c. Send second requests after ten days.
    d. Confirm information in replies to cash receipt detail.
        1) *Note time lag between customer payment and deposit.*
            a) Investigate and explain unusual time lapses.
    e. Perform alternate procedures on non-replies.

D. Audit A/R as per section C. under *I. All Operations.*
1. Review A/R write-off procedure with person responsible.
    a. Select random sample of W/O's, from your listing taken from headquarters, and *verify proper support and approval for W/O.*
    b. Trace to invoices and shipping documents proving receipt.
    c. Confirm selected write-offs on a positive basis.
    d. *Examine customer files to see if any subsequent sales were made to the customer after write-off.*
    e. Discuss collectibility of old accounts with person who normally collects. Confirm all of these on a positive basis.
2. Test check collection agencies used to recover delinquent debts. Obtain list from agency of collections they made since last audit.
    a. *Trace recoveries of accounts written off to cash receipts.*

E. Audit inventory as per section D. under *I. All Operations*
1. Pay particular attention to potential cutoff problems.
    a. Check all paperwork of trucks on route during audit counts.
        1) Determine that truck returns are handled correctly.
    b. Be certain that loads put up for tomorrow delivery, are correctly included in count.
        1) Visually determine that product is not moved.
2. Review salesperson's car stock controls. Ascertain that these products are included in the inventory count.
    a. Physically verify some of these car stocks.
3. Review branch controls over unsalables.
    a. Determine that records are maintained by salesperson and/or customer; and that supervisor reviews the records.
        1) *Investigate those that appear excessive.*

F. Audit branch warehouse sales systems and controls.
1. Determine that all charge outs to customers are posted to A/R.
2. Audit numerical sequence of warehouse sales tickets.
    a. Determine that all tickets are accounted for.
    b. *Compare warehouse copies to copies on file in office.*
3. Send questionnaires to selected warehouse customers to obtain a listing of product picked up at branch during a specific period.

a. Base selection on review under 2. above. Particularly choose customers who buy large quantities irregularly, or who pay cash.
1) *Trace each acknowledged purchase to covering collection.*

G. Review sales of XYZ products to employees. They should be priced as listed on the employees price list, be on a cash basis and the sales should be restricted to established periods.
1. Make notes of *any* exceptions to policy that you observe.

H. On test basis, count coupons on hand and tie-in to branch record. Verify coupon destruction reports by review of redemption records.
1. Test several days local coupon receipts against credit memos.
a. Verify that supervisors compare detail of coupons to C/Ms.
1) Test a few C/Ms to attached coupons.
2) Trace total of C/Ms issued to the entry for the day.
a) Trace to see where customers took their credits.
2. View summary of coupons redeemed for accounting period; compare to destruction reports. Difference should be inventory on hand.
3. Review coupon redemptions by selected customers to verify that *redemption is reasonable compared to total purchases by account.*
a. Discuss standard verification procedures with salesmen.
4. Review procedures for processing clearinghouse billings and for determining that coupon amounts are correct and controls adequate.
a. Review for excessive redemptions from any one customer.
1) *Follow up on any coupons that appear fictitious.*
5. Review consumer complaint procedures over premiums and coupons.
6. Review controls over stocks of coupons held in branch.

I. *Review files of consumer and customer complaints.* Determine that supervisors follow up on every one in conformance with directives.

J. Determine that prizes issued to customers or sales personnel were legitimate and were received by the party that earned them.
1. Check branch records to verify that prizes were actually earned.
2. Examine proof of delivery to winners.

K. For expenses, reimbursed by salespeople's drafts, review supporting vouchers for several reimbursement periods.
1. Determine that supervisor and manager review and approve.
2. Review supporting documents for validity and reasonableness.
3. For the period tested, tie-in to recap of expenses and reports.

INTERNAL AUDIT PROGRAM—INTERNAL CONTROL QUESTIONNAIRE

The following internal control questions are intended to direct your attention to the high risk areas of these operations. Some of these points are covered in the audit program and are included here to ensure that they receive adequate attention.

Answer these control questions as your audit progresses. For section II, write in the names and job titles of the various employees who perform the listed functions. Be certain to note any conflicting duties that could jeopardize internal control.

I. The following are indicative of good internal control.

A. All operating systems and procedures are set by Headquarters.

B. All inventory transactions are processed by computer.

C. Local records and reports are accurately maintained and are reviewed by personnel in the Headquarters office.

D. All operations are regularly visited by Headquarters' supervisors.

II. Following lists functions performed by named employees.

Function:	*Name/Position*	*Conflicting Duties*
A. Collects cash.	________	________
B. Consolidates inventory counts.	________	________
C. Enters inventory data.	________	________
D. Distributes paychecks.	________	________
E. Enters time summaries.	________	________
F. Approves vendor's bills.	________	________

III. Internal Control Questions:

A. Are all records and accounts adequate for nature of the business?
   1. Are local operating statements regularly reviewed by responsible local officials?
   2. Is there good control over inventories?
   3. Are miscellaneous supplies adequately protected?
   4. Are all reports and vouchers sent in to Headquarters, properly and adequately supported?
      a. Are they properly reviewed and approved?
   5. Are all movements of materials or supplies to outsiders properly documented and followed up?
      a. Are accounting records adequate and timely in recording affect on costs?
   6. Are all changes of materials or supplies inventory levels properly approved before change is made?

B. Are safeguards adequate to prevent loss of critical assets?
   1. Are records tagged, filed and destroyed as per schedule?
   2. Are all manuals kept current?
   3. Is security over visitor control adequate?
   4. Are perimeter guards alert at all times?
      a. Is security over the complex adequate?
      b. *Is a section supervisor assigned to challenge anyone that attempts to enter a restricted area?*
         1) Is confidential equipment protected from visitor's view?
         2) *Are formulas adequately safeguarded?*
   5. Are there good controls over inventory cutoffs, safeguarding of inventory count sheets, etc.?
   6. Are accounting records accurate and complete for any material in our plant that is owned by others?

C. Are miscellaneous sales transactions well controlled?
   1. Is there an adequate program to notify the proper employee of any incurred losses that should be charged to outsiders?
   2. Do we require that checks, not cash, be received in payment?

D. Are property items classified as "Idle, awaiting disposition" adequately protected in storage?
   1. Have all surplus, or idle, assets been reported to Headquarters?
      a. Are these items frequently reviewed for action?
      b. *When "Junked," are they properly cannibalized?*
      c. When sold, do systems ensure proper handling?
      d. After disposition are records promptly posted?
   2. *Is any company equipment being used in the home of any employee?*
   3. Is any XYZ equipment being rented out?
E. Are cash receipts and funds properly safeguarded at all times?
   1. Are they readily available for verification?
   2. *Is an independent list of mail receipts prepared by mail clerk and checked to deposit records by a disinterested party?*
F. Is preventative maintenance program in use?
   1. Is it effectively followed? Should it be continued?
   2. Do maintenance procedures ensure that all items of property are examined and checked periodically?
G. Are quality control requirements rigidly adhered to?
   1. Is the materials and product testing program followed closely?
      a. Are statistical sampling techniques properly used in quality control sampling?
      b. *Is testing adequate at all hours of day or night?*
      c. Are all items that fail quality control standards discarded?
         1) *Is unsatisfactory product destroyed beyond recognition?*
      d. Are vendor evaluation reports periodically prepared by quality control on a scheduled basis?
   2. *Is there quality control supervision at all times, day or night?*
   3. Does the cleaning crew conform to quality specs and directions?
   4. Are all scales regularly checked for accuracy?
H. Do make-ready sheets used by workers conform to formulas and instructions issued by the Research and Production Departments?
   1. Do foremen ensure that all old procedure sheets are destroyed?
   2. *Are old-timers checked to see that they follow new formulas?*
I. Does cost section adhere rigidly to cost manual of instructions and User's Manual for EDP system?
   1. Do National Standard Cost Reports accurately reflect conditions?
   2. Do standard cost systems and reports serve as a useful tool for plant operating management?
   3. *Is overhead spread fairly over all items, including by-products?*
      a. Are by-products controlled in the same way as major products?
   4. Do all employees punch the time clock or prepare time report?
      a. *Do all employees continue working until quitting time?*
   5. Are computer-controlled production lines operating properly?
   6. Does the computer program produce a satisfactory production schedule?
      a. Is the schedule followed meticulously?

7. Do personnel handling plant materials attempt to minimize demurrage charges?

J. Do deliverypeople or drivers have access to any products or materials in the warehouse area?
   1. Are deliverypeople rotated to various routes?
   2. *Do loaders know in advance the identity of scheduled drivers for orders they are filling?*
   3. Are computer Over and Short Reports used to ensure the proper billings to customers for delivery overages of product which they accepted?
      a. Do procedures insure that Overs and Refused are brought back?

K. Does manager approve all distress sales and credit memos?
   1. *Is control adequate over disposition of salvage merchandise?*
   2. Is the amount of product dumped in the warehouse reasonable?
      a. Is more than one employee involved in the physical destruction of unsalable product?
      b. Is proper management approving all dump tickets?
      c. Do dump tickets contain proper explanations?
      d. Are tickets accumulated and reported correctly?
   3. *Do supervisors check salesmen's car stock and approve all credit memos issued by personnel?*
   4. Are customers notified of invoice errors?
      a. Are customers' signatures obtained on refunds?
   5. Is control adequate over the redemption of cents-off coupons by location personnel.
      a. *Are coupons mutilated and destroyed as per directives?*
         1) Are proper reports of destruction prepared and approved?

CRITICAL POINTS

Plants, Distribution Centers and Branches all carry inventories and therefore experience the same type of problems that were outlined in the critical points described at the end of the chapter titled Auditing Inventory Transactions. They all handle cash and accounts receivable, in varying degrees. The following discussion contains some repetition of material, but you may benefit from rereading the critical points described in the earlier chapters on cash and accounts receivable.

Be on the lookout for illegal acts that relate to thefts of cash or products, for you will encounter many ingenious methods for such acts. In sales branches, lapping of customer accounts is common, and false credit memos are often issued to cover withholdings. Most of these illegal practices are discovered by routine audit verification contact with customers. Some cases are so blatant that it seems that the perpetrator is begging to be caught.

FOURTEEN ILLEGAL PRACTICES TO WATCH OUT FOR

Receiving

1. A critical area of concern is the receipt of merchandise. Clerks who act as receivers should only sign a bill of lading which shows the quantity of product actually received. Any overages, shortages, substitutions or damages should be noted on all pertinent documents.

   Shipments are often made on pallets, usually full ones, and the receiving location may well acknowledge receipt based on full pallet loads. Accepting full pallets reduces the work of the receiving clerk and frees up the space on the receiving dock. However, these pallets may be *stacked incorrectly or dishonestly, with cases removed from the center of the pallet. Or some inside cases may have been opened and all or part of the product removed.* If this occurs the location will later turn up short of product.

   To detect such discrepancies, the receiver should use a test check system, that breaks down a sampling of full pallets, and checks to insure that the stacking is correct and that interior cases are full. **TIP:** *Another method, equally effective, is to test weigh full pallets and compare to ideal weights.* The system must consider the average weight of the pallet itself and the tolerance factor per case or per package. If a pallet's gross weight is not within tolerance, a supervisor, after checking the accuracy of the scales, should witness that all the cases are removed and individually checked.

   All discrepancies should be documented, and witnessed, with sufficient product identification noted, as well as witnesses and the date the check was made. **CAUTION:** *The entire pallet should be set aside and the shipper immediately notified of the discrepancy.*

   Ideally, this procedure should be a part of the receiving routine that can disclose differences before any documents are signed.

   If receipt has already been acknowledged, the shipper may contend that product was removed by receiver personnel and may refuse to issue credit. In such situations the auditor must make certain of the facts and then cause all future receipts from a specific company, or from a specific truck driver, to be minutely examined at time of receipt and in the presence of the driver and supervisory personnel.
2. In the receiving function, product is unloaded from a truck and often placed on the receiving platform. There it is counted and stays until a fork lift operator moves the product to its proper place in the warehouse. When this practice is followed, cases, or even full pallets, may be removed

before they can be moved in to the storage area. **CAUTION:** *These stolen cases of product, or full pallets, may be placed in an empty truck that has already been unloaded and is cleared to leave the dock area.*

This type of theft can be discouraged by requiring that empty trucks be inspected by a responsible party after they have pulled away from the dock, but before the truck doors are closed. If a truck has been only partially unloaded, the *checker must enter the body to check for unauthorized product among the remaining load.* This system will not be effective if like product is being dropped off, and similar product remains aboard for delivery elsewhere. When this occurs, a receiving clerk must be certain of the count of product received, and must ensure that all receipts are moved into storage.

3. Inter-company shipments may be received from company locations to be stored until they can be combined into economic loads. Transfers between a company's locations are ideally carried in full truckload quantities. *The trucks carrying such product are sealed to discourage theft or to provide evidence that tampering has occurred.*

Truck seals are numbered, and when affixed to a truck, the seal number is recorded on the Bill of Lading. It is essential that the receivers enforce a system that requires careful examination of the truck seals to determine that the number is as recorded, and that the seal has not been broken. **IMPORTANT:** *This verification must be performed before the truck driver is issued a dock number and allowed to bring the truck into the dock.* Many docks are so constructed that a truck's doors must be opened *before* it backs into the dock space.

Receiving clerks frequently assign space and permit drivers to bring in the seal after opening their doors and backing into the dock. *This procedure sabotages the concept of sealing trucks.* The driver, who is familiar with all calls, and knows their systems and controls, can remove product at leisure while retaining the broken seal to turn over to the receiving clerk. **CAUTION:** *The receiving location may not be concerned since any shortage is the responsibility of the shipping location, and does not effect the receiving operation.*

Receiving supervisors should be instructed to carefully check each seal before it is broken. Many drivers have devised a variety of ways to remove and then replace a seal in a manner that makes it difficult to detect that it has been tampered with. Some glue the seal back together, others merely insert the tongue back in the groove so that, unless the checker pulls hard on the seal, it appears that the seal is intact. Still others throw away the old seal and merely apply a new one, knowing that most receivers will not check the numbers unless the seal appears to have been tampered with. **NOTE:** *Some locations check the seals at the guard gate* leading into the premises, which is better than no check at all. *However* *this does not preclude transfer of product from the truck to a nearby parked vehicle.*

KEY POINT: *If a truck's seal has been broken, a supervisor must be notified who can verify the facts and take appropriate action. The driver and the driver's company must be informed of the infraction. The facts should be noted on the B/L and R/R.*

All product received from the truck must be carefully counted and accurately recorded. If it is an inter-company shipment, the shipping location should immediately be informed of the infraction. If it is an outside shipper, a factual letter should be sent to the vendor. **IMPORTANT:** *Tampering with a seal may be a federal offense,* depending on the locations of the parties concerned. However it is dangerous to file charges in such cases because drivers who habitually steal product from their loads always have a ready explanation for the infraction. They may claim that an emergency required that the truck doors be opened or that the doors had to be opened for inspection by a state policeman. In many cases they plead ignorance and contend that the seal must have been tampered with by someone at the last gas station or truck stop they used. Any excuse is hard to disprove unless the truck had been under observation during its entire run.

4. Full shipments frequently arrive carrying more product than ordered. This often occurs when the *receiving location* has a good system for checking the security of truck seals. The overage may be an honest mistake by the shipper, or may result from a *deliberate overloading of product that WAS TO BE taken off by the driver for later disposition.* In any event, the bill of lading, and receiving report, should both be noted with the details of the overage, and its disposition. **IMPORTANT:** *If some of the overage is accepted, and some refused, the receiving documents should list the identity and quantity of product refused, as well as the product accepted.*

   On inter-company overages, which are delivered by a common carrier, the best system is to require that the receiving location accept all products on the vehicle. If the location cannot use the product, it should be held until an economic shipment can be made to an appropriate company location. *If the items are not removed from the common carrier truck, they may never be returned to the company, or the shipping costs may be greater than the value of the product.*

5. Receipt of raw materials into a production plant can present a high risk opportunity for loss. Through error, negligence or collusion, the plant may be charged for more materials than actually received. **CAUTION:** *Such overcharges frequently occur when tanks of product are received that require accurate weighing before and after unloading to determine the true delivered quantity.*

Losses can occur because viscous product clings to the delivery vehicle. Where tankers are washed out to insure complete delivery, this wash water may be erroneously included in the report of received weight. The best protection against this type of error is to weigh the vehicle immediately before and after delivery, and only pay for the difference in weight.

When collusion occurs, the receiving clerk reports receipt of a greater quantity than was actually delivered. The difference in quantity may represent product dropped off somewhere else. In many cases the supplying company may not know what has transpired, and may be shocked to learn of the conspiracy. However, when full loads are received with seals intact, and an overstatement is made of the quantity delivered, the shipper should detect the overcharge and should issue a correcting credit memo.

Procedures for plant receipts of raw materials, condiments, and supplies should be personally observed by internal auditors. Where applicable, samples of incoming materials should be taken and tested for correct quality. Packages should be test weighed to be certain that marked weights are correct. For bulk items, the carrying vehicle should be weighed both before and after materials are unloaded. All incoming items should be counted *before* agreeing and signing the R/R.

6. Sometimes, itinerant truckers, who sell farm products to plants for cash, use ingenious methods to cheat the buyer. When items are purchased on the basis of weight, they find illegal ways to increase the weight of the materials they deliver. **TIP:** *A common method is to place sand or stones at the bottom of product containers.* Plants that buy truckloads of eggs from passing truckers may find that the lower row of many egg crates contain rocks instead of eggs.

   Milk may be watered to increase weight. Sometimes the addition of water comes about because the dairy farmer washes the residual milk from the containers into the milk tanker. Grain products will contain a quantity of husks, or dirt, that adds to the delivered weight but must be removed before processing. Normally, a sample is taken and analyzed, and the percentage of extraneous matter is applied to the total load to determine usable product. Receivers might also accept "seconds" as top quality or accept reconditioned machinery as new.

Shipments

The other primary activity relating to product handling is the shipping procedure that is used by an operation. All product that has been produced or received will, in one form or another, be shipped out. In a large operation millions of pounds of product move over the docks in a never ending flow, perhaps twenty-four hours per day and seven days a week.

Control over movements is difficult and costly. *Lack of control might save manpower, but it will ultimately result in greater costs.* A variety of control procedures are useful, depending on complexity of the operation, available resources, risk factor, and value of product.

7. Some large shipping centers have adopted a system of controlling product movements through weight analysis. Under such a system a truck scale is located near a guard station at the truck gate. All trucks are routed through the control gate and they are weighed upon entering and departing the premises. The difference in weight should be equal to the weight of incoming product dropped off, or outgoing product picked up for delivery.

   Under a weight control system, actual weighing of vehicles can be reduced by establishing a standard cab and trailer tare weight for vehicles that regularly move about the premises. When the guard knows that the vehicle is empty, the tare weight is used to make the product settlement, and if it checks within tolerance, there is no need to weigh the vehicle. **CAUTION:** *Tare weights can be affected by quantity of gas carried, variance in number of spare tires, empty pallets, snow, amount of dirt on the vehicle, the placing of the vehicle on the scale or even the wind direction and velocity during the weighing process.*

   These variables make weighing an inexact science. But it will detect substantial errors of omission and commission, and can be used to deter gross theft. Reconciliations of weights must also consider the number and average weight of any pallets used to carry a load.

8. Distribution activities require a detailed operating procedure spelling out actions to be taken to assure the accuracy of loads. The procedure must name a specific supervisor responsible for investigating variances during each shift. All pertinent data concerning each problem shipment should become a matter of record. Cab and trailer number, the driver's name, the date and time, the facts concerning the problem, the operating decision and the name of the supervisor who made the decision should all be recorded. **IMPORTANT:** *Any repetitive questionable data should be the subject of an in-depth audit review.*

   If a weigh control system is being used, any discrepancy over a preset tolerance requires that the trailer be reweighed, preferably after being detached from the cab. If the discrepancy is still evident, the guard responsible for the weighing should call the loading foreman and disclose all of the facts.

   The best system of control is to require the truck to return to the loading dock. The truck should immediately return to the dock, and the dock supervisor should be on the lookout for it. **TIP:** *The supervisor* *should examine the truck door seal to be certain that it hasn't been tampered with and then strip and recount the load.*

If the recheck shows that there was no loading error, then the information as to standard weight of product may be wrong and should be investigated. **CAUTION:** *It is important that standard weights be correct, because they serve as the basis for computing load weights and therefore become the basis for invoicing of some products and for freight billings by common carriers.*

Unloading and reloading of trucks is time consuming and costly and should only be used as a last resort. *But it must be used if the weighing system is to be an effective tool.* A load may have to be detained for hours before a discrepancy can be resolved, and many supervisors are loathe to authorize such action, choosing instead to believe that an error has occurred in the weighing process. Guards who make the weight reconciliations are reluctant to order a truck to return to the loading dock. They know that if the load checks out they will be criticized for weighing improperly.

There must be a firm, clearly stated policy that spells out the actions that the guard performing the reconciliation must take in the event of a discrepancy. Such policies reduce the exposure to criticism, and offer the guard no choice. A firm policy also relieves the dock supervisor of potential criticism for ordering the recheck of a load.

9. Storage places for products are critical points in the control process. Employees, and outsiders, devise ingenious ways to take possession of items without paying for them. Petty theft, and thefts of trucks carrying full loads, occur everyday. Such events vary in location, people involved, and the extent and method of theft.

The author recalls an unusual method of stealing from a transport truck that was a puzzler, for a while. Here's what happened:

> **EXAMPLE:** Shortages from a particular truck, with a particular driver, were occurring on each shipment. A decision was finally made to take the time to resolve the matter.
>
> A load was closely checked to ensure that shipping documents were correct, and the doors were carefully sealed with a seal that required a special cutter to open. The vehicle was met at the delivery point and carefully checked. The seal was intact and the doors had not been opened but the load checked ten cases short. All missing items were taken from a pallet of small cases that had been stacked on the top of the load.
>
> After intensive investigation, it was discovered that the refrigeration unit at the top of the front of the trailer had been removed and then put back. The action had provided just enough space for the

driver's nine-year-old son to crawl into the trailer and pass the small cases through the opening.

Miscellaneous

10. In production plants, thefts of finished products, raw materials, supplies, and tools are common. Some of these activities may be uncovered by surprise locker checks, or by searches of lunch pails or vehicles by security guards at the exit gate. But some thefts involve knowledgeable employees and sophisticated methods. **NOTE:** *When a conspiracy is involved in thefts of product, the quantity taken must be large enough to distribute the proceeds among all the conspirators.*

    This large a theft does not normally go unnoticed.

    However, if an office employee is among the conspirators, the thefts may not be detected until they are large enough to produce noticeable losses. **TIP:** *Product thefts may be hidden by increasing the quantity of reported dumps, faulty manufacture or product reworks.*

    If the thefts are hidden by merely *decreasing* the quantity of production, it should show up in variances in raw materials, supplies and direct labor. But a cost clerk may adjust production cost standards to hide the thefts. **CAUTION:** *A very small adjustment in standards can hide regular, consistent thefts of product.*

    Removal of the items taken becomes the major problem for the conspirators. If a good security system is operational, with weight control as an important element; then removal is the main obstacle.

    When manipulated standards are used to hide thefts, the standard used for costing may be different than the formula used in production processing. Production uses the required quantity, but the standard shows a slightly higher quantity or includes an excessive shrinkage, trim or waste factor. *The difference appears negligible, but in mass production a minute difference can translate into a lot of product.*

    The key to good control is an airtight production recording system that employs a dual count procedure in which counts are independent and cannot be altered. A TV camera can be a good control mechanism if the film is checked regularly. If the production counting system is foolproof, any theft of product will show up as an inventory shortage.
11. Another area of risk, which occurs when many people are employed, is the possibility that company employees may be used to work on a manager's personal property. Executives have been known to use employees to improve or build new homes or other structures. Building supplies and equipment are purchased and charged to company expense.

    Be aware that service type employees are used for such purposes.

Pay particular attention to the whereabouts of maintenance personnel during the normal work day. Also examine overtime reports for these employees. Such overtime might be spent at the manager's property.

12. Cash from warehouse sales is particularly vulnerable to theft. In outlying locations, the office staff is frequently small, and all clerical routines are controlled by and rely on the office manager.

    If a manager succumbs to temptation, a difficult problem is created. The manager may merely destroy the office copies of selected cash sales tickets and pocket the proceeds. **CAUTION:** *This type of manipulation can go undetected and unnoticed* until the amounts involved produce a noticeable inventory shortage.

    When that occurs, a detailed study of all related procedures will lead you into the cash sales area. Upon deciding that cash sales is the likely problem area, the audit approach is to identify customers who regularly pick up product at the warehouse; determine their buying patterns and then look for exceptions to the pattern. For noted exceptions, ask those customers to supply a record of purchases for a set period, which includes the unusual lapses. A comparison of this information to branch reported sales should disclose the manipulation.

13. Failure to accurately record transfers between departments or company locations is often the cause of inventory variances. This is particularly true when product is produced by a plant and immediately transferred to distribution. Since this is not a true loss to the company, employees in these areas are often careless. **IMPORTANT:** *These errors distort location operating results and efficiency reports and can lead to incorrect product cost computations.*

    These situations can be found through a comparison of variances between associated locations, and spotting offsetting variances between the related operations. But remember that any breakdown in internal control can be the result of, or can produce, real losses through theft. **CAUTION:** *Where people are engaged in stealing products, they frequently manipulate records to give the appearance of offsetting errors or unrelated mistakes, in order to hide the thefts.*

14. Other problem areas in production plants can include preparation and production areas. **NOTE:** *If too much of an expensive material is used in place of a cheaper item, such as water or air, or if packages are over filled, losses will occur.*

    If quality controls and testing procedures are adequate, all of the above problems will be spotted and quickly corrected. However, if the laboratory is negligent in their testing, the product will move into the trade, and the company will bear the loss. In such cases the substantial raw material variances created by the errors should come to management's attention in a reasonable period of time. Once the cost reports show raw material variances, a review by production analysts or internal auditors should locate the source of the problem.

SUMMARY

This completes the section of this manual that contains specific audit programs designed for the examination of particular operations. These programs should provide a skeleton approach to an audit review of selected business activities. They are not all-inclusive and do not cover all aspects of every operation that must be examined. Every business company is unique and requires individualized analysis to determine the best internal audit approach.

The next section of this manual, Part IV, deals with the special types of problems that an internal auditor encounters when practicing the profession. These items are not approached in the same methodical fashion as a review of an operating department. But every problem that is encountered can be approached systematically, using as a basis the audit programs that are contained in this manual.

The following problems are not presented in the audit program fashion, but we still use the basic audit approaches, just described, to analyze a problem. Our solutions often are found by using standard audit techniques.

Part 4

Special Items

Chapter 29

Fraud, Outside Interests and Special Assignments

Some of the unusual challenges that exist in internal auditing are frauds and special investigations. These types of transactions or events are not the highly repetitive, high volume activities that an internal auditor normally encounters.

Audit investigations often center on isolated transactions that may only involve one, or a small group of individuals. Each problem has unique characteristics that require special analyses.

Let's consider employee defalcations, frauds and thefts involving outsiders, conflicts of interest and outside interests of employees. We will also discuss special investigations or projects that an internal auditor may be called upon to perform.

Definition of Fraud

Legally, fraud is defined as containing seven important, necessary and distinct elements. If any one of the seven elements is lacking, then no fraud has been perpetrated. The elements are the following:

1. There must be a MISREPRESENTATION
2. Of a PAST or PRESENT
3. MATERIAL FACT,
4. Made KNOWINGLY or RECKLESSLY
5. With the INTENT of inducing a party to act.
6. The injured party must have ACTED on the MISREPRESENTATION
7. To his/her DETRIMENT.

Legal distinction aside, in this chapter we will use the term FRAUD in it's broadest commonly accepted usage. It will include manipulations, malfeasance, peculations, withholdings, defalcations, thefts, embezzlements and any other misdeeds by an individual that might cause a financial loss to an organization. Fraud and dishonesty will be used interchangeably.

Fraud and Internal Controls

There are many more ways to perpetrate a fraud than devices to prevent it. Many of the checks and audit steps covered in this manual are designed to protect against fraud and to detect its occurrence.

A good set of internal controls protects an organization against dishonesty and enables early detection of a violation of procedures or an irregularity which may indicate that fraud is present. In reviewing the financial painting of an enterprise, an auditor familiar with an operation can easily spot flaws in the picture. Having once noted a flaw, it then becomes the auditor's job to investigate and determine whether those problems were brought about through errors of omission or commission or are the signs of fraud.

When an internal control procedure has been eliminated, bypassed, or disregarded, then an immediate question must be posed, *"Why were those controls not followed?"*.

Sometimes, as when an enterprise is on a cost control program, internal controls that are believed to cost more than they are worth are put aside either for a short time or permanently. Controls cost money, and any duplication of effort costs money, therefore the elimination of some of these steps can produce savings. A routine internal control may become outdated and useless through the passage of time or changes in the business. **KEY POINT:** *Elimination of such controls benefits the firm, and it is therefore imperative that the internal auditor be familiar with the reasons behind all of the internal controls that are used in a company.*

Recognizing the purposes of controls, the auditor is able to evaluate whether their elimination has created a risk, and if it has, in what areas of an operation. If a risk element is involved, audit effort should emphasize the review of related transactions to determine whether the elimination of controls had produced a fraudulent act.

REMEMBER: *Deliberate bypassing of a control is often associated with an act of fraud.* The elimination of an important control is an inducement for someone to perpetrate a fraud, but if the control never existed, then perhaps no one has taken advantage of the oversight.

CAUTION: *But when an existing control is bypassed, the auditor should be alerted to the possibility that someone chose to ignore the procedure in order to commit fraud.*

Potential for Fraud

Let's look at a simple and obvious example of what can occur when an auditor notices that an established internal control is discarded:

EXAMPLE: An auditor finds that incoming checks are no longer pre-listed in the mail department, but are delivered directly to the accounts receivable bookkeeper so that they can be compared to open invoices before they are turned over to the cashier.

The elimination of the prelisting has reduced the work load in the mail department and also in the cashier's department. (The cashier no longer needs to compare the checks that were deposited to the mail room pre-listing.)

It has not increased the work in the accounts receivable department, since bookkeepers now work with the actual checks instead of the transmittal notices and remittance advices.

The receivable clerk now removes and retains the check stub and other remittance advice and turns the checks over to the cashier for listing and deposit.

The operation has been streamlined and made more efficient and the only thing that has been given up is a small element of internal control. *However, a good opportunity now exists for a receivable clerk to misappropriate a check that pays an account already written off, or a disputed amount which has been cleared out of the open file.* If a money order or currency is received in the mail, then the bookkeeper may be tempted to create bogus credits to an open account to offset an amount that is illegally withheld.

These manipulations are common, and they usually come to light during a verification of accounts written off or credit memos, or a comparison of first party checks to the amounts of the invoices that the checks purportedly pay.

KEY POINT: *(Repeat) Any bypassing of an essential internal control should be viewed with suspicion by an internal auditor.*

Danger Signals

There are certain danger signals that an internal auditor should recognize as accompanying an illegal act. When a clerical cover-up is not used, the act is begging to be noticed. *Employee Defalcations* may be indicated by one of the following:

1. Missing records that may identify the manipulator or the action.
2. Altered records. The signs of alteration might be evident, or there may have been an attempt to hide it. Changes in records are frequently accomplished to hide an illegal transaction.
3. Losses or variances in assets. Sometimes assets are taken, but the thief is not in a position to alter records to cover the thefts.

4. Variances in production usage reports. These may show up even when some production records have been altered.
5. Unusual or frequent adjustments to asset accounts. Dishonest acts are often covered by a series of relatively small adjustments.
6. Unsupported credit memos. Either unsupported, fictitiously supported or overstated credits are frequently used to hide employee withholdings or thefts of assets.
7. Excessive labor costs. High labor costs for a specific operation may be caused by padding a payroll.
8. High materials or supply costs. Cause may be theft or collusion.

Outsider Fraud may result in the following:

1. Write-offs or write-downs of assets. Items delivered may have been inferior to materials specified.
2. Overcharges for services or materials. Many times a deliberate overcharge is attributed to clerical errors.
3. Fictitious invoices for goods or services. May be a mistaken billing sent to the wrong company, or may be a fraudulent act.
4. Lack of support for a payment for goods or services. Billing may be completely fictitious or worded in a way that induces payment but is really a solicitation.
5. Unusually large orders. These may be a scam, particularly if they are from newer customers that formerly ordered small quantities.

Employee Misdeeds

Employee frauds usually involve the removal of assets from the employer. Sometimes this is a direct act of theft or manipulation. *At other times it occurs in a roundabout way* such as increasing payouts by the company to cover items procured for the employee's personal use. Sometimes the peculations take the form of kickbacks that do not appear to be a direct cost to the company, but in reality represent overpayments for purchased items. Other defalcations occur in which the thief proudly contends that the employer lost nothing, such as when a salesperson or deliveryperson uses a position of trust to steal from or defraud a customer.

In these cases, a key employee betrays the trust and confidence that was erroneously bestowed. These culprits defraud the innocents who trust them as creditable representatives of a reputable company. The time that they spend in dreaming up their illegal acts, hiding them by altering reports and original documents, and the time required to investigate, prove and then discharge the thieves and locate and train replacements, are all direct or indirect costs to their employer.

NOTE: *Employee misdeeds all have one thing in common; the employer at some point loses something of value.* Funds, which should have gone into the company's accounts, may be diverted. Thefts or manipulations may involve inventory or items of property, but the bottom line is the dollar disappearance in one form or another.

All assets are subject to manipulation and the most common motive is to produce cash income. Thefts of cash can occur at any level of a business. They can occur either directly or through other means such as excess payments for payroll or the purchase of items from outsiders who kickback funds to the dishonest employee.

Products may be stolen to be retained by the thieves or sold for cash. Receivables offer an opportunity for potential manipulation, but these only have value when converted into cash. It is rare that receivables are illegally written off as a personal favor to a debtor, though such activities have occurred.

Thefts of miscellaneous goods and services are another problem area. Here we find fraudulent expense reports, which produce cash for the defrauder. There is also the fraudulent inducement to make company payments to outsiders for personal items purchased by employees. This does not produce incoming cash to the manipulators, but it results in their receiving free merchandise. The same benefit occurs when company labor is used for personal purposes.

Preemployment Misrepresentations and How to Prevent Them

Employee dishonesty may start with the employment application that is submitted by a prospective worker. Many prospective employees fabricate their educational background and prior experience, and do not give an accurate report of their criminal record. Some companies don't bother to investigate employment applications because of the cost involved in checking, and because there is no assurance that the applicant will be offered a job, or will accept.

Some employees are hired at low level jobs that do not warrant an intensive investigation of their application. Once hired the form is filed in the Personnel department and forgotten. The employee progresses through the firm based on individual initiative, ability and luck. That is why it can sometimes come as a shocking surprise to discover that a responsible executive has a background that would have prevented the hiring, had the facts been known.

As a prevention your company may opt to adopt certain procedures:

1. Issue a statement of policy decreeing that any false or misleading information written on the application form is cause for immediate dismissal. This

policy can eliminate the individual problems of deciding what to do about employees who lied on their applications.

2. Require the applicant to show any diploma or degree that has been earned. A call to the registrar of the school can confirm the validity of the document.
3. Require that a thorough check be made of any employee who is about to be offered a position. To reduce investigative costs, a check need not be instigated until an interest in the applicant has been expressed. It might be more economical to check out all prospects before even wasting executive's time in visiting with them.
4. Require a series of tests as evidence of the applicant's knowledge, personality, psychological make up and perhaps veracity.

INDICATIONS THAT PROBLEMS EXIST

Some fraudulent acts will not be immediately evident in a lowering of profits; such as when idle property is stolen. Theft of property might have the reverse effect if it results in a decrease of the depreciation write-off. However the asset account is also reduced.

The diversion of recoveries from bad debts for accounts written off will also not be reflected in current operating statements, even though such thefts represent losses to the company. **KEY POINT:** Despite exceptions of this nature, *major defalcations usually result in an ultimate lowering of profits.*

The Signals

There are various signals that indicate that fraud may be occurring in a company. Some of these warnings are evident by the following:

1. Reported profits not up to expectations.
2. Variances in finished goods, raw materials or supplies.
3. Unexplained increases in specific or total operating costs.
4. Unexplained increases in costs of materials, supplies or labor.
5. Reports, anonymous or otherwise, of questionable transactions.

Any of the above indications may be the result of operations which though not efficient, are not fraudulent. But let's see how fraud can result in creating each of these warning signs.

1. Profits Not Up to Expectations. Companies compile much statistical information which is designed, prepared and used to indicate whether any activity is failing to perform up to expectations. Failure can be caused by a number of factors, one of which is an employee defalcation.

In a large operation, minor thefts will not usually be noticeable in statistical analyses since the total volumes are so great that small peculations may not have an effect on reported figures. Or an operation may be improving at the time that thefts are initiated, and the improvement may completely hide the thefts. This is not to say that statistical analyses is not useful in locating employee defalcations; far from it, but you *may have fraud occurring in an operation that is not readily apparent from statistical reports.*

When major problems arise, a statistical comparison may disclose a problem immediately. It then becomes the job of management to find out where the problem exists and what is causing it.

Let's consider an example in which the statistical profits of an operation declined for no apparent reason.

> **EXAMPLE:** A major distribution center's statistical operating profits have decreased during the past year. Though the decrease is not earth shaking, it is an unexpected surprise and the center has become the company's highest cost operation. The Distribution Department does not know the reason for the high costs at this location. Internal Auditing is asked to investigate to learn the reasons for the failure to achieve planned profits.
>
> An analysis discloses that the per hundred weight costs of shipping product is the highest in the company. All other costs are in line. Auditing studies the pertinent areas and determines the following:
>
> 1. There were no general salary increases, and union labor contracts in the center are the same as many other operations.
> 2. Overtime payments are not excessive.
> 3. Vacations and illnesses are not excessive.
> 4. Volumes of product handled have remained fairly constant for a long period of time.
> 5. Product returns and breakage are at a low level, consistent with past experience.
>
> Based on an analysis of statistical data, the problem is narrowed down to an audit of the payroll at the center. Payroll costs have increased, above what might be normally expected from the passage of time. Auditors take possession of paychecks, and find that several checks are not claimed. Since pay envelopes are customarily placed in employees' personal message center boxes, it is not possible to determine who might regularly take the checks.
>
> Personnel records are checked, and the questionable employees are

found to be fictitious, with all papers being forged. All supervisors deny any knowledge of the fictitious employees. The padded payroll is corrected, improving the operating results.

Payroll fraud had been perpetrated for over six months. Obviously, someone in the center is involved since paychecks are sent to the location for insertion into the employees' boxes. A study of the cashed paychecks discloses that they were all cashed at a currency exchange that charges a high fee but does not ask for identification. The exchange is unable to provide assistance, since many of the center's employees use the exchange's services.

A decision is made to employ an outside investigating agency. They take the canceled paychecks, and the false personnel records and timecards, bearing employees' signatures and supervisory approvals, and give them to a handwriting expert, together with sample writings of all supervisory, and office personnel. The handwriting expert identifies the culprit as the office payroll supervisor, who stoutly denies any knowledge. The employee is offered a polygraph test as a method of establishing innocence.

The outside investigators learn that the payroll supervisor has been spending large sums of money in recent months for new cars, a new home, and other large purchases. The supervisor claims to have inherited money, which cannot be substantiated.

The supervisor fails the polygraph test, and during subsequent interrogation admits to fabricating the records and profiting from the payroll padding. The supervisor agrees to repay the full amount taken and appropriate arrangements are made. The employee is terminated and the case is closed.

2. Reported Variances in Asset Accounts. When items are stolen, the theft will appear as a variance in the appropriate asset account, unless the culprit can adjust records to hide the shortages. When variances are reported, rather than hidden, it may indicate that office employees are not involved in the frauds.

Such losses, when they involve raw materials, supplies or finished goods, may be caused by acts of employees or of outsiders. Shortages in delivery of raw materials or supplies will show up as variances in the cost reports. These shortages may be deliberate short-shipments which are accepted as full compliance to the quantity ordered. The false receiving reports may be the result of carelessness, or more likely the acts of conspirators on the dock who receive remuneration from the shipper. **CAUTION:** *Keep in mind that there is always the possibility that variances are caused by an error in a cost standard.*

Variances in finished goods can result from under billings, mistakes in reporting movements or in counting inventory, or from theft by employees or outsiders. All of these possibilities must be explored when attempting to track down a finished product variance. Consistent losses of product are almost always a sure sign of theft.

3. Unexplained Increases in Total Operating Costs. When your records show that an operation is experiencing increases in operating costs, which local management is unable to explain, it is likely that fraud is contributing to the problem.
KEY POINT: *Sometimes costs increase because unusual disbursements are charged to an operation without the knowledge and consent of local management.* Fictitious invoices, or those for personal purchases, may be processed on the basis of forged approvals. These illegal acts might be initiated by local employees, or might be perpetrated by personnel at the paying office. **CAUTION:** *Where payments are processed through the computer, errors in data entry might cause the wrong location to be charged with expenses incurred at some other point.* These errors can be either accidental or deliberate.

When auditing a location that is experiencing unexplainable operating cost increases, every significant element of cost must be minutely confirmed. This is a tedious task, but if the information is in the computer data base, you can get a printout of all the detail as a starting point toward tracking down the problem. Remember that any disbursement, honest or otherwise, must be charged out. **TIP:** *Accounts that show increased costs may be a dumping ground.*

4. Unexplained Materials or Labor Cost Increases. Unexplainable increases in labor costs are frequently the result of payroll padding. Where materials are concerned, increases may be the result of overpayments because of poor purchasing practices, or there may be collusion between purchasing agents and suppliers. This differs from 3 above in that a specific cost has been identified.

When an employee in a position of decision, conspires with an outsider to pay inflated prices, the vendor usually kicks back part or all of the overpayment. Sometimes these situations are not readily apparent, as when bids are obtained that are allegedly competitive.

When you suspect bid rigging, you should consider using an outside agency to learn the fair price for the item in question. Any inquiries you make, as a representative of your company, will be viewed with suspicion; and your information may be valueless, particularly if a group of suppliers are involved in the rigging.

5. Reports of Questionable Transactions. You will, from time to time, receive reports from fellow workers or outsiders of employee misdeeds. Some of these will be anonymous while others will be from people you know. They may demand that you protect their identity before they disclose anything. Perhaps the people you are acquainted with will be confident that you will handle the matter discreetly. If you make any promises, be certain to keep them. If you are forced into an untenable position, discuss the matter with your source before you give out any names. **IMPORTANT:** *Information from any source should be viewed with caution.* Often such information is self serving, but it is frequently accurate even in such circumstances. Sometimes the information will be specific as to what is going on and where, while at other times it will be vague. Employees may tell you of things that they have heard or seen which would be known as perfectly proper if the whole story were disclosed. *Learning just a small part can often be misleading.*

Where detailed information is not available, but a location or operation has been named as a potential problem area, your best approach is to schedule a routine audit. Alert the staff to be on the lookout for any danger signal. Examine every discrepancy carefully, and be suspicious of everything no matter how minor it may appear.

Sometimes a major fraud is uncovered as the result of a minor oversight that was investigated by an auditor. Convince your staff to resist the temptation to ignore apparently minor discrepancies.

Every internal control should be dissected, and all employees questioned as to the meaning and application of each control that affects their job. Discussions with employees often disclose that some type of irregularity occurs from time to time. The employee may believe that these are minor infractions and hardly worth mentioning. **IMPORTANT:** *These are the infractions that should be studied minutely.* You must find out what they are, how often they occur and which employees are involved in the violations. **NOTE:** *You may learn that the main culprit is someone in a supervisory position who has the authority to instruct clerical workers to ignore certain controls.* Or the employee may be told that the supervisor will perform the control action. This is an area that presents a potential danger.

Even when conducting an investigation that is based on solid, specific information; your approach should still take the form of a routine internal audit. This is particularly so if you want to protect the identity of your informant. You may move to the problem area rapidly, but too much haste may alert the thief and make your job more difficult.

Methods of Manipulation and Warning Signs

Here are a few of the more common dishonest practices.

1. *Payroll padding or other types of payroll manipulation.*

   Warning signs are (a) increased labor costs, (b) decreased labor efficiency, or (c) elimination of certain internal control procedures.

2. *Thefts of products.*
   Warning signs are (a) inventory shortages reported as a result of inventory settlements, (b) out of stock conditions that are not reflected in daily stock status reports, (c) increases in samples, spoils, scrap, dumps or salvage, and (d) high levels of adjustments to inventory figures.
3. *Diversion of accounts receivable payments.*
   Warning signals are (a) an out of balance condition between the detail records and control accounts, (b) a spate of customer complaints about inaccuracies in billing or statements, (c) heavy issuance of credit memos, (d) an abundance of adjustments to control accounts, and (e) replies to audit confirmations that indicate problems.
4. *Diversion of cash.*
   Warning signs are (a) diminishment of profits, (b) failure to reconcile bank accounts, (c) missing deposit slips, collection reports or sales invoices, (d) excessive credit memos adjusting sales, and (e) significant adjustments to the cash control accounts.
   A list of common methods of defrauding is printed in this section.

WHAT TO DO WHEN YOU ENCOUNTER FRAUD

Handling a Fraudulent Act

When you encounter a fraudulent act, there are certain precautions to follow. Some things you must do, and others you must not. **KEEP IN MIND:** *An auditor's job is to determine what happened, how it happened, and what can be done to prevent it from happening in the future.* Recovery of company assets and punishing the culprits are activities that *may* be decided by Legal and/or other departments.

KEY POINT: *If you discover that a company record has been manipulated, you must proceed with caution.* Before discussing the matter with anyone other than audit supervisors, you should do the following:

1. *Recheck* all data to ensure your information is correct and provable.
2. *Keep your information, and suspicions, confidential.* Make complete and accurate notes of everything you do, but handle these work papers carefully. You should not discuss the investigation with anyone but your boss and the assigned auditors that are concerned.
3. Obtain and safeguard, *in your personal possession,* all documents that relate to the transactions.
4. For a selected period, *carefully review all similar transactions* to see if there are other instances of manipulation.

5. For a selected period, *carefully review all transactions that involved the individual(s)* who are the principle suspects in the current investigation.
6. Gather your information together and carefully study the acts, your proof, and *ALL POSSIBLE conclusions.*

KEY POINT: *There are a number of things that, at this point in time, you should not do:*

1. *You should not jump to a conclusion.* Remember that truth is often stranger than fiction, and bear that in mind as you listen to explanations that are offered to you.
2. *You should not accuse anyone of anything.* Until you have absolute, irrefutable proof, you cannot be certain of anything.
3. *You should not venture an opinion that any specific individual has been involved in a wrongdoing.* Until it is legally provable, you should not even imply that an illegal act has been committed.
4. *You should not use any of the information as the basis for casual conversation,* even with other members of the audit staff.

Assuming there is very good evidence that an individual has manipulated company records and committed a fraudulent act, what is your next step?

You must make certain to obtain all pertinent facts. When you know all there is to know, you will then be in a position to make a decision about the incident.

Handling Interrogations

The most logical, direct approach to resolving a fraud problem is to interview the employee(s) who are involved. You may elect to do the following:

1. Use an outside agency in order to obtain the services of a professional interrogator.
2. Discuss the matter with your company's Security Department who may have someone trained in the art.
3. Elect to have someone on the audit staff conduct the questioning.

Let's consider each of the options.

If you decide to use an *outside agency* to interrogate the suspects, be certain that a member of the audit staff is present during the entire session. Many outside agencies prefer that the actual questioning be conducted by a company employee, while they sit in as witnesses, offering support and counsel. Depending on the particular circumstances, this approach can be effective.

If the agency conducts the interrogation, the employee may be frightened into cooperating, or may decide to remain silent and accept the consequences; feeling that the matter is out of the company's hands. **TIP:** *When feasible, and where there is no possible connection, have the employee's immediate or higher level supervisor present at the interrogation.* The supervisor can insure proper treatment for the employee and can also promptly verify or rebut any procedural defenses that the subject may offer. Some employees will talk more freely in front of their friendly supervisor, while others may be more likely to tell the truth without such witnesses.

If you elect to use your company's *Security Department* for the interrogation of suspects, you should handle these sessions in much the same way as those conducted by outside companies.

A knowledgeable auditor should sit in on all the sessions, even if the matter has been turned over to the Legal Department and sworn depositions are being taken. The auditor probably is in the best position to evaluate the truthfulness of any statements made by the subject. Knowing the operating systems and controls, the auditor can steer questions into areas that need to be considered.

When such sessions are scheduled, there should be preliminary discussions among the planned interrogators so that appropriate questions will be asked. The group should also plan how they will follow up to determine the truthfulness of any information offered by the subject. **TIP:** *It is advisable to continue an interrogation until all matters have been resolved.* Once the meeting has started, the session should not be interrupted.

If you decide to handle the questioning *within the Auditing Department,* you should use an auditor who has some experience in conducting interrogations. This is a complicated procedure that all professional internal auditors face from time to time. In the normal audit, routine audit questioning to obtain necessary information sometimes comes very close to a true definition of interrogation. **KEY POINT:** *To question and accept an answer is one thing; to question and challenge the reply is another.* Following are some important precepts that should be considered:

A. Preparation

A prime requisite to a successful interrogation is adequate preparation. **IMPORTANT:** *The better the preparation, the greater the probability that the session will be a success.*

Good preparation means that you will not interrogate anyone without sufficient evidence to justify the procedure. If your evidence is irrefutable, and you are trying to learn the extent of a defalcation, you are on solid ground and will probably be able to learn what you want to know.

Before starting your questioning, learn as much as you can about the suspect, and the acts that prompted the investigation. The discussion may get out of hand, and you may be forced to take action on the spur of the moment without an opportunity to study all detailed information. In these situations you will be forced to make a decision based on whatever information you have at hand, and the *chances of a mistake are high.* With adequate preparation you should be prepared to control any situation.

B. Environment

The environment in which an interrogation takes place can also be of prime importance. It should not be held out in the open where other employees can witness the procedure, but rather in a private office, with as few witnesses as practical.

The room should be *free of distractions,* with a minimum of furniture. *If a recording device is used, the subject should agree that the proceedings be recorded.* The suspect should be seated in a position that allows *free unblocked movement to an exit door* and be assured of freedom to leave the room at any time.

C. Conducting the Session

The questioning itself should be conducted in a calm, clear voice. *Be sure the subject completely understands each question.* If there is the slightest doubt, ask the question again so that there is a clear understanding of its meaning. Keep calm and mask your emotions, no matter what answers are given to your questions.

For critical information, repeat the answers for confirmation and to be certain that you and the subject are thinking alike. **CAUTION:** *Be certain to do this for incriminating answers; you don't want to jump to a conclusion, only to later learn of a misunderstanding in the language used by one party or the other.*

You will encounter all types of people in these interrogation sessions, but the major distinction lies in their reaction to you.

A. Most of those will be people who are basically honest.

- They have become involved in a situation that got out of hand.
- They don't like what they've done, and feel guilty about it.
- They will be relatively easy to interrogate.
- They will tell you about anything that they think you already know.
- They will hesitate to reveal any other incriminating evidence that they believe is not known to you.

B. You may find yourself facing the street-hardened type.

- They have been questioned by the police in criminal investigations.
- They know that they cannot be forced to incriminate themselves.
- They will usually be uncooperative if they are guilty. When you encounter this type of person be prepared to shorten the session and terminate their services.

Here are some tips for dealing with a theft problem:

1. Try to get positive proof of several instances before starting your questioning. If you spotted one case of theft, the chances are good that there were other thefts committed by the same individual. With proof of several, you are in an excellent position to interrogate.
2. Concentrate your questioning on one incident and demonstrate your knowledge of the surrounding facts so that the subject believes that you know everything that has occurred. **TIP:** *Once you convince the thief that the illegal acts are known, you may receive complete cooperation.* This will occur if the culprit realizes that full cooperation may resolve the matter in-house.
3. When a subject first breaks down and agrees to tell everything, it means that he or she will tell the truth about everything that you already know. Ask the employee for a recap of every occurrence.
4. State that you *know about other illegal acts committed,* and if the statements are not completely and fully honest the matter will be out of your hands. At that point you merely ask for the full story, and then sit back and listen.

If a subject states that you have cited the only incident in which an illegal act was committed, that is the time to admit that you have proof of other misdeeds. **IMPORTANT:** *Do not specifically mention the details of other cases that you can prove,* but say enough to demonstrate that you are speaking with knowledge.

At that point the employee must decide whether to be completely candid, or to try to bluff it through. If the decision is complete honesty, some transactions will be mentioned that you knew nothing about. Listen carefully to every word, observe the body language and judge whether the subject is being cooperative.

If it is clear that the culprit is not yet prepared to cooperate, your next step will depend on your evaluation of the employee.

For the A type, basically honest person, you might do the following:

- Leave the office so that the suspect is left alone to contemplate the dilemma. Perhaps even give the subject a cup of coffee, or a soft drink, to toy with while thinking the matter over.
- After about ten minutes, reenter the room and announce that you are offering one last chance for cooperation.
- Assure the subject that a complete detailed examination will be made of every transaction in which the employee participated, and that all mishandlings will be referred to the proper parties for appropriate action. If the individual still refuses to cooperate:
- Fire the thief and have your staff examine all activities in which the subject had a hand.
- Follow legal advice as to further action that must be taken.

When dealing with street hardened type B individuals, your approach may be somewhat different.

- You must be certain to have *at least one indisputable case in hand* before scheduling a meeting.
- *Be prepared for the thief to refuse to answer questions,* contending that you are not the boss.
- Call in the appropriate supervisor, to be seated in the rear of the room while you ask your questions.
- The employee may ask that the union steward be present. Stop your questioning and call in the steward.
- Explain that your *questions will relate solely to the employee's work,* and that you are all on company time and being paid.
- If the subject still refuses to answer questions, your best action is to fire the culprit.

If the problem is significant, you may decide to call the police, sign a complaint and have the subject arrested. Such actions require prior agreement with Legal and perhaps Personnel and Security people. **IMPORTANT:** *Before going into an interrogation where a quick decision might be required, it is advisable to have prior discussions with interested and concerned department executives,* so that all options are discussed and a course of action tentatively set. The location manager and the local personnel manager should be advised and perhaps participate in the meeting. **IMPORTANT:** *You should receive advance carte blanche authority to do whatever you think best in the circumstances. If not, the executive who has final authority should be available at the time you are holding your meeting.* You may then step out of the room, make a phone call to discuss the matter and receive an immediate decision.

The decision will probably be to support whatever course of action you advise if you have first obtained the agreement of local management. However, in many of these cases, the final decision will rest with the internal auditing department.

Termination Procedures

When a person is discharged, or permitted to resign under these conditions, you must ensure that a *trustworthy supervisor remains with the departing employee every second that the person remains on company property.* This includes all movements up to the company's exit gate.

Some of these people will demand a paycheck, and depending on the laws governing the location involved, their demands should be honored. If it is not possible to issue an immediate check, they should be assured that a paycheck will be promptly prepared and mailed to them.

When the check is prepared, operating and financial management must decide whether the final paycheck should be for all monies earned, or should be reduced by the amount of provable theft. **TIP:** *In cases involving a fidelity bond claim, it is wise to talk to the bonding company before the final paycheck is released.*

1. Statements. When an employee admits to wrongdoing and agrees to make restitution, it is advisable to get a statement from the individual *at that time.* The statement can be handwritten by the subject. It should be dated, name the defaulter and the position in the company. It should describe the manipulation, the inclusive dates involved, and the total amount taken. It should also state how the funds are to be repaid. The statement should be signed in the presence of witnesses, and the witnesses should also sign.

Following is a sample statement containing the basic information:

> I, __E.V. Doer_____, office manager at XYZ's Anycity, Anystate branch, hereby make this statement on June 15, 19__, of my own free will, having received neither promises nor threats.
>
> For a period from Jan. 1, 19__, to May 30, 19__, I withheld cash receipts from warehouse sales in the amount of $5,000. I destroyed office copies of the covering invoices. No other employee was aware of my acts, and no one else benefited.
>
> I will repay the $5,000, which I owe to XYZ within a twelve-month period, at interest to be determined by XYZ.
>
> Signed in the XYZ office at 237 N. Bay Drive, at 5:30 P.M.
>
> Signed ____________________ Date ____________
>
> Witnessed: __________ Date ______ Witnessed __________ Date ______

A copy of this statement should be retained in the confidential audit files and the original turned over to the controller responsible for seeing that the company receives restitution as promised.

2. Resignations. When an interrogation is successfully completed and the employee has cooperated, it is a common practice to permit the thief to resign rather than be fired. Where acceptable, the subject should be asked to submit the resignation at the time that the statement of withholding is written. It should be handwritten, dated, and signed by the employee. It need merely state:

> I, _E.V.Doer_, office manager at XYZ's Anycity, Anystate sales branch, do hereby tender my resignation for personal reasons.
>
> This resignation from XYZ Corp. is to take effect immediately.
>
> Signed ______________________ Date ______________

The original copy of the resignation should be turned over to the personnel department for filing in the employee's personnel file. A copy should be retained in a confidential Audit Department file.

USING OUTSIDE INVESTIGATIVE AGENCIES

In much investigative work that is outside of the routine verification field, the internal auditor may turn to outside experts for guidance and perhaps assistance. It is often advantageous to use outsiders to gather information that rests outside of the company.

More frequently, the necessary information is available in company records, and an outsider would have more difficulty in obtaining it than the internal audit staff. In these cases, when outsiders are used, they must work very closely with the internal audit staff and use the audit staff to obtain critical company information.

There are many private investigative agencies that are competent in assisting in special investigations and in the tracking down of thieves or dishonest employees. Many of them are international companies that can provide services almost anywhere in the world.

When using such agencies you should keep a close check on their assignments and actions. Do not permit them to do anything without your prior approval, even if your approval merely consists of agreeing to let them do anything they believe necessary at the time. After you have worked with specific people over a period of time, you will learn how much leeway you can give your agent. **NOTE:** *No matter the size of the agency, the outcome of an* *assignment rests with the investigator.* You will actually be dealing with an individual, not a company.

But remember that when you employ them they act as your agents and your company is responsible for any of their improper acts.

Outside agencies can be very helpful in the following areas:

- Obtaining information from public records, or outside sources.
- As a source of trained manpower to perform certain types of tasks.
- As specialists or experts in the following areas:

(1) fingerprinting, (2) handwriting analyses, (3) polygraph operations, (4) voice stress analyses, (5) surveillance, (6) checking public records, (7) interviewing and interrogating, (8) photographic work, and (9) communication, including testing for listening devices.

In short, there are companies that can help you in almost any type of problem that you encounter.

The problem is to locate the right agency for a particular job and to be reasonably sure that a good investigation will be conducted. The large international agencies have grown through their ability to both attract good investigators and supervise them. They are usually able to perform assignments without getting themselves or their clients into trouble. These firms have learned to do *exactly what the client asks.* No more, no less. They also perform their services in the manner that the client suggests.

Let's look at areas in which these agencies may assist you:

- *Interviewing personnel of outside companies.* If the people are employees of vendors or suppliers of your company, they might be more cooperative when questioned by members of your audit staff.

  Outsiders would have difficulty conducting an investigation in your company, unless they are accompanied by an internal auditor. Honest dedicated employees will not hesitate to cooperate with an internal auditor, but may be reluctant to talk to an outsider.
- *Questioning antagonistic employees* who are engaged in acts of conspiracy against your company. Every investigation must be evaluated individually to determine the best approach and how best to obtain the information required.
- *Surveillance services.* This is useful when you know the identity of a location or an individual involved in an illegal movement of product. It can be costly, and when dealing with street hardened types is not always successful.
- *Security services.* This is the standard security guard service used to control movements in designated areas.

- *Check of public, and perhaps private records.* If you need information that is a matter of public record, an expert knows where it is and how to get it. They can obtain data promptly.
- *Preemployment verifications.* A background check can be conducted, with a minimum of effort by an outside agency.

  However, your department, or internal security personnel, can easily obtain certain information. A call to a previous employer can establish that the applicant worked for the concern, the dates of employment and the job titles. Any missing dates require an explanation. Education can be checked by a phone call to the applicant's school to verify graduation dates and degrees granted.

Whatever agency you choose, be sure that you check the company out first and then meet with the manager of investigations and learn how they operate. Read their brochures and be certain that you understand their rate structure. It is best to establish a rapport with the agency's local management and then work on an open-end basis, so that you can use their services whenever you require them.

Don't expect these agencies to do your thinking for you; they don't know your company a fraction as well as you do. You should objectively evaluate any suggestions they may give you. Listen to their advice and counsel, and *then make up your own mind.* Your decision will likely be influenced by the confidence you have in the expert that you employ. **IMPORTANT:** *No matter what tests or checks are used, or who performs them, outside companies that supply information should submit a formal report that draws a clear cut distinction between known facts, and supposition or rumor.*

The report should state if information is from public record or from talks with individuals. If conversations, the persons should be specifically identified. Ignore reports claiming an individual has a bad reputation if it fails to supply any supporting documentation. The investigator should state the reasoning. **KEY POINT:** *When a person's reputation is at stake, YOU cannot afford to be careless.*

Billings from outside agencies should read, "For services rendered to ________________, Internal Audit Manager." Names or locations involved should not be mentioned. Agency billing are viewed by many employees and you don't want to broadcast that auditors are checking an employee or specific location. Attach a copy of the invoice to a copy of the agency's report as evidence of services provided.

FIFTY COMMON ILLEGAL ACTS

Following is a list of illegal acts that are frequently discovered during an internal audit. This list is by no means all inclusive, it is based on actual cases reported by many internal auditors. The following merely reports the acts without going into detail.

1. Stealing merchandise, equipment, tools or supplies.
2. Cashing checks made payable to the thief's company.
3. Forging endorsements and cashing checks made payable to suppliers.
4. Conspiring with suppliers to increase amounts of their invoices.
5. Conspiring with suppliers to pay false invoices that they submit.
6. Accepting kickbacks from contractors or suppliers.
7. Using forged approvals to cause payment of invoices to culprit.
8. Using a properly approved voucher of the prior year, that was not canceled, and merely changing one figure.
9. Using carbon copies of previously used original vouchers.
10. Using personal expenditure vouchers to support paid-outs.
11. Increase amount on paid-out receipts when reporting disbursements.
12. Charge personal purchases to company, through misuse of P/O's.
13. Carrying fictitious "extra help" on payroll.
14. Carrying employees on payroll beyond actual severance date.
15. Falsifying additions to payroll.
16. Causing fictitious overtime payments to employees.
17. Paying employees a rate in excess of agreed rate. Excess kicked back to supervisor.
18. Fail to record sales of merchandise and pocket the cash.
19. Creating overages in cash funds or registers by under recording, and removing overage when convenient.
20. Failing to make bank deposits daily, or depositing only a part of collections and using the other funds for personal purposes.
21. Making round sum deposits, withholding the balance and attempting to catch up at the end of the month.
22. Altering dates on deposit slips to cover withholdings.
23. Stealing small amounts from cash funds or registers.
24. Holding a cash receipts box open beyond the normal time, and retaining late receipts.
25. Making erroneous footings of cash receipt and disbursement books.
26. Withholding cash sales monies by using false charge accounts.
27. Void cash sales tickets through fictitious explanations.
28. Alter cash sales tickets after handing copies to customers.
29. Destroying sales tickets.
30. Misappropriating tax refunds or quantity rebates.

31. Lapping collections on customers' accounts.
32. Pocket payments on customers' accounts, issue false receipts.
33. Collecting on old accounts, pocketing the money and charging the accounts off as uncollectible.
34. Collecting charged-off accounts, but not reporting the collection.
35. Issue credits for false returned goods or customers' claims.
36. Recording unwarranted cash discounts.
37. Billing merchandise to fictitious accounts.
38. Falsely deliver merchandise to an employee or relative's home.
39. Falsifying inventory records to cover thefts.
40. Deliberately delaying the reconciliation of a customer's account.
41. Deliberately confuse postings to detail and control accounts.
42. Creating or rewriting a ledger sheet to hide thefts.
43. Diverting traveling or other business expenses to personal use.
44. Overloading expense accounts—false mileage, entertainment.
45. Sell scrap materials and pocket the proceeds.
46. Sell idle equipment and retain part, or all, of the proceeds.
47. Using company employees for personal projects.
48. Selling keys or combinations to safes or vaults.
49. Placing undated checks and IOU's in a change fund.
50. Pilfering stamps or miscellaneous supplies.

EMPLOYEE OUTSIDE INTERESTS

Few positions in modern business require an employee's full time, energy and mental resources. Many successful managers have spare time to devote to other interests. Some of these activities involve business ventures, and in this section we will discuss such matters.

Outside interests are not of themselves dangerous to the internal control of an organization. Much depends on the nature of the outside interest, and the position of the employee involved. Many companies have a formal policy that permits outside interests upon proper supervisory approval, providing that such an interest does not interfere with the efficient performance of the employee's normal duties and that it does not involve the use of other company personnel during business hours.

To get new business, or to insure a continuing relationship, some business people offer incentives to customers' employees who select suppliers or handle complaints against vendors. Part time jobs or jobs for relatives, interest in a business, commissions, vacation trips, country club memberships, or gifts of money or property are frequently dangled before the eyes of susceptible employees.

Many find these lures impossible to resist. The employee is often deluded into believing that such gifts are presented out of friendship, and that the employer is not losing anything through the employee's acceptance of such gratuities.

KEY POINT: *Employees owe employers loyalty, initiative and dedication.* An employer has the right to expect their employees to arrive at their jobs on time and in a condition to perform their assigned tasks. Some people must work at two jobs to meet their financial obligations, and this arrangement can be accepted providing the hours and the job responsibilities are not in conflict.

It is possible that two jobs may be held without actually presenting a conflict of interest, but both jobs should be clear of decision making responsibilities. Even then, problems can develop. A two-job employee will, sooner or later, be faced with a decision that will affect one or the other employer. Here is a case in point:

> **EXAMPLE:** The job performance of an excellent secretary began to decline. The secretary was frequently late, and always seemed tired and sleepy. The secretary's boss enquired as to the reason and was told that that there was a second job that was performed during the evening hours. The boss stated that she would have to select one or the other since it was obvious that the night job was interfering with the day job.
>
> The secretary stated that the choice was clear, since she earned over twice as much in her evening job and worked less hours. Her boss found this difficult to believe until she stated that she worked as a Playboy Bunny and her tips as a waitress far exceeded her salary as a secretary. She had not sought advance approval for the waitress job, because she was convinced that there could not possibly be a conflict of interest.
>
> While there was no apparent conflict, the action of holding down two jobs was detrimental to the daytime job.

There are situations where the distinction between an outside interest and a conflict of interest is a fine line. For example:

> **EXAMPLE:** One of your Traffic Department rate clerks, who audits your company's freight bills, takes a part-time job with a freight audit bureau. The part-time job is performed over weekends and does not interfere with the principal job. The clerk seeks and is given permission to hold the part-time job, since the bureau does not audit your company's bills. If they did, this would clearly be a conflict of interest, but for now this

merely represents an outside interest. If the clerk later induces your company to use that particular audit bureau, then the outside interest would turn into a conflict.

CAUTION: *A part-time job with a supplier, or potential supplier, of the principal employer will often create a conflict of interest.*

Other hazy areas often occur in normal business operations. Many people desire a business of their own, and many are attracted to franchising and distributing opportunities. Consider the following:

> **EXAMPLE:** An employee decides to become an independent distributor for a consumer goods company. If related activities are confined to evenings and weekends, and if no sales effort is made while on the job, or on the premises, there should be no problem. But when the employee uses company time to solicit business or make deliveries, then a conflict begins to develop.
>
> Often, these conflicts are unintentional, or even unknowing. A supervisor, during coffee break, talks to an employee about the products that the supervisor is distributing. Without considering intent, there is the possibility of coercion because the employee may order products out of fear, or the hope of currying favor.
>
> These same elements enter into the common practice of soliciting contributions to charitable organizations. Though the motive is pure, and probably good, the element of coercion enters into even this worthwhile activity.

Each company must evaluate the good and the bad factors and develop a policy that its employees can live with. **KEY POINT:** *Once a policy is formulated, it must be made known to all employees, and to all new hires.* This policy must then be enforced across the board and should apply to all employees without exception.

Administrative and management people must not only avoid conflicts, *they should avoid even an appearance of a conflict.* They must be careful to discourage outsiders from offering gifts of any type, and they must make these people realize that they are not interested in such offers.

Some conflicts of interest are apparent, as when a purchasing agent is dealing with a company in which the agent holds a proprietary interest. The interest may be represented by shares of common stock, but the buyer knows that the success of the company will have an effect on the value of the stock. The more business the buyer can give to the company, the greater that company's chance for success.

Even though transaction prices are fair, there is still a question of propriety in such dealings, since the objectivity necessary in an arms length business deal has been breached. Despite the best of intentions, the buyer will not treat all suppliers alike and is bound to favor the company in which the buyer has an interest.

Many companies have formulated policies to apply to conflict of interest situations. Since an employee who has a family member working for a supplying company will be tempted to route business to that supplier, it is vital that a policy apply not only to employees but to all members of their immediate family. It is also important that the policy cover all likely occurrences, and spell out those actions that require prior management approval. Let's examine a sample of such a policy statement.

Sample Policy Statement

A sample of an outside interest policy statement follows. After the customary heading the statement appears, followed by definitions and procedural requirements for approving outside activities. The policy statement's subject matter reads:

> POLICY: No employee, nor a member of the employee's immediate household, may hold a position with, or have an interest in, another company, if such position or interest may result in a conflict with the interests of the XYZ Corporation.
>
> A. If such interest, or service, may in any way subordinate or be adverse to our company's interest, no employee may, without the PRIOR APPROVAL OF MANAGEMENT:
>   1. Serve as a member of the Board of Directors of another company;
>   2. Serve as employee, advisor or consultant of another company;
>   3. Accept any benefit or any form of gratuity or compensation from another company or company agent;
>   4. Transact any business for or with our company as an individual apart from the role as an employee;
>   5. Invest in another company.
>
> B. Management will approve of outside interests only if such interest or service is not contrary to our stated policy.
>
> C. We do not encourage non-management people to hold other jobs. However, if other jobs are held, such secondary employment shall not interfere in any way with primary job performance. Prior approval is required whenever the secondary job is of such a nature as to constitute a conflict with our interests.

NOTE: *During your routine audits, the Outside Interest files should be reviewed.* Carefully scrutinize company transactions with any other organization named in any of these reports. Make certain that there are no irregularities where executives' interests are concerned.

SPECIAL ASSIGNMENTS

Internal auditors frequently are called upon to resolve special problems. When normal operating routines fail to correct apparent deficiencies, top management often turns to the internal audit department. Let's consider a case example:

> **EXAMPLE:** Top operating management meets to discuss a major location that is operating at a loss. The location was very successful for many years, but operating results have been deteriorating for the past nine months, and in the last three months the location has lost money. The possibility of closing the operation is even considered, since local management admits that they have no idea how to turn the operation around and, indeed, cannot even identify the problems.
>
> Top executives call in the Internal Audit manager, and explain the situation. They agree to give the audit manager carte blanche power to do whatever is necessary to correct the problem.
>
> The location houses three distinct, independent operations, each with its own manager. All managers are informed of the special audit study and instructed to cooperate completely.
>
> An internal audit team is assigned to conduct a special profit oriented study of the operation. An examination of statistical analyses comparisons to similar operations reveals variances in all areas. Auditors decide to use the audit program designed for Plants, Distribution Centers and Sales Branch operations, and proceed with an audit that concentrates on the high risk areas.
>
> The team learns that problems began after major management changes were made at the start of the year when one of the former managers retired and another was transferred to a different location. Everywhere that the auditors turn they find violations of procedures, policies and good business practices. As discrepancies are noted, they are called to management's attention and corrections are made as per auditor suggestions.
>
> Auditors discover several minor cases of fraud, such as salespeople withholding collections from customers, and deliverypeople selling products for cash and retaining the proceeds. But the amounts involved are minor. They also note some more serious problems, such as the failure to check the accuracy of outgoing shipments. When there are shortages on these loads, the documents are properly noted and the sales people make certain that their customers receive proper credit. When the loads are over, there is no attempt to trace product or to bill customers.
>
> Some overages had been accepted by customers, but were never billed. In other instances the common carrier took the overages, but they were never returned to the location. Contact with customers who had

accepted product and had not been billed indicated that they had expected to be billed, and were not aware that proper billings had not been submitted.

Billings are prepared for all such overages that auditors can document; but this only covers a portion of the product actually delivered. Many records are incomplete or fail to note overages or shortages on receipt. However, substantial recovery payments are received from customers.

Attempts to collect from carriers for overages that their drivers had taken, but which were never returned to the shipper, are not very successful. Carriers contend that products may have been moved to their storage points, but they disappeared after waiting for disposition instructions that never came. Products being held in carrier warehouses are recovered.

Auditors also learn that reconciliations had not been made between product reported as produced by the plant, and product reported as received by distribution. Each operation used its own unverified count to prepare its inventory reconciliation.

Physical security at the location is almost nonexistent. No check is made of trucks entering the premises and the security guard merely acts as an information center to tell people where various activities are located. Loads are pulled and allowed to sit on the dock until a truck arrives to pick them up. It is obvious that a substantial quantity of product has been stolen.

The two new location managers, a former sales supervisor, and a former plant superintendent, had been assigned higher management positions without any formal training in managerial skills or how to handle management problems. The three managers ran their own operations and rarely spoke to one another.

The audit manager held a series of meetings with the local managers, and emphasized the importance of internal controls and of cooperation between all managers at the location. The local managers knew that their jobs were in danger. Meetings were also held with staff people and line supervisors and important company systems, procedures and controls were explained and justified.

All of these actions turned the operation around and several months later at an executive staff meeting the financial vice-president was asked what had been wrong at the location. The VP replied that this was not a case of where one thing was wrong, but one in which there were many minor problems. The situation was likened to a radio that would not play. "So you replace all of the tubes, then a new dial, then a new lamp light, then a condenser; but the radio still won't work. So you soundly slap the thing a few times and it suddenly starts to play."

It is rare that one single type of omission, or commission, can affect a total operation. It usually takes a combination of factors to turn a successful operation into a problem area. However the following case illustrates a special assignment where one major activity caused upheaval. Here is a case in point:

> **EXAMPLE:** A major plant in an international operation was having serious problems. The president of the international division sought help from the vice-president of international operations in the headquarters office. At the request of the International V.P., the internal audit manager visited the division and supervised the local internal auditors in a profit oriented study.
>
> A review of cost accounting reports indicated that the operation was losing large quantities of expensive raw materials. The losses could occur through short deliveries, errors in processing, or theft of the raw materials or of finished product. To isolate the problem it was decided to conduct a twenty-four hour settlement of the production processing area to verify that product cost standards were accurate.
>
> During the wee hours of the morning, the audit manager entered the plant to see how the study was progressing. All of the plant supervisory, and many workers, were in the cafeteria playing cards.
>
> The audit manager and the sole auditor on duty visited the laboratory and noted a shocking piece of information. The reports of finished product's lab tests had been filled out for the entire period of the shift, which still had several hours to go. Tests were prelisted for all scheduled times and test results posted; all of which fell into the acceptable range.
>
> In the processing area they found that one isolated section was not following prescribed procedures. All employees assigned to that section were in the cafeteria, and no one was minding the shop. As a result high priced raw materials were being added to products in larger quantities than the formula required. This oversight should have been noted by the laboratory had that job been done properly. The oversights were costly, but the problem was limited to the night shifts and was therefore not spotted.
>
> Corrective action was immediately taken and the operation returned to profitability.
>
> The audit manager, upset that such an obvious problem had not been discovered by local management, discussed the matter with the division controller. When asked if the controller was aware that the cost reports clearly indicated a problem in the raw material area, the controller acknowledged that the information was quite obvious. When asked why the division president had not been informed, the controller told the following story:

At a staff meeting of top management to discuss the problem, the controller had volunteered the information that the problem was located in plant raw materials usage, and was strictly a production problem. The division president was irate because he had not asked the controller to speak, and asked, "Who appointed you Jesus Christ?". Then, using an age old joke, the president said, "When I want your opinion, I'll give it to you." After that the controller chose not to say anything unless asked a direct question.

The controller had been carefully scrutinizing the want ads in a financial paper when the audit manager walked into the office. The controller had decided to leave the organization after working up from an entry level job to one of the top jobs in the division. This particular assignment ended with the termination of the international division president. The controller eventually became one of the top international officials in the headquarters office.

Problems relating to headquarter's operations are also the frequent subject of special audit assignments. Here is a case in point:

EXAMPLE: The president of a corporation called the director of internal auditing into the office to discuss a problem. A good friend of the president, whom we shall call Mr. X, had spoken of an experience illustrating that something was wrong with the way that the company's Purchasing Department procured certain items. Mr. X had learned that his friend's company was paying more for some products than Mr. X's company had bid to supply them.

The audit manager agreed to look into the problem. Purchasing had instituted a bidding procedure, recommended by Auditing, that would have made such an action impossible. Bid records of the contract award were studied, and everything appeared to be proper.

The audit manager took possession of the bid in question and called Mr. X to verify the information. Mr. X confirmed that though they had indeed submitted a higher bid; they had called in and reduced their prices. Although told that is was contrary to company policy, Mr. X didn't believe the statement. Verbal changes in bids was an accepted practice in the industry.

When assured that only written bids, submitted at the proper time, were given consideration, Mr. X pleaded for another chance to save money for his friend's company. The audit manager agreed to ask Purchasing to request new bids for the products involved.

About a month later new bids were solicited, and the entire process

> was carefully monitored by auditors. The low bidder, a new company headed by a former representative of a major company, was low on all items. All the other low group of bidders' prices were exactly the same, at about ten percent above the low bidder.
>
> The buying company had a practice of using two suppliers for major purchases. Purchasing elected to use, as the second supplier, the company that had formerly been the primary supplier and had demonstrated excellent quality and service. The bulk of the business was allocated to the new low bidder.
>
> Shortly after the bids had been opened, Mr. X called the audit manager to enquire as to the results of the bidding. Mr. X's bid was identical to the earlier one submitted, that had allegedly been verbally reduced. Mr. X was surprised to hear that his company was not a successful bidder. He asserted that he knew for certain that no one had bid a lower price than his company. He was told, "You may feel certain that you know, but you are wrong. Your company was not the low bidder." The audit manager refused to discuss the matter further.
>
> Several years later, Mr. X's company, and the entire industry was sued by the federal government for price fixing. Many major corporations received millions of dollars as compensation for losses incurred as a result of such illegal actions.

Other special assignments may involve any activity that occurs at any location or level of company operations. These assignments can include a study to determine whether there had been any insider trading in company stock, to an examination of personnel operations to determine if any personnel people are prejudicial in their hiring practices.

Any special assignment is approached in a routine audit fashion, whenever possible. All available audit tools are used as required, and personal computer applications are frequently helpful. When possible, the normal audit staff is used to aid in an assignment, but some assignments require a great degree of confidentiality and may be restricted as to disclosures to any employee other than the head of the auditing department.

The above-cited cases represent a few samples of the type of special assignments that internal auditors are asked to perform. They demonstrate the wide scope of business activities that an auditor may be called upon to examine and analyze. Hopefully some of the pointers and programs in this manual may help you to successfully perform some of the special assignments that you are called upon to undertake.

Chapter 30

Audit Tools: Computer, Statistical Sampling and Contract Auditing

USING THE COMPUTER AS AN INTERNAL AUDIT TOOL

This chapter deals with computers, statistical sampling, outside agencies and contract auditing. We'll start with the computer, a machine that tirelessly analyzes a maze of information by working continuously, processing millions of items, and extracting and printing requested data.

The major problem with the computer is that it is a machine that merely follows orders and does *not* do any original thinking. *An audit program designed to use the computer as an audit tool must be exact in its instructions.* It must, in minute detail, consider and provide for all possible conditions that the computer might encounter.

Internal auditors, computer analysts and programmers all use the same basic business problem approach when seeking a satisfactory computer software program. Programs should be so designed that if the data being processed does not fall within the programmed restraints, the information can be treated as an exception and be printed out for the auditor's special handling. **NOTE:** *In order to have an effective internal auditing function, the audit staff must be aware of all pertinent computer operations.* Many internal audit staffs have separate sections that specialize in computer auditing and have experts in computer programming and systems analyses. Such groups can either design original audit programs or can modify available standard programs for staff use.

A computer audit program can be designed to perform many routine audit tasks in areas of operations where manual examinations are limited by time constraints. Generally the in-house programs are designed to aid in auditing high volume, high risk areas and are most useful in operations which would otherwise require a great deal of manual audit work. Areas frequently programmed are (1) accounts receivable, (2) accounts payable, (3) cash, (4) inventories, (5) production, (6) billings, (7) shipments, and (8) property.

When an internal audit staff decides to use the computer as an audit tool the EDP experts on the staff must work with and review the work of the software programmers and analysts who design the specific computer programs that are used within a particular company.

Printing a hard copy program listing is almost meaningless without documentation and unless the reviewer is versed in the programming language. Even if an auditor understands the program there are still problems to be solved, such as ensuring that the following are true:

- Data contained therein is adequately protected;
- Program conforms to company policies and procedures; and
- Program contains sufficient internal controls and internal security features to ensure the integrity of the system.

TIP: *The use of well-commented, high-level programming language, as opposed to assembly language, will make the program easier to analyze.*

Internal auditors who are also computer experts can ensure that programs contain line checks for errors, as well as built-in internal and security controls which limit accessibility to the computer and reduce the possibility of unauthorized revisions to a program. They also have the knowledge required to extract special or exception reports of transactions that field auditors can use for their reviews.

1. Cash Application

As a device for extracting and reporting unusual transactions, the computer is unmatched for speed, accuracy and dependability. For example, in a company that requires all cash collections to be deposited intact, a computerized audit program can direct the machine to list all transactions in which reported collections do not exactly match the covering reports of receipts. This gives the auditor information relating to events that require detailed examinations.

At the same time the program can screen all cash transactions and report any transfers from a depository account that did not move to an approved account. It can report movements out of transfer accounts that exceeded a set dollar value or that did not go to an approved disbursement account, or to other authorized financial institutions.

If all petty cash transactions are entered into the data base, an audit program can list all payments to specific persons or accounts, of a particular type, or all those exceeding a specified amount.

2. Accounts Receivable Application

In A/R, the computer can preselect accounts for verification, and prepare the statements to be verified. Some applications print the customer's statement with an overprinting of the audit confirmation request and an audit identification number. Such programs are simple and use the open invoice file as the data base. Other programs print audit verifications on specially designed audit forms, which are then manually processed and mailed. These also use the open invoice file.

A/R computer programs are also frequently designed to do the following:

- Provide a list of delinquent accounts,
- Print aging schedules,
- Report discrepancies between amounts credited to A/R and the amount of cash deposited showing differences by day and account,
- Report all adjustments by type, customer, and/or dollar value,
- Compute the A/R audit confirmation statistics.

3. Accounts Payable Application

Specially constructed computer audit programs can be helpful in a review of accounts payable operations. You can use optical scanners connected to a host computer to input disbursement data, and the computer can then list all payments:

- Over a predetermined amount,
- To named suppliers, or
- Charged to specific accounts.

You can extract credits, adjustments or unusual charges appearing on all invoices or just those from specific suppliers. You can print out all P/Os by date and by vendor. You may wish to determine outstanding commitments at any point in time, and can print a list of all canceled P/Os and all P/O change notices.

During an audit of A/P the computer can provide a list of the following:

- All invoices waiting payment,
- Comparative purchase price information,
- Payments for specific items,
- Lost cash or other discounts, and
- Exceptional transactions approved by management for payment.

You may want to study a listing of all charges to a specific account or sub account, or a report on payments pending for items that have been received and not yet billed. You can obtain a list of P/Os issued for specific goods or services that have not yet been received.

4. Inventory Application

For an internal audit of inventories, the computer can do the following:

- Provide a location record of class, type or individual items,
- Compare physical counts to book records and print variances and value of each exception,
- Report special handling of items by type of disposition and the locations involved,
- Review inventory transactions and report by specified location the products that are overstocked and not turning over as expected,
- Provide a list of close dated, past dated or obsolete products on hand as well as the products sold as salvage or junked,
- Provide current and previous inventory cost information for specific products, classes or for the total inventory.

5. Production and Quality Control Application

For an audit of production operations, the computer can provide the following:

- Production reports of items produced on each line, at every producing location, and totals for the entire company;
- Reports that show when, where and how much was produced of any particular item or class of items;
- Line down time and its effect on efficiency;
- Costs of production, and allocations, broken down in many ways;
- Quality control costs and results;
- Reports showing quantities and costs of product taken for quality control tests and samples; And,
- Amounts and types of products faulty, spoiled, and junked.

6. Sales and Marketing Application

An audit of a sales operation can be assisted by sales analyses reports prepared by the computer. Special programs can be helpful:

- In auditing the invoicing operations, by tracing sales to specific customers and reporting exceptional transactions.
- In providing sales information by product, location, and customer.
- By listing exceptions from correct pricing after giving consideration to all factors affecting prices.

- In reporting all canceled billings and any sales adjustments granted to any customer.

The computer audit program approach assures the auditor that an accurate and timely pricing file was used for invoice processing.

KEY POINT: *If a special file had been introduced for selected accounts, the independent audit run would list all exceptions.*

Internal audits of Marketing Departments or marketing programs can be assisted by computer provided information. Specific program costs and results can be analyzed. Information on coupon, rebate or premium offerings and redemptions can be obtained. Programs can also summarize and analyze customer complaints about products or services, and can report on the associated costs of these complaints.

7. Miscellaneous Operational Applications

For an audit of *distribution* the computer can provide total sales tonnage carried and total dollars paid to selected carriers or for selected vehicles. It can also provide a list by company and/or carrier of products reported short on delivery.

Rate data can be at the auditor's fingertips as well as a track record of the delivery results of each carrier and/or vehicle. The computer can calculate statistical efficiency reports of man hours spent in unloading or loading at specific locations, and can compare these statistics to the national average and print a list of locations that do not fall within an acceptable predetermined range.

For use during an audit of *property* transactions, the computer can provide a record of all additions or dispositions of company property by location and/or type. It can provide a record of all adjustments to property records and verify depreciation and depletion calculations and accumulations. You can get a list of all property assigned to a given location and see the value by item and/or total, or you can identify all locations using a special item of property.

Though the computer can help to design and prepare basic plans and specs for repetitive types of *engineering* projects, the internal auditor must handle such information with caution. The computer can provide a guide to the amount of board time required to draw up some architectural or mechanical plans, but it cannot judge how long it takes an engineer to design an acceptable new machine or process.

However, computers are of great value in planning and carrying out construction schedules. And they aid internal auditors in reviewing and controlling progress and final completion payments.

For an audit of a *construction* project you might request reports of all payments made and charged to the project, or for all payments exceeding a stipulated amount. Or you may want total payments to selected vendors, or for specific materials or equipment.

Summary of Applications

The computer can be used as an audit tool in the review of any activity that has already been computerized. *If the information HAS NOT already gone through the computer, there is an economic question to be considered.* All information to be analyzed must be input into the computer and even optical scanners have restrictions in that input data must be adjusted to conform to a preset pattern for use by a computer program. This could require many hours and dollars to accomplish. **IMPORTANT:** *Entry of information into a computer data base for use by an audit program might be economically justified if the alternative was a complete detailed manual audit required in connection with a major lawsuit or employee defalcation.*

Computers can aid you in analyzing data and can present requested exceptions for your follow-up and action. Using a computer, you can examine a much greater portion of business activity than is possible in a manual review. What the human mind can conjure or analyze, the computer can be programmed to accomplish. The limiting factors in business use are the capacity of the computer, ability of the programmers, cost of program design, maintenance costs and the availability of Central Processing Unit time.

Once a program has been developed, many of the routine, and some of the complicated audit tasks can be performed by the computer. With a good computer program, properly constrained and directed, it would be possible to analyze all of selected types of transactions on a continuing basis. In a large organization, where millions of transactions occur each year, it is impractical to analyze each individual action. *Even if the computer only reported a small percentage of the records as exceptions,* the auditors would have an immense job in trying to run down every discrepancy.

Developing a Program

Most audit programs are designed to report any discrepancies found in a run through the company's data base. You then take over and decide on future actions. You may call for a computer analysis of additional information, of the same data using a different approach, or you may decide to manually study the information.

There is difficulty in trying to develop a computerized internal audit program. The time and costs of development are a small fraction of the problem. *The most difficult items to obtain are the expertise of the programmer and the internal auditor who together must design the system.* These difficulties induce many audit staffs to use commercial audit programs, which they modify to suit their particular operation. The problem with *modifying most existing commercial packages* is that the in-house computer programming staff must be familiar with and have access to the source language used to write the program. Some commercial programs can be customized by the user without changing the source code.

The fact that commercial computer audit programs need to interact with the main data base can sometimes be a major hindrance to their use. *These programs must be able to communicate with the mainframe computer and have free access to the information therein.* One obstacle is that the data being audited may not be on-line. If this is the case then running the audit program could cause your company's normal data processing to be delayed.

Another difficulty is that the computer audit program must be written in a manner consistent with the Data Base Management System being used to control the main data base. This requires additional costs in training personnel and maintaining the program, which may not be justified if hardware changes are in the offing.

You must make certain that the program is run against the most current applicable version of the file being examined. Two or more copies of files are customarily prepared for security purposes, so that if one is destroyed the other is still available. Updating of files may not have been completed on all copies, so you must be *certain that the correct file is loaded for the run.* You could be easily misled if information were added or deleted from the file that you intended to use. **CAUTION:** *Don't overlook the possibility that a tampered or outdated file is being used.* This area is covered in more detail in the chapter titled, Auditing Data Processing.

Commercial Computerized Audit Programs

Most commercial programs are designed to be modified, and they provide facilities for entering variable information. You should consider using such programs when they are applicable because they are usually less expensive than the cost of designing a custom program. **IMPORTANT:** *But you must be certain that your available equipment is capable of running the program.* You should also be aware of all the facets of the program's design so that any area that the program overlooks can be manually reviewed.

An uncertainty in using a commercial program is the ease of modification. This factor, though a good selling point, also contains an element of risk. **TIP:** *To protect against unauthorized changes, you must keep possession of the program, and be present when it is run.*

Technical Considerations

With the advent of smaller, more powerful, and cheaper computers, the immense fixed costs of rented or purchased main frame computers has dropped dramatically. With reasonable development and usage costs, specific computer audit applications are now a reality for many internal audit staffs. As costs are further reduced, it may well pay for auditors to take the time required to design complex programs that can really delve into audit problems. The evolving expert system technology from the computer research field of Artificial Intelligence may speed up the development of these types of audit programs.

In order for an audit program to function properly, the working data base must be available and the audit computer program must do the following:

- Enable interaction between auditor's terminal and the data base,
- Have built-in controls to prevent the auditor's terminal from entering or changing information in the data base, and
- Be able to look at information and obtain reports upon request.

This means that an audit review of data base records may have to be scheduled by the computer department in the same fashion as their normal production runs; unless the audit program has the ability to extract information during a normal on-line production run of particular transactions. For example, at the same time that the main computer is processing A/R transactions, you might do the following:

- Print account verification statements,
- Obtain a list of delinquencies or accounts written off, or
- Make comparisons and print exceptions that require an examination.

Before you spend a great deal of money in creating a custom audit program you should look into the future. Consider that your present computer might be replaced due to technological improvements or to take advantage of more efficient and cheaper computers on the market. **CAUTION:** *If the mainframe is changed, the custom audit program might not be of use as originally conceived and designed.*

There are other dangers in using an audit program to review company transactions if you rely on regular telephonic channels to interact with company data bases. *There is a chance that information might be intercepted, and perhaps changed or sections obliterated, without your knowledge.* To learn if such things were occurring, you could use a manual tie-back of total information received to total information sent to insure that all information had been received. You would add all amounts involved in each transaction received to be compared to the total batch figure reported as sent by the computer.

In addition, because of the broad access to the data base that an audit program must be granted, *there is the possibility that confidential company information may be disclosed.* One solution to this problem is the use of call back feature modems. These modems require users to sign on to register, and it then disconnects the call. The caller hangs up the phone and waits for the computer to call back, which occurs if the caller is an authorized entry.

Future Role

The time will come when audit staffs will have computer specialists working on cash, A/R, A/P, distribution, property, production, sales, purchasing, and other major activities that occur within a company. These computer audit specialists will spend time each day sitting at a terminal using a custom program to interact with the main computer as it processes the transactions that the auditor is assigned to review. The program will extract all exceptional events, and the auditor will take the printout and follow up on significant discrepancies.

The internal audit staffs may well be reorganized and structured along those lines. These specialists will work closely with the field audit teams that visit each location to perform various audit checks that can only be performed on the job site. As exceptions occur, the specialist will call these transactions to the attention of auditors at the site for their follow-up and action.

Under such an arrangement, the audit specialist could learn of troubles or impending problems before management at the location even had a hint. The auditor might forestall an employee manipulation or detect it at an early stage; or the auditor might note that serious errors were being made and could alert local management to take corrective action.

This is similar to the type of continuous audit customarily used in certain operations where a department auditor reviews paperwork to spot errors before the work is released. These reviews are usually manual operations under the control of the department supervisor.

KEY POINT: *With custom software programs, interacting with the computer operation and the central data base, internal auditors would be in a better position to discharge their explicit responsibilities.*

STATISTICAL SAMPLING

Benjamin Disraeli is credited with a brief definition of statistics, he is purported to have said, " There are lies, damn lies and statistics." What may have been true over a hundred years ago, has not changed too much over that period of time. Statistics can be misleading, and findings can still be distorted and abused. However, in more recent years statistics have gained credence and reliability when used properly in a homogeneous environment; that is, when the elements being measured have a high degree of commonality.

Usage of the Technique

Statistical sampling is used to verify transactions within predetermined limits of accuracy. Use of the technique requires the auditor to decide in advance the percentage of error acceptable under a given set of conditions. The technique is most useful when there are large numbers of transactions to be audited.

The tremendous volume of transactions and associated paperwork involved in daily operations of a large enterprise makes it impractical for an audit staff to review every record and report. *All auditors, in the normal course of reviewing an operation, use sampling techniques either consciously or subconsciously.* When so used, auditors do not know what degree of reliability to expect from the selected sample.

In predicting the outcome of political elections, statistical sampling has achieved a high degree of acceptance and confidence even when only a very small percentage of the votes have been counted. Final counts are usually within a few percentage points of the early projections. In this area the reliability factor of any sampling technique is directly related to the number of choices, and to the *known economic, social and political history* of the sample that is used as the basis for the projection.

Unfortunately, this historical relationship does not apply in the field of internal auditing. *What has happened in the past does not ensure that it will happen in the future.* A change in personnel might lead to complete disruption in the orderly processing of routine transactions. A management change could dictate that paperwork be handled in a manner completely unacceptable to home office directives. A respected and long term honest employee may steal at any time without any apparent reason and without showing any outward sign.

Application to Internal Auditing

Internal auditors use a form of statistical sampling in their everyday verification work. Very rarely will you examine every act of a particular type for an extended period of time. Such in-depth study is usually only performed when important errors, or frauds have been found in materials already examined. A minute examination of every transaction for a long period of time is sometimes required to prove the amount of loss for a fidelity bond claim, or the amounts to be charged or credited to customers for previous pricing errors.

Any statistical sampling technique should be modified when you feel that a change is in order. Intuitive feelings may be founded on observations or information stored in the subconscious mind. Though unable to recollect the specific information, you may have a feeling that something is amiss, and *that feeling should not be ignored.* In such instances the sampling approach should be modified to encompass the touchy area; or the selected sampling system may be abandoned in favor of a complete study of all data in a particular field.

Sampling is an audit tool used for collecting and evaluating data. An auditor forms an opinion about a group of items by studying a small sample of the total group. Auditing is built around the principle of test checking, in which the auditor uses personal judgment in selecting the sample to be examined. But purists, and mathematicians, are bothered by the fact that there is no practical way of measuring the results of judgment sampling. They prefer statistical sampling which is based on the "laws" of probability. The statistical approach provides an objective evaluation, and a means of measuring the reliability of the results of the sample examination.

Objectivity is essential in extracting an effective sample and in selecting an appropriate sampling method. Selected samples must be representative of the whole, and have a behavior that is measurable under the theory of probabilities: the normal curve or the "law" of large numbers. There must be no bias exercised in the selection of the samples or the method.

Statistical sampling establishes the size of an appropriate sample and it appraises results mathematically. Under this system you can achieve a set degree of confidence that the results obtained from examining the sample are within a certain percentage of the total universe. The universe being the total items being studied.

Overview

For the benefit of readers who only want a brief overview, we will list and briefly explain some of the commonly used statistical terms.

1. *Universe.* The total of all items to be studied. For example, all paychecks written in a given period of time.
2. *Population.* A group of items from which samples are taken for statistical measurements. Very similar to Universe, but commonly thought of as a part of the universe which is to be subjected to statistical sampling.
3. *Sample.* A set of values taken from the population to be studied.
4. *Random sample.* A set of values selected without bias and at random from the population to be studied.
5. *Strata sample.* A group of samples having something in common. All items in a specified layer; such as all disbursements exceeding a stipulated value.
6. *Range.* The distance between the low point and the high point in a series of values. The value between the least and greatest value of a normal curve.
7. *Average.* Something that represents the middle point between extremes within a sample or population.
8. *Mean.* A mathematical calculation made by adding all of the values within a sample and dividing the sum by the number of values.
9. *Median.* The value of the middle element in a sample. Half way between the high and low value.
10. *Error.* A value that deviates from a studied characteristic of the other values in the sample.
11. *Reliability.* The likelihood that a sampling program will produce identical

results. The extent to which a statistician can depend on the accuracy of test results.

Factors Affecting Use

Following are some important factors to keep in mind when using statistical sampling techniques. There are sampling tables to help you select sample sizes for designated populations under specified conditions. The table to use depends on the *confidence level* and *precision* that you desire. **IMPORTANT:** *These concepts are interdependent and must be considered together.*

Confidence level is the degree of certainty that the sample examined indicates the true value of the universe from which the sample was taken. It is ordinarily expressed as a percentage.

Precision is the range within which the sample should fall at a specified confidence level. It is comparable to a specified tolerance in tooling machinery, and is ordinarily expressed as plus or minus a stated number of percentage points.

You also must determine the sampling plan to use. The nature of the transactions that you are studying, and the purpose of the audit test will often dictate the most appropriate sampling approach. The plans frequently used by internal auditors are the following:

- *Judgment sampling* covers those actions in which the auditor uses personal judgement to determine sample size and method of selection in place of statistical sampling tables. This sampling plan is commonly used by internal auditors.
- *Sampling for attributes* is used to determine a particular characteristic of a population. This statistical sampling plan is useful when an auditor is trying to learn the estimated number of a specific type of error that occurs in selected transactions. There are various tables available for determining sample size.
- *Sampling for variables* is used to determine the quantity of the population through an examination of a sample. Special tables and estimating methods are available for use when using this plan. For example, this type of sampling can project, within a given range and with a stipulated reliability, the total dollar value of errors contained in the sampled universe.
- *Discovery sampling* is used in investigating fraud where evidence of a single irregularity is needed to justify an all out investigation. This plan utilizes special tables which show the probability of finding at least one occurrence in a given population. The population size must be determined, and a designated occurrence rate must be specified.

- *Acceptance sampling* is used to evaluate quality of purchased items. A good quality level is set and a random sample of material is tested. The number of errors in a sample dictates the action.
- *Stop and go sampling* uses progressive evaluation of test findings to prevent over sampling.

Having determined the sampling plan that you intend to use for a particular examination, you must then decide how to select the samples to be audited. Some of the common techniques are the following:

- *Cluster sampling* is a sampling technique frequently used in auditing in which the universe is divided into clusters of documents. Then all items within selected clusters are examined. In internal auditing, these clusters are usually all transactions of a particular type that occur within a specified time.
- *Random sampling* means that all samples are drawn completely at random from the entire universe or from selected strata within the universe. Random sampling is best applied when each item that makes up the universe has a unique identifier, such as checks or vouchers. A table of random numbers is used in selecting samples.
- *Stratified sampling* separates items into two or more classes. Then each of these classes are sampled independently. This system is often used by auditors in sampling items that have a wide range of dollar values. The higher dollar value items might be entirely examined, and the lower strata sampled statistically.
- *Interval sampling* is the technique that separates samples into regular intervals. For example, every tenth voucher is selected as a sample. The starting point should be selected at random.
- *Mechanized sampling* merely refers to the use of a computer to select the items to be sampled. The computer may contain lists of random numbers which are used to select samples for examination.

IMPORTANT: *Human errors should be considered in any sampling plan.* No matter how many samples are taken, or how valid the sampling plan, auditors can make errors during their examinations. These human errors can occur in any examination, no matter how the samples are selected.

Using the Technique as an Audit Tool

Statistical sampling is used by an auditor to locate violations of policies and procedures, clerical errors and frauds. Violations of policy and clerical type errors are often caused by misinterpretation of procedures or policies. **TIP:**

This type of discrepancy will occur often and regularly and will show up rapidly regardless of the sampling plan selected by the auditor.

Clerical errors caused by carelessness or stupidity will not necessarily repeat with any degree of regularity. A change in personnel might lead to complete disruption in the orderly handling of routine transactions. A management change could dictate that that paperwork be handled in a manner that is entirely irreconcilable to home office policies and procedure directives. Any of these events could produce an unexpected deviation from the historical pattern of a particular operation. These possibilities cannot be built into a judgement sampling program designed in advance for a particular audit. This is one reason why statistical sampling is a valuable audit tool.

When used in internal auditing the sampling problem is complicated by the variety of discrepancies that might occur. An auditor is concerned with the validity and accuracy of the following:

1. Transaction dates,
2. Product or service identities and quantities,
3. Pricing, extensions and footings,
4. Authorizations and approvals,
5. Legitimacy and legality, and
6. Appropriateness and justification.

The law of large numbers applies across a wide spectrum of business activities and is useful in selecting an efficient sampling technique. It can help select a quantity of data for review that will provide a preselected degree of assurance that the sample taken is representative of the universe under review. The number of errors found in the sample provide a basis for estimating the total number of such errors that are contained in the total number of transactions that are being audited.

Frauds or employee defalcations are difficult to project. Some frauds are perpetrated at regular intervals, when circumstances are favorable. The occasion may occur once or several times a day, week, month or year. When conditions are right, the defaulter will take advantage of the situation to perform the misdeeds.

During an audit visit, a major decision is the determination of what records to examine in detail. This is a difficult decision if the possibility of fraud is considered. **KEY POINT:** *Some manipulators are office supervisors who can fairly well predict when the internal auditors will visit their operation and what records they will audit.*

These employees commit their acts during periods when they are certain that auditors will not examine any transactions. Many embezzlers ruefully admit that they thought they knew what records would be examined and for what period of time. These thieves believed that auditors would not look at transactions which occurred during the period immediately following the completion of an internal audit.

When using a cluster sample technique, audit staffs generally review transactions that occurred within the last month or two before the current audit. This system has some merit if the audit schedule staggers the time interval between visits. **TIP:** *If time lag between audit visits vary from three to eighteen months,* it would be difficult for anyone to predict the arrival time of an internal audit team.

If the audit interval is known to be a year or more, and the review of records is limited to transactions that occurred within the current months, a knowledgeable thief will limit illegal activities to the months immediately following the completion of an audit, and will stop the acts several months before the expected audit visit. These people are caught when they become dependent upon their fraudulent income and must continue their thefts longer than normally intended.

When another source of income becomes available to a dishonest employee, there is an urge to take full advantage of the situation. However, there are some thieves who only take their employer's funds for specific purposes. Periodic large bills produce the need, such as rent, insurance premiums or car payments; and the employee taps the company till to meet these obligations.

Thieves who regularly and frequently steal are soon caught, but the culprit that steals for a single purpose, and at lengthy intervals, is less likely to be detected. The infrequent thief usually takes a fairly large sum of money at each misappropriation, perhaps thousands of dollars per act, while the frequent manipulator may be satisfied with less than a hundred dollars each time.

To detect the various types of manipulations, the internal auditor uses a combination of strata and random statistical sampling. Larger samples may be required from the higher values than from the lesser ones because of the infrequent occurrence of the larger thefts. The more frequent occurrences in the lower dollar value range, reduces proportionately the number of samples that need to be examined.

Statistical sampling can be helpful in the following areas:

A. *Accounts receivable* verification work. Many organizations carry thousands of open accounts on their books, and the internal auditor is expected to verify the accuracy of account balances. Using computers, it is possible to prepare confirmation requests for every open account; but this could be quite expensive and time consuming. Each reply must be sorted, examined, recorded, analyzed and followed up. Postage charges would be substantial, though they can be reduced by using monthly statements as the basis for verification requests. Under this system, the reply is the only additional postage cost, and this can be reduced by using a negative response system, in which only customers who disagree with the statement are requested to reply.

Statistical sampling can appreciably reduce the number of accounts to be verified. An auditor would normally narrow the verification field, instinctively, using common sense and intuitive knowledge of the business to select accounts or group of accounts to be verified. This is called judgement sampling.

A statistical sampling approach performs this function in a mathematically scientific manner to achieve a predetermined degree of certainty desired by the auditor. Samples may be selected at random, by strata, cluster, interval, or any other criteria.

B. *Cash* transactions. The volumes of paper work associated with cash receipts presents a fertile field for applying statistical sampling techniques. Such applications can materially reduce the number of transactions needed to be reviewed to determine that prescribed procedures had been followed.

Statistical techniques can be profitably applied to an audit of bank reconciliation work as well as the examination of drafts submitted for acceptance. Another possible application lies in the procedure for verifying large quantities of paper money.

C. *Inventory* audit work. Statistical sampling can be useful in verifying the physical count of products in storage. It is particularly useful when dealing with large quantities of small items, such as nuts and bolts, screws and tapered pins, small tools, transistors and the like.

When using these techniques for inventory verification, the auditor is interested not only in quantity, but also in quality. Not only must the sample counts be accurate, but the samples must also truly represent the condition of the products relative to age, obsolescence, short weights and other qualities.

Pricing of inventories can also be appropriately confirmed through statistical techniques. The extensive use of computers has led to a decrease in the use of statistical sampling as an audit tool. For example, the computer can check all pricing in a relatively short period of time. There is little advantage in selecting a sample for a detailed price check. The computer can check prices and print out any exceptions for audit examination.

D. *Property* verifications. Statistical sampling is useful in a property audit at a location that contains thousands of property items. An assignment that might require many audit weeks to accomplish manually can be substantially shortened through the application of a sampling technique.

E. *Quality control* programs. Statistics play an important role in the quality control checks performed on production line output. Samples for weight, contents, proper fill, color and similar audit requirements are extracted at specific intervals and examined for conformance to preestablished specifications.

Application to Specific Cases

Here's an example showing how it works:

EXAMPLE: You suspect that some landscaping services are overcharging and kicking back part of the overcharges to company employees. Your company owns over a hundred branch locations, all of which are of similar size and design and use contracted landscaping services that are awarded out of the main office.

Through the cooperation of your EDP audit staff, you receive disks containing all accounts payable transactions for the past six months. Using your personal computer, you extract all disbursements charged to branch miscellaneous expenses, and break these down to extract all charges made to landscaping services.

You then arrange the service payments in value order, and analyze the data. The monthly costs range from $30 to $250, with the median cost being $65. You note that there are only a few payments that exceed $150, and so you decide to audit each one of those disbursements. You have selected a strata sample. You use a random sampling approach for the remaining payments.

You run a list of all payments made to suppliers that look suspicious, as well as all payments made at branches that appear to be out of line. Your computer calculates the average monthly cost per branch, and lists the branches in cost order.

Now you can determine which branches appear to be overpaying. You discuss the type of plants and the local climatic conditions with an auditor who has visited the questionable branches.

Based on this analysis and discussions with staff auditors you can now select the branches to visit to evaluate the reasonableness of the landscaping charges. You have used your computer as an audit tool and a combination of judgement, strata, cluster and random sampling in your study of the problem.

Now let's look at a case that demonstrates several techniques:

EXAMPLE: A friend enters your office with some interesting information. At lunch, in the company cafeteria, several supervisors were debating the merits of internal control procedures. One manager stated that disbursement checks could be obtained without submitting any supporting documentation.

Your friend acknowledges that the statement may have been pulled out of thin air, but thought it something that might interest you. You learn who made the statement and visit him.

You are told that a general statement was made at a bar, after a company bowling session had ended. A man made it after a few drinks, and might have been merely trying to get attention. The supervisor had never seen the man before, and since he was not wearing a company T shirt he was probably one of the hundreds that fill in when a regular is unable to bowl. The conversation had occurred over a month ago, but the supervisor had not paid attention to it, and it had just popped into his mind when the group at the lunch table started to discuss internal controls.

You believe it wise to explore the possibility. Knowing that A/P writes about ten thousand checks per month, you decide to limit your universe to the past year, which is 120,000 checks.

Considering your universe, and the type of problems that could possibly exist, you use your personal judgement and limit your study by applying the strata principle. You know that any check for $1,000 or over requires a manual signature, and you are personally acquainted with the people that manually sign these checks. You feel certain that they would not approve any payment that did not have adequate and valid documentation. So you decide to limit your population to all checks issued for an amount less than $1,000. This reduces your field by about 20%, you now are faced with 8,000 checks per month, which might have as little as one example of what you are seeking.

You decide to use a cluster sampling approach, and since the original conversation occurred over a month ago, you elect to review all checks written that month and the previous month. Your population has been narrowed to 16,000, and you decide to use a stop and go sampling technique.

Up to 16,000 checks would have to be studied to be 100% sure of the results. That would require a great deal of audit time, so it seems prudent to settle for something less. The attribute sampling table shows that for a 95% confidence level, and an expected error rate of not more than 2%, a very high degree of precision can be realized by examining a sample of 2534 checks.

The entire project may be completely unfounded, so you decide to use a precision rate of plus or minus one percent, and a confidence level of 90% which requires that a sample of 513 checks be examined. You check your Discovery Sampling Table and find that this sample size is close to the number in that table.

The next problem is to select the sample transactions. The EDP audit group provides a print out of all disbursement checks issued for the two months that you selected. This list contains check numbers, dates and amounts. You receive about one hundred pages, printed on both sides, with three separate checks listed on each line. You decide to use a mechanized random selection process and obtain a computer generated table of random numbers for the 20,000 items in the population. A line is drawn through each item over $999.99 on the computer listing of payments.

Now the random starting point is selected. The sheets are shuffled and turned, and with closed eyes a pencil is placed on a spot on one of the sheets that becomes the random starting point.

About a fourth of the way through your study you find a questionable payment. An examination of this disbursement gives information for narrowing the search for more examples. Stopping your present sampling, you obtain a printout of all payments made to a specific payee, or charged to a particular account.

Using the discovery sampling table and the random sampling approach to select samples, you find more examples of the same type of manipulation that was originally noticed. After the third example you stop the study because there is enough evidence to ensure that the employee involved will tell the full story.

You learn from interrogating the subject that there were three instances in the two-month period selected for study. Only one of those three was contained in the sampling list that had been randomly assembled. You are upset by the fact that the sample used might not have contained any of the three instances; but you are forced to acknowledge that there are advantages to statistical sampling. The statistical sampling technique did succeed in materially reducing the internal auditing time that could have been spent on such an examination.

SUMMARY

A professional auditor should never substitute statistical tables for audit judgement, nor should the professional ever reject methods that may improve audit performance. *No matter what form of sampling plan you elect to use, you will still have to evaluate test results.*

If you use statistical sampling, you will find mathematical tables available to help judge the results obtained from your review of the samples. Evaluation of results is a means to an end, not the end itself. You are attempting to form an overall opinion about the transactions being audited, and this opinion must give appropriate consideration to all relevant facts.

KEY POINT: *In the final analysis, you must use personal judgement as to when and where to apply any internal auditing technique.* Statistical sampling is a technique that falls into this category.

CONTRACT AUDITING

Many audit staffs do not have auditors who are qualified to review some of the professional activities and operations that may be carried on in a large enterprise. A successful internal audit staff must often face new problems that arise from recent acquisitions, or the introduction of new systems, procedures or product lines. At such times the audit manager may seek assistance from outside experts.

Many services are available to audit groups. The major source of outside audit expertise is from public accounting companies. In addition, there are a variety of consulting companies, who offer their services. Many of them have been formed by internal audit specialists.

Audit of Utility Billings

Some audit groups perform their services with the understanding that they will receive a percentage of everything they save for a company. There are specialized audit companies that review utility bills on this basis. Utility service companies use rates established by various public agencies, and the established rate structure can be complicated. **TIP:** *A company that is a large user of energy can benefit from learning what factors affect their billings from utilities.*

Utility audit companies identify areas of overcharges, or they may suggest ways that their clients can reduce costs by making changes in operations or by requesting different classifications. These audit agencies operate by reviewing utility bills paid by a company and comparing the charges to the rate schedule authorized for the utility involved. They usually receive a fixed percentage of savings for the first full year after their suggestions are implemented. Example: they may illustrate that by changing working or production schedules by an hour, the power usage would fall into a lower rate class.

Audit of Suppliers' Billings

In the same genre are the audit companies that review bills from selected suppliers in the hope of detecting overcharges. These agencies concentrate on suppliers that offer frequent quantity rebates, sales promotions and special discounts. The agency reviews all payments made to certain suppliers and compares the payments to promotions and rebates offered. They locate payments that did not receive all of the full discounts offered, and then either prepare, or assist the company in preparing, claims for all provable overcharges. These agencies are paid a percentage of the money actually recovered from suppliers as a result of their work.

Freight Bill Audit Agencies

Freight bill audit agencies review payments of freight bills in the hope of detecting overcharges. They compare the rates and the classifications of product shipped and detect errors in rates, classifications or arithmetic. They receive a percentage of all recoveries that result from their activities.

These audit agencies can actually work in two directions; they may spot undercharges by a carrier as well as overcharges. But their major source of revenue is derived from helping shippers recover overcharges from carriers. These freight audit agencies are mentioned in the chapter titled Auditing Distribution and Traffic.

Construction Audits

There are agencies that specialize in auditing construction work. They may assign a full time auditor as the owner's representative on a construction site, or may perform post audits of construction charges.

Some agencies use computers to determine and prepare quantity estimates of all materials required for a specific job. They apply experience labor standards to the various trades to arrive at reasonable estimates of labor hours required. They process all billings against their estimates and determine areas of potential overcharges which are explored in minute detail. Much of the success of a post audit in these areas is dependent on the nature and language of the construction contract that covered the project work.

These audit companies usually work on an hourly or flat fee plus expenses basis, rather than a percentage of savings. For some jobs, where the construction contract is well written to protect an owner, an audit company may take an assignment on a percentage of savings when the square footage cost of the building is obviously excessive.

Investigative Agencies

Internal auditors also have access to all of the investigative services that were discussed in the previous chapters dealing with Security Departments and Fraud. Of course, public police agencies are always available to assist in problems that fall in their jurisdiction.

Private investigative services are usually paid for on an hourly basis, since there are rarely any positively identifiable savings involved. There are frequent recoveries of funds stolen by employees, but pay backs can take a long time and private investigative agencies can't survive waiting for their fees.

Outside Expertise

In addition to the above mentioned agencies, the public accounting and management consultant firms offer a wide range of expertise that can be useful to an audit function. They are most useful in areas in which an internal audit staff does not have the know how to properly perform a specific audit review. These are commonly referred to as operational or management audits. For example, they may include studies in Engineering, Research, Banking, Advertising, Marketing, Distribution, or Computer operations.

These specialized management advisory services from management consulting and public accounting firms are usually contracted for in one of two ways. You may add an outside expert to the audit staff for a review of a particular department. The expert operates as a member of the audit team. After the review is completed, the expert writes up the salient points noted, documents the comments with appropriate reference material and submits a report to the audit manager. The expert may be requested to participate in the audit windup meeting.

Another approach is to use outside experts to independently conduct a review of a specific department or operation. An audit supervisor may work with the outside experts as a liaison service to obtain required company information. Under such an assignment the experts work directly for and report to the audit manager who closely supervises the review.

Contract audits differ from management advisory or consulting services in that they deal with examination of transactions which have already transpired, whereas the true consulting service provides aid to management in making decisions as to future actions. Management consultants usually help executives decide what to do about a specific problem or situation, while the contract audit expert is used to evaluate actions that have already taken place and to determine if there have been any improprieties.

Peer Reviews

Another type of assistance available to an audit manager is the peer review, which has been described in an early chapter. Peer reviews take many forms, the more common of which are the following:

1. A study, *made in the home office,* of the audit department's work schedules; programs; training methods; methods of reviewing work papers; audit report writing, their processing and the follow-up work; filing systems and auditors' work evaluations.
2. In a study of the *field audit work,* the reviewer travels with an audit team and evaluates their approach and work. The study covers audit techniques, preparation of working papers, interview procedures, reviewing

audit work papers, conducting the windup meetings, obtaining management comments, writing and circulating the final report, discussions with top operating management, and the follow-up work performed as a result of the audit.

3. Peer reviews *may be directed toward the audited employees* to get their view of the conduct, ability and approach of the audit group. These studies often includes employee comments relating to the advantages, and disadvantages, of the internal audit function. This type of audit operation review is often conducted by the audit manager through a questionnaire submitted to employees in a recently audited department. It may be conducted by an outsider who obtains information through personal interviews.
4. Some peer reviews concentrate on the *evaluation of the audit function by top executives of a company*. Through personal interviews the reviewer seeks to learn the executive's evaluation of audit services performed by the internal staff. The executives are given an opportunity to express their feelings toward the merits of the audit reports received and the follow-up work performed by the audit function.

Peer reviews can be a valuable tool for an audit manager, when the review is conducted by a knowledgeable internal auditing expert who is completely objective and free to express professional observations.

Chapter 31

General Comments and Helpful Hints

Starting with the organization of the auditing department, we considered many of the technical aspects of administering an internal auditing function, including audit manuals, programs and instructions. We outlined procedures for conducting an audit, for reviewing the audit work performed by staff members and for winding up the review, and preparing and issuing the audit report. We presented many examples of workable audit programs and discussed some of the special problems that are encountered when performing internal auditing work.

The checklist programs can lead into the significant areas of an operation and should be used as examples to assist your thinking; they are not a substitute for your creative imagination. The audit checklists relate to most of the common operations that exist in a business organization. Interpretation of audit points and the method of approaching a particular problem lies with you who are accustomed to working within the framework of your organization.

If you are faced with an operation that is not covered by one of the audit programs in this manual, design your own using the procedures outlined in the chapter dealing with the creation of an audit program.

A. REQUIREMENTS FOR AN INTERNAL AUDITOR

Internal auditing is not an exact science, there are no great truths or absolute principles. Like any other profession, the *quality of the work is largely dependent upon the ability, initiative, drive, perceptiveness and persistence of the individual internal auditor.*

One auditor may ignore signs that another recognizes immediately. There is no way to separate the individuality of an auditor from the approach to the profession, nor is there a single correct way to handle a particular problem. But there are a few requirements, and above all an internal auditor's integrity and honesty must always be above question or suspicion. An auditor's words must always be true, and all promises honored.

Important characteristics of successful internal auditors are (1) good business judgment, (2) intelligence, (3) common sense, and (4) a good formal education or extensive field experience. Experience is a good teacher and knowing that something has worked is a good basis for trying it again under similar circumstances. But experience also teaches us that there is no absolute assurance that when dealing with human beings, what has worked once will necessarily work again.

Good auditing management requires the following:

1. *Imaginative leadership* of a competent staff.
2. A *clear understanding* of the operation being audited.
3. A *manageable scope* of work.
4. An *evaluation of crucial operations* and alternative ways of doing business.
5. The *ability to produce* meaningful results.
6. *Major conclusions clearly presented* in a formal report.
7. Getting out from behind your desk and *talking with people* who are actually doing the work.
8. Letting the *people concerned know what you are doing.*
   (a) Solicit their ideas.
   (b) Ask about their problems and needs for information.

B. GETTING THE JOB DONE

Auditors sometimes grow impatient when things are not done as promised or when supervisors are reluctant to take obviously necessary actions. **TIP:** *It's said that patience is a virtue, but in a business environment impatience is also a virtue.* Auditors should become impatient, if that's what it takes to get people to act. The law of inertia applies to business people as well as to inanimate objects. **KEY POINT:** *Business managers, particularly if their operations are successful, are reluctant to make changes.* They are usually too occupied with day to day challenges to want to create new problems by making changes; even when a revision will obviously be an improvement.

A major loss or an employee misdeed is frequently the catalyst that stirs management to action, and when so stirred the action is often extreme. The old adage that "a stitch in time saves nine" is not appreciated by some business people. They usually assume that "an ounce of prevention is worth a pound of cure," only applies to others.

C. ATTITUDE AND BEHAVIOR

1. Be a Good Listener

A good internal auditor is a good listener. As an auditor you should have a genuine interest in people and a dedicated interest in your profession. The art of listening is a difficult one to master.

KEY POINT: *Your job requires constant attention during all your interviews. It is essential that you pay strict attention because the critical information that you seek may be conveyed in a split second.* A person you are talking to will give a hint that there really is more to be said but the individual does not feel free to discuss it. You must be constantly on the alert for a signal that indicates the presence of knowledge that the individual is reluctant to disclose. Your fellow employees will reveal these things if properly pressed.

During your conversations, if you are continually on the alert, you will learn to spot telltale signs. Your interviewing technique should enable you to get as much information from body language, tonal inflections and innuendo as you do from the spoken word. **CAUTION:** *As an auditor, it is your job to determine the facts. Ask yourself: What is the truth? How do I know it's the truth?*

You do not visit an operation to entertain or to provide a distraction from the everyday monotony of performing a repetitive job. You must maintain a questioning attitude, but you should *not* make this apparent. No one likes to be questioned or to feel that their motives or actions are under suspicion. Avoid a belligerent or authoritative attitude, even when you are convinced that something is wrong. **TIP:** *Look for a reasonable explanation for every discrepancy. If you do not fully accept an offered explanation, do not show your distrust.*

Through your questioning, make it apparent that you are seeking a reasonable, valid and truthful explanation. Learn to control your facial expressions, your body language and the tone of your voice. Those elements can betray your true inner feelings. If you give a message of mistrust to someone you are interviewing, be assured that they will be ultra careful in every word they say to you.

The art of conducting a successful interview is learned through experience. Use the first few minutes to gain the confidence of the subjects and ease their minds so that they will relax and want to cooperate. It is important that there be a clear understanding of every word uttered at the meeting. Remember that you are approaching the conversation from different perspectives. Some words may have different meanings to both of you, so it is important to reword important questions so that any problem of semantics is resolved.

2. Working With Your Fellow Employees

It is important that you treat everyone with respect, even those guilty of wrongdoing. Remember that you are not a judge, but a representative of the top management of your company. Your attitude, your behavior, your treatment of the employees you contact will affect the employees' reaction toward you.

Watch out for the few people who are natural con artists and engage in illegal acts. These people believe that they can mislead you into either bypassing their area of operations or into overlooking their illegal acts. Or they may ask that you come to them directly for explanations of discrepancies that relate to their actions. By being friendly toward you, they hope that you will skim over their work and miss the signs of their wrongdoings that you might otherwise normally note.

3. Remember That Your Work Is Confidential

KEY POINT: *All the work that you do as an auditor is considered to be of a confidential nature and should not be discussed with anyone other than audit supervisors.* Some things that you may note while reviewing an operation may have a greater impact upon local employees than you can possibly imagine. You have no way of knowing what information the local managers may not wish their employees to know.

Be discreet in your conversations with your fellow auditors. When among staff members who are working on the same assignment, you may freely mention observations and ideas, but avoid discussing classified information with other staff members unless instructed to do so by audit management. You may freely talk about audit approaches and techniques and company rules and regulations with all staff members, but don't volunteer information about audit observations unless you are in a training session where such items are being discussed.

An auditor may observe certain procedures or actions that must be written up as audit points, and the auditor may never learn the outcome of the observations. A write-up may be included in the audit report and covered at the windup meeting, but an auditor who does not attend the meeting will be left in the dark. Much of the basic audit work performed during an audit is never discussed or mentioned unless it serves as the basis for a subject at a training session.

Remember that organizations do not publicize their failures or problems. Any employee defalcation is a failure. It means that management did not install the right controls or take proper action or give the type of consideration that might have prevented the illegal act. When an employee goes wrong, the company loses not only whatever the culprit may have misappropriated, but also a valuable employee for whom they have spent a lot of training time and money. **NOTE:** *Companies do not broadcast such losses and neither should you.*

4. Recognition of Accomplishments

Everyone likes to have their work recognized and to be complimented for a job well done. Such recognition is rare in our profession. You must learn to accept this oversight as a condition of employment.

Within the internal audit function, audit supervision should be diligent in giving credit where due, among staff members. It is customary for the department head to accept the plaudits for good work performed by the staff. But where a single auditor, or a small group, is responsible for accomplishing a notable act, the department head should acknowledge the actions of staff members. Special recognition, awards, dinners or even a specific mention during training sessions can encourage auditors to be constructive and original in their auditing approach and suggestions.

If you note a method or practice that is inefficient and costly, and suggest corrections that are put into place and save a great deal of money, the credit for the accomplishment will rightfully go to the manager that authorized the corrective action. Your contribution may not even be mentioned. You may receive recognition from fellow staff members and supervisors, and perhaps from the executive to whom the internal audit function reports.

If you are called upon to perform a special study for the Chairman of the Board, the President or any other top executive, and you do a good job you may receive special recognition. An increase in your paycheck is really the best recognition.

D. Handling Errors

Every active human being makes errors. In the natural course of performing internal auditing there are a great many errors observed. **REMEMBER:** *The important thing about an error is that there is a positive side to its detection.* The defect should be corrected if there is any benefit in doing so, and *ways should be devised to prevent its recurrence.* It is also important not to overemphasize the importance of an error or to dwell on the subject.

If one puts a hand in front of a whirling blade, a finger will be cut off. Such an act demonstrates what happens if one makes this type of error. Those who have knowledge of the event are careful when they see the danger sign of a whirling blade. Responsible supervisors will try to devise ways of preventing the error from recurring and may well design and install preventive guards. The operation has then profited from the error in that it probably will not be repeated. An attempt at correction might be to sew back the part that had been cut off.

The same approach applies to the auditing field. If, during an audit, an error is noted, such as charging a wrong price for an item sold, the error can be corrected by rebilling for the correct amount. The oversight can be kept from being repeated by carefully checking the price lists and initiating a system that requires all invoices to be double checked for correct pricing. Other errors might not be correctible. An error in a production process, that uses too much of a valuable raw material in the product, cannot be recovered.

Perhaps the most important audit problem relating to errors is the determination as to whether an oversight was inadvertent or deliberate. Inadvertent errors can be forgiven and forgotten, and corrected where practical. The deliberate act can be the result of an employee's dissatisfaction with the job and just a way to get even with the employer. A deliberate oversight might give advantage to a person or group that the employee happens to like. Or, it might be the method used by miscreants involved in defrauding the company.

KEY POINT: *Every time you spot a mistake you must mentally evaluate to determine what category the miscue fits into.*

Repetition of an error does not necessarily mean that fraud is involved, but it could well be an indication that such is the case. Repetition could occur from a variety of innocent reasons.

E. Don't Jump to Conclusions

Be wary of jumping to conclusions. Sometimes a preponderance of evidence can indicate that it is staged or false. However, there are many cases where someone who commits a wrongful act is not fully aware of the systems or controls in effect to prevent such acts, and therefore leaves a blazing trail that leads to the culprit.

When outside experts are available to assist in the determination of actions or motives, the internal auditor would be well-advised to take advantage of such professional assistance.

F. Use Outside Agencies Judiciously

CAUTION: *Much wining and dining and alcohol consumption goes on amongst suppliers and employees who direct company business.* Auditors are not expected to act as policemen, but unhealthy business relationships may create reasonable grounds for suspicions that cannot be ignored. In such cases the auditor may decide to employ outside investigators to learn where and how frequently these people get together. Payoffs frequently take place over a lunch table, when the payer drops an envelope or a big bill and then picks it up and hands it to the dinner partner with the statement, " You just dropped this."

Before deciding to tail an employee, be certain that the matter is thoroughly discussed with top management, including other departments that have a responsibility in the area. **TIP:** *Order such surveillance only after all executives concerned agree that it is appropriate.*

G. Evolution Versus Revolution

The following case demonstrates a significant point:

> **EXAMPLE:** An auditor was asked to study the organization and operating systems used in a major department. At the completion of the study the recommendations were brought into the office of the executive vice-president and a verbal report was presented.
>
> Five major recommendations were offered for reorganizing and improving the operation. The executive vice-president listened carefully, read the suggestions and nodded his head in agreement. He agreed completely with the findings and recommendations, and implied that the meeting was at an end.
>
> The auditor asked if directives should be prepared for signature and issuance by the VP, as the first step toward implementing the recommendations. The VP shook his head and indicated that he would handle the matter in his own way, commenting that the first moves would be made within the month, and the others would follow in time.
>
> Reminding the VP of his agreement that all recommendations were necessary, the auditor wondered why they all weren't to be acted upon immediately. The VP replied, "We'll get it all done in time, but we'll *accomplish it through evolution not revolution.* This way we won't rock the boat and we'll gain everyone's cooperation."
>
> Of course, that approach was followed and all recommendations were implemented within four years. The reorganization was very successful and all of the executives involved in the changes felt that they had initiated and were responsible for them, and they, therefore, made them work. If the changes had been forced on the executives, there would have been antagonism and resentment, and the program may not have been successful.

The moral of the above story is that an auditor can accomplish more by working with executives than against them. A good auditor sells ideas and then walks away, permitting executives who accept and implement the program to get full credit for the accomplishment. This is not to say that auditors should completely ignore their part in an operation. Audit work papers and the preliminary report should contain all the information relating to these acts and the decision to eliminate something from the final report should be well documented.

The internal auditor often must make a choice. Decide to make the auditor look good by making other people look bad, or help the company by making others look good.

H. Strange Things are Happening

Computer experts operate under the philosophy that anything that can happen, will. Or anything that can possibly go wrong, will, at one time or another. This seems like a pessimistic outlook, but there is enough history to justify the assumption. Similarly, in internal auditing you will probably run into situations that will lead you to believe that, anything that can possibly be manipulated, will be. That doesn't mean that it will be done on every occasion, but you will find many instances where odd manipulations have occurred. **IMPORTANT:** *When you look at any documents that makes you feel that something doesn't look right, something that you can't put your finger on, don't pass it by.* Let your imagination run free and try to think of the most remote activities that could explain the inconsistencies. Then follow up to see if those improbable events actually occurred.

> **EXAMPLE:** There was a situation where a bookkeeper prepared a completely new set of books, covering a five-month period, over a long weekend. Of course, not all records were doctored, but there were substantial entries and the books had to be made to balance with the manipulated figures. Records did tie-in, and might have escaped detection had new sheets not been used, and if all entries had not been made with the same pen. If old paper and different colored ink had been used, and if coffee had been spilled and mopped up on some of the pages, the records might have been accepted as originals.

Also, you should never stake your reputation that a machine is operating correctly. Even machines that are normally very accurate may develop a quirk, or may miss some entries because of a power failure. When working with computers, a fractional second loss of power can result in the loss of much information. Some losses are obvious, but others can require many hours of research to discover the problem. **TIP:** *When you are working with machine-generated information, you should use mental logic checks where practical.* If not practical and a report is questionable, run the report again, and then if necessary, use a different machine or different system to verify accuracy. It may be necessary to check each individual number since the problem may be caused by a misplaced decimal point.

I. International Considerations

Differences in cultures result in differences in mores, business character or philosophy and may require different approaches to apparently identical problems. I recall a visit to an international division that was experiencing losses in a particular operation.

> **EXAMPLE:** The problem appeared to be centered in any one of a group of four employees. I remarked that we would consider offering a polygraph test to any of the employees who requested it, in order to remove them from suspicion. The chief financial officer was aghast at the approach, saying, "We would never consider such a thing; we couldn't put any of our employees through that type of thing."
>
> Later in the conversation, the executive blandly stated that all plant employees were regularly put through a thorough body search as they exited the plant, to insure that they weren't stealing something and secreting it on their person. Such a body-search was routine and was accepted in that community.
>
> There was also a conversation with the top financial executive of a European subsidiary operation whose internal controls over one area of operations left much to be desired. External security was totally lacking; creating a situation that was an open invitation to theft.
>
> When this was pointed out, the executive stated that his workers were not Americans and didn't behave like Americans. Hearing this, I recognized a mistake in failing to take cultural differences into account. None of the security suggestions were accepted and the operation continued as before.
>
> The original approach to the problem was vindicated several months later when the location began experiencing large losses. The executive called and asked for advice. Remembering the obvious weaknesses, I repeated some of the earlier suggestions, and added a few designed to apprehend the culprits. A few days later a group of workers were caught in the act of stealing. The same executive called to admit, "People are pretty much the same the world over."

1. Use a Unique Audit Program

Just as every operation or department requires an individualized audit program, so too does each international division. *Laws and business practices* differ from country to country, so it is necessary to modify internal auditing procedures and approaches to suit the culture. Where an international division has been set up in the image of the home office, a standard audit program can be used as the basis for an audit approach. Sometimes, only minor modifications are required to prepare a program that covers the operation.

Some countries have *tax laws that necessitate the keeping of multiple sets of ledgers,* such as those sometimes set up to take advantage of accelerated depreciation of specific types of equipment under U. S. tax laws. In such cases the local books are prepared to conform to existing laws and customs, and the audit program should test to determine that local laws are obeyed.

National mores also may affect the audit program. In some countries certain concessions are given to employees that might not conform to home office directives. Some countries have a shortage of certain types of labor, and to offset this shortage many part-time people are employed in production line positions, which creates certain operating problems. One country requires that employers grant employees a six-month vacation after a set number of years of employment, and this is in addition to the normal annual vacation.

2. Adapting the Program for Use

Internal audit programs must be fine-tuned to national mores and business customs. Each audit point, and every instruction, must be rethought with the particular country in mind. After a revised program is tentatively decided upon, it should be reviewed and evaluated by the top financial executive in the operation concerned. After necessary revisions, the program is ready for trial.

For original application, the program might best be tested by auditors from the head office. After they have used, revised and approved the program, it is then ready for use by the local staff.

If a new local audit staff is being hired and set in place, their training might be enhanced by having them visit the home office to participate in internal audits with the corporate audit staff. After they become familiar with audit techniques and approaches used by the headquarters staff, they can assist in drawing up an audit program that applies to operations in their home country. Or members of the corporate staff might lead them through an audit of their operations, using the corporate audit program. As the audit progresses the program could be modified to fit the particular country's operations.

3. Reporting on Audits of International Divisions

An audit report should normally be addressed to the party that has the authority and desire to take appropriate action. However, in an international operation the president of the division frequently wants to be informed of everything that occurs, and in such cases the audit report might best be addressed to the president.

Implementing audit recommendations in an international division depends upon the organization's structure. In many divisions the top financial executive or the president of the operation assumes the responsibility for implementing audit recommendations.

The corporate audit staff has a role to play in this area. A copy of every audit report written in the international division should be transmitted to the Director of Internal Auditing who should take an active part in following up to learn of actions taken to correct audit deficiencies. To facilitate such corporate activity a procedure should be installed that requires a copy of all follow-up correspondence and directives be sent to the office of the Director of Internal Auditing. Any major audit points that are not resolved within a reasonable time should be explored. A letter from the Director to the President of the derelict international division, with a copy to the International VP will usually produce prompt action.

HELPFUL HINTS

Even the simplest routines can be easily forgotten or overlooked. It pays to spend a few moments to review the practices that we generally take for granted. There is no logic governing the sequence in which these random thoughts are presented.

A. Audit Forms

1. Audit forms are designed to aid an auditor in conducting routine examinations. Every auditing department should create audit forms to fit its own special company operations. These should be designed by the experienced, knowledgeable auditors who have gained expertise in reviewing particular operations.

   If the form is well-designed, it calls for the information to be presented in a methodical fashion that helps analyze transactions and leads to logical conclusions. Standard forms are usually preprinted and contains blank spaces large enough to accommodate the varying information that is to be inserted. The variable factors may be stamped, typed or handwritten onto the document.
2. Internal auditors working in a familiar environment soon learn what repetitive information they need to work with. They become aware of the high volume areas to be examined. One routine phase of audit work is the review of work standards and efficiency. Applying these concepts to the time-consuming audit tasks leads into the use of forms to meet recurring needs. Here's a common example:

   A/R verification forms are designed to meet a specific audit activity. Sample A/R verification forms are shown in the chapter dealing with Receivables. In one of the samples the heading may be stamped but all other information is written by the auditor. The form was designed so that the customer's name is positioned to fit a window envelope so as to eliminate rewriting the name and address.

Statements are prenumbered to be used sequentially so that they all can be accounted for and be held in sequence to readily locate the proper form when replies are returned by customers.

Forms are printed in triplicate: the first copy is mailed to the customer; the second copy (with the words "Second Request" printed in red across the face of the copy) is the second request and is mailed to customers who have not responded; the third copy is retained as the audit file copy of the verification request.

This type of verification approach is used when the number of open accounts is relatively small. Companies that have all of their receivables on computers generally use the data base to draw off statements selected for verification.

Standardized audit forms can be designed for any repetitive audit examination. Your audit staff requires its own special types. The forms printed throughout this book may serve as a guide and a reminder.

3. In Chapter 28, there is an Internal Audit Check-Off Form which enables a material reduction in the size of the audit program. This checkoff form replaces the space on the audit program that is used to record the period covered by the review, and the initials of the auditors that performed the work. The form is very adaptable.

   Carefully control the copies of this form; make your auditors responsible for safeguarding the working copies in their possession. A copy of the completed forms should be attached to the department copy of the final audit report, and originals filed in the audit workpapers.

B. Flow Charting

1. In order to study any operation an auditor must learn what is done, by whom and in what sequence. The individual work steps are written up by the auditor in some fashion, so that they can be studied and analyzed. The auditor may use a narrative write-up approach, or can speed up the recording process by using a flow charting technique.

   For preparing flow charts of operations, systems analysts have adopted a standard set of symbols. This standardization, used by most analysts, enables an immediate interpretation by any other analyst.

   These symbols are used by many internal auditors, depending upon their individual desires. The symbols, consisting primarily of circles, triangles, squares and rectangles have specific meanings.

Storage, transportation, operations and inspections are determined by noting the type of symbol used. Number of copies and distribution is also discernable. Any auditor could benefit from reading printed material describing systems and procedures flow charting.

2. Before you start an audit review of a particular area, *review the flow charts of that activity and of related areas* and attempt to combine audit work required in those areas that overlap or are interrelated.
   KEY POINT: *Audit steps often overlap, and if you approach an audit task with the sole intent of satisfying only one specific requirement, you may find yourself looking at the same record several times during the course of your review.* Each time you will examine a different aspect of the record. This of course is a waste of audit time.

C. Unique Identifying Marks

Auditors must leave trail marks that enable them to retrace their steps when and if necessary. Audit trail marks are called tick marks and are placed next to words or numbers that have been traced or compared to reports or records.

Use a distinctive check mark to identify your audit work, and a unique signature to identify your audit work papers. On complex audit work, where several verifications are performed, use a different tick mark and/or colored pencil for each type of verification. For example:

- A black tick mark opposite a first party check listing on the audit schedule of incoming cash could signify that the check had been properly applied to the correct account;
- Red tick marks show that checks had been properly deposited; and
- Blue tick marks might signify that the amount of the check had been correctly included in the schedule total of cash deposited.

When items must be traced to many records or schedules, a large number of distinctive tick marks may be required. In such instances a variety of marks should be used, such as a check, a double check, a circle, a double circle, etc. and several colors may be needed. **TIP:** *When using multiple tick marks, be sure to inscribe a legend on the first page that clearly identifies the meaning of each mark.*

D. Checking for Accuracy

1. When attempting to locate an error in a column of figures, be alert for a figure inversion. A figure may easily be transposed and may be written as 49, when it should be 94.

- When attempting to verify that a column of figures has been added properly and while using a machine to accomplish the task, it is wise to make a fast logic check so that you will recognize a gross machine error. **TIP:** *If you are adding pages of figure treat each page individually, and arrive at a total per page.* Then add up the pages. If an error is made you may only have to re-add one page.

2. If there are fifty figures on a sheet and no figure has more than two numbers to the left of the decimal point, the sheet total cannot *logically* exceed 5000; any figure in excess of that amount would be an obvious error. If every figure on the sheet contained at least two numbers to the left of the decimal point, then the lowest *logical* figure would be 500; any figure lower than that would be an obvious error. The range would logically fall between 500 and 5000.

    - Your logic check may consist of scanning the largest numbers in the column and mentally adding up these figures. You might add a one for remaining sums that are over 1/2 the value if you want to get close to the correct figure. This is a fast way of checking columns in which pennies have NOT been eliminated. Your total should be close to the machine calculated total. If the machine figure is different, carefully reenter the figures into the machine.
    - When running a logic check of multiplied figures, use a decimal approach to get into the ball park. For example, if a large number is being multiplied by 151, merely add two zeros to the figure multiplied and then add one half of the total to arrive at a logic figure. If you want to be exact, add the original figure to your total. Using the decimal logic check, you can get a fast estimate of the correct figure.
    - Machines sometimes develop quirks or errors that are disturbing. The author has mentioned an adding machine that printed figures over ten thousand but did not pick up that round amount in the total.

      When working with computers or calculators you should always run a rough logic check, recognizing that any machine error will be a large one. **TIP:** *Comparing previous months figures for comparable operations will often serve as a rough logic check.*

3. Values for specific types of operations are often fairly close to one another. For example a payroll audit would show pay rates, or gross pay, as fairly consistent and close when reviewing a particular operation. Sales figures in some operations may have a degree of consistency. Such similarities should be readily noticeable.

    In such cases, you should be on the lookout for the oddball. Any figure that is noticeably excessive or too low should be singled out for examination. An additional random sampling of the items within range should suffice. **TIP:** *In your audit work look for the odd item.*

4. In high volume operations fractions can mount up to large numbers. In inventory transactions, where individual products are packaged in cases, a part case might be valuable. Fractional cases are often written in their decimal equivalent. Alterations in part case figures are frequently overlooked, though they can represent a lot of dollars.

   If an inventory clerk has access to product, a theft can be easily covered by changing these fractional figures. Whole numbers can be altered in the same fashion, but such obvious changes are more likely to be noticed and questioned than are fractional alterations.

   The following increases are difficult to spot and are the most frequently used. A 1 can become a 4,6,7 or 9. A 3 can be made into an 8. A 4 can be made into an 8 or 9. A 5 can become an 8. A 6 can become an 8. A seven becomes a 9. And a 0 can also become an 8. Going downward, the possible alterations are not as numerous. A 9 may be changed to an 8. A 7 becomes a 4 or a 0. And a 1 is changed to 0.

   If you notice any such alterations, consider the consequences and act accordingly. Your company should adopt and enforce a policy that requires any figure change to be made by drawing a line through an incorrect figure and writing in the correct one. Under this system any alteration as described above becomes a noted discrepancy.

E. Problems with Signatures

1. The use of signature stamps present a problem to internal auditors. Authorized signatures are key internal control features, assuming that an official signature means that a supervisor has examined and approved a transaction. Many executives have the onerous tasks of signing many documents. After a short period of diligent pursuit of their duty, most executives resort to another means of satisfying this requirement. Some obtain a signature stamp, while the more efficient opt for a signature plate. In the former the executive applies the stamp to each document, in the latter the name is signed mechanically. Both eliminate the executive's manual signature.

   The job of stamping documents is often assigned to a secretary or an assistant. The location of a signature stamp, or plate, becomes generally known and its safeguarding is forgotten. **CAUTION:** *At that point the approval signature loses most of its control value.*

2. During an audit review, you should assume that a signature applied by such devices are meaningless. Therefore if something out of the ordinary has occurred relative to a specific transaction, the matter should be discussed with the executive whose signature has been applied. If it's some-

thing the executive has seen and recalls, no harm is done. If it is something that the individual does not recall, the executive should be pleased to have it presented for review.

3. Even if a signature is manually applied by the executive in question, it does not mean that every little detail has been studied. Most executives rely on their assistants to perform the necessary accuracy checks and verifications before presenting documents for signature. Some executives are reluctant to question assistants about details relating to routine documents, unless there is a clear obvious discrepancy that requires explanation.

   KEY POINT: *In effect, the signature of approval, no matter how applied, does not of itself assure that a transaction is legitimate and proper.*

F. Audit Work Sheets

1. When you are reviewing a particular operation that almost always presents some problems, you should prepare an audit work paper with sufficient columns to contain much variable information. Start by reviewing (scanning) several of the documents in the file to be audited. This will give you an idea of the areas in which there are oversights, discrepancies or questionable items. Once this is done, go back to the first document and enter pertinent information. Start your schedule by heading up the columns to provide sufficient data that would enable anyone to find the document you are examining.
2. When preparing such a schedule for an accounts payable review, the work paper should be sufficiently wide to enable you to add columns as you encounter different types of discrepancies. Be sure to allow several columns on the right end for comments, where you can note any unusual information relating to a particular listing.

   For example, in reviewing accounts payable, start the schedule by listing the disbursement check number, the date of the transaction or the A/P document; or perhaps the batch number and date on which the document was entered into the computer system. Following that, list the name and address of the payee and the amount of the disbursement. Using this information you can be certain that you are looking at the same document if it must be referred to at a later time.

   Next on your audit schedule are columns for questionable items:

   - For documents not properly approved; label a column "Approvals," and note in that column the lack of approval or the name of the individual who had approved the document in question. ("Approved by JCL, not authorized" or "No proper approval").

- For missed discounts; set up a column labeled "Terms" in which you note the terms that had been overlooked in the payment. ("2% earned discount not taken"; or "2% discount missed by 2 days"; or "5% quantity discount missed by two dozen"; or "5% quantity discount if this order combined with one issued 3 days earlier.")

- For late payments. List dates (1) of the invoice, (2) received in accounts payable, and (3) of payment. This will help locate the problem, perhaps caused by mail room or by the time taken to travel from vendor to your office. **TIP:** *Such problems can be corrected by working through Purchasing to persuade the vendor to consider such delays when stating the last date for taking a discount.*

3. If you are studying payments to a specific vendor and are only listing those that have exceptions, be sure to also list the check numbers, or other identification, of all payments reviewed that were proper. In the event that a later question arises, you can return to your schedule to find out whether you had seen a particular payment. If the payment had not been in file, or had been extracted, your work papers would clearly show that you had not examined it.
4. In the normal routine audit checking of prenumbered documents, the auditor checks to insure that all numbers are accounted for. **NOTE:** *A missing document might be a serious danger signal.* If documents are voided and thrown away, they would not be found. On the other hand, if the printer had erred, you could be misled into believing that a problem existed. **TIP:** *In order to minimize the possibility of needless auditor excitement when missing numbers are noted, you should install company systems that explain missing numbers in a sequence.*

   When receiving prenumbered documents, the receiver must check the first few numbers and the last numbers and note the starting and last number on the R/R. If there are missing numbers, the receiver must note all missing numbers, keep a copy for receiving department files, and send a copy to the department that uses the forms.
5. Anytime a mistake is made in preparing a prenumbered document, all copies should be voided, and the document should be filed in a "Voided" file folder. This file is a part of the active file in your audit examination. Any number that is missing in your audit study should be contained in the "Voided" file.

   If you are auditing voucher files, the filing system should require that a marker be placed in the files when a voucher is removed. These markers should show who removed the file and the date and time.

G. Handling Major Problems

1. Work at developing the ability to differentiate between a major and a minor problem. Don't waste any of your valuable time on insignificant items, use as little time as possible on the minor problems that *might become important.* Hoard your time, and then spend whatever is necessary to get to the bottom of the serious problems that you will regularly encounter.
2. When you are faced with an important problem, make certain that no information is ignored. Even the slightest detail can materially change a picture, so explore all factors, all facets, all related consequences of the problem before you reach a final decision.
   KEY POINT: *Any discrepancy, no matter how small, can become important.*
3. When a cash fund is being verified, it is a good idea for the auditor to enter the cashier's cage without carrying any personal cash. A custodian might contend that there was no shortage when the auditor started counting the fund. Such contention is difficult to dispute unless the auditor takes certain precautions. It is always best to have a disinterested observer present during the counting of a cash fund. **IMPORTANT:** *Anytime the custodian or the witness must leave the area, the auditor should stop the count and move away until the witness or custodian returns.*
4. Following are some brief tips for handling fraud investigations:

   - When a major fraud occurs, management frequently goes overboard in their attempt to prevent that type of incident from recurring, though they originally did nothing to forestall it. It always shocks management when an auditor states that certain control measures are unnecessary or that they are too expensive to implement. **NOTE:** *But there are times when an internal auditor must do just that.*
   - When people engage in a fraudulent act they usually start out with a minor amount. If successful, they try it again and if it continues to work they then go all out in their thefts. They usually repeat a successful manipulation, and this can lead to discovery.

     When reviewing records, pay particular attention to those that are similar or exactly alike in explanations, approval signatures, amounts, ink color and writing, and that occur at the same time. These may be at times that the manager goes to lunch or on break or when a management meeting takes place. When questionable activities are noted, study records to see if identical events have occurred. **TIP:** *If a repeat pattern is noted, regard the matter with suspicion.*

- Often a number of similar transactions are used to bypass an internal control that starts operating at a set dollar value. For example, if every transaction exceeding $100 requires a manager's approval, a dishonest employee might insert half a dozen fraudulent documents, each one of which only amounts to $85 to $95. The thefts may all occur on the same day, and maybe at the same time.

  By extracting all similar records that were processed over several months and placing them side by side, any odd similarities become readily apparent. Investigation of each transaction often leads to disclosure and to the identity of the perpetrator.

- Communicating with a suspect can be very touchy. If you notice a discrepancy that raises the strong possibility of fraud, you must be very careful in following up on the item. If you immediately take it straight to the responsible individual, that employee will offer some excuse that is intended to explain the act.

  To prepare for such an eventuality you should dig deeper and obtain several pieces of evidence, hopefully all of a different nature. Having discovered a pattern, and the method used, you are now ready to question the culprit. Only discuss one or at most two of the items known, so that the individual is not aware of the full knowledge that you possess. The discussion will let you know the employee's attitude and whether there is any merit to the offered explanations, and will dictate your further actions.

  Refrain from making accusations. Ask questions to learn the facts, but don't accuse. **NOTE:** *Ask for explanations and give the employee a chance to tell you what you want to know.*

- When questioning fraud suspects, be certain to have witnesses present. Always advise interviewees, in the presence of witnesses, that they are free to get up and and leave the room at any time. **TIP:** *Place their chair near the door, free of obstructions.*

- Before reaching a final conclusion in a fraud case, be certain that you have considered every other remote possibility. Sometimes the most impossible explanation will turn out to be the right one.

- One problem that you and your staff should be wary of, is that some auditors relax if they discover a dishonest act. There is often a tendency to assume that this one fraudulent act is the only one that occurred during the period being examined. Auditors may then skim over the rest of the papers they intended to examine, or they may even decide to discontinue the search. They then devote all of their efforts to document and prove the one event which drew their attention. But frequently an early disclosure of fraud or a major discrepancy may occur because there are many similar instances in the papers that were scheduled for examination.

If you've made up your mind to examine transactions for a set period, study all of the documents for the period of time that you selected. Don't pull up short because you found one major example. It is not unusual to find that a group of employees use the same method for perpetrating a fraud. Many people who believe they have found an easy way to cheat the company, tell their friends, who tell their friends. The result is that a number of employees may engage in the same type of theft. **TIP:** *If you discover an employee using a unique method of defalcation, check people working in similar jobs to see if they have used the same methods for the same purpose.*

For example, if you find that a salesperson has found a unique way of covering withholdings of collections; check all salespeople at that location to see if any others are using the same technique.

5. It is wise to pull many more records than you have time to examine, and make it obvious to office employees that you intend to study all the data. Pull records for the first few months after the last audit, and for several months in between, as well as for the current month that you plan to audit in detail. **KEY POINT:** *Lead office supervisors to realize that you can, and will, look at transactions for any period of time, not just the few months before your current visit.*
6. In the control of a competent, experienced operator, the polygraph can be a useful tool for determining the innocence of an individual placed under a cloud of suspicion. I recall a case:

   EXAMPLE: There was a mysterious disappearance from a safe. Only two people had a key, and one was on vacation. The other, the office manager, was in the office the day that the incident occurred. The obvious suspect asked for and received a polygraph test, which cleared him completely.

   Shortly thereafter an office employee was noticed in the room containing the safe, although there was no reason for the individual to be in that area. Subsequent investigation disclosed that the employee had made a copy of the key and had used it to extract money from the safe. If the polygraph had not been available, the office manager would have had difficulty proving his innocence.

7. Farfetched explanations of unusual transactions may be true.

   I remember a situation in which collections from a group of customers had not been turned in to the company. When the salesperson was questioned he acknowledged receiving the monies and stated that the collections had been mailed in to the home office.

   The alleged mailing had occurred several months before the start of the audit. Fortunately, I believed that the salesperson was telling the truth, and checked with the PO station located in a small town where the salesperson usually mailed in collections.

After some persuasion the local PO employees searched the premises and discovered the readily identifiable envelope. It had fallen behind a radiator in the office. In this case we accepted the salesperson's explanation, because there had been no attempt to wipe out the charges that were allegedly paid.

H. Handling Confidential Materials

1. Don't completely trust your central files. Keep critical papers in your personal confidential file under controlled lock and key.
2. When handling secret papers, such as formulas or drawings, be certain that at least two executives are present during the full time that the documents are out of the vault.
3. If you seal confidential material in an envelope which you do not wish anyone else to open, seal the flap and place your initials so that they occupy both the flap and a portion of the envelope. Place a piece of scotch tape over your initials. Do this at both flap ends of the envelope. If the scotch tape is removed and the envelope opened, the improper entry will be evident.

I. Auditing Procedures

1. When attempting to learn the truth of a matter, seek independent and objective corroboration, before accepting something as fact. Keep your eyes and ears open and be wary lest false facts lead you astray.
2. Listen to your intuition, but act only upon facts. Consider many conclusions from your review of facts and select one you can prove. A decision tree approach can be a useful way to evaluate your answer.
3. Beware of giving an opinion of the ability or character of any other employee. Your opinion of managers, supervisors and employees will be frequently sought. In such cases, state facts or observations that you personally witnessed, and note that your information is limited to the short time that you spent in an operation, and may not be fully representative of the character or ability of an individual.
4. Try not to offer suggestions until all elements of a problem have been considered. If you are forced to evaluate suggestions, your best approach is to request time and permission to explore the validity and appropriateness of all suggestions that are being considered.
5. Keep your audit reports brief and to the point. At your windup meetings

ensure that all present have a copy of the report and read each point aloud. Be sure your important audit correspondence shows the name of every person who receives a copy. **NOTE:** *Every reader will want to know who else has seen your letter.*

- When you find mechanical errors or oversights that are not devices used to conceal frauds; discuss the matter with employees concerned. If corrective measures are taken, do not include comments on such minor matters in your final audit report. Your operation will be more successful if you work *with* people rather than against them.
- Use a camera when a picture will more clearly and concisely describe a condition. Photographs may tell a better story than several pages of description. When using photographs be certain that the picture contains positive identification and a time reference, when applicable, such as placement of a clock, newspaper or calendar.
- During windup meetings, don't ramble or go off on a tangent. Confine topics and discussions to the items considered important enough to include in your report. After all items in the report have been covered, if time allows you may want to discuss some of the less important matters that you decided to omit from the report.
  TIP: *These are best left out of the report after discussing them with local management and getting their agreement to changes.*
- Your audit findings and reports are confidential and not to be discussed with unauthorized employees. If employees are discharged or forced to resign because of dishonesty, and you are asked why the employee is gone, your standard reply should be, "Ask him." Don't explain how you caught someone with their hand in the till.

6. It is better to sell management on an idea so that it is accepted as their own, rather than the auditor's. Bear in mind that most managers feel that they have an open-door policy toward any of their assigned employees. Many are erroneously convinced that their people tell them everything. They are upset when they discover that employees tell auditors things that they would not dare to tell their boss.

   It is foolhardy for auditors to tell managers that employees do not feel that they can level with them. It is also touchy to suggest to a manager that a suggestion box be set up to encourage anonymous suggestions. The manager might consider it an insult.

J. Managing the Audit Staff

1. Remember that as an auditor you are a representative of top management. Anything you say or do has an impact on people around you. Treat everyone with respect and kindness, and don't criticize an individual in any of

your reports or comments. **TIP:** *Where possible, use names of positions rather than names of individuals.*

2. Work to gain the respect and confidence of all your staff. Be truthful and forthright with them, and don't tell them lies to spare their feelings. People don't like to have their feelings hurt, but they prefer it to learning that their supervisors had lied to them. News gets around quickly, and your entire staff may learn to doubt your word. Your staff people are professionals; treat them as such.
3. Let your employees know what type of expenses they are permitted to charge to the company, and the permissible dollar value or range. **IMPORTANT:** *If an expense report is submitted that you consider out of line, talk to the staff member about it and consider the reasons before you reach a final conclusion.* Make certain that the staff member knows your final decision in the matter.
4. It might sometimes be better to use a training session as a method of pointing out the type of mistakes that your staff people make. At these sessions do not name the individual that made the error, but rather point out the consequences of the mistake and the way to prevent the oversight from occurring in the future.
5. Don't hesitate to advise a member of your staff to transfer to another department. A person who can't quite hack it as an auditor, might turn out to be an excellent salesperson or accounting manager.
6. Encourage your people to improve themselves through continuing education and participating in outside professional organization activities. Don't stand in the way of people who have an opportunity to improve their position. Moving auditors into executive positions benefits your operation and attracts new graduates to your staff.
7. Encourage your staff to participate in professional conferences and seminars. Participation as an instructor is particularly helpful.

   In addition, the social activities give your staff a chance to become acquainted with auditors who work for other companies. The possibility that your people might come away with an original idea or two is well worth the price of admission. One good idea might pay back thousands of dollars in future audits, and the conference registration fee is usually only a fraction of that amount. Becoming acquainted with auditors from other companies can pay off when a situation arises in which there is an advantage in communicating with another company.

   If your people know the auditors of that other company you can easily discuss the problem and perhaps elicit their support in resolving the matter. Personal contacts can be very valuable. Knowing other auditors may help understand how their company operates its business and help evaluate a transaction that your crew is studying.

8. Regular social gatherings of audit personnel can be very helpful in encouraging an exchange of ideas and experiences among staff members. These informal conversations usually register more concretely than classroom instructions. Some choice bits of information, heard during a social gathering, come to mind when an auditor is faced with a situation that had been described by a fellow staff member. Earlier conversations may point out pitfalls or potential solutions.

K. General

1. Some people may have unusual reasons for doing things, some of which may not occur to a financial-minded auditor. I remember an instance where there was an irregular pattern in the cashing of checks written to a supplier. The supplier was visited to try to find out what was going on, since there were many old checks still outstanding, while current checks were frequently cashed.

   The supplier, a one-man operation, had the checks lying on a bench, and selected a check written for the exact amount of an outstanding bill. He would then send that check in payment. It reduced the number of company checks that the supplier had to write. The disclosure also explained the unusual endorsements that appeared on many of the checks.
2. There will be times when your company fails to achieve planned profits, or when economic conditions demand a reappraisal of all company operations. Cost controls programs will be initiated, and even the most insignificant savings will be considered. The auditing department will be a focal point in such programs.

   When you begin to look for areas in which costs may be trimmed, you may find the list of *cost cutters* at the end of this chapter to be of value. Even when a cost control program is not in effect, you might periodically review the list. Some of these items are intended for extreme conditions, while others should be considered at all times. Use this list of items as a basis for preparing your own list that applies to your company's operations.

CONCLUSION

Most of the material in this manual is designed to serve as a guide, and perhaps as a catalyst to stimulate your thinking. Internal auditors are aware that an approach that may have worked very well in one area, or at one time, may not work as well in other places or at other times. However, there are some routines that are generally successful. This book contains many of the time-proven concepts that can be useful.

While there is no guarantee that it will make you a better analyst, if read carefully, it will make you more knowledgeable and it should provide enough information to improve your auditing performance.

COST-CUTTERS
Some Things to Think About

A. Planning
   1. Review operating statements and identify areas that offer best cost reduction potential.
   2. Flow chart all major functions.
   3. Group related functions under same supervision.
   4. Shorten the chain of command; it improves communications and eliminate excess levels of supervision.
   5. Define responsibilities and authority; eliminate overlaps.
   6. Consider decentralizing and/or centralizing operations.
   7. Consider a profit planning program.
   8. Try to measure benefits before spending.
   9. Make employees plan major jobs in advance.
   10. Defer all new actions until true needs are determined.
   11. Reduce the number of committees and length of meetings.
   12. Have an annual cost reduction suggestion program.
B. Analyses of Departments and Activities
   1. Are all departments necessary? Should any be added?
   2. Are all officers and jobs necessary?
   3. Is the company magazine necessary?
   4. Are company sponsored organizations necessary?
   5. Establish a word processing center.
   6. Reduce central filing.
   7. Centralize office services.
   8. Evaluate all major cost programs.
   9. Review the need for institutional type advertising.
   10. Eliminate duplicate records. Put a price tag on each report issued. The information will be surprising.
   11. Review all scrap, see if any salvage value can be realized.
C. Personnel
   1. Set a good example for your staff.
   2. Promote from within to improve morale.
   3. Institute a hiring freeze for short periods.
   4. Review manpower requirements periodically.
   5. Review all educational and training programs.
   6. Have periodic performance reviews.
   7. Request periodic time distribution reports from employees.
D. Efficiency
   1. Start and leave work on time.
   2. Utilize people to full capacity and qualifications.
   3. Permit carry-over of work load and level out peaks.
   4. Reduce overtime by better scheduling and prioritizing work.

5. Review all form designs for efficiency.
6. Review quality of office equipment.
7. Standardize equipment.
8. Use more estimates in accounting.
9. Have cycle billings.
10. Close books quarterly; use estimated P/L statement monthly.
11. Reduce quantity of reports.
12. Use handwritten instead of typewritten memos.
13. Eliminate federal and trade reports where not required.
14. Make a periodic review of files for retention necessity.
15. Establish convenient "libraries" for manuals.
16. Use combination requisition, purchase order, receiving report.
17. Route reports rather than prepare multiple report copies.
18. Use microfilm files to save space.
19. Use computer to assist auditors.
20. Use cheaper paper in duplicating machines.
21. Use better machines for duplicating to cut down on wastage.
22. Reduce necessity for duplicating by use of common files.
23. Do more internal printing of forms.
24. Utilize copiers at strategic locations.
25. Establish a form control manual; control quantities of forms.
26. Review all forms for necessity and simplicity.
27. Review all stationery costs.
28. Reduce the size of annual reports, and number of colors.
29. Purchase and issue office supplies in economical quantities.
30. Reduce kinds of accounting paper carried in inventory.
31. Control supplies and sundries.

E. Office Facilities
1. Have forward planning of office layout.
2. Have more modest offices.
3. Eliminate offices for lower supervisory personnel.
4. Use proper wattage and voltage.
5. Use florescent lighting.
6. Turn out lights when not in use.
7. Establish janitorial procedures that cycle the work load.
8. Remove materials from desk nightly to reduce janitorial work.
9. Set standards for floor space allowances by classification of office employee.

F. Outside Services
1. Hire temporaries for emergencies; no overtime.
2. Utilize a supplier's free technical services.
3. Cut out professional services where possible.
4. Do your own building or garden maintenance.
5. Use bank facilities to accumulate and pay freight bills.
6. Use bank facilities to mechanically reconcile bank accounts.

7. Self-produce costly supplies or materials needed.
8. Send paid freight and utility bills to outside audit agencies.

G. Communications

1. Review all communication facilities.
2. Start a telephone expense reduction campaign.
3. Reduce switchboard hours; close board earlier.
4. Use one central mail room only.
5. Install intra-office mail and messenger service.
6. Mechanize mail processing.
7. Use lowest class mail rate where feasible.
8. Use lighter paper and envelopes.
9. Don't use separate envelopes on inter-office mail.
10. Mail dividend check with annual report.
11. Eliminate the second proxy mailing.
12. Don't mail statements to *all* customers.
13. Reduce size of mailing lists.
14. Don't use express mail unless necessary.

H. Meetings and Travel

1. Strictly regulate all travel.
2. Cut out executive cars.
3. Cut out company airplanes.
4. Use coach instead of first class air fare.
5. Use the airport bus instead of cabs.
6. Stagger company hours to relieve congestion problems.
7. Lease company cars instead of purchasing, and use compacts.
8. Set up our own transport fleet.
9. Reduce meeting and travel expense by a set percentage.
10. Eliminate or reduce convention attendance.
11. Use lower priced hotels.
12. Make contract travel arrangements with hotels in cities that are frequently visited by our employees.
13. Control moving expenses of people transferred.
14. Eliminate expensive stockholders meetings.
15. Eliminate special stockholders meetings by better planning.
16. Cut down on lunch time meetings.
17. Have management meetings in corporate offices.

I. Payroll and Fringe Benefits

1. Schedule overtime by priority.
2. Dock employees for being late.
3. Have shorter lunch hours.
4. Eliminate oddball deductions for employees.
5. Eliminate paychecks; have pay deposited in employee's bank account.
6. Schedule varying pay dates to level load in payroll department and reduce staff.
7. Eliminate fringe benefits: picnics, golf outings, etc.

8. Review employee stock option plans.
9. Eliminate Christmas gifts to employees.
10. Eliminate or reduce coffee breaks.
11. Have suggestion award system.

J. Funds
1. Raise capitalization limits.
2. Use lockbox banking.
3. Keep petty cash funds to a minimum.
4. Minimize number of bank accounts.
5. Have bills paid by sight draft.
6. Use idle funds.
7. Speed up billings.
8. Review discount procedures.
9. Hold payables for maximum time but pay for discount.
10. Have salesmen and drivers deposit collections directly into banks.

K. Taxes and Insurance
1. Move to lower tax areas.
2. Renegotiate real estate taxes on idle facilities.
3. Control inventories to reduce property taxes.
4. Don't pay tax installments until due.
5. Establish subsidiary corporations for branches in areas that tax on total company business.
6. Review all insurance costs.
7. Extend the use of "self-insurance."
8. Negotiate insurance rates on a "package" basis.

L. Subscriptions and Dues
1. Reduce memberships in outside societies, clubs, associations, etc.
2. Eliminate duplicate memberships in organizations.
3. Buy industrial and trade magazines at wholesale rates.
4. Centralize magazine services.
5. Reduce number of magazine and newspaper subscriptions.
6. Develop bibliography of current periodicals to ensure review of latest ideas.

M. Miscellaneous
1. Assemble all reports (internal) into a single book.
2. Establish greater security to avoid inventory thefts.
3. Obtain competitive bids for purchases of materials and supplies.
4. Review purchase frequency for supplies and materials.
5. Review technical magazines systematically for cost saving ideas.
6. Distribute useful "cost-cutters" to all personnel who might use them.

Appendix

THE INTERNAL AUDITING PROFESSION

The IIA

The Institute of Internal Auditors (IIA) is an organization formed by internal auditors to foster an interchange of ideas among internal auditors. The organization grew and now has chapters in many of the major cities in the United States and in many countries overseas. The IIA has been very active in the field of internal auditing education, and sponsors regional and international conferences that feature multiple day seminars on internal auditing subjects. All chapters hold meetings at which subjects of interest to internal auditors are discussed. Chapters also frequently hold one- to three-day seminars for chapter members and guests.

The IIA also sponsors classes for auditors and publishes papers on internal auditing subjects. The institute prints a magazine titled *The Internal Auditor* which contains worthwhile information for members of the internal auditing profession.

The CIA Program

In recognition of the importance of standardizing and gaining acceptance of the internal auditing profession, the IIA developed and implemented a program for the certification of internal auditors. In the same fashion as the certification of public accountants, the IIA developed a Code of Ethics, and a written examination for determining which internal auditors should be permitted to identify themselves as Certified Internal Auditors. Any internal auditor that meets the stringent requirements may take the four-part examination and, upon successful completion of the test and acceptance of the Code of Ethics, is awarded the Certificate. The Code of Ethics follows.

THE INSTITUTE OF INTERNAL AUDITORS

Code of Ethics

PURPOSE: A distinguishing mark of a profession is acceptance by its members for responsibility to the interests of those it serves. Members of The Institute of Internal Auditors (Members) and Certified Internal Auditors (CIAs) must maintain high standards of conduct in order to effectively discharge this responsibility. The Institute of Internal Auditors (Institute) adopts this Code of Ethics for Members and CIAs.

APPLICABILITY: This Code of Ethics is applicable to all Members and CIAs. Membership in The Institute and acceptance of the "Certified Internal Auditor" designation are voluntary actions. By acceptance, Members and CIAs assume an obligation of self-discipline above and beyond the requirements of laws and regulations.

The standards of conduct set forth in this Code of Ethics provide basic principles in the practice of internal auditing. Members and CIAs should realize that their individual judgment is required in the application of these principles.

CIAs shall use the "Certified Internal Auditor" designation with discretion and in a dignified manner, fully aware of what the designation denotes. The designation shall also be used in a manner consistent with all statutory requirements.

Members who are judged by the Board of Directors of The Institute to be in violation of the standards of conduct of the Code of Ethics shall be subject to forfeiture of their membership in the Institute. CIAs who are similarly judged also shall be subject to forfeiture of the "Certified Internal Auditor" designation.

STANDARDS OF CONDUCT

I. Members and CIAs shall exercise honesty, objectivity, and diligence in the performance of their duties and responsibilities.

II. Members and CIAs shall exhibit loyalty in all matters pertaining to the affairs of their organization or to whomever they may be rendering a service. However, Members and CIAs shall not knowingly be a party to any illegal or improper activity.

III. Members and CIAs shall not knowingly engage in acts or activities which are discreditable to the profession of internal auditing or to their organization.

IV. Member and CIAs shall refrain from entering into any activity which may be in conflict with the interest of their organization or which would prejudice their ability to carry out objectively their duties and responsibilities.

V. Members and CIAs shall not accept anything of value from an employee, client, customer, supplier, or business associate of their organization which would impair or be presumed to impair their professional judgment.

VI. Members and CIAs shall undertake only those services which they can reasonably expect to complete with professional competence.

VII. Members and CIAs shall adopt suitable means to comply with the Standards for the Professional Practice of Internal Auditing.

VIII. Members and CIAs shall be prudent in the use of information acquired in the course of their duties. They shall not use confidential information for any personal gain nor in any manner which would be contrary to law or detrimental to the welfare of their organization.

IX. Members and CIAs, when reporting on the results of their work, shall reveal all material facts known to them which, if not revealed, would either distort reports of operations under review or conceal unlawful practices.

X. Members and CIAs shall continually strive for improvement in their proficiency, and in the effectiveness and quality of their service.

XI. Members and CIAs, in the practice of their profession, shall be ever mindful of their obligation to maintain the high standards of competence, morality and dignity promulgated by The Institute. Members shall abide by the *Bylaws* and uphold the objectives of The Institute.

(Adopted by the Board of Directors July, 1988)

The above formal code is properly applicable to every internal auditor, certified or not.

Index

A

D

H

I